THE PRENTICE-HALL SERIES IN MARKETING

Philip Kotler, Series Editor

COMPETITIVE MARKETING STRATEGY

John A. Czepiel

Leonard N. Stern School of Business
New York University

PRENTICE HALL, *Englewood Cliffs, NJ 07632*

Library of Congress Cataloging-in-Publication Data

Czepiel, John A.
    Competitive marketing strategy / John A. Czepiel.
        p.   cm.
    ISBN 0-13-143082-3
    1. Marketing--Management.   2. Strategic planning.   3. Competition.
    4. Technological innovations.   I. Title.
    HF5415.13.C94   1992
    658.8'02--dc20

                                                                91-44622
                                                                   CIP

Acquisition Editor   *Jennifer Young*
Production Editor   *Maureen Wilson*
Copy Editor   *Patricia Daly*
Cover Designer   *20/20 Services, Inc.*
Prepress Buyer   *Trudy Pisciotti*
Manufacturing Buyer   *Bob Anderson*
Supplements Editor   *Lisamarie Brassini*
Editorial Assistant   *Ellen Ford*

 © 1992 by Prentice-Hall, Inc.
A Simon & Schuster Company
Englewood Cliffs, New Jersey 07632

Printed in the United States of America
10 9 8 7 6 5 4 3 2 1

ISBN 0-13-143082-3

Prentice-Hall International (UK) Limited, *London*
Prentice-Hall of Australia Pty. Limited, *Sydney*
Prentice-Hall Canada Inc., *Toronto*
Prentice-Hall Hispanoamericana, S.A., *Mexico*
Prentice-Hall of India Private Limited, *New Delhi*
Prentice-Hall of Japan, Inc., *Tokyo*
Simon & Schuster Asia Pte. Ltd., *Singapore*
Editora Prentice-Hall do Brasil, Ltda., *Rio de Janeiro*

To my wife
A. Dawn Lesh
and my son
John Jason

CONTENTS

3
A FRAMEWORK FOR THE STRATEGIC
ANALYSIS OF PRODUCTS   65

4
MARKET-BASED PRODUCT CONCEPTS   110

8

CREATING STRATEGIC CHANGE IN EVOLUTIONARY MARKETS   254

9

ANALYZING COMPETITION   283

10

ANALYZING COMPETITORS 331

11

DEVELOPING AND ANALYZING STRATEGIC OPTIONS 373

12

STRATEGIZING: UNDERSTANDING THE PROCESSES OF STRATEGY FORMULATION AND STRATEGIC THINKING   411

13

EVALUATING, VALUING, AND IMPLEMENTING STRATEGY   449

PREFACE

This book is the result of a fifteen year odyssey into the world of competitive marketing strategy. It represents this author's attempt to make sense of the concept of strategy for himself, for MBA students, and for working managers and executives. The book is a working document because the very conceptual foundation on which it rests is still actively evolving and expanding, as is the author's ability to understand and internalize its concepts, processes, research, insights, and implications.

The goals out of which the project grew are to have a book that:

1. emphasizes strategic content over strategic planning,
2. captures the underlying essence of pure competitive strategy concepts,
3. stresses the centrality of the concept of value creation as the dominant force in marketplace competition,
4. explains to marketing strategists how to analyze and incorporate technology into their strategies, and
5. is applicable and understandable to all businesses, be they consumer, industrial, product, or service.

In addition, the goal is to emphasize empirical reality over normative prescription. For this reason the book links concepts with empirical research which measure their existence and magnitude whenever possible.

An interesting sidelight is that this process parallels the transformation to a competitor of an individual whose earliest training in music (from the age of 8) stressed cooperation over competition—since there is not much of a payoff to competing when making music in an orchestra, band, or choir. That transformation to the competitive mode was given a boost by three additional formative factors. The first was the need to make sense out of what concepts and tools MBA students needed and how they could be best acquired. The second was the opportunity to test and apply those concepts and tools as a consultant who actively participated in a wide range of strategic decisions. The third was the need to hone personal level competitive instincts in order to successfully participate in a weekly seminar on Probability Estimation and Competitive Strategy. The seminar was, in reality, a poker game involving members of the Stern School faculty. You really learn to understand the push and shove aspects of competitive advantage when it's your own money on the table.

ORGANIZATION OF THE BOOK

Competitive strategy is marketplace driven. It matters little whether the source of the strategic advantage comes from advertising, R&D, raw materials sourcing, information systems technology, competitive failure, or selling effectiveness. The goal is to have a competitive advantage in creating value for customers. Two major forces—the laws of economics and the laws of strategy—dominate the competitive game. Those are the focus of the first two chapters in the book, *The Concept of Strategy in Marketing* and *Competitive Advantage*. Chapters 3 and 4 analyze the focus of those rules, the product offering. Chapter 3 provides *A Framework for the Strategic Analysis of Products* while Chapter 4 presents *Market-Based Product Concepts*.

Chapters 5 and 6 cover the two most potent competitive advantages, the creation of technology that provides valued benefits and the productive capacity that allows the firm to supply products that actually deliver the benefit. Chapter 5 is about *Analyzing Production Operations and Cost Behavior for Strategic Decision Making*. Chapter 6 provides *A Framework for Incorporating Technology into Product Strategy Decisions*. The next two chapters take the analysis of competing into a dynamic mode—how all of the forces evolve over time and how and when strategic moves can pay off. Chapter 7 discusses *The Dynamic Nature of Competition and Competitive Strategy;* Chapter 8 is about *Creating Strategic Change in Evolutionary Markets*.

Chapters 9 and 10 are about competition itself. Chapter 9 provides the tools for *Analyzing Competition* and Chapter 10 those that are needed for *Analyzing Competitors*. Chapters 11, 12, and 13 provide the analytic tools and processes useful in creating strategy. Chapter 11 provides analytic techniques useful in *Developing and Analyzing Strategic Options*. Chapter 12 explores *Strategizing: Understanding the Processes of Strategy Formulation and Strategic Thinking*. Chapter 13 concludes the book by presenting concepts for *Evaluating, Valuing, and Implementing Strategy*.

ACKNOWLEDGMENTS

The MBA students in my Product Strategy course at the Leonard N. Stern School of Business stimulated this book. Their enthusiasm for the value of the insights that the competitive approach to strategy gave them, together with their persistence in demanding clear exposition of those concepts, were the carrot and stick that kept me at the project. To this day, I gain new insights into the analysis of strategic situations as we discuss their assigned cases in small groups or as they formally present and defend their recommended strategies in front of their peers. I would not have and could not have done it without them.

There is a group of managers who taught me what it meant to be competitive, who gave me the opportunity to play in their sandbox, and who helped me to internalize what an unfair advantage was. In alphabetical order these include Keith Atkins, Bob Boysen, Joe Byck, Ron Cottle, Pat Gallo, Bill Joyce, Tom Lawrence, Lee McMaster, Stan Norwalk, Lou Ongchin, Don Ryan, Dan Scheid, Don Schober, Roger Staub, and John Yimoyines. Working with these individuals provided me with intellectual challenges equal to any I have ever experienced. Their influence permeates this book.

I received invaluable support from a series of loyal research assistants. They chased citations, drew figures and charts, spent time in the library and in front of copying machines, tied up loose ends, and were premier masters of footnote style. In chronological order they were Bob Cullinan, Carole Mercorella, Maria Sekas, Alison Mason, Elena Fletcher, Kevin Rockoff, and Cheryl Taylor.

In addition, I need to thank the Leonard N. Stern School of Business at New York University for providing me the students and the support necessary to the project and my colleagues in the Marketing Area for tolerating my eccentricities not only over the period in which this book was written but in general. Like a good family, they accept individuals as they are. That acceptance is important and appreciated.

Finally, I thank my mother, Genevieve Czepiel, for the ambition to start this project and my wife, A. Dawn Lesh, and son, John J. Czepiel, for the emotional support and love needed to finish it.

1

THE CONCEPT OF STRATEGY
IN MARKETING

In 350 B.C., Sun Pin, recognized as a great thinker and strategist, was in the employ of T'ien Chi, the commander in chief of the Chinese province of Ch'i. Sun Pin's employer frequently raced his horses against those of the other Princes of Ch'i. On one occasion Sun Pin noticed that the opposition's horses did not differ greatly in performance from those of his employer but had been divided into three groups according to their speed. This showed him how he could be sure his prince's horses would win. He was so sure, in fact, that he advised T'ien Chi to bet heavily on the races, but only if he followed Sun Pin's instructions to the letter. His instructions were simple. He had T'ien Chi match his third-string horses against the opposition's first string, his best horses against the opposition's second string, and his second string against the slowest of the opposition's. T'ien Chi's horses lost the first race, but they won the next two and a substantial sum of gold.[1]

Hannibal, the great Carthaginian general, used a similar idea to win the battle of Cannae in 216 B.C. against superior forces led by the Roman general, Varro (see Figure 1-1). While his infantry was outnumbered by the Romans 70,000 to 20,000, both sides' cavalry were equal at 2,000 apiece. Hannibal's idea about how to win in this unwinnable situation was based on this equality in cavalry. Hannibal's key was to divide his cavalry into two *unequal* halves, which he then positioned partway up the foothills that flanked the two sides of the valley in which his infantry was centered.

Terrain is an important element in battle, and a defender who forces attackers to fight uphill has the advantage of gravity. Varro, the Roman general, expecting that Hannibal's forces would be evenly divided, sent half of his cavalry to attack each position. With the advantage of terrain, the smaller of Hannibal's two forces was able to defend and hold its position against the Roman unit, which outnumbered it, while Hannibal's larger unit (with the assistance of its larger numbers and the terrain) overwhelmed its opposition.

---

[1] Sun Tzu, *The Art of War*, translated by Samuel B. Griffith (London: Oxford University Press, 1963), pp. 60–61.

Figure 1-1   The battle of Cannae

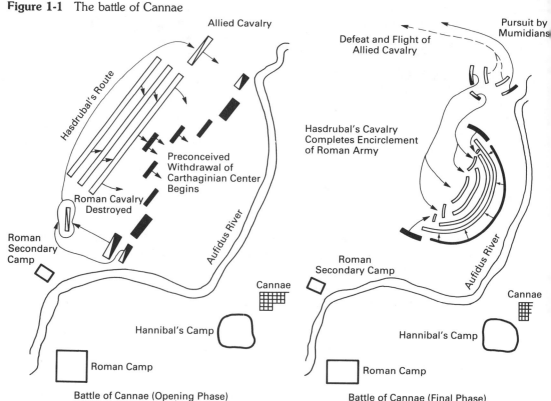

Battle of Cannae (Opening Phase)   Battle of Cannae (Final Phase)

SOURCE: From *The Encyclopedia of Military History from 3500 B.C. to the Present* by R. Ernest Dupuy and Trevor N. Dupuy. Copyright © 1970 by R. Ernest Dupuy and Data Memory Services, Inc. Reprinted by permission of HarperCollins Publishers.

This was the key to the battle. As soon as it won, Hannibal's victorious larger cavalry unit rushed downhill and across the narrow valley to assist the smaller cavalry unit, which was holding off the other half of Varro's cavalry. Attacking the now outnumbered Roman cavalry from the rear, Hannibal's forces were able to defeat them quickly and assist the infantry.

Hannibal had arrayed his 20,000 infantry troops in a convex array pointed at Varro's 70,000 troops, which were arrayed in conventional rank and file. While the cavalry units were involved in battle, Hannibal allowed his infantry troops to be pushed back slowly by Varro's infantry—with the apex of the convex array retreating the most and the outer edges not at all. When this occurred, the Roman troops sensed victory in Hannibal's apparent retreat and rushed forward into what they thought was the collapsing center of Hannibal's formation. However, as it was pushed back, the center of Hannibal's formation became the apex of a *concave* array of troops—a net-shaped array which surrounded Varro's army on three sides. At this point, Hannibal's by-now-victorious cavalry came up to close the circle, trapping Varro's infantry into such a tight mass that they could not raise their swords.

EXHIBIT 1-1

The Incan King Uses His Unfair Advantage

In one sixteenth-century battle between Spanish Conquistadors and the Incas of Peru, General Pizzaro planned to capture King Manco, disperse his army, and destroy his cattle. But Spanish horses were useless in the steepness and high altitude of the Andes Mountains. The soldiers therefore attempted to raid the Incas on foot. But altitude sickness, which affected the Europeans at altitudes over 13,000 feet, weakened Pizzaro's men. Pizzaro's soldiers were ambushed and nearly wiped out by Incan troops, who were accustomed to high altitudes. The Incan army exercised their unfair advantage.

SOURCE: Hiram Bingham, *The Lost City of the Incas* (New York: Macmillan, 1963).[2]

THE LAWS OF PHYSICS AND THE UNFAIR ADVANTAGE

These examples demonstrate that the race need not go to the swift nor the battle to the larger army. Neither of the two deserved to win. An objective analysis shows that the physics of the situations favored the eventual losers. Hannibal was outnumbered, and T'ien Chi could not have expected to do better than to tie, win, or lose based on purely random factors. The laws of physics were on the losers' side—they should have won—but they lost.

In both examples the victory resulted from an idea about how to gain an "unfair" advantage. It was unfair in the sense that, once it was put into effect, the opposition could not effectively counter it. It altered what the natural outcome would have been had the idea not been applied. It gave one side an advantage—the fight was no longer between equals, nor was it on a level playing field.[3] Exhibit 1-1 shows how an Incan king gained an unfair advantage over the Spanish Conquistadors.

Where one's own life or death is at stake, most conventionally rational minds would not accept that an equally matched, fair competition be used to decide the outcome. I would not want to be in a fair fight if *my* life were at stake. But one need not speak of life-and-death situations to understand the point. Most outcomes in life are not determined in fair fights.[4] The laws of physics of life say that the big win over the small, the smart over the dumb, the resource rich over the resource poor. This concept of the laws of physics is explained more fully in Exhibit 1-2.

---

[2] I am indebted to a student for bringing this example to my attention.
[3] Someone once noted that the concept of unfairness seems, in general, to be defined by the losing side.
[4] As a friend of mine consistently explains to her daughters, "Life is not fair."

EXHIBIT 1-2

A Note on the Laws of Physics

The phrase *the laws of physics* is here used to refer to the natural laws that determine the outcome of situations or competitions. In the physical world, for example, physics says that the stronger force will overcome the lesser. In economic competition, the product that provides better value to the user will sell more than those providing less value, *all other things being equal.*

Strategy cannot overcome natural laws; in fact, strategy depends on the existence of natural laws which govern the outcomes of situations. Strategists' knowledge of those laws allows them to use the laws to their advantage. For example, physical laws determine the likely winner of physical fights. All other things being equal, the larger, bigger, stronger will win—after all, that is why boxing puts fighters into weight classes. Yet these same laws allow the small person who is skilled in the techniques of judo to overcome much larger opponents. These techniques involve using opponents' own momentum and force against themselves through the skillful use of leverage.

The strategist who does not understand the laws of physics governing his or her situation is at a disadvantage, for those laws will determine the outcome.

Biological competition has at its core the idea that the strong prey on the weak. Species with an advantage over others in acquiring and processing food multiply and expand at the expense of others, which shrink in population. That's not fair at all, is it? But to say "well, that's life" is to oversimplify and perhaps to miss the point. There is a reason that language recognizes certain separate categories of activity as play and sport. In these two activities, the concept of fairness has moral legitimacy. Such activities are not work or war, and the concept of fair competition makes sense since it is the game and not the outcome that is of greatest importance. In work and war, on the other hand, moral legitimacy is determined by the physics of the situation which determines the outcome—the advantage one has that increases the probability of one's winning. This discussion can be summarized simply as "fight fair, but avoid fair fights."

Economics is built on the premise that some producers have, can gain, and indeed are motivated to seek an unfair advantage over others. The concept of specialization of labor is built on the reality that we each have different abilities and that by doing those things in which we have an inborn or acquired advantage, we and society both win.

How then did Sun Pin and Hannibal win? What allowed them to set aside the laws of physics that said they should not have won? As noted earlier, they had an idea about how to use the physics of the situation to their advantage. In war, the laws of physics dictate that the larger army wins. Hannibal's victory was actually based on that same law—for at the initial point of contact Hannibal's cavalry actually outnumbered Varro's even before gravity assisted them. In the second cavalry engagement Hannibal's forces had a clear size advantage. The subsequent infantry engagement was designed to nullify Varro's numerical advantage in two ways. First and most important, the encirclement reduced the number of effective infantry—those able to fight—to just those on the periphery of the circular mass, a number far smaller than the total. Second, the encirclement forced Varro's infantry into such close quarters that they could not raise their weapons to strike. Both factors turned the laws of physics to Hannibal's advantage. In a similar manner, Sun Pin's sacrifice of one race enabled him to win the next two, in which he could position his employer's stronger horses against weaker opponents.

Both Sun Pin's and Hannibal's ideas about how to win are at the core of the concept of strategy. The ideas developed because they knew the physics of their specific situations, both in general and specifically. In general, they knew that the physics favored larger armies and faster horses. In specific, they each knew about the strengths of their opponents. Sun Pin knew how his employer's opponents had arranged their horses; Hannibal knew that Varro's cavalry was approximately equal in size to his and would most likely be divided into equal halves in such a situation. Both facts set the stage for creative thinking that turned a potential loss into victory.

Sun Pin and Hannibal were both able to create their respective ideas because they were strategists, accustomed to thinking strategically. Sun Pin's ancestor was the great Sun Tzu, author of the earliest book on strategy, *The Art of War*. Sun Pin was hired by T'ien Chi because he was known to be a great thinker and strategist. As a general, Hannibal had been accustomed to analyzing strategic situations. He, too, was known for his strategic abilities.

Four lessons can be learned from these examples and the discussion so far:

1. Strategy is about seeking an unfair advantage in those situations where it's the outcome and not the game that counts;
2. Doing strategy requires that you know the laws of physics that govern the outcomes of the particular competition;
3. Specific knowledge of the competitors and the situation are needed to produce real, implementable strategies;
4. Creating strategies that win is a skill that can be learned.

This chapter is about the concept of strategy. Its first task is to explore more thoroughly the idea of strategy itself, what it means, and how to think about it. Second, the chapter imbeds the concept of strategy in the context of economic competition. Since most of the concepts used in strategic analysis and formulation come from the study of warfare, it is necessary to understand how such concepts translate into the business sphere. Third, the chapter introduces the strategic thought process and positions strategy making as a managerial task at several levels in a business.

THE CONCEPT OF STRATEGY

The aforementioned contests were not won with actions, resources, or people. In each case they were won on the strength of the strategist's idea about how to use the resources at hand within the context of a specific situation to offset the balance that the laws of physics seemed to dictate. Strategy is an idea, a concept, a plan. As Sun Tzu wrote in 500 B.C. in his classic treatise *The Art of War*, "All men see the tactics by which I fight, but what none see is the strategy out of which victory is evolved."[5] He meant that while it was possible for the observer to see the size of his army, the number of its weapons, the courage of its soldiers, and the actions it took on the battlefield, he could never see (at least in the physical sense) the overall concept which led Sun Tzu to choose when, where, how, or even which battles to fight.

There are many definitions of strategy, as a look through several dictionaries will show. Most of these concern the use of military forces in battle. In fact, the word derives from the Greek words meaning generalship and "to think."[6] One particularly insightful definition is that "strategy is the science of planning and directing large-scale military operations, specifically of maneuvering forces into the most advantageous position prior to actual engagement with the enemy."[7] According to another definition, "strategy is the plan, method, or series of maneuvers or stratagems for obtaining a specific goal or result."[8] In the military sense, again, the concept of strategy is encompassing: the utilization of all of a nation's forces, through large-scale, long-range planning and development, to ensure security or victory.

The concept of strategy is sometimes better understood if it is compared with the idea of tactics. The word *tactics* comes from the ancient Greek word meaning "to arrange." In military terms, tactics is concerned with the use and positioning of troops in battle. In a sense, tactics involves the best playing out of a hand chosen by a prior strategic-level decision. In contrast, and somewhat simplistically, strategy is about what battles are worth fighting in the first place. Second, strategy is about the thinking before the battle that determines how troops will be used to best advantage. Third, strategy is about the translation of those ideas into action plans that incorporate the result of that thinking—ultimately, it is real action that wins the battle.

Basic Strategy Concepts

Strategists have developed concepts and ideas with which to analyze situations. These concepts are reflected in the specific terminology of strategists—words

---

[5] Sun Tzu, p. 100.
[6] I am grateful to a former student for this meaning.
[7] *Webster's New World Dictionary*, Second College Edition (New York: Simon and Schuster, 1984).
[8] *Random House Dictionary of the English Language*, Second Edition (New York: Random House, 1987).

that capture the ideas, discriminate between the ideas, and allow strategists to communicate with each other. This section introduces that terminology and the ideas it expresses. While the ideas are most important, we cannot speak about them without the words.

Strategy versus Tactics.   Strategy is about the best way of achieving some objective. In this sense, it is a simple concept. If one wants to travel from one city to another, there are a few strategic choices available: One can walk, hitchhike, bicycle, drive, take a bus, train, or plane. In this example (illustrated in Figure 1-2), each strategic choice can indeed allow one to achieve the objective. The choice in this example will not depend on whether the strategy will work but on which strategy is best. To determine which is best will depend on the criterion or criteria used. Speed, cost, comfort, and safety are all possible criteria by which one can evaluate which is best.

Tactics are about the choices one has in implementing a strategy. If one chooses to drive, the tactical choices involve whether one rents, borrows, or uses one's own car, the route taken, and the time of day one departs. At the tactical level there are also choices that will or will not work and that are better or worse depending on the criteria used. However, no matter how well one chooses, the outcomes of any given tactical choice can never exceed those inherent to the strategy (although chance or poor implementation can reduce outcomes to a level less than what was expected). For example, driving will never allow one to arrive faster than the limit imposed by the top speed of the car, although driving could be faster than taking a plane if one chose an unreliable carrier or if chance intervened (coastal fog closed the airport but did not hamper driving conditions). Moreover, even superb tactical choice and implementation cannot make a wrong strategy work. If, for example, we had listed *typewriter* as one of the strategic choices available in Figure 1-2, we would never get to Boston no matter what make of typewriter we used or how fast we typed.

Let us deal with the distinction at a more abstract level. Strategic-level alternatives are those which require choices that are enduring, not easily changed, and involve the very structure of the situation. A strategy is a decisive allocation of resources in a particular direction. A white-tablecloth restaurant strategy requires a vastly different set of investments in real estate, equipment, skills, and people than does a fast-food strategy. The two have totally different financial pictures; the white-tablecloth restaurant has high prices, high margins, and low turnover whereas the fast-food restaurant has low prices and margins coupled with a high customer count.

Once a choice is made for one or the other, there is little one can do to redeploy those assets in another direction. Neither operation can be readily converted to the other, although each can be changed within its type. A white-tablecloth restaurant can be changed from continental to Italian but not to a Burger King. The difference is at the structural level, so the choice is important.

Figure 1-2 Relationship between strategies, tactics, objectives, and goals

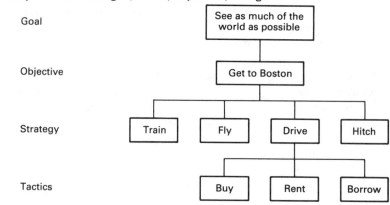

The things that make it difficult to change a strategy are the same that make it difficult for competitors to counter.

Goals and Objectives. In the preceding example, the objective of getting to Boston was never questioned. It was simply a given. The questions "Why go anyplace at all?" or "Why Boston?" were never asked. Equally interesting, the availability of the strategic alternatives (perhaps the existence of a free ticket) seemingly never affected whether the goal was set in the first place or what it was. These are not academic questions but serious concerns to those who must make strategy decisions, whether business, personal, or for national security. The relationship between goals, objectives, strategy, and tactics is depicted in Figure 1-2.[9]

Goals are generally defined as expressions of long-run ends that are generally desirable—survival, security, and similar open-ended attributes such as profit maximization. These are considered open ended because they are not bounded. There is no true limit to profit maximization—there can always be more. Similarly, survival and security can never be truly achieved since the future can always bring new threats.[10]

Objectives are more concrete. They are the accomplishments that are necessary (but never sufficient) to reaching the goal. If the goal in Figure 1-2 was to see as much of the world as possible, then Boston would be a reasonable objective; achieving the objective would bring one closer to the goal. Objectives are generally quite specific, they are and need to be capable of being measured. Objectives frequently involve the setting of targets and time frames (Boston by tomorrow).

There is an uneasy relationship between the level of the ends (goals and objectives) and the means (strategy and tactics). In one sense the means should

[9] While the specific terminology used here is common, it is by no means universal and there are other ways of expressing these same relationships.
[10] Charles W. Hofer and Dan Schendel, *Strategy Formulation: Analytic Concepts* (St. Paul, MN: West Publishing Company, 1978), pp. 20–21.

be subservient to the ends, and the ends exist independently of the means. For example, a nation does not enter a battle or a war just because it is possible to win it. The existence of a strategy should not dictate goals. On the other hand, goals and objectives must be influenced by the opportunities available.[11]

This is especially important when the strategizing takes place not in a one-person, static mode (as in Figure 1-2) but when it involves more than one player and becomes both interactive and dynamic. In the pursuit of goals, one should be prepared to jettison a given set of objectives for another set as the opportunity arises because of chance or the mistakes of the others in the game. While the physics of a situation at one point in time may dictate certain objectives, the fact that the others in the game do or (perhaps more importantly) do not want the same set of objectives suggests that one change one's objectives.

It is not realistic to have a model of strategy which does not allow for goals and objectives to be influenced by the availability of strategies and tactics. One could argue against goals being as strongly affected as objectives, but one should be open to the possibility of a strong feedback between the ends and means levels.

Effectiveness versus Efficiency.   Some of the biggest arguments among those making strategic decisions are over the issue of effectiveness—will it work?—and efficiency—what will it cost? Nowhere is this trade-off seen more clearly than in the military. At war there is seldom a margin for error. A general who calculates that 10,000 soldiers are needed to achieve a given objective may none-theless send in 15,000, reasoning that if he miscalculated on the 10,000 and lost as a result, the outcome would be worse and more costly than sending in 15,000 soldiers in the first instance. The waste incurred by sending in the extra 5,000 was small in comparison to the waste incurred by the possible loss of the entire 10,000 if the battle had been lost. Of course, once the battle was won the general knew that a corps of bean counters from headquarters would show up and question the decision. If 10,000 were what the situation required, they would say, then maybe 9,000 or even 8,500 would have done the job.

Strategy concerns the relationship between the actor (the person taking the action) and the outside world. It specifies the cause-and-result relationships between what the actor does and how the external world responds. "This strategy will cause that set of results" is the statement the strategist makes. If those results are the desired results, then the strategist can say that the strategy is effective; it did what it was supposed to do.

Since most situations that require strategic analysis are not static but inter-active and dynamic, the cause-and-result relationship is neither fixed nor invari-ant as in the physical sciences, and what will really happen when the 8,500, 9,000, 10,000 or 15,000 soldiers are sent in is open to interpretation, argument,

[11] For a discussion of this point, see Robert H. Hayes, "Strategic Planning—Forward in Reverse?," *Harvard Business Review*, 63, no. 6 (November-December 1985), 111–119; B. H. Liddell Hart, *Strategy*, 2nd rev. ed. (New York: Frederick A. Praeger, Publishers, 1954), chapter 19, 333–346; and James Brian Quinn, *Strategies for Change: Logical Incrementalism* (Homewood, IL: Richard D. Irwin, 1980), chapter 5.

and conjecture. The opposition could act differently than one expected, for example, as Hannibal did to Varro. The outcome is always arguable, and serious strategists invite others to test the strategy, to point out its flaws or weaknesses. Almost by definition, then, to talk about strategy is to talk first about effectiveness. Strategy concerns the degree to which the actual results correspond to the desired results.

Tactics, on the other hand, are the actual actions that the actor takes—they are totally under the actor's control. Of course, the actions may be frustrated by the outside world, but they are not taken in the first place unless the actor wills them. In contrast to strategy, then, tactics are internal and the criterion by which they are judged is not effectiveness but efficiency: Are these tactics the most cost-effective way of implementing a given strategy?

The effectiveness/efficiency argument is frequently put into a useful catch phrase, first used by Peter Drucker.[12] He suggested that the first question to be asked was "Are we doing the right things?" The first concern must be with effectiveness—obtaining the desired outcome. Only then will the question "Are we doing things right?" make sense. Drucker's point is that efficiency in the absence of effectiveness is nonsensical.

Decisions and Implementation.   The nineteenth-century military strategist Carl von Clausewitz was concerned that strategy be real—that the ideas about how to use troops be translatable into actions that produced what the ideas promised. But he also realized that there was, inevitably, slippage between the actions as the strategist conceived of them and the reality of what was achieved in the field. He used the term *friction* to describe the cause of the difference between the strategic idea and its actual achievement.[13]

This insight into what actually happens (von Clausewitz had years of actual battle experience) led him to understand that effective strategy grows out of the tactics that are implementable. If the strategy did not direct the soldiers into situations where the advantage was on their side, then it was a bad strategy. The general must have a deep understanding of what the tactics are capable of to create strategies that work.

The concept of friction also led von Clausewitz to understand that, to be good, a strategy must work even if its implementation is only ordinary. A strategy is flawed if it works only when superbly executed. When superbly executed, the long bomb pass in football can put points on the scoreboard faster than any other play. However, the play works only when the timing and skills of all involved are at their highest. No coach can build a game strategy on such a play. A game plan within the competence of mere mortals is better.

A strategic decision is nothing without implementation. Strategy depends on the possibility and potential of tactics. It must be capable of achieving its goal—to win by placing those who implement in a position where the odds are in their favor, even if they are ordinary mortals with average skills.

---

[12] Hofer and Schendel, *Strategy Formulation*, p. 2.
[13] Carl von Clausewitz, *On War*, edited and translated by Michael Howard and Peter Paret (Princeton, NJ: Princeton University Press, 1976).

Content versus Process.   General Eisenhower once said that plans were worthless but that planning was everything. The first known book ever written on strategy devotes considerable space to the *process* of strategizing. At the end of the first chapter in his book *The Art of War*, Sun Tzu says,

> Now if the estimates made in the temple before hostilities indicate victory it is because calculations show one's strength to be superior to that of his enemy; if they indicate defeat, it is because calculations show that one is inferior. With many calculations, one can win; with few one cannot. How much less chance of victory has one who makes none at all! By this means I examine the situation and the outcome will be clearly apparent.[14]

Sun Tzu says that the creation of strategy depends on a weighing of each side's strengths beforehand. His statement "With many calculations, one can win" does not mean that by adding up the same numbers many times the total will somehow change and turn sure defeat into victory. He means that if one has the data and thinks about it enough, one may be able to devise a winning strategy. This is the first known description of the strategic planning process. More of Sun Tzu's thoughts about strategy are summarized in Exhibit 1-3.

It is not possible to learn strategy, per se. One can only learn how to *create* strategy. This is why the strategic planning process is important.[15] The strategist is the prisoner of the way the strategic problem is presented and of the information provided. If the process is flawed, if it does not bring the right data to the strategist at the right time, it is unlikely that the result will be right either.[16]

While it is possible to analyze strategy without examining the process by which it was created, one cannot criticize the strategist's plan unless one starts the process with only that information available to the strategist at the time. The rightness of a strategy can be interpreted in several ways.[17] One is through the eyes of the strategist when the strategy was devised—given what knowledge was available at that time, was the strategy chosen a reasonable choice? By this view one can say that Varro made a reasonable choice in dividing his cavalry equally. A second interpretation is based on objective reality (and perhaps hindsight). In retrospect, was the strategy right? Varro's even division of his cavalry was, after all, the key to his loss of the battle that he should have won; therefore, it was objectively wrong. A third interpretation considers the adequacy of the strategic planning process. This interpretation says that Varro failed because his planning process was flawed in not providing him with the intelligence he needed to make the correct decision. Varro failed not because he was not a good strategist but because he did not set up a good strategic planning system!

---

[14] From *The Art of War* by Sun Tzu, translated by Samuel B. Griffith. Copyright © 1963 by Oxford University Press, Inc. Reprinted by permission.

[15] The strategic planning process is examined in depth in chapter 12.

[16] "Clausewitz: Man of the Year," *New York Times*, January 28, 1991, p. A23.

[17] Chapter 13 discusses the means by which strategy is evaluated.

EXHIBIT 1-3

Sun Tzu: *The Art of War*

The Art of War was likely written between 500 and 400 B.C. by an individual called Sun Tzu (scholars dispute his exact identity) who, by the nature of the textual material, must have had considerable experience in war. War in China had, by that time, already become a sophisticated and large-scale undertaking with armies numbering in the hundreds of thousands. Such large armies demanded careful planning just to maintain let alone wield as an effective force in battle. Generals and their strategists were professionals in the service of their lords and gave much time over to the study of fighting and strategy.

Sun Tzu's book consists of some thirteen short chapters with titles such as "Estimates," "Terrain," "Marches," "Offensive Strategy," and even "Employment of Secret Agents." The book is written in the form of short statements or verses, averaging perhaps 30 to 40 per chapter. As the following selections will show, Sun Tzu's approach to winning was simple: enter only those battles that you are sure of winning beforehand. To know if you will win requires that you do your homework and that homework must include a lot of calculating. The following give the flavor of his analysis and insight:

> Victory is the main object in war . . . we
> have not yet seen a clever operation that was
> prolonged . . . for there has never been a
> protracted war from which a country has
> benefited. (p. 73)

> Generally in war the best policy is to take a
> state intact; to ruin it is inferior to this . . .
> To subdue the enemy without fighting is
> the acme of skill . . . Thus, what is of
> supreme importance in war is to attack the
> enemy's strategy . . . Next best is to attack
> his alliances, the next best is to attack his army.
> (pp. 77, 78)

> This is the art of offensive strategy . . .
> When ten to the enemy's one, surround him . . .
> When five times his strength, attack him . . .
> If double his strength, divide him . . .
> If equally matched you may engage him . . .
> If weaker numerically, be capable of
> withdrawing . . . And if in all respects
> unequal, be capable of eluding him, for a
> small force is but booty for one more powerful.
> (pp. 79, 80)

> Know the enemy and know yourself; in a
> hundred battles you will never be in peril . . .
> When you are ignorant of the enemy but

EXHIBIT 1-3 (cont.)

---

know yourself, your chances of winning or
losing are equal . . . If ignorant both of
your enemy and of yourself, you are certain
in every battle to be in peril. (p. 84)

Invincibility depends on one's self; the
enemy's vulnerability on him . . . It follows
that those skilled in war can make themselves
invincible but cannot cause an enemy to be
certainly vulnerable . . . Invincibility lies
in the defense; the possibility of victory in
the attack . . . One defends when his
strength is inadequate; he attacks when it is
abundant. (p. 85)

To foresee a victory which the ordinary man
can foresee is not the acme of skill . . .
the skillful commander takes up a position in
which he cannot be defeated and misses no
opportunity to master his enemy . . . Thus a
victorious army wins its victories before
seeking battle; an army destined to defeat
fights in the hope of winning. (pp. 86, 87)

SOURCE: Sun Tzu, *The Art of War*, trans. by Griffith. Reprinted by permission.

THE RULES OF COMPETITIVE STRATEGY

To contend that there are specific rules of strategy may be presumptuous. Those
who have studied strategy, whether in war, games, or sports, have a surprisingly large amount of overlap in their thinking. The following rules are by no
means comprehensive but do offer insight into the areas about which most
strategists agree.[18] Exhibit 1-4 presents the essence of strategy as distilled by
B. H. Liddell Hart, a twentieth-century military strategist.

THINKING MUST PRECEDE ACTING.   All strategists are united on this point. To
rush off and compete without thinking first about whether this is a fight worth
fighting or how it should be fought contradicts every insight that innumerable
soldiers, generals, and game players throughout the centuries have gained.

---

[18] Quinn provides a comprehensive listing of principles in chapter 5 of his book *Strategies for Change:
Logical Incrementalism*; see also William A. Cohen "War in the Marketplace," *Business Horizons*, 29,
no. 2 (March-April 1986), 10–20; and W. A. French, J. B. Ford, P. Heil, and G. Schultz, "The Military
Strategy behind Japanese Market Dominance," in W. D. Guth, ed., *Handbook of Business Strategy:
1985/1986 Yearbook* (New York: Warren, Gorham & Lamont, 1985).

EXHIBIT 1-4

Liddell Hart's Concentrated Essence of Strategy

   B. H. Liddell Hart wrote over twenty books on warfare and the history of war. He is best known, however, for his book *Strategy*, which, along with the works of Sun Tzu and von Clausewitz, is one of the most read works on the topic. In his chapter 20, Hart attempts to distill what he terms the fundamental and universal truths of experience with respect to strategy. Prior to giving his list, however, he further states that all of the principles of war can be condensed into the single word *concentration*, by which he means the concentration of strength against weakness. Furthermore, after listing his eight principles, Hart cautions the reader that two other problems must be solved before and after the eight principles are used in battle. These he terms *dislocation* and *exploitation*. Dislocation precedes battle and, in Hart's concept, is the action taken by the strategist that creates the opportunity to win. Exploitation is what the commander does after winning to exploit the win before the enemy can recover. In Hart's view, forgetting these is the cause of much of the indecisiveness of warfare. One must make the enemy do something wrong in the first place to make the principles work.

   "Adjust your end to your means." Hart warns that it is "folly to bite off more than you can chew." Objectives must take account of the limitations of one's means.
   "Keep your object always in mind." It is okay to adapt a plan as circumstances evolve, but opportunism should never lose sight of the object.
   "Choose the line of least expectation." Look at yourself through the enemy's eyes and think about what actions it is the least probable that the enemy will try to prevent.
   "Exploit the line of least resistance." If the results of such a strategy take you in the direction of your goal and it is the most easily achieved strategy, do it.
   "Take a line of operation which offers alternative objectives." Current usage would suggest that all strategies have a positive fall-back position. Hart argues more positively, reckoning that if you can win in more than one way by a particular strategy you put your opponent in a dilemma. Your opponent may not be able to guard against more than one objective and has to choose what to defend.
   "Do not throw your weight into a stroke whilst your opponent is on guard." This is the source of one of Hart's most quoted phrases: "No commander should launch a real attack upon an enemy in position" unless his or her power of resistance has been "paralyzed."
   "Do not renew an attack along the same line (or in the same form) after it has once failed." Hart clearly notes that this holds true even if the second attack is with a much larger force. He estimates that any attack will cause the defender to analyze the results and strengthen himself or herself on that front in the interim.

QUANTITATIVE KNOWLEDGE IS KEY.   Whether it is the number of soldiers in an army or the average height of a basketball team or the number of home runs an individual hit, some quantitative measure of strength is essential. Sun Tzu used some sort of primitive abacus to compare the relative strengths of his and his enemy's armies.

FAST-ACTING STRATEGIES DOMINATE SLOW ONES.   All competition requires resources and willpower, both of which are consumed by time. A strategy which requires a long time to achieve its objective is likely to run out of resources and willpower. In addition, time brings new factors into the competitive equation that were not present at the beginning—factors just as likely to favor the opponent as oneself. This changes the nature of the competition from one of strategy based on known or estimated probabilities to a gamble with unknown probabilities.

VICTORY MUST PRESERVE THE VALUE OF THE OBJECTIVE.   The only true victory is one in which the prize is still worth winning. A scorched-earth policy in war, for example, brings the victor little but a population without the human, agricultural, or economic means to feed itself.

ATTACK ONLY THOSE YOU CAN BEAT.   Poker players are fond of saying that the only way to win consistently in poker is to play with players worse than yourself. When the competition is for life and death, either directly or over the economic resources that maintain it, to do otherwise is to court death or poverty.

DEFENSE IS THE STRONGER FORM OF COMPETITION.   The concept of defense is the parrying of a blow characterized by waiting for the blow.[19] This waiting time allows the defender to gain the advantage of position and inertia. To win, the attacker must apply a stronger force to dislodge the defender than the defender needs to hold its position, so defense must be the stronger form of competition.

SUPERIORITY IN THE ESSENTIAL COMPETITIVE FACTOR IS ALL.   In his analysis of war, von Clausewitz's contribution was to reduce war to its essential competitive factors, the laws of physics that controlled its outcome: force and violence. In his terms, then, the goal of military strategy is to put a larger and more violent army than the opponent has *at the point of attack*. If you do, you win; if not, you lose. One must understand the essence of competition—the laws of physics—in the specific situation and gain superiority in these essentials. To do otherwise is to lose.

INVINCIBILITY IS THE ONLY TRUE DEFENSE.   To base a strategy on an assumption that a competitor will not attack is to trust fate. The essence of strategy is to build a defense that can withstand any possible attack. One must assume the worst of the competitor and build strategy on that basis.

STRATEGY REQUIRES THE EXPLOITATION OF UNIQUE STRENGTHS.   Successful strategy is built on using one's unique characteristics. To base a strategy on strengths which others also possess or can easily acquire is to play from a

---

[19] von Clausewitz, *On War*, p. 357.

position of equality or inferiority, for one's opponents can easily duplicate and neutralize one's advantage.

STRATEGY IN ECONOMIC COMPETITION

Economic competition is obviously not the same as warfare. While business strategists may speak of killing their competitors, for the great majority the term is only a metaphor. While the metaphor may give some insight into the issues facing business strategists, for many people that metaphor neither illuminates nor communicates. This section begins by exploring the basic idea of economic competition and then explores the relevance of several alternative metaphors by which the strategic principles relevant to economic competition can be better understood. In a sense, this section begins the search for the laws of physics which govern economic competition.

Basic Economic Competition

When a good or service is produced and consumed, utility is created which has a value. Competition determines who gets that value. Contrary to the usual conception, this competition takes place not only among the members of an industry as they compete with one another for the patronage of customers, but between the industry and its customers, its suppliers, substitute products, and the firms that seek to enter the industry as well. Consider, for example, the competition that exists between any buyer and seller. The buyer always wants to pay as little as possible for the product, while the seller wants to get as high a price as possible. Both are competing for the value created by the production and consumption of the product. One of the major structural determinants of the profitability of an industry (and therefore of the firms that exist within it) is a function of its bargaining power with respect to its customers. The impact of this position is felt even before the firms in the industry begin to compete for the value the industry is able to capture. Figure 1-3 illustrates this more complete view of economic competition. It depicts the five forces that affect competition and profitability in the ethical (e.g., prescription) drug industry and for the firms that compete within it. The following paragraphs expand on this approach to analyzing economic competition. The analysis that follows takes the viewpoint of the existing competitors in the industry. In Figure 1-3 they are located in the center box labeled "Competitor Rivalry."[20]

Competition along the Supplier-to-Customer Dimension. The industry (box in center of Figure 1-3) buys raw materials, labor, and other inputs from suppliers (box on left) and transforms them into a product or service that delivers utility and therefore has value to customers (box on right). The three form a "chain" that

---

[20] This section draws on the ideas of Michael Porter. See, for example, his article "How Competitive Forces Shape Strategy," *Harvard Business Review*, 57, no. 2 (March-April 1979), 137–145; or *Competitive Strategy* (New York: Free Press, 1980).

Figure 1-3 Competitive forces at work in the ethical drug industry

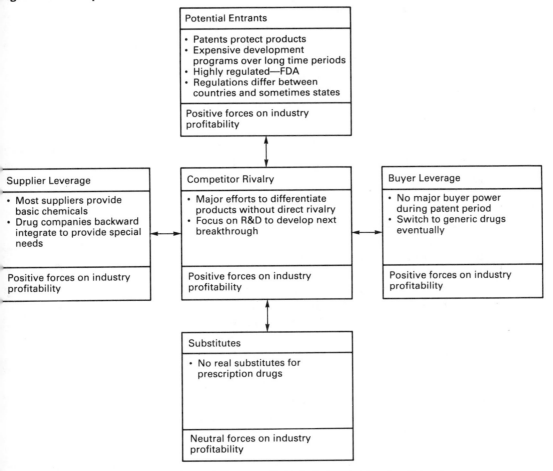

Summary: Concentration of favorable forces defines a profitable industry structure for ethical drugs.

SOURCE: Roland L. Roehrich, "The Relationship between Technological and Business Innovation," *Journal of Business Strategy*, 5, no. 2 (fall 1984), p. 64. Reprinted from *Journal of Business Strategy* (New York: Warren, Gorham & Lamont), Copyright © 1984 Warren, Gorham & Lamont Inc. Used with permission.

transforms raw materials into something useful to consumers. The value to the customer (as in the answer to the question "What's it worth to you?") constitutes a ceiling on the value which is available to the entire chain. The customer will be happy to pay a lower price if it becomes possible or available, however. That value will be distributed among all three members of the chain (suppliers, firm, customer) depending on the bargaining power of each.

As an easy case, assume that a pharmaceutical manufacturer obtained a patent on a new miracle drug. The drug is manufactured out of ordinary chemicals freely available on the open market from a large number of suppliers, and the drug manufacturer has no particular power over the suppliers. However, the drug maker does have the bargaining power compared to its customers in two ways: (1) When it comes to their health, consumers are little concerned with price; and (2) by virtue of the legal monopoly conferred by the patent, consumers have no alternative but to buy from that company. In this instance the value created in the chain will be captured primarily by the drug manufacturer. There is no competition from other drug manufacturers, so the price will begin to approach the value it delivers to the user. This kind of analysis can tell us how the value created by the production and consumption of the good is divided on the horizontal dimension.

Competition with Substitutes and New Entrants.   The vertical axis in Figure 1-3 deals with another dimension of competition. In brief, it can be seen as placing a limit on the value that a given industry can appropriate. First, the existence of substitute goods (box on bottom in Figure 1-3) puts a limit on the price an industry can charge customers. As the price of any product approaches the product's utility to the consumer, the attractiveness of lower-priced substitutes increases and consumers switch purchases to the more economically attractive alternative. The competition among alternate sources of energy provides a good example of this. When oil prices rose after the oil embargo of the mid-1970s, many people who heated with oil retrofit their boilers to burn gas and coal as well as oil. As a result, whenever the price of any of the three gets out of line, the customer quickly switches to the lowest-priced substitute. The drug industry, however, is in a favorable position in this respect—it has no real substitutes until the patents expire and generic drugs emerge.

Moreover, as any industry increases the amount of value that it can capture (either by the high prices it charges its customers or because of the low prices it pays its suppliers), its profitability becomes attractive to firms not currently in the industry but capable of entry. These potential entrants are shown as the top box in Figure 1-3. The entry of these new firms into the industry adds to its productive capacity and actual output, and as supply increases relative to demand, the industry's relative bargaining power with customers diminishes. For example, within five years of the date that the CAT scan machine was introduced as a medical device, some seventeen competitors had entered the business. In the first several years before their entrance, however, demand was so high that the few existing suppliers were able to demand and receive $100,000 deposits from customers. Later entrants, however, were willing to forgo those deposits and offered better-performing machines for the same price as the earlier entrants' machines.[21] Patents, the long development time, and the intensive Food and Drug Administration (FDA) regulations of safety and efficacy deter potential new entrants in the drug industry.

Competition within the Industry.   When output expands to exceed demand as a result of the aforementioned processes, the bargaining balance between industry and customers is reversed. Competitors vie with each other for customers, and

---

[21] "International Systems CT Scanners," *Harvard Business School Case* 9-578-182 (1978).

customers reap the major share of the value created in the form of lower prices produced by such competition. The lower-prices form of competition may also take the form of competitors offering higher quality, better performance, or even larger quantities of a product for the same price. Anyone who has moved and noted the differences in apartment rental practices between two cities can testify to the effect that supply and demand can have. In a city with limited supply (in New York City in recent years, for example, the vacancy rate has averaged less than 1%), there are no free months and the tenant may have to pay a fee to a broker to find an apartment. Alternatively, in a city like Houston which overbuilt housing and office space during the oil boom in the late 1970s and early 1980s in advance of demand that was never realized, a prospective renter will find owners willing to make any concession necessary to attract a renter.

There are two concerns at the industry level: (1) the *intensity of competition* within the industry, and (2) the *division of the value among the competitors* that the industry captures. The intensity of competition within an industry is a function not only of its relative bargaining position vis-à-vis the four external forces (suppliers, customers, potential entrants, and substitutes) but of the number and relative size of the firms within the industry, especially as compared to the level and growth of demand for the industry's output. Other factors, such as the cost structure of the business, the nature of the products, and the goals and objectives of the competitors, also contribute to the intensity of competition. Consider, for example, the aforementioned Houston rental market. It is an industry which attracted a large number of competitors. But because of high growth expectations which failed to materialize, competition is intense. Commercial and residential building owners fight each other for scarce customers in an attempt to get some positive return on their sunk investments instead of the zero return if they just shut their doors and abandoned the buildings.

Competition within the drug industry, on the other hand, is less directly cutthroat. It is focused on the use of research and development (R&D) to create unique products, so direct, head-to-head product competition is reduced. This makes it possible for each producer to win without necessarily causing a competitor to lose. In 1984, for example, return on equity (ROE) in the drug industry was 18.5%.[22] On the other hand, in the tire industry, which resembles the Houston real estate market with vast amounts of production overcapacity and directly comparable products, median ROE was only 5.1%.

Competition within an industry determines which of the industry's competitors gets the larger share of the value the industry itself captures. If one competitor, for example, is not able to produce a product up to the quality level of the others in the industry, or it has poor cost controls, or its sales methods are just not as winning as its competitors', then its share of the value in the form of sales and profits will be less than its competitors' shares. A superior competitor, one able to more accurately and efficiently produce and sell those satisfactions valued by customers, will obtain a larger share. Com-

---

[22] Roland L. Roehrich, "Relationship between Technological and Business Innovation," p. 63.

petitors with essentially equivalent products and resources should receive approximately equal shares.

Implications for Strategy

This view of economic competition identifies the factors that determine the
success of firms. First, *successful firms choose their battles carefully.* They analyze
the present and potential future attractiveness of an industry as determined by
the forces of the five factors (suppliers, customers, potential entrants, substitutes, and other competitors) that operate on it. Some industries are simply less
attractive arenas in which to operate. The structural characteristics are such that
the industry as a whole is not able to capture and hold much of the value created
in the chain. The American steel industry has been generally unprofitable for
much of the last twenty years, while industries such as pharmaceuticals and
electronics have consistently produced profits.[23]

Second, *successful firms seek situations in which they can gain unfair advantages
over their rivals.* The competitive position that the individual firm has relative to
the other firms in the industry is the factor that determines the firm's profits.
Because of its long history as a marketer of mechanical accounting machines and
systems, IBM knew more about the firms and the applications where computers
would be economically valuable than did those who invented them. This proved
to be its unfair advantage, since IBM found it far easier to acquire the computing
technology that it needed than its technologically sophisticated competitors
found it to acquire the applications knowledge and customer relationships and
trust they needed to sell their machines. This head start has enabled IBM to earn
consistently higher profits than its rivals.

GM's unfair advantage over its rivals had it source in its large market share.[24]
This large market share gave it scale economies in both manufacturing and
marketing, as shown in Table 1-1. Because of its significantly lower manufacturing and administrative costs, GM consistently outperformed all other American automobile companies for years. It earned an average 18.3% return on
equity for the period from 1951 to 1975, while its closest rival, Ford, earned only
12.2%. GM's return was over twice that of Chrysler, which earned an average of
only 8.2% over the same period.[25]

Third, *successful competitors compete wisely.* Since profitability is determined
by competitive intensity, wise competitors seek ways of competing that do not
lead to destructive types and levels of competition. For example, they seek to
focus competition onto product benefits rather than onto price, since price competition is more volatile; they seek to gain strong positions that deter competi-

[23] Lacy Glenn Thomas, "The Economics of Strategic Planning: A Survey of the Issues" in Lacy Glenn
Thomas, ed., *The Economics of Strategic Planning: Essays in Honor of Joel Dean* (Lexington, MA: Lexington Books, 1986).
[24] The question about how GM achieved that share in the first place is an equally important strategic
question, but the advantage it gave GM versus rivals cannot be denied.
[25] Thomas, "The Economics of Strategic Planning," p. 4.

TABLE 1-1 *Economies of Scale in Production, Marketing, and Product Development, U.S. Automobile Industry, 1966*

	MARKET SHARE	RATIO OF COST OF GOODS SOLD TO SALES	RATIO OF SELLING, GENERAL, AND ADMINISTRATIVE COSTS TO SALES	RETURN ON EQUITY
General Motors	50.1%	80.0%	1.3%	21.2%
Ford	26.1	84.8	2.7	13.0
Chrysler	15.4	85.7	5.2	11.1
American	2.9	87.9	13.4	−5.9
Studebaker	exit	89.1	15.6	−21.9

NOTE: Market share data, *Automotive Industries*; other data, corporate annual reports. All figures are from 1966, except Studebaker-Packard figures, which are from 1963.

SOURCE: Reprinted with the permission of Lexington Books, an imprint of Macmillan, Inc., from *The Economics of Strategic Planning* by Lacy Glenn Thomas III.

tors from attacking; they seek to satisfy customers' needs so customers have no reason to seek competitive suppliers and potential competitors can find no weakness to attack. Wise competitors remember that the object of the game is profitability, not dead competitors.

Fourth, *successful competitors seek to change the competitive structure.* Firms that find themselves at the mercy of powerful buyers or sellers seek alliances or moves that allow them to integrate forward or backward to reduce vulnerability. They seek to establish the strong patents, brand identification, customer loyalties, and technological leadership positions that discourage the entrance of new competitors, which increases competition and reduces profits. They understand that changing the rules can be more advantageous than following them.

A SOCIOBIOLOGICAL MODEL OF ECONOMIC COMPETITION

Bruce Henderson has been a leading thinker in the field of strategy. He founded The Boston Consulting Group, the first firm to specialize in business strategy. In his constant search for models of competition by which to analyze issues in competitive strategy, he has suggested that the concepts of natural competition as developed in biology and especially as advanced by sociobiologists may provide a better model than models based on purely economic bases.

Natural Competition

Henderson describes natural competition as the basic form of competition between living organisms for their necessary life resources. Organisms that more effectively obtain sustenance and that more efficiently process it preempt those resources from their competitors, thereby weakening the competitors at the same time those resources are strengthening the organism. Over time, this process leads to the extinction of the less effective competitor through the process known as *natural selection.*

In such a system, the continued existence of two seemingly similar competitors requires that there be some differences between them. If there were not some difference, then over time the superior would gain at the expense of the inferior (even if that superiority were only slight). Continued coexistence requires that each have some difference that gives it a unique and significant advantage over the other (and any other competitor, for that matter) in some subsection of the environment in which it can preempt the required resources.

This process of natural competition produces two kinds of competition: (1) *horizontal* (among similar organisms for resources needed in common), and (2) *vertical* (between levels of organisms in the ecological food chain). As the biological landscape demonstrates, over long periods of time natural competition creates a large and complex diversity of organisms with a wide variety of individual characteristics. However, for this to occur, there must be diversity in the resources and environmental conditions that can be traded off one for the other. If not, then each competitive group would not be able to become superior in some way by specializing in some segment.

The processes of biological competition and natural selection can be seen to parallel the model of economic competition described earlier.[26] Horizontal competition takes place among the competitors within an industry and with substitutes and potential new entrants. Vertical competition is similar to that which occurs between suppliers to an industry and between the industry and its competitor industries. Vertical integration in business is the parallel to the ecological food chain in biology. As a metaphor for understanding competition in business, the concept of natural competition can offer real insights. Exhibit 1-5 lists the business implications of natural competition.

Strategic Competition

There is a difference between natural selection as observed in nature and strategic competition between human beings individually and as those individuals combine to form organizations and businesses. Natural competition just happens. Through natural selection and mutation, those organisms that possess the characteristics needed for continued existence prosper and survive. Those that do not eventually disappear. Strategic competition, on the other hand, is conscious—it recognizes and acts on the factors that are affecting the organism's viability rather than awaiting the generations required for natural selection to filter out those with the requisite characteristics (or for spontaneous mutation to occur); it can change itself by itself. In Henderson's words: "Strategic competition is not an alternative or substitute for natural competition. It is the deliberate

---

[26] The natural *selection* perspective is not universally accepted. Some would take an *adaptation* perspective in explaining the relationship between organizational change and the environment. See Michael T. Hannan and John Freeman, "The Population Ecology of Organizations," *American Journal of Sociology,* 82, no. 5 (March 1977), 929–964.

EXHIBIT 1-5

Major Implications of the Sociobiological Model
of Natural Competition

- *Businesses which continue in existence over time have a unique advantage over all others with which they compete.* If this were not the case, then those other firms would have crowded the business out of existence.
- *Businesses which are most similar to each other will compete most severely.* This is the key insight made by Darwin in his work.
- *Effective competition produces a wide range of sizes among competing businesses.*
- *Where one competitor has a clear and visible superiority, there will be a very low level of competition from others.* This insight is predictable based on the analyses of military strategists.
- *The smaller the number of key strategic variables in an industry, the smaller the number of competitors that will exist.* This is so because each competitor needs a unique differential advantage if it is to succeed. There is a relationship between the number of competitors and the number of key strategic variables.
- *Entry sequence is a critical factor.* The successful entry of a new competitor requires a clear superiority over all existing competitors in some part of the market.

SOURCE: Based on the work of Bruce Henderson, "Understanding the Forces of Strategic and Natural Competition," 11–15; and "The Anatomy of Competition," *Journal of Marketing*, 47 (spring 1983), 7–11.

prediction and management of the higher orders of the controlling variables."[27]

In these terms, then, natural competition is expedient and evolutionary while strategic competition is deliberate and revolutionary. Natural competition, on a moment-to-moment basis, seizes on any adaptation that offers the opportunity for bettering the organism. It is expedient in that sense. It is evolutionary in that these trial-and-error changes are always small and incremental since they occur within the framework of the existing organism. In opposition, strategic change is deliberate. Chance certainly plays a role, as does trial and error, but strategic competition is marked by carefully considered and tightly reasoned actions. As a result, the change that strategic competition can realize is not as constrained as that which natural competition can produce—it is able to make very large changes in the competitive relationships that determine the viability of the organism.

Strategic competition is not without its drawbacks, however. Along with the opportunity to alter its characteristics significantly and to determine its fate comes the opportunity to fail. As a strategic competitor is able to make larger

[27] Bruce Henderson, "Understanding the Forces of Strategic and Natural Competition," *Journal of Business Strategy*, 1, no. 3 (winter 1981), 11–15.

changes, it is also able to make larger mistakes. Moreover, in strategic competition the competitors are not unthinking or unaware. They are able to discern the changes that are taking place and respond to them. Most important, since the change that strategic competition seeks to bring about is offensive, almost by definition, the defenders have the major competitive advantage. Success depends on the actions of the defenders as well as on the actions of the strategic competitor.

DEVISING STRATEGY

Getting started in strategizing is not difficult. It is, however, a different task than many have encountered previously. As a result, some find it difficult to envision how one goes about strategizing. This section is intended to help the strategist get started. It begins with a description of a simplified model of the strategic thought process. It reviews some common strategic moves and postulates several simple principles by which to develop strategy.

The Basic Model of Strategy Development

The basic strategic thought process is not difficult. As shown in Figure 1-4, it has four phases: intelligence, analysis, alternative generation, and evaluation. As with any such model, this representation is a simplification and abstraction of a more complex process, discussed in detail in chapter 12.

Intelligence.   A competitor needs knowledge of the three factors in the strategic situation: the environment, the competitors, and itself. Think about the situation with Hannibal and Varro. Hannibal needed to be fully conversant with the terrain on which the battle was to be fought, he needed to know how many troops Varro had and his likely attack plan, and he needed to know what his own capabilities were.

The economic competitor needs the same knowledge. The economic, technological, political, market, and social environments have the same impact on developing business strategy as the weather and terrain have on developing battle strategy. The strategist needs to know the capabilities of the opponents as well as those of his or her own firm. While this may sound obvious, the apparently impersonal nature of the marketplace—especially for those in large organizations—leads many to think that they can compete without specific knowledge of their competitors' resources and capabilities.

Analysis.   The second phase of the process is to compare these factors to obtain an understanding of the opportunities and threats posed by the environment and competitors and to identify the firm's strengths and weaknesses compared to those of competitors. Since the environment and competitors are constantly changing, this process is a continual one.

A declining birth rate is a threat to a toy maker just as the increasing prev-

Figure 1-4 A basic model of the strategic thought process

alence of word processing is to a maker of typewriters. On the other hand, the growth in computer literacy is an opportunity to those who make computer diskettes just as the financial difficulties of one's competitor are an opportunity. The ever-increasing capacity of computer memory chips is an opportunity to makers of notebook and laptop computers at the same time that it poses a threat to the makers of mainframe computers.

Comparing one's own internal capabilities and resources with those of competitors is a critical step in the strategic thought process. The ability to win over competitors is not a function of what a business is capable of but of the difference in those capabilities compared to those of competitors. Since one of the key strategic principles is to position one's strength against the weaknesses of competitors, this is a critical step. It reflects the concept of competitive advantage.

Alternative Generation.   The most difficult step in the process of developing strategy involves generating alternatives that are capable of creating strategic advantage. The processes of intelligence and analysis can be broken down to techniques that can be learned and that, if followed mechanically, will yield reasonable results. Generating alternatives capable of creating strategic advantage can be approached similarly, but ultimately success at this stage comes from a creative leap (which itself may be the result of serendipity, accident, or pure insight).

On the principle that chance favors the prepared mind, however, there are processes which can help to bring together the ingredients necessary to the creative leap. Exhibit 1-6, for example, lists the basics of the military moves of attack and defend. Strategists can use this list to find analogies to their own situation or to spark ideas. Even the most creative individuals will often mechanically list the implications of such moves for their business.

It sometimes seems that getting started in devising strategy is a hopeless

EXHIBIT 1-6

Using the Military Principles of Attack and Defend to Generate Strategic Options

The concepts of attack and defend exist in every competitive situation. There are a number of well-defined types of attack and defense which translate into the wider, nonmilitary competitive sphere. In some sense, the strategist can find the seeds of any strategy within these forms.

Attack. The positive returns that come from competition come from attack. To attack means to seek more than one has, specifically to take that which another possesses. There are two general rules to remember about attack: (1) One should not attack unless the objective cannot be reached in any other way; and (2) attack is weaker than defense, so the attacker must gain superiority over the defender if an attack is to be justified. There are five types of attack:

Frontal: In a frontal attack, one's forces are massed directly opposite those of the opponent. This form of battle would be chosen when one's forces are superior in number to those of the opponent. Sun Tzu suggests that a factor of five to one is needed for a successful frontal attack; Napoleon estimated that a three-to-one advantage was needed.

In the 1970s, three electronics powerhouses—General Electric, RCA, and Xerox—each launched a head-on attack against IBM's stronghold, its mainframe computer business. All three failed. RCA lost $500 million in its quest; at its departure, Xerox noted that its business would have needed another $600 million just to hold the small position it had attained. A head-on attack fails because it strikes at the defender's strength.

Flank: A flank attack directs one's forces against the sides of the enemy's forces where it is weaker. It is a classic strategy for allowing an aggressor that does not have overwhelming superiority to concentrate force and gain superiority of force at the point of attack.

In the mid-1970s, Xerox owned an overwhelming 88% of the plain-paper copier market. By the mid-1980s, it had lost more than half of the market to Japanese copier companies who attacked Xerox's weak flank—the small-size copier market aimed at businesses that could not afford Xerox's large- and medium-size copiers, its only offerings. Had Canon, Sharp, and Ricoh attacked Xerox head on, they would have lost. The flank attack wins because it pits the attacker's strength against the defender's weakness.

Encirclement: In those few instances when one truly has overwhelming and unequivocal superiority, encirclement demonstrates to the opponent the futility of defense. Encirclement attacks the enemy on all fronts simultaneously. A ten-to-one superiority is needed for this strategy, according to Sun Tzu.

Smirnoff vodka used an encirclement strategy in defending itself from Seagram's Wolfschmidt brand vodka, which was introduced and positioned directly against Smirnoff, but at a price $1 lower. Rather than defend, Smirnoff chose to

EXHIBIT 1-6 (cont.)

counterattack using an encirclement strategy. It first raised the price on its Smirnoff brand by $1, putting $2 between it and Wolfschmidt, thereby preserving Smirnoff's premier image. It then introduced a fighting brand (Relska), positioned head-to-head against and at the same price as Wolfschmidt, and to close the circle it then introduced still another brand (Popov) at a price $1 lower than Wolfschmidt. In effect, the moves enveloped Wolfschmidt, which had not anticipated a war on three fronts. As of the mid-1980s, Smirnoff was number one of all domestic and imported vodka in the U.S., and Popov was in the number two spot.

Bypass: A bypass attack succeeds by avoiding direct battle with the enemy. Instead, it wins by attacking areas that are not being defended.

The concept of the bypass strategy is more difficult to envision in business. Diversification moves, such as those followed by Colgate-Palmolive in the 1970s as it sought to position itself in businesses (nonwoven textiles, health care) and markets (international instead of domestic) in which it did not have to fight Procter & Gamble's strengths is one frequently cited example of the bypass strategy.

Guerrilla: Guerrilla attacks produce small victories that, over time, can add up to a reasonably substantial gain. This type of attack works first by reason of the unconventional nature of the tactics used, which make it difficult for the defender to counter. Second, guerrilla attacks are directed at small and weak portions of the defended territory and gain concentration of force in that manner.

In the mid-1980s, IBM became concerned that the success that Japanese companies had exhibited in their invasions of the U.S. markets for cars, cameras, copiers, and electronics could be duplicated in computers. IBM's opportunity for a guerrilla warfare strategy came when it won a lawsuit against Hitachi, Inc., for allegedly stealing IBM software, after which IBM decided to stop disclosing its source codes (which describe the operating system of software needed to run applications programs). This guerrilla-style move put the Japanese computer manufacturers on the defensive by forcing them to divert vast amounts of money and scarce software R&D personnel to rewriting old programs and developing others that would not infringe on IBM's intellectual property rights. The time (estimated by some to be more than five years) and money spent in this manner could not be used to further their attack on IBM and the U.S. market. IBM took advantage of this dislocation to intensify its efforts in the Japanese market itself, further forcing its competitors to protect and defend rather than to expand and attack.

Defense. Defense lacks the well-developed typology of strategies that characterize the attack mode. Nonetheless, there are several types of defense.

Fortification: The classic defense strategy rests on the concept of the protected fort. The idea is to leave no weakness for an attacker to exploit. While it is the

EXHIBIT 1-6 (cont.)

best form of protection against most forms of attack, this strategy is vulnerable to bypass attacks, which win without directly confronting the defender.

General Foods practices market fortification in the coffee business by having strong entries in all physical, price, and perceptual positions in the marketplace. Its Maxwell House brand occupies the center of the market, Sanka the decaffeinated segment, and it has premium and economy brands which complete its market coverage. Key brands are offered in both ground, soluble, and ready-to-brew filter packs. This leaves competitors with few unserved or poorly served consumer needs to capitalize on in an attack.

Preemptive defense: In an apparent reversal of logic, it is often said that a strong offense is the best defense. A preemptive defense is one in which the defender ensures the security of his or her defense by attacking those that are potential adversaries before they become strong enough to pose a threat.

Texas Instruments illustrated the power of the preemptive defense in the early 1970s with the emergence of the first generation of computer memory chips, the 4-K random access memory (RAM). The competitors followed suit during the summer of 1974, announcing product availability and prices. First in was Mostek, quoting a price of $45 on July 10. It was followed by Intel on July 22, with a price of $38, and Motorola on August 6 at $26.25. Texas Instruments then instituted its preemptive defense by pricing its entry at $11.66—one quarter of Mostek's opener and less than half of Motorola's—and effectively capturing the market for TI.

Counterattack: The object of this defense is to preserve, which is a negative objective (especially in comparison to attack). The counterattack, however, allows a defender to capitalize on the mistakes of the attacker or the weaknesses that are demonstrated during his or her attack.

Both the Smirnoff vodka and IBM moves demonstrate elements of counterattack. One frequent form of counterattack is to aim the counterattack at the aggressor's source of cash for the attack, whether that source be a product or a geographical region. The counterattack therefore succeeds two ways: (1) It cuts off the aggressor's cash supply needed to fuel the attack; and (2) it produces gains for the counterattacker at the same time because the attacker cannot defend and attack simultaneously. In one recent example, a European-based firm attacked an American firm in its U.S. market. The U.S. firm had no presence in the European market but quickly established one there, threatening the attacker in its home market and forcing it to moderate its assault on the U.S. market.

SOURCE: Adapted from material in Philip Kotler and Ravi Singh, "Marketing Warfare in the 1980's," *Journal of Business Strategy*, 1, no. 3 (winter 1981), 30–41; and Norton Paley, *The Manager's Guide to Competitive Marketing Strategies* (New York: AMACOM, 1989), chapter 1.

task. There is always that moment when everything and anything seems important and the flash of insight that will illuminate the problem seems to have suffered from a power outage. At such times the following three principles will serve to get the process moving.

THE PRINCIPLE OF OPPOSITION.   Every strategy contains the seeds of its own destruction. Those very factors that give a strategy its strength are the same that give a competitor the means to counter that strategy. Consider, for example, the defensive strategy based on the fort described earlier. The impregnability of the fortress is a function of the solidity of its construction, which also makes it immobile. That very immobility makes it vulnerable to competitors, who literally run around it. One could postulate a principle of opposition for strategy that says simply, "You can win against almost any strategy by pursuing a strategy which takes an opposite approach to competitive advantage."

If the leaders in a market, for example, are succeeding by producing large volumes of a generic product at low prices, then the principle says that you might be able to win by producing small volumes of special-purpose or differentiated product at a high price to meet the needs of those for whom the generic variety is insufficient. Will such a strategy beat the biggies? Probably not, but it will enable its practitioner to win and profit when a strategy of going head-to-head against the existing leaders would have certainly lost.

THE PRINCIPLE OF THE VOID.   At the heart of any strategist's arsenal of ideas is the avoidance of competition. The principle of the void suggests that a business build its strategy around filling needs that others are not serving or, better yet, have not even discovered. The U.S. television market in the 1960s is a good example. At that time, all of the domestic producers of television sets were producing sets with ever-larger screen sizes. Since TVs in their infancy had small and hard-to-see screens, most of the product's evolution had been to increasing screen size. Bigger was better to customers, or so it seemed at that time to the producers in the market.

Sony, the Japanese electronics manufacturer, in looking for a strategy which would allow it to enter the U.S. market successfully, found the void which the domestic producers had overlooked (and perhaps had even created by their own actions): the absence of truly compact, truly portable television sets. These were small (9- to 11-inch screens) and very lightweight sets that anyone could easily pick up and carry around from room to room. By the time domestic producers recognized that there was a void that could be served profitably, Sony already owned it. It had come in during the night (so to speak) and seized territory that the existing competitors were not protecting because they were unaware of it and its value. Sony competed by not competing. In simple terms, strategies based on the principle of the void succeed because the existing competitors do not recognize the competition until it has succeeded, too late to respond effectively.

THE PRINCIPLE OF STRENGTH.   The idea of an unfair advantage is central to the concept of strategy. The principle of strength says simply that the unfair advantage should be based on some characteristic inherent in the strategist's business or which the strategist's firm can acquire but which others cannot easily acquire, if at all. A strategy must recognize and incorporate the strengths of the business for which it is being devised. If it is not based on the *unique* strengths of the business, then any other firm can quickly duplicate the strategy.

As simple as this concept is, it is frequently violated. The idea of fighting on one's own turf has its roots in this principle. Strategists often make the mistake of starting the strategy process by identifying and correcting their weaknesses versus competitors instead of building on their strengths. Correcting a weakness is useful in strategy only if the weakness is detracting from a strategy built on the business's strength.

Peters and Waterman make this point well in their book *In Search of Excellence*; their principle is to "Stick to the Knitting."[28] They note that 3M's success is due to its unique skill in solving problems for industrial customers with products based on 3M's technology. They note how this skill is enshrined in its management, almost all of whom spend some time in the sales force working on the practical application of the firm's technology to market needs. They cite other firms, like Hewlett-Packard and Texas Instruments, which have failed in most of their forays outside the technical, industrial markets in which their expertise and ability to think like their customers marked their strengths.

Evaluating Strategy.   Evaluating strategy involves two steps: (1) determining its probability of success by comparing its idea to the basic principles of strategy and strategic advantage; and (2) comparing its probable results against the objectives at which it is aimed. If the strategy idea is based on a sure knowledge of the laws governing the particular competition and meets the basic principles of strategic competition (for example, it pits two strong, well-armed soldiers against one weak, poorly armed enemy soldier), then it should be effective. Table 1-2 provides a checklist of strategic principles cast in a business context.

The second step considers whether the strategy attains the goals set for the business. In a business competition, for example, it is not enough that the strategy win sales away from competitors but that those sales be profitable. Ultimately, every business strategy must meet the objective of contributing to profitability.[29] One of the curious aspects of the real world is that many who devise strategy are often unclear as to just what their business's goals and objectives are. As the saying goes, "If you don't know where you're going, any road will get you there."

STRATEGY AS A MANAGERIAL TASK

In an army, one can conceive of three levels of managerial work. On the firing line are the several levels of officers who are responsible for ensuring that the

---

[28] Thomas J. Peters and Robert H. Waterman, Jr., *In Search of Excellence: Lessons from America's Best-Run Companies* (New York: Harper & Row, 1982), chapter 10.
[29] Chapter 13 discusses at length the evaluation and valuation of strategy.

TABLE 1-2 *A Checklist for the Principles of Marketing Warfare*

	YES	NO
1. Concentration Are resources concentrated at the strategic center of gravity, where they will have decisive effects?	———	———
2. Objective a. Are clear overall objectives specified for the project? b. Are objectives specified for each organization involved in the project? c. Does everyone understand each objective?	——— ——— ———	——— ——— ———
3. Initiative a. Are we dominating the environment and the competition by acting rather than reacting? b. Will the competition have to play "catch-up" as the result of our operations?	——— ———	——— ———
4. Economy of force Are resources allocated to secondary and other nondecisive areas the minimum necessary in order to accomplish their objectives?	———	———
5. Maneuver a. Is positioning of our resources accomplished in such a manner that the overall strategy and objectives are supported? b. Is the positioning of resources being accomplished in a coordinated fashion?	——— ———	——— ———
6. Unity of command Is a single manager assigned responsibility for every task in support of the overall strategy?	———	———
7. Coordination a. Are required tasks of different divisions of the organization coordinated for maximum output? b. Are required tasks of different division of the organization coordinated to avoid optimization of a single division at the expense of the overall organization? c. Is the timing of actions by different divisions of the organization coordinated and in the correct sequence?	——— ——— ———	——— ——— ———
8. Security a. Are precautions being taken to avoid premature exposure of our plans and strategy? b. Are the consequences of the competition's learning of our plans being considered and allowed for?	——— ———	——— ———
9. Surprise Is the factor of surprise built into the strategy so that by the time the competition can react, it will be too late?	———	———
10. Simplicity Are our strategy, tactics, and tasks to be accomplished screened for complexity so that what remains can be realistically accomplished by those required to execute what we have planned?	———	———
11. Flexibility a. Are alternative actions planned should the environment change or should the competition react in a way other than we have planned? b. Do the necessary resources for alternative actions exist?	——— ———	——— ———
12. Exploitation a. Do plans exist for additional actions after our strategies succeed? b. Do resources exist to implement additional actions during the exploitation phase?	——— ———	——— ———

SOURCE: William A. Cohen, "War in the Marketplace." Reprinted from *Business Horizons*, March/April 1986, Figure 3, p. 16. Copyright © 1986 by the Foundation for the School of Business at Indiana University. Used with permission.

fighting is done right. These are the officers whose duty it is to see that the task they have been assigned is achieved. The next level of managerial work is performed by the planners, who see to it that the front-line officers have the soldiers and materials at the right time and in the right place so they can discharge their obligations. The third level is the strategists, who decide what battles are worth fighting and how the army should use its resources to ensure that those battles are winnable and, indeed, won. The strategists' task is to direct the army into those situations in which their victory is a foregone conclusion.

The division of managerial work and responsibilities in a business organization is similar. However, the responsibility for strategic work is often more diffused and, without the impetus of an immediate competitive threat, frequently postponed in favor of a continuation of past policies. In such an environment, strategies may be made and communicated in a rudimentary form. As one manager put it during an interview about the strategic planning process in his company,

> When I was younger I always conceived of a room where all these [strategic] concepts were worked out for the whole company. Later I didn't find any such room . . . The strategy [of the company] may not even exist in the mind of one man. I certainly don't know where it is written down. It is simply transmitted in the series of decisions made.[30]

The lack of a formal process that can be observed and the output of which is written in formal documents does not mean that strategy does not exist or is not important, however. Whether conscious or unconscious, every firm does have a strategy in that it will have made choices about the areas in which it will compete and how it will compete. Those choices may reflect a less than optimal strategy, but they are choices nonetheless. This text, of necessity, presupposes a conscious strategizing process. This does not necessarily require a formal planning system, written documentation, or even presidential-level managers.

As can be seen in Figure 1-5, there are several levels at which strategy is devised in a business organization. At the corporate level, a basic strategy issue is to optimize the returns from a portfolio of businesses—at this level the strategic issue is the choice of the industries in which the corporate capabilities can gain strategic advantage. The business then must select the markets within that industry in which it can best gain advantage versus existing and potential competitors, and then narrow the target down to the segment, niche, and customer levels. Looked at in this manner, one can see that strategy is indeed made and played out at a number of levels. Every participant, therefore, needs to understand strategy in general and the strategy of the business in specific if he or she is to contribute.

The rationale for this approach is both simple and basic: Competition occurs

---

[30] Quoted in James Brian Quinn, "Strategic Change: 'Logical Incrementalism,' " *Sloan Management Review*, 20, no. 1 (fall 1978), p. 7.

Figure 1-5 The market selectivity hierarchy

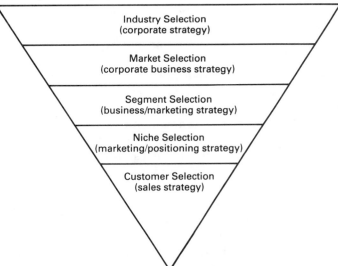

SOURCE: From James M. Hulbert, *Marketing: A Strategic Perspective* (1985), p. 31. Reprinted by permission of James M. Hulbert.

at the point at which a specific product or service is offered to a specific market, segment, niche, or customer. Competitive choices exist at every one of these levels. The advantages a business brings to a specific product or market-level situation may arise in the broader business or corporate framework, but it is the knowledge of the specific needs of a specific market with specific competitors following specific strategies that is needed to devise a winning strategy. The individual responsible for the management of the offering at a given level, therefore, is the one best informed about the threats and opportunities at that level, whether it is the value of the product's franchise with its customer base or distribution channels, or the competitive interactions that have occurred over time.

While the focus of this text is on the individual product and market entry, the same strategy constructs, techniques, perspectives, and methodologies are used at the business level and at the corporate level. But this text is not about strategic management per se or about corporate strategy. It is for those who manage and direct the activities that ensure that a product succeeds in the marketplace. This position exists in many firms under such titles as product (or brand) manager, market manager, business manager, marketing manager/ director, or even vice president or president.

SUMMARY

Strategy is about obtaining an unfair advantage in a competitive situation in which the outcome is more important than the play of the competition. It is the idea about how to use the laws of physics that determine the outcome of a given situation to one's own advantage. The concepts of strategy as developed by military strategists have almost direct application to business competition, especially in the dictum "fight fair, but avoid fair fights."

At the heart of economic competition is the assessment of the relative attractiveness of competitive situations and the relative advantage that the business has within a given situation. Some settings are not conducive to profits, no matter how much advantage a firm has relative to competitors. Profitability is a function not only of the competition that occurs among direct competitors but of the competition that occurs along the supplier-firm-customer dimension for the value created by exchange, as well as with potential new entrants and substitute products all vying to share in that value. This competition is not very different in kind from biological competition, in which only those that match their environment and are advantaged with respect to their competitors survive.

Creating strategy is the task of the individual who relates the firm to the marketplace. This is the point at which strategizing must take place because it is the only point at which the strategist will have full knowledge of the tactics available—the critical resource necessary for good strategy in von Clausewitz's view.

2

COMPETITIVE ADVANTAGE

Military strategists made two great contributions to the idea of strategy. First, one should not enter into a battle unless one knows beforehand that one is certain to win. Second, the strategist must understand the basic principles which determine the outcomes of battles and wars. The concept is the same in business: Do not compete unless you are sure you can win, and to do that you need to know the basic rules that determine the outcome of the competition.

The factor which allows the strategist to say, "We can win that battle" is termed *competitive advantage*—the unfair advantage described in chapter 1. This chapter is about the basic forces which determine the shape and winners of economic competition. It begins by isolating the underlying principle that determines who wins in business competition. This principle concerns *value*. Next, the chapter discusses how firms use value to compete and how, unless they obtain competitive advantage, they cannot earn true economic profit. It then examines three generic routes to delivering value and gaining competitive advantage: low cost, differentiated product, and focus. The chapter closes by examining the factors important to choosing the target of strategic action.

VALUE: THE BASIS OF ECONOMIC COMPETITION

The modern, sophisticated marketplace is, at its roots, no different from primitive barter systems or even two children trading toys or comic books. In none of these settings do participants enter into a transaction, an exchange, unless they feel that they are getting more than they are giving up. Because the exchanges are voluntary, participants may back out at any time they choose before the consummation of the exchange simply by saying, "It's not a good deal."

Since the marketplace exchanges are, for the most part, free of familial or other similar noneconomic contaminants, their only motivation is to make both parties better off than before the exchange. In other words, exchanges are motivated by value. That value may be functionally utilitarian (does something of measurable physical or economic worth) or psychosocial (provides a psycholog-

35

ical or social utility), but for the exchange to occur, each party must perceive the utility he or she will receive. Bargaining and negotiating in this framework are nothing more than the two partners deciding how the value the exchange creates for each will be divided between them.[1]

Since an exchange is a value-creating process (both parties are better off after the exchange than before), there is frequently competition over who gets to be one of the exchange partners. Seldom is the number or relative attractiveness of the buyers and sellers in the marketplace equal, such that each buyer and each seller is satisfied with the number and quality of the transactions completed. For example, we are used to seeing sellers compete among themselves for scarce customers by offering a lower price for the same product performance or, alternatively, better product performance at the same price. Either tactic results in more utility per unit of exchange for the customer (in other words, better *value*), making that seller's exchange offer more attractive than competitors' and more likely, therefore, to be accepted by a potential customer.[2]

But buyers compete, also. At auction sales, for example, buyers compete among themselves by offering increasingly larger sums of money for a given product. In effect, each potential buyer is saying to the seller, "If you trade with me, I'll share with you a larger part of the value the exchange creates for me."[3] Industrial buyers frequently act to establish ongoing relationships with their suppliers so they become preferred customers. Even those who attend the most popular nightclubs cultivate the doormen, who determine which of those waiting in line are allowed entrance.

WINNING IN THE COMPETITION
FOR ECONOMIC EXCHANGE

There is seldom any question about what it means to win in war. Winning in the competition for economic exchange, however, has two aspects. One aspect of winning is the number of exchanges completed. A firm must first entice buyers to exchange with it in preference to competitors (or to no exchange at all) if it is to win. From a seller's perspective, winning in this sense means higher absolute sales and profits. A second aspect of winning is the proportion of the value created by the exchanges that the seller gets to keep. The seller with the highest relative profitability rate per exchange is also said to win.

A firm can win in any of three ways, then. An overall winner would be the firm with the greatest number of transactions completed at the highest relative

---

[1] Richard P. Bagozzi, "Marketing as Exchange," *Journal of Marketing*, 39, no. 4 (October 1975), 32–39; and Franklin S. Houston and Julie B. Gassenheimer, "Marketing and Exchange," *Journal of Marketing*, 51, no. 4 (October 1987), 3–18.

[2] Since value can be defined as the amount of satisfaction one receives per unit of expenditure (value = satisfaction/price), value can be increased either by increasing the numerator or reducing the denominator. This point is discussed further in chapter 3.

[3] See Kotler and Levy, "Buying Is Marketing Too!," *Journal of Marketing*, 37, no. 1 (January 1973), 54–59.

profitability rate. However, one can also speak of a firm with a large volume of transactions as winning, as one can of the firm which keeps a large proportion of the value created by the transactions it completes. Losing could mean that a firm has a smaller than desired number of exchanges or keeps a smaller percentage of the value as profits.

The preceding discussion of winning, however, neglected the firm's asset base and the return those transactions gave relative to the size of the investment base necessary to support them. From the viewpoint of financial theory, one wins in economic exchange when one's actions increase shareholder wealth.[4] One does that by increasing the value of the business's assets over and above what they cost by maximizing the future stream of earnings that their use can generate as measured by the net present value of that income stream. If one assumes an efficient equity market, then that value is reflected in the relationship between the market's valuation of the firm's equity to the book value of the firm's assets. This is termed the firm's *market-to-book ratio*. If it is greater than one, then the market's consensus is that the future will add to the value of the assets.[5]

This is important because there are many ways of winning in the competition to complete exchanges which do not add to a firm's long-run value. In the simplest terms, one could win in the competition for exchanges by selling at an amount lower than the firm's marginal costs of production. The firm could win in the competition to complete exchanges with customers but lose by having to give up all of the value created in the exchange and then some to entice the customer away from competitors. Less drastically, one can win exchanges by selling at an amount which does not capture enough value to yield an economically profitable return on the firm's investment base.

Figure 2-1 portrays the relationships just described. If ultimate winning is measured in return on investment (ROI), then there are four main routes to improvement. Starting from the top of the diagram, one can (1) decrease costs, (2) increase price, (3) increase the number of units sold, or (4) reduce the size of the investment (thereby reducing investment intensity). Assuming that one can create marketplace exchanges—create actual sales transactions—then these four are viable routes. However, this analysis assumes that competitors are pursuing the same objective (ROI) in the same time frame and possess the accounting and managerial reward systems that measure and shape managerial behavior. The competitor who lacks good cost accounting or managerial control systems or who does not need to produce profits today can make it difficult for one to complete any sales at a price above costs, making the rest of the analysis moot. Even worse, of course, is the competitor who by nature of his or her skills has lower costs or investments or is able to garner

---

[4] See Alfred Rappaport, *Creating Shareholder Value* (New York: Free Press, 1986).

[5] See Marcus C. Bogue III and Elwood S. Buffa, *Corporate Strategic Analysis* (New York: Free Press, 1986), chapter 1; and Arnoldo C. Hax and Nicolas S. Majluf, *Strategic Management: An Integrative Perspective* (Englewood Cliffs, NJ: Prentice-Hall, 1984), chapter 10.

Figure 2-1   The sources of return on investment

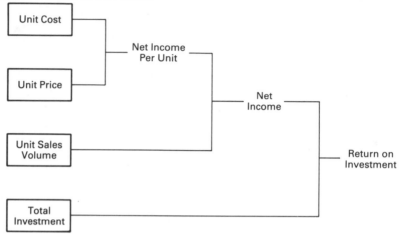

higher prices or unit sales. This competitively advantaged competitor is the subject of the following section.

THE NEED FOR COMPETITIVE ADVANTAGE IN ECONOMIC EXCHANGE

Imagine a boxing match in which the two boxers were evenly matched: same age, height, weight, reach, training, skill, experience, and ambition. There is no appreciable difference in any of the essential characteristics that could differentiate between the two. Which wins? One's best guess is that the fight will end up as a draw unless some purely random factor intervenes. Both will stand up in the ring and bloody each other in equal measure. The real winner, of course, would be the audience, which received full value in those things that fight fans seem to value, a long and violent battle which either competitor could win.

Imagine two sellers in the marketplace with identical offerings based on the same design and technology, raw materials sources, fixed and variable costs, inventory availability and delivery time and distance, selling and advertising costs, and capital structure and borrowing costs. There is no appreciable difference in any of the characteristics that could differentiate between the two. Which wins in the competition for customers? As in the boxing match, one's best estimate is that it will end up a draw. Both sellers will stand out in the marketplace and try to win customers by increasing the value they offer. Since their offerings are identical, that value is ultimately enhanced by their willingness to accept a lower price for their offering. Since both have the same cost structure, however, the result is much the same as the boxing match—two bloodied competitors both much the worse for wear. The real winner, of course, is the market of customers which, as a result of the competition between the sellers, receives the greatest share of the value created by the exchanges. As a *Fortune* magazine article about Pepsi and the cola wars put it, "The real victor in PepsiCo's . . . battle for industry supremacy will be the consumer. That's because when marketing giants fight it out, you're bound to see lower prices, better products, and improved service amidst the fray."[6]

Without collusion, the most the sellers can earn in such a situation will be the risk-adjusted rate of return—essentially the cost to each of the capital invested plus a risk premium equal to the risk investors perceive in the business when compared to a risk-free investment.[7] In economic terms, such a return is not profit per se. Such a return is nothing more than the cost of an essential raw material, capital, corrected for its actuarial risk. Economic profit is a return which exceeds this value. If there is effective competition, there can never be true economic profit.

In other words, the two equally matched businesses in our example may be able to survive, but neither can *win*. This is because any action one seller takes to enhance its offer and thereby gain customers will be matched by the other seller (if the other seller did not match the enhanced offer of its competitor it would lose all of its customers). In terms of what *winning* means, both sellers will have completed an equal number of transactions. In those transactions they will have each captured the same amount of the value created, but that value capture rate will not be sufficient to create economic profit.

Winning and Competitive Advantage

True winning means the ability to offer sufficient value to buyers to attract them, yet keep enough of the value created to yield an economic profit on the firm's asset base. To attain this, however, the firm must be able to avoid or mitigate the effects of competition. This can be achieved only if the firm possesses a competitive advantage which competitors cannot match or neutralize.[8] In the boxing example, if one of the fighters had an arm reach two or three inches longer than the opponent, then he could be said to have a competitive advantage. He could strike his opponent without being hit back as hard—he would have an unfair advantage in the competition.

In economic exchange competition, the equivalent of the boxer's longer arms must be related to the firm's ability to offer superior value to the marketplace as described in Exhibit 2-1. The firm that is uniquely able to provide superior value has an unfair advantage that allows it to avoid or mitigate the effects of compe-

---

[6] Patricia Sellers, "Pepsi Keeps on Going After No. 1," *Fortune*, March 11, 1991, p. 70.

[7] See Bogue and Buffa, *Corporate Strategic Analysis*; and Hax and Majluf, *Strategic Management*.

[8] The basic concept of competitive advantage is still ill defined. An excellent discussion of its definitions can be found in Lacy Glenn Thomas, "The Economics of Strategic Planning: A Survey of the Issues," in Lacy Glenn Thomas, ed., *The Economics of Strategic Planning: Essays in Honor of Joel Dean* (Lexington, MA: Lexington Books, 1986). For more of a business-level perspective on the concept, see George S. Day and Robin Wensley, "Assessing Advantage: A Framework for Diagnosing Competitive Superiority," *Journal of Marketing*, 52, no. 2 (April 1988), 1–20.

EXHIBIT 2-1

The Benefits of Competitive Advantage

   Competitive advantage provides a business with the ability to create a self-sustaining position. Look at the dynamics of the situation shown in Exhibit Figure A. The cycle starts with the attainment of competitive advantage—the ability to deliver superior value to customers. The competitive advantage may be due to initiating factors such as competitive failure, or luck, or they may stem more directly from the superior skills or resources of the business. The interesting result is what happens once the firm has gained competitive advantage.

   With the ability to deliver superior value to customers, the business will obtain several outcomes. First, it will have more satisfied customers than competitors, making customers less vulnerable to competitors' offers. Second, the business will gain market share by its ability to provide better value. Third, this market-share advantage will translate into larger and better profits, which can be fed back into providing the business with the resources needed to sustain its position: the funding of R&D for improved products, investing in better manufacturing facilities, and acquiring and improving the human and organizational skills necessary to produce superior value. In effect, the competitively advantaged business becomes and has all of the advantages of an entrenched competitor. It owns the market and earns the resources that allow it to maintain that position.

   In contrast, the competitively disadvantaged business loses in this cycle. Its

---

tition. In other words, competitive advantage exists when customers value a business's products or services in preference to competitive alternatives and buy enough of them at a price high enough over cost so the business unit creates shareholder value. The greater the business's competitive advantage, the greater its profitability relative to the industry average.[9] Two routes are available to achieve this:

1. *The ability to offer product performance benefits that others are unable to match.* One sure way to avoid the effects of competition is to avoid competition itself. By offering benefits others are unable to provide, there can be no effective competition. Polaroid is the only firm offering instant photography. If a customer wants the benefits of instant photography, he or she must buy from Polaroid. There are no competing sellers.

   In most marketplaces, however, there are few opportunities to gain advantages of the strength that Polaroid possesses. Moreover, the benefit proposition

---

[9] Cathy Anterasian and Lynn W. Phillips, "Discontinuities, Value Delivery, and the Share-Returns Association: A Re-Examination of the 'Share-Causes-Profits' Controversy" (Cambridge, MA: Marketing Science Institute Report No. 88-109, October 1988), p. 5.

EXHIBIT 2-1 (cont.)

customers receive lesser value and therefore are less satisfied and vulnerable to competitors' offers, causing a fall in market share and volume and, ultimately, the profits that are available for reinvestment in the business. With lowered resource levels, the firm finds it difficult to invest in the R&D, plant facilities, people, and organizational skills necessary to maintain its value position, let alone to catch up with the leader. Catching up with the leader is equivalent to attacking, which requires greater resources—but the defender is the one with the greater resources. This is a no-win situation for all but the advantaged.

EXHIBIT FIGURE A
The self-sustaining nature of competitive advantage

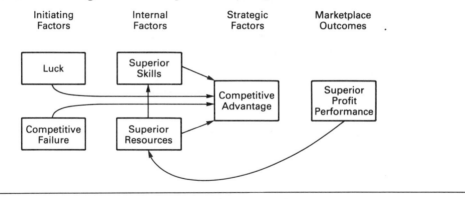

that customers are seeking is not always as obvious. In some markets there may be as much competitive advantage in knowing what the customer values as there is in delivering that value. The marketer needs to be skilled in understanding what it is that customers value—why they select one competitive product or service over another. Exhibit 2-2 expands on the concept of value delivery.

2. *The ability to provide equivalent product performance benefits at a price that others are unable to match.* If one cannot avoid competition per se, then one can try to avoid the effects of competition. If a firm's costs to deliver benefits equivalent to those of competitors are the lowest of the competing firms, then it will always be the most profitable. In fact, it can still profit even after the others have competed away their profits through price competition. This is because those competitors will have stopped lowering their prices when they reached the level of their manufacturing costs, a point *still above* the costs of the low-cost producer. Competition will have occurred, but the firm was able to avoid its effects.

EXHIBIT 2-2   Understanding Business Skills at Value Delivery

---

A key question in creating competitively advantaged offerings is understanding why some businesses are more skillful than others in profitably delivering superior value to customers. Whether through the benefits or cost route, a business needs to convince a target group of customers that they are receiving a net value superior to alternatives. This requires *choosing the value* the business will offer to some set of target customers, managing activities involved in *providing the value*, and *communicating the value* to customers. These three steps are pictured in Exhibit Figure A.

EXHIBIT FIGURE A
Value delivery sequence

Choose the Value			Provide the Value					Communicate the Value			
Customer Value Need Assessment	Select Target(s)	Value Positioning (Benefits/ Price vs. Competition)	Product/ Service Develop- ment	Sourcing and Making	Distribution	Service	Pricing	Application Engineering	Advertising	Selling	Promotic PR

Notes:
Value	=	Benefit − price
Benefit	=	Attribute(s) desirable to customer (in customer's eyes)
Price	=	Total costs to customer (as perceived by customer)
Superior perceived value	=	Customer believes buying/using the product or service gives a net value superior (more positive) than alternative's value

SOURCE: From Cathy Anterasian and Lynn W. Phillips, "Discontinuities, Value Delivery, and the Share-Returns Association," p. 8.

Choosing the value involves deciding on the precise benefits, price, target customer groups, and costs versus some set of competitive offerings. In marketing terms, this is often termed the *value proposition*. IBM's proposition, for example, is to provide superior reliability at modestly higher prices. Firms that are superior in providing the value attain that result by reflecting the value proposition in every activity of the business unit. Competitive advantage is often found in the thoroughness with which the value is provided and communicated by subunits and managers throughout the business unit. Building marketing capability and competitive advantage entails integrating all the functions of the business around a common vision of how to deliver superior value at a profitable cost, and helping every employee understand the role he or she must play.

SOURCE: From Cathy Anterasian and Lynn W. Phillips, "Discontinuities, Value Delivery, and the Share-Returns Association: A Re-examination of the 'Share-Causes-Profits' Controversy." Cambridge, MA: Marketing Science Institute, Report No. 88-109.

In sum then, the key to competitive advantage lies in the firm's ability to achieve an unfair advantage in delivering superior value to the marketplace.[10] The importance and appropriateness of that advantage depends on the nature of the marketplace in question. The next issue concerns the firm's ability to maintain its competitive advantage. An advantage that can soon be matched by competitors offers little in the way of protection and is certainly not a basis on which to build a business.[11]

Competitive Advantage and Strategic Advantage

There is a difference between competitive advantage and *strategic* competitive advantage. A strategic competitive advantage is one that others cannot or cannot easily duplicate.[12] A boxer with a 2- or 3-inch longer reach than others has an advantage that others cannot duplicate or even offset. A firm such as Polaroid with a patent on its product or manufacturing process has a legally enforceable competitive advantage that lasts for seventeen years. Only Mercedes-Benz can sell cars with its name on them; only General Foods can sell Kool-Aid® powdered soft drink mixes or Maxwell House® coffee. These are the kinds of advantages that are strategic in nature. The patent and the brand name are assets unique to their owners.[13]

Strategic advantages find their basis in the very structure of a situation, not in its detail. Strategic advantages have substance. Minor differences in costs or product performance are seldom strategic. If one has to look hard or calculate to the fifth significant digit, it is not a very important advantage.

Another way to define a strategic competitive advantage is as the ability to deliver superior value to the market for a sustained period of time. How long is that? One answer is that it must, at a minimum, be longer than the industry's design/manufacture/market cycle.[14] If, on seeing another's competitive advantage, a firm is able to duplicate it within the time frame of its design-to-market cycle, the advantage is certainly not sustainable. This is one of the reasons why there is so much volatility in the fashion business. The creator of a design that captures the market's fancy soon finds it being knocked off by competitors.

Another answer to the sustainability question might be that it should be sufficiently long enough for the firm to enjoy its benefits in terms of the time

---

[10] Roger C. Bennett and Robert G. Cooper, "The Misuse of Marketing: An American Tragedy," *Business Horizons*, 24, no. 6 (November-December 1981), 51–61.

[11] Stephen E. South, "Competitive Advantage: The Cornerstone of Strategic Thinking," *The Journal of Business Strategy*, 1, no. 4 (spring 1981), 15–25.

[12] Pankaj Ghemawat, "Sustainable Advantage," *Harvard Business Review*, 64, no. 5 (September-October 1986), 53–59.

[13] The word *unique* means that something is the only one of its kind. There are no degrees of unique—something is not more or less unique.

[14] An industry's design/manufacture/market cycle simply means the time that it would take for a firm in the business to deliver a new offering to the market, starting with the time it takes to design and develop the product through the time it takes to manufacture, sell, and deliver the product.

necessary for it to recoup its investment. Since the concept of winning is linked to the firm's ability to earn a profit on its investment base, an advantage which does not at least offer the potential to recoup that investment before others duplicate or neutralize the advantage cannot be said to be sustainable.

In this text, the terms *sustainable competitive advantage* and *strategic competitive advantage* are used interchangeably. This is because, by definition, a strategic advantage is a sustainable advantage. Alternatively, if it cannot be sustained, it cannot be strategic.[15]

KEY COMPETITIVE PRODUCT STRATEGIES

From this understanding of economic competition, Michael Porter has developed the concept of three generic competitive strategies which confer a sustainable competitive advantage.[16] As shown in Figure 2-2, the strategies are based on the particular form of strategic advantage the firm brings to the market. As noted earlier, a firm can either (1) avoid head-to-head competition by providing unique benefits to the marketplace, or (2) mitigate the effects of competition through its low-cost production position. Porter terms the first of these a *differentiation* strategy, the second a strategy of *overall cost leadership*.

The second strategic insight that Porter brings is that the strategic target is as important as the strategic tool. Accordingly, he notes that the strategic advantage may be used either industry-wide or only in a particular segment of the market. That is, the firm has a strategic choice about how much of the market it will choose to serve. Such a choice depends on the resources the firm has available (large targets require substantial resources) as well as on the nature and strength of the competitors (larger markets have larger and more committed competitors) and, ultimately, on the relative attractiveness of the whole of the market versus its various segments. Porter terms a strategy (whether low-cost or differentiated) aimed at one part of the market a *focus* strategy.

Generic Strategies and Sustainability

What makes each of these choices (source of competitive advantage and target) strategic is that each represents structurally different business types—each honed to provide the highest level of either type of value, whether low prices or differentiated benefits. The type of assets, people, location, R&D—the very nature of the businesses that choose to provide the different value propositions—is different. This structural difference provides one source of sustainability in that it reduces imitatibility. A K-Mart or Caldor or Wal-Mart type of

---

[15] Not all industries allow competitors the ability to gain a sustainable advantage. See Amar Bhide, "Hustle as Strategy," *Harvard Business Review*, 64, no. 5 (September-October 1986), 59–65.

[16] The following section is based on the ideas contained in Michael E. Porter's books *Competitive Strategy: Techniques for Analyzing Industries and Competitors* (New York: Free Press, 1980) and *Competitive Advantage: Creating and Sustaining Superior Performance* (New York: Free Press, 1985).

Figure 2-2   Three generic competitive strategies

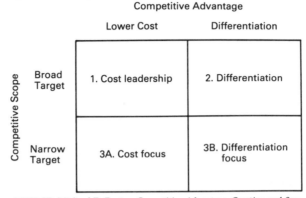

SOURCE: Michael E. Porter, *Competitive Advantage: Creating and Sustaining Superior Performance*, p. 12.

retail operation is structurally different from a Macy's, Nordstroms, Bloomingdale's, or Saks Fifth Avenue. The physical assets used for the one type of business cannot be used for the other; the people in the business are not interchangeable; the buyers deal with different merchandise suppliers and do not understand what the others' customers value; even the financial structures and economic formulas differ.

This same state of affairs exists between firms that choose to serve broad markets versus those that choose to serve selected segments (i.e., different focus strategies). The firm that chooses to serve a segment must gain a structural advantage versus its more broadly targeted rivals if it is to gain strategic advantage. *Advertising Age* is insulated from competition by *The Wall Street Journal* or *Business Week* because it has a far larger number of reporters covering the advertising industry, all of whom are specialists in the advertising business. Its competitors cannot deliver the same value to those who need news of the advertising business. The same holds for cost focus strategies. The focused firm must gain a structurally based lower cost by focusing on the segment that its more broadly aimed competitors cannot duplicate.

Generic Strategies and Competitive Forces

As noted in chapter 1, profitability is determined not only by the competition that occurs among direct competitors but also by (1) the relative power of suppliers and (2) customers, (3) the threat of new competitors' entrance, and (4) of substitute products. Porter's three strategies not only confer competitive advantage vis-à-vis direct competition but also provide additional strength against the above four competitive forces that determine industry and firm profitability. The following sections discuss how these strategies give the firm a defensible position against all competitive forces.

OVERALL COST LEADERSHIP

As noted earlier, the low-cost producer in an industry with a product perceived to be equivalent to others' is insulated from the effects of direct competition. Such a business will always do better than the other firms in the industry because, as long as it has a parity product, it will receive prices equal to those of its competitors but realize higher profits because of its lower cost structure.[17] Of course, if the basic structure of the industry is unfavorable, those profits may not be acceptable, but they will always be better than those realized by competitors. This insulation from the effects of competitive rivalry is the biggest benefit enjoyed by the low-cost producer.

The Effect on Competitive Forces

The low-cost producer in an industry also gains some power to offset the other four competitive forces that shape industry and firm profitability. The power of buyers is reduced because they can only move prices to the level of the firm with the next lowest costs. Since the low-cost producer in an industry is also frequently the largest, it will have more power than others in its industry to resist cost increases from suppliers. The threat of entrance of new firms into the business is also reduced. Potential entrants realize the difficulties to be incurred in obtaining a competitive cost structure, reasoning that if the other established and experienced competitors cannot achieve cost parity, the likelihood of the new entrant's attaining favorable costs is unlikely. Finally, the low-cost producer is in the best position to defend against substitute products by virtue of its lower costs. The price advantage required by a substitute product to replace the lowest-cost incumbent is greater.

The Low-Cost Producer Wins in Efficiency

In effect, the low-cost producer gains because it fulfills the dictates and goals of economic competition. It is the most efficient producer and therefore the last firm in its industry to be affected by competition, whether that competition comes from within the industry or without. Consider a worst-case example. The demand for the product produced by an industry (e.g., automobile tires in the U.S.) has been permanently reduced as a result of technological change (radial tires last twice as long as bias ply tires), customer needs (small, "donut" spare tires reduced original equipment from 5 tires per car to 4.5), and economic change (30 + % of automobiles are now imported).

---

[17] The concept of a parity product is defined as a product which is perceived by the marketplace to be comparable to those offered by competitors. In some instances (e.g., in the chemicals industry), this may require the product to be chemically identical. In other settings, it may allow the firm to offer a slightly different set of product features as long as the total is perceived to be as attractive as competitive offerings.

As the industry begins the necessary contraction, competition becomes cut-throat. There is just too much capacity available relative to the number of tires needed. Rather than shutting down, in which case a firm obtains a zero return on its sunk investment, all firms use price in an attempt to capture customers from competitors. The first firms to experience losses are the least efficient producers. As a result of their higher costs, they will be the first to feel the effect of the lower prices and, in time, are generally the first to exit, be bought out, or simply go under. Just as in biological competition, the weak and unfit are quickly weeded out. If the industry has been truly obsoleted (e.g., vacuum tubes by semiconductors), then theoretically the most efficient producer—the low-cost producer—should be the last to exit. In such an instance, the last producer, whether of buggy whips or vacuum tubes, frequently finds its business to be profitable although much smaller in size than before. In effect, the firm has no competition and, by definition at least, is both the low-cost producer and has the differentiated product.

Achieving Low-Cost Producer Status

The concept underlying the advantages that accrue to the low-cost producer requires that (1) the firm be the only low-cost producer, not one of several with equally low cost; (2) the cost difference be significant versus contenders; and (3) the advantage be sustainable. Together, this means that the firm has created a structural basis for its low-cost position, not one which came about simply by working smarter and harder than competitors.

Chapter 5 examines operations and production costs in depth, but basically there are seven strategic sources for gaining a cost advantage:

1. *Process technology.* A firm which has a superior method of manufacturing (or operating, in the case of services) is in the best position to have lower costs. Union Carbide, for example, invented a new process for manufacturing low-density polyethylene plastic which required only 50% of the capital investment and which could be operated for a quarter of the energy required by competitors' manufacturing techniques.[18]
2. *Product design.* A "plain vanilla" offering is one route that many take to achieve the low-cost position. This means designing the product offering to contain only those features and services necessary to deliver the basic, highest-value benefits desired by the market. While frill cutting is one way to accomplish this, the true low-cost position comes from designing products and product lines to optimize product performance and production costs. Texas Instruments, for example, has a managerial philosophy of design-to-cost, "designing the product and the equipment for producing it to meet both cost and performance goals . . . unit

---

[18] *Business Week*, "Carbide's Polyethylene Coup," December 5, 1977, p. 44.

cost is a primary design parameter. It is a specification equal in importance to functional performance, quality, and service."[19]

3. *Changing the value chain.* The value chain is the sum of the individual activities the firm performs as it designs, produces, markets, and distributes its products. Most firms in an industry do business in a certain way; their value chains are similar. By breaking with the traditional way of doing business, a firm can gain substantial advantages over competitors. For example, Federal Express changed the way that the air freight business was conducted. By limiting itself to small packages, using its own planes to fly them to a central sorting hub and then on to their destination cities, and finally delivering them in company-owned trucks, Federal Express gained a major cost advantage over Emery and Airborne Express, which accepted any size shipment and forwarded them to their destination on scheduled airlines.

4. *Low-cost inputs.* A business can gain significantly lower costs if it can gain a strategic advantage in sourcing major input costs. The chemicals and plastics businesses of the major oil companies are able to use the byproducts of their gasoline refineries as a source of raw materials at a lower cost than free-standing chemicals or plastics companies, which must either manufacture those same inputs or buy them on the open market. The no-frills airlines gained a substantial cost advantage over the traditional carriers because they were able to buy used airplanes (then in excess supply) and use nonunion labor.

5. *Location advantage.* Locating a business to reduce raw materials or finished product shipping costs significantly or, alternatively, near a plentiful supply of low-cost labor can give a strategic cost advantage. The initial success of the Japanese, Korean, and other Far Eastern countries in steel, automobiles, and consumer electronics was due in large part to their lower wage structures. Electronics manufacturers in the U.S. have had to move their assembly operations offshore to remain competitive.

6. *Scale economies.* Economies of scale can be a significant source of advantage in lowering production and overhead costs in many industries. The R&D costs to design new mainframe computers are immense, ranging into the billion-dollar territory. These costs must be spread out over the number of units produced, and IBM, with its current 70% share of the mainframe computer market, has a real advantage over its nearest competitor, Unisys, which sells only one sixth as many units.[20] GM has a similar advantage over Chrysler and Ford in the automobile market for the same reason.

7. *Experience curve.* The experience curve says that costs are a function of the cumulative experience a firm has in producing a product.[21] It is the total financial result of the many changes—small and large—the firm has learned about how best to design, manufacture, and distribute its product. This cumulative effect is not available to new entrants or to smaller-share competitors, according to the

---

[19] J. Fred Bucy, "Marketing in a Goal-Oriented Organization: The Texas Instruments Approach," in Jules Backman and John A. Czepiel, eds., *Changing Marketing Strategies in a New Economy* (Indianapolis, IN: Bobbs-Merrill, 1977), pp. 137–138.

[20] Stuart Gannes, "Tremors from the Computer Quake," *Fortune*, August 1, 1988, pp. 42–60.

[21] Boston Consulting Group, *Perspectives on Experience* (Boston: MA: Boston Consulting Group, 1972).

theory, because the changes are each incremental and are learned only as a function of the cumulative volume of production experience.

Becoming the low-cost producer is more than simply instituting one of the seven sources of cost advantage, however. Being the low-cost producer is frequently achieved by combining more than one source of advantage. More important, however, is that low-cost producers build organizations designed to pursue efficiency. That is, the dominant value of the culture of the firm is efficiency and cost control. This ethos differs from firms following other strategies. (This point is pursued further in chapter 5.)

Risks of a Low-Cost Strategy

No strategy is riskless. The business that follows a low-cost strategy can be beaten even though it follows the book in its pursuit of the strategy. Three of the more common risks to the strategy are technological change, changes in consumer demand, and structural changes in major input costs.

Technological change in production or product technology can negate the cost advantage. For example, a competitor which innovates a new generation of product or production technology can leave the previously low-cost producer with outmoded production equipment. When Union Carbide announced its new low-cost technology for manufacturing low-density polyethylene, one of its competitors complained, "They've effectively shut everyone else out of expanding . . . Who can afford to go ahead and start building what may be an obsolete plant?"[22] The producers of integrated circuits and memory chips have found that being the low-cost producer of one generation of chip does not ensure that the firm will be the low-cost producer of the next. There is sufficient difference in both the product and in its manufacturing technologies that the race to become low-cost producer begins anew with each chip design.

Changes in consumer demand can also affect the strategy. By its disciplined focus on achieving low cost, a firm may neglect to pay sufficient attention to changes in what customers want, reasoning that there is no feature that price cannot offset. Texas Instruments fell into this trap in its ill-fated foray into digital watches. It relied on simply styled plastic cases and bands to help it achieve a very low price when what consumers wanted was more stylish timepieces, even though they had to pay more for that styling. TI thought it could win the game in the factory but found out that it was more important to win in the marketplace. Interestingly, General Motors used a similar styling strategy in the 1920s to unseat Ford's dominance of the automotive market with its low-cost but plain black Model T. GM offered a variety of models, body styles, and colors, which allowed consumers to satisfy their higher-level social and aesthetic needs as well as their basic utilitarian need for transportation.

Structural changes in major input costs are a constant risk to the strategy.

---

[22] *Business Week*, "Carbide's Polyethylene Coup," p. 44.

The high petroleum price legacy of the oil embargo in the mid-1970s completely changed the economics of the petrochemical industry. Whereas operating costs were once the major cost of production, the price of raw materials became the major determinant of a firm's costs. This resulted in the displacement of the purely chemical firms from their positions of cost leadership by firms that had access to low-cost feedstocks. In electronics, firms that set up offshore assembly operations to take advantage of cheap labor have changed the economics of that business. And, as the locus of the lowest-cost labor has sequentially shifted from Japan to Taiwan to Korea, Singapore, Malaysia, and Thailand, competitive positions have changed rapidly. The shifting of international exchange rates, of course, further complicates the economics. Japan's position of low-cost producer in many businesses was threatened by the strong yen in the latter half of the 1980s.

DIFFERENTIATION

Differentiation works to provide a sustainable competitive advantage because, in delivering unique benefits valued by the market, the firm effectively removes itself from direct competition. The business which follows a differentiation strategy positions itself to meet needs that are widely valued by buyers and which it has a competitive advantage in supplying. In other words, it supplies superior value to its customers and, since other firms cannot effectively compete with it for customers, is able to price on the basis of that value.

The Effect on Competitive Forces

In addition to insulating the business from direct competition, a differentiation strategy also gives it power to offset the remaining four competitive forces that shape industry and firm profitability. Buyer power is reduced considerably since buyers lack directly comparable alternatives. If the benefits are of value to them, there is only one source. Since a differentiated product is a closer fit to customer needs, it is better able to compete against substitutes. New entrants are discouraged because satisfied customers are one of the stronger barriers to entry. If the customer's needs are fully satisfied, what reason is there to buy a competitor's product? Finally, the higher margins the firm realizes allow it more room to offset the actions of powerful suppliers.

The Differentiated Producer Wins in Effectiveness

A firm following a differentiation strategy gains because it fulfills one of the goals of economic competition: Its offering is effective in satisfying customer needs. By being the only one to create an offering which delivers a valued benefit and to have invested the capital necessary to produce and deliver that benefit, the firm is rewarded by sales and profits which reflect the absence of direct competition. Customers buy differentiated products because they value the benefits, not because of their price.

An offering may be differentiated along many dimensions, and because of this a market may allow for more than one successful differentiation strategy. Perhaps the most extreme examples of this are to be found in the branded candy segment of the confection industry and in the toy industry, both of which seem to be best described as infinitely differentiable. Except for the plain chocolate bar in the former and for some sporting goods in the latter, both industries create unique products identified by brand name. A Cabbage Patch lookalike doll will not satisfy a child who wants a *real* Cabbage Patch™ doll. Neither M&Ms® nor Snickers® nor any of the other branded candy bars have competition in the sense that directly comparable products exist to challenge them for sales. Imitation Monopoly® games and Barbie® dolls are seldom successful because, although many attempt to imitate their physical characteristics, none can adopt the same name as the original.

Although it is often termed a product differentiation strategy, the source of differentiation may be any element of the total offering which delivers value to the customer.[23] In photo finishing, for example, many customers are willing to pay a premium for one-hour service. Federal Express succeeded in part because its control of the customer's package from pick-up to delivery allowed it to offer guarantees of on-time delivery its competitors could not match. Its advertising slogan, "When it absolutely, positively must be there," communicated the advantage perfectly. In other instances, such nonproduct variables as just-in-time delivery, field service facilities, design assistance, back-up support, credit, sales assistance, or supplier dependability may provide the benefits customers value.

Achieving Differentiation

The routes to achieving differentiation are many. They may begin in the R&D laboratory or in an understanding of the needs of the marketplace, but all must deliver value to the customer to provide the business with a price premium that exceeds the added cost to the firm of being unique. A differentiation strategy does not mean that the firm merely creates a *different* offering or product. The point of differentiation must be substantive, not cosmetic. It must be perceived as offering more value to the customer than its competitors' standard offerings, and it must not be easily copied—it must be sustainable.

Value has two aspects for customers: A differentiated product can either (1) lower the buyer's costs to perform a desired function or (2) provide superior

---

[23] The concept of the offering says that a customer buys more than just the physical product—the firm's reputation, product guarantees, ability to supply repair services, credit terms, and a whole host of similar augmentations to the bare physical product make up the total offering. See chapter 3 for a complete description of the concept. See also Theodore Levitt, "Marketing Success through Differentiation—of Anything," *Harvard Business Review*, 58, no. 1 (January-February 1980), 83–91.

benefits.[24] A truly differentiated offering allows a customer to do both. There are three main routes to providing that superior value: (1) provide new functional capabilities not previously possible, (2) provide a major improvement in product performance, and (3) tailor or fine tune a product so it more closely satisfies customers' needs. These benefits may be made possible by new or improved technology directed at either the product itself or at its production process, or by changes in the value chain (the way the company organizes its activities in the business).

New Functional Capabilities.   The most potent differentiated offering allows customers totally new capabilities—the ability to satisfy needs previously unsatisfied. Edwin Land did it by creating a new technology. His invention of instant photography allowed people the satisfaction of immediately seeing the pictures they took. That capability was powerful enough to found a company called Polaroid. However, there was no radically new technology in the Sony Walkman®. It was just the ability to envision a new configuration of already available technology which enabled users to enjoy superb sound reproduction anywhere and anytime. Federal Express changed the way the air freight business was conducted and was thereby able to offer an unheard-of guarantee of next morning delivery performance.

New functional capabilities are sustainable to the extent that they can be legally protected through patents or trade secrets or through the head start that the innovating firm enjoys over subsequent competitors. Polaroid has continued to develop its instant photography technology, gaining a long list of patents which have allowed it to continue its legal monopoly. Neither Sony nor Federal Express received patents on their innovative products, yet both have managed to retain leadership positions in the categories they created. While others were racing to match their innovative offering, both were solidifying their position by improving their own product performance. By the time the competitors' products were on the market, Federal Express and Sony already had second-generation offerings with superior performance in the marketplace. Both have continued to present a moving target to competitors.

Performance Improvement.   It was possible to copy documents before the Haloid Corporation (Xerox's original name) developed electrostatic copying technology. But it was the ability of that new technology to do it quickly and cleanly on plain, dry paper that gave the important performance advantage on which the fortunes of the Xerox Corporation were based. The Japanese, on the other hand, brought no really new mechanical technology to the automotive business. But they did bring about a change in product performance and manufacturing costs. Their absolute dedication to quality as measured by the number of defects

---

[24] Porter, *Competitive Advantage*, p. 131, uses the term *raises buyer performance* to mean "provides superior benefits." Allowing the buyer to accomplish a task better (buyer performance) must result in benefits that the customer perceives to be of value. The phrase *provides superior satisfaction* could also be substituted.

on delivery and, especially, as measured by durability and low maintenance over extended usage periods set standards which U.S. and European manufacturers are still struggling to match. Most importantly, customers still pay premiums for Japanese cars.

The sustainability of Xerox's position is due to its strong patents, but there are none that cover the Japanese auto makers. Nonetheless, it has taken years for the traditional automotive powers to begin to catch up. Although there was no new mechanical technology involved, the statistical approach to achieving quality and the managerial systems and relationships with suppliers which were necessary for its implementation have proven formidable obstacles to imitation. In the meantime, powerful impressions and associations are formed in buyers' minds linking the idea of quality to Japanese automobiles. In time, this association and reputation will be harder for competitors to match than the physical quality itself.

Product Tailoring.   Tailoring an offering to meet the exact needs of customers is a more market-driven approach to achieving differentiation than the former two approaches. When such differentiation involves attributes that are widely valued across an industry, it is termed a *differentiation strategy*. This is a different strategy from one in which products are tailored to fit more closely the needs of one particular segment or application. This latter approach is termed a *differentiation focus strategy* and is discussed later in this chapter.

Caterpillar is a prime example of a differentiation strategy which is pursued industry-wide through tailoring the total product offering. Its products are really not greatly different from those of its competitors; it has simply tailored every aspect of the offering more closely to market needs than its competitors. First, it offers more models than competitors, thereby increasing the fit between the product performance characteristics and individual customer needs. Not only does this increase user satisfaction, but fewer customers need to overbuy or underbuy relative to actual performance requirements. Second, the major design criterion for Caterpillar's equipment is durability. Since an equipment breakdown can idle many workers and even delay an entire construction project, equipment buyers are willing to pay a premium for durability. Downtime is more expensive than the price premium. Third, to further reduce the costs of downtime, Caterpillar's spare parts inventories are the largest and most geographically dispersed in the industry.[25] Fourth, its dealer network is the largest and best managed. The field service capability Caterpillar offers further reinforces the overall value of the offering. Individually, these advantages are not overwhelming, but together they represent an offer that more closely matches customers' needs than those of competitors.

The interconnections among all aspects of Caterpillar's offering strategy

[25] According to one source, Caterpillar guarantees delivery of repair parts anywhere in the world within forty-eight hours. See David A. Garvin, "Competing on the Eight Dimensions of Quality," *Harvard Business Review*, 65, no. 6 (November-December 1987), 101–109.

make it difficult for competitors to imitate, and this increases Caterpillar's sustainability.[26] Only large competitors can match its broad product offerings, and because of the years of experience the marketplace has with its products, competitors find it difficult to match either the substance or reputation it enjoys for durability. Spare parts inventories are scale sensitive. The existence of a large equipment population makes it possible for Caterpillar to maintain more extensive inventories than competitors at a lower cost. Finally, good dealerships require equal parts of financial strength on the part of the dealer and mutual trust in the relationship between dealer and manufacturer. Competitors find it almost impossible to breach this combination of barriers.

Short of patents and trade secrets, there are few strategies as sustainable as one which results in a fully satisfied customer. Products tailored to the specific needs of the market, application, or the customer are more likely to satisfy than those which are not. To win such a customer away, a challenger must offer an improved level of performance than offered by the incumbent. If the incumbent has consistently matched the offering with customer needs, then there is little for the challenger to improve on. Such is the strength of the entrenched competitor.

Risks of a Differentiation Strategy

No strategy is riskless. The more successful a strategy is in attracting customers, the more competitors will try to share in that success, even though a differentiation strategy leaves as little as possible for competitors to improve on in terms of customer satisfaction. There are four major risks that a differentiated-product business faces.

1. *Commoditization of the offering* is the first of these risks. The risk is that a competitor will simplify and standardize the product and, by using high-volume manufacturing techniques, achieve costs so low that customers will be willing to forgo some of the benefits of the differentiated offering for the overwhelming price advantage of the adequate, generic offering. This is a risk that all new product markets share. Although it can happen at any time, it is generally seen when a market first begins to become a large market and economies of scale can begin to affect costs significantly. The commoditization of a market is a constant and real risk to a differentiation strategy. As one strategy consultant put it, "Over time all products tend to become commodities."[27]

   Amstrad is an English company that has reached $1 billion in sales in less than ten years by that strategy. It specializes in delivering established technology at prices so low that specialty markets are transformed into mass markets. For example, it was the first European company to clone the IBM PC. It sold its

---

[26] Pankaj Ghemawat, "Sustainable Advantage," 53–59.
[27] Seymour Tilles, "Segmentation and Strategy," in *Perspectives on Experience* (Boston MA: Boston Consulting Group).

model for less than half the cost of comparable IBM models, doubling the size of the British PC market by its actions.[28]

2. *A more differentiated product* is the second major risk faced by the differentiated producer. In the market for vodka, Smirnoff was long the differentiated product at the upper end of the scale. Although produced in the United States, its name and image as communicated in its advertising was Russian and decidedly upscale. It was the brand to serve guests, and it commanded a premium price. But Smirnoff was leapfrogged by the emergence of Stolichnaya, which was even higher priced and clearly unique as the only true Russian vodka. The effect of "Stoli's" introduction was to relegate Smirnoff to ordinary (or closer to commodity) status in the vodka world. Although the performance criteria in the vodka market are ephemeral—image and exclusivity—the same kind of performance leapfrogging is a feature of every market. Portable computer makers are all racing each other to produce the smallest and lightest portable with the longest-lived batteries, brightest screen, largest resident memory, and fastest processor. Today's differentiated offering is tomorrow's commodity.

3. *Imitation* is the third threat to a differentiation strategy. For example, Stolichnaya's success in leapfrogging Smirnoff did not go unnoticed. Stoli's claim to being the most prestigious vodka by virtue of its unique Russian origin was quickly imitated by brands from two other heavy vodka-consuming countries: Absolut (from Sweden) and Finlandia (from Finland), both of which were also premium priced and cultivated a sophisticated image. Stoli's response was to begin importing specialty vodkas to reclaim its status as the differentiated product. At last count, Absolut has countered with a pepper-flavored vodka. Imitation may be the most sincere form of flattery, but it is also a constant threat to a differentiated product.

4. *Creative segmentation* of the leader's market is the fourth risk to a differentiation strategy. The challenger which focuses its resources on one segment of the leader's market and devises an offering which performs better in meeting that segment's special needs for product performance can win away that segment. Most importantly, it may be difficult for the leader to retaliate. The following section describes this focus strategy in greater detail.

FOCUS

In pursuing a focus strategy, a firm has determined that a strategic advantage is as much a function of the target as it is of the firm's capabilities. The key to the strategy is that the focus on a particular application or segment allows the firm to gain a sustainable competitive advantage against its more broadly focused competitors. That advantage may be based on cost to serve the segment (cost focus) or on special product needs of buyers in that segment (differentiation focus), but the important point is that there is a substantial difference between the target segment and other segments in the industry in either their needs or in the costs to serve them.

Segment boundaries, in fact, are best defined by such differences. With

[28] Richard I. Kirkland, Jr., "Pile 'Em High and Sell 'Em Cheap,' *Fortune*, August 29, 1988, pp. 91–92.

commodity-like products, the basic segment boundary is the cost differential for serving different customers.[29] If there are substantial differences in the production, operations, distribution, or even marketing costs to serve different segments, then the firm that focuses its efforts on a specific segment may be able to gain a structural cost advantage over those who do not focus.

Discount stock brokers are one easy-to-understand example of a cost focus strategy. They succeeded because of the existence of a substantial segment which did not value the personal service and advice of a broker or the credit facilities, stock research, and administrative support offered by the broker's firm. By eliminating these services, discounters were able to gain a substantial, structurally based cost advantage, which they were able to share with customers. Equally important, the cost structure of these firms was such that the full-service brokers could not match the low prices without losses. What makes this a focus strategy is that the low-price offering strategy appeals to only one segment of the brokerage market, unlike discount department stores whose price appeal is widely valued in that market.

Differentiation focus strategies are generally based on the tailoring concept, and their basis of segmentation is the combination of the features built into the product and their cost/price ratio. The segmentation of markets for differentiated products rests on the relationship between the cost features to the producer and the value of the features to the customer.[30]

In the computer industry, for example, Tandem Computers makes large mainframe computers, like IBM and Unisys. However, rather than making general-purpose computers that must serve a wide variety of customers, Tandem has chosen to focus on meeting the specific needs of firms which use their computers to provide on-line transactions processing and which cannot afford computer downtime. It sells fail-safe systems for a few critical jobs in which vital data must be captured second by second—running a network of automated teller machines, for instance.[31] Tandem's computers use a technology known as parallel processing to achieve that result, and they obtain a premium price because they solve their customers' needs exactly. Customers could save on their initial purchase cost by buying general-purpose computers, but their real needs for fault-free performance would not be met. Convergent Technologies, the maker of powerful small computers bought by Unisys in 1988, has focused its business on providing computers to special markets like law firms and auto dealers.[32] Nixdorf, a European computer company, follows a similar service-intensive strategy. It sells its minicomputers by providing software tailored to specific markets and top customer service.[33]

The magazine and newspaper businesses offer another good example. Gen-

---

[29] Tilles, "Segmentation and Strategy."
[30] Tilles, "Segmentation and Strategy."
[31] *Business Week*, "Why Tandem Struggles While Its Market Sizzles," August 22, 1988, pp. 88–90.
[32] Andrew Pollack, "Unisys Says It Will Buy Convergent," *The New York Times*, August 11, 1988, p. D3.
[33] *Business Week*, "A Rude Shock for One of Europe's High-Tech Successes," August 22, 1988, p. 51.

eral business magazines such as *Business Week* and *Fortune* cannot offer the industry specific news that *Chemical Week* does or the functionally oriented information *Plant Engineering* can. National shelter magazines such as *Better Homes and Gardens* face stiff competition from regionally oriented magazines such as *Sunset*, which more closely reflects the climate and lifestyles of the Western audience.

The businesses in all of these examples are choosing to focus on meeting the needs of market segments rather than the overall market. In this way they use their limited resources to beat out the larger firms, which dominate the broader market. In comparison to those larger firms, they win by offering their chosen segments superior value. In line with the insights of the military strategists, by focusing their limited resources on small targets they achieve a higher effective resource level per targeted customer unit than their competitors. This is demonstrated by their ability to deliver exact answers to the segment's needs while more broadly focused competitors are only able to deliver approximate answers.

Risks of a Focus Strategy

A focus strategy faces many of the same risks as other strategies. These risks can be summarized as follows:

1. *The advantages of size regain potency.* The initial advantage the focuser attained against its larger targeted opponents can be neutralized or reversed if the sheer volume of the larger business gives it the resources to pursue programs that the focuser just cannot afford. Consider an instance in which the initial absolute size difference between the segment and the overall market is not sufficiently large to give the more broadly focused firm a resource advantage compared to the smaller. This initially safe situation for the focuser can change over time to favor the larger. For example, if both the overall market and the market segment grow at the same percentage rate, the absolute value of the difference in size between the two markets will widen steadily. In the case of R&D, for example, this widening difference can give the larger firm the dollars to advance its product technology at a rate that the smaller firm is incapable of duplicating, even for its smaller segment. Over time, the larger might even be able to obsolete the focuser's product. But the effect need not be restricted to R&D. It could involve marketing programs, levels of customer service, or the firm's ability to use scale-sensitive technology.

   In businesses where production or operations are experience or scale sensitive, the effect of the widening absolute size difference could be to reduce the larger firm's manufacturing costs and prices to a level that the smaller firm cannot match. The resulting widening of the price difference between the average differentiated product and the exact differentiated product can become so large that customers can no longer justify buying the focused offering in terms of its additional benefits. The price/value ratio, in other words, is no longer favorable.

2. *Competitors can out-focus the initial focuser.* In the same way that the focused firm gained an advantage in its chosen segment against its larger competitors, another firm can segment the focuser's market. This is not unlikely when markets

are growing. As what was initially a small and homogeneous segment becomes larger with time, the diversity in the needs of its members also grows. Just as the unfocused firm gave the initial focuser the opportunity to steal some of its customers by its inability to satisfy the exact needs of the customers in that segment, the initial focuser also risks losing out if it does not recognize the growing variance in the needs of customers within its segment.

OPERATIONS AND ECONOMIC PROFILES OF THE STRATEGIES

To implement the three strategies—cost leadership, differentiation, and focus—most firms follow similar conceptual approaches. Those approaches involve a combination of product, marketing, operations, and financial components which work together to attain the desired effect. A good example involves comparing a discount store (Caldor, K-Mart) to a department store (Macy's, Rich's) or a manufacturer of commodity electronic components (Texas Instruments, Intel) with a manufacturer of electronic test equipment (Hewlett-Packard, Textronics).

The firm following a stereotypical low-cost strategy produces (or sells) a limited variety of "plain vanilla" products in high volumes at a low price, yielding a small gross margin (in percentage terms) but with a high inventory turnover. Since customers are expected to know what they want and to buy in large quantities, selling costs are low on a per-unit basis. The business has typically replaced labor with capital equipment to reduce variable costs and, consequently, has high fixed overhead costs and a high breakeven point (typically at 60% to 70% of capacity or greater).

Typically, firms pursuing a differentiation strategy offer a greater variety of performance-oriented products in smaller volumes at premium prices, yielding a large gross margin but with a slower inventory turnover. Selling and service costs are significant in this strategy because customers need and expect help in selecting the correct product for a given application. Because of lower volumes or its need for a greater variety of products, the firm typically has more general-purpose production equipment. Such an operation is less capital intensive, resulting in a lower breakeven point (less than 50% to 60% of capacity). Businesses built around a focus strategy have profiles similar to this.

Profitability and the Generic Strategies

Evidence suggests that there may be a difference in profitability rates among the generic strategies.[34] In sum, differentiated-product businesses may yield higher profitability rates (percentages, not absolute dollars) than those pursuing commodity markets, and those aiming at segments may gain over those aimed at the broad market. These indications are tentative, however, and need to be exam-

---

[34] The capital-intensity argument is discussed in Robert D. Buzzell and Bradley T. Gale, *The PIMS Principles: Linking Strategy to Performance* (New York: Free Press, 1987), chapter 7.

ined carefully on a case-by-case basis for their validity. The primary argument against this tendency says that returns will always be equated in the long run—that if differentiated-product businesses are earning a higher rate of return than commodity-like businesses, additional entrants will be attracted to the business, competition will intensify, and returns will be lowered. This is the essence of the structural forces argument presented in chapter 1. It is a strong argument.

The Capital-Intensity Argument. However, the concept that returns may remain different between commodity and differentiated businesses has its points, too. One of the strongest arguments for this contention is that those pursuing low-cost strategies frequently use capital-intensive processes to obtain low variable costs.[35] Once that investment is made, the argument goes, it leads the business (and the others in the same industry) to aggressive and often destructive competition to obtain the volume necessary to reach the high breakeven point the investment creates. Further, the heavy capital investments themselves create a barrier to exit, and firms that ought to exit hang on hoping that the situation will turn around.

Industries such as airlines, aluminum, paper, and corrugated boxes are some examples cited in support of this view. The data in support of this argument show that instead of increasing (as would be necessary to offset the increasing investment base), return on sales (ROS) actually decreases as capital intensity increases, leading (mathematically) to lowered returns on that investment (ROI). This argument applies to those who are participating in commodity-like markets, not necessarily to those who achieve lowest-cost status in such markets.

The Market- and Product-Differentiation Argument. Figure 2-3 graphs the ROI contours obtained in an analysis of the PIMS database portrayed as a function of the amount of market differentiation (on the vertical axis) and the relative quality (on the horizontal axis) of the offering of the individual product entry.[36] What is of concern here is that ROI varies directly with market differentiation, the extent to which the buyers in the market differ (or do not differ) on the benefits and attributes that they value. Commodity markets are the least differentiated (almost by definition), and competitors with offerings of average quality in such markets are lucky to receive ROIs in the 10% to 20% range. One reason for this is that the buyers have forced all suppliers to compete on the most restricted set of variables, essentially centering on price.

Viewed from another angle, it may be that differentiated products offer values that are more difficult to duplicate or offset, thereby allowing the possessor to maintain that advantage longer. The highest returns shown in Figure 2-3 are earned by those offering the highest-quality products in the most differentiated markets—those in the upper right-hand corner. While one can dupli-

---

[35] Buzzell and Gale, *The PIMS Principles.*

[36] PIMS stands for Profit Impact of Market Strategy. It is a program of the Strategic Planning Institute, a not-for-profit organization which collects and analyzes data on business strategy and profitability. A full explanation of the PIMS program can be found in chapter 11.

Figure 2-3   How differentiation and quality drive profitability

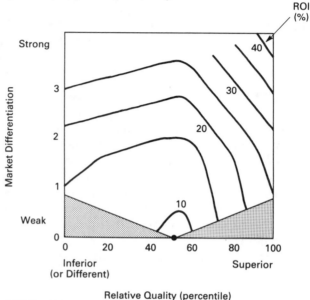

Relative Quality (percentile)

SOURCE: Robert D. Buzzell and Bradley T. Gale, *The PIMS Principles*, p. 124.

cate low cost in the factory and laboratory by technological and physical means, such benefits as buyer trust in a supplier and the psychological and social meanings that branded products possess exist in the minds of buyers and society and are not easily duplicated. The Lexus and Infinity luxury cars have been able to match and even surpass the physical performance of their targets, cars such as Mercedes-Benz, Jaguar, and BMW. However, it will take time for society and individuals to accord them the same symbolic meaning as that possessed by their targets. Until that time, they will sell at a discount to those cars because they do not offer the important social performance that buyers want and value highly.

THE IMPORTANCE OF THE TARGET MARKET

Choosing the correct target market—where to compete—is as important in devising strategy as the question of how to compete. First, not all targets are equally attractive. Second, the size of the opportunities differ. Third, while the impression given visually in Figure 2-2 is that there are two choices, broad market or segment, the choice of market is far more complex. In reality, the choice is between the largest market and a literal cascade of consecutively smaller markets, culminating in the smallest market unit—an individual customer. In effect, one can envision in Figure 2-2 a large number of successively smaller boxes as one moves down from the broad market.

This reality gives firms of almost any size the opportunity to concentrate their resources on an appropriately scaled target. The business that is trying to devise its strategy needs to examine both the inherent attractiveness of the markets available and the size of those opportunities relative to its and its competitors' resources.

All Markets Are Not Equally Attractive

In the 1920s there was a famous bank robber in the United States by the name of Willy Sutton. When asked why he robbed banks, Sutton replied, "Because that's where the money is!" The choice of target market has similar strategic import. If you choose a market in which the prospects for profits are inherently poor, even if you win there will not be anything to show for it. For example, one company's internal new-business development team chose to examine the profitability of the customers in the target market as one measure of their relative attractiveness. They reasoned that customers whose own profitability was poor would likely put pressure on their suppliers to reduce prices, just as the Chrysler Corporation demanded of its suppliers during the early 1980s when it faced losses.

Table 2-1 lists some of the factors that determine industry and market attractiveness. These factors are the same as those discussed in chapter 1 that define the structure of an industry or market. Attractive markets are those in which there are some barriers to entry but in which competitors are not locked in forever. In attractive markets, customers have little bargaining power because the amount of their purchase is small, the item's functional performance is critical to them, and they have few if any alternatives. Finally, markets are attractive if competition is not intense, as is the case when there are few competitors, each producing differentiated products in the face of fast growth in customer demand.

The market for the electronic telephone switchboards used in businesses and institutions, known as PBXs (private branch exchanges), is an example of the competitive forces at work.[37] In the five-year period from 1986 to 1991, sales of new PBXs declined by over one third from $3 billion annually to about $1.75 billion, and product differentiation declined as all manufacturers imitated each others' features—making one indistinguishable from the other. Yet because the technology continues to develop and is of strategic importance to all of the players (AT&T, Northern Telecom, Rolm, Siemens, NEC, Fujitsu), manufacturers continue to spend heavily on R&D. However, to pay for that R&D they routinely sell PBX hardware at a loss, hoping to make it up later with more profitable sales of added capacity and specialized gear for voice mail, telemarketing, and the like. Because of that future potential, no one is exiting the market and it's a bloody turf war in which competitors are routinely discounting as much as 40% of list price to get business.

---

[37] *Business Week*, "For PBX Makers, the Future Is Later," February 25, 1991, pp. 88–89.

TABLE 2-1   *Characteristics of Attractive Industries and Markets*

	WILL DECREASE PROFITABILITY	WILL INCREASE PROFITABILITY
Ease of entry	*Easy to enter*	*Difficult to enter*
	Low-scale threshold	High-scale threshold
	Little brand franchise	Brand switching difficult
	Common technology	Proprietary know-how
	Access to distribution channels	Restricted distribution channels
Ease of exit	*Difficult to exit*	*Easy to exit*
	Specialized assets	Salable assets
	High exit costs	Independent business
	Interrelated businesses	
Power of suppliers	*Suppliers powerful*	*Suppliers weak*
	Credible forward integration threat by suppliers	Many competitive suppliers
		Purchase commodity products
	Suppliers concentrated	Credible backward integration threat by purchasers
	Significant cost to switch suppliers	
		Substitutes available
		Concentrated purchasers
Power of customers	*Customers powerful*	*Customers weak*
	Buyers concentrated	Producers threaten forward integration
	Buyers purchase a significant proportion of output	Significant buyer switching costs
		Buyers fragmented
	Buyers possess credible integration threat	Performance is critical to customer's functional product
	Product cost is large portion of customer's total cost	Typical purchase amount is small
	Low buyer switching costs	
	Typical purchase amount large	
Availability of substitutes	*Substitution easy*	*Substitution difficult*
	Low user switching costs	High user switching costs
	Substitute producers profitable and aggressive	Substitute producers unprofitable and passive
Industry conditions	*Many competitors*	*Small number of competitors*
	Competitors equal in size	Diversity of competitor size
	Slow demand growth	Industry leader
	High fixed costs	Fast demand growth
	Excess capacity	Low fixed costs
	Commodity products	Differentiated products
	Diversity of approach and historical background	Commonality of approach and historical background

SOURCE: Adapted from Roger Kerin and Robert A. Peterson, "Strategy Formulation," in *Perspectives on Strategic Marketing Management* (Boston, MA: Allyn & Bacon, 1983), p. 98.

Market Size Is Important

Although the statement that market size is important may sound trite, its implications are not obvious. A market can be too large both in an absolute sense and in a relative sense. In an absolute sense, very large markets seldom allow their participants high rates of return. Large competitors with large capital investments in large, slow-growing markets too frequently get locked into competitive battles in which brute force seems to be the main weapon. Larger markets tend to be older and therefore have become more efficient in the economic sense. Rates of return decline with the age of a market.

Small markets attract fewer competitors and allow early entrants to shape the market to fit their own distinctive competencies. For the business looking for a growth vehicle, small markets offer a better opportunity than large markets. Small markets find rapid growth easier mathematically, whereas it is more difficult to obtain large percentage increases on an already large market base.

Market size is important in a relative sense also. An important strategic factor in all marketplace competition is the size of the firms involved. Larger firms tend to have more resources than smaller ones. Since strategy can be defined as the attempt to maximize the return from a given set of resources, the issue is for the strategist to find the largest target capable of being captured—and held—given the resources available.

This analysis works in two directions. First, it indicates that the small firm should not attempt to capture large pieces of territory because, even if it succeeds in its initial attack, the resources available to larger competitors will defeat it eventually. In the early 1980s, for example, New England Digital, which was a pioneer in digital synthesis of music, had the opportunity to extend its technology lead from the professional markets it had created to the newly emerging consumer market but wisely chose not to do so. It reasoned that the large potential there would favor consumer electronics companies like Casio and Yamaha, which had the resources to develop and serve markets worldwide. The rapidly falling prices and the proliferation of product models and forms proved the correctness of that decision. The skills needed to succeed in the consumer market—large-volume production capacity and broad distribution capability—already existed in the large consumer electronics companies, whereas New England Digital would have had to develop that capability from scratch.

Second, the large firm which chooses to bring its resources to bear on small targets (initial and long run) is not using its full potential. It is as much of a strategic mistake to underutilize resources as it is to attempt too much with them. While it may be true that in the former case there is no out-of-pocket financial loss, nonetheless the shareholders have lost. The failure to use shareholder equity to its maximum is just as real a loss in economic terms.

SUMMARY

Wise competitors pick fights in which they have the competitive edge that allows them to feel confident about their chances of winning. In economic competition, that edge comes from the ability to offer, at a profit, superior value to the market. In the absence of competitive advantage the only true winners in economic competition are the customers, who benefit from the lower prices, better products, and improved service.

Sustainable competitive advantage comes from the ability of the business to use its unique characteristics to create superior value, thereby preventing competitors from duplicating its success. Sustainable or strategic advantage is typically located in the structure of the situation and results in enduring advantage for its possessor. The retail competitor who is located on the most desirable piece of real estate has it; the holder of a major product or process patent has it; the owner of a respected and trusted brand name has it. Competitive advantage should be self-sustaining if its possessor nurtures it. The superior returns it brings should allow the business to out-invest its rivals and to reinforce those skills which allow it to deliver superior value, thereby reinforcing its positional advantage.

When one takes the two key strategic questions—how to compete and where to compete—and crosses them in a matrix, one obtains the key generic strategy choices. *How to compete* typically requires the strategist to choose between two incompatible operations and organizational system types—that of pursuing a strategy to be the low-cost producer in a price-oriented commodity market or to produce uniquely differentiated products in a market whose customers value product performance over price. *Where to compete* offers the strategist a wider choice, ranging in size from the broadest market to the smallest unit consisting of a single customer. The strategies in the broadest markets are termed either a *low-cost producer strategy* or a *differentiated-product strategy*. Those who choose smaller segments of the market on which to focus their resources are said to pursue *focus strategies*—either differentiated focus or cost focus. The generic strategies work not only because they provide superior value to customers but because they allow those who pursue them to avoid the effects of the competitive forces that act to lower returns.

The choice of where to compete is equally important as the choice of how to compete. First, not all markets are equally attractive, and the wise competitor chooses targets that promise profitability. Second, since strategic advantage comes from the ability to bring more resources to bear on a target than do competitors, the choice of the proper size target market allows every firm, from the smallest to the largest, to choose a market in which it has an opportunity to win. That is the essence of wise competitive product strategy.

3

A FRAMEWORK
FOR THE STRATEGIC ANALYSIS
OF PRODUCTS

The product strategist's task is simple in concept: to create and manage the firm's offerings so the firm gains and maintains a strategic competitive advantage. This means managing the resources of the firm and choosing customers so the firm's products deliver value that cannot be duplicated by competitors. To do this, the strategist must be able to see the product as customers see it, think about it as the firm's product designers and operations people think of it, calculate its cash flow as the financial vice president does, understand its strategic role in the business as top management understands it, and find its flaws as only competitors can.

This chapter and chapter 4 present a framework for the strategic analysis of products. Both chapters discuss concepts—useful frameworks that assist thinking about products and that generate viable ideas for their strategic management. This chapter concentrates on products as free-standing entities; chapter 4 views products in relation to their competitors. Products can be conceptualized in a variety of ways. This chapter first presents the key concepts that customers and managers use to examine and describe products. Second, it presents frameworks which enable the manager to analyze the central rationale for the existence of a product: its ability to create value. Third, it examines the importance of product performance and quality.

CONCEPTUALIZING PRODUCTS

Anything that can be offered to a market to satisfy a want or need is a product. This includes what we traditionally think of as products (physical objects like books or pens) as well as those we call services (checking accounts, insurance, theatrical performances). Other categories of products include the marketing of people (celebrities, politicians),[1] places (for vacations or as places to locate busi-

---

[1] Elizabeth C. Hirschman, "People as Products: Analysis of a Complex Marketing Exchange," *Journal of Marketing*, 51, no. 1 (January 1987), 98–108.

nesses), organizations (corporate recruiters sell their companies to potential employees), and ideas (Mothers Against Drunk Driving).[2]

The product is the central focus to any business. The product is what the firm does. Individuals unite to design products, set up production and operations systems to make and deliver products, and create the marketing programs, sales forces, channel systems, and advertising that sells them. To customers, the product is the firm. To competitors, the product is the target that must be beaten to win.

Each of the functions within the firm views the product in a different way. Each has different insights into what the product is, why it sells (or does not sell), what needs to be done to sell more, or how its profitability can be improved. Not one of these conceptualizations of what the product is and why it sells is either the dominant or the correct one. The product must not only satisfy customers but must satisfy and build on the strengths of the firm's various functional groups (sales, operations and manufacturing, finance, top management) if it is to win in the marketplace.[3]

Figure 3-1 presents the constellation of key product concepts that link customers and the firm. To the firm, a product is a causal promise made to customers via a marketplace offering of some physical action or object made possible by an investment in technology. To the customer, a product is the causal promise of some functional, experiential, or symbolic satisfaction created via a real physical object or action. The following section discusses in depth each of these aspects.

Products as Physical Actions and Objects

The easiest way to think about a product is in terms of its physical reality. As a physical product, a telephone consists of electronic parts and components contained in a housing. As a service product, telephone service is the transmission of voices through a system of cables, microwave towers, switching stations, computers, and telephone operators. Both the telephone and the telephone service can be described in terms of their physical characteristics: the range of frequencies they transmit, sensitivity to tone and volume, noise and static levels, the frequency of disconnects, and a host of other physical and performance specifications.

The success of any firm is simultaneously a function of and constrained by its ability to make and do. If the product or system does not have a needed feature or the operations unit lacks the capacity to serve, sales will be less than desired. Marketers implement their strategies through the physical realities of the objects and actions their businesses bring into being. Even the most image-laden product has a physical reality that must be produced and managed.

---

[2] Philip Kotler, *Marketing Management*, 6th ed. (Englewood Cliffs, N.J.: Prentice-Hall, 1988), pp. 445–446.

[3] Paul F. Anderson, "Marketing, Strategic Planning and the Theory of the Firm," *Journal of Marketing*, 46, no. 2 (spring 1982), 15–26.

Figure 3-1 Key product concepts

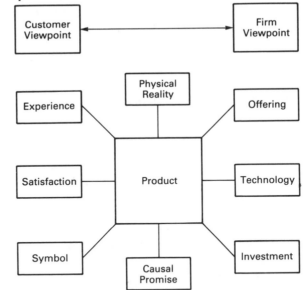

Products as Satisfaction-Generating Systems

Businesses make physical objects; customers buy benefits. As Charles Revson, founder of Revlon cosmetics, put it, "In the factory we make cosmetics. In the stores we sell hope." To the customer, a physical product is nothing more than the necessary evil required to attain some satisfaction.[4] Theoretically and practically, the customer cares little about the physical attributes of a product except as those attributes contribute to delivering the benefits the customer desires.[5] Building managers do not care what fuel they burn. They switch between fuels depending on their relative cost per BTU. When it comes to getting a good night's sleep, people do not care what it is that gives them comfort. They buy futons, waterbeds, air mattresses, and foam rubber mattresses interchangeably with the traditional inner-spring mattress and box spring.

As Theodore Levitt pointed out years ago, firms that define their business in terms of what they do rather than in terms of the satisfactions or utilities their customers buy are myopic.[6] People's wants and needs do not change as much as do the products and technologies available to satisfy those needs. It is marketing's responsibility to define the benefits that customers value. It is the strat-

---

[4] Harvard Business School Professor Theodore Levitt stated, "Purchasing agents don't buy quarter-inch drills, they buy quarter-inch holes."

[5] Professor Levitt also stated, "Everybody sells intangibles in the marketplace, no matter what is produced in the factory." See Theodore Levitt, "Marketing Intangible Products and Product Intangibles," *Harvard Business Review,*" 59, no. 3 (May-June 1981), 94–102, at p. 94.

[6] Theodore Levitt, "Marketing Myopia," *Harvard Business Review,* 38, no. 4 (July-August 1960), 45–56.

egist's task to identify and understand the real source of competition for satisfying customer needs, whether that competition be from similar or dissimilar product offerings.

Products as Psychosocial Symbols

It is difficult to justify the purchase of sterling silver flatware on any functional basis. The difference in price between sterling and stainless for a service for eight is easily more than $1000. Both materials transport food from plate to mouth equally well. Sterling requires more maintenance (it must be polished) and it is doubtful that it is a good financial investment unless one expects a rapid rise in silver prices. Yet sterling sells. Why? One answer is that more than anything else, sterling silver flatware is symbolic of a gracious, traditional lifestyle.

Products and brands have symbolic content.[7] At the product level, there is the general meaning that society attaches to objects and activities. At the object level, for example, station wagons do not mean the same thing that two-seat sports models do. The wagon means family and practicality, while the sports car symbolizes youth and playfulness. At the brand level there is the finer tuning of that symbol as the firm consciously or unconsciously positions itself among the available brands of that same product. The Mercedes-Benz roadster and Porsche 928 are both sporty, imported two-seaters but symbolize quite different things to their owners. Exhibit 3-1 discusses how the automobile market continues to match its products to customer needs.

Marketers need to understand not only the symbolic attributes of their product but to recognize that the symbolic content can itself be the major satisfaction or benefit sought. Marketers must therefore manage the symbolic aspects of their products as carefully as they manage the physical realities.[8] The symbolic content of a product may be ascribed or acquired. Ascribed content is that which society assigns to objects and actions. Many objects carry meaning independent of what any business might do. For years, California's prune farmers have tried to disassociate prunes from their unfortunate symbolism.[9] Acquired symbolic content, on the other hand, is that which the firm fosters and develops. The Marlboro brand of cigarettes has skillfully added symbolic content to its brand over the years through the masculine images and associations it uses in its advertising. Virginia Slims took the opposite approach to obtain its feminine identification.

---

[7] For the classic exposition of this idea, see Sidney J. Levy, "Symbols for Sale," *Harvard Business Review*, 37, no. 4 (July-August 1959), 117–124. Levy expands on his ideas in *Marketplace Behavior—Its Meaning for Management* (New York: AMACOM, 1978); appendices A and B are especially relevant. A broader perspective is given by Mihaly Csikszentmihalyi and Eugene Rochberg-Halton, *The Meaning of Things: Domestic Symbols and the Self* (Cambridge: Cambridge University Press, 1981).

[8] See, for example, C. Whan Park, Bernard J. Jaworski, and Deborah J. MacInnis, "Strategic Brand Concept-Image Management," *Journal of Marketing*, 50, no. 4 (October 1986), 135–145.

[9] "California Prune Advisory Board (A)," Harvard Business School Case 9-576-046.

EXHIBIT 3-1

The Evolving Definition of Performance
in the Automobile Industry

"Back in the 1950s, U.S. automakers turned out cars in one size—big. Today full-line manufacturers produce five basic sizes (mini, subcompact, compact, midsize, and full-size), with several variations of each (two-door, four-door, three- and five-door hatchback, fastback). 'We have learned that universal mass production is not enough,' says Kazuo Morohoshi, head of Toyota's Tokyo Design Center. 'In the 21st Century, you personalize things more to make them more reflective of individual needs.' The winners will be those who target narrow customer niches most successfully with specific models."

SOURCE: From Alex Taylor III, "Why Toyota Keeps Getting Better and Better and Better," *Fortune*, copyright © 1990 The Time Inc. Magazine Company. All rights reserved.

Products as Causal Concepts

A product contains a cause-and-effect promise: "Buy me and use me and you'll be satisfied." A product concept contains the essential elements of that promise—it identifies the key benefits the product will provide to its customers, as explained in Exhibit 3-2.[10] Before the potential customer will buy the product, he or she must first understand and believe that promise. Marketers and others within the firm understand their product and its promise so well that they may find it difficult to understand that the promise is not obvious to others.

Communicability and credibility are the two aspects of the product concept with which marketers need to be concerned. Communicability refers to the ease with which the basic concept can be communicated. Some promises are simple and apply to all consumers in all situations. A new battery that lasts twice as long as others might be such an idea. More complex promises, those which hold only in certain situations or only for specific consumers, are more difficult to communicate. Many financial products seem to fall into this category. They promise, "This financial investment product is good if inflation is _____, interest rates are _____, you are in the _____ tax bracket, are married, and your spouse does/doesn't earn over $_____ per year."

Some concepts are easily communicated but are not credible. When semi-moist food technology was first applied to pet food under the Gainesburgers® brand, the underlying concept was easy to communicate.[11] The product con-

[10] C. Merle Crawford, *New Products Management*, 3rd ed. (Homewood, IL: Richard D. Irwin, Inc., 1991), chapter 8. Some term this the *product's core benefit proposition*. See Glen L. Urban and John R. Hauser, *Design and Marketing of New Products* (Englewood Cliffs, NJ: Prentice-Hall, 1980), pp. 155–157.
[11] "General Foods Post Division (A)," Harvard Business School Case 9-510-008, (B) 9-510-009, (C) 9-564-001.

EXHIBIT 3-2

The Product Concept

A product concept is a verbal description of a product that communicates all of its essential elements. These elements include the product's attributes—the technology that makes it possible and the form that the product takes—and the benefits that it delivers users, as shown here:

Form ⟶
Technology ⟶ Attributes + Benefits = Product concept

Complete concepts:

- Slager Beer: A new brewing technique brings a completely different enjoyment to beer. (This is technology plus benefit, with form unstated.)
- Slager Beer: A double-strength beer that recaptures the taste enjoyment of the 1800s. (This is a form plus benefit, with technology unstated.)

Incomplete concepts (cannot be evaluated):

- Slager Beer: A beer that tastes good. (Benefit only)
- Slager Beer: A beer darker than other beers. (Form only)
- Slager Beer: A beer made by a totally new process. (Technology only)

SOURCE: Adapted from C. Merle Crawford, *New Products Management*, 3rd ed. (Homewood, IL: Richard D. Irwin, Inc., 1991), p. 75.

---

tained 100% beef, had one third the bulk of canned dog food, was packaged in cellophane for ease of use, did not smell, needed no refrigeration, and supplied all of a dog's nutritional needs. People understood the concept and promise and even liked it. The trial rate of the product in test market, however, was low, indicating that most potential consumers did not find the idea credible. Its advertising program had to deal with the credibility issue head-on. Educating the consumer about the product was a major task.

The causal promise is the key element that links the customer to the firm and that links the marketing, manufacturing, and product development activities within the firm. A clearly enunciated causal promise is a performance standard which marketing can give to product development and manufacturing by saying, "Design and build a product which matches this promise." The customer, of course, is the ultimate arbiter of the extent to which the promise is fulfilled.

Products as Experiences

There is an old adage, "The proof of the pudding is in the eating." While simple ownership may be the key benefit in some instances, the *experience* of the product is an important aspect for most products, and in some instances the experience *is* the product.[12] Service products, for example, are frequently highly experiential. Plays, movies, and musical performances are more than the story or the music. They involve experiencing the aesthetics of the surroundings, the pulse of the audience, the interaction between performers and audience, and the conscious or subconscious recognition of the ephemeral nature of the event.[13] But one need not go so far afield for the experience to be important. Christopher B. Hemmeter, the developer of the $750 million, 850-room Westin Kauai resort hotel in Hawaii, defined his business as follows: "We're not in the hotel business. We build experiences, not buildings."[14] Dissecting the product into its experiential components is an important aspect of analyzing and comparing products.

The experiential aspect of service products as compared to physical products is both their strength and weakness. It is a strength in that experiences are powerful satisfiers—life is an experience, after all. The experiential aspect of a service, however, is also its main weakness from a managerial viewpoint.[15] An experiential service is a process in which the customer participates along with the firm's employees—the service providers. The service product itself is the interaction that occurs between the two.[16] Since both customer and provider vary in mood, temperament, and energy in general and from day to day, the result is that the service product varies. It is never quite the same. In contrast, a box of breakfast cereal varies little from day to day or even year to year. Managing experiential products demands that management identify the key dimensions of experiential satisfaction and design operations systems which naturally shape the "spontaneous" interaction to deliver on those key dimensions.[17] Exhibit 3-3 examines further the characteristics of services as product offerings.

---

[12] See Morris B. Holbrook and Elizabeth C. Hirschman, "The Experiential Aspects of Consumption: Consumer Fantasies, Feelings, and Fun," *Journal of Consumer Research*, 9, no. 2 (September 1982), 132–140; and Morris B. Holbrook, Robert W. Chestnut, Terence A. Oliva, and Eric A. Greenleaf, "Play as Consumption Experience: The Roles of Emotions, Performance, and Personality in the Enjoyment of Games," *Journal of Consumer Research*, 11, no. 2 (September 1984), 728–739. Variety seeking is another experiential aspect of products. See Leigh McAlister and Edgar Pessemier, "Variety Seeking Behavior: An Interdisciplinary Review," *Journal of Consumer Research*, 9, no. 3 (December 1982), 311–322.

[13] See, for example, Sidney J. Levy, John A. Czepiel, and Dennis W. Rook, "Social Division and Aesthetic Specialization: The Middle Class and Musical Events," in Elizabeth C. Hirschman and Morris B. Holbrook, eds., *Symbolic Consumer Behavior* (Ann Arbor, MI: Association for Consumer Research, 1981).

[14] "A Hawaiian Developer Builds the Untraditional," *The New York Times*, September 16, 1987, p. D2.

[15] John A. Czepiel, "Managing Customer Satisfaction in Consumer Service Businesses" (Cambridge MA: Marketing Science Institute Report No. 80-109, September 1980).

[16] See Peter G. Klaus, "Quality Epiphenomenon: The Conceptual Understanding of Quality in Face-to-Face Service Encounters," in John A. Czepiel, Michael R. Solomon, and Carol F. Surprenant, eds., *The Service Encounter: Managing Employee/Customer Interaction in Service Businesses* (Lexington, MA: Lexington Books, 1985).

[17] See Christopher H. Lovelock, "Managing Interactions between Operations and Marketing and Their Impact on Customers," in David E. Bowen, Richard B. Chase, Thomas G. Cummings, et al., eds., *Service Management Effectiveness* (San Francisco, CA: Jossey-Bass, 1990); and Valarie A. Zeithaml, A. Parasuraman, and Leonard L. Berry, *Delivering Quality Service: Balancing Customer Perceptions and Expectations* (New York: Free Press, 1990).

EXHIBIT 3-3

Services as Products

Are services the same as products? How can one equate an action with a hard, physical object? Isn't managing a service business a lot different from managing a product business? The answers? Yes. Easily. Definitely!

Products and services both are promises of satisfaction. While a service is a deed, act, or performance and products are physical objects, insofar as customers are concerned both are offers of future benefits.[18] It is true that a customer cannot pick up a service, turn it around, and look at it from all angles prior to purchase, but then neither can the purchaser of a car evaluate the kind of service the dealership will extend after purchase or the manufacturer's willingness to authorize in-warranty repairs. Clearly, managing a service business is different from managing a product business, but from the strategic viewpoint both act the same.[19]

However, in studying services offerings for strategic insight, there are useful concepts. Lovelock suggests that five questions will allow one to isolate the critical conceptual issues in service products:

1. What is the nature of the service act?
2. What type of relationship does the service organization have with its customers?
3. How much room is there for customization and judgment on the part of the service provider?
4. What is the nature of demand and supply for the service?
5. How is the service delivered?[20]

The first of these questions is perhaps the most useful. Lovelock suggests that the nature of the service act be categorized as tangible versus intangible and

The Product as Offering

The product that a firm offers in the marketplace may vary in its exact content. It may, for example, consist of little more than the bare minimum necessary to fulfill a narrowly defined benefit promise. In the case of physical products, this bare-minimum offering might consist of the basic physical product in the most simple protective packaging, sold for cash on the basis of a product specification sheet,

[18] Theodore Levitt, "Marketing Intangible Products and Product Intangibles," *Harvard Business Review*, 59, no. 3 (May-June 1981), 94–102.
[19] Leonard L. Berry, "Service Marketing Is Different," *Business*, 30, no. 3 (May-June 1980), 24–29; Ben M. Enis and Kenneth J. Roering, "Services Marketing: Different Products, Similar Strategies," in J. H. Donnelly and W. R. George, eds., *Marketing of Services* (Chicago: American Marketing Association, 1981).
[20] Christopher H. Lovelock, "Classifying Services to Gain Strategic Marketing Insights," *Journal of Marketing*," 47, no. 3 (summer 1983), p. 10.

EXHIBIT 3-3 (cont.)

then analyzed against the act's recipients, whether people or things, as shown in Exhibit Figure A. His schema allows one to answer such questions as "Does the customer need to be physically present? Does the customer need to be mentally present during service delivery? In what ways is the target of the service act 'modified' by receipt of the service?"[21]

EXHIBIT FIGURE A

Understanding the nature of the service act

WHAT IS THE NATURE OF THE SERVICE ACT?	WHO OR WHAT IS THE DIRECT RECIPIENT OF THE SERVICE?	
	PEOPLE	THINGS
TANGIBLE ACTIONS	SERVICES DIRECTED AT PEOPLE'S BODIES: • Health care • Passenger transportation • Beauty salons • Exercise clinics • Restaurants • Haircutting	SERVICES DIRECTED AT GOODS AND OTHER PHYSICAL POSSESSIONS: • Freight transportation • Industrial equipment repair and maintenance • Janitorial services • Laundry and dry cleaning • Landscaping/lawn care • Veterinary care
INTANGIBLE ACTIONS	SERVICES DIRECTED AT PEOPLE'S MINDS: • Education • Broadcasting • Information services • Theaters • Museums	SERVICES DIRECTED AT INTANGIBLE ASSETS: • Banking • Legal services • Accounting • Securities • Insurance

SOURCE: Christopher H. Lovelock, "Classifying Services to Gain Strategic Marketing Insights," in *Journal of Marketing*, 47, no. 3 (summer 1983), p. 12. Reprinted with permission of the American Marketing Association.

requiring customer pick-up, and with no warranty. On the other hand, the offer may consist of that same product loaded with extra features and packaged in a permanent protective carrying case with accessories, available for lease with no down payment, and selected on the basis of a lengthy consultation which determined whether the product was suitable for the customer, how to use it, and which exact model to buy. The offer may even have included a warranty covering both manufacturing defects and the application of the product.

Clearly the two offerings differ. While both may offer the same core benefit or generic product, the total package of benefits the customer receives is different for each.[22] Levitt suggests that product offerings such as these can be ana-

---

[21] Lovelock, "Classifying Services," p. 12.

[22] Theodore Levitt, "Marketing Success through Differentiation—of Anything," *Harvard Business Review*, 58, no. 1 (January-February 1980), 83–91. Kotler uses slightly different terminology, which is compared to Levitt's in Figure 3-2.

Figure 3-2 Generic, expected, and augmented product concept

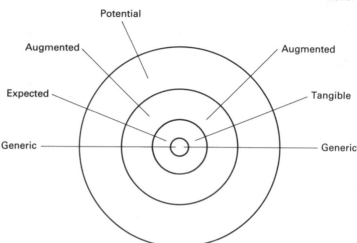

SOURCE: Adapted from Philip Kotler, *Marketing Management: Analysis, Planning Im-plementation and Control*, 6th ed. (Englewood Cliffs, NJ: Prentice Hall, 1988), p. 446; and Theodore Levitt, "Marketing Success through Differentiation—of Anything," *Harvard Business Review*, 83–91.

lyzed by reference to the generic (or core) product, the expected product, the augmented product, and the potential product, as shown in Figure 3-2.

The *generic* product consists of the bare-minimum, substantive object or actions necessary to fulfill the core of the basic benefit proposition. In automotive terms this is a chassis, engine, transmission, four wheels, a seat, and protective body. It is the bare minimum necessary to satisfy customers' basic needs. As shown in Figure 3-2, this is the center of the offering.

The *expected* product is the minimum of everything that a customer considers an essential value component to purchase the offering. It would be difficult to categorize, let alone list, all that could be expected and valued. Packaging, applications advice, delivery dates, credit, repair service, trust, and security of supply are just some of the things that may be in the expected product. The expected product may be less *or* more than offered.

The *augmented* product is one in which the seller has added value to the offering beyond what was expected. One of the reasons for the success of Japanese automobiles in the U.S. is that the models they exported included as standard equipment many items that had been optional on U.S.-made cars. The value additions of the augmented product may take many forms. Guaranteed, scheduled delivery may offer the buyer great value but cost the supplier little. Burger King's "have it your way" slogan illustrated how it had augmented the standard McDonald's hamburger.

The *potential* product includes all that might be done to add value to the offering. For some products, the list may be long and include everything from governmental lobbying on customers' behalf to the provision of advertising support. In other instances, there may be little that might be done to add value. Nonetheless, the marketer, as judge of what customers value, must keep the potential in mind lest a more savvy competitor preempt the opportunity by adding value.

Products as Technology

It is easy to overlook the technological content of products. As consumers we buy benefits, and once the products which deliver them are on the market, we care little about how they are created or delivered. Yet without the technology neither the product nor the benefit would be possible. A product is not so much the result of technology as the physical embodiment of technology. Inherent in objects and actions is the knowledge of how and why the product works.

Technology is the knowledge of how to do or make something which yields benefits to users. That ability is an asset. Patent laws and the laws governing trade secrets and intellectual property attest to that fact.[23] For example, the firm which possesses such knowledge can get a return on it in two ways. It can pass the benefits on to customers in the form of products or services which embody the technology, or it can sell the technology directly to customers so they can use it.[24] Many firms license others to operate under patents they own or pass on trade secrets and know-how they have developed.

The returns obtained on a product can be allocated to two sources: (1) the monopoly profits that accrue as a result of knowing how to do something that few others can, and (2) the returns that flow as a result of the investment in the physical assets that embody the technological principles. This understanding yields several strategic insights. First, the knowledge and ability to do or make controls the supply function. Patents are time limited and trade secrets difficult to keep. Over time, therefore, the value of technology as an asset decreases as others learn how to make the product or perform the activity. Sooner or later imitators catch up to innovators.

Second, the state of technology does not remain static either in the short or the long run. In the short run, one way that products compete is by leapfrogging each other in terms of performance—whether measured in taste, styling, speed, or durability. In any industry in which the technology advances over time, the competitor with the newest product in the market often has the best product. That is why IBM's competitors have such a hard time competing—IBM's superior R&D resources enable it to bring out more new products, faster, than its competitors. Figure 3-3 shows how the Japanese are winning over the U.S. auto

[23] See Louis W. Stern and Thomas L. Eovaldi, *Legal Aspects of Marketing Strategy* (Englewood Cliffs, NJ: Prentice-Hall, 1984), chapter 2.

[24] Noel Capon and Rashi Glazer discuss this option in their article "Marketing and Technology: A Strategic Coalignment," *Journal of Marketing*, 51, no. 4 (July 1987), 1–14. For a particularly informative exposition of current practices and the profitability of licensing technology, see Andrew Pollack, "A Chip Maker's Profit on Patents," *The New York Times*, October 16, 1990, pp. D1 and D19.

Figure 3-3   How Toyota is beating U.S. auto makers

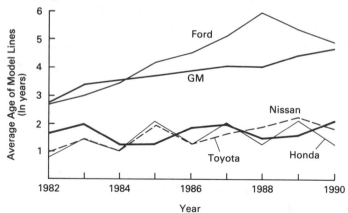

SOURCE: Alex Taylor III, "Why Toyota Keeps Getting Better and Better and Better," *Fortune*, November 19, 1990, p. 69.

makers as measured by the average age of the models in their product lines. Ford and GM have average product ages of approximately five years in comparison to the one- to two-year average age of the products of their Japanese competitors.

Technology is even more dynamic and competitively dangerous in the long run. In the long run, it is not just improvements within an existing technology regime but entirely new technologies which compete. Ballpoint pens obsoleted fountain pens, which had obsoleted steel-nibbed stick pens, which had obsoleted quill pens.[25] As soon as one technology is on the market, somewhere there is someone working to obsolete it. In fact, the more technological a product the more likely it will be replaced by a better technology for producing the same benefit. R&D is the ultimate marketing tool, for it creates the ability to supply benefits.

Third, the financial returns that come from a firm's investment in physical assets which embody the technology can be destroyed overnight by the emergence of a new technology which obsoletes the existing asset base. All of the plant and equipment owned by the Swiss watch industry was rendered useless as an earning asset by the emergence of electronic timekeeping technology. There was simply no profitable use for the machinery which made the tiny precision parts that drove mechanical watches. The technology and the capital assets which embodied it were obsolete. Evidence suggests that the personal computer is doing the same to typewriters.[26]

The strategist must understand the role that technology plays in the business. Just as customers must be constantly replenished through advertising and selling, so too must the firm's technology base—the source of its core

---

[25] See the many examples cited in Arnold C. Cooper and Dan Schendel, "Strategic Response to Technological Threats," *Business Horizons*, February 1976, pp. 61–69.

[26] "Smith Corona's Market Is Tapping Out: Its Typewriters and Word Processors Are Losing Out to PCs," *Business Week*, July 16, 1990, p. 31.

competence—be constantly invigorated and advanced through R&D.[27] Technology is a more important and basic tool in the marketer's arsenal than many recognize. There is no more valuable advantage than the ability to solve customer problems with products that competitors have yet to learn how to make.

Products as Investments

To the firm, the product is an investment on which a return should be earned.[28] Individual products often require physical investments in plant and equipment (even if only at the margin) and always involve the ongoing expenditure of managerial and sales-force time (which, if not technically an investment, could always be expended on another product). At the least, the firm has working capital invested in the form of work-in-process, finished goods inventories, and accounts receivable.

Many managers have little understanding of the financial aspects of their products, and they delegate all financial questions to their resident number crunchers. This phenomenon has always seemed curious since those same managers are often intensely competitive individuals who would never think about playing a game without knowing the rules about how to score in the game. To manage a product or product line properly, the manager must understand the economic formula by which the actions taken on behalf of a product, and the marketplace results of those actions, are translated into profits. This means understanding the product's value chain and cost structure (discussed in chapters 2 and 4), its cost behavior with time and experience (discussed in chapter 5), and cash flow (discussed in chapters 7 and 11).

USING PRODUCT CONCEPTS

The concepts we have discussed so far are not the only ones by which the strategist can gain insights useful in formulating strategy. Every product category has some ways of thinking about products that are particularly relevant to that business. (Exhibit 3-4 defines some of the more common slang phrases and terms used.) In some categories, for example, it may be useful to think about the product as an element in a use, consumption, or lifestyle system. In a system, the individual elements must be coordinated for the system to work. For example, a strategist gains a different insight by viewing laundry detergents as an element in a household cleaning system than as stand-alone products.[29] Product performance is defined in broader terms than simply "cleaning power." Cloth-

---

[27] C. K. Prahalad and Gary Hamel, "The Core Competence of the Corporation," *Harvard Business Review*, 90, no. 3 (May-June 1990), 79–91.

[28] Harper W. Boyd, Jr., and Jean-Claude Larreche, "The Foundations of Marketing Strategy," in Roger A. Kerin and Robert A. Peterson, eds., *Perspectives on Strategic Marketing Management*, 2nd ed. (Boston: Allyn & Bacon, Inc., 1983), pp. 24–41.

[29] Harper W. Boyd, Jr., and Sidney J. Levy, "New Dimension in Consumer Analysis," *Harvard Business Review*, 41, no. 6 (November-December 1963), 129–140.

EXHIBIT 3-4

Plain Vanilla—A Glossary of Terms

Marketers in industry use many shorthand terms to refer to the products in their markets and industries. These terms capture the essence of the products' physical characteristics or market situations. The following are some of the more colorful terms.

- *Plain vanilla* refers to a product which contains only the most basic features necessary to perform some function, such as a car without a radio, air conditioning, or other options. Typically referring to the product aimed at the middle of the mass market (vanilla ice cream comprises 80% of the ice cream market), a plain-vanilla product seldom has "bells and whistles."
- *Bells and whistles* describes the optional features that may be hung on a plain-vanilla product to satisfy the dreams of the buyer who wants it all. A product with every possible option is loaded. The term *loaded* originated in the automotive industry to describe the cars a dealer bought for inventory which carried all sorts of expensive options, forcing the buyer who wanted immediate delivery to pay top price.
- *Parity product* refers to a product no better or worse than the average product in the market or than some specific comparison product. Usually used in a derogatory sense as nothing to be proud of, as in "It's a parity product, at best."
- The term *me too* concerns the order of entry into a market. A me-too product is one that is rushed into the marketplace by a competitor afraid of being shut out. It frequently imitates the original entrant but need not be a parity product. This term suggests a younger sibling saying, "Me too, mommy!" and is not necessarily a complimentary term.
- *Drop-in* products are the quintessential me-too products. A drop-in product is one that is so identical to that of competitors that the customer can drop it into his or her production machinery without altering any settings or affecting in any way the production process.
- *Mummy dust* refers to the stuff that many manufacturers add to their products in minute quantities that is necessary to make the products work but for which no scientific basis can be found. Natural and synthetic rubber manufacturers frequently have formularies which call for up to a dozen different ingredients to be added to the base material in quantities so small that they are expressed in parts per million (ppm). *Whiffle dust* (derivation unknown) is a term frequently used interchangeably with mummy dust.
- *Jelly beans* is a term used in the electronics, communications, and computer industries to refer to the now ubiquitous integrated circuit chips which are the heart of those products. Memory chips, used in great quantities in computers, are especially commodity-like products to which the term was originally applied. Can be used to refer to any technically sophisticated small product bought in large quantities.

ing and furniture are often sold on the basis of coordinated lifestyle settings that show customers how to put together individual items in ways that match and create a pleasing ensemble.

Often, the market situation suggests the way the product should be conceptualized. For market leader products, the strategist will find great insight by viewing the product as competitors do, as a performance target to be beaten. The leader's competitors have it easy, after all. All they need to do is to beat the performance of the leader's offering. By adopting the competition's perspective, the analyst can begin to anticipate competitive actions and plan to preempt them. The way the product's performance is perceived across different market segments is of particular interest to the leader. Major differences across segments suggest ways the product may be vulnerable to competitive actions. Gaining an equal understanding of competitive products on the same dimensions is also valuable. Products do not stand alone but exist in relationship to competitive products. A discontinuity between the ways in which two competing products are conceptualized is a frequent source of strategic insight.

Characterizing products in conceptual terms frees one from the immediate situation to recognize the forces that drive the product's success. The next section continues this approach by exploring the ideas of value and product performance.

MEASURING AND MAPPING VALUE

Adam Smith noted long ago that the purpose of production is consumption. Restated from a customer's viewpoint, the purpose of purchase is consumption. Basic economic theory is predicated on the concept of utility and assumes that buyers seek to maximize the utility they receive from their purchases. This assumption is not unreasonable. The alternatives are that buyers either act randomly or are economic masochists who seek out products they do not like.

At the core of marketplace exchange is the concept of value: the acquisition of so many units of satisfaction per unit of expenditure in dollars and personal effort. Marketers who deliver satisfaction (their products are *effective*) gain sales over those who do not, and marketers who deliver greater value (their products are *efficient* providers of satisfaction) win over those who deliver lesser value.

These concepts are at the core of the Procter & Gamble product strategy. While outsiders frequently marvel at P&G's marketing prowess and the hundreds of millions it spends on advertising and selling its products, P&G insiders know that the "key to successful marketing is superior product performance."[30] They know today that the words in an 1891 advertisement for Ivory® soap still retain their truthfulness: The homemaker "does not try a poor soap twice."

[30] Speech by Edward G. Harness at the Annual Marketing Meeting of the Conference Board, 1977. P&G is four times larger than Colgate-Palmolive but spends more than seven times in R&D than Colgate-Palmolive, according to "R&D Scoreboard," *BusinessWeek*, June 15, 1990, p. 203.

Equally important is P&G's use of product performance as a strategic variable in a strategic manner. For P&G, ties or slight edges in product performance compared to competitive products do not represent a true competitive advantage. P&G's strategy is to enter markets only when it possesses what it terms a "big product edge." This defines a product that is perceived by consumers as "clearly better than anything else in the marketplace."[31] Such a strategy also explains P&G's preference for product sampling as a promotional technique. With truly outstanding product performance, sampling would have to be superior to advertising; the reality of actual personal experience with a product is a stronger motivator than the brief impersonal communications that comprise advertising.

Value, value-in-use, and perceived value are the basic variables that define the utility or satisfaction that customers derive from purchase and consumption and that are under the strategist's control.

Measuring Value

Value is not a difficult concept. It is the ratio of utility or satisfaction compared to the cost to obtain that utility.[32] Since products are satisfaction-generating systems (as described earlier in this chapter), one can compare two products on the basis of the satisfaction they deliver per dollar.

Physical Measures of Value. In markets where the satisfaction desired can be measured physically, value can indeed be expressed in numerical terms. In simple consumer terms, unit pricing in supermarkets is a measure of physical value. With standardized products, the amount of product provided on a per-dollar basis is the appropriate measure of value. One can also make such comparisons when the products are not identical. For example, one can compare the current carrying capability of aluminum versus copper wires. Laboratory tests can determine the inherent electrical resistance of both materials for different gauge wires and then express each as a function of their price. The result is a number that is useful in comparing the relative value of the two materials in an application where the capability to carry current is the major consideration. In this context, value is the price-versus-performance relationship that engineers speak of when designing (or buying) products. We discuss this relationship next.

Value-in-Use. Value-in-use is simply the calculation of the economic answer to the question, "What's it worth to you?" Sometimes termed the economic value to the customer, or EVC, value-in-use measures the economic cost to a user to satisfy a given need with one product or service versus another. In simple terms,

---

[31] John Smale, "Behind the Brands at P&G," *Harvard Business Review*, 63, no. 6 (November-December 1985), p. 88.

[32] In mathematical terms, value can be defined as $V = U/P$ where V = value, U = utility, and P = price. Value can be increased either by raising the utility level and holding price constant, or by lowering price while holding utility constant.

igure 3-4   Value-in-use

Economic value to the customer (EVC) is
life-cycle costs of the current product less start-up and
postpurchase costs of the new product plus incremental value

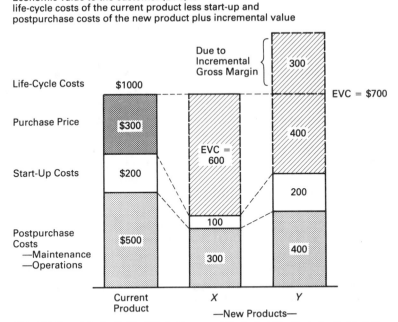

SOURCE: From John L. Forbis, "Market Leverage," in *Product Line Strategies*, Earl L. Bailey, ed., *The Conference Board* no. 816, 1982, p. 57. Reprinted by permission of The Conference Board, Inc.

for example, a newly formed household might compare the out-of-pocket cost of doing its laundry by taking it to a laundromat versus the purchase of a washer and dryer over some given period of time.

Figure 3-4 shows the total life-cycle cost to a customer for performing a certain function with an existing industrial product. That cost includes a purchase price of $300, $200 in installation and start-up costs, and $500 in postpurchase costs for operations and maintenance, for a total life-cycle cost of $1000. The answer to the question, "What's product X worth to the customer?" is easy to calculate. With postpurchase costs of only $300 and start-up/installation costs of $100, the buyer could pay up to $600 for the product. At $600, the buyer would be indifferent between the current product and product X. The value-in-use of product X is $600—the economic value of the product's performance to the customer in terms of the customer's current best way of performing the function.

The customer can also buy product Y, which has slightly different costs ($400 postpurchase and $200 start-up) and enhanced performance. For example, product Y is a retail terminal that, because it captures additional billing information, can boost revenues and reduce losses, and the increased profit it brings to the user is valued at $300. The total economic value of Y, then, is the $400 it is worth for performing the same function as the current product with lower postpurchase costs *plus* the $300 in additional profit it creates for its user, for a total of $700.

EXHIBIT 3-5

Steps in Calculating Value-in-Use

1. Define or diagram the consumption system or application in which the incumbent product is used. Draw a boundary around the portions of that system that might be changed or replaced if the candidate product were substituted.
2. Develop a general-use cost equation for the incumbent product which reflects the user's total cost of accomplishing the function within the defined boundary for the appropriate time period.
3. Create the similar equation for the candidate product, letting the candidate's price be an unknown, V, which is the value-in-use of the candidate. Equate the incumbent- and candidate-use cost equations and solve for V to obtain the candidate's value-in-use by using actual data for the application.

SOURCE: Adapted from Donald D. Lee, "Value-in-Use and the Opportunity Concept" from *Industrial Marketing*, p. 60. Copyright © 1978 Technomic Publishing Co., Inc.

Value-in-use counts both contributions to gross margins as well as savings in costs. Exhibit 3-5 details the three basic steps in calculating value-in-use.

Figure 3-5 demonstrates some of the thinking that management can go through in deciding how to price product X, or how it can understand the economics that must prevail if it is to beat the economics of the current product. To be successful at comparable performance levels, the life-cycle cost of any new product cannot exceed the total life-cycle cost of the incumbent. With the life-cycle costs for product X at $400 and those same costs plus purchase price for the incumbent totaling $1000, the highest price a customer would pay is $600.

If the manufacturer's costs are $250, then it can theoretically charge a price anywhere between $250 and $600. If it prices at the high end of the region, then it gives the customer little reason to switch from the current product, whereas at prices close to $250 it makes very little profit—it gives all of the value created to the customer. The object is to choose a price that shares enough of the value created with the market to induce customers to buy the new product, while keeping enough value for the firm to profit.

In reality, of course, there is a range of values-in-use in the market. Just as the value-in-use of owning a washer and dryer versus going to a laundromat increases as a function of the size of the family, so too does value-in-use for any product vary with end use, application, or customer characteristics. In a market, then, one observes a range of values-in-use, as shown in Figure 3-6. Setting the price at A will yield only small volumes, whereas pricing at B increases the volume substantially and a price at C captures all of the market.

A skimming price strategy (price set at A) is one that sets the price high to capture only the segments or applications that have a high economic value for a product. A penetration price, on the other hand, sets the price at C initially, and

Figure 3-5   Customer savings in context of value-in-use

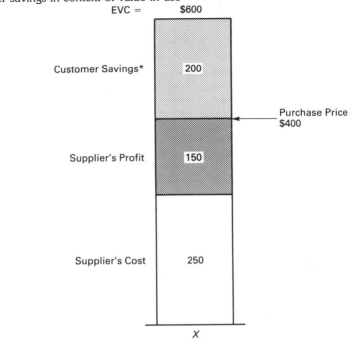

Note: Customer savings is defined as EVC less the product price.
SOURCE: John L. Forbis, "Market Leverage," Conference Board no. 816.
Reprinted by permission of The Conference Board, Inc.

by sharing (or giving away) much of the value it creates for users with higher values-in-use for the product, induces them to buy. For a buyer whose value-in-use is higher than price point B, the product at a price of C is a real bargain. In economists' terms, it creates a large amount of consumer surplus.

Value-in-use is not always apparent to customers. In industrial markets, firms frequently help potential customers estimate the value to be obtained by using their products in the customer's application. In the early days of computer use, it was common for the selling firm to survey a customer's system and to calculate how many clerks would be replaced, to justify the purchase of a computer.

The manager or strategist who does not understand the value a product brings to customers is at a great disadvantage. At the bottom of all marketing issues is the question, "What's it worth to you?" Value-in-use allows one to calculate the real economic answer to that question in many situations and to segment markets according to the differences in each segment's value-in-use.

Perceived Value.   Not all performance attributes, however, have economic impact(s) that can be measured directly. To a consumer, for example, a better taste or pleasing product appearance has value but has no economic impact in the traditional sense. In business-to-business markets, the reliability or trustworthi-

Figure 3-6   Range of values-in-use

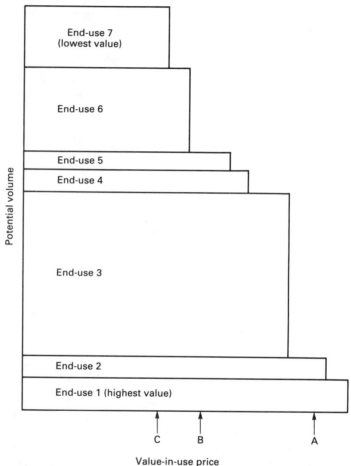

SOURCE: From John B. Frey, "Pricing and the Product Life Cycle," given at the annual Marketing Conference of The Conference Board.

ness of a supplier has some assumed long-run economic value to a buyer, but there is no economically objective measure of that value. If one believes that differential value is the key element in successful strategy, then it is important to understand the value that such performance variables contribute.

For example, a businessperson needs to travel to Paris, and considers the following flight descriptions:

> A B-707 flown by British Airways that will depart within two hours of the time you would like to leave and that is often late in arriving in Paris. The plane will make two intermediate stops, and it is anticipated that it will be 50% full. Flight attendants are "warm and friendly" and you would have a choice of two movies for entertainment.
>
> A B-747 flown by TWA that will depart within four hours of the time you would

TABLE 3-1 *A Comparison of Flight Offerings*

VARIABLE	FLIGHT 1	FLIGHT 2
Carrier	British Airways	TWA
Aircraft type	B-707	B-747
Flight type	Two intermediate stops	Nonstop
On-time performance	Often late	Almost never late
Courtesy	Warm and friendly	Cold and curt
Entertainment	Choice of two movies	Magazines only
Crowding	50% full	90% full
Departure time	Within two hours of desired	Within four hours of desired

like to leave and that is almost never late in arriving in Paris. The flight is nonstop, and it is anticipated that the plane will be 90% full. Flight attendants are "cold and curt" and only magazines are provided for entertainment.[33]

Many product offerings are similar to the foregoing. As shown in Table 3-1, they are characterized by the presence of many performance attributes whose values are categorical rather than quantifiable in the traditional sense. While a flight on one carrier rather than another (TWA vs. British Airways) or service type (warm and friendly vs. cold and curt) may certainly have differential value to a customer, there is nothing intrinsic that one can measure. Since consumers make such choices daily, they are able to calculate subjectively the complex trade-offs entailed and estimate their relative value. The manager who understands what customers value is in a good position to create valued offerings.

One measurement technique has been developed that does perform such measurements with a high level of validity and reliability. It is called *conjoint analysis* or *trade-off analysis*. Based on work in mathematical psychology and psychometrics, the technique allows the manager to compute consumers' utility functions for individual variables and to understand how they are combined, traded off, and valued. Exhibit 3-6 presents a brief example describing the essential elements of the technique.[34]

The issue here is not with the research technique but with the insight into people's value structure that the technique can provide. Since the key variable in any competitive situation is the offering, the ability to understand the value that customers place on the different elements of an offering provides managers with helpful insight.[35]

[33] This example is given in Paul L. Green and Yoram Wind, "New Way to Measure Consumers' Judgments," *Harvard Business Review*, 53, no. 4 (July-August 1975), p. 107.
[34] The best technical reference to conjoint analysis is Paul E. Green and V. Srinivasan, "Conjoint Analysis in Marketing: New Developments with Implications for Research and Practice," *Journal of Marketing*, 54, no. 4 (October 1990), 3–19.
[35] For those seeking insight into current methodological considerations, see Green and Srinivasan, *op. cit.* Joel Axelrod and Norman Frendberg provide a less technical explanation in "Conjoint Analysis: Peering behind the Jargon," *Marketing Research*, June 1990, pp. 28–35.

EXHIBIT 3-6

Measuring Customers' Judgments of Perceived Value

Conjoint analysis is a technique that allows managers to find out (1) what elements in an offering are valued by customers, (2) how much they are valued, and (3) how the customer trades off the different values to maximize the perceived value he or she obtains from a purchase. It is useful to think about the technique as having the seven steps outlined in the Exhibit Table A.

Steps 1 and 2 are often performed together. The objective here is (1) to learn from customers what attributes/benefits in an offering are important or relevant to them as they make their purchase choices, and (2) what levels or type of performance on those attributes those customers consider to be high or low (or good/poor, acceptable/marginal, etc.). These attributes are typically identified using qualitative techniques such as focus groups or unstructured personal interviews. To give a simple example, you might find that for customers of overnight express shipping services, delivery time and price were the two relevant attributes that defined the value of a service to customers. Further, in these interviews, it was found that customers identified delivery by 9:00 A.M. to be a high level of performance, noon to be an average level, and 3:00 P.M. to be the lowest acceptable level of performance. On the price issue, it was found that price should be examined at two levels—the usual price and a 20% premium versus the usual.

The third step in the process is to develop the conjoint questionnaire, which will elicit customers' evaluations of offerings with the different levels of the attributes identified. The object of the questionnaire is to force respondents to choose among offerings in which a sufficient number of attribute types and levels are presented. When this is done, the choices that the respondent makes contain information content, which allows the analyst to assess how much utility each attribute and its level provides customers and how they trade off one utility type for another. Exactly how this is done is the subject of some complex technical questions. These questions involve the exact task presented to respondents and how many of the possible attribute-level pairings are presented. A complex offering with many attributes and levels could have so many possible permutations that no respondent could reasonably be expected to choose among them.

EXHIBIT 3-6 (cont.)

EXHIBIT TABLE A

Conjoint analysis procedure

Stage 1.	Identify relevant attributes of the product/service.
Stage 2.	Specify the levels of each attribute to include in the study.
Stage 3.	Develop conjoint questionnaire.
Stage 4.	Select respondents and administer conjoint questionnaire.
Stage 5.	Estimate utility of each level of each attribute for each respondent. Examine attribute importance weights.
Stage 6.	(Optional) Develop preference segments by clustering or grouping customers having similar attribute preferences.
Stage 7.	(Optional) Simulate choice share among alternative company and competitor product/service offerings described by the attributes under study. May be for total market or selected segments.

EXHIBIT FIGURE A

Conjoint questionnaire alternative

1. *Full concept approach:* Each alternative contains one level of each attribute

Alt. 1	Alt. 2	Alt. 3
Price: Usual	Price: Usual	Price: Usual
Delivery: 9 A.M.	Delivery: Noon	Delivery: 3 P.M.

Alt. 4	Alt. 5	Alt. 6
Price: 20% premium	Price: 20% premium	Price: 20% premium
Delivery: 9 A.M.	Delivery: Noon	Delivery: 3 P.M.

2. *Trade-off matrix:* Rank order each cell in the matrix such that 1 = first choice, . . . , 6 = last choice.

Price \ Delivery	9 A.M.	Noon	3 P.M.
Usual	1*	2	5
20% premium	3	4	6

*Hypothetical customer answers.

    Exhibit Figure A presents two ways in which the possible choices in the overnight express freight service example could be presented to respondents. The full concept approach presents a set of alternatives, each of which contains one level of each attribute, whereas the trade-off matrix presents a series of matrices taking the attributes two at a time (in this simple example, the two are identical for all practical purposes). The choices are often presented to respondents using interactive PC-based questionnaires which present the trade-offs. Exhibit Figure B illustrates the trade-offs presented to respondents in a study concerning microcomputers.

EXHIBIT 3-6 (cont.)

EXHIBIT FIGURE B
Conjoint questionnaire trade-offs

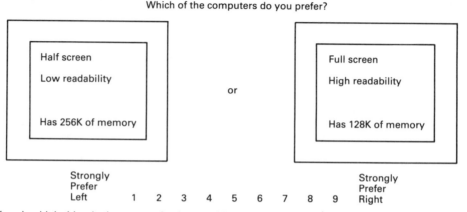

Which of the computers do you prefer?

Half screen									Full screen
Low readability			or						High readability
Has 256K of memory									Has 128K of memory

| Strongly Prefer Left | 1 | 2 | 3 | 4 | 5 | 6 | 7 | 8 | 9 | Strongly Prefer Right |

You should decide whether you prefer the portable computer described on the left, or the one on the right. If you prefer the computer on the left, type a number from 1 to 4. If you prefer the computer on the right, type a number from 6 to 9. '1' means that you strongly prefer the left. '9' means that you strongly prefer the right. A '5' indicates that you have no preference.

Type your preference to proceed.

SOURCE: John Morton Company, Chicago, IL, Company Literature.

The answers to the questionnaires have a high level of information content. If you look at the trade-off data matrix for the overnight express example, the customer unsurprisingly prefers earliest delivery at the lowest price and prefers least the offering of a late delivery at a price premium. The choice that is made between these two reveals this customer's relative preferences between price and delivery time. For this customer, a price premium for a morning delivery is not worthwhile if noon delivery is available. On the other hand, the customer would rather pay a 20% premium than have the shipment arrive at 3:00 P.M.

The fourth step in the process is to sample the relevant population and to obtain its responses to the questionnaire. This might imply separately sampling different segments in the market, across various user categories, or different decision-making levels. In the simple example we are using, there are only four respondents.

Given a completed data collection process, the fifth step is data analysis. The goal of the analysis is to estimate the utility (termed *part-worth utility*) each customer has for each level of each attribute. The analysis does not aggregate the data to obtain averages for the sample but rather calculates each customer's utility function separately. The process by which these utilities are obtained is another technical step in which the analyst has choices to make. Among the techniques used are dummy variable regression analysis and monotonic analysis of variance. The result of the analysis is like that presented in Exhibit Table B for the price and delivery attributes in our simple example.

EXHIBIT 3-6 (cont.)

EXHIBIT TABLE B
Customer Utilities and Importance Weights for Air Freight Example

ATTRIBUTE	CUSTOMER			
	1	2	3	4
Price utility: Usual	.6	.5	.2	.1
20% premium	−.6	−.5	−.2	−.1
Price importance weight	1.2	1.0	.4	.2
Delivery utility: 9 A.M.	.4	.8	.3	.4
Noon	.1	.4	.2	.1
3 P.M.	−.5	−1.2	−.5	−.5
Delivery importance weight	.9	2.0	.8	.9

In step 6, which is optional, the importance weights (shown in Exhibit Table B) are used to form clusters or segments of customers based on the similarity of the importance the attributes have for them. The importance weights reflect the range of utilities obtained for each customer for a given attribute. The utility range for customer 1 on price ranges from 0.6 to −0.6 for a total of 1.2, whereas for customer 4 the range is only from 0.1 to −0.1 for a total of 0.2. In this simple example, customers 1 and 2 appear to be the most price sensitive, while customer 2 is even more delivery sensitive. If there is a cluster here, it consists of customers 3 and 4, who appear to form a preference segment that is not terribly price sensitive and is medium high on delivery sensitivity.

The reason that conjoint analysis is so seductive is what can be done with the data in step 7. Recall that the technique has estimated each customer's utility function separately. In effect, the database is a small population of people for whom we can calculate the utility any given offering will create. This means that it is possible to simulate customers' choices of (or responses to) various product offerings and competitive scenarios. To do so, one calculates the utility created by each of the offerings—the firm's and the competitor's—and predicts which of the two the customer would choose based on their relative ability to create value for that customer.

In the simple example used here, utility would be the sum of the utilities for the delivery and price attributes. Let's look at a scenario in which we offered 9:00 A.M. delivery at a 20% price premium and the competitor offered 3:00 P.M. delivery at the usual price. Using the utilities presented in Exhibit Table B, customer 1's utility for a 9:00 A.M. delivery at a 20% price premium would be $(.4) + (−.6) = (−.2)$. Utility for the competitive offering would be $(−.5) + (.6) = (.1)$. Our prediction is that customer 1 would choose the competitor's offering in this scenario. By calculating the utility for each customer in the database, we can estimate the market share that each competitor would

EXHIBIT 3-6 (cont.)

obtain in the simulated market scenario. In this scenario, the firm would obtain a 75% market share—customers 2, 3, and 4 would choose our firm and only customer 1 would choose the competitor.

But the analysis assumes that the competitor holds to its current offering. What would happen if the competitor, rather than lose its share, responded by holding price and improved delivery to noon? In that scenario, our share would drop to 25% as only customer 4 would find that our offering created more value for it than the competitor's offering. It is this type of customer-based "war gaming" that makes the conjoint analysis procedure so useful.

SOURCE: From David B.Montgomery, "Conjoint Calibration of the Customer/Competitor Interface in Industrial Markets." Cambridge, MA: Marketing Science Institute, Report No. 85-112. Table A is from p. 4; Figure A from p. 5; Table B from p. 7.

Mapping Value

If we assume for illustrative purposes that we can express product performance or quality as a single number (such as current carrying capacity), then a simple plot of product performance or quality versus price indicates the value positions

Figure 3-7 Value map: five generic product/service positions

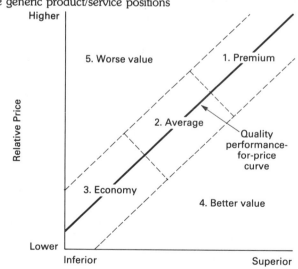

SOURCE: Robert D. Buzzell and Bradley T. Gale, *The PIMS Principles*, p. 112.

EXHIBIT 3-7

Three Value-Based Strategies,
Their Sources, and Their Advantages

Exhibit Figure A shows that from the starting point labeled A, the competitor seeking to improve its relative value position can either hold performance and reduce its price (point B), improve performance while holding price (point C), or simultaneously improve both performance and price (point D). Each move requires different capabilities and has different strategic implications.

The ability to offer improved value can come from three sources: *process* (or product) technology that reduces product costs, *product* (or process) technology that leads to performance improvement, or *financial* advantages that let a competitor deliver shareholders an acceptable return with smaller profit margins.

The strategic advantage of holding performance while reducing price (point B) depends on the magnitude of the reduction achieved by the new process. If the new process (or product) technology provides the competitor with knockout economics (the ability to price below existing opponents' variable costs while still achieving an acceptable return itself), then the strategy is viable. The competitor can achieve and hold a sustainable value advantage. If the cost reduction is more moderate, however, then competitors will simply match the lower price and the attacker's value advantage will be neutralized. A price advantage can be neutralized instantly.

The strategic advantage of improving performance while holding price (point C) follows a similar analysis except that its success depends on the importance of the performance improvement to customers. If the performance improvement obsoletes current performance levels (such as antibiotics did), then the value advantage will yield the desired results. If customers are satisfied with current performance levels, however, then threatened opponents can neutralize the value advantage by reducing their prices. In this way they reposition their product to offer a comparable price/performance ratio. Situations in which the performance improvement to customers lies between these two positions offer the competitor some advantage depending on the time it takes opponents to respond. At the least, the competitor achieves a temporary monopoly with customers who value the extra performance in the interim period.

The competitor who is able to improve both price and performance simultaneously is in an enviable position, for it is difficult for opponents to offset both sources of the value advantage. The new Japanese luxury imports, for example, are delivering what some would term superior physical performance in comparison to the European makes at prices almost $20,000 lower. It is reported that the prime reason behind this is the advanced manufacturing technology used by the Japanese. It supposedly takes Mercedes-Benz nineteen labor hours simply to correct assembly-line defects on its automobiles, while it

EXHIBIT 3-7 (cont.)

takes the Japanese a total of nineteen labor hours to make its cars.[36] Advantages of such a magnitude are not easily or quickly matched.

EXHIBIT FIGURE A
Technological advances can increase product value in two ways

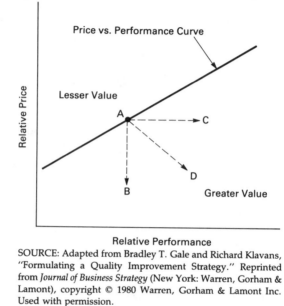

Relative Performance

SOURCE: Adapted from Bradley T. Gale and Richard Klavans, "Formulating a Quality Improvement Strategy." Reprinted from *Journal of Business Strategy* (New York: Warren, Gorham & Lamont), copyright © 1980 Warren, Gorham & Lamont Inc. Used with permission.

that are available in any market.[37] As shown in Figure 3-7, there are five positions that an offering can occupy. Offerings lying along the diagonal all offer the same relative value per dollar, although those closer to the origin offer less absolute performance and those farther away offer greater total performance. The three basic positions along the diagonal correspond to the three common product offerings: economy, average, and premium.

A product with average performance at an average price would fall into the middle range. If a product delivered superior performance and was priced correspondingly higher, it would fall into the premium range. A product offering a smaller absolute amount of performance but at an appropriate price would be

[36] The labor-hour numbers are cited in Alex Taylor III, "New Lessons from Japan's Carmakers," *Fortune,* October 22, 1990, pp. 165–168. Additional data on this point can be found in Steven Prokesch, "Jaguar Battle at a Turning Point," *The New York Times,* October 29, 1990, pp. D1 and D4; and Doron P. Levin, "European Luxury Cars Fade," *The New York Times,* February 27, 1989, pp. D1 and D7.

[37] Buzzell and Gale term the performance dimension *relative quality.* An economist might term it *utility. Satisfaction* could also be substituted. See Robert D. Buzzell and Bradley T. Gale, *The PIMS Principles: Linking Strategy to Performance* (New York: Free Press, 1987), chapter 6.

Figure 3-8   Perceived performance of four analgesics

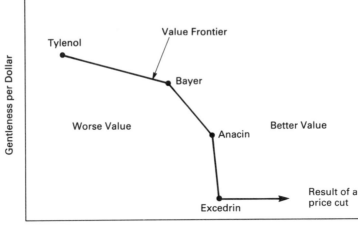

SOURCE: From John R. Hauser, "Theory and Application of Defensive Strategy." Cambridge, MA: Marketing Science Institute, Report No. 85-107.

designated as economy. All offer comparable value per dollar—the consumer need only decide how much performance is desired. In reality, of course, there is a band within which the products fall, both since markets are never perfect and due to minor variations in individuals' definitions of performance.

Products can also lie off the diagonal. A product located in the upper left-hand quadrant in Figure 3-7 offers worse value (a lower amount of performance at the same or higher price), whereas a product in the lower right-hand corner provides better value (a greater amount of performance at an equal or lower price). Over time, products in better value positions tend to induce customers to move their definition of acceptable value (the price-versus-performance curve) down and to the right. Exhibit 3-7 describes the three different strategies a competitor can take in pursuing better value.

Empirically, customers' purchase behavior and competitors' actions tend to force most products to align along the diagonal shown in Figure 3-7. Offerings which lie on the diagonal tend to hold share because they offer similar perceived value, and therefore there is no force which would cause customers to buy more or less. Products offering better value, on the other hand, tend to gain share since the better value they offer provides customers with the incentive to change their purchase behavior. In fact, the greater the difference in relative value offered, the greater the driving force behind the move toward the better-value product and the bigger the share effect. Similarly, products delivering worse value tend to lose share.

Mapping Perceived Value.   Consumers base their purchase behavior on their perceptions of product characteristics, and it is possible to represent products by how consumers perceive their characteristics or performance on dimensions important to their purchase. The value map shown in Figure 3-8 depicts the

Figure 3-9   Preference trade-offs

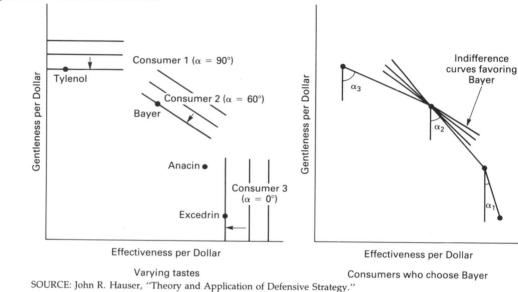

SOURCE: John R. Hauser, "Theory and Application of Defensive Strategy."

perceived performance on a per-dollar basis of four analgesic products (circa early 1970s) on two key product attributes—gentleness and effectiveness.[38]

Products which lie beneath the value frontier linking the three brands offer less value on either of the two dimensions and are unlikely to be purchased by a knowledgeable consumer. Analogous to the terminology used on the value map in Figure 3-7, the region beneath the curve in Figure 3-8 offers worse value and the region above offers better value. Also similar is the ability of a product to move in that space based on changes in price and/or performance (assuming that performance improvement is perceived by the market). A price cut, holding performance constant, will move a product out from the origin, as would an improvement in real or perceived performance (as shown for Excedrin in Figure 3-8). The depiction is useful because, in addition to showing how a value map with two independent performance variables can be constructed, it also allows one to understand consumer choice behavior in value terms. This mode of analysis also allows one to better analyze competitive actions and reactions, as described in Exhibit 3-8 on p. 98.

Consumers vary in their tastes. Some prefer gentleness; some effectiveness. By using indifference curves to show consumers' relative utility for the two attributes of analgesic performance, it is possible to understand their behavior (see Figure 3-9). The angle of the indifference curve for consumer 1, who valued only gentleness, will be a horizontal line (90 degrees), and that consumer will buy Tylenol. Consumer 2 values gentleness somewhat more than effectiveness (the an-

---

[38] This analysis is based on John R. Hauser, "Theory and Application of Defensive Strategy" (Cambridge, MA: Marketing Science Institute, August 1985), Report No. 85-107.

Figure 3-10 Distribution of consumer tastes

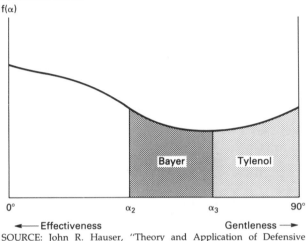

SOURCE: John R. Hauser, "Theory and Application of Defensive Strategy."

gle of the indifference curve is 60 degrees) and will choose Bayer. Consumer 3, on the other hand, who values only effectiveness (0 degree angle) chooses Excedrin. Consumers whose taste angles fall between α_2 and α_3 will choose Bayer. Consumers with taste angle α_2 will be equally likely to choose Bayer or Anacin.

If we know the distribution of consumers' tastes (expressed as the angle of their indifference curves), then it is possible to compute market share. As shown in Figure 3-10, the market share for any product (Bayer, for example) is simply the area under the taste distribution (the area between α_2 and α_3). The market share for Tylenol is the area between α_3 and 90 degrees. This analysis assumes that all brands have equal awareness and distribution in the marketplace. If a consumer is not aware of the Tylenol brand—it is not in the consumer's evoked set, the set of products of which a consumer is aware and can evaluate—then it does not exist as a choice for that consumer and its share will be lower accordingly. The same analysis holds for distribution—if a product is not available for sale in the store which the consumer frequents, then its share will be lower.

For example, in the early 1970s Tylenol had a reasonable share of the analgesic market even though it was not advertised. The awareness it achieved was obtained through doctors' recommendations (which themselves were strongly influenced by the sales force of McNeil Laboratories, the division of Johnson & Johnson responsible for the product). Figure 3-11a shows how Figure 3-10 would be modified to account for how the low general awareness level of Tylenol would affect its share, especially among those for whom gentleness was not an important attribute.

Bristol-Myers saw Tylenol's unique performance position and the opportunity available to the marketer who used advertising to increase awareness of the availability of the gentleness performance benefit and the existence of a brand to satisfy that benefit (and thereby increase the market). It launched its own prod-

Figure 3-11 Tylenol vs. Datril

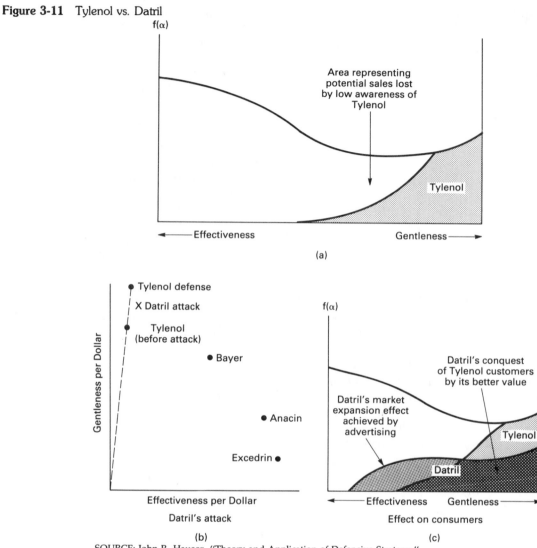

SOURCE: John R. Hauser, "Theory and Application of Defensive Strategy."

EXHIBIT 3-8

Value and Defensive Marketing Strategy

The analysis of the Tylenol case presented in the text led Hauser (of MIT) and Steve Shugan (of the University of Chicago) to wonder if the analysis could be generalized.[39] In their work, they assumed that the defending firm was behaving rationally before the attack (maximizing long-term profit) and that it would react to achieve the best profit after the attack. Further, they assumed that the attacker enters with perfect foresight as to the defender's reaction. They simplified the analysis by focusing on the primary defender and holding all other firms' strategies constant. In effect, they tried to analyze what would be an equilibrium result. They published fourteen theorems based on their work. This exhibit examines a few of the more interesting theorems.

> If consumer tastes are uniformly distributed, then profits after the attack can be increased by lowering price from its before-attack level.

Since the price decrease causes the brand to move out from the origin (and offer more product per dollar), this value enhancement has a share-increasing effect that offsets the decrease in margin that comes from the lowered price. In terms of total profit, the firm that lowers price and holds or gains share is better off than the firm that holds margins but loses share.

> There exist distributions of customer tastes for which the best defensive pricing strategy requires a price increase.

If the consumer taste distribution is multimodal rather than uniform (is characterized by several peaks rather than being even across the performance attribute distribution), then one can infer that those peaks represent market segments. In such a case, a brand's position gives it something akin to a local monopoly. If this is the case and (1) before the attack it paid for the defender to have a low price to allow it to compete in more than one segment and (2) the attacker outpositions the defender in one market segment but not in others, then (3) after the attack, the firm may pay the defender to raise price and, in effect, exploit the local monopolies not under attack.

> If market size does not increase dramatically, optimal defensive profits must decrease if a new brand enters competitively, regardless of defensive price, distribution, and awareness advertising strategy.

[39] John R. Hauser and Steven M. Shugan, "Defensive Marketing Strategy," *Marketing Science*, 2, no. 4 (fall 1983), 319–360. More recent work in this area can be found in John R. Hauser, "Competitive Price and Positioning Strategies," *Marketing Science*, 7, no. 1 (winter 1988), 76–91.

EXHIBIT 3-8 (cont.)

Hauser and Shugan demonstrated this by asking the reader to consider the argument, "If we can increase profits after the attack when the market is more competitive, why did we not do so before the attack?" It is from this insight that one understands the importance of proactive strategies which prevent a competitor from getting a foothold in a market. Once in, the defender loses profits. That is why Tylenol fought so hard versus Datril.

Product improvements in response to attacks are shown in Exhibit Figure A. The terminology used refers to the defender's strength as that dimension on which it is strongest (dimension 1 in the figure). The upper adjacent attack shown is one that positions the attacking brand on the side away from the defender's strength, between it and the next brand to its left. The pure defensive movements that the defender may take are shown by the dotted lines as toward the attack or away from the attack. Since movements in reality are seldom pure, the movement net of the two pure directions is shown by the solid line.

> At the margin, if consumer tastes are uniformly distributed and the competitive brand chooses an upper adjacent attack, then profits are increasing for product improvements away from the attack (or, alternatively, toward the defender's strength).[40]

This finding is bolstered by the strategy dictum, "Play to your strength." Defending brands, like A or C, frequently seem to have obtained their share by being the dominant brand on a key dimension. Probably because of pioneer advantage, the attacking products do not choose a parity position but rather an upper or lower adjacent attack. Hauser and Shugan found an unambiguous result that movements toward the defender's strength pay off.

> If the market size does not increase dramatically as a result of the new competitor, the best advertising strategy includes decreasing the budget for awareness advertising.
>
> If consumer tastes are uniformly distributed and the competitive brand chooses an upper adjacent attack, then at the margin, profits are increasing in spending advertising dollars on positioning messages that reinforce the defender's performance on attributes away from the attack (toward the defender's strength).

These two results, for unsegmented markets, combine to give useful insights on the role of advertising in defensive situations. Together they suggest

---

[40] Under certain conditions, profits can improve for product improvements toward the attack (and, with respect to the advertising discussion to come, for advertising positions toward the attack). The conditions under which these findings hold, however, are not easily interpretable. The reader can find the discussion in Theorem 9 of Hauser and Shugan, "Defensive Marketing Strategy" (1983).

EXHIBIT 3-8 (cont.)

that spending on advertising aimed at strengthening the brand's image along its strength is a more effective strategy than spending on advertising that simply increases consumer awareness about the brand. In the Tylenol example, this would mean favoring advertising copy that stresses gentleness rather than just its name.

EXHIBIT FIGURE A
Defender's options under an adjacent attack

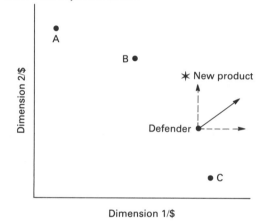

SOURCE: From John R. Hauser, "Theory and Application of Defensive Strategy." Cambridge, MA: Marketing Science Institute, Report No. 85–107

uct, Datril, which it advertised as "just as good as Tylenol, only cheaper" using direct price comparisons to illustrate the message. Since the amount of acetaminophen each brand contained was identical, the effect of the Datril strategy was to position the product as shown in Figure 3-11b.

This positioning had the potential to change Tylenol's share dramatically. While Datril could not reach all of Tylenol's customers by its national advertising, it could reach some of the customers of the other entrants who had interest in the gentleness benefit but were unaware of a product with which to fulfill it. Since it offered better value than Tylenol, Datril was better positioned to compete for those customers than Tylenol. The effect of this would have been for Datril to capture the area shown in Figure 3-11c.

In a strategy formulated at the highest levels of the firm, Tylenol's management decided to fight to maintain Tylenol's dominance. On the product front, Tylenol cut the price to the level of Datril, thereby neutralizing the Datril value advantage, as shown in Figure 3-11b.[41] Since Datril's advertising strategy was to compare its price to Tylenol's to demonstrate its value, that comparison no longer held, enabling Tylenol's managers to charge Datril with false advertising. Since Tylenol had some prior awareness and a strong image based on doctors' recommendations, it was able to win once Datril could no longer advertise a differential value benefit. Tylenol then initiated national advertising to sustain its dominance and added a flanker product, Extra Strength Tylenol, to capture customers with a greater interest in effectiveness.

PRODUCT PERFORMANCE AND QUALITY CONCEPTS

Products and services sell most easily when they deliver value. Value comes from performing the customer's desired function over some expressed time period. Three concepts are contained in that statement: performance of a function, the quality of that performance, and the satisfaction that customers experience as a result of that performance. There is little agreement among product designers, engineers, operations and production managers, economists, and marketers about a common conceptual terminology with which to communicate about product performance.[42] This section gathers together the common threads in their thinking about product performance, beginning with the two key concepts of perceived quality and conformance quality.

Quality Concepts

Most authorities use the term *perceived quality* to describe products and services which closely fit customer needs.[43] What this means is that the basic product design—the combination of technical features, aesthetics, and symbolic qualities—is a better fit to the customer's desires for benefits than others products. The customer wants a sports car, and car A more closely delivers on the customer's concept of sports car than does car B. As one scientist who designs complex polymer materials put it, "It's not simply that a polymer is best on all physical measures of performance. It's the overall balance of prop-

---

[41] Tylenol utilized the full strength of both the McNeil Laboratories and Johnson & Johnson sales forces to do this—giving rebates to wholesalers and retailers and even changing the prices of product already on the shelves. It was able to accomplish this in a few weeks.

[42] Two articles which seek to bridge that gap are John R. Hauser and Don Clausing, "The House of Quality," *Harvard Business Review*, 66, no. 3 (May-June 1988), 63–73; and Genichi Taguchi and Donald R. Clausing, "Robust Quality," *Harvard Business Review*, 68, no. 1 (January-February 1990), 65–75.

[43] Buzzell and Gale, in *The PIMS Principles*, use this terminology. Others use it to mean customers perceptions of an offering's quality based on experience and indirect measures such as image, brand names, and the like. For example, see David A. Garvin, "Competing on the Eight Dimensions of Quality," *Harvard Business Review*, 65. no. 6 (November-December 1987), 101–109.

erties linked to a specific application in terms that matter to customers that defines what material is best." Perceived quality as it is defined here captures the essence of that idea. Perceived quality is a market-derived definition of quality.

The second term used to describe a product is *conformance quality*. Conformance quality measures how well the firm does in producing products or delivering services that conform to the design standards. In one sense, if the appropriate specification to meet customer needs is "one inch," conformance quality measures how well the firm does in making products that measure one inch. Conformance quality would be considered to be better if production is within one tenth of an inch (0.9 to 1.1 inches) than if it is only within one half of an inch (0.5 to 1.5 inches). Conformance quality is an internally derived definition of quality.

In many instances, perceived quality can be copied (witness the quick "knock off" of hot styles in the fashion business) and many products are identical in general design, so conformance quality then becomes one of the key attributes in the customer's buying decision. However, many firms pay more attention to conformance quality than perceived quality because it is easily measured in physical engineering terms.

Discussions of quality can frequently become confused unless the participants are careful. Merely to refer to a *quality* product communicates little, for quality has many underlying aspects.[44]

Application Fitness.   Similar to perceived quality, application fitness describes the extent to which the product/service is appropriate to the needs of the market. Application quality is achieved by an overall integration of the physical and economic aspects of a product—the combination of attributes that determine how well the product fits the dominant mixture of customer needs.

Ford's Model T and Mustang models, Honda's Accord, the Douglas DC-3 and Boeing 727 airplanes, Levi's 501® jeans, Apple and IBM PCs, the IBM 360 computer series, the Lotus 1-2-3 spreadsheet program, the Waring blender and Cuisinart® food processor, M&M® candies, the basic Hershey's chocolate bar, and Kraft's Philadelphia brand cream cheese all exhibit such an appropriateness. When such a product emerges in a market which previously had numerous design configurations, it is termed the *dominant design*.[45] Dominant designs are seldom legally protectable and are frequently "cloned" by competitors. Exhibit 3-9 explains more fully the concept of the dominant design.

Performance.   The product does what it is designed to do better than other products designed for the same application. Performance is often a multifaceted

[44] The following discussion is suggested by David A. Garvin, "Competing on the Eight Dimensions of Quality," pp. 101–109.

[45] William L. Moore and Michael L. Tushman, "Managing Innovation over the Product Life Cycle," in W. L. Tushman and M. L. Moore, eds., *Readings in the Management of Innovation* (Boston, MA: Pitman Publishing, 1982), pp. 131–150.

EXHIBIT 3-9

The Dominant Design

Michael Tushman, William Moore, and James Utterback have advanced the idea of the emergence of the "dominant design" as an optimal product configuration which does not undergo any major changes for some time. As they see it, the dominant design is usually an evolutionary design in that each of its major features may have been incorporated in previous models, but the particular combination of features has not been present in any single previous model. They note, for example, that a number of features that were embodied in virtually all cars between 1920 and 1970 were present in the early 1900s: longitudinally mounted engine in front connected to rear-wheel drive via torque tube, steering wheel on the left, H transmission, water-cooled engine, independent body and chassis design, and the essential driver controls of today. Yet no single car contained all of these design features until the popularity of the Ford Model T, which did, made it a dominant design. Based on the number of experimental designs before the Model T and the similarity of all designs after it, this design combination appeared to be optimal.

Tushman, Moore, and Utterback cite the DC-3 as another example. It was not the largest, or fastest, or longest-range aircraft; it was the most economical large fast plane able to fly long distances. All of the features which made the design so completely successful had been introduced and proven in prior aircraft. After the DC-3's introduction in 1936, no major innovations were introduced until new jet-powered aircraft appeared in the 1950s.

Similarly, the Lotus® 1-2-3™ program was not the first spreadsheet program available. Visicalc, among others, preceded it on the market, but the Lotus version was the first to incorporate all of the best features of its predecessors. That combination made it the dominant design.

SOURCE: Adapted from material in William J. Abernathy and James M. Utterback, "Patterns of Industrial Innovation" (pp. 97–108) and William L. Moore and Michael L. Tushman, "Managing Innovation over the Product Life Cycle," (pp. 131–150), both in Michael L. Tushman and William L. Moore, eds., *Readings in the Management of Innovation* (Boston, MA: Pitman Publishing Inc., 1982).

---

concept. The product is faster, performs more accurately or at a higher level, is better tasting, smoother, more forgiving, easier, more economical, more consistent, or serves more applications/sizes. Product markets frequently advance the definition of average or acceptable performance over time based on changes in economics, technology, or simply the actions of the competitors as they seek advantage over rivals.

Poor product performance can be disastrous. In the mid-1970s, Schlitz substituted extra corn syrup for some of the expensive barley malt in its brew, and at one point was brewing beer in eleven days compared with the twenty-one days or more standard at most major brewers. The reduction of its quality and taste led customers to abandon the product. As one customer said, "Schlitz has cut quality to cut costs and now the stuff tastes like seltzer water. I don't intend to buy Schlitz again."[46] As a result, Schlitz beer lost one half of its market share, from 16.2% in 1976 to 8.5% in 1980, through poor-quality and poor-tasting suds. While the company said that it had never made bad beer, it admitted that it had to make changes to improve its quality. The company was never able to recover the lost share and was ultimately purchased by the Heileman Brewing Co. in 1981.

Measures of performance can be difficult when they involve benefits that not every consumer needs. Consider the following example. Two power shovels possess identical capacity—60 cubic yards per hour—but achieve it differently: one with a 1-cubic-yard bucket operating at 60 cycles per hour, the other with a 2-cubic-yard bucket operating at 30 cycles per hour. The capacities of the shovels would then be the same, but the shovel with the larger bucket could handle massive boulders while the shovel with the smaller bucket could perform precision work. Which is the superior performer depends on the task.[47]

Features. Features can sometimes be logically included in performance, and at other times are conceptually separable from performance. Garvin, for example, suggests that there are times when the availability of features is part of the definition of performance, such as free drinks on an airplane.[48] Other times, the added features allow the performance of more functions by the product rather than better performance of its core function. Does a coffee maker that automatically grinds coffee beans and then brews them perform better than one which requires ground coffee? The issue is not whether a concept is subsumed under another but whether it gives the manager a useful insight into how to describe a product's performance and quality.

Durability. Durability concerns the length of a product's useful life and is an aspect of product quality not measured by conformance quality. Although durability is sometimes difficult to sell because the benefits are both hard to judge and delivered in the future rather than immediately, evidence suggests that consumers do respond to it. The experiences of friends and neighbors with Japanese automobiles have alerted many Americans to the worth of durability. The differences in the estimated useful lives of major appliances indicate that

---

[46] Quoted in Paul Ingrassia, "Schlitz Seeks to Brew Better Image, but Sales Are Still Lacking Gusto," *The Wall Street Journal*, August 30, 1979, pp. 1 and 27, at p. 27. For further information on Schlitz's problems, see "Heileman's Super Suds," *Newsweek*, August 10, 1981, pp. 53–54, and "Schlitz's Brew of Old and New," *Business Week*, May 12, 1980, pp. 31–32.

[47] Garvin, "Competing on the Eight Dimensions of Quality," p. 104.

[48] Garvin, "Competing on the Eight Dimensions of Quality," p. 104.

durability is within management's control. Based on 1981 data, Gibson washing machines were expected to last 5.8 years, while those built by Maytag were estimated to have a useful life of 18 years; Westinghouse refrigerators had a useful life of 9.9 years compared to Frigidaire's 13.2 years.[49]

Reliability.   Reliability is related to durability, but it is possible to have products that are durable but not reliable. Reliability concerns the frequency with which a product malfunctions. At about the time that the Japanese entered the market for dry paper office copiers, Xerox machines were not known for their reliability. They jammed frequently and were often simply out of adjustment. Xerox repair engineers frequently seemed to live in customer offices. Ricoh and Savin, among others, seized this opportunity to design machines in which reliability was the dominant design criterion. They were able to use reliability as the lever with which to enter the market.[50]

Reliability is frequently foretold by more basic measures of quality. In March 1980, Hewlett-Packard reported that after testing 300,000 RAM (random access memory) chips from three U.S. and three Japanese manufacturers, it had discovered wide disparities in quality. At incoming inspection the Japanese chips had a failure rate of zero; the comparable rate for the three U.S. manufacturers was between 11 and 19 failures per 1,000. More important was what this initial measure foretold about reliability. After 1,000 hours of use, the failure rate of the Japanese chips was between 1 and 2 per 1,000; U.S. chips failed up to 27 times per thousand.

Consistency.   Consistency is an important aspect of quality in many markets. Business or industrial customers who use a product in their business or production system frequently place a high value on consistency. Federal Express, for example, based its business on the slogan "When it absolutely, positively has to be there." Many production managers will tell you that they care less about the exact number that describes some aspect of a purchased input as long as that number is the same from unit to unit, batch to batch, shipment to shipment, year to year. As long as they do not have to readjust their production equipment each time a new batch of the material is delivered, they will be happy. McDonald's fast food chain has long stressed consistency among units. Holiday Inn used the phrase "no surprises" to characterize the consistency it concentrated on delivering to travelers.

Satisfaction and Quality

The key element in all of these aspects of quality is a satisfied customer. The customer's experience and his or her evaluation of that experience is what mat-

---

[49] David J. Curry, "Measuring Price and Quality Competition," *Journal of Marketing*, 49, no. 2 (spring 1985), pp. 106–117.
[50] Bro Uttal, "Xerox Is Trying Too Hard," *Fortune*, March 13, 1978, pp. 84–94.

ters. In fact, this is the major shortcoming of all of the aforementioned measures of quality—all seek hard, physical, factual data to measure something that ultimately takes place in a customer's head, heart, and gut. Because satisfaction is defined (and can be measured) as the discrepancy between expectations and perceived reality, a firm can change its customers' satisfaction without changing its offering at all. For example, a firm which consistently overpromises in its advertising will have less satisfied customers because the reality of the product's performance will never measure up to the performance expectations the firm's advertising created in the customer. The firm could have more satisfied customers if it reduced the level of its advertising's promises to be closer to reality.[51]

Since satisfaction is what product performance and quality seek to achieve, direct measurement of customer satisfaction is theoretically superior to physical measurement of product properties. Many firms which once had internally devised physical specifications for quality now measure satisfaction directly. GTE regularly measures customer satisfaction and reports that declines in satisfaction rates have led to the creation of several high-level multifunctional task forces to improve service quality in its direct-distance dialing and its billing procedures.[52] Several airlines which once had set time standards and timed how long it took for baggage to arrive at the carousel now measure customer satisfaction with waiting time instead. If customers are satisfied, no action is necessary. If they are not satisfied, then the airline speeds up the process.

To make satisfaction measurement useful, measures are necessary which are sufficiently *diagnostic* to allow the firm to identify corrective measures. That is, the survey instrument items should map customer satisfaction or dissatisfaction onto product or service features. This is important because the firm does not manage satisfaction directly. It manages manufacturing and operations, which produce physical products and services that yield satisfaction.

Quality and Profitability

Because competitive advantage is achieved through the delivery of superior value, offerings with superior perceived quality should be superior profit performers. The data show this to be so.

---

[51] Holiday Inn dropped its "no surprises" campaign when it determined that it could not control its quality sufficiently to deliver on its promise. One definition of quality posits it to be the gap between customer expectations and perceptions. See Valarie A. Zeithaml, A. Parasuraman, and Leonard L. Berry, *Delivering Quality Service: Balancing Customer Perceptions and Expectations* (New York: Free Press, 1990).

[52] John F. Andrews, James H. Drew, Michael J. English, and Melanie Rys, "Service Quality Surveys in a Telecommunications Environment: An Integrating Force," in John A. Czepiel, Carole A. Congram, and James Shanahan, eds., *The Services Challenge: Integrating for Competitive Advantage* (Chicago: American Marketing Association, 1987), pp. 27–31.

Figure 3-12 How quality drives profitability and growth

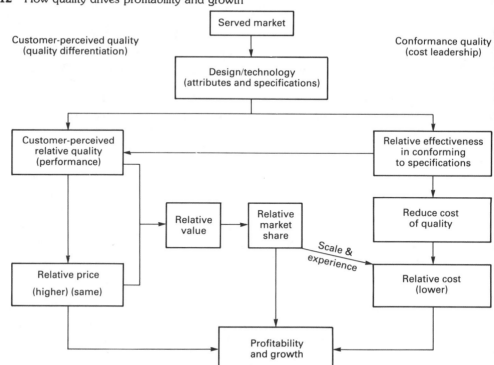

SOURCE: Robert D. Buzzell and Bradley T. Gale, *The PIMS Principles* (New York: Free Press, 1989), p. 106.

Figure 3-12 explains the different ways by which perceived quality and conformance quality drive business performance. On the left-hand side of the figure, high relative perceived quality has two effects: a higher relative price, which contributes directly to profitability, and a higher relative value, which contributes indirectly to profitability through the effect of market share on relative costs. On the right side, conformance quality achieves superior performance by being more effective than competitors in conforming to the appropriate product specifications and service standards.

Figure 3-13 shows the relationships between relative quality and both return on sales (ROS) and return on investment (ROI) found in the businesses in the

Figure 3-13   Relative quality boosts rates of return

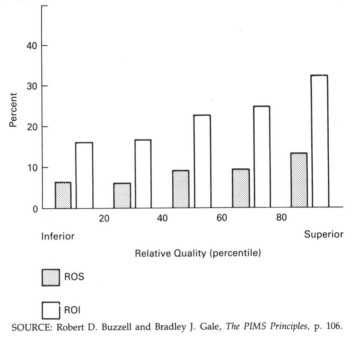

SOURCE: Robert D. Buzzell and Bradley J. Gale, *The PIMS Principles,* p. 106.

PIMS database.[53] As can be seen, both increase substantially with relative quality. The intuition behind the data is as follows: ROS benefits from increases in relative prices without increases in costs. ROI benefits because in most businesses investment is no different for higher-quality than lower-quality offerings. So, with equivalent investment bases, the higher margins that accompany quality products translate directly into higher returns on that investment. These data and findings have been subjected to rigorous, state-of-the-art tests, which find them to be valid.[54]

The PIMS findings have also been applied to the positions on the value map, (ROA) for makers of heavy-duty trucks shown in Figure 3-14. Based on analyses as illustrated by the relationship between relative quality and Return on Assets of the entire database, businesses which offer average value at the premium end of the market show the highest rate of profitability (in ROI terms), and better-

[53] For a complete description of the PIMS program and its database, see chapter 11.

[54] Only for capital goods manufacturers has relative product quality been found to raise relative costs. See Lynn W. Phillips, Dae R. Chang, and Robert D. Buzzell, "Product Quality, Cost Position and Business Performance: A Test of Some Key Hypotheses," *Journal of Marketing,*" 47, no. 2 (spring 1983), 26–43; and Robert Jacobson and David A. Aaker, "The Strategic Role of Product Quality," *Journal of Marketing,* 51, no. 3 (October 1987), 31–44.

Figure 3-14   Value map: heavy-duty trucks

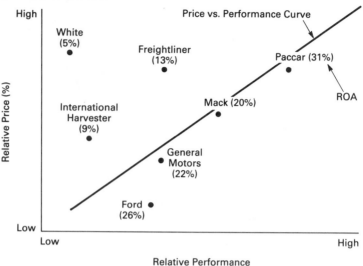

SOURCE: Bradley T. Gale and Richard Klavans, "Formulating a Quality Improvement Strategy." Reprinted from *Journal of Business Strategy* (New York: Warren, Gorham & Lamont), copyright © 1980 Warren, Gorham & Lamont Inc. Used with permission.

value businesses (superior performance with no price premium) are nearly as profitable. These firms grow rapidly. The worse-value businesses experience disastrously low rates of profitability.[55]

SUMMARY

The purpose of a business is to create technology, invest in assets, and operate them to provide products and services that satisfy chosen customers. A business does so by delivering true value, as defined by those customers, either better or more efficiently than do its competitors. The product is always the central focus of competitive strategy.

Customers need to understand and believe the causal promise—the relationship between some physical or action-based reality and the satisfaction of their needs. That satisfaction may be functional, symbolic, or purely experiential. But whatever its type, customers will purchase based on the performance they perceive. Managers need to understand customers' perceptions of the products they manage because those perceptions are often at variance with those of individuals inside the firm.

Products that succeed have high perceived quality—the overall balance of properties enables the product to deliver the mix of benefits that most closely fits the mix of customer needs. The key is to understand those dimensions of per-

[55] Buzzell and Gale, *The PIMS Principles*, p. 113.

ceived quality and performance and the trade-offs that consumers make between product performance and economic efficiency in arriving at their judgments of the product's value. Seeking to satisfy customers is more than being nice. It is the best strategy for achieving a sustainable competitive advantage.

4

MARKET-BASED PRODUCT CONCEPTS

Strategically, the most important characteristic of products is how they fit in the competitive marketplace. Analyzing products in terms of the characteristics of the markets in which they compete adds insight that cannot be gained in any other way. It is frequently more strategically useful to think about a product in terms of generic market descriptors than in specific industry and business terms. For example, in the small computer market, IBM PC clones have come to be described as a commodity. This means that the market and the actions of the competitors in it can be understood by studying commodity markets in general. In commodity markets the physical characteristics of the products are nearly identical, the price level is generally determined by supply and demand, and the competitor with the lowest price gets the order.

The first part of this chapter presents two useful approaches to understanding products in terms of their markets. The first approach describes products in physical terms on a continuum whose end points are termed raw materials and consumable products. The second approach holds that the competitive situation creates a commodity/specialty product continuum, a key concept in understanding a product's strategic position.[1] These discussions lead directly into the second part of the chapter, which introduces the concept of product positioning. Product positioning, whether in terms of physical features, perceived benefits, or competitive offerings, is the key product strategy decision.

RAW MATERIALS TO CONSUMABLE PRODUCTS

A relatively simple way of conceptualizing products that frees them from their specific industry context is to position them along a continuum which stretches

---

[1] Other approaches to classification are possible. An excellent review of many existing schemes, including the SIC (standard industrial classification) code can be found in Yoram Wind, *Product Policy: Concepts, Methods, Strategy* (Reading MA: Addison-Wesley Publishing Company, 1982), chapter 4. A more recent scheme is offered in Patrick E. Murphy and Ben M. Enis, "Classifying Products Strategically," *Journal of Marketing*, 50, no. 3 (July 1986), 24–42.

from raw materials through intermediate products to consumable products, as shown at the top of Figure 4-1. A *raw material* is material in its natural or original state before processing or manufacture (e.g., wheat). *Intermediate products* are those in which some processing has taken place. Flour is the next step away from wheat, for example, and refrigerated dough is yet one step further toward a consumable product. A *consumable product* is capable of free-standing use or consumption—it does not become physically incorporated into yet another product (e.g., bread, cake, or muffins).

A consumable product need not be a *consumer* product. Machine tools and computers are both products used in the manufacture of other products, but they are not intermediate products since both are capable of free-standing use. The important factor is that for strategic purposes each acts similarly whether the buyer or user is a household or organization.

Three things happen at each stage of the continuum. First, value is added to the raw materials by processing. It costs money, in the form of capital investment and operating costs, to effect each transformation. At each stage, the manufacturers invest cost into the raw materials with the expectation that the output will have a higher value than its cost. Second, at each stage the form of the product becomes more closely aligned to the needs of a specific market, making it more useful and valuable for that application and less useful for others. Further, rather than the few large markets at the raw materials end, each move to the right creates a larger number of smaller markets. As one might expect, the investment required for plant and equipment at each stage is also reduced in absolute terms and on a per-unit-of-output basis.

Third, it is important to understand the differentiation that occurs at each stage. Whether crude oil or wheat, commodities tend to be generic products in the sense that the core physical product accounts for all but a tiny proportion of the total offering. Nonetheless, some differentiation of raw materials can and does occur. At the far left, most differentiation occurs at the customer interface where distribution logistics, supply security, and similar supplemental services differentiate among suppliers. As one moves to the right, the potential for supplier and product differentiation increases.

Adding value and differentiation, however, does little for the firm if customers place little value on the result. There are intrinsic differences among markets, market segments, and product applications in the ways that customers define performance and the extent to which they value and are willing and able to pay for it. At the commodity end of the spectrum, for example, being unique is frequently a liability. Since the product will be used as an input into the customers' production process, buyers require that all suppliers deliver identical

Figure 4-1 The raw material/consumable product continuum

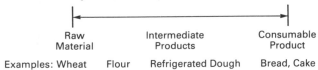

products. Further, since the input is incorporated into the customer's product, the need is for a specific, established level of some performance characteristic, and more is not always better.

The computer manufacturer wants all of the memory chips it buys from all suppliers to have the same electrical, thermal, and mechanical characteristics so they all can be dropped into the automatic inserter machine without adjustment and so all the computers it makes have a consistent performance level. In the chemical industry, some production processes are extremely sensitive to impurities even when their presence is expressed in parts per million (ppm). Raw materials which contain impurities exceeding such limits can cause a customer's plant to reduce its output or even shut down entirely.

In other instances it is not the exact composition that is important so much as the consistency in composition from one supplier to another and from shipment to shipment. Commercial bakeries want the flour they buy to be consistent in gluten content so they do not have to experiment with each shipment of flour to determine the exact amount of kneading necessary to produce a high-quality loaf of bread. Customers for products toward the left end of the continuum may even be unwilling to incorporate a product with desirable superior performance into their operations unless a second source for the identical item is available. They are unwilling to risk their business on the performance of a single supplier.

Such constraints in the definition of performance are relaxed considerably as one moves toward the right end of the continuum. In clothing, music, and food, for example, variety can become a positive virtue. Some objects are desired solely because they are unique. Freed of the necessity for physical conformance, buyers are able to concentrate on obtaining satisfaction performance. Satisfaction can range from real physical or financial results to psychosocial benefits. The customer for a consumable product cares not about the physicals of the product but about the benefits.

COMMODITY/SPECIALTY CONTINUUM

The raw material/consumable product continuum is inherent in the physical form of the product and the ways customers necessarily define and value performance. The concept of the commodity/specialty continuum, on the other hand, arises out of market factors. The intuition of the concept is simple. Commodity products are those for which there is effective competition in the market such that entrants compete away any monopoly profits.[2] Specialty products are those for which there is no effective competition, so price is determined by the value of product performance to the customer. A commodity can just as easily be a finished consumer product or a raw material by this definition. The key is the presence or absence of marketplace competition.

[2] The economists' concept of perfect competition is the ideal-case commodity product. However, as described in chapter 9, recent research suggests that a market does not require either perfectly homogeneous products or a large number of competitors to achieve effective competition.

A specialty product—a differentiated product—remains a specialty product only until the emergence of the first imitator. After that it begins to act like a commodity.[3] The market for IBM PC clones acts just like a commodity market, as do the markets for plug-compatible computer system disk drives and add-on memory units or steel office furniture. If a market acts like a commodity market, there is effective competition.

Effective competition means that (1) the production technology is sufficiently diffused, (2) enough capital has been available and invested in production facilities so the capacity to supply can meet the quantity demanded, (3) suppliers have accurate knowledge of customer needs, and (4) customers are not naive about technical or market factors.[4] In this instance, barring collusion, entrants will compete away any monopoly profits that had accrued to the possession of proprietary technology (no longer proprietary) or to the possession of productive assets (no longer in short supply) or to a lack of knowledge on the part of either customers or competitors.

If we accept this explanation, then the reason for the higher than normal gross margins of specialty (differentiated) products is the absence of truly effective competition. If we rule out collusion among competitors, then we come to the conclusion that specialty products are delivering benefits that their market (and society) values highly and no others have been able to duplicate. In a positive sense, this is what the price mechanism in the economic system is designed to do; it acts as a carrot to reward those who supply the needs it values. A product with high gross margins and profits can be said to be an *effective* product, not an *efficient* product. It is effective in satisfying needs; otherwise the market would not pay the high margin over the actual direct costs that it currently pays. It is not efficient because that would mean reducing price to the level necessary to bring the returns to the risk-adjusted rate.

The concept of a commodity/specialty continuum means that there are many offerings which are neither pure commodity nor pure specialty. There are gradations in the presence (or absence) of competition. Economists speak of oligopoly (duopoly as a special case) as a competitive state between perfect competition and monopoly. There are no generally accepted classifications beyond that, however, and the strategist must work as much by intuition as by science.[5] Some industries have coined terms like *pseudocommodities* (used in the chemical industry) or *engineered commodity* (used in assembled electronics and office equipment businesses) that suggest the combination of product and market characteristics between competitive situations. But the important issue is not

---

[3] Seymour Tilles, *Segmentation and Strategy* (Boston: Boston Consulting Group, 1972). Or, as one economist stated, "In the long run all specialty products become commodities."

[4] These conditions are similar to those discussed by Benson F. Shapiro in "Specialties vs. Commodities: The Battle for Profit Margins," Harvard Business School Case Services Case No. 9-587-120, Rev. 4/20/87.

[5] Robert J. Dolan, "Models of Competition: A Review of Theory and Empirical Evidence," in *Review of Marketing* (Chicago: American Marketing Association, 1981), pp. 224–234.

exactly where a product falls on the continuum so much as identification of the forces that allow or constrain effective competition.

In sum, one can characterize a specialty market as one in which the market has a greater need to be satisfied than those with the ability and resources have been able to satisfy. By necessity the market buys and values *effectiveness*—the actual satisfaction of its needs or the ability to supply. Commodities, on the other hand, are a category in which the technology and assets needed are widely available—there is enough for everyone, in simple terms. Since in the commodity market all of the products are perceived to be interchangeable in terms of benefits, society bargains for improvements in the cost/benefit ratio that the product delivers, and the producers have no choice but to compete on that basis. The market buys *efficiency*.

Sources of Market Power

It is helpful to envision the various forms that specialty products or services can take, especially since the theoretical source of their market power is not always readily apparent. There are four categories for most of the important sources of differential advantage: proprietary products, performance products, market franchise products, and systems and services products.

Proprietary Products.   A proprietary product is one in which the firm enjoys a unique supply position. The most common barrier to imitation in this case is the existence of strong patents on the product or its manufacturing process. Since patents have a fixed term, however, trade secrets may be even more valuable if that secrecy can be maintained. Patents are the only protection in those instances where the products may be reverse engineered (i.e., taken apart to see what makes them work so that they can be copied).

Polaroid, since its emergence in 1949, has been eminently successful in continuing to extend its patent shield over its instant photography technology. Its 1986 patent infringement victory over Kodak forced Kodak to withdraw from the instant photography business. Since the cameras it sold could no longer be used without film (the subject of the suit), Kodak offered to exchange the cameras it had sold for a share of stock or $50 in rebate coupons on Kodak film. Some 2.7 million people called to take advantage of the exchange offer.[6] As another example, DuPont's U.S. patent on its Kevlar brand of aramid fiber was found valid in 1986. This allowed DuPont to exclude the Dutch producer, Akzo, from exporting its aramid fiber into the U.S. market, although the two later reached an agreement which allowed Akzo some access.[7]

Other sources of a unique supply position are possible. People-based services are perhaps the most extreme example of a proprietary position. There is, after all, but one Luciano Pavarotti (operatic tenor), William Kunstler (defense lawyer), or Madonna (singer, actress).

[6] *Business Week*, "Potpourri: Kodak Rebate, Hotel Extras, Scouting," May 19, 1986, p. 168.
[7] *The New York Times*, May 11, 1990, p. D1.

Performance Products. Performance products also offer a high value-in-use but enjoy no legal or other insurmountable barriers to competitive imitation and entry. Several routes are available that allow the firm to maintain its quasi monopoly. The first is that the volume in the business may simply be too small to attract competitors. That is, competitors recognize that entry into the market could not be achieved without destroying the very profits that made the market attractive. Curiously, the worst thing that can happen to a performance product is for the market to grow rapidly to a large size, for that inevitably brings with it competitive entry and, ultimately, the price competition that ends the product's specialty status.

A more common path to the maintenance of specialty status for a product is continued product and applications R&D, which continues to move the performance standard that competitors must meet. The firm continues to keep two steps ahead of me-too competitors and in so doing positions itself in the better value zone of the value map. Hewlett-Packard follows such a strategy in its scientific and medical instrumentation products businesses. It continues to incorporate state-of-the-art technology to provide increased performance and thereby stays several years ahead of its competitors. The rule concerning performance products is to have the first-generation product in the market, the second generation on the shelf, with R&D work being performed on a third-generation product.

Market Franchise Products. One of the most difficult barriers for any competitor to breach is a strong brand name or trademark. Brand recognition gives products wider distribution and the strong market position necessary to obtain higher unit prices. Most market franchises are outgrowths of earlier proprietary or performance positions. Sometimes simply being first into a market may give the firm a position that its later competitors cannot match.[8]

Pyrex® brand heat-resistant glass and Prestone® antifreeze once had unique patent or manufacturing positions. Tylenol® brand acetaminophen, Realemon® brand reconstituted lemon juice, and Tang® brand instant breakfast beverage, on the other hand, had no such protection. Their positions came from being first in their markets. Such recognition can also exist in nonconsumer markets. Loctite's brands of anaerobic and instant adhesives in industrial markets, and innumerable prescription drugs in medical markets, are examples.[9] However, since industrial markets are more able to measure objectively and judge physical product performance and quality, market franchise products are a somewhat less likely phenomenon there.

The power that a trusted brand has to stave off commodity-like competition and the advertising that maintains the brand's value is one of the most intriguing aspects of marketing strategy. One explanation of this power centers around the concept that the brand and its psychological or social symbolic content may itself be the performance attribute that competitors cannot duplicate. For exam-

---

[8] The value of market pioneering is explored in chapter 8.
[9] *Business Week*, "Loctite: Home Is Where the Customers Are," April 13, 1987, p. 63.

ple, a Federal Trade Commission (FTC) administrative law judge once proposed allowing the Realemon brand to be used by all of the product's competitors as a remedy in a predatory pricing case.[10]

Would someone buy a Mercedes-Benz automobile if it could not be identified as such? The social value of the Mercedes name is likely as important to customers as the reality of its quality and durability. Levi's, Gloria Vanderbilt, and Guess? brands of denim jeans wouldn't be the same without their brand names either. Clearly, the physical performance differences among cigarette brands is less than the differences their brand names and advertising suggest. It has been suggested that if all of the plants and inventories of the Coca-Cola Company were to go up in smoke overnight, the company could acquire funds to rebuild by using the inherent goodwill (or equity) in the marks alone as security.[11]

Systems and Services Products.   Offerings in this category sell pure results; the supplier does whatever is necessary to deliver the customer-specified benefit. This category of specialty products is based on identifying customer needs or problems and solving them with a complete system of expertise, services, and physical products. The problem is normally outside the customer's area of expertise, and it is cheaper to have an expert guarantee its solution than it is for the customer to acquire (or hire) the expertise and to accept the technical and financial risk of delivering the desired result.

Chem-Lawn lawn services in the consumer market and Nalco Chemical's industrial water treatment services are two clear examples. Both companies price their systems on the basis of the results obtained rather than the labor and materials expended. The customer relies on the supplier to manage current and future problems. The physical product is incidental, since only solving the problem is important to the customer. If the customer elects to buy the components from an outside source to solve the problem, then he or she must provide the expertise and service. This is not generally cost effective or even possible.

Much of IBM's success in computers is due to this aspect of its business. In fact, some would say that for many of its customers, IBM's computers are incidental. As long as IBM provided the data when and where it was needed for the quoted price, the customer would be happy. IBM salespeople solve customers' problems first and sell products second. Thomas Watson, Jr., who ran IBM from 1955 to 1971, put it this way: "The secret of my father's sales approach was what we called systems knowledge. . . . What IBM offered its customers was not just *machines* but *services:* business equipment plus the continuing assistance of IBM's staff."[12]

---

[10] Clement G. Krouye, "Brand Name as a Barrier to Entry: The ReaLemon Case," *Southern Economic Journal*, 51 (October 1984), 492–498.

[11] For more on the concept of brand equity, see Lance Leuthesser, "Defining, Measuring, and Managing Brand Equity: Summary of an MSI Conference" (Cambridge, MA: Marketing Science Institute Report No. 88-104, May 1988). Dorothy Cohen provides a good overview of the issues in managing brand names and trademarks in her article "Trademark Strategy," *Journal of Marketing*, 50, no. 1 (January 1986), 61–74.

[12] Thomas J. Watson, Jr., "The Greatest Capitalist in History," *Fortune*, August 3, 1987, p. 26.

The market-based commodity/specialty continuum offers insights into the performance of products that go beyond those yielded by the raw materials/consumable product continuum or the concepts described in chapter 3, such as value-in-use or the product as psychosocial symbol. None of the three perspectives, however, is superior to the other, for each approach gives the strategist a different perspective on the strategic issues faced by a product. Next we complete the picture by discussing positioning—the selection by the strategist of the exact mix of benefits, attributes, and quality relative to customer needs and competitors' offerings.

PRODUCT POSITIONING

The concept of product positioning has been an integral part of the discussion in this chapter. The discussion of a firm's choice to provide a certain level of physical performance at a specific price could have been described as its choice of a *position* on the value map described in Figure 3-7. The decision to offer an analgesic product which delivers more gentleness than effectiveness could have been described as a choice to position the product to better fit the needs of those who prefer gentleness to effectiveness.

Positioning involves determining the exact configuration of the complete product offering (physical, psychosocial, and economic benefits across all aspects of the offering from advertising through postsales service) to compete most effectively. The concept of positioning is based on the understanding that

1. There are multiple sources of value in any product offering (physical, social, economic);
2. Because of the nature of at least some of those values, seldom can one offering provide outstanding performance across all value sources (exclusivity is incompatible with ubiquity);
3. Markets are segmented based on the similarities in consumers' needs for various bundles of those benefits; and
4. There are differences in firms' abilities to supply those values.

In strategic terms, the positioning decision is the one that chooses the exact value basis on which the firm will compete. Implicit in the positioning concept is the understanding that exact fits to customer needs win over average fits at comparable economics; that a product which offers the best average performance across all segments will generally lose out to products which are tuned to fit the specific needs of specified segments.

The positioning decision is strategic because it **targets the customer group** for whose patronage one will compete. Not all segments offer equal opportunity. Some are large but unprofitable; others are ill fitted to the capabilities of the firm. The positioning decision is strategic because it is a **choice of the competitors** against whose products the firm's will be compared. To the extent that winning or losing resembles a zero-sum game, winning against a stronger competitor known for its competitive vindictiveness could be the equivalent of a death wish. Finally, the positioning decision is strategic because it represents the firm's decision of **how and where to use its distinctive competence to gain competitive advantage.**

Good positioning decisions require accurate knowledge of four factors already discussed in this chapter and chapter 3: (1) What are the performance attributes (or dimensions) which consumers use to evaluate competitive offerings—how many are there and what are they called? (2) What is the relative importance of each of these in the customer's decision process? (3) How does the offering compare to those of competitors in view of the attributes? (4) How do consumers make choices based on this information?[13]

Good competitive positioning decisions also require an understanding of the dynamic gaming nature of competition; specifically: (1) From which of the existing competitive products will the offering draw its customers? (2) What are the possible competitive countermoves to which the positioning decision is vulnerable? (3) Which countermove will the affected competitor(s) likely implement?[14]

Physical Performance Positioning

The basic level of product positioning takes into account the basic functional performance attributes of products. In product categories in which core or generic performance provides most of the utility desired by customers, performance positioning is the dominant positioning issue. Financial products, for example, get positioned along risk and yield dimensions, as shown in Figure 4-2a. Since these two dimensions capture so much of the utility delivered, the exact identity of the issuer is relatively unimportant.

Similar analyses exist in many markets in which specific performance criteria must be met. Figure 4-2b shows the positioning of elastomers (synthetic rubbers) along their two most critical performance dimensions—heat resistance and oil resistance. Since prices increase as one moves along the diagonal, and since buyers' needs for heat and oil resistance can be accurately specified based on the specific application in which the elastomer will be used, buyers choose products that deliver just the amount of performance needed. While there are other attributes that contribute value in this market (supplier reliability, speed of delivery, etc.), they contribute nothing if the product cannot fulfill the basic needs for specific physical performance.

Even in product categories in which performance is more ambiguous or in which nonproduct attributes make large contributions to the total value of the offer, R&D or product designers still need direction concerning the types and levels of performance required. Understanding the functional dimensions along

---

[13] Glen L. Urban and Steven H. Star, *Advanced Marketing Strategy: Phenomena, Analysis, and Decisions* (Englewood Cliffs, NJ: Prentice-Hall, 1991), p. 134.
[14] Tools for the dynamic analysis of competition are presented in chapter 12.

Figure 4-2   Positioning products based on objective or physical performance

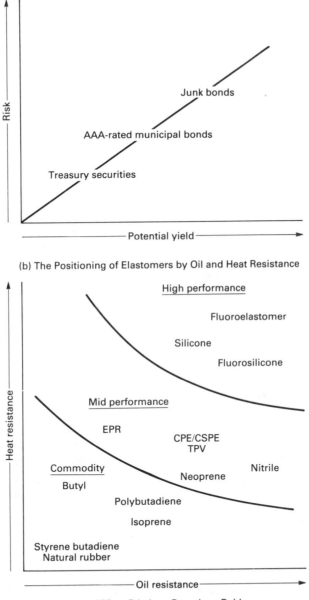

(a) The Positioning of Debt Offerings by Risk and Yield

(b) The Positioning of Elastomers by Oil and Heat Resistance

Notes: EPR = Ethylene Propylene Rubber
       CPE/CSPE = Chlorinated Polyethylene
       TPV = Thermoplastic Vulcanates

Figure 4-3   Perceptual map of office communication methods

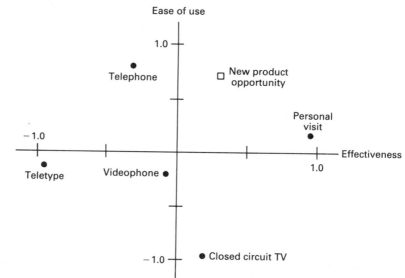

which product performance is evaluated and how the offerings in a market perform on those terms is essential to any positioning decision.

Perceptual Positioning

Even in those instances in which they are appropriate, one of the key shortcomings of positioning maps based on physical attributes or performances is the assumption that customers or the market accurately perceive the physical reality. This is not always the case. Telephone customers, for example, regularly overestimate the cost for extension phones, resulting in a poor value position on a comparison of convenience and cost. The Peugeot 405 is perceived by owners of the Peugeot 505 to be smaller than it actually is, causing them to eliminate it as a possible replacement purchase.[15]

Perceptual maps avoid this difficulty by locating products based on the market's perceptions (for anyone, of course, perception is reality). In addition to avoiding the perception-versus-reality problem, perceptual maps have the ability to portray performance on attributes which have no direct physical measure, such as convenience, effectiveness, or friendliness. Figure 4-3 shows a map of consumers' perceptions of various office communication methods.[16] The dimen-

---

[15] The 405 model actually offers more interior passenger and trunk space than the 505 model.

[16] This discussion is based on an example presented in Glen L. Urban, John R. Hauser, and Nikhilesh Dholakia, *Essentials of New Product Management* (Englewood Cliffs, NJ: Prentice-Hall, 1987), pp. 107–110.

sions which differentiate among the potential offerings are effectiveness and ease of use. As the map shows, there is an opportunity for a product which is as easy to use as a telephone but as or more effective than a closed circuit TV.

Figure 4-4 shows a "snake plot" of the original twenty-five dimensions on which each product was originally rated on a scale from 1 to 5, measuring performance as perceived by the respondent. When the data were analyzed statistically by a technique known as factor analysis, it was determined that two independent dimensions could adequately represent the perceptions of these product options. How this was achieved can be seen by looking at the correlations between the average perceived performance on each of the attributes and the two dimensions as portrayed in Figure 4-5. Dimension 1 had higher correlations for such individual items as "effective information exchange," "persuade," "all forms of information," "control impression," "monitor interaction," "solve problems," "feelings," "group discussions," and "idea development." Based on these items, it was determined that "effectiveness" captured the essence of the idea represented by those responses. Dimension 2 was termed "ease of use" based on the high correlations it had with items such as "no real hassle," "inexpensive," and "quick response." Exhibit 4-1 (p. 124) describes the techniques most frequently used to create perceptual maps.

Using Perceptual Maps to Design Offerings.   If effectiveness and ease of use are the essential elements, why not just ask consumers to rate products directly on those two dimensions? One answer is that one could do so; however, that rating would give the firm little information about the individual attributes which together contributed to that overall evaluation. To be useful, perceptual mapping must enable designers and marketers to understand how physical features and performances of the product and total offering map onto evaluations and perceptions of utility and value.[17]

The concept of quality function deployment used by Japanese automobile manufacturers (such as Toyota) incorporates this idea. Figure 4-6 demonstrates how the knowledge about how customers' perceptions of relative competitive performance on such customer benefit attributes as "easy to open and close door" are the result of individual performance items like "easy to close from outside" and "stays open on hill." Knowing this relationship enables marketers to communicate with engineers, who are able to specify the engineering characteristics such as "energy required to close door" that deliver the benefit, and to compare the car door's physical performance with that of competitors.

Attribute Importance, Segmentation, and Strategy.   In our earlier discussion of the use of conjoint analysis in Exhibit 3-6 we stated that the customers' impor-

---

[17] There is a body of work which seeks to extend the perceptual positioning and physical characteristics linkage to determine the most profitable position. See John R. Hauser and Patricia Simmie, "Profit Maximizing Perceptual Positions: An Integrated Theory for the Selection of Product Features and Price," *Management Science*, 27, no. 1 (January 1981), 33–56; and Paul E. Green, J. Douglas Carroll, and Stephen M. Goldberg, "A General Approach to Product Design Optimization via Conjoint Analysis," *Journal of Marketing*, 45, no. 3 (summer 1981), 17–37.

Figure 4-4 "Snake plot" of average consumer ratings of five office communication methods

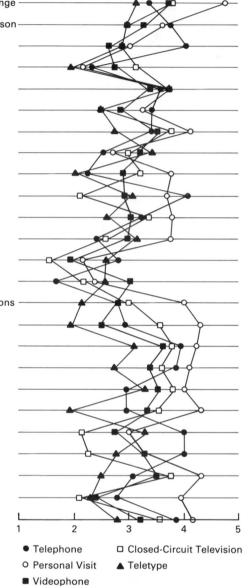

1. Effective information exchange
2. Find and reach the right person
3. Save time
4. Not need visual aids
5. Not get trapped
6. Eliminate paperwork
7. Persuade
8. Focus on issues
9. All forms of information
10. No hassle
11. Control impression
12. Good for security/privacy
13. Must plan in advance
14. Eliminate red tape
15. Monitor people and operations
16. High level of interaction
17. Solve problems
18. Express feelings
19. Not misinterpret
20. Good for group discussion
21. Inexpensive
22. Quick response
23. Enhance idea development
24. Works well for commitment
25. Can maintain contact

1   2   3   4   5

● Telephone   □ Closed-Circuit Television
○ Personal Visit   ▲ Teletype
■ Videophone

SOURCE: Glen L. Urban, John R. Hauser and Nikhilesh Dholakia, *Essentials of New Product Management*, © 1987, p. 107. Adapted by permission of Prentice Hall, Englewood Cliffs, NJ 07632.

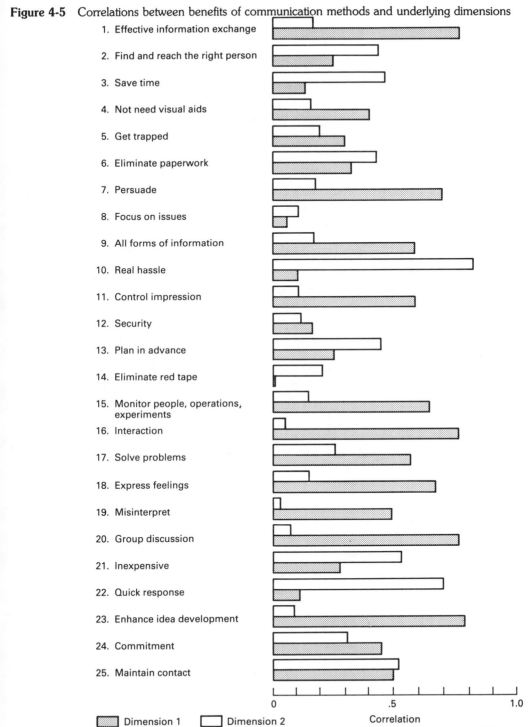

Figure 4-5 Correlations between benefits of communication methods and underlying dimensions

1. Effective information exchange
2. Find and reach the right person
3. Save time
4. Not need visual aids
5. Get trapped
6. Eliminate paperwork
7. Persuade
8. Focus on issues
9. All forms of information
10. Real hassle
11. Control impression
12. Security
13. Plan in advance
14. Eliminate red tape
15. Monitor people, operations, experiments
16. Interaction
17. Solve problems
18. Express feelings
19. Misinterpret
20. Group discussion
21. Inexpensive
22. Quick response
23. Enhance idea development
24. Commitment
25. Maintain contact

0   .5   1.0

▨ Dimension 1   ☐ Dimension 2   Correlation

SOURCE: Urban et al., *Essentials of New Product Management*, p. 107. Adapted by permission of Prentice Hall, Englewood Cliffs, NJ 07632.

EXHIBIT 4-1

Techniques for Producing Perceptual Maps

Perceptual maps are representations of the way consumers think about (the image of) different products. Two techniques exist for capturing and reproducing these images.

In one method, termed *factor analysis,* consumers are first asked to rate the product on a listing of attributes which could be used to describe the product. The office communications example shown in Figure 4-3 is an example of such a rating scale. The scale data is then statistically reduced from the large number of individual items to a smaller number of underlying dimensions (or factors) by a technique known as factor analysis. Figure 4-5 shows how the information in the twenty-five items can be represented by the two underlying dimensions of effectiveness and ease of use. Each product receives a factor score based on the way it was rated on the twenty-five items, and this score is used to reproduce the relative image that respondents held of it as a position on the two-dimensional map. The naming of the dimensions on the map is based on the items that correlate highly with each dimension. This technique requires that the rating scale be reasonably complete and representative of the ways that customers actually think of the products to generate valid positioning maps.

A second method, termed *multidimensional scaling (MDS),* does not require rating scales at all. In this technique, consumers are asked simply to compare products, one pair at a time, and to make judgments about the similarity of those products. Exhibit Figure A shows how simple this task can be. What the multidimensional scaling technique does is to work backwards from the similarity data to infer the number of underlying dimensions necessary for customers to

EXHIBIT FIGURE A
Similarity judgment scales for pairs of soft drinks

	VERY SIMILAR 1	2	3	4	VERY DIFFERENT 5
Coke/Pepsi	____	____	____	____	____
Coke/7-UP	____	____	____	____	____
Coke/Tab	____	____	____	____	____
Coke/Fresca	____	____	____	____	____
Pepsi/7-UP	____	____	____	____	____
Pepsi/Tab	____	____	____	____	____
Pepsi/Fresca	____	____	____	____	____
7-UP/Tab	____	____	____	____	____
7-UP/Fresca	____	____	____	____	____
Tab/Fresca	____	____	____	____	____

SOURCE: Glen L. Urban, John R. Hauser, and Nikhilesh Dholakia, *Essentials of New Product Management,* © 1987, p. 115. Adapted by permission of Prentice Hall, Englewood Cliffs, NJ 07632.

EXHIBIT 4-1 (cont.)

have seen the products in the way they did. Look at Exhibit Figure B, for example. It presents one customer's similarity judgments for the five products. Although the customer need not have been aware of the reasoning underlying the similarity judgments made, one explanation of this particular ordering could be the relative perceived "lightness" of the brands.

MDS computer programs try to make sense of the similarity data by trying to find the number of dimensions and product positions that best fit the data. Exhibit Figure C shows a hypothetical map for soft drinks generated using this technique. One major difference as compared to factor analysis is that the naming of the dimensions is far more judgmental. In the absence of rating scale data, the analyst must look at the array of products on the map and, based on the characteristics of the products, infer what the underlying dimension is. For the map shown, the interpretation is that the horizontal dimension represents the lightness of the drinks based on the presence of light drinks (Tab, Fresca) on one end and heavy drinks (Coke, Pepsi) on the other. A similar reasoning applies to the vertical dimension.

The factor analysis method of producing positioning maps is useful when much is known about the exact benefits that customers want and the attributes that provide them. In that instance, not only does the technique provide maps of the product's perceived position, but it also provides diagnostic information about the benefits and features that caused customers to perceive it that way.

MDS, on the other hand, provides customer-defined measures of the extent to which two products are in competition with each other. Products which customers perceive to be very similar compete more directly than those which are perceived to be quite dissimilar. The technique is especially useful when the benefits are difficult to specify exactly. Consider, for example, comparing such psychologically and socially complex products as perfumes. Trying to capture on rating scales the subtle differences in nonverbal symbolic meaning which discriminate among brands is difficult, yet customers can easily provide input about their similarity. On the negative side, the MDS analyst needs extensive knowl-

EXHIBIT FIGURE B
A one-dimensional illustration of similarity judgments

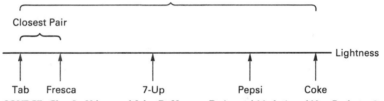

SOURCE: Glen L. Urban and John R. Hauser, *Design and Marketing of New Products,* © 1980, pp. 198, 221. Adapted by permission of Prentice Hall, Englewood Cliffs, NJ 07632.

EXHIBIT 4-1 (cont.)

edge of the market to interpret the psychological dimensions—and this task is not always as easy as with the soft drink map.

EXHIBIT FIGURE C
A hypothetical MDS map for soft drinks

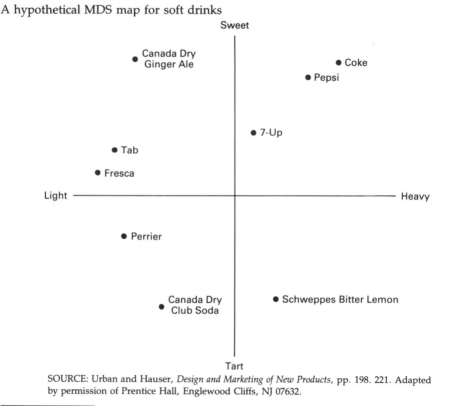

SOURCE: Urban and Hauser, *Design and Marketing of New Products*, pp. 198. 221. Adapted by permission of Prentice Hall, Englewood Cliffs, NJ 07632.

SOURCE: Glen L. Urban and John R. Hauser, *Design and Marketing of New Products*, © 1980, pp. 111–118. Adapted by permission of Prentice Hall, Englewood Cliffs, NJ 07632.

tance ratings of each attribute were used to understand how markets were segmented. In the example used in Exhibit 3-6, Figure B, the weightings showed the relative importance each customer placed on delivery and price. One can imagine three basic segments: one segment for which delivery time is all important, another for which price rules, and a third which values both equally. Understanding the different mixes that customers seek and the relative number desiring each mix is critical in determining positioning strategy.

Figure 4-6 Mapping benefit perceptions onto engineering characteristics to guide physical product design

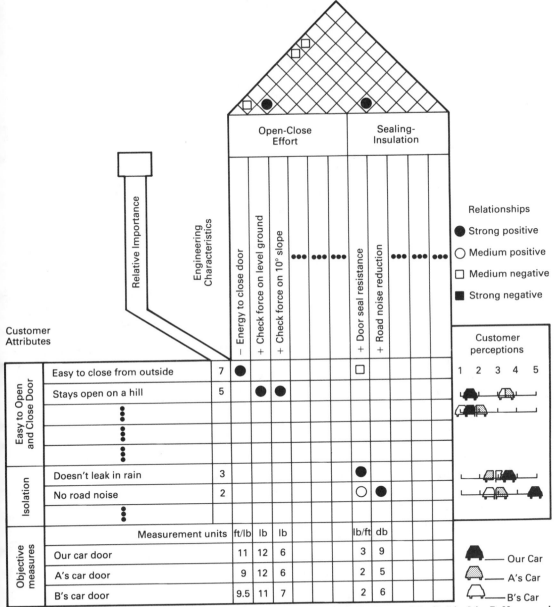

Let us represent the relative importance that an individual consumer has for a benefit mix by an arrow.[18] As shown in Figure 4-7 which presents a per-dollar map for bathroom tissue, arrow A represents a customer with a high utility for absorbency, arrow C a customer with a high utility for softness, and the 45-degree arrow (B) one who values both equally. For example, someone whose utility function was represented by the 45-degree arrow would choose the offering farthest out on the arrow if he or she multiplied the ratings on each dimension by their importance weights and and chose the brand that offered the highest total value. This is represented in Figure 4-7 by drawing a perpendicular line from each offering to the arrow on the map. The brand that intersects the line the farthest out would be predicted to be that individual's choice. In the case of the customer represented by arrow B, that choice would be predicted to be Northern. Given these performance perceptions, we would predict that customer A would choose Scott and customer C White Cloud.

Figure 4-8 shows why it is so important to understand how markets are segmented on the basis of benefits and their relative importance. The preferences of the market are shown as a collection of arrows, each of which represents the importance of 10% of the market. In Figure 4-8a most people want a more or less equal mixture of absorbency and softness. If that is what actual preferences are like, then such brands as Soft 'N Pretty, Charmin, and Northern are well positioned. If the market is segmented as shown in Figure 4-8b, however, then the best-positioned brands are White Cloud and Scott.

Positioning and Distinctive Competency.   At the beginning of our discussion of positioning, one of the understandings underlying the concept was that typically no single product could be superior across all desired benefits. This incompatibility could either be purely perceptual—the desire for exclusivity conflicts with the need for conformity—or technological—an internal combustion engine can be designed to deliver either high torque or high horsepower, but there is no way to design it to deliver the highest level on both. A second key understanding underlying the importance of positioning is that there are differences in competitors' abilities to deliver on the different values.

Consider the case of bathroom tissue. Technological constraints prevent any one brand from being superior on all brand attributes.[19] The success of Charmin, for example, was not due to its advertising and Mr. Whipple, but to the ability of Procter & Gamble to devise a production process which produced a product considerably softer than prior manufacturing processes. Once committed to that technology, moreover, P&G was constrained in its ability to produce highly

---

[18] This use of an arrow to demonstrate the customer's relative utility for the two attributes is mathematically identical to the indifference curves used in chapter 3 in the section entitled "Mapping Perceived Value" (p. 93). Figure 9 in chapter 3 could have represented customers' relative preferences by arrows rather than by the angle of their indifference curves. The use of arrows is found in Glen L. Urban and Steven H. Star, *Advanced Marketing Strategy* (Englewood Cliffs, NJ: Prentice-Hall, 1991), pp. 136–137.

[19] Steven M. Shugan, "Brand Positioning Maps from Price/Share Data: The Case of Bathroom Tissue" (Chicago: University of Chicago Graduate School of Business, September 1984, revised July 1986), p. 13.

Figure 4-7   Brand positioning maps

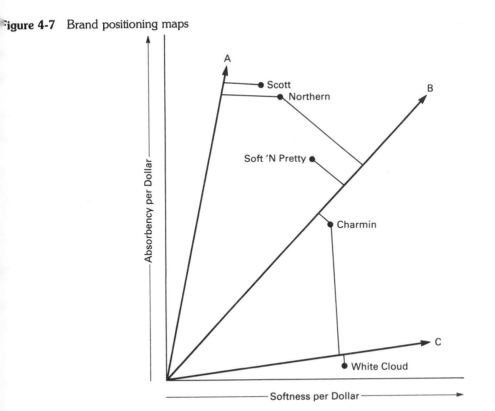

absorbent tissue like Scott Tissue. Should P&G attempt to pursue greater absorbency, it will move away from its own distinctive competency—the basis on which it delivers better value than its competitors. This may explain why Procter & Gamble's second entrant is White Cloud, an even softer product than its Charmin brand tissue.

A key strategic issue in positioning is the need to stay with one's own distinctive competencies. This requires that competency be replenished and maintained. Since competence is the underlying rationale for a company's ability to deliver superior value, any diminution in that competence represents a weakening in competitive advantage. The rule for positioning, therefore, is to play your own game and resist temptations to try to be all things to all people.

SUMMARY

The strategist's task is to configure the firm's technological capability to position physical and service products so the promise and offer the firm makes to customers cannot be matched by its competitors. In this way, the return on the

Figure 4-8   Importance vectors (each vector represents 10% of the market)

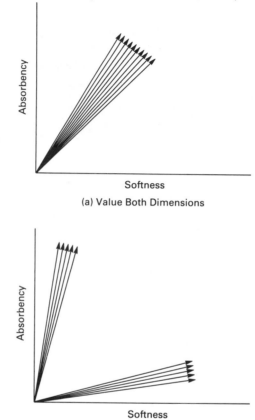

(a) Value Both Dimensions

(b) One Dimension Dominant for Each of Two Subgroups
SOURCE: Glen L. Urban and Steven H. Star, *Advanced Marketing Strategy: Phenomena, Analysis, and Decisions,* © 1991, p. 137. Adapted by permission of Prentice Hall, Englewood Cliffs, NJ 07632.

firm's investment in the product is maximized. Accomplishing this, however, requires that the strategist understand the product not only as the customer or firm sees it but as an entry in a dynamic competitive marketplace that prizes long-run economic efficiency as much as it rewards performance and technological superiority.

Key to this task is understanding where the offering stands in marketplace terms, on the commodity/specialty continuum, and the ability to identify the specific source of whatever market power it has. Positioning the offering is the second task. Choosing the combination of physical attributes and benefits that both satisfy the needs of customers while gaining competitive advantage versus competitors is the major creative task facing the strategist.

5

ANALYZING PRODUCTION OPERATIONS AND COST BEHAVIOR FOR STRATEGIC DECISION MAKING

The marketing success that Japan has had with VCRs is one of the business coups of all time. It is a coup not only because of the worldwide dominance Japan has been able to achieve (no VCRs are produced in either the U.S. or in Western Europe) but because the situation is such that one would be tempted to say, "It shouldn't have happened." The Japanese did not invent the base technologies involved. Video recording, videotape, and videocassette technology originated in the United States. The physical and mechanical product secrets inherent in the VCR itself are all open to reverse engineering by competitors. Matsushita, the holder of the patents on the VHS process, has been willing to license that technology to others. Because VCRs are produced oceans away from their major markets in the U.S. and Europe, the units incur high shipping and working capital costs. Yet no VCRs are produced in these markets. Why? The answer is that no one can manufacture them with the same combination of cost and quality that the Japanese have attained. The Japanese have won in the marketplace because of their strength in the factory.

This chapter discusses the use of manufacturing (in a goods business) and operations (in a service business) to gain competitive advantage.[1] Since few businesses are ever able to gain the absolute monopoly on benefits necessary to avoid all competition and to be able, therefore, to ignore costs, manufacturing must be an intrinsic element of every strategy. Three aspects of manufacturing are discussed in this chapter. The first is the basics of manufacturing from a strategic viewpoint: the trade-offs among costs, quality, variety, versatility, and volume that determine the strategic strengths and weaknesses of a given manufacturing configuration. The second is the concept of the value chain. The value chain is a method for understanding the contributions to value and cost of each of a business's activities. The third is the experience curve, the behavior of operating costs as a function of cumulative manufacturing volume over time.

---

[1] In this chapter, the terms *manufacturing* and *operations* are used interchangeably because although the physical processes are clearly different between goods-manufacturing and services-producing businesses, the strategic choices each faces are the same. They are the trade-offs among cost, quality, variety, versatility, and volume.

PRODUCTION OPERATIONS AND STRATEGY

Central to the success of any business, central to the success of any competitive strategy, is the ability of the firm to make and perform. The relationship between strategy and operations is two directional, as depicted in Figure 5-1. In one direction, a firm's competitive strategy sets the goals and objectives that manufacturing must meet for the strategy to succeed—goals such as cost and quality levels, volume and timing targets, product mix, and order response time. In the opposite direction, the firm's operating capabilities—the kinds and levels of costs, quality, and mix of products it can produce—set the limits of the competitive strategies available to the firm.

Inherent in all strategic problems is the tension between what the strategist wants to be able to do and what he or she can do. The strategist Liddell Hart said to adjust your end to your means; von Clausewitz said that the only good strategy was one that was achievable. Every strategic problem is constrained, and seldom is the strategist given the unlimited time and funding to design the perfect, grassroots, green fields[2] operating system, technology, and facility. The ability to operate in both directions, to specify to manufacturing the parameters that it must deliver on to meet strategic ends as well as to design strategies that work within the constraints of existing manufacturing systems and facilities, is essential to the strategist's tasks.

This means that the strategist must be a master of the possible. The strategist must have the same understanding of manufacturing that the general has of hand-to-hand fighting, that the architect has of masonry, that the interior designer has of the upholsterer's art.

GAINING A STRATEGIC VIEW OF TECHNOLOGY

Wickham Skinner, Professor of Production and Operations Management at Harvard Business School, has focused on helping managers understand production technology so it can be managed strategically.[3] In his view, there are three understandings about equipment and process technology that a manager must acquire:

1. *The systemic influence of a technology.* The specific equipment and process technology (EPT) at the heart of an operation influences every other element in the operating system, from the number and skill level of those who operate the technology to the kind of product mix it will support. The manager must know the scope and reach of these influences and the centrality of the EPT to the entire operating system and the business.

---

[2] *Grassroots* in this case refers to starting from the most basic level. *Green fields* is a special case and refers to building a brand new facility in a location where only green fields had existed before.
[3] Wickham Skinner, *Manufacturing in the Corporate Strategy* (New York: John Wiley & Sons, 1978). This discussion is based on his chapter 7, "Technology and the Manager."

Figure 5-1   The strategic role of production operations

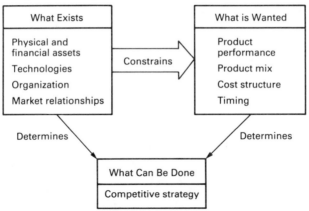

2. *The managerial view of the technology.* There are four basic facts about a given EPT a manager needs for decision-making purposes: (1) what it costs, (2) what it will do, (3) what it requires, and (4) the degree of certainty of that knowledge.
3. *The strategic implications of the technology.* Any given EPT sets the economics of the operation, determines the types of strategies it can support, and generates the key factors for achieving operational success with a given strategy.

Systemic Influence of the EPT

Professor Skinner likes to use the word *pervasive* to describe the extent of the systemic effects that any given EPT has on an organization. Compare two simple systems for producing moderately priced wooden furniture. In one system the heart of the process is the individual. Each worker assembles and finishes complete pieces at his or her work station. The alternate EPT is built around a conveyor which carries furniture past workers, each of whom specializes in performing some small number of tasks on it. In the former process, wages were based on a system of individual incentives, workers had a fairly high skill level, supervisors scheduled and kept records, product flexibility was high, and quality control resided in each assembler.

In the conveyor system, because of the costs involved in stopping and starting the line, scheduling and inventory control become very important tasks. While the system can operate with a lowered worker skill level, supervisors must now direct the workers and at the same time keep the line moving and identify and rectify quality defects. Since the line paces the work in this system, the individual incentive system is inappropriate and worker motivation becomes an issue. Finally, the product mix is more constrained and product changeovers take time to effect. While the system produces large quantities at a low cost, it can no longer easily, quickly, or economically produce just two units of a given model.

As the preceding example illustrates, the core EPT clearly affects not just how the work gets done but the entire business. For either EPT to perform as it should, the business (what is sold) and the rest of the operating system (work-ers, pay system, supervision, facilities, order entry) needs to be congruent with it and mutually consistent. This is neither automatic nor easy. The manager needs to recognize this pervasiveness and the critical role that the choice of an EPT has on the business system.

Managerial Knowledge of the EPT

To make decisions about EPTs, managers must be able to understand the phys-ical actions and transformations that take place within the technology and to visualize how they vary among the different choices. EPT choices involve four characteristics: (1) size and capacity, (2) general versus special-purpose technol-ogy, (3) precision and reliability, and (4) the degree of mechanization.

Size and capacity decisions involve not only whether to plan for future growth but, more importantly, whether to do it with one big piece of equipment or several smaller ones. *General-purpose versus special-purpose* technology asks about the EPT's ability to handle a broad range of products or materials and to change over among them (general purpose), or alternatively its ability to perform at a high level on one task or material (special purpose). *Precision and reliability* is concerned with the need for the technology consistently to produce certain product specifications and the degree to which it does that time after time. *Degree of mechanization* refers to the fact that the more mechanized or automatic a technology is, the more it will cost initially and the lower will be its direct labor costs, but with higher overhead costs. Each of these decisions requires that the manager be able to understand the trade-offs between operating costs and per-formance capabilities and the implications they have on the entire administrative structure of the firm.

Consider a hypothetical size and capacity decision. One large piece of equip-ment costs less than three small ones and can be operated by one third the number of workers. But product changeovers produce three times the amount of scrap material and take three times as long. Taking this into account, the minimum run length is three times as long as with the small-size machine. These factors require the firm to implement a sophisticated forecasting and scheduling system to max-imize output. Because of the equipment's sophistication, it requires highly skilled operators who are paid rates substantially higher than the rest of the workers. The manager-strategist must be able to visualize how a technology works and to trace through the implications that it has for the business.

The understanding of an EPT that the manager needs, however, is not the same understanding that a scientist or an engineer needs or is capable of. As noted earlier, the manager must be able to understand enough of what is going on to be able to answer four questions: (1) what it costs, (2) what it will do, (3) what it requires, and (4) how certain that information is.

What It Costs.   Two categories sum up the cost question: investment costs and operating costs. On the investment side, these include purchase and installation costs and their associated depreciation or capital cost charges based on the estimated life of the EPT. Operating costs can be divided into those which are direct and those which are overhead, such as maintenance or scheduling.

In our hypothetical example, while the business gains lower investment costs and higher margins (assuming the product sells for the same price as the current output), which singly or together work to increase the rate of return, the company has had to add additional overhead costs for the scheduling system (which reduces margins) and may end up with larger average inventories (which increases the amount of the capital invested in the business).

What It Will Do.   What kind of physical activities can the EPT perform, on what kinds of inputs, and with what kind of results? The key measures are output related: the instantaneous, hourly, or annual output rate; the rate over average or special product mixes; the quality or tolerance range; the mean time between shutdowns.

The key implications of the system described in the example relate to the product mix strategy of the business. Under the old production method, each of the machines could be producing a different variety and, because the minimum run length was but one third as long, the business could economically produce the small volume needed by small customers and niches. Since the run length is now three times as long, the firm will be constrained to selling only to the larger segments of the market. Furthermore, the system will not be able to accommodate rush customer orders or respond as quickly to the small, constant changes in market tastes and needs. Together, this might mean a lower average selling price than before and, depending on the importance of a wide and varied product mix on sales volume, perhaps some reduction in the overall attractiveness of the firm's offering to the market.

What It Requires.   An EPT creates a set of raw materials, utilities, people, administrative, space, and waste disposal requirements which must be met for it to operate. The availability and the extent to which these requirements differ from that which currently exists are important criteria for selecting an EPT.

In our example, this new production equipment requires a wide set of corollary changes. Work-in-process and finished goods inventories will increase, requiring more storage space for the latter. Marketing will have to direct the sales force to concentrate more on high-volume customers; the sales force will have to be trained to encourage customer ordering farther in advance; and the human resources people will have to deal with the potential pressure for higher wages that may arise among the rank and file.

Certainty and Uncertainty.   The risk of a technology can be estimated by its newness and the extent of the experience the firm or other firms have had in operating it. Major risk categories include *reliability* (that it works, that it delivers a specific quality, specification, or output level), *knowledge* (the numbers and costs that describe the technology are accurate, there are no new problems not anticipated), and *timing* (the EPT will remain economically viable for some period—the company is not building the last plant based on an about-to-be-displaced technology).

In our example, with the old production system there were three production machines. If one went out, the business was still producing at two thirds capacity. When this new machine goes down, the whole plant goes down. In effect, to end up even in output over the year, the new machine must be three times as reliable! However, since none of the production staff have firsthand experience with the machine, there is no database about how exactly it will perform in this particular environment. Worse yet, the new machine will be installed in the same space as occupied by the old, precluding hedging the risk by keeping both going at the beginning. Only a very large inventory prior to the changeover can reduce the risk.

Strategic Implications of the Technology

Any given EPT creates strategic limits—things that cannot easily be changed—on the firm's ability to act and succeed. It (1) sets constraints on the competitive product strategy it can support, (2) creates the set of basic economics that rule the operation, and (3) determines the set of key operational success factors.

Competitive Product Strategy.   There is no single EPT that can support all possible product strategies. Because every product strategy alters the tasks of a manufacturing system, any given EPT is optimal only for some small range of strategies, acceptable for some others, and inappropriate for the rest.[4] An EPT composed of general-purpose machinery that produces a wide range of products in many varieties, for example, would likely have too high variable costs for the firm to pursue a low-cost strategy.[5] An EPT is a strategic choice that narrows the range of alternatives open to the firm, and the manager must understand the strategic limitations on product strategy that each EPT choice entails.

Economics of the Firm.   An EPT creates the set of basic economic parameters for the firm. Of these, the two most important for operating management is that it (1) sets the gross margin level (assuming some going market price), and (2) sets the ratio of fixed to variable costs, thereby affecting the firm's breakeven point. Both control the firm's ability to operate at different price levels.[6] For

---

[4] Robert Stobaugh and Piero Telesio, "Match Manufacturing Policies and Product Strategy," *Harvard Business Review*, 61, no. 2 (March-April 1983), 113–120.

[5] For more on the constraints that traditional production systems face, see David Lei and Joel D. Goldhar, "Multiple Niche Competition: The Strategic Use of CIM Technology," *Manufacturing Review*, 3, no. 3 (September 1990), 195–206. The marketing aspects of this trade-off can be found in Benson Shapiro, "Variety versus Value: Two Generic Approaches to Product Policy," Harvard Business School Case No. 9-587-119 (1987).

[6] During tough times, for example, the firm with the lowest variable costs can take the price down farther than others, if necessary, to generate business. Such action may seem uneconomic in the sense that it results in a very low ROI measure; however, that action is not so bad in comparison to competitors who must either sell at an actual variable cost loss or suspend operations until the market recovers and prices increase.

higher-level management, the EPT is generally the major element in the investment base of the business and therefore the primary determinant of ROI, Return on Assets (ROA), and other measures of investment performance. Together, these economics direct attention to the critical operating factors that management must attend to if financial success is to be achieved.

Key Operating Factors.   Every EPT, through the constraints it creates and its economics, directs management attention to the operating factors critical to the successful implementation of its strategy. A high-volume producer of plain-vanilla products, for example, likely achieves its low cost through the use of capital-intensive, difficult-to-control, special-purpose equipment which can economically produce only a small product range. On the operating side, such an EPT demands good forecasting, scheduling, and inventory control, high-quality raw materials, and skilled operators to maximize output from the expensive equipment. On the marketing side, it requires managers who can create programs that direct demand to its plain-vanilla strengths. It also requires a sales force that can seek out customers for those few products it can profitably produce. If it does these things well, the strategy succeeds—they are the key operating factors. The manager must understand what the strategic operating implications are for any given EPT, how they match what the firm is good at, and how those affect the business's competitive strategy.[7] Exhibit 5-1 lists the five steps to take to ensure that product strategies and manufacturing strategies match.

VALUE CHAIN ANALYSIS

Competitive advantage comes from the activities a business performs. Being the low-cost producer in a market can be a result of a variety of factors: low physical distribution or labor costs, products designed for easy manufacturing, efficient raw materials procurement, or low-cost manufacturing process technology. Similarly, a business's position as producer of differentiated product offerings may stem from its ability to fill orders quickly, create unique product aesthetics, invent new technologies, or consistently deliver physical quality and durability. Competitive advantage comes from being able to create value for customers that others cannot. This means that the business performs some activity better, at lower cost, or simply differently than competitors. The value chain is a methodology for identifying those activities.[8]

---

[7] A framework by which to examine the fit between business and manufacturing strategy is offered by Suresh Kotha and Daniel Orne, "Generic Manufacturing Strategies: A Conceptual Synthesis," *Strategic Management Journal*, 10, no. 3 (May-June 1989), 211–231.

[8] The value chain is a concept used by Michael Porter in his book *Competitive Advantage: Creating and Sustaining Superior Performance* (New York: Free Press, 1985). This discussion is based on his chapters 2 and 3.

EXHIBIT 5-1

Linking Manufacturing Policies
to Product Strategies

A failure to match manufacturing policy and product strategy can have disastrous results. A product strategy defines the tasks that a manufacturing system must accomplish—requirements for cost, product flexibility, volume flexibility, product performance, and product consistency. As product strategies shift over time, so too must manufacturing's policies. Five steps ensure that the match remains acceptable:

1. Define a product strategy.
2. Identify the critical tasks of a manufacturing system geared to serve that strategy.
3. Set up, adapt, and control the manufacturing system to perform these tasks.
4. Periodically reevaluate the ability of the manufacturing system to perform the required tasks.
5. Stay abreast of changes in product strategy to modify the manufacturing policy accordingly.

SOURCE: Reprinted by permission of *Harvard Business Review*. "Match Manufacturing Policies and Product Strategy" by Robert Stobaugh and Piero Telesio, March/April 1983. Copyright © 1983 by the President and Fellows of Harvard College; all rights reserved.

The Value System

Businesses are seldom the sole determinants of the value they create for customers. The business's value chain is, in reality, typically just one step in a chain of activities that extend from raw materials extraction to the ultimate consumption (and even waste disposal) step, as shown in Figure 5-2. Figure 5-3 depicts the entire value system for the titanium industry.

Suppliers to a firm have their own value chains that create and deliver the inputs that the firm uses as raw materials in its chain. This is termed *upstream value*. The firm's value chain and its success is dependent on many dimensions of its suppliers' performance. For example, any success in fabrication experienced by Titanium Industries is dependent on the quality of the raw materials it obtains from its suppliers.

Downstream of the firm are the channels by which its products reach the ultimate consumer. In addition to creating place value by virtue of their distribution activities, channels perform additional activities (applications assistance, training, assortment) that provide value to the ultimate buyer. This component of the value system creates what is termed *channel value*. The ultimate member of the value system is the consumer, and the role that the product plays in the consumer's value chain determines its worth. Competitive advantage depends

Figure 5-2   The value system

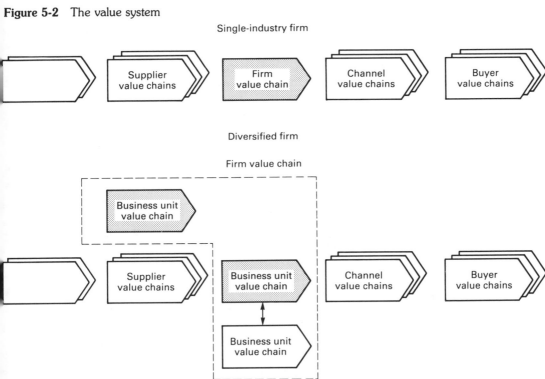

SOURCE: Michael E. Porter, *Competitive Advantage: Creating and Sustaining Superior Performance* (New York: Free Press, 1985), p. 35

on two factors in these terms: (1) the firm's value chain, and (2) the role played by the firm in the overall value system.

Seldom are the value chains of even directly competitive businesses identical. They are each the product of their individual history, strategy, and successes. One reason is that no two firms have the same competitive scope—few serve the exact same range of customer classes, customer segments, or even geographical territories. A firm serving a broad geographic market has the opportunity to gain scale economies and low cost, whereas a firm which has restricted its scope to a particular customer segment has the opportunity to tailor its activities to meeting the needs of that particular segment better than others. Either way, both have different value chains.

Scope also refers to the extent to which a firm is forward or backward integrated or competes in related industries which give it the opportunity to gain advantages through interrelationships in manufacturing, selling, or distribution (see the bottom half of Figure 5-2). Such broadened scope can also be gained through strategic alliances with other firms such as joint ventures, long-term supply agreements, or shared R&D. Differences and activities such as these give rise to differing value chains among competitors and to the potential for competitive advantage.

Figure 5-3   Titanium industry valued-added structure, 1981

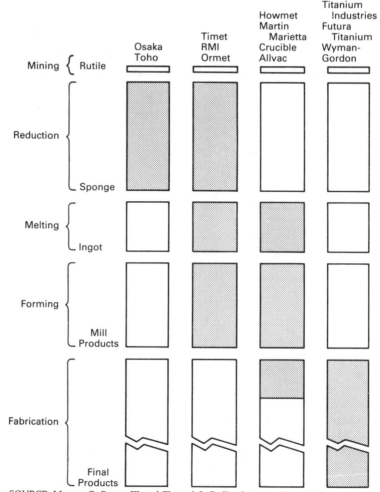

SOURCE: Marcus C. Bogue III and Elwood S. Buffa, *Corporate Strategic Analysis* (New York: Free Press, 1986) p. 41, as found in *Mineral Facts and Problems* (U.S. Bureau of Mines, 1980), Annual Titanium Supplement to *American Metal Market*, Fairchild Publications (various issues), and conversations with industry sources.

The Value Chain

The value chain looks at the activities the firm performs by aggregating them into nine generic categories, as shown in Figure 5-4. The value chain reflects what the business does to create value for its buyers. That value, of course, is ultimately measured in the firm's total revenue—price × units. In a competitive sense, value is the price that buyers pay for what the firm provides them—the price the product is able to command in the marketplace. If that total revenue exceeds the cost involved in creating it, then the firm is profitable. That is the goal of any competitive strategy.

Figure 5-4   Generic value chain activities

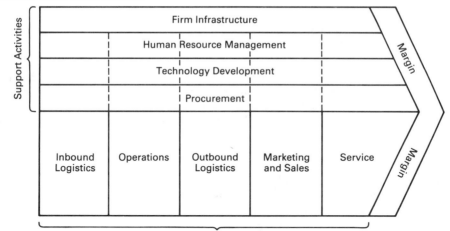

SOURCE: Michael E. Porter, *Competitive Advantage: Creating and Sustaining Superior Performance*, p. 37.

It is useful to think of the area within the arrow shape in Figure 5-4 as consisting of the total value (revenue) of the firm, some portion of which is expended in the value activities the firm performs and the rest of which is termed *margin*, the difference between total value and the cost of producing that value. The figure is divided horizontally into two major activity types, primary activities and support activities. The primary activities are the five generic categories involved directly in the physical creation of the product or service and its sale and transfer to the buyer, including any assistance provided the buyer before, during, or after the sale.

Support activities are the four activities which support the primary activities (and each other) by providing the technology, human resources, and procurement activities they need to function. The vertical dotted lines in Figure 5-4 indicate that some portion of these activities can be directly tied to specific primary activities. The horizontal segment at the top (labeled "Firm infrastructure") represents those activities that support the entire value chain and whose costs cannot be associated with any particular primary activity (true overhead).

By analyzing the business's value chain and comparing it to the value chains of competitors, one can identify the sources of competitive advantage. The absolute and relative economics of each value activity determine whether a business is high or low cost relative to its competitors. While value per se is determined outside the business's value chain (inside the buyer's value chain), how and how well the firm performs each value activity is the source of that value and any differentiation the firm may experience. The following discussion first defines the terms used in Figure 5-4 and then describes how to construct a value chain for a given business. Finally, it suggests how to use this value chain to gain strategic insight.

Primary Activities

Every firm performs the following generic activities, although in different form
and proportion:

1. *Inbound logistics.* This category includes all of the actions involved in physically
   receiving, storing, and handling the firm's inputs up to the point at which they
   enter operations.
2. *Operations.* This includes all of the activities traditionally identified as manufacturing, including the cost of operating the facilities, packaging, assembly, and
   testing.
3. *Outbound logistics.* Finished goods inventory, warehousing costs, distribution
   costs, materials handling, and even order processing costs are included here.
4. *Marketing and sales.* This includes all of the activities associated with making it
   possible for buyers to purchase the product and those activities designed to
   entice them—advertising, promotion, sales force, etc.
5. *Service.* This includes such activities as product installation, user training, repairs, parts supply, and technical or other assistance provided to the customer.

A major strategic question at this level is identification of the activities most
critical to customer value and competitive advantage. In fashion retailing, for
example, it is the buying/merchandising function—locating sources of unique,
high-style fashions.[9] This differs from supermarkets and mass merchandisers,
where the critical functions center on inbound and internal logistics and operations.

Support Activities

There are four generic support activities in any business. Each encompasses a
number of separate, discrete activities.

1. *Procurement.* The function of purchasing the firm's needed inputs usually represents a small and perhaps insignificant portion of a business's total costs. It
   has, however, a large impact on the firm's overall costs and differentiation.[10]
   While there is generally a purchasing department in most businesses, procurement activities are spread throughout a firm. Improved practices can have a
   significant effect on a firm's ability to compete both in terms of quality and
   differentiation as well as costs.
2. *Technology development.* Every activity involves technology—the knowledge of
   how to perform some task or function. While this may seem fundamental, every
   firm is constrained by what it knows how to do. Technology development is that

[9] In fashion retailing, buying/merchandising is not a support function like procurement is in other
organizations, but the central act of choosing and creating the products to be sold. It is a primary
activity.

[10] An often-used example cites the profit leverage that procurement has on a business with a 20%
gross margin. In such a business, the savings of $1 in purchased inputs has the equivalent profit
impact of a $5 increase in sales, since the gross margin on those sales would be $1.

range of activities that the firm pursues in improving its product or its process for making it (including all of the support activities involved).

While the possession of technology is the price of entry in all businesses and its development important to the maintenance of competitive position in most, for some it is the key to competitive advantage.[11] Firms operating on the cutting edge of technology (lasers, computer software, telecommunications) ultimately compete by offering new benefits to the marketplace made possible by R&D. Once new product technology has been developed, the locus of competition frequently moves to the manufacturing process arena. Process technology development is the key to success in such large-volume industries as chemicals and plastics, integrated circuits, and steel.

3. *Human resource management.* Human resource management, like procurement, is frequently dispersed throughout an organization. It involves obtaining, training, and compensating all the personnel of the firm. Its effect, although not always recognized, is pervasive in every business. It is of critical strategic importance in many industries such as direct selling (Avon Products), construction engineering (Bechtel, Brown and Root), temporary help (Manpower, Kelly Services), and consulting (Boston Consulting Group, McKinsey). Of course, its traditional importance to such industries as steel and automobiles remains.

4. *Firm infrastructure.* While generally thought of as overhead in the most pejorative meaning of the word, such activities as accounting, legal, planning, and finance can provide significant competitive advantage. Patent lawyers can be a potent force in protecting a business's proprietary product or process technology. Astute financing decisions can reduce the firm's capital costs but, more importantly, can also profoundly affect basic strategy decisions. The proper financial structure with an appropriate amount of leverage, for example, can alter a firm's reinvestment economics and change what had been a harvest strategy into one in which aggressive growth is called for.[12]

Defining and Analyzing the Value Chain

The goal in defining the firm's value chain is to identify those activities that give it a competitive advantage in either cost or differentiation. There are four broad steps to take in that analysis.

Step 1: Defining the Chain. The nine generic activities that comprise the value chain are composed of a large number of discrete activities. The first step in defining the value chain is to identify those specific activities that are significant to the chain. The basis for this division is that the activities (1) have different economics, (2) have the potential to affect differentiation significantly, (3) represent a high proportion of present or future costs, or (4) are performed differ-

---

[11] See, for example, Alan L. Frohman, "Technology as a Competitive Weapon," *Harvard Business Review*, 60, no. 1 (January-February 1982), 97–104; and John E. Butler, "Theories of Technological Innovation as Useful Tools for Corporate Strategy," *Strategic Management Journal*, 9, no. 1 (January-February, 1988), 15–29.

[12] For an extended discussion, see Marcus C. Bogue III and Elwood S. Buffa, *Corporate Strategic Analysis* (New York: Free Press, 1986), pp. 33 and 34 and especially chapter 7. See also "Learning to Live with Leverage," *Business Week*, November 7, 1988, pp. 138–143.

ently among competitors. Marketing and sales, for example, could be broken down into five discrete activities: marketing management (general administration, product management, and market management), advertising, sales management, personal selling, and promotion.

Second, these activities can be classified by type: whether they are direct, indirect, or quality assurance in nature. *Direct* activities directly create value for the buyer. Direct manufacturing operations, personal selling, personnel hiring, and the like are examples. *Indirect* activities support direct activities—administrative marketing management and equipment maintenance are two examples. *Quality assurance* is represented by such direct actions as inspecting and testing, as well as any that involve determining whether a product or action is as it should be.

These distinctions are useful for two reasons. First, the interrelationships between direct and indirect activities frequently involve trade-offs such as those between equipment maintenance policies (an indirect activity) and direct manufacturing costs. Improved equipment maintenance can lower direct costs and improve product quality in many instances. Second, direct and indirect costs have different economics. Differentiation or cost reduction can sometimes be more economically achieved through the indirect activities the firm performs than through changes in direct activities. Quality assurance can have a major impact on differentiation and cost for the firm able to identify and isolate all of the trade-offs and interrelationships that affect quality.

Step 2: Identifying Linkages in the Value Chain.   One thing that the value chain cannot easily display are the *linkages* among the discrete activities. The business acts not only by performing the discrete activities but by coordinating them. A linkage is the relationship between the way one value activity is performed and its effect on some other activity. Such impacts were discussed earlier as one reason for distinguishing between direct and indirect activity types, but linkages exist among all types of activities. While most attention is given to gaining competitive advantage through the activities a firm performs, sustainable competitive advantage can also be gained by improving the linkages among the activities.

Optimization of the linkages between activities is one form of gaining competitive advantage. One chemical firm, for example, significantly improved product quality while simultaneously reducing direct manufacturing costs and total output as a result of a more expensive raw materials purification system. Understanding the systemic effects of changes in the activities is essential to optimization. *Coordination* is another way linkages can be improved. For example, better coordination among the many operations in multistep manufacturing processes can reduce work-in-process inventory (reducing working capital and therefore increasing ROI) by reducing the need for the buffer stocks that each work station accumulates. The so-called just-in-time manufacturing systems are the result of tight coordination and scheduling between suppliers and customers.[13]

Linkages can be found in three locales: internal, vertical, and with buyer-

[13] Gary L. Frazier, Robert E. Spekman, and Charles R. O'Neal, "Just-in-Time Exchange Relationships in Industrial Markets," *Journal of Marketing,* 52, no. 4 (October 1988), 52–67.

users. *Internal linkages* are those found within the firm itself—most of the preceding examples were of internal coordination and optimization. *Vertical linkages* are those that tie the firm's value chain to the value chains of upstream suppliers and downstream channels. Firms frequently view their relationships with suppliers and channels in an adversarial vein—as a zero-sum game in which one can gain only at the expense of the other. But, properly managed, such relationships can become win-win for both. IBM, for example, does not use its bargaining power to extract the lowest price out of its suppliers because it feels that would cause them to skimp on quality and lag on delivery. Instead, it tries to make its business profitable for suppliers. In the channel direction, many firms have found that by coordinating sales programs with their channels, both win.

User-buyer linkages are the most important. User-buyers view the firm's product as an input to their value chain. It is generally not too difficult to understand the role that the product plays in the value chains of industrial or institutional buyers. Their value chains, after all, are frequently similar to the firm's. Individuals and households have value chains also, however, even though their objective functions include psychological and social benefits not easily quantified.

Customers, whether organizations, households, or individuals, buy products that create value because of the impact it has on their value chain. Value, in this instance, is defined as the lowering of the customer's costs or improvements in the customer's performance (whether economic or personal). The better the firm understands its customers' value chains, the better it can link its activities to creating value through not only its product but through the myriad of activities that the customer must perform to learn about, select, order, finance, receive, install, use, and maintain that product. Mail-order firms with 800 numbers, 24-hour ordering, and knowledgeable sales staffs, for example, deliver added value to customers.

Step 3: Assigning Costs and Assets.   Once the discrete activities and the linkages among them that operationally define the firm's value chain have been identified, a cost analysis can be performed. The starting point is to identify the actual (as opposed to accounting) operating costs for each activity and the assets used in that activity, including both the real, physical assets and the working capital.[14] Inventory, for example, requires both physical storage facilities as well as the working capital represented by that inventory. The assignment of asset values to activities is integral to strategic cost analysis because of the typical interrelationship between assets and direct costs (asset intensity frequently implies lower operating costs) and because of the importance of asset utilization to return calculations.

While simple in concept, assignment of costs and assets is not always easy. Accounting records frequently need to be restated to represent the activity de-

---

[14] For information on these issues, see Michael Hergert and Deigan Morris, "Accounting Data for Value Chain Analysis," *Strategic Management Journal,* 10, no. 2 (March-April, 1989) 175–188; "Costing the Factory of the Future," *The Economist,* 314, no. 7644, pp. 61–62; and Alfred Rappaport, *Creating Shareholder Value* (New York: Free Press, 1986).

lineation used in the analysis rather than the classifications of the accounting system. Asset valuation is seldom easy. Whether to use original cost, book value, or replacement cost is not a simple question. Indeed, differences among competitors in an industry may reflect how the firms value and assign assets to activities and business units. For example, a manager whose unit is assigned a capital charge (an assigned overhead amount designed to reflect the interest cost that would be incurred if the unit had to borrow money for its assets) based on a replacement-value estimate of the unit's physical assets will act very differently than one whose asset base reflects only a totally depreciated plant.

Three rules of thumb apply. First, the analyses should be done in several ways and the results of each method analyzed for their implications. Second, the most intense focus should to be on those areas where the firm differs in its activities from those of its competitors. Third, the analysis should be strategic in nature and level. Strategic differences are structural in nature. They are seldom found in the number precision financial accountants require (it cannot be very strategic if the differences are only apparent in the fourth or fifth significant digit). Once determined, cost and asset values can be visually displayed on the value chain diagram either in their absolute or relative amounts.

COST BEHAVIOR.   The preceding cost discussion was static in nature—it assumed that operating costs are fixed. In reality, costs change as a function of a number of factors. The term that is used to describe the dynamics of costs is *cost behavior,* and the term used to describe the factors that determine those changes is *cost drivers.* Porter identifies a number of major cost drivers such as scale economies, learning, and capacity utilization.[15] Cost drivers are the structural causes of the cost of an activity that a firm can control in some manner.

Key to understanding cost behavior at the product or business level is understanding cost drivers at the activity level. Activity costs generally reflect the effect of several interacting drivers, and the relative contribution of these will vary among the different activities in the value chain. No single cost driver is ever the sole determinant of a business's cost position. The experience curve, which postulates that costs decline as a function of accumulated production experience, is one such oversimplification. How cost drivers work is discussed later in this chapter in our presentation of the experience curve.

Step 4: Assessing the Impact of Scope.   Once the firm has defined the *what is* and *what it costs* of its value chain, it can begin to assess the effect of the structural factors that set that configuration. Competitive scope is a function of the following factors:

1. *Segment scope.* The range of product types and varieties and the different customer or application types served by the business.

---

[15] Porter, *Competitive Advantage,* chapter 3.

2. *Vertical scope.* The extent of backward and forward integration as well as the extent to which the firm makes versus buys the services, components, and other inputs it incorporates into its product.
3. *Geographic scope.* The breadth of the area in which the business competes in a coordinated manner—cities, states, regions, countries, etc.
4. *Industry scope.* The amount to which the business competes in related industries or product markets under a coordinated strategy.

The implications of the firm's present scope can be explored by examining the impact that a broadened or narrowed scope would have on competitive advantage. Consider, for example, a firm with a broad scope, such as IBM. It serves a wide variety of customer segments and applications; makes many of its own components down to the semiconductor and integrated circuit level as well as the production equipment it uses; sells directly to most of its customers; coordinates its strategy on a worldwide basis; and manufactures and sells some related office equipment. All of its business units benefit from its extensive technology development efforts and large-scale manufacturing experience, broad advertising umbrella, worldwide service operations, and customer relationships. Some of these interrelationships, such as technology and manufacturing, allow the firm simultaneously to gain differentiation and low cost.

Procter & Gamble similarly gains from its broad scope. As Figure 5-5 shows clearly, P&G is able to share experience in manufacturing, marketing, distribution, and R&D across broad sectors of its wide mix of seemingly different products and businesses. None of its businesses are totally free-standing; all benefit from the interrelationships.

A narrow scope, on the other hand, such as that pursued by Tandem computers (which specializes in computers for firms that cannot afford to have even a momentary computer outage), has compensating benefits. What the firm loses in scale economies, it gains by being able to tailor its value chain specifically to serve the one, clearly defined set of customer needs. Its R&D and manufacturing, for example, can be clearly focused on the narrow range of products it produces, as can its sales force, for whom the potential customers are small in number and clearly identified. Regionally oriented business publications (*Crain's Chicago Business, Crain's New York Business*) do not require the extensive national or international coverage that broader business publications do and can therefore reduce fixed costs. Editorial direction is also clear: serve the local market, interpret for the local market.

There is a wide variety of implications for the firm's value chain and the cost position or differentiation it can achieve as a result of the scope of its business. Of itself, however, scope means little. The implications come (1) from capitalizing on the opportunities scope creates, (2) from the differences in the value chains among competitors with different scopes, and (3) from the differences due to narrowing or broadening the firm's scope.

Figure 5-5   Procter & Gamble's scope

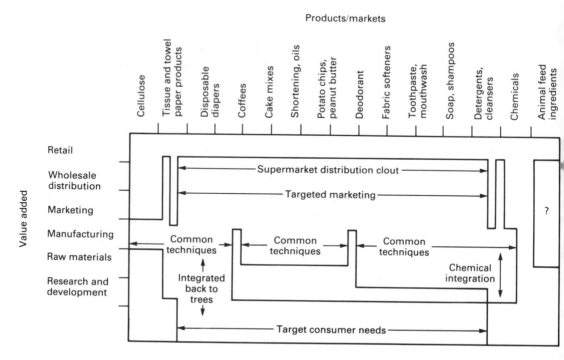

SOURCE: Arnoldo C. Hax and Nicolas S. Majluf, *Strategic Management: An Integrated Perspective* (Englewood Cliffs, NJ: Prentice-Hall, 1984), p. 39.

OPERATIONS COST BEHAVIOR
AND THE EXPERIENCE CURVE

Cost behavior, as discussed earlier, is about what happens to a firm's costs over time. The experience curve is a tool for understanding the behavior of costs as a function of the firm's experience in manufacturing a product, expressed in terms of the cumulative volume of production. In brief, the experience curve says that the direct costs of producing a product decline by a fixed percentage with every doubling of the firm's cumulative production. The intuitive appeal of the concept lies in its implication that the firm that grows the fastest and has the largest market share will therefore have the lowest costs and a sustainable competitive advantage.[16]

In this discussion, the basic idea of the experience curve is explained first, including some caveats concerning its use. Next, the sources of the experience effect are explored. Finally, the discussion closes with the strategic implications of the experience effect and suggestions concerning its use.

[16] This intuitive implication is an oversimplification that must be qualified in almost any particular setting. It is more fully stated and qualified later in this discussion.

Figure 5-6   Experience curve variation by product

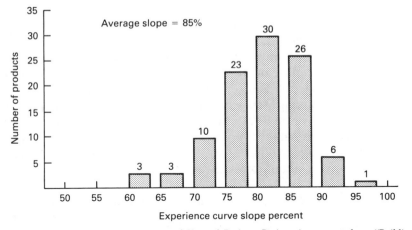

The Experience Curve

The experience curve has its roots in a commonly observed phenomenon called the learning curve. In simple terms, the learning curve states that as people repeat a task they learn how to do it better and faster. The learning curve applies to the labor portion of manufacturing costs. The first reported measurement of the effect concerned the manufacture of airplanes and was reported in the 1930s.[17] The studies showed that as the cumulative output of airframes was doubled, there was a 20% decrease per unit in labor costs.

By the 1960s, the Boston Consulting Group and others had generalized and extended the learning effect to cover all of the value-added costs (not including purchased inputs) related to a product—manufacturing plus marketing, sales, administration, and the like. The studies on what came to be termed the *experience curve* showed that the total unit costs in real terms (constant dollars) of a product can be reduced by a constant and predictable percentage with each doubling of cumulative production.[18]

That percentage decline in costs typically ranges from 10% (termed a 90% curve) to 30% (a 70% curve), although greater and lesser declines are observed, as shown in Figure 5-6. The experience curve is the result of learning plus other economic and technological factors (termed cost drivers) that range from econ-

[17] T. P. Wright, "Factors Affecting the Cost of Airplanes," *Journal of the Aeronautical Sciences*, 3 (1936), pp. 122–128.
[18] Barry Hedley, "A Fundamental Approach to Strategy Development," *Long Range Planning*, 9, no. 6 (December 1976), 2–11. For a complete history of the phenomenon, see John M. Dutton and Annie Thomas, "Treating Progress Functions as a Managerial Opportunity," *Academy of Management Review*, 9, no. 2 (April 1984), 235–247; and John M. Dutton, Annie Thomas, and John E. Butler, "The History of Progress Function as a Managerial Technology," *Business History Review*, 58 (summer 1984), 205–233.

omies of scale to product redesign. These causes are discussed later in this chapter.

An 80% experience curve is plotted in Figures 5-7a and 5-7b. Cumulative units of production are on the *x* axis, and cost per unit in constant dollars (except for the first unit) on the *y* axis. On an 80% experience curve, costs decline 20% with each doubling of cumulative experience, so if the first unit cost $100, the second would cost $80 (0.8 × $1.00), the fourth $64 (0.8 × $80), the eighth $51.20, and so on. Most experience curves are plotted not on arithmetic paper, as shown in Figure 5-7a, but on log-log paper, as shown in Figure 5-7b, which converts the constant percentage reduction into a straight line. Exhibit 5-2 describes the steps that need to be taken to obtain the cost data. Three observations must be made about experience curves:

1. *The largest absolute costs savings are realized in the initial stages of production experience.* This is purely an arithmetic effect—take out a calculator and continue the calculation of the absolute value of the reduction in costs in dollars with each doubling of experience for the 80% curve example. The amounts of the cost savings are very large initially ($20, $16, $12.80, etc.) and then begin to level off, as the arithmetic experience curve (Figure 5-8) graphically demonstrates. While the cost of the 1,000th unit is $10.80, the cost of the 2,000th is $8.64—a reduction of only $2.16 compared to the earliest $20 and $16 reductions.[19] This suggests that the greatest absolute difference in costs among competitors is achieved early in a product's life cycle.

2. *Cumulative production is doubled most easily in the early stages of production experience.* Again, this is an arithmetic effect. Doubling experience from one to two units is easy, from 1,000 to 2,000 more difficult, from 1,000,000 to 2,000,000 more difficult yet, and at the mature stage of the life cycle it is a long-term proposition.[20] In fact, as shown in Figure 5-8, over the first ten years cumulative volume grows at a faster rate than volume grows (for growth rates of less than approximately 20%). In that example, annual volume took over eight years to double while cumulative volume has doubled over three times in the same period. These effects mean that competitive cost positions are determined early in a product's life cycle by those firms that are able to grow the fastest—doubling their cumulative experience when it is easiest to do so. The only way to do this, of course, is by increasing market share.[21]

3. *Cost reductions are not automatic.* Increasing experience provides management with the opportunity to reduce costs through pure learning and for other reasons (discussed later in this chapter). Management must work to achieve that result. Some suggest that the effect be termed organizational learning because

---

[19] Nonetheless, the effect is still important. If one assumes that a mass market develops, the unit cost for the 500,000th unit would be only $1.50—about 14% of the cost of the 1,000th unit and 1.5% of the cost of the initial unit.

[20] Both the Colgate-Palmolive and Procter & Gamble companies have been producing bar soaps since the late 1800s. While the two still undoubtedly achieve experience effects, it is probably not easy for either to double the almost 100 years of cumulative experience each has.

[21] This again is a mathematical truism, since if all firms grew at the same rate their market shares would remain equal. If one assumes that all firms are on a common experience curve, the cost position of the firm that grows the fastest moves down the experience curve faster than the others.

Figure 5-7   The 80% experience curve plotted on arithmetic and log-log scales

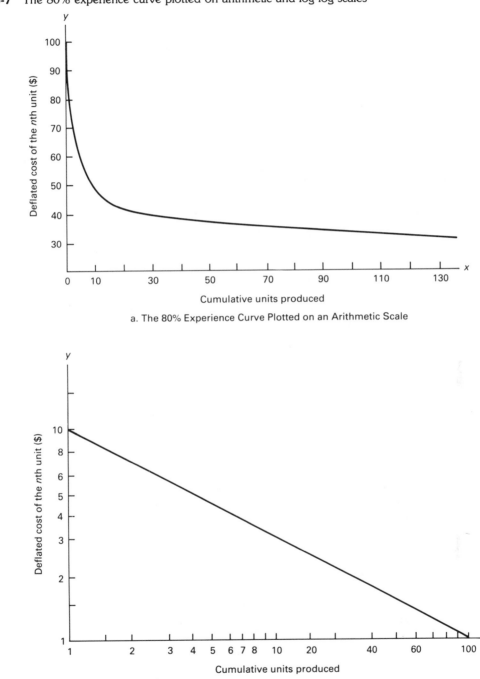

a. The 80% Experience Curve Plotted on an Arithmetic Scale

b. The 80% Experience Curve Plotted on a Log-Log Scale

EXHIBIT 5-2

Steps in Analyzing the Experience Effect[22]

- Determine the unit of analysis. How narrow or wide shall the competitive set be for comparison purposes? Against what set of competitors is it important to maintain a cost advantage or parity?
- Gather relevant historical cost data for the various cost components over a time period covering many doublings of experience. Accounting cost data must be restated and the determination made of the standard unit for counting purposes to account for mix and design changes.
- Determine which of these costs should be actually allocated to the unit of analysis. Joint costs (overhead) are frequently allocated on a percentage basis; special circumstances may have affected certain time periods.
- Group cost components that will be likely to behave similarly with respect to experience, isolating those that have significantly different amounts of prior experience, different learning rates, or shared experience.
- For each group, determine and plot (on log-log paper) short-run average unit costs at various points in time.
- Fit a line through the plotted points, judiciously selecting a slope which appears to be most representative of how future costs will behave.
- Use the fitted line to project future costs of each cost component, allowing for shared experience with other units of analysis.
- Combine the projections of the separate cost components to obtain total unit costs.

SOURCE: Derek F. Abell and John S. Hammond, *Strategic Market Planning: Problems and Analytical Approaches,* © 1979, pp. 131–132. Adapted by permission of Prentice Hall, Englewood Cliffs, NJ 07632.

"when all of the experience effects are added together, it is a measure of the quality of management of a firm."[23] In fact, it is possible for a fast-growing firm to experience increases in unit costs due to its inability to control its growing operations.

Sources of the Experience Effect

As noted earlier, the experience effect has many sources. It is important to note that the experience effect observed at the product level is, in reality, a build-up

---

[22] Bogue and Buffa, *Corporate Strategic Analysis,* pp. 22–23. See also Barbara Levitt and James G. March, "Organizational Learning," *Annual Review of Sociology,* 14 (1988), 319–340.

[23] Performing an experience curve analysis involves many important technical issues and trade-offs. For a comprehensive review of these, see J. P. Sallenave, *Experience Analysis for Industrial Planning* (Lexington, MA: Lexington Books, 1976).

Figure 5-8 Cumulative production grows faster than annual production

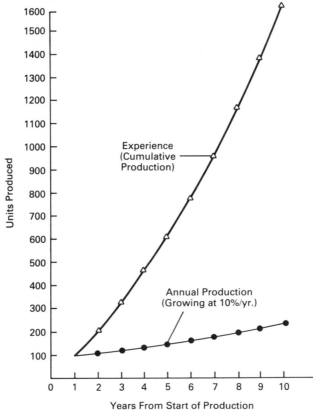

Years From Start of Production

SOURCE: Derek F. Abell and John S. Hammond, *Strategic Market Planning: Problems and Analytical Approaches,* © 1979, p. 123. Adapted by permission of Prentice Hall, Englewood Cliffs, NJ 07632.

based on the configuration of individual activities in the firm's value chain and their relationships. Experience accumulates at the level of the individual activity, not at the product level. Each activity has its own associated cost drivers, and it is at the activity level that better technology, worker learning, improved materials utilization, and so on occur.

Figure 5-9 shows how each activity in the value chain can have its own experience curve of differing slope. The overall observed experience curve for the firm will be the combined effect of these different curves. But not only do experience curves differ at the activity level, they differ for the separate operations that are performed within each activity. For example, Table 5-1 shows the range of learning curves and cumulative experience for each of the nine different production operations involved in the manufacture of semiconductor diodes. The labor content for a new diode and its learning curve will be a mathematical combination of the different production operations used in its manufacture.

Figure 5-9   Experience curves of value chain activities

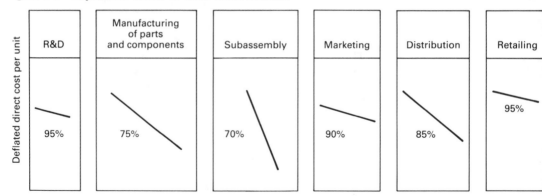

Accumulated volume of production in each stage (units)

SOURCE: Arnoldo C. Hax and Nicolas S. Majluf, *Strategic Management: An Integrated Perspective,* © 1984, p. 121. Adapted by permission of Prentice Hall, Englewood Cliffs, NJ 07632.

Analysis on a component-by-component basis produces valuable insight for managers. Table 5-2 contains a hypothetical analysis for a product consisting of three components with differing experience and usage rates. Item A, which started out comprising 70% of total unit costs, accounts for only 11.7% at 1 million units of cumulative experience, whereas component C increases from 10% to almost 54% of total unit costs. By understanding how costs will change in the future, management can divide its attention appropriately.

This is an important point. The rate of cost improvement that is observed as an apparent function of cumulative experience at the product, firm, and indus-

TABLE 5-1   *Representative Production Processes and Their Approximate Historical Data*

PRODUCTION OPERATIONS	% LEARNING CURVE	CUMULATIVE NUMBER OF TIMES THIS OPERATION PERFORMED TO DATE	DIRECT LABOR HOURS PER UNIT (CURRENT)
Diffusion	85%	8,000,000	1.7×10^{-4}
Photolithography	80	6,000,000	0.6×10^{-4}
Varnish passivation	65	2,000,000	10.0×10^{-4}
Glass passivation	70	100,000	3.3×10^{-4}
Evaporation	75	1,000,000	5.0×10^{-4}
Contact plating	70	6,000,000	1.1×10^{-4}
Scribing	80	20,000,000	4.2×10^{-4}
Soldering	95	20,000,000	11.0×10^{-4}
Machine sealing	90	20,000,000	8.3×10^{-4}

NOTE: The data in this table were gathered during interviews conducted in 1973. The approximations are rough and meant to be used for illustrative purposes only.

SOURCE: Reprinted by permission of the publisher from "Estimating Learning Curves for Potential Products," by Louis E. Yelle, in *Industrial Marketing Management, 5,* p. 150. Copyright © 1976 by Elsevier Science Publishing Co., Inc.

TABLE 5-2 *Relative Contribution of Various Cost Components Changes with Experience*

| | COST COMPONENT | | | | | | | | | |
| | A (75% CURVE; 1 ITEM PER UNIT) | | | B (80% CURVE; 1 ITEM PER UNIT) | | | C (80% CURVE; 2 ITEMS PER UNIT) | | | |
EXPERIENCE WITH THE PRODUCT	COMPONENT EXPERIENCE	COST PER UNIT	% OF TOTAL UNIT COST	COMPONENT EXPERIENCE	COST PER UNIT	% OF TOTAL UNIT COST	COMPONENT EXPERIENCE	COST PER UNIT	% OF TOTAL UNIT COST	TOTAL UNIT COST
100 units	100	$70.00	70.0%	10,100	$20.00	20.0%	1,060,200	$10.00	10.0%	$100.00
1,000 units	1,000	26.92	47.8	11,000	19.46	34.5	1,002,000	9.99	17.7	56.37
10,000 units	10,000	10.35	28.4	20,000	16.05	44.2	1,020,000	9.94	27.4	36.34
100,000 units	100,000	3.98	17.5	110,000	9.27	40.9	1,200,000	9.43	41.6	22.68
1,000,000 units	1,000,000	1.53	11.7	1,010,000	4.53	34.6	3,000,000	7.02	53.7	13.08

SOURCE: Abell and Hammond, *Strategic Market Planning*, p. 126. Adapted by permission of Prentice Hall, Englewood Cliffs, NJ 07632.

try levels is first the result of the combination of improvements taking place at the activity level, and second as much or more a function of management's behavior regarding the cost drivers as it is of cumulative experience. To focus purely on aggregate accumulated experience and market share as the key measure of the relative cumulative experience of competitors is to obscure the real causes of cost improvement. The following discussion identifies some of the most common cost drivers.

Scale.   Economies of scale are one of the largest components in the observed historical behavior of costs.[24] As a product market grows from its initial, small-volume beginnings to become a large industry, annual volume may grow many-fold. In 1975, 119,000 VCRs were produced. In 1986, production approximated 32 million units and cumulative production totaled almost 120 million. That first year's volume has doubled almost 1,000 times over eleven years.[25] The production facilities and technologies appropriate for producing units whose output is counted in the hundreds or thousands is seldom appropriate when that volume is in the millions or billions. Scale has two subcomponents: true scale effects and volume-induced technology changes.

True scale effects work on investment, operating, and administrative costs. The capital investment required for a plant (or a piece of production equipment) does not double as its size (as measured in terms of output) doubles. In process industries such as chemicals and petroleum (and, increasingly, semiconductors), for example, the rule of thumb is that investment costs increase by 2^a where a varies between 0.6 and 0.8. At a value of 0.6 for a, the cost of a facility double in size would be only 1.52 times the cost of the smaller. The investment per unit of output, therefore would be approximately 25% less than with the smaller facility (1.52/2 = 0.76 vs. 1/1 = 1). Such a facility could generate an adequate return on its investment at a lower price than the smaller facility. In extreme cases in the process industries, such facilities can sometimes be operated with no more direct operating labor in the larger than in the smaller, in effect reducing the labor cost component per unit by half. While operating cost reductions resulting from scale changes are seldom as large as this example, or in general as large as the investment cost savings per unit, they are real.

Administrative and overhead costs are also scale sensitive and, in industries where such costs form a large proportion of total costs, an important effect of scale. Consider R&D costs, for example. IBM has approximately 70% of the mainframe computer market, and its nearest competitors each have about 8%. With R&D for a new computer estimated at $1 billion, IBM's cost of R&D

[24] Economists have estimated that the manufacturing costs of Portland Cement would rise by 26% if the plant were only one third the size of one at the minimum optimal scale. Costs at integrated steel and glass bottle plants would have risen 11% under the same conditions. To put these numbers in perspective, many firms consider a 5% or 10% return on sales a respectable figure. See F. M. Sherer, Alan Beckenstein, Erich Kaufer, and R. D. Murphy, *The Economics of Multi-Plant Operation: An International Comparisons Study* (Cambridge, MA: Harvard University Press, 1975), pp. 80, 94.
[25] *Business JAPAN*, "New VCR War Heating Up," December 1986, pp. 87, 89, and 91.

on a unit basis is but one ninth its nearest competitors'. Advertising costs for automobiles in the United States total over $1 billion per year. In 1986, Chrysler spent $503 million ($232 per vehicle); Ford spent $650 million ($187 per vehicle); and General Motors spent $838 million (only $133 per vehicle).[26] But it is not only the per-vehicle figure that is important—the fact is that General Motors has 1.66 times as much total advertising as Chrysler. The ability of IBM and GM to spend more (and obviously do more) than competitors on key strategic factors in their business yet to have lower costs for those activities on a per-unit basis is a good working definition of a strategic competitive advantage.

Volume-induced technology changes are another effect of scale. Many major technology types are economically sensitive to the volume of an operation. This is frequently true of automated equipment, whose costs include a large component of such things as computers, electronic sensors, and programming, which do not change at all as a function of the machine's size or output. To use such technology, therefore, the firm needs to be above some volume minimum if it is to be able to achieve low unit costs.

Even marketing technologies show this effect. National television time is a communications technology that is too expensive (in absolute dollars) for small-market-share advertisers, but it enables the larger-share businesses that can afford it to reach their large audiences at a lower cost per thousand (CPM) than the small-share businesses are able to achieve.

Capital Investment. The substitution of capital for labor frequently occurs as part of the cost-reducing effects that scale is able to achieve and should not be confused with scale per se. One can distinguish between two types of capital investment, in addition. The first is that of the major investment that accompanies plant expansions, new facilities, and what are called retrofit or de-bottlenecking projects. Some economists hold that much of the cost reduction experienced over time is due to such investment.[27] But that investment need not be major to accomplish similar results. The accumulation, over time, of small "working budget"[28] improvements to a plant's stock of capital equipment can produce equally impressive savings, as a study of DuPont's rayon plants showed.[29] The cumulative effect of the many smaller and incremental changes over time was greater than those from major technological change.

Process Technology Development. Seldom is the initial way a firm makes or sells its products the lowest cost. Firms that invest in process R&D (research into

---

[26] "U. S. Auto Advertising per Unit Sold," *Advertising Age*, September 28, 1988, p. 150.

[27] K. J. Arrow, "The Economic Implications of Learning by Doing," *Review of Economic Studies*, 29 (1962), 155–173.

[28] "Working budget" items are those capitalized additions to a facility's asset base that a local plant manager is able to make without capital budget approval from higher-level management. In one large business, for example, local production managers are able to institute individual capital improvement projects designed to improve quality or productivity up to $300,000.

[29] S. Hollander, *The Sources of Increased Efficiency: A Study of DuPont Rayon Plants* (Cambridge, MA: MIT Press, 1965).

how to make a product) can significantly lower production costs and gain a strategic advantage over competitors, as shown in Figure 5-10. The curve for the new process technology is below the curve for the existing technology. This means that its costs are structurally lower at any experience level. Texas Instruments develops and manufactures its own integrated circuit manufacturing equipment to keep competitors from being able to benefit from its advances.[30]

Learning.   Labor learning was the original focus as the source of cost reduction with production experience. The learning effect was well documented in a study of the Horndal iron works in Sweden, which had no new investment in a fifteen-year period. The lack of investment ruled out new capital equipment or technology as the source of any savings. Nonetheless, over this period productivity in terms of output per man-hour rose about 2% per year.[31]

Labor learning, while the most obvious form of cost reduction, is only one example of this cost driver. A business learns in all of its activities. Changing the layout of a plant and finding lower cost or more reliable raw materials suppliers are just two examples. Over time, firms find ways of operating production equipment and facilities that can significantly increase the output of that equipment beyond that for which it was designed. Exxon Chemicals, for example, recently reported that it consistently had been able to operate a facility at 130% of its designed nameplate within three years of its start-up.

The learning effect also extends to administrative learning. In a recent publication, the consulting firm of Booz, Allen, and Hamilton reported study results that showed that the cost of introducing new products declined along a 71% curve as firms gained experience with the new product development process.[32]

Product Design Advances.   Although technically a form of learning, improvements in product design can be a major source of cost improvement. In the earliest stages of a product technology's development, engineers and designers are concerned primarily with effectiveness—making a product that performs and does not fail. This means that initial models are typically overengineered. Once the technical staff is convinced that they have product performance in hand (and perhaps because competitors have begun nipping at their heels), the focus turns to efficiency. Long-term use tests identify parts and materials that are stronger and more costly than they need be to function reliably. Reverse engineering of competitors' products identifies different and less expensive technical approaches to the solution of design problems. Production engineers propose design changes that will allow them to produce the product at lower cost. Suppliers of parts for the product obsolete themselves and propose newer,

---

[30] J. Fred Bucy, "Marketing in a Goal-Oriented Organization: The Texas Instruments Approach," in Jules Backman and John Czepiel, eds., *Changing Marketing Strategies in a New Economy* (Indianapolis, IN: Bobbs-Merrill Educational Publishing, 1977), pp. 129–144.

[31] E. Lundberg, *Produktivet och Rantabilitet* (Stockholm, Sweden: P. A. Norstedt and Soner, 1961).

[32] Booz, Allen, and Hamilton, *New Products: Best Practices—Today and Tomorrow* (Cambridge, MA, 1982).

Figure 5-10   The impact of new process technology

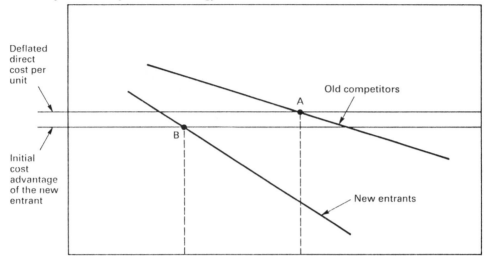

Accumulated volume of production (units)

SOURCE: Hax and Majluf, *Strategic Management*, p. 118. Adapted by permission of Prentice Hall, Englewood Cliffs, NJ 07632.

better-performing, and lower-cost components.[33] Together, these product design iterations produce significant cost reductions.

Sony's Walkman® line of personal tape players has benefited greatly from such design improvements. The first Walkman had 232 parts; by 1989 that number had been halved to 118 as had the time it took to assemble a unit. In addition, Sony has created a design that allows it to add preferred features easily and without total redesigns.[34]

Product standardization is one form of product design change that can significantly affect costs. The emergence of a dominant design, discussed in Exhibit 3-9, frequently enables a firm to produce a much smaller set of products to fill consumer needs than before. More proactively, a visionary may see the cost savings that can be achieved through simplification of product variety and understand the firm's ability to shape and expand market demand through offering a basic product form at the very low cost that simplification made possible. That is basically the strategy that Henry Ford followed in the early 1900s with his Model T. Over fourteen years, he was able to reduce price following an 85% experience curve, as shown in Figure 5-11.[35] As price was lowered, volume grew

---

[33] Suppliers do not do this out of the goodness of their hearts. The underlying force pushing suppliers to improve performance is the realization that if they do not offer their customer the most cost-effective component, their competitors likely will.

[34] "Tinkerers versus Dreamers," *The Economist*, December 23, 1989, p. 73.

[35] William J. Abernathy and Kenneth Wayne, "Limits of the Learning Curve," *Harvard Business Review*, 52, no. 5 (September-October 1974), 109–119. To underline the contrasts in price, all of the prices quoted are in constant, 1958 dollars.

Figure 5-11 Price of the Model T, 1909–1923 (average list price in 1958 dollars)

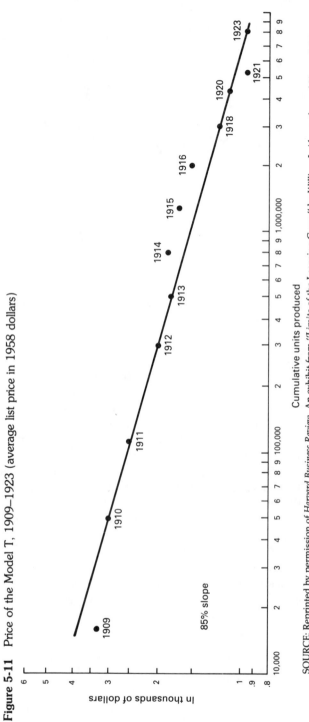

SOURCE: Reprinted by permission of *Harvard Business Review*. An exhibit from "Limits of the Learning Curve" by William J. Abernathy and Kenneth Wayne, September/October 1974. Copyright © 1974 by the President and Fellows of Harvard College; all rights reserved.

Figure 5-12 Matching major stages of product and process life cycles

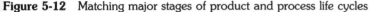

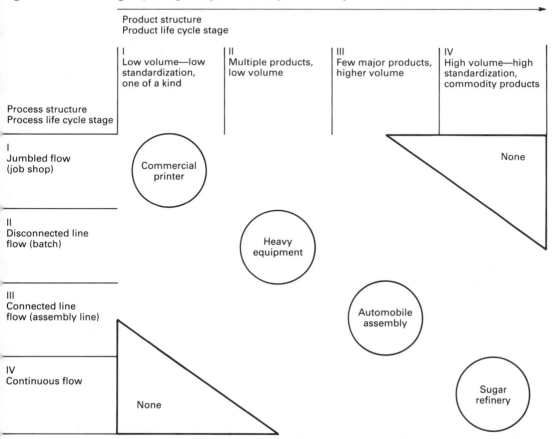

SOURCE: Reprinted by permission of *Harvard Business Review*. An exhibit from "Linking Manufacturing Process and Product Life Cycles" by Robert H. Hayes and Steven C. Wheelwright, January/February 1978. Copyright © 1978 by the President and Fellows of Harvard College; all rights reserved.

as more people could afford the product, and as they bought more, Ford was able to produce at lower cost.

Ford may have been one of the first to move down what has been called the process life cycle. Figure 5-12 reproduces some of the steps that Ford went through in achieving low cost. As it gained in volume, it moved from what was essentially a job-shop process technology to an assembly-line technology. Figure 5-12 shows how a firm is able to change its major production process type as a function of product volume and standardization. As firms and industries grow over time, this progression from labor-intensive to increasingly capital-intensive but more efficient production technologies is one major reason for the observed experience effect. Exhibit 5-3 elaborates on how this interaction worked in the office copier business.

Integration.   As time progresses and volume grows, it frequently becomes economically possible for the firm to integrate backwards and/or forwards and improve raw materials supply reliability, lower costs, and improve performance. For example, in pursuing his strategy of cost reduction, Ford integrated backwards into steel production, logging, and saw mills, and operated a railroad, paper mill, and glass and cement plants.[36] Data from the PIMS database validate this tendency, indicating that "large share businesses tend to be more vertically integrated than small-share businesses. They tend to carry out more stages of the value adding chain. . . . They do more 'make' and less 'buy.' "[37]

Location.   In the early stages of a product's life cycle, volume is small, margins high, and transportation costs seem unimportant. As volume grows, however, the opportunity to reduce those costs by moving closer to raw materials, labor, or markets (depending on which offers the better or more important economics) becomes real. This is often stimulated by later entrants seeking ways of gaining competitive advantage over earlier entrants, for whom transportation advantage was not a factor in the initial location decision. The importance of seeking the lowest-labor-cost location for the assembly of electronics products has led many firms to open facilities in Southeast Asia.[38]

Shared Activities.   The ability to share an activity in the value chain with other products or business units within the firm can be another source of savings. While not a direct cost driver (the sharing of the activity allows the firm to reduce costs—it does not reduce costs in and of itself), it is an important result of differences in scope between competitors and a contributor to observed reductions in cost. Figure 5-13 shows how shared activities increase cumulative experience and thereby affect costs.

Determinants of the Slope of the Experience Curve

There are no known theories which, a priori, allow one to predict the slope of an experience curve. Actual empirical evidence and comparisons with known activities and products appears to be the norm for estimating the expected slope, at least based on the literature. Several simple questions, however, can help the analyst to understand whether the slope of the curve will be steep or shallow.

How Old Is the Base Technology and Key Raw Materials?   Manufacturing technologies that have been around for long periods of time allow their users to start far down the curve. There is not much that is not known about arc welding, die casting, or the assembly of mechanical products, for example. Much the

---

[36] Abernathy and Wayne, "Limits of the Learning Curve."

[37] Robert D. Buzzell and Bradley T. Gale, *The PIMS Principles: Linking Strategy to Performance* (New York: Free Press, 1987), pp. 82–83. See also Robert D. Buzzell, "Is Vertical Integration Profitable?," *Harvard Business Review*, 61, no. 1 (January-February 1983), 92–102.

[38] Labor costs for General Electric's motor business in the U.S. totaled $16.16 per hour (wages and benefits) in comparison to a total for the low-cost Emerson Electric in the U.S. of $10.15. In GE plants in Singapore and Mexico, however, total labor costs are $2.26 and $1.23 per hour, respectively. See William Glaberson, "An Uneasy Alliance in Smokestack U.S.A.," *The New York Times*, March 13, 1988, Section 3, pp. 1 and 11.

EXHIBIT 5-3

The Impact of Product Design
on Cost and Performance

Ricoh benefitted from Xerox's pioneering of the copier business by being able to improve on Xerox's basic manufacturing product design philosophy. By choosing a slightly different design route, it was able to halve both its basic manufacturing and its field service costs concurrent with an increase in the mean time between failures, a major measure of product performance, by 70 to 180%.

The two basic design choices allowed Ricoh this advantage: (1) It elected to base its machines on existing, mass-produced components wherever possible. This enabled it to share in the scale economies enjoyed by those components in contrast to Xerox, which designed its machines from the ground up and used many unique (and therefore higher cost) components. (2) It elected to use liquid toner instead of the dry powder Xerox used. This enabled it to eliminate the mechanisms necessary to apply and fuse the toner to the paper, saving $60 per machine and avoiding a major source of unreliability and complexity.

But the impact of these changes extended far beyond direct manufacturing costs. Not only did the simplified design reduce the mean time between failures to 17,000 copies (versus Xerox's 6,000 to 10,000), it also reduced repair time to 30 minutes. The result? A Ricoh repairman could support some 100 machines in the field, a Xerox technician about 50. Service charges, one of the largest components in a copier's total cost to the user, are reduced accordingly.

Competitive effect? Xerox was forced over a 22-month period to reduce the price on its flagship model by 63%, from $12,000 to $4,400 just to hold its market share position. However, because its service charges were still twice those of Ricoh's, customers who kept the Xerox copier for more than a year and a half offset the benefits of that lower price in the service charges they paid.

same can be said about raw materials. The older either is, the likelier the curve will be shallow. The reverse is also likely true: The newer either is, the steeper the slope. Carbon-Carbon composites, an exotic carbon material that has enormous structural strength and can withstand temperatures as high as 3,000 degrees Fahrenheit, likely has a very steep curve since it is based on complex and newly developing fabrication processes.[39]

What Percentage of the Product's Cost Is Accounted for by Purchased Materials?   The firm can only control those costs that are incurred within its direct

[39] John Holusha, "Withstanding 3,000-Degree Heat," *The New York Times*, November 23, 1988, p. D7.

Figure 5-13   Cumulative experience effects

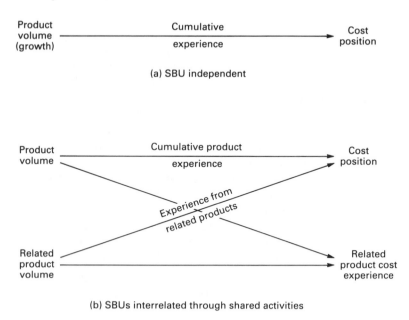

(a) SBU independent

(b) SBUs interrelated through shared activities

Note: SBU = Strategic Business Unit

SOURCE: Marcus C. Bogue III and Elwood Buffa, *Corporate Strategic Analysis* (New York: Free Press, 1986), p. 26.

control, the value-added portion of manufacturing costs. The higher the proportion of total costs accounted for by purchased materials, the shallower the total cost curve will necessarily be. If 70% of a product's initial costs are purchased materials, the firm cannot reduce its costs any lower than just over that 70%, because that would mean it had somehow reduced its costs to zero, an unlikely event.

How Difficult Is the Technology to Control?   Manufacturing technologies differ in their innate stability—and therefore the ability to control what they produce, at what quality level, and at what rate. Learning to control a technology better can increase yield or aim grade rates substantially, contributing to a steep experience curve.[40] Until they learn how to control the manufacturing process for a given chip, semiconductor manufacturers sometimes have yield rates as low as 10 or 20%. Once under control, however, yield rates average over

[40] A yield rate is the number of acceptable quality units that a process makes expressed as a percentage of the number of units that entered the manufacturing process. Aim grade refers to the percentage of the total output of a manufacturing process that met the intended specifications. Processes that involve curing, baking, annealing, or chemical transformations are frequently hard to control exactly and not infrequently produce products that are usable but of other than the desired characteristics.

95%, drastically reducing costs. Some technologies, however, remain intractable. While the Cabot Corporation has been making carbon black (the pure carbon that makes ink black and is a basic ingredient in tires) since 1882 and using its newest furnace since 1970, it still admits that there is a lot of art to running that furnace. To control quality, workers scoop up samples and bicycle them to an on-site lab where tests take forty minutes. "Only then do the people know enough about what they have been making to adjust the controls properly!"[41]

Where Is Production Currently on the Process Life Cycle? A firm which is at the job-shop or batch stages of production still has room to lower costs by moving to an assembly-line or continuous-flow process. A facility which is at either of those stages has no further room for improvement in its basic process.

The Strategic Impact of Experience on Prices

The laws of economic competition are ever present and, in the long run, always work. These laws say that the competitor that gains a competitive advantage will use it and that higher than normal profits attract new entrants. What this means with respect to the lowering of costs that accompanies experience is that, in the long run, prices will track experience, as shown in Figure 5-14. That result, however, is not always seen in the short run.

In the early stages of a new product's life, prices and costs frequently exhibit a relationship similar to that shown in Figure 5-15. After the development stage when average costs reach their anticipated level and profits begin to flow, prices do not always fall as quickly as costs. There are two reasons for this: (1) Supply is less than demand and there is little need to do so and (2) the competitors are all anxious to begin recovering development costs. The effect of this is that the spread between costs and prices widens, in effect creating a price umbrella under which production efficiency is rewarded by exceptional profits but under which inefficient, high-cost producers are not penalized.

The self-correcting mechanisms inherent in economic competition mean that this state of affairs is not a stable one, however. At some point, the umbrella will be folded and a shakeout phase will begin. Inefficient producers will be shaken out by rapidly falling prices, and only those whose costs are competitive will remain. The folding of the umbrella may be precipitated by an ambitious competitor seeking to gain share—either the low-cost producer using its advantage or a higher-cost entrant seeking to improve costs by moving down the experience curve faster than competition. It might also be prompted by the entrance of new competitors attracted to the high profits who bring additional capacity to the market, causing prices to tumble faster than costs.

---

[41] Stratford P. Sherman, "The Smutty Story of Cabot Corp.," *Fortune*, December 5, 1988, p. 138.

Figure 5-14   An idealized price/cost relationship when profit margin is constant

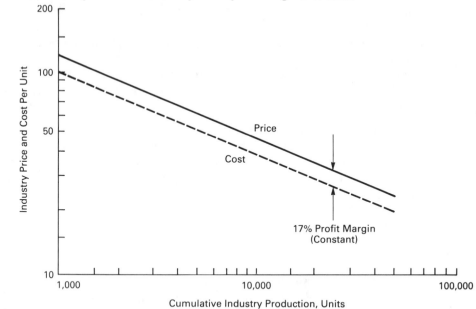

Cumulative Industry Production, Units

SOURCE: Abell and Hammond, *Strategic Market Planning*, p. 115. Adapted by permission of Prentice Hall, Englewood Cliffs, NJ 07632.

This is the likely explanation of what happened to Kodak in the amateur photographic film business. As shown in Figure 5-16, Kodak's costs have been following a 78% experience curve since the 1950s, but its prices, until 1965 at least, followed only an 86% curve. Given Kodak's dominant worldwide position in that period, it may have felt safe in the widening margins that produced. That indeed may have been a safe assumption on a short-run, year-to-year basis, but short runs do have a way of totaling up to the long run. As competitive theory predicts, the high profits did attract competition. The entrance of aggressive competitors such as Agfa and Fuji and even Polaroid forced Kodak to reduce prices faster than costs in the latter half of the 1960s through 1979. At that point, the margins were back to where they were in 1952.

Was Kodak's decision not to reduce prices earlier and thereby possibly forestall the entrance of competition a wise move? There is little doubt that competition is vastly more intense today. Would the company have been better off to reduce prices earlier to reduce the industry's attractiveness? Was the value of whatever additional profits were accrued then worth today's more intense competition? Is there a manager alive who would have done differently given the acknowledged weaknesses of the firms that had any potential to compete in that period? Everyone knows that all price umbrellas will fold sooner or later. The strategic question is when to do it and whether to do it preemptively or defensively.

Figure 5-15   Price/cost relationship

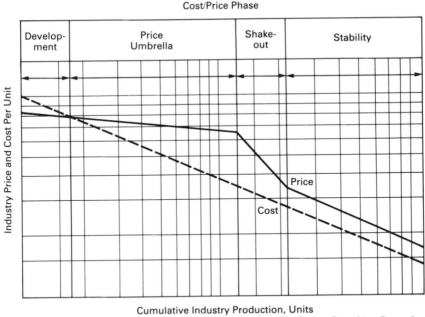

Cost/Price Phase

SOURCE: *Perspectives on Experience.* Adapted by permission from The Boston Consulting Group, Inc., 1968, p. 21.

Using the Experience Curve Argument Correctly

The classic argument for incorporating experience curve effects into business strategy states that market share is the key to profitability through its effects on accumulated volume, which produces low unit costs and high profitability. Although the argument has face validity, it cannot in any way be considered an unambiguous principle or truth. It is just too simple in light of concepts such as the value chain and cost drivers. Especially dangerous in the argument is the implication that market share is the magical secret to profitability.[42] There are a number of arguments which demonstrate how that simple argument can produce bad strategic choices:

1. *Market share/cumulative volume is not a causal variable.*[43] As discussed earlier, neither market share nor cumulative volume are the causal variables operating to reduce costs. While volume may be a necessary condition to enable management to operate on the actual cost drivers at the activity level, it does not lower costs in and of itself. It is management's actions on the cost drivers that are the causal variables.

[42] The market share argument is especially complex and is discussed extensively in Exhibit 11-1 (p. 388).

[43] For an extended discussion of this point, see William W. Alberts, "The Experience Curve Doctrine Reconsidered," *Journal of Marketing*, 53, no. 3 (July 1989), 36–49.

Figure 5-16   Kodak's price and cost experience curves

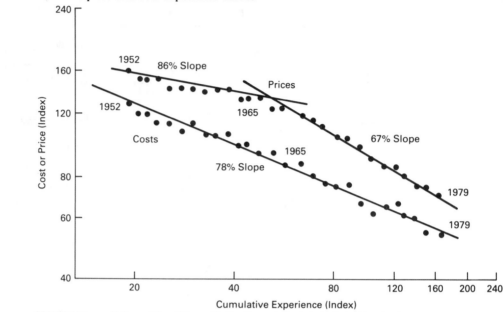

SOURCE: Marcus C. Bogue III and Elwood Buffa, *Corporate Strategic Analysis* (New York: Free Press, 1986), p. 28.

2. *Value chains differ among competitors.* The argument assumes that all competitors have the same value chain. This is unlikely. Some may be competitively advantaged (or disadvantaged) by virtue of differences in scope, location, technology, or any number of similar factors. For these reasons, a high-share firm may have higher costs than a low-share firm (Exhibit 5-4 gives a numerical example).

3. *Quality differences may outweigh costs.* The argument assumes that all competitors are perceived to offer the same quality and therefore receive the same price in the marketplace (or, at least, their prices are not proportionately lower than their cost advantage). Firm reputation or the use of a trusted brand name may allow smaller-share competitors to receive higher prices that offset any cost penalties their share position could cause. In the PC market, IBM has been able to receive a consistent price premium for technically comparable products compared to other competitors.

4. *Competitors do not start from the same position.* Assuming that all competitors enter from the same position on the cost curve is unlikely to be true. Later entrants to a business are frequently able to learn from the experiences, successes, and failures of earlier entrants. One route might simply be to build a facility that takes advantage of the scale economies possible in the larger available market in comparison to the smaller market available to the pioneer on its entry. The experience gained by earlier entrants may be obtained by reverse engineering their products, purchased in the form of the improved capital equipment they helped to develop, or by the hiring of competitors' technical and operating people.

EXHIBIT 5-4

The Effect of Differences in Value Chains
on Actual Experience Effects

Assume a business type with two primary activities—manufacturing and distribution—in which each activity contributes 50% of the value added. Assume further two competitors, Business A with an 80% market share and Business B with a 20% market share; a 4 to 1 advantage for A over B. The apparent experience effect is as shown in the left-hand graph in Exhibit Figure A.

However, if we now learn that Business B, as a subsidiary of Megacorp, shares in Megacorp's distribution system in which it has a 3 to 1 advantage over Business A (Megacorp's total distribution share is 75% versus A's 25%), the result is considerably different. If we assume that the experience effect is the same for both activities (to simplify calculations), calculating a normalized market share will give the true relative standing of the two businesses. This normalized market-share figure is calculated as follows:

Market Share = Manufacturing Share × Manufacturing Value Added + Distribution Market Share × Distribution Value Added

or,   for Business A, $0.8 \times 0.5 + 0.25 \times 0.5 = 0.525$,
and   for Business B, $0.2 \times 0.5 + 0.75 \times 0.5 = 0.475$.

EXHIBIT FIGURE A
Changes in competitive position of two firms when using market share of value-added stages

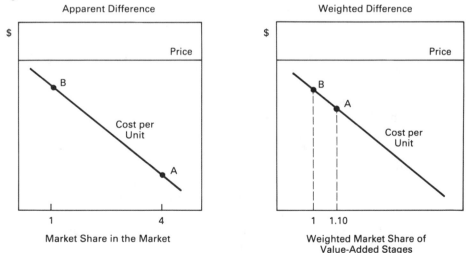

SOURCE: Hax and Majluf, *Strategic Management*, p. 122. Adapted by permission of Prentice Hall, Englewood Cliffs, NJ 07632.

EXHIBIT 5-4 (cont.)

The difference in relative market share of Business A over Business B (and experience effects, therefore) in terms of this normalized market share (really a weighted measure of experience) is not 4 to 1, as market share showed, but 1.1 to 1 (0.525/0.475). The difference shows clearly by comparing the right-hand experience curve in Exhibit Figure A with the left.

Source: Arnoldo C. Hax and Nicolas S. Majluf, *Strategic Management: An Integrative Perspective,* ©️ 1984, p. 120. Adapted by permission of Prentice Hall, Englewood Cliffs, NJ 07632.

Strategic Weaknesses of Experience-Based Strategies

There is little doubt of the potency of experience-based strategies. They are not only potent but frequently appropriate. The business graveyard is full of small, innovative companies that pioneered innovative technologies and products but failed to make the transition to high volume and cost efficiency that was needed to stay competitive. However, while following an experience-based strategy keeps the firm viable, it concurrently exposes it to other risks. In fact, the longer and more successful the firm has been in pursuing an experience-based strategy, the more vulnerable it is to competition. At the core of the strategic weakness of an experience-based strategy is that the factors that contribute to low cost are frequently incompatible with product innovation and organizational flexibility.

Most manufacturing and operations technologies require that one trade off product innovation to obtain low cost. Economies of scale, learning, and the other cost drivers require the emergence of something approximating a dominant design that will stay relatively unchanged in its underlying technological structure for some period of time if costs are to be reduced. The technologies and the capital investments in which those technologies are imbedded are different for fountain pens than for ballpoint pens; different for vacuum tubes than for semiconductors; different for half-inch VCRs than for 8-millimeter VCRs. Each new product technology starts the experience curve anew. Ask the Swiss, who lost most of the watch business to the Japanese with the advent of electronic timekeeping technology, or DuPont, whose dominant position in cellophane became obsolete with the emergence of plastic film in the early 1960s.

Most manufacturing and operations process technologies achieve low variable costs through maximizing output and restricting product variety. Time spent in changing tooling and the like to accommodate different models or varieties reduces output and increases costs. Although the emergence of computer-aided design and computer-aided manufacturing and the growth of robotics promise to ameliorate the cost penalty that a wide product mix incurs in comparison to a narrow one in traditional bend, weld, and assemble operations, there will likely still be a penalty.[44] The penalty will still be there in large batch and process industries like semiconductors and chemicals, which depend heavily on maximizing output from large pieces of capital equipment to obtain low unit costs. Even airlines (where flight frequency is the direct analogy to product variety) are subject to these limitations. Low cost comes from reducing schedules to fill big, wide-bodied aircraft. Costs go up as flight frequency increases.

The organizations and cultures that foster low-cost production are inimical to innovation. A central element in the concept of culture is shared values and beliefs. The organization that has won by the pursuit of low cost has built an organization that values cost efficiency because that is associated with winning. The unwritten beliefs are that process R&D is more important than product R&D and that when there is a choice to be made and no direct guidance available, one should choose the low-cost alternative. Over time, the very structure of the organization solidifies into a form by which these dominant values and beliefs are achieved. Innovation, variety, and change are inimical to an organization whose success has been built on stability and standardization. The inability of such an organization to change is known as "adaptive failure."[45]

Three factors determine if and when the aforementioned factors become crippling or fatal to the firm: (1) the market's demand for product change and variety, (2) the rate of technological innovation in the industry, and (3) competitors' ability to use product performance as the basis for competing.[46] Two things happen as markets become larger and larger. The first is that the firm's ability to reduce costs constantly by doubling its cumulative experience slows—gains in market share come hard and the sheer size of cumulative volume makes it difficult to double. The firm's cost leadership, therefore, rests on ever-smaller absolute competitive differences. Second, the probability that one or a restricted range of products can satisfy the needs of the entire market becomes less and less likely. Larger markets simply have greater variances in their tastes and needs.

This means that the business becomes increasingly vulnerable to competition on the basis of product performance at the very time that its ability to compete against that performance difference via cost/price reductions is lessened. Further attempts by the firm to reduce costs aggravate the situation by diminishing the firm's ability to respond in kind to the new competition. Its strategy has backfired, for only by widening its range of offerings can it compete, in effect abandoning the volume basis for its low costs and its competitive advantage. Exhibit 5-5 lists the questions that need to be asked when thinking about using an experience-based strategy.

Abernathy and Wayne analyzed the first known example of this strategic trap, the Ford Motor Company's experience with the Model T, and noted that it

---

[44] See Lei and Goldhar, "Multiple Niche Competition"; and Patricia Nemetz and Louis Fry, "Flexible Manufacturing Organizations: Implications for Strategy Formulation and Organization Design," *Academy of Management Review*, 13, no. 4 (October 1988), 627–638.

[45] Raymond E. Miles and Charles C. Snow, *Organizational Strategy, Structure, and Process* (New York: McGraw-Hill, 1978).

[46] Abernathy and Wayne, "Limits of the Learning Curve."

EXHIBIT 5-5

Nine Questions to Ask When Considering an
Experienced-Based Strategy

1. Does my industry exhibit a significant experience curve?
2. Have I defined the industry broadly enough to take into account interrelated experience?
3. What is the precise source of cost reduction?
4. Can my company keep cost reductions proprietary?
5. Is demand sufficiently stable to justify using the experience curve?
6. Is cumulated output doubling fast enough for the experience curve to provide much strategic leverage?
7. Do the returns from an experience curve strategy warrant the risks of technological obsolescence?
8. Is demand price sensitive?
9. Are there well-financed competitors who are already following an experience curve strategy or are likely to adopt one if my company does?

SOURCE: Reprinted by permission of *Harvard Business Review*. An exhibit from "Building Strategy on the Experience Curve" by Pankaj Ghemawat, March/April 1985. Copyright © 1985 by the President and Fellows of Harvard College; all rights reserved.

probably also explains the difficulties that Volkswagen experienced as a result of the long and overwhelming success of its "Bug" models.[47] From 1909 to 1926, Ford was able to reduce the price of a Model T (the dominant design of the time) from $5,000 to less than $900 (in 1958 constant dollars) while expanding output and sales some 300 fold. However, as Ford pursued cost reduction, it became less and less innovative and increasingly constrained by its manufacturing technology. Its low-cost strategy demanded it respond to the market by saying, "You can have any color you want as long as it's black."

GM's response to the new, emerging market demand for increased comfort, closed car bodies, and improved styling was considerably different. In contrast to Ford's one-size-fits-all strategy, GM's strategy was to produce a car for every purse and every purpose. Ford was unable to respond to this performance-based competition. Its sales fell, and the volume base on which costs depended evaporated. In two years, the Model T became noncompetitive as an engineering design. Worse yet, the company which had introduced eight different models in the four-year period prior to the Model T's introduction was so technologically tied to the Model T that it had to shut down its plants for one year to retool. The model change caused Ford to lose $200 million—it had to replace 15,000 machine tools, rebuild an additional 25,000, and lay off 60,000 workers in Detroit alone. That move left GM's low-priced Chevrolet model

[47] Abernathy and Wayne, "Limits of the Learning Curve," p. 117.

unopposed in the market and also opened the window for Plymouth's successful entry. Abernathy and Wayne concluded that "the unfortunate implication is that product innovation is the enemy of cost efficiency, and vice versa."[48]

The Core Message of the Experience Curve

The preceding discussion, when combined with what is known about strategy and economic competition, contains a powerful core message:

1. *Cost competitiveness is always an issue.* Whether in a differentiated or commodity product market, competitors' costs must always be within competitive distance to remain viable.
2. *Time, cumulative volume, and volume growth provide firms the opportunity to reduce costs.* The firm which does not act on those opportunities is at a strategic disadvantage.
3. *Manufacturing costs in competitive markets always go down with time and cumulative volume.* The business that does not reduce its costs at least at the same rate as its competitors will soon be uncompetitive.[49]
4. *The early stages of a technology's practical application offer the greatest potential for absolute cost differences among competitors.* Small differences in experience and volume level among competitors can produce large differences in absolute costs and, therefore, competitive advantage.
5. *A low-cost competitor will ultimately use its cost advantage to gain strategic advantage.* The competitor with a cost advantage will lower price to gain additional volume and further lower costs while crippling the ability of higher-cost competitors to compete.[50]
6. *Low-cost producers are not invulnerable to shifts in basic technology or consumer tastes.* Competitors can beat them by exploiting new process technology which reduces costs below those of the existing cost leader and new product technology which delivers improved product performance and which starts a new experience curve, or by responding to changes in consumer needs and tastes for variety or uniqueness.

SUMMARY

Few strategists are ever given a blank check and the ability to create an organization and operating and manufacturing facilities from scratch. This means that

---

[48] Abernathy and Wayne, "Limits of the Learning Curve," p. 118.

[49] Strictly speaking, the statement should read, "The unit quantities of a product's factor inputs in physical terms are always reduced with time, cumulative volume, and volume growth." Increases in the prices (in constant dollars) of a product's inputs, such as raw materials or labor, can indeed raise a product's price in constant dollars over time. Nonetheless, competitors are always operating on the cost drivers and reducing the physical units incorporated in their products.

[50] It does not matter that, to date, the cost leader has not used that strategic advantage. From the viewpoint of the advantaged firm, to delay the use of a strategic competitive advantage is to allow competitors (or chance) that amount of time to neutralize the advantage. Further, the high profits attract new competitors, increasing long-run competitive intensity and ultimately hastening the inevitable shakeout.

strategy must, more than anything else, be interpreted as the art of the possible—creating strategies which confer competitive advantage out of what is. At the root of that strategic problem is the ability to understand and capitalize on the business's existing technological base.

Central to that understanding is the concept of the EPT, the equipment and process technology that a firm has or is capable of creating within the constraints of its financial and human resources. The influence of EPT pervades every corner of the organization, from the basic economics of the firm to the crucial operating criteria, human resources, and competitive strategies. The strategist needs to understand the strategic implications of current and prospective EPTs. These can be summarized as understanding not only the impact of investment and operating costs but the implications for product mix, product quality, and the ability to change in the future.

The value chain is a powerful concept for analyzing the strategic impact of existing and potential operating systems, especially as compared to different kinds of competitors. Key ideas include the concepts of primary and support activities, the impact of scope and linkages, and identification of the key factors which drive dynamic costs—the cost drivers.

Understanding how cost drivers contribute to the lowering of costs as a function of cumulative operating volume is at the base of the experience curve. Based initially on the learning curve (which states that as people repeat a task they learn how to do it better and faster), the experience curve states that the same effect is observed if one relates the total costs of manufacturing a product to the firm's cumulative experience in manufacturing that product. Costs are observed to be reduced by a constant percentage with each doubling of cumulative experience.

Of key strategic importance is the fact that the competitor who reduces costs faster than competitors can gain a competitive advantage—low cost. Equally important is market share as both a means and measure of experience, and speed in acquiring it. It is crucial that management identify the key cost drivers in the business and utilize those drivers consistent with the opportunities that volume and growth present. But the opportunities that experience-based strategies give a firm to gain the strategically valuable position of low-cost producer can be offset by the rigidities that accompany the pursuit of low cost. As markets grow large, they increasingly offer opportunities for competitors to segment them and to offer improved product performance as a means to beat the cost leader, whose very ability to respond to such competition is constrained by its cost focus.

In this way, strategy is like the children's game of paper, stones, and scissors. Paper wins because it covers stones. Stones win because they break scissors. And scissors win because they cut paper.

6

A FRAMEWORK
FOR INCORPORATING TECHNOLOGY
INTO PRODUCT STRATEGY DECISIONS

Technology, the knowledge about how to do something practical, is at the base of every business. New technologies create new products (computers, VCRs) and new industries (solid-state electronics, bioengineering), create complementary businesses (prerecorded videotapes, computer software), make other products possible (cash management accounts, home banking), and destroy others (mechanical cash registers, typewriters, watches, electronic vacuum tubes, and discrete electronic components). New or different technologies provide the opportunity for competitive advantage—new benefits, differentiated products, or lower-cost products are some of the ways this can happen.

Managers are constantly called on to make technological decisions. They are asked whether they will fund research that affects their products, and whether to aim that research to attain superior or parity performance, new benefits or lower costs, research on the product itself, the process by which it is manufactured, or the computer system that controls its order entry, inventory control, and customer fulfillment processes.

To make these decisions, managers must know about how technology is created and destroyed, managed, and used strategically. The first part of this chapter focuses on the process of technology creation and application to attain strategic advantage. The second part outlines the basics of a technology strategy by which the firm can direct and control its technology efforts.

TECHNOLOGY CREATION AND UTILIZATION

Figure 6-1 presents an overview of the role of technology in competitive strategy and the processes by which it is created, evaluated, measured, and applied. Essentially, it shows that R&D creates technology that produces a strategic advantage for the firm. R&D can be described in terms of what is done, by whom it is performed, and in terms of the resulting output. The R&D and technology steps can be explained by several theoretical frameworks that allow one to understand, predict, and manage the processes. The results of the processes are

Figure 6-1   Technology creation and strategic advantage: An overview of types, processes, and theories

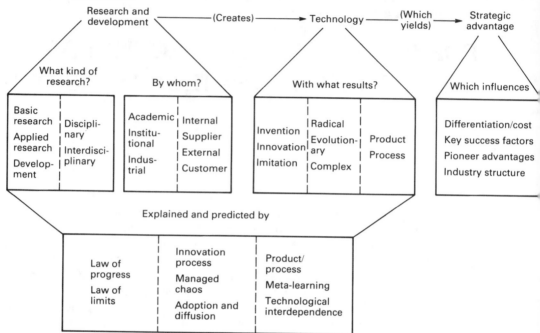

ultimately measured by the degree to which they give the firm a strategic advantage, either by enhancing the firm's ability to (1) differentiate its products or produce them at lower cost, (2) excel at the key success factors in the industry, (3) gain pioneer advantages, and/or (4) improve the structure of the industry in which it competes.

This discussion first describes the processes of R&D (the *what* and *by whom*) and technology (the resulting output). It then explores the theories that have been proposed to explain the pace of technology development and technology acceptance.

Research and Development

Research and development activity is the key part of the process of technology creation. The strategist who can gain an intuitive feel for the process—its pace, potential, and probabalistic nature—is able to make decisions not only on the basis of what is but on the basis of what can be. At its most basic level, R&D is the process by which knowledge is created. Knowledge is frequently classified on a continuum, with one end characterized as that which is basic or scientific and the other as that which is applied or technological.

As shown in Figure 6-2, the term *research and development* is based on this distinction. The closer one is to the basic end of this continuum, the more the

Figure 6-2   The R&D continuum

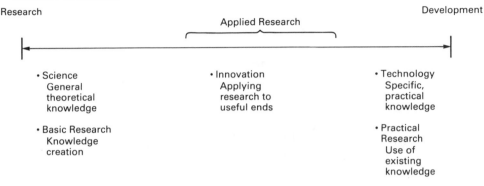

activity is termed research. The more one moves to the right, toward the applied end, the more the activity is termed development. Activities on the research end of the continuum attempt to develop scientific or general knowledge—the goal is to establish principles or theories which explain and predict phenomena at the broadest possible level. At the far right, on the other hand, is applied or technological knowledge. This specific know-how or information is required to produce and/or sell a product or service.[1] Three levels of the knowledge production activity are typically distinguished: basic, applied, and development. As shown in Figure 6-3, the largest amounts are spent on development activities, the smallest on basic research.

Research.   Basic research is synonymous with scientific research. Sometimes called pure or scholarly research, it is pursued essentially for its own sake, generally within a given disciplinary framework. Biochemists, chemists, biologists, and medical researchers, for example, all study living organisms but from sometimes vastly differing perspectives. Each discipline has its own journals, techniques, and agendas which do not necessarily overlap. An individual researcher is generally conversant (and sometimes competent) only within his or her discipline. Because of this, interdisciplinary research is generally performed by teams of researchers from different disciplines. Basic research is pursued primarily in universities and independent, nonprofit research institutes. Only a few, large businesses sponsor basic research in-house, although larger numbers support general or directed research at universities and research institutes.

Little is known about the process of knowledge creation. While there are many studies of creativity per se, few observers are able to point with certainty to the factors that control or cause the creation of new knowledge. Some kinds of new knowledge, of course, are simply the result of time and effort and result in the build-up or accretion, over time, of a substantial body of knowledge about a topic.

Truly new knowledge, however, is both more important and far less con-

---

[1] Noel Capon and Rashi Glazer, "Marketing and Technology: A Strategic Coalignment," *Journal of Marketing*, 51, no. 3 (July 1987), pp. 1–14.

Figure 6-3 Industrial R&D expenditures for basic research, applied research, and development, 1960–1978 (in $ millions)

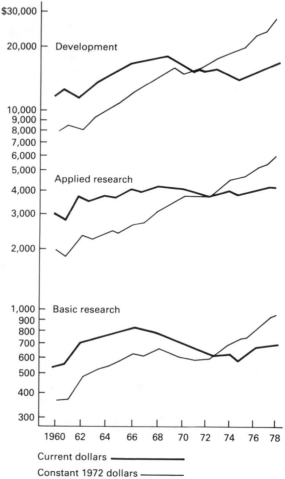

Current dollars ⸺⸺⸺⸺

Constant 1972 dollars ⸻⸻

SOURCE: Robert H. Hayes and William J. Abernathy, "A Drastic New Loss of Competitive Strength," in Michael L. Tushman and William L. Moore, eds., *Readings in the Management of Innovations* (Boston: Pittfield Publishing, 1982), p. 87.

trollable or predictable. The breakthroughs in superconductivity in the late 1980s, for example, were neither predicted nor expected. They seemingly just happened. True invention, which is typified by major breakthroughs (such as superconductivity, the transistor effect, and xerography), is unpredictable and rare.

The management of research activity is, therefore, a difficult task. While one knows that the breakthrough will not come unless resources are applied to an area or problem, the application of resources does not in any way assure that a solution will come sooner or even whether a positive outcome will indeed be achieved. For although it may be that not enough work has yet been done in an area, it may also be that the solution of a problem requires development of techniques or knowledge in other areas before it can be solved. In the latter case, one might say that its time has just not come. A third explanation is also possible—it may be that it just cannot be done. The problem is that one never knows which is the case.

Accordingly, those who fund and manage basic research aimed at invention—true technical breakthroughs—follow a rather simple decision rule: Allocate resources to problems and issues where progress is being made. In following this rule, managers fund a large number of probes—small-scale projects designed to establish the probability that effort in an area will bring rewards—and then allocate further and increasingly larger budgets to those areas and researchers that produce results while shrinking funding to those that do not. Philosophically, these managers seem to regard the frontiers of knowledge in physical or geographical terms: If there is a path at the edge of knowledge, take it. But if the frontier seems to lack a path, appears to have a brick wall in fact, do not waste your time trying to batter your way through it.[2]

Basic research is not a significant *direct* source of innovations (the practical, economic use of new knowledge to accomplish useful ends).[3] Its contribution to innovation is through the educational channel. This results in a substantial lag between the time research is performed and the time its findings appear in an innovation. These lags have been estimated to be as much as eight to fifteen years.[4] For example, it took some twenty-three years for xerography to find its way into the market. The basic finding that led to the development of the birth control pill, which received FDA approval and its first marketplace sales in 1962, took place between the late 1930s and 1944 when Syntex, the firm that pioneered the pill, was founded.[5] More recently, Merck introduced a revolutionary cholesterol-lowering drug named Mevacor. Although the active ingredient in Mevacor was discovered in 1956, it was not until 1987 that the drug reached the market. It had taken thirty years and $125 million to commercialize that initial discovery.[6] Exhibit 6-1 examines the impact that R&D has on business success in general.

Development.   At the other end of the spectrum is technology development. While still a knowledge-producing activity, development is concerned with the production of technology, the ability to reproducibly create products, processes,

---

[2] Donald G. Marquis, "The Anatomy of Successful Innovations," in *Readings in the Management of Innovation*, pp. 42–50; and James Brian Quinn, "Innovation and Corporate Strategy—Managed Chaos," in Mel Horwitch, ed., *Technology in the Modern Corporation: A Strategic Perspective* (Elmsford, NY: Pergamon Press, 1986), pp. 167–183.

[3] Invention and innovation are not the same. This distinction is explored in a later section.

[4] James M. Utterback, "Innovation in Industry and the Diffusion of Technology," *Science*, 183 (February 15, 1974), 658–662.

[5] James Brian Quinn, "Innovation and Corporate Strategy," p. 169.

[6] *Business Week*, "The Miracle Company," October 19, 1987, p. 85.

EXHIBIT 6-1

Does R&D Work?

R&D is a business-expanding expenditure just as much as is advertising or sales-force expenditures. Results of empirical research into the relationship between measures of R&D input and the growth of the firm typically show positive relationships. One researcher who has recently performed research on the impact of R&D on worldwide market share and competitive advantage made the following points:

- Corporate-level resource allocation with respect to R&D does indeed matter, to the point that it is one of the most important factors underlying recent changes in shares of world markets by the world's leading firms.
- The R&D intensity of individual firms . . . is positively and significantly related to subsequent relative worldwide corporate sales growth, and thus to company gains in world market share . . . across a broad, and seemingly heterogeneous range of industries.
- R&D spending relative to sales is generally more closely related to corporate performance than are absolute levels of corporate R&D spending . . . the eventual product or process output of R&D activity is not just a matter of "dollars or yen spent," but also of how highly firms value R&D activity relative to other claims on their resources.

This last point is emphasized by the researcher. He notes that R&D is not just an activity—it is not something that one simply does, but rather it is a part of an organizational culture, one of the internalized values of people in successful organizations.

SOURCE: Lawrence G. Franko, "Global Corporate Competition: Who's Winning, Who's Losing, and the R&D Factor as One Reason Why." Copyright © 1989 John Wiley & Sons Limited. Reproduced by permission of John Wiley and Sons Limited.

and services.[7] Perhaps the best example would be to examine the developmental activities that are undertaken to produce and sell a simple thing such as a new candy. The following are just some of the things that must be accomplished:

- The generation and refinement of the exact recipe to be used,
- Testing and approval of the raw materials to be used and the qualification of suppliers of those materials,
- Learning how to make the product in 1,000-pound batches (rather than the 2-pound batches made in the test kitchen) and establishing the optimal manufacturing procedures to reproduce the desired result reliably,

[7] John Friar and Mel Horwitch, "The Emergence of Technology Strategy: A New Dimension of Strategic Management," in *Technology in the Modern Corporation: A Strategic Perspective*, p. 50–85.

· Developing and specifying the exact mixing and packaging machinery needed.
· Establishing the specific quality control tests for the product's taste, color, and texture,
· Testing and final specification of the wrapper and packaging materials,
· Testing the product for shelf life,

While no new scientific principles are involved, the process involves the creation of a large amount of specific knowledge and entails considerable technical skill, time, and money. New processes and machinery may be required, raw materials shortages may force the development of alternate product formulation recipes, and a host of other unforeseen (and unforeseeable) problems will likely emerge that must be solved under tight deadlines.

Development activities involve a close association between a business's R&D personnel (if such exist) and its operating and line business people. Its focus is on real projects for implementation in the real-time future, whether tomorrow, next week, next month, or next year. The majority of such activities are tied to specific business activities and projects—very little is unallocated overhead in budgetary terms. Product, market, and business managers typically sponsor development projects related to their products. Product performance or quality improvement and various cost-reduction projects probably account for most of the development work done on existing products and businesses.

In opposition to basic research, seldom are any new principles or truly new knowledge created in development activities. For this reason, brute force works to produce results where it does not in basic research. The basic knowledge needed to solve the problems is there; all that is needed is the time, effort, and funds to develop and apply it. For this reason, bigger budgets bring bigger, better, or faster results; and larger, more profitable, or better-financed firms can out-innovate smaller, less profitable, or less cash-rich firms.

Applied Research.   Applied research is not as well defined as the end points of the continuum. If theoretical physics is at one end of the continuum and the engineering design for a specific manufacturing process or product is at the other end, then applied research bridges the two. Applied research is done primarily at the institutional and industrial levels. Seldom is it conducted in universities or other pure research centers. Such organizations as Batelle, IIT Research Institute, and SRI, Inc., do applied research under government and industry grants.

At the level of the firm, applied research is best defined as the development of the in-house capabilities, skills, and knowledge necessary to support the continued technological viability of a business in an environment in which technology is continually changing. Very little applied research is done in industries where the technological environment is stable. Why, after all, would a mattress maker want to do applied research?

Producers of integrated circuits, such as Intel, Texas Instruments, NEC, and AT&T, on the other hand, face a rapidly changing technological environment, and accordingly all are doing applied research. A major research focus for all chip makers is on gallium arsenide as the substrate for their chips.[8] Silicon, the present material, appears to be approaching the theoretical limits of its capabilities and may soon be obsoleted by gallium arsenide, just as silicon obsoleted germanium as the material of choice during the late 1950s and early 1960s. When that transition occurred, Hughes, Sylvania, and Clevite were displaced as industry leaders (and ultimately from the business) by Motorola and a then-small firm known as Texas Instruments. It is possible for that scenario to repeat itself, because a new transistor design made possible by the use of gallium arsenide—the resonant tunneling transistor—would make it possible for one transistor to do the work of twenty-four conventional transistors. The firm that first masters this new technology, if any of them ultimately do, can deliver higher performance *and* lower cost to the marketplace. Such an advantage would allow that firm virtually to obsolete competitors' products and take over the market.

Applied research, while clearly directed toward the needs of the business, seldom has the same project orientation that development activities do. It is not expected (nor can it be) to produce a specific salable product within some given time frame. While all semiconductor manufacturers are focusing on gallium arsenide, for example, it is still not a successful technology. Furthermore, it could be that it never will be. Working on the frontiers of science and technology is like that. In the late 1970s and early 1980s, for example, early applications of magnetic bubble memory technology for computers got as far as the marketplace before certain insoluble limitations stopped further applications. Try as they might, proponents of the technology just could not improve the state of the art sufficiently to remove those limitations.

Nonetheless, in the long run one expects that such activities and expenditures will benefit the business. The crux of the problem at the business level revolves around that issue—how much to spend, on what technologies, and with what economic payback. Since those are almost insoluble questions, applied research is typically a risky overhead item in business budgets.[9]

One reason applied research is risky is that the relationship between resources and results is much more like that found in basic research than the model found in development. That is, while nothing happens without resources, more resources do little to speed up or guarantee results. Savvy business managers, therefore, operate as if they were funding basic research. They fund numbers of probes and then, once the crucial invention is made, pour the resources into the successful area. The difference here is that the additional resources go not so much toward adding more knowledge as to the exploitation of the breakthrough. The idea is to begin moving the new knowledge toward

---

[8] Andrew Pollack, "New Chips Offer the Promise of Much Speedier Computers," *The New York Times,* January 4, 1989, pp. A1 and D6; *Business Week,* "The Chips of Tomorrow May Have Finally Arrived," November 19, 1990, pp. 89 and 92.

[9] George F. Mechlin and Daniel Berg, "Evaluating Research—ROI Is Not Enough," *Harvard Business Review,* 58, no. 5 (September-October 1980), 93–99.

commercialization and to funnel additional funds to that research necessary to develop the idea into something salable.

The failure of industry in the United States to make the essentially risky decision to fund applied research is a frequently cited cause of the loss of international competitiveness. One reason for the failure may be that the ability to perform sophisticated financial analyses outran the ability of managers to forecast the returns to research as opposed to development. As one R&D director said, "It's much more difficult to come up with a synthetic meat product than a lemon-lime cake mix. But you work on the lemon-lime cake mix because you know exactly what that return is going to be. A synthetic steak is going to take a lot longer, require a much bigger investment, and the risk of failure will be greater."[10]

R&D Sources.   A complete view of the R&D process must recognize that the firm is seldom the source of all of its own technology. Most managerial systems technology, for example, is done by communications and computer suppliers. Suppliers are a frequent source of technology for many firms—production equipment manufacturers do R&D to enhance the performance of their own machinery, which they then make available to all of their customers. While such a strategy allows the firm to focus its technology development resources on its own products, it also means that the firm accepts parity with its competitors with respect to its production technology. Most manufacturers of plastic parts, bags, bottles, and other small parts, for example, all have the ability to be exactly equal in their production costs because they all share the same few machinery suppliers. Much the same can be said for the airlines and innumerable other businesses.

In some industries there are firms whose business it is to sell or license technology. Engineering contractors such as Lummus, Kellogg, Bechtel (in the U.S.) and Snambergetti (in Italy) and IHI (in Japan) are the frequent source of technology for petroleum refining and petrochemicals. Sometimes such technology is included in the price of the facility the contractor builds for a client; in other instances the technology is licensed for fees and royalties.

Firms in other industries such as pharmaceuticals and computer software also license their technology and patent positions to other firms. Whether to externally source technology or to license out one's own technology is a critical question in determining a firm's technology strategy.

Technology

Technology—useful knowledge—is the output of R&D. This section discusses the many ways one may characterize, describe, and evaluate that result. One useful distinction is that made among invention, innovation, and imitation.

Invention.   An invention is the creation of new knowledge which promises some useful potential. One way of defining an invention is to base the definition

---

[10] Quoted in Robert H. Hayes and William J. Abernathy, "Managing Our Way to Economic Decline," *Harvard Business Review*, 58, no. 4 (July-August 1980), p. 68.

on the ideas used in determining patentability. In patent terms, then, an invention is an idea that has usefulness (vaguely defined, but at least in the abstract) that derives from a fundamental new combination of scientific principles. This latter distinction is made when the "differences between an invention and the prior art are substantial and . . . the invention would not have been obvious to someone reasonably skilled in the art."[11] In patent language, the idea is both novel and nonobvious. Not all inventions are patented, nor are all patented inventions used. In fact, of the some 30,000 inventions that have been made under U.S. government funded research and patented, only about 1,500 have been licensed.[12]

Invention allows one to do something that one could not do before. That "something" might be a new material with useful characteristics (such as superconductors), a new product (such as disposable contact lenses), a new way of making something (recombinant DNA), or a new way of doing something (computer speech recognition technology). Most invention occurs as the result of basic and applied research, but some still comes from practice. For example, the surgical procedure known as radial keratotomy used to correct certain eyesight problems resulted not from basic research but from the clinical experience of eye surgeons. It was not until several thousand practitioners were using it that it was "scientifically" evaluated.[13] But, as noted earlier, inventions rarely appear in well-developed or fully useful form. Much work is needed to bring the potential benefits into reality. Invention is creation; the application of invention is termed innovation.

Innovation.   Innovation can be an act or a thing. The first practical use of new knowledge is termed innovation (the act); the new knowledge used (or its product) is termed the innovation; and the person or organization introducing it is termed the innovator. The economist Joseph Schumpeter termed innovation "as the setting up of a new production function."[14] He used the term *innovation* to distinguish the act of application from that of invention because he recognized that, from an economic viewpoint, it was the act of applying new knowledge that created economic wealth.

The innovator in Schumpeter's view is as creative as the inventor, taking the risks inherent in doing something practical for the first time. An innovator takes technical risks and market risks. Technical risks involve the product (if that is the innovation) and its manufacture. Will it reliably and regularly work as it is supposed to, and can it be regularly and economically produced? Market risk is concerned with market acceptance. Is there a market for the product at the current price/performance ratio? Can I find a way to create sufficient value to attract customers and still profit?

---

[11] Louis W. Stern and Thomas L. Eovaldi, *Legal Aspects of Marketing Strategy* (Englewood Cliffs, NJ: Prentice-Hall, 1984), p. 29.
[12] Everett M. Rogers, *Diffusion of Innovations*, 3rd ed. (New York: Free Press, 1983).
[13] Cited in Rogers, *Diffusion of Innovations*.
[14] Joseph Schumpeter, *Business Cycles* (New York: McGraw-Hill, 1939), p. 87.

Imitation.   Imitation is as important a result of R&D as are invention and innovation. The imitative process has long been observed. In fact, the early French sociologist Gabriel Tarde published a book in 1903 titled *The Laws of Imitation*.[15] Some of his observations concerned the speed of imitation and which kinds of ideas were widely imitated and which were not.

Schumpeter saw imitation as the third step in the invention-innovation-imitation chain. In his words,

> whenever a new production function has been set up successfully and the trade beholds the new thing done and its major problems solved, it becomes much easier for other people to do the same thing and even to improve upon it. In fact, they are driven to copying it if they can, and some people will do so forthwith . . . innovations do not remain isolated events and are not evenly distributed in time, but . . . on the contrary, they tend to cluster, to come about in bunches, simply because some, then most, firms follow in the wake of successful innovation.[16]

Imitation is more than simply copying someone else's idea, as Schumpeter observed. As one manager in a highly technological industry explained it, the success of one new technological breakthrough seems to spur competitors' researchers to finding alternative technological routes to the same result (inventing around the innovator's patents). Knowing that the act of invention in an area can be accomplished leads competitors to manage applied research as they do development—they pour resources into the area to accelerate the invention they now know is possible.

Since January, 1986, for example, when IBM scientists announced that they had observed superconductivity in a copper oxide, the pace of discovery has accelerated rapidly, raising the critical temperature required for superconductivity from IBM's announced -406 degrees Fahrenheit to -28 degrees Fahrenheit (and perhaps even $+76$) in the period from 1987 to 1988. But although scientists had first observed superconductivity as early as 1911 (at -452 degrees Fahrenheit), it wasn't until IBM showed the way to more practical routes that substantial amounts of effort were expended.[17]

Product and Process Research.   There are but two areas to which R&D may be directed: product or process. Since research spending on product research reduces the funds available for process research and vice versa, the balance between the two is a critical choice for the manager. Some see the choice as reflecting an expansionary or conservative philosophy on the part of management.

Product-oriented research is typically aimed at expanding or improving on the benefits that a product delivers to consumers. Since it is directed toward the improvement of the basic value equation by increasing the utility delivered,

[15] Gabriel Tarde, *The Laws of Imitation*, translated by Elsie Clews Parsons (New York: Holt, 1903).
[16] Schumpeter, *Business Cycles*, p. 100.
[17] *Business Week*, "Will the Results Be as Hot as the Rumours?," January 9, 1989, p. 42.

product research is frequently seen as expansionary in philosophy. This is because the managers who fund product research do so to gain sales at the expense of competitors or by expanding the size of the market.

In contrast, research on manufacturing process improvements is often characterized (often wrongly) as conservative because it is seen as directed inward to solving the business's problems rather than customers'. Whether this is so depends on where the technology is relative to the state of the art and the linkages between product design and manufacturing process.

Semiconductor manufacturers, for example, know what their new generation of integrated circuits will look like—the products are designed conceptually. The problem is to learn how to make them. To do this, semiconductor makers are now experimenting with a process known as molecular beam epitaxy, which allows them to lay materials down on each other—atomic layer by atomic layer—almost like high-tech spray painting. In many instances, product characteristics are a function of such manufacturing breakthroughs. Procter & Gamble's Charmin® brand toilet tissue, for example, won in the marketplace because it was the first to deliver a new standard of softness. All of the competitors knew that customers valued softness; the problem was the none of them knew how to produce it. P&G's research into manufacturing technology provided it with the breakthrough needed to produce softness and gave it many years of sales without direct competition.

On the other hand, process research is conservative when it is aimed at improving production of existing products and existing benefits. The process research that a manufacturer of consumer electronics products, automobiles, or commodity plastic resins does is generally aimed at cost reduction; knocking a few cents or so off costs to improve profitability. To the extent that funding for this type of research displaces funding for product research, it is conservative.

Types of Innovation.   As may be obvious by now, there are many types of research and many types of invention and innovation. Three types of invention and innovation are typically distinguished: radical, evolutionary, and complex.[18]

Radical innovations mark what can be called a step change in either or both the *means* of accomplishing some useful purpose or some *measure of performance,* in either technical or economic terms. It is not smooth or incremental change. It is a qualitative jump, a discontinuous change with the past. It is synonymous with such terms as *major* or *breakthrough.*

Radical innovation is the kind of discovery that changes the whole character of an industry.[19] One of the reasons it changes industries is that the breakthrough frequently is based on scientific principles and technologies different from those in use in the industry. Radical innovation, therefore, favors the newcomers who are basic in the new technology and have no vested interest in

[18] Donald G. Marquis, "The Anatomy of Successful Innovations," in Michael L. Tushman and William L. Moore, eds., *Readings in the Management of Innovations* (Boston: Pittfield Publishing, 1982), p. 44, as reprinted from *Innovations* (Technology Communications, Inc., November 1969).

[19] Francisco-Javier Olleros, "Emerging Industries and the Burnout of Pioneers," *Journal of Product Innovation Management,* 3, no. 1 (March 1986), 5–18.

protecting the old technology or the productive assets embodying that old technology.

Consider, for example, the difference between mechanical timekeeping technology and the digital and quartz analog electronic timekeeping technology made possible by microelectronic circuitry. Clearly, the means by which the two keep time are radically different. Mechanical watches use mechanical technology, springs, gears, and levers, which use physical motion to accomplish timekeeping. In a digital watch, electron flow does it all. Nothing moves, therefore eliminating friction, the largest user of energy and the basic cause of wear in any mechanical device.

In terms of performance, the electronic technology attains an equivalent step change improvement, whether measured in terms of absolute accuracy, the reliability of that accuracy, the reliability of the mechanism, the reduction in maintenance, or the economics of achieving that result. A $10 or $20 digital watch can now keep time at a level of accuracy that formerly only very expensive chronometers were able to achieve.

The emergence of electronic timekeeping technology changed the face of watch manufacturing. Before the mid-1970s, for example, mechanical watches held close to 100% of the watch market. By 1984, that share had dropped to about 10% as quartz analog and digital watches took over. In 1975, some 35% of watch production was held by Switzerland, with the rest of Western Europe holding close to 20% and the U.S. a little over 10%. In contrast, these three players' shares in 1982 were 14%, 6%, and 2%, respectively. Hong Kong and Japan, which in 1975 together held only 15% of the output share, were the big gainers, achieving a combined share of over 50% by 1982.[20]

Incremental innovation, in contrast, tends to refine the existing, established technology. Typically, it is the kind of innovation that extends the frontiers of a technology's usefulness (or economics), as longer battery life and improved chargers have broadened the market for battery-powered hand tools. "Nuts and bolts" innovation is what Marquis calls it because

> modest as it is, such innovation is absolutely essential for the average firm's survival. So long as your competitors do it, so must you. If your competitor comes out with a better product, you must make a technical change in your own—innovate—to get around the advance in his.[21]

Since incremental innovation generally takes place within the existing technologies used in the industry, it favors incumbent firms—reinforcing the status quo. After all, the incumbents know the existing technology base better than anyone else and have already made their investments in the plant and equipment that uses the technology. These head starts reduce considerably the prob-

---

[20] *Business Week*, "Price Wars and a Glut Have the World's Watchmakers in Chaos," February 20, 1984, p. 102D.
[21] Marquis, "The Anatomy of Successful Innovations," in *Readings in the Management of Innovations*, p. 43.

ability that a newcomer could compete as well as the existing, incumbent firms.

Complex systems innovation is the third type of innovation.[22] It is involved in the creation of large-scale communications or computing systems, such as AT&T's installation of a data communications network based on packet-switching technology or IBM's new Sierra series of large mainframe computers. New weapons systems for the government or space systems for NASA are other examples. Complex systems innovation takes years to create and requires careful planning to ensure that the needed technologies will all be ready, available, and will work together in the target time frame.

While such projects seldom are begun without a clear idea of their technical feasibility, planners frequently need to "bet-on-the-come"[23] in the expectation that during the project's long life applied research and development will indeed deliver the many state-of-the-art technologies needed. Success, in such a case, depends on the ability of technical managers to know how far they can go beyond that which is technically possible at the time the project is planned. Their intuitive sense of what research can achieve, which yet-to-be-proved new technology will deliver on its promises, and where the roadblocks are likely to occur is a key skill.

Evaluating New Technology.   Not all inventions are worthy of being put into practice. Managers need more than an intuitive sense about what R&D can produce and when. Managers need to be able to direct R&D and to evaluate the contribution that a technical breakthrough can make to the business—for that is where its ultimate worth is measured.[24]

There are two key determinants of that success: (1) the inherent technical power of the new technology, and (2) its implications for business practice.[25] As shown in Figure 6-4, four major constructs contribute to that technological potency and business advantage: inventive merit, embodiment merit, operational merit, and market merit.

Inventive merit is the extent to which the new technology avoids the major constraints of the prior technology. The transistor, for example, improved on vacuum tube technology in three independent and significant ways: size, power consumption, and reliability. In size it was approximately one tenth the size of a vacuum tube (or even smaller). Vacuum tubes consumed most of their power in the heating of the cathode to speed the electron flow to the anode with a glowing filament much like that found in incandescent lightbulbs. By using a different scientific principle, the transistor was able to avoid the use of the heater, thereby reducing power consumption manyfold. Finally, like the fila-

---

[22] Marquis, "The Anatomy of Successful Innovations."

[23] A poker term meaning to bet on the expectation that the player will get the card needed to complete a winning hand. In business, to make plans on the assumption that certain results can be achieved even though the company has not yet demonstrated that fact.

[24] For more on this aspect of innovation, see Edwin Mansfield, "How Economists See R&D," *Harvard Business Review*, 59, no. 6 (November-December 1981), 98–106.

[25] George B. White and Margaret B. W. Graham, "How to Spot a Technological Winner," *Harvard Business Review*, 56, no. 2 (March-April 1978), 146–152. This discussion is based on their ideas.

Figure 6-4   The characteristics of successful innovations

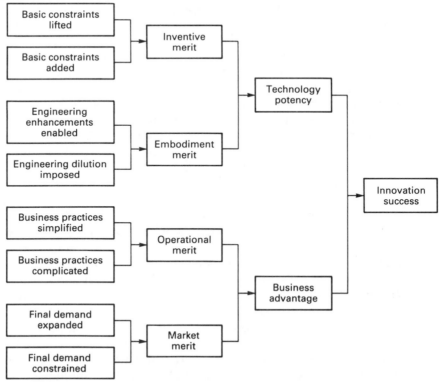

ment on a lightbulb, the heating filament gave off heat and broke (either from long use or mechanical shock). Neither happened with the transistor technology. With no heater filament to break or burn out, the transistor would work almost indefinitely and gave off very little heat.

But every technology introduces its own constraints. Inventive merit is the net of the pluses and the minuses. Transistors had two minuses of their own. One was cost. Until manufacturers were able to improve the yields from their early and crude manufacturing processes, transistors were very expensive. Second, transistors could not handle as much power as vacuum tubes. This required engineers to design new circuits specifically for transistors or to use them in parallel. The net of the merits, however, was so positive that the entire industry known as solid-state electronics was born.

Embodiment merit is concerned with the extent to which the merits of the core inventive concept can be incorporated into a physical product without dilution. The transistor was the perfect component for use in portable radios. Its size, low power consumption, and immunity to shock damage made it the component of choice. But it would not have been as valuable if manufacturers were not also able to reduce drastically the size of the other electronic components needed to make a finished product. Had they not been able to reduce the size of the antenna, speaker, and tuning capacitor, the transistor radio would not have been as impressively smaller. Of course, sound quality and sensitivity suffered, but on the whole the promise of the inventive concept was delivered.

Not all innovations are able to capture the fruit that their inventive merit promised. One chemical manufacturer, for example, spent millions in developing a new core chemical process that was able to manufacture its products to tolerances far more stringent than any competitor's process—an important characteristic to customers. However, it found that heating the product in the downstream physical processes necessary to put the product into a form that could be handled and shipped introduced so much variation that the entire benefit of the core innovation was lost. Embodiment merit is the net of the pluses and minuses in the finished product.

Operational merit is the effect that the innovation has on the company's existing business practices. Truly potent new technologies have far-reaching effects on existing business practices or constraints. Electronic watches, for example, require virtually no maintenance in comparison to mechanical watches, and that maintenance which is needed requires a different kind of skill than watch makers possess. While this required central service facilities to which customers mailed their watches for repair, it also freed manufacturers from the need to sell only through franchised jewelers capable of providing service. Watches could be, and soon were, sold through every kind of outlet. The impact of the widened distribution was to increase sales and to reduce the cost of distribution. While the difference in maintenance for electronic watches was apparently but one less constraint, it had a significant impact on sales strategy and distribution costs.

Market merit is the effect that the technology has on the creation of value-in-use, the real benefits to the end user that create demand. The highest form of market merit is exemplified by innovations such as the transistor, jet aircraft, and electronic watches. These three brought both improved benefits and economics to users, not just better performance at parity economics or parity performance at better economics. Jets were quiet, fast, and flew above the weather—passengers liked them in preference to propeller aircraft. They provided the air carriers with greatly lowered maintenance costs and improved fuel economy. The analyses for electronic watches and the transistor are the same—simultaneous improvements in performance and economics.

This combination of performance and economics grows markets. Lesser innovations, those that improve only costs or performance, clearly grow share for the innovator, make the new product the one of choice for replacement, but seldom have the power to increase overall demand.

THEORIES OF TECHNOLOGICAL INNOVATION

Technological progress and innovation does not just happen. There is a substantial theoretical and empirical literature which provides a solid basis for technology forecasting and assessment.[26] While these theories and techniques cannot accurately predict the exact timing or content of radical, discontinuous invention, they do enable one to gain a good, working understanding of the forces driving efforts at the technological frontier. The two basic phenomena underlying technological innovation are known as the law of progress and the law of limits. These two concepts are discussed first. Next, several views of the innovation process are presented, including those relating to the adoption and diffusion of innovation. Finally, several theories of innovation are presented which will help to put the process into a managerial perspective.

The Law of Progress

Henry Adams made the initial observations that led to what is known as the law of progress and *S*-curve analysis.[27] He saw in the ever-increasing pace of human progress through history the same rate of progression observed in such mundane phenomena as increases in the world's output of coal and the steadily increasing power of ocean-going vessels. By his calculations, these all improved at a similar rate—they doubled every ten years. The shape of the curve this produced—a period of slow growth followed by an exponentially increasing rise—seemed to him to explain the increasing rapidity of technical progress.

Applied as a technological forecasting tool, Adams's law of progress worked. Figure 6-5, for example, shows an exponential projection of the ton-miles per hour achieved by civilian and military transport aircraft since 1935. The earliest point on the plot represents the DC-3 and the last a Boeing 747F. While trend extrapolation seems an overly simplistic approach, technology forecasters explain that their central concept is one of continuity:

> If, in some area of technology, there has been a continuous progression of technical approaches, each one surpassing the limitations of the previous one, it is not unreasonable to expect the rate of innovation to continue. . . . To argue the contrary, in fact, is to say that the present is a point of discontinuity; that despite the fact that there has been more or less regular innovation in the past, this innovation is coming to a halt at the present level of functional capability.[28]

The Law of Limits

If one adds a ceiling to the performance that can be achieved, perhaps by reason of some physical (or chemical, electric, etc.) limit, then the curve takes on an S shape. The speed that electrons travel, for example, puts limits on the speed of

---

[26] See, for example, Edwin Mansfield, "Technological Forecasting," in T. S. Khachaturov, ed., *Methods of Long-Term Planning and Forecasting* (New York: Halstead Press, 1976); and Marvin J. Cetron and Christine A. Ralph, *Industrial Applications of Technological Forecasting and Its Utilization in R&D Management* (New York: John Wiley and Sons, 1971).

[27] H. Adams, *The Education of Henry Adams* (New York: The Modern Library, 1931). Reprinted by Heritage Press, New York, 1958. Cited in Michael J. Cleary and Horace W. Lanford, "The Evolution of Technology Assessment," *Industrial Marketing Management*, 7, no. 1 (February 1978), 26–31.

[28] James R. Bright and Milton E. F. Schoeman, eds., *A Guide to Practical Technology Forecasting* (Englewood Cliffs, NJ: Prentice-Hall, 1973), p. 107.

Figure 6-5   The laws of progress in aircraft productivity

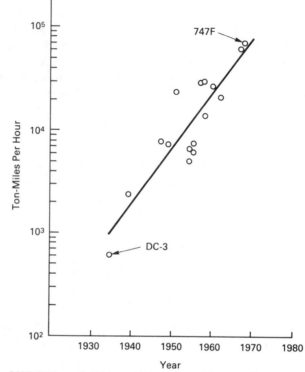

SOURCE: James R. Bright and Milton E. F. Schoeman, eds., *A Guide to Practical Technological Forecasting*. Reprinted by permission of James R. Bright. Published by Prentice Hall, Englewood Cliffs, NJ 07632, p. 18.

semiconductor devices, so there is a limit to the improvement that the law of progress would otherwise have forecast. Then, by transforming the *x* axis from time to some input measure (e.g., research funding, or man-years of technical effort), one has a forecasting tool that closely approximates the kinds of problems facing technological decision makers.

Known as the law of limits or simply the *S* curve, this has become the basis for many technological forecasting and management techniques. The law says that initially, as funds and effort are invested into research on a new technology (whether product or process), results are slow to come. Then, at some point a critical mass of knowledge is acquired and the rate of progress accelerates—"all hell breaks loose" is the phrase one experienced consultant uses to describe what happens.[29] At some point, finally, progress comes more slowly and at higher and higher costs as the technology begins to reach its limits. There is only so much that can be done to make a better-performing detergent or pocket calculator, after all.

[29] Richard Foster, *Innovation: The Attacker's Advantage* (New York: Summit Books, 1986), p. 31.

But if technologies reach physical limits, then how can a curve like that shown in Figure 6-5 be explained? Figure 6-6 represents the way that most technologists think of progress, as a series of S curves composed of short periods of linear progress separated by discontinuities. The discontinuities represent the points of invention or market acceptance of a new technology regime. The law of limits requires that managers address two questions, discussed next.

The Law of Limits or the Law of Progress?   The first question is to know how close or how far one stands from the present technology when looking at the curve (as shown in Figure 6-7). From the viewpoint of the operating manager charged with maximizing the day-to-day return from a business based on a given technology, the S-shaped law of limits dominates, and he or she must stand close to the curve. The manager must concentrate on using and improving the present technology to beat present competitors (who are generally using the same technology regime). If a firm cannot stay technically abreast or ahead of competitors in a given technology, it seems unlikely that it will be around long enough to fend off competitors who are using a newer technology.

A higher-level manager, say a corporate-level R&D person (or the same operating manager wearing a long-term strategic hat), would probably be standing farther back from the curve. In this role, the law of progress dominates. The manager would be evaluating alternate technologies, trying to decide which new technology has the best chance of being the regime of the future, when it would achieve that promise, and how much it would cost for the company to be the innovator. This might be as mundane as the technology manager of an appliance business trying to decide when microprocessor controls would overtake and replace electromechanical relays in washers and dryers. Or it could be as esoteric as IBM's chief scientist (or AT&T's, etc.) deciding about how to allocate research funding among Josephenson junction technology, gallium arsenide technology, and ballistic transistors. One of those technologies will dominate in the future—the question is which one.

Invention, Innovation, or Acceptance?   The second question the manager faces concerns the timing of the new technology. Which is the critical, controlling concern? Is the problem one of invention, with innovation and acceptance sure to follow, or is it innovation—who will be the first to commercialize the new technology? Or is the major concern with acceptance? When will market acceptance become reality? Will sales ever take off? It is easy to forget that market acceptance of VCRs, for example, was a long time in coming. It took five years to reach a disappointing 2 million unit level of annual sales. However, in the long run the VCR did achieve success, with sales in the tenth year reaching 28 million units annually.

Long-run success is sometimes too late for the managers who struggled through those lean early years. One researcher describes the way that many industries emerge as "over the dead bodies" of the early pioneers, as shown in Table 6-1. In his words,

Figure 6-6   The law of progress as a family of *S* curves

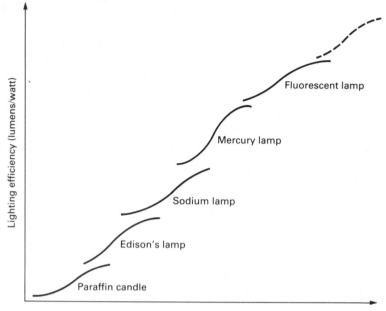

SOURCE: Reprinted by permission of the publisher from "Trends in Technology Fore-casting," by J. G. Wissema in *R&D Management*, 12 , 5–18. Copyright © 1986 by Elsevier Science Publishing Co., Inc.

Figure 6-7   The operating manager's view of technical progress

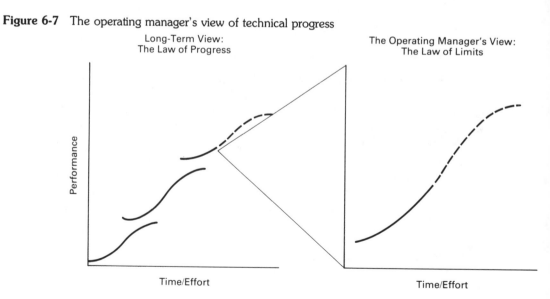

TABLE 6-1   *Unsuccessful Pioneers of Radically New Technologies*

PIONEER	TECHNOLOGY	YEAR
Robert W. Thompson	Pneumatic tire	1845
Thomas Saint, Walter Hunt, etc.	Sewing machine	1790–1851
The Stanley Brothers, Colonel Pope, etc.	Automobile	1897–1905
Henry Mill, Xavier Projean, etc.	Typewriter	1714–1878
Valdemar Poulsen	Magnetic tape recorder	1899
Alexander Parkes and Daniel Spill	Artificial plastics	1866–1869
Juan de la Cierva	Helicopter	1930
John Baird and Francis Jenkins	Television	1924
Frank Whittle	Jet engine	1930
Transitron, Philco, and Germanium Products	Transistor	1952–1955
Biologicals	DNA synthesizing machine	1981

SOURCE: Reprinted by permission of the publisher from "Emerging Industries and the Burnout of Pioneers," by Francisco-Javier Olleros in *Journal of Product Innovation Management*, no. 1, pp. 5–18. Copyright © 1986 by Elsevier Science Publishing, Inc.

Many people think that Edison pioneered ("invented") electric lighting, that Sony pioneered video-tape recordings, that Apple pioneered the personal computer, or even that Henry Ford pioneered the automobile. . . . Few people seem to remember the *true* pioneers, simply because the pioneers often didn't survive.[30]

To be able to deal with the timing issue, the manager has several theories which provide useful insight. One is a descriptive theory of the innovation process, the second a managerial theory of the same process, the third a theory of market acceptance termed the *diffusion of innovations*.

The Innovation Process

The innovation process has been widely studied. Researchers and managers agree that the process involved is the same regardless of the company, industry, or technology. Figure 6-8 shows one commonly accepted way of conceptualizing the process.[31] The figure is composed of two parts. On the top is a time line identifying the major stages in the process from problem recognition to the utilization and diffusion of the innovation. In reality, the process is not strictly linear but full of feedback loops. What is learned at a later stage may require the firm to recycle back to an earlier stage and to reformulate the task. Beneath the time line is a box representing the firm and the activities which take place inside it at each stage. Figure 6-8 sandwiches the firm between two conceptual (but real) forces: the external technological environment and the external market environment.

---

[30] Olleros, "Emerging Industries and the Burnout of Pioneers," p. 8.

[31] The process described here is essentially that described by Donald G. Marquis, "The Anatomy of Successful Innovations." See also James R. Bright, "The Process of Technological Innovation—An Aid to Understanding Technological Forecasting," in *A Guide to Practical Technological Forecasting*, for additional insight.

Figure 6-8   Model of the innovation process

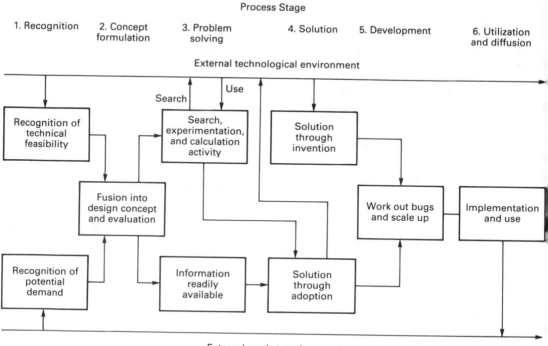

Process Stage

1. Recognition   2. Concept   3. Problem   4. Solution   5. Development   6. Utilization
                    formulation   solving   and diffusion

SOURCE: Donald G. Marquis, "The Anatomy of Successful Innovations," in *Readings in the Management of Innovations*, p. 44.

Recognition is the first phase. It can start from either the technology (supply) side or from the market (demand) side. In the former case, the progress of technology may make something feasible that could not be accomplished before, which the firm is able to evaluate based on its knowledge of the market's needs and wants. If real or potential demand exists, then the process would move to the next stage. Alternatively, the process may be initiated from the market side—demand for some benefit may be so obvious that the firm actively searches the technological frontier for potential technical approaches. In many industrial market cases, innovation is actively stimulated by users who approach potential suppliers with their needs and (sometimes) solutions.[32]

Concept formulation takes the combination of feasibility and demand and *creates* a design concept. This is an essentially creative act because the form in which the benefits promised by the technology can be delivered to the market is an open question at this point. The same benefits can frequently be delivered via a physical product, a service, by outright sale or rental, in person, or by telephone, videotape, etc. The initial design concept requires that the firm under-

[32] Eric von Hippel, "Novel Product Concepts from Lead Users: Segmenting Users by Experience" (Cambridge, MA: Marketing Science Institute Report No. 84-109, December 1984).

stand enough about what can be developed (both in the laboratories and in the marketplace) to evaluate whether the costs of developing the technology and the market are worthwhile. Since the next stage requires greatly increased out-of-pocket expenditures, strong judgment is required here.

Problem solving is the third stage of the process. In some simple instances, recognition of technological feasibility is sufficient to provide all of the information needed for a finished solution. More frequently, however, there is much to learn and master, and therefore research, development, and inventive activities are required. Unanticipated problems pop up that need to be solved: a manufacturing process proves sensitive to raw materials quality, the tolerances in a product need to be closer than conventional technology can provide, there is a shortage of some component of choice, and so on. In some unknown percentage of projects, the problems cannot be solved and the project is canceled or put on hold.

Solution is the result of successful problem-solving activity. It matters little whether the solution came about as a result of the adoption of someone else's technology or through invention, although in the inventive case this is the point at which one would apply for a patent. The solution may be the exact match to the original design concept or, more likely, the answer to a modified concept developed as a result of an earlier iteration through the process.

Development is the stage in which the technical and business (or market) solutions are verified and the bugs worked out of both before the scale-up process begins. Since out-of-pocket investment and operating costs escalate at and beyond this stage, it is as critical an evaluation as the evaluation that occurred earlier at the concept development stage. Many technical and marketplace problems typically occur here. A new manufacturing process which worked on a small scale may not scale up well—perhaps its quality cannot be controlled. On the market side, competitors may have beaten the firm to the market with similar or different products, forcing a reevaluation of the product's launch plan. The possibilities for difficulties at this stage are immense.

In the *utilization and diffusion* stage, innovation is actually achieved. The inventive, creative idea is put into actual use. Risks, however, do not necessarily decline. Marketplace risks are primary at this point. One study estimates, for example, that four of ten consumer products and approximately one of five services and industrial products fail in the marketplace.[33]

Even if the marketplace proves tractable, however, the technology is still not necessarily proven. The kinds of day-to-day use to which the market subjects a product provides a statistically more powerful test of its basic technology and construction than any laboratory testing ever can. Production technology, operating on a 24-hour-per-day basis with three different shifts of operators, also gets a different testing than that which occurred in the clean environment of the laboratory.

---

[33] David S. Hopkins and Earl L. Bailey, "New Product Pressures," *Conference Board Record*, June 1971, pp. 16–24.

It is at this stage that the benefits and drawbacks of innovation by invention versus innovation by imitation become evident. The imitator knows more about the nature and level of market demand, about the failure rates and user acceptance of different product designs, and innumerable other questions than did the pioneer at any comparable stage of the process. This substantial reduction in risk accounts for the popularity of imitation.

The Innovation Process as Managed Chaos

While the innovation process seems realistic and useful as an aid to understanding how innovation occurs, the idea of the innovation process as an orderly, linear flow is a gross oversimplification of reality. The facts seem to indicate a process quite the reverse; that historically most major technological advances did not occur within a well-planned and controlled linear process. Instead, they came out of

> a relatively chaotic sequence of events typically involving an early vision; numerous fits, starts and lapses in progress; random interactions with the outside world; frequent intuitive insights and personal risk-taking; and even some lucky breaks which ultimately led to success.[34]

This statement describes a process that is not easy to control or to manage. It does not have the kind of characteristics that managers typically deal with—certainty of output and timing are not the hallmarks of innovation. One observer noted that it was "more akin to a fermentation vat than a production line" in that "initial discoveries tend to be highly individualistic and serendipitous, advances chaotic and interactive, and specific outcomes unpredictable and chancy until the very last moment."[35]

A better conceptualization of the innovation process needs to incorporate this reality. The process should be conceived as one in which several technical approaches to the problem are pursued simultaneously because of the probabalistic nature of innovation. Since prediction is difficult, multiple approaches increase the probability of a breakthrough. As someone once noted, if theory can predict everything, you're at the production stage, not in development.

Champions. A second insight provided by reality is the importance of individuals who champion the new technology.[36] Most organizations seem to be designed to become more and more efficient at some predefined task, and innovation, by its very nature, is contrary to that goal and threatening to those supported by the old order. Only by overcoming the inertia inherent in the

---

[34] Quinn, "Innovation and Corporate Strategy," p. 168.

[35] Quinn, "Innovation and Corporate Strategy," p. 173.

[36] Many have observed the impact that champions have had. The clearest statement is by Modesto Maidique, "Entrepreneurs, Champions, and Technological Innovation," *Sloan Management Review*, 21, no. 2 (winter 1980), 59–76.

TABLE 6-2 *Key Personal Roles in the Innovation Process*

Gatekeeper	An individual who acts as a clearinghouse for external information for those within the firm. There may be technical, marketing, or manufacturing gatekeepers.
Creative scientist (technical innovator)	The individual who is the major creative technical contributor to the design or development of the innovation.
Business innovator (technological entrepreneur)	The organizer of a technological venture who exercises control of the venture (typically by owning a significant percentage of the equity) and assumes the risks of the business. Usually the chief executive officer.
Product champion	A member of the organization who creates, defines, or adopts an idea for a new technological innovation and who is willing to risk his or her position and prestige to make possible the innovation's successful implementation.
Executive champion	An executive in a technological firm who has direct or indirect influence over the resource allocation process and who uses this power to channel resources to a new technological innovation, thereby absorbing most, but usually not all, the risk of the project.

SOURCE: Modesto A. Maidique, "Entrepreneurs, Champions and Technological Innovators," in Michael L. Tushman and William L. Moore, eds., *Readings in the Management of Innovations* (Boston: Pitman Publishing, 1982), p. 569.

organization can the new emerge. As Quinn describes the process, "For a high probability of success an innovation needs a mother (champion) who loves it and will stay with it when others would give up, a father (authority figure with resources) who can support it, and pediatricians (experts) who can see it through technical difficulties."[37]

Based on research done in a number of settings, five personal roles seem important: (1) gatekeeper (either technical or market), (2) creative scientist, (3) business innovator, (4) product champion, and (5) executive champion. These roles are described in Table 6-2. They seem to have different kinds of inputs depending on the stage of the innovation process, as shown in Figure 6-9. Thinking of the innovation process in these terms provides greater insight into the creation of innovation as well as the process of managing it.

The Innovation Acceptance Process

The process by which innovative technology, products, and practices receive acceptance, are adopted by individual potential users and spread throughout a market or social system, is termed the *diffusion process*. Not all innovations are accepted. While some spread quickly (hand-held calculators, for example, took eight years to become ubiquitous), others diffuse slowly (robotics in manufacturing plants) and some nose dive quickly into oblivion (videodiscs).[38]

[37] Quinn, "Innovation and Corporate Strategy," p. 177.
[38] William Duals, Richard W. Olshavsky, and Ronald E. Michaels, "Shortening of the PLC—An Empirical Test," *Journal of Marketing*, 45, no. 4 (fall 1981), pp. 76–80.

Figure 6-9   Key personal roles at the different stages of the innovation process

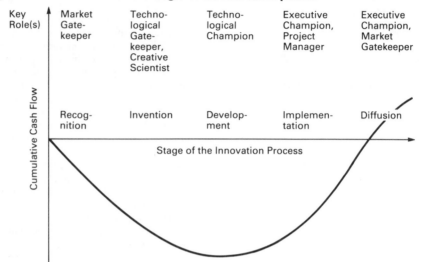

SOURCE: Modesto A. Maidique, "Entrepreneurs, Champions and Technological Innovators," in *Readings in the Management of Innovations*, p. 569.

Those who study the diffusion of innovation are concerned with answering questions about why and how the process works, what factors speed up or retard diffusion, and so on. Figure 6-10 provides an overview of the questions diffusion addresses. The framework used for the study of diffusion has four main elements. According to one author, "*Diffusion* is the process by which (1) an *innovation* (2) is *communicated* through certain *channels* (3) *over time* (4) among the members of a *social system*."[39]

The Innovation.   The basic idea of an innovation is that it be a product, process, or idea that is perceived as new by the individual or organization considering adopting (or buying) it. Newness is inherent to the study of innovation diffusion; otherwise the field would simply be the study of decision making. Newness brings with it two aspects: (1) that somehow one must become aware and learn about the new, and (2) that the risk of the new is different in kind and quality. How people become aware of the new is discussed later in this chapter. This discussion deals with the characteristics of innovations that affect the risk they present to those who adopt them and therefore the speed with which the innovation is adopted and spread.

RISK AND THE DEGREE OF NEWNESS.   Newness is not always synonymous with goodness. In fact, the greater the degree of newness, the greater the likelihood that there will be severe drawbacks. Radical, discontinuous technological innovations are "typically crude, costly, and unreliable when they first appear

[39] Everett M. Rogers, *Diffusion of Innovations*, 3rd ed. (New York: Free Press, 1983), p. 10. Most of this discussion is based on Rogers's work.

Figure 6-10   The cumulative diffusion curve

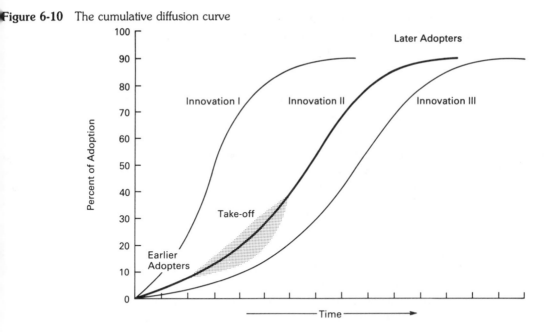

Diffusion is the process by which (1) an *innovation* (2) is *communicated* through certain *channels* (3) over *time* (4) among the members of a *social system.*

SOURCE: Everett M. Rogers, *Diffusion of Innovation*, 3rd ed. (New York: Free Press, 1983), p. 10.

on the market. It is only after a series of follow-up improvements that their superiority and attractiveness will be asserted."[40] Early ballpoint pens leaked and blotched. Incandescent lights were expensive, sensitive to shock, and short lived. Pneumatic tires punctured frequently. Computers were economically useful only for simple but large-scale number crunching. Airplanes could fly only in good weather and were uncomfortable and dangerous.

Radical technologies pose two special risks: early user externalities, and rapid obsolescence. *Early user externalities* mean that the first to buy pay for the privilege of early use by their acceptance of the initially poor cost/performance ratio and by forgoing the typically rapid improvement that occurs in that offer. In addition, early users frequently share in the burden of discovering and correcting the bugs in the new technology. This costs first users, but much of the benefits their participation with the technology creates is appropriated by the supplier and later users.

Rapid obsolescence is a potentially costly risk. When radically new technologies emerge, there are often several competing suppliers offering incompatible alternatives. Those who chose Sony's Beta system for their VCR paid for not waiting until the battle for dominance with Matsushita's VHS system was resolved. Further, first-generation technologies are frequently improved on at

[40] Olleros, "Emerging Industries," p. 11. This discussion of radical innovation is based on his research.

such a pace and degree that they are frequently quickly obsoleted. Had the first few purchasers of digital watches, hand-held calculators, or laptop computers waited but a year or so, they could have bought products with vastly more favorable price/performance ratios as a result of increased performance and lowered prices.

This means that the more radical an innovation is, the slower it is likely to diffuse. The root cause of this slow diffusion is in the radical newness itself. As one researcher puts it,

> In view of these deficiencies, uncertainties, and penalties surrounding radically new emerging technologies, the wait-and-see attitude of many potential users is eminently rational. Without needing to be especially conservative or risk-averse, most potential users will determine that it would not pay for them to be pioneers in the adoption of a technology of this kind, regardless of its superior promise. In fact, the greater the promise, the greater the incentive for potential users to delay their purchases.[41]

RELATIVE ADVANTAGE.   The greater the degree to which an innovation is perceived to provide benefits, the faster it will diffuse. The key words here are *benefits* and *perception*. Newness is not what users seek—benefits are. And of course, the greater the real benefits the more likely they will be perceived. On the other hand, objective benefits that are not perceived as such do not count at all.

COMPATIBILITY.   Some innovations are fully compatible with buyers' existing technologies, systems, values, and needs. The user need not change to use the new. The more a new technology is compatible with existing practices and investments, the faster it will be accepted.

COMPLEXITY.   Some ideas are easily grasped; some are not. Those which are complex and require long, patient explaining for the potential user to grasp diffuse more slowly than those which are easy to understand. It is easier for people to understand how to make money in a rising (bull) stock market than in a falling (bear) market, and both are easier to understand than how options trading works.

TRIALABILITY.   The greater the degree to which a potential user can try out an innovation prior to full adoption, the more rapidly it will diffuse. Trial is an important risk assessment and reduction strategy, and the real experience of the benefits provided by trial use is more convincing than any amount of explanation or data. Conversely, all-or-nothing and especially nonreversible innovations diffuse much more slowly.

OBSERVABILITY.   Observability is an important factor in the imitation process, as it allows the observer an opportunity for vicarious trial and learning. The more an innovation and its results are visible to others, the more likely they are to be adopted. Agricultural seed producers provide signs to mark fields planted with their products so passing farmers can assess the results. Industrial salespeople make sure potential buyers know about the success of other firms' use of new technology and encourage and arrange for them to visit and see for themselves.

---

[41] Olleros, "Emerging Industries," pp. 12–13.

Communication of the Innovation.   Key to any of this, of course, is learning about the existence of the innovation and evaluating its benefits. While the mass media are perhaps the most efficient communications channel, interpersonal channels are generally considered to be more effective in communicating and persuading about innovation. Interpersonal communication involves direct, personal communication between and among individuals. This is considered to be the heart of the diffusion process:

> The results . . . show that most individuals do not evaluate an innovation on the basis of scientific studies of its consequences, although such objective evaluations are not entirely irrelevant, especially to the very first individuals who adopt. Instead, most people depend mainly upon a subjective evaluation of an innovation that is conveyed to them from other individuals like themselves who have previously adopted the innovation.[42]

A key feature in this communication is the extent to which the two involved in the communication process are similar (homophilous) or dissimilar (heterophilous). The more two people are like each other, the more effective the communication. This suggests that there is almost always some degree of mismatch between a salesperson (change agent) and client, and also why word of mouth is so much more effective. For one, a salesperson does not share the same job, problems, and life of his or her clients. Second, the salesperson is generally much more technically competent—at least with respect to the innovation. To some extent, it can be said that the two do not speak the same language. To cope with this, it appears that individuals often seek out those who are like themselves but are slightly more technically competent for information about innovations. *Opinion leaders* is the term used to describe these individuals.

Figures 6-11 and 6-12, for example, show how this worked in the diffusion of the continuous casting process (a major and costly innovation) in the steel industry. At the time of the study, the steel industry was composed of two kinds of firms: the traditional big steel companies and a rapidly growing group of smaller firms termed *mini mills*. As the sociometric diagram in Figure 6-11 shows, homophily works.[43] Two communications networks linked the industry: one composed of the small firms, another linking the large firms. Each group communicated more within itself than with the other group. Opinion leadership seemed to rest with the big firms, moreover, as the arrows linking the two groups show. It was the small firms who sought out the large firms' opinions and advice (six arrows from the right-hand cluster to the left-hand cluster, one arrow from left to right) and not the reverse.

Figure 6-12 demonstrates the actual seeking out of personal information

---

[42] Rogers, *Diffusion of Innovations*, p. 18.
[43] Sociometry asks individuals with whom they communicate and displays that information in the form of arrows linking the two (depicted by circles). The direction of the arrowhead indicates the direction (from, to) of the communication. In the case of Figure 6-11, respondents were asked to indicate the specific other firms from whom they sought opinion and advice.

Figure 6-11   Communication networks in the American steel industry

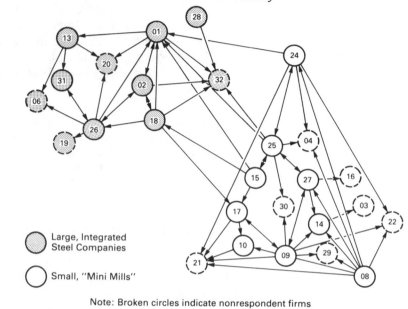

Note: Broken circles indicate nonrespondent firms

SOURCE: Adapted from John A. Czepiel, "Patterns of Interorganizational Communications and the Diffusion of a Major Technological Innovation in a Competitive Industrial Community," in *Academy of Management Journal*, 18, no. 1, p. 14. (March 1975).

with respect to the innovation. The main effect shown in the figure is the extent of active information seeking directed at early adopters. One can only speculate what the result would have been had the information received been uniformly negative.

The second effect seen is the extent to which that information seeking was directed to firms similar in size. Of the two early adopting firms, one (27) in Figures 6-11 and 6-12 was a mini mill. The other (28) was a large, integrated steel maker. While there was initially more cross-group communication in this specific instance, within a short period the prior networks reasserted themselves. As Figure 6-12 demonstrates, the big steel firms are primarily clustered on the right in this network; that is they tended to seek their information more from the large firm adopters than from the small firm adopters.

Time.   Two aspects related to time are of concern in diffusion. The first is the time it takes for an innovation to diffuse. This is a primary interest of diffusion researchers and innovators. Second, the time at which an individual or organization adopts an innovation is a primary measure of innovativeness. Since diffusion time is partially a function of the point at which the first adoption decisions are made, identifying potential early adopters is an important activity.

INNOVATIVENESS.   Adopters of new technology are frequently classified on the basis of their time of adoption relative to others in the same market or social

Figure 6-12 Actual personal information seeking in the diffusion of the continuous casting process

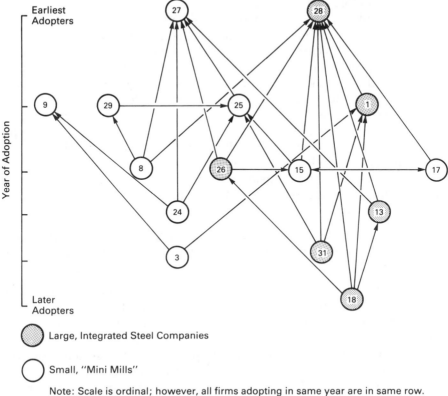

Note: Scale is ordinal; however, all firms adopting in same year are in same row.
SOURCE: Adapted from Czepiel, "Patterns of Interorganizational Communications and the Diffusion of a Major Technological Innovation in a Competitive Industrial Community," p. 20.

system. Typically, five adopter categories are recognized: innovators, early adopters, early majority, late majority, and laggards. Innovators or earlier adopters are typically contrasted with laggards or later adopters. Rogers has described innovators succinctly:

> Innovators are active information seekers about new ideas. They have a high degree of mass media exposure and their interpersonal networks extend over a wide area, usually reaching outside of their local system. Innovators are able to cope with higher levels of uncertainty about an innovation. . . . As the first to adopt . . . they cannot depend upon the subjective evaluations of the innovation from the other members of their system.[44]

[44] Rogers, *Diffusion of Innovations*, pp. 22–23. Recent empirical work has examined the characteristics of organizations as innovators. See John A. Czepiel, "Word-of-Mouth Processes in the Diffusion of Major Technological Innovation," *Journal of Marketing Research*, 11, no. 2 (May 1974), 172–180; and Hubert Gatignon and Thomas S. Robertson, "Technology Diffusion: An Empirical Test of Competitive Effects," *Journal of Marketing*, 53, no. 1 (January 1989), 35–49.

THE RATE OF DIFFUSION.   The curve (see Figure 6-10) which shows the cumulative frequency of the adoption of an innovation is S shaped like the law of limits. In early time periods, only a few innovators adopt the innovation. As the number of these innovators reaches about 10 to 25% of the target population, the diffusion curve takes off as the interpersonal communication networks come into play. As the percentage of adopters in the market begins to approach the upper limits, however, the rate slows and fewer remain who have not adopted.

Two factors determine the diffusion rate. First is the characteristics of the specific innovation. An innovation which is not perceived to be radical, has high relative advantage, is compatible, simple, and easily tried or sampled will diffuse more rapidly than one which is opposite in one or more of these factors. These factors are under the control of the innovator to some extent. The second factor which affects the diffusion rate, however, is not under the control of the innovator: the characteristics of the social system or market into which the innovation is being introduced.

The Social System.   Three aspects of a social system can speed or retard the diffusion of an innovation: (1) the social structure, (2) the norms established by the society, and (3) the role of opinion leaders.

SOCIAL STRUCTURE.   Of greatest interest to innovators seeking to introduce an innovation into a market is the communication structure that links the members. Some markets can be envisioned as having dense networks in which the actions of one member are soon known to the others. Others may be characterized by the patterns formed by the networks: a system, for example, may be characterized by the existence of several distinct cliques, as those seen in the steel industry. Those introducing an innovation into a market composed of highly competitive and secretive business firms (such as in Silicon Valley) may well wonder what kind of communication takes place among them. It is clearly a different social structure—one with deficiencies that the innovator must overcome.

NORMS.   The norms in a society influence the behavior of its members by defining acceptable behavior. Norms cover both the general and the specific. There may be general norms relating to innovation and change, for example. Not too long ago, the banking business was a conservative one in which newness was not a valued attribute. Specific norms relate more to content. Telecommunications engineers and operating managers place a high value on system integrity and reliability. The norms that guide behavior, therefore, require that change in operating systems be thoroughly tested and proven before implementation. This is in contrast to engineers and designers of advanced semiconductors and computers, where technical change and advancement are sought out as the wellspring of growth and profits.

OPINION LEADERS.   The role of opinion leaders is interesting. First, they are often not true innovators—those who are the most innovative—because innovators are often perceived as somewhat deviant and of low credibility. Opinion leaders are typically in a central position in the system's informal, interpersonal communications network. They are able to influence others' attitudes and behavior because of their technical competence, social accessibility, and because they exemplify the system's norms. This is important to recognize because opinion leaders are just as able to retard innovation (if that is the norm of the system) as to promote it.

One way to think about opinion leaders is as social role models whose behavior is imitated by others. As with all informal leadership roles, however, the leader cannot get too far out in front of his or her followers. This is one reason that opinion leaders are generally not the most innovative members of their societies.

Theories Explaining the Pattern of Innovation

Innovation is not a random process. Sophisticated observers of industrial innovation perceive patterns in the content and timing of innovation which suggest that it is an evolutionary process. That is, in profit-seeking industrial organizations there is a link between industry evolution, the strategies needed to compete, and the nature of the technological innovation that occurs. The manager who can perceive how these will interact in the future may be able proactively to position his or her firm by shifting the focus and timing of its research. One researcher has suggested that the combination of three theories of innovation could provide such insight.[45] The three theories are (1) the product/process life cycle, (2) meta-learning, and (3) technological interdependence and improvement. These are summarized in Table 6-3.

Product/process Life Cycle.   In this view, the type and amount of technological innovation that occurs is related to the stages of a product's life cycle.[46] The theory separates innovation into two main types—product innovation and process innovation—and the life cycle into three main stages: uncoordinated, segmental, and systemic, as shown in Figure 6-13.[47]

In the *uncoordinated stage* there is a great deal of fluidity in the firm. Product changes are frequent as the new product seeks to increase demand by satisfying customers' needs. The primary form of competition is based on product performance, and the typically nonstandardized production processes used at this early stage allow (and perhaps encourage) frequent product changes. At this stage, product innovation is frequent. Process type innovation which might tend to make the system more rigid is discouraged.

At some point, as demand grows, the industry moves into the *segmental*

---

[45] John E. Butler, "Theories of Technological Innovation as Useful Tools for Corporate Strategy," *Strategic Management Journal*, 9, no. 1 (January-February 1988), 15–29.
[46] William J. Abernathy and James M. Utterback, "Patterns of Industrial Innovation," *Technology Review*, 80 (June-July 1978), 40–47.
[47] Abernathy and Utterback originally used the terms *fluid, transitional,* and *specific* for the three stages.

TABLE 6-3 *Three Theories of Technological Innovation*

1. *Process/product (Abernathy and Utterback)*[a]
   Overall: The quantity and type of innovation varies with the stage of the life cycle.
   Specific: The rate of innovation initially increases and then decreases as the life cycle
              progresses. Earlier innovations are dominantly product innovations; later innova-
              tions concern process.
2. *Meta-learning (Sahal)*[b]
   Overall: The laws of progress and limits result from learning by *scaling, doing, planning,* and
              sharing at equipment, plant, firm, and industry levels.
   Specific: The laws of progress and limits can be used to predict and assess technological ev-
              olution at each !level.
3. *Technological interdependence (Rosenberg)*[c]
   Overall: Technology progress is a function of expectations of technological advancement, the
              availability of value-enhancing complementary technology, and learning by using.
   Specific: Expectations of rapid technology advancement retard adoption; examination of re-
              lated technology sets identifies constraints to an innovation's value; user interac-
              tion with innovation enhances its value.

[a] William J. Abernathy and James M. Utterback, "Patterns of Industrial Innovation," *Technology Review,* 80 (June-July 1978).

[b] Devendra Sahal, *Patterns of Technological Innovation* (Reading, MA: Addison-Wesley, 1981).

[c] Nathan Rosenberg, *Inside the Black Box: Technology and Economics* (Cambridge: Cambridge University Press, 1982).

stage. A dominant design may emerge which standardizes (relatively speaking) expectations of product performance and form across segments. Since volume is now higher, firms attempt to differentiate their products from those of competitors while simultaneously reducing the number of variations to gain the benefits

Figure 6-13   The product process of innovation

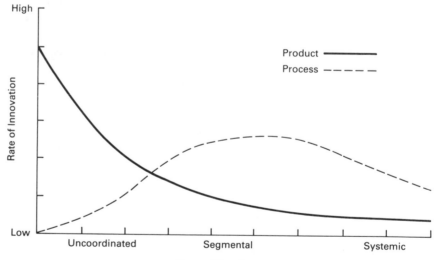

SOURCE: James M. Utterback and William J. Abernathy, "A Dynamic Model of Process and Product Innovation," *Omega,* 3, no. 6 (December 1975), p. 645.

that come from standardized production equipment. Together, these developments act to reduce the desirability of change for producers (and sometimes consumers) and therefore to reduce the number of product innovations that occur. At the same time, there is an increase in process innovation which, because of the volume increases, is now cost justified. Relative to the prior stage, the proportion of innovation between the two types is balanced.

At the *systemic stage*, the amount of innovation, both product and process, is reduced. Standardization is the byword as competitors seek to standardize products and production systems to reduce costs and improve quality. The cost of any change is high, and only incremental innovation is economic. A new product design or production process must offer significant advantages to overcome the strong economic flywheel effect exerted by fully depreciated, sunk investment. The probability that innovation will occur is low.

Table 6-4 provides another view of the same process as seen from the viewpoint of industry evolution. The segmental stage has been divided in two, but the process is the same.

In summary, the theory is that innovation type and quantity will vary with differences in (1) the firm's environment, (2) the firm's competitive and growth strategies, and (3) the development of the firm's and the industry's process technology.

Meta-learning. Meta-learning is based on the laws of progress and limits discussed earlier in this chapter. Rather than simply extrapolate to forecast improvement, however, it says that innovation is based on learning. Specifically, it posits that learning takes place via *scaling* at the *equipment* level, *doing* at the *plant* level, *planning* at the *firm* level, and *sharing* at the *industry* level.[48]

In this view, however, probability is more dominant than in the product/process model. One central idea is that innovation is probabalistic and operates across firms. This means that while innovation is a function of R&D expenditures, it is also a function of the total pool of expenditures. In other words, if the industry is spending on R&D, something will come out of it; it is just that one cannot predict which firm will make the breakthrough. This may explain why much research fails to find a statistically significant relationship between expenditures on R&D and the firm's profit performance. A second key idea in this theory is that product and process technology are strongly linked and that the association between the two becomes stronger over time.

At the equipment level, scale increases provide benefits—technological improvement, in other words—up to some point beyond which the present technology can no longer deliver. This limit then becomes the stimulus for the development of the next generation of technology. Similarly, at the plant level, experience is accumulating as a result of learning by doing, and this process is also creating new technology. At the level of the firm and industry, learning by sharing is taking place as firms learn of and imitate others' innovations through the diffusion process. Scientists and engineers associated with each level or

[48] Devendra Sahal, *Patterns of Technological Innovation* (Reading, MA: Addison-Wesley, 1981).

TABLE 6-4   *Stages in the Technological Development of a New Industry around a Radical Innovation*

STAGE IN THE TECHNOLOGICAL DEVELOPMENT OF A NEW INDUSTRY	REPRESENTATIVE INDUSTRIES
1. *Innovation,* a period of very high uncertainty in which trial-and-error problem solving leads to the innovation, with makeshift production in a small facility.	1. Bioengineering industry, in which the basic invention of recombinant DNA is applied.
2. *Imitation,* when there is decreasing uncertainty as many new firms enter the industry and develop their own variants of the basic innovation, which is gradually improved through R&D and by closer attention to marketing.	2. Solar-collector industry, built around the basic idea of the solar flat-plate collector.
3. *Technological competition,* where R&D laboratories improve the innovation through process changes, while smaller firms find it difficult to enter the industry and competition eliminates existing firms that cannot succeed in making important improvements on the basic innovation.	3. Semiconductor industry.
4. *Standardization,* where the ideal product has been found and R&D activities concentrate on improving production and on prolonging the product life cycle, and where technological competition has shifted to price competition.	4. Pocket calculator industry.

SOURCE: Everett M. Rogers, *Diffusion of Innovation* (New York: Free Press, 1983).

activity can predict each of these types of learning, and by comparing their predictions with those obtained from a technological forecasting perspective, managers can obtain a more accurate concept of the future.

Technological Interdependence and Improvement.   The third theory is based on technological expectations and "learning by using."[49] The theory says that the market's expectations about the rate of future technological progress and improvements in the cost of the technology affect the time of adoption and both the present and future direction of the technology. Expectations of rapid improvement may slow adoption as potential buyers perceive that delaying an immediate purchase in anticipation of even better technology in the near future is a more profitable action.[50] This action, however, perversely reduces the producer's incentive to produce more sophisticated models.

Expectations about performance are functions not only of the technology itself but of complementary technologies. The value of a VCR to potential adopters, for example, increased greatly after the introduction of prerecorded movies

[49] Nathan Rosenberg, *Inside the Black Box: Technology and Economics* (Cambridge: Cambridge University Press, 1982), p. 122.
[50] Recent empirical work supports this observation. See Allen M. Weiss and George John, "Leapfrogging Behavior and the Purchase of Industrial Innovations" (Cambridge, MA: Marketing Science Institute Report No. 89-110, July 1989).

and other software and the easy access to that software that video rental outlets provided. By examining the interactions among the elements in a related set of new technologies, one can better understand its pace and direction. Especially important is to understand the constraints that related technologies place on users as they attempt to maximize the value they receive from a new technology.

Learning by using refers to the changes and modifications that occur (technology improvements) as a result of user experiences. It is the user, not the producer, who identifies a product's (or technology's) maximum performance capabilities and the minimum service support needed. Computer software, for example, has benefited greatly from strong user input. Semiconductor manufacturers experience similar inputs. As one observer noted about a new microprocessor, "As Intel's customers learn what's in the N-10, they're envisioning applications Intel had not thought of."[51] User improvements are another explanation of the large numbers of innovations observed during the early stages of a product's life.

This theory suggests that there may be a limit to the initial success that an innovative technology may have because of buyer expectations. Further, it suggests that attempts to extend the technological shelf life of a product by designing it to incorporate technology far beyond the forecast performance horizon will be self-defeating since the market will likely lack the complementary technologies that increase the innovation's value to the buyer.

The Elements of a Technology Strategy

The goal of technology strategy is to help the firm obtain a sustainable competitive advantage. As was shown in Figure 6-1, technology can contribute to competitive advantage in four ways:[52]

1. *The technology directly lowers cost or provides unique and desired customer benefits, and that advantage is sustainable.* Either result is the goal of competitive strategy, but sustainability is the key. Easily imitated results bring no real long-run advantage.
2. *The new technology changes the factors that drive costs or product differentiation in a direction in which the firm is advantaged.* Neither the innovative electric furnace nor continuous casting technologies were as scale sensitive as the old open-hearth furnace and ingot technologies in the steel industry. The new technology favored the small, specialized firms which directed their output into special applications or small geographical markets away from the center of steel-making activity.
3. *Being first to use or introduce the technology provides the firm with first-mover advantages.* The first into a market with a new technology can reap advantages such as the ability to set competitive rules, preempt positions, or establish product stan-

---

[51] *Business Week*, "Intel Introduces a Superfast RISC Chip," January 30, 1989, p. 69.
[52] Michael E. Porter, *Competitive Advantage* (New York: Free Press, 1985), chapter 5. This discussion is built on his insights.

dards which favor the pioneer, act against followers, and sometimes outlast the technological lead.

4. *The technology being introduced or used improves overall industry structure.* Industry structure, the product of the five competitive forces, can be improved or worsened as the result of technological change. Intel's new microprocessor technology (the logic heart of small computers) is pitting personal computer (PC) makers against the makers of the previously more powerful workstation computers used by scientists and engineers—in effect doubling the number of competitors each faces.[53] The change is good for Intel but bad for its customers.

Tests such as these distinguish between basic and applied research and between science and business. Technologists are concerned with inputs, the skills needed to create a product or service, and the advancement of those skills (and the technology they embody). As shown in Figure 6-14, an underlying motivation for technologists (especially young technologists) is some notion of the essential worth of technological advancement. In technologists' eyes, business is just one subset of that notion.

For business types, however, technology and its skills are often seen as simply another functional capability and, as such, just part of a business.[54] Business managers are interested in output—and that output is not of interest for what it is but for what it can do for the business. This means that technological accomplishments are academic if they do not contribute to strategic advantage. They may bring patents, they may bring awards. But if they do not bring business advantage, they are of little use. The firm needs a technology strategy to ensure that the two views reinforce rather than cancel each other.[55]

Technology Strategy[56]

The choice of a strategy by which the firm will obtain a sustainable competitive advantage sets the stage for the firm's technology strategy. The technology strategy must support that competitive strategy. Two questions are key to that strategy: which technologies to support, and whether the firm should seek to lead or follow in that technology. Exhibit 6-2 lists the steps that need to be taken to link the technology strategy to the business's larger competitive strategy.

Which Technologies to Support?   This question can be answered at several levels. At the broadest level, the technology strategy should support the generic strategy which the business is pursuing. Table 6-5 describes the basic direction that R&D should take in support of the four generic competitive strategies.

---

[53] *The Wall Street Journal*, "PC and Workstation Makers Square Off," January 18, 1989, p. B1.
[54] Graham R. Mitchell, "New Approaches for the Strategic Management of Technology," in *Technology in the Modern Corporation*, ed., Mel Torwitch pp. 132–144.
[55] For further insight into this process, see Ralph E. Gomory, "From the 'Ladder of Science' to the Product Development Cycle," *Harvard Business Review*, 67, no. 6 (November-December 1989), pp. 99–105.
[56] The technology strategy field is surveyed in Paul S. Adler, "Technology Strategy: A Guide to the Literatures," *Research in Technological Innovation, Management and Policy*, 4 (1989), 25–151.

Figure 6-14 Technology strategy reconciles the two views of technology

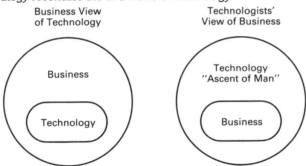

SOURCE: Reprinted with permission from Graham R. Mitchell, "New Approaches for the Strategic Management of Technology" in *Technology in the Modern Corporation*, Mel Horwitch, ed. Copyright © 1986 by Pergamon Press PLC.

In reviewing those prescriptions, the reader should note that they do not apply only to the firm's primary, product technology. Competitive advantage can come from any of the activities a firm performs. The information systems area, for example, has allowed many firms to improve customer service to a level that customers perceive as providing differential value.[57] American Express, for example, was among the first to adopt digital image storage and processing in its travel credit card business. The technique allows it to provide superior service to customers at the same time that the technology lowered its costs.

THE TECHNOLOGY PORTFOLIO.   The prescriptions contained in Table 6-5, however, are still quite broad. To begin to fine tune its technology strategy, the firm needs to construct and analyze its technology portfolio. Figure 6-15 presents one such technology portfolio.[58] The technology portfolio positions the firm's key technologies along two dimensions, importance and position:

- *Technology importance* is a measure of the role that a specific technology plays in the competitive viability of a given product area or business segment. It may be important because of the rapidity of change that the technology is undergoing, the proportion of the product or service's cost it accounts for, or because of its contribution to the differentiated benefits consumers experience.
- *Technology position* is a measure of the relative position the firm holds in that technology. One question is whether the firm leads, follows, or is at parity with competitors. Current funding levels compared to competitors may give a different view than that obtained by patent counts, firsts, and other historical measures.

Analysis of such a portfolio is not unlike that of various other portfolios. The upper left-hand quadrant in Figure 6-15, for example, is a generally strong position, with a technology lead in a business where that technology is key. The

---

[57] Marc S. Gerstein, *The Technology Connection—Strategy and Change in the Information Age* (Reading, MA: Addison-Wesley, 1987).

[58] Chris Pappas, "Strategic Management of Technology," *Journal of Product Innovation Management*, 1, no. 1 (January 1984), 30–35.

EXHIBIT 6-2

The Six Steps in Determining
a Technology Strategy

1. *Identify all of the distinct technologies (and subtechnologies) in the value chain.* This analysis should include the technologies used by the firm and its competitors—making sure to identify those which are interdependent with technologies used by the firm's suppliers and customers.
2. *Identify existing and developing technologies in use or under development in other industries.* Discontinuous innovation often uses technologies from outside one's own industry. The development of new materials from the chemical industry, new processes from genetic engineering, devices from the electronics industry, and systems from the computer industry have the potential to bring new value to many industries.
3. *Forecast the direction and rate of change of relevant technologies.* The paths of key technologies in the firm's industry, its supplier and customer industries, as well as key technologies outside the industry need to be understood if the firm is to be able to assess their potential.
4. *Identify the technologies and changes which are most likely to affect competitive advantage.* A technology which promises a strategic differentiation or cost advantage, shifts industry cost drivers, promises first-mover advantages, or could affect industry structure needs to be watched carefully.
5. *Evaluate the firm's ability to participate in important technologies and the cost of doing so.* The firm's competitive abilities in key technologies and the costs of making gains are important inputs.
6. *Formulate a technology strategy which addresses the key technologies affecting the firm's competitive advantage.* The strategy should rank technologies and projects relative to their competitive effect and specify in which technologies the firm will lead.

SOURCE: Adapted from Michael E. Porter, *Competitive Advantage* (New York: Free Press, 1985), pp. 198–199.

upper right-hand quadrant is a dangerous position—the firm has a weak technological position in a business that rewards technology. Such a position demands that the firm either invest heavily to attain at least a parity technology position or, alternatively, to withdraw in some way from that sector. To continue to participate without correcting the technology deficiency goes against every rule of strategy.

In the lower left-hand quadrant, the firm has a strong position in a sector where that leadership is unimportant to business success. In the early stages of the market for electronic watches, for example, the basic electronic componentry was the highest-cost element and the one that was changing continually. At that time, it was very important to success to be at the forefront of that technology. At this point in time, however, the technology is cheap and fairly mature—it is

TABLE 6-5 *Technology Strategy and the Four Generic Strategies*

	COST LEADERSHIP	DIFFERENTIATION	COST FOCUS	DIFFERENTIATION FOCUS
		Illustrative Technological Policies		
Product technological change	Product development to reduce product cost by lowering material content, facilitating ease of manufacture, simplifying logistical requirements, etc.	Product development to enhance product quality, features, deliverability, or switching costs	Product development to design in only enough performance for the target segment's needs	Product design to meet the needs of a particular segment better than broadly targeted competitors
Process technological change	Learning curve process improvement to reduce material usage or lower labor input Process development to enhance economies of scale	Process development to support high tolerances, greater quality control, more reliable scheduling, faster response time to orders, and other dimensions that raise buyer value	Process development to tune the value chain to a segment's needs to lower the cost of serving the segment	Process development to tune the value chain to a segment's needs to raise buyer value

SOURCE: Michael E. Porter, *Competitive Advantage* (New York: Free Press, 1985), p. 178.

no longer the key to competitive success. Investing further funds in technology development will likely bring few rewards. Being positioned in the lower right-hand corner may or may not prove problematic. The firm is behind technologically, but that shortcoming is not critical to success in the business.

Capon and Glazer have developed a variant on the technology portfolio which offers additional insights.[59] Shown in Figure 6-16, the circles represent technologies; the vertical axis represents time, from research to development in the premarket phase and the high- and low-growth stages of the life cycle in the postmarket phase. Technologies are positioned along the horizontal axis according to their relative technology strength in the premarket phase and according to relative market share in the postmarket phase. The size of the circles represents the relative resource flow and its direction (shaded = cash user, open = cash generator).

In Figure 6-16, the entries, both top and bottom, represent technologies, not products. The lower entries, therefore, represent the weighted average performance of the totality of the products dependent on (or possessing) the technology. Such a portfolio highlights both the cash implications of the firm's technology decisions and the number and balance of its different technology efforts. A firm, for example, can be attempting to develop too many separate tech-

[59] Capon and Glazer, "Marketing and Technology, 1–14.

Figure 6-15   The technology portfolio

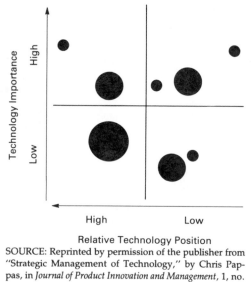

Relative Technology Position

SOURCE: Reprinted by permission of the publisher from "Strategic Management of Technology," by Chris Pappas, in *Journal of Product Innovation and Management*, 1, no. 1, 33–35. Copyright © 1984 by Elsevier Science Publishing Co., Inc.

nologies, thereby providing each with too few resources to achieve significant or timely results. Portfolio approaches can help the firm determine which technologies to support.

Seek Technology Leadership?   Whether to seek technological leadership is a question equal in strategic importance to the choice of the technologies the firm will work on. However, there is no clear criterion by which to choose between the leadership or follower roles, for each is capable of gaining the firm a sustainable advantage. There is agreement, however, on what it means to be the technological leader. Technological leadership means that the firm allocates sufficient resources to ensure that it is the first to introduce the key technological changes that support its generic strategy.

The technology follower strategy, contrary to its seeming implications, is an equally active, conscious strategic choice. A follower strategy should not be thought of as that which happens to those who try and fail or to those without a conscious technology strategy. As can be seen in Table 6-6, both leadership and follower strategies are capable of sustaining either a low-cost or differentiation strategy.

Timing and time are the key elements of difference between the two strategies and, logically, the source of competitive advantage (or disadvantage) each can confer.[60] Time issues are central to each of the three questions one should ask in choosing between the two strategies:

[60] George Stalk, Jr., "Time: The Next Source of Competitive Advantage," *Harvard Business Review*, 66, no. 4 (July–August 1988), 41–51. See also Brian Dumaine, "How Managers Can Succeed through Speed," *Fortune*, February 13, 1989, pp. 54–59.

Figure 6-16 A technology portfolio showing development and market phases

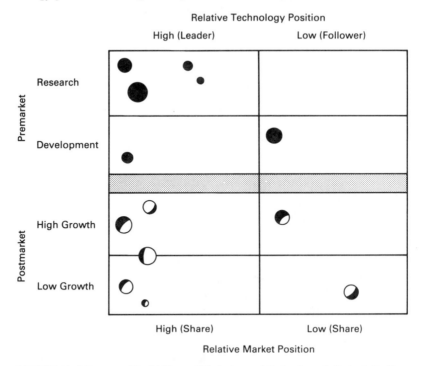

SOURCE: Noel Capon and Rashi Glazer, "Marketing and Technology: A Strategic Coalignment," in *Journal of Marketing*, 51, no. 3 (July 1987), p. 10. Reprinted by permission of the American Marketing Association.

1. Does leadership improve sustainability?
2. How important are first-mover advantages?
3. What risks and disadvantages does the first mover assume?

SUSTAINABILITY. Leadership can yield sustainable advantage if, by being first, it means (1) that competitors cannot duplicate the technology, or (2) that they cannot catch up technologically. Patents are one obvious source of sustainability in which being first is key. The performance product category described in chapter 4 obtains its competitive advantage from technological leadership. By always being first, the product has a monopoly on its unique benefits until competitors are able to duplicate it. By staying out in front of competitors, the firm can sustain its advantage.

FIRST-MOVER ADVANTAGES. First movers benefit in two broad ways: (1) by being the rule setters, and (2) by the across-the-board preemption of preferred positions. By its selection of product form, channels, customers, selling methods, service policies, etc., the leader is able to set the rules of competition to match its strengths.

The first mover also has the ability to define the technological standards for the category, thereby forcing competitors to play by its rules and on its own turf.

TABLE 6-6   *Technological Leadership and Competitive Advantage*

	TECHNOLOGICAL LEADERSHIP	TECHNOLOGICAL FOLLOWERSHIP
Cost advantage	Pioneer the lowest-cost product design Be the first firm down the learning curve Create low-cost ways of performing value activities	Lower the cost of the product or value activities by learning from the leader's experience Avoid R&D costs through imitation
Differentiation	Pioneer a unique product that increases buyer value Innovate in other activities to increase buyer value	Adapt the product or delivery system more closely to buyer needs by learning from the leader's experience

SOURCE: Michael E. Porter, *Competitive Advantage* (New York: Free Press, 1985), p. 181.

This is important in many industrial markets where customers standardize their production (or other processes) around the first entrant's product. Philips, for example, was the first plastic resin producer to make a resin specifically designed to work in the high-speed, automated blow-molding machines that dairies use to make plastic milk bottles. As a result, the machine's manufacturer standardized its molds to meet the characteristics of Philips's resins. Since those molds are very expensive, the dairies buy only the resins that work in those molds. As a result, other resin manufacturers must incur additional manufacturing costs to do what Philips's resins do naturally. Had one of the other resin manufacturers been first, Philips would have had to bear the additional cost.

Preemption is another major category that allows the leader significant advantages. Like chess or checkers, there are many areas important to competitive advantage where only one player may occupy a square on the gameboard. Being first to market preempts others from the unique advantages that accrue to a leader's reputation, recognition, and image. The leader has the opportunity to choose the most favorable positioning(s) for its product, forcing competitors to choose less attractive ones. This is especially important in image products.

The leader can frequently effectively lock up the most attractive customers, suppliers, and channel members when switching costs are important. It can choose the most attractive manufacturing or retail sites and discourage followers by adding enough stores (or production capacity) so there is not sufficient room for the competitor to enter profitably. Finally, a leader can enjoy the higher profits that come from being the only one to be able to offer the value created by the new technology (before others follow) and the advantages that accrue to being the first down the learning curve.

FIRST-MOVER DISADVANTAGES.   First movers face a host of disadvantages, however. Being the pioneer brings with it a substantial burden not unlike that faced by the pioneers in settling a new territory. The pioneer must create its own infrastructure, as shown in Table 6-7. These are real, significant costs that followers do not incur.

Like pioneer settlers, moreover, first movers also face risks that followers do

TABLE 6-7   *The Costs that Pioneers Bear*

MARKET DEVELOPMENT: Identifying and educating consumers; developing and training channel members; subsidizing development of complementary products and services.

MANUFACTURING AND MATERIALS: Creating methods and machinery for manufacture; bearing costs of experimentation and inefficiencies due to learning.

REGULATORY: Running experiments for safety and efficacy; creating new certification and compliance standards.

---

not. Foremost among these is demand uncertainty. The first mover's investment decision is made in the absence of sure knowledge about the certainty of the product's acceptance or the level of demand that will be generated if it is accepted. In general, the more radical the innovation, the greater the market uncertainty faced by the pioneer.[61]

The videodisc, for example, simply failed to generate demand. Consumers did not perceive sufficient value in the technology to buy it instead of the initially more expensive videotape technology then emerging. RCA's pioneering and failed investment in videodisc technology was probably its last chance to play in the big leagues of modern consumer electronics. It lost $580 million (1983 $) and its reputation in the trade as a strong and wise consumer electronics supplier whose products always sold.[62]

The second primary risk faced by first movers is technology risk, which goes with investing in a moving technology. The first mover may invest in a technology that is quickly superseded by a second generation. Its pioneering introduction of the new technology may be the stimulus for a change in buyers' needs, which obsoletes its technology. The technology it chooses may turn out to be second best. All of these situations are common to radical technological innovation:

> It is typical of the period of early emergence that a multiplicity of incompatible, alternative core technologies appear (e.g. electric vs. steam-powered vs. gasoline-powered engines for early automobiles, Sony's Betamax vs. Matsushita's VHS vs. Philips' system 2000 for video tape recorders) and struggle for preeminence.[63]

The greatest risk, however, is that the first mover opens the way for followers to imitate its innovation at a lower cost than it incurred and thereby walk away with the prize that should have been the pioneer's. Apple and IBM were both late entrants into the personal computer industry, which they have come to dominate at the expense of the original pioneers.

---

[61] Olleros, "Emerging Industries and the Burnout of Pioneers."
[62] *Business Week*, "The Anatomy of RCA's Videodisc Failure," April 23, 1983, p. 89.
[63] Olleros, "Emerging Industries and the Burnout of Pioneers," p. 12.

SUMMARY

Technology is at the bottom of every value-producing activity that a firm pursues. Understanding technology and the role that technology plays in obtaining and sustaining a competitive advantage for the firm is a key element in every manager's knowledge base.

Technology is the product of research and development, whether or not R&D is a formally recognized activity in the firm. The process must occur for change to take place. Technology includes not only the product or service the firm offers but also the manufacturing or operating process by which the product or service is created and the systems by which the product is promoted, sold, and distributed.

As specific, practical knowledge, technology is the last, practical step in the knowledge creation process that begins with basic research and ends with development. Innovation is the application of new technology to practical ends—it may be continuous, as seen in the incremental improvement in performance that takes place within a given technological regime (better and cheaper mechanical watches), or discontinuous, as seen in the step change in performance and economics brought about by new technological regimes (electronic watches vs. mechanical watches).

The pace of technological change is just one part of what some have seen as the continual ascent of humankind. The law of limits that constrains the cost and performance of any given technology is overridden by the law of progress, by which totally new technologies emerge to solve the problems humans face. While one cannot pinpoint the exact time and place that the new will emerge, to act and bet that it will not emerge is a poor strategy based on retrospective analysis.

But the new is seldom perfect when it emerges, and the manager must be able to manage the risks of pioneering with the advantages it confers. It is as important for the manager to understand the process by which innovations are accepted, imitated, and diffused as it is to understand the process of innovation itself. For while the innovation process can sometimes be called managed chaos, the processes of imitation and diffusion are more predictable. What was unpredictable *research* for the innovator becomes predictable *development* for imitators. Adopters, those who use new technology, are overwhelmingly rational. They base their decisions on the basis of risk and economic advantage and the expectations about the pace of technological improvement. Perversely, radical innovations are often shunned initially because of expectations about the forthcoming rapid improvement in performance.

Technological change can have dramatic effects on existing competitors and industries. It can allow some to differentiate products or lower the costs of producing those products; it can shift the cost or differentiation drivers in favor of some firms and not others; it can change the structure of an industry, strengthening its profitability or plunging it into destructive competition; and it can reward or punish those who are first or last to adopt the new technology.

7

THE DYNAMIC NATURE
OF COMPETITION
AND COMPETITIVE STRATEGY

Strategy must be based on a dynamic, not a static, model of the environment. The general strategizing over a map marked with the enemy's positions does not assume that those positions will remain fixed for the duration of the battle, let alone for the war. The general's own attack, among other changes in the enemy's environment, will cause the enemy to take action, shift position, move, strengthen, weaken, or withdraw from those positions. As an abstraction of the world of war, the game of chess illustrates how a good strategy takes account of the sequential unfolding of a series of competitive moves and countermoves.

Understanding the dynamic nature of the competition itself and the enemy's likely moves is critical to the general's and the chess player's success. The term *product life cycle* has been used to refer to the pattern of the changes that occur over time in the engagement of a product with a market.[1] Its focus is on explaining and predicting how competitors and the bases of the competition evolve, how customers mature in their responses, and how the size of the prize and what it takes to win it change with time and the actions of those involved.

As the experience base with large, modern markets has increased with time, so has the understanding of the forces that shape their evolution. The classic product life cycle (PLC), which is a first-generation model of the process, starts off this chapter. A second-generation model is the product evolutionary cycle (PEC).[2] This model is especially useful in understanding the changes that product offerings undergo as product markets develop and mature, and it is the second model presented in this chapter. A third-generation model gives a population ecology perspective to the process. This model yields a supply-side perspective of competitive entry and success and is also covered in this chapter. Next, two specific models which give insight into the dynamics of competitive

[1] More simply, the product life cycle is "the curve(s) that represent the sales history of a product class, product, or brand over the life span of a given product class, product, or brand." See David M. Gardner, "The Product Life Cycle: A Critical Look at the Literature," in Michael Houston, ed., *Review of Marketing* (Chicago: American Marketing Association, 1987), p. 164.

[2] Gerard J. Tellis and C. Merle Crawford, "An Evolutionary Approach to Product Growth Theory," *Journal of Marketing*, 45, no. 4 (fall 1981), 125–132.

strategy are presented. The chapter ends with a review of the key insights provided by the various models.

AN OVERVIEW OF THE CLASSIC LIFE-CYCLE CONCEPT

The idea that products experience some predictable form of competitive development began to surface in the 1950s. Some authors credit Joel Dean with its development—his 1950 *Harvard Business Review* article introduced the concepts of penetration and skimming price strategies for new products.[3] The first actual use of the term *product life cycle* appeared in an article authored by the manager of new product planning at Booz, Allen and Hamilton in 1957.[4] In describing the forces behind the drive for new products, he noted, "There is a life cycle that is characteristic of many—if not most—products. Since all products are 'new' at their outset, we can call it the basic life cycle for new products."[5]

The classic product life cycle is shown in Figure 7-1. It is based on the biological birth-growth-maturity-decline sequence in life. At the introduction stage, sales grow slowly as the product is introduced. Profitability is low or nonexistent because of the expenses of the introduction. In the growth stage, the product achieves rapid market acceptance and profits improve substantially. The maturity stage is characterized by a slowdown in sales growth as most potential buyers have accepted the new product. Profits stagnate or decline because of an increase in the level of competition. The decline period sees a downward drift in sales and an erosion of profits.[6]

Authors agree that this classic cycle can be characterized by five statements:

1. Products have a limited life.
2. Their sales history follows an *S* curve until annual sales flatten, when penetration of the potential market is achieved, and eventually decline.
3. The inflection points in the sales history identify the stages known as introduction, growth, maturity, and decline. Some life cycles add more stages, including a period of shakeout or competitive turbulence once growth begins to slow.
4. The life of the product may be extended by finding new uses or users, or getting present users to increase their consumption.
5. The average profitability per unit rises and then falls as products move sequen-

---

[3] Joel Dean, "Pricing Policies for New Products," *Harvard Business Review*, 28, no. 6 (November-December 1950), 28–36.

[4] According to William Muhs, Conrad Jones was the first to use the term in an article titled "Product Development from the Management Point of View," in Robert L. Cleweth, ed., *Marketing's Role in Scientific Management* (Chicago: American Marketing Association, 1957). William F. Muhs, "The Product Life Cycle Concept: Origin and Early Antecedents," in Stanley Hollander et al., eds., *Marketing in the Long Run,* Proceedings of the Second Workshop on Historical Proceedings in Marketing (East Lansing: Michigan State University, 1985), pp. 413–419.

[5] Jones, "Product Development," pp. 41, 42.

[6] Philip Kotler, *Marketing Management: Analysis, Planning, Implementation and Control,* 7th ed. (Englewood Cliffs, NJ: Prentice-Hall, 1991), p. 350.

Figure 7-1   Classic product life cycle

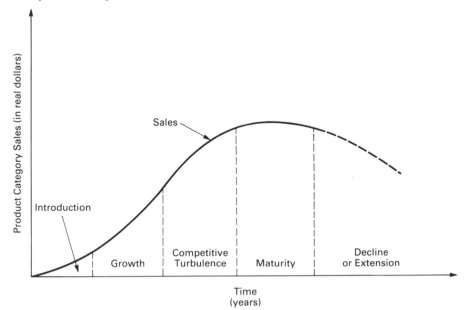

SOURCE: Philip Kotler, *Marketing Management: Analysis, Planning, Implementation, and Control*, 7th ed., ©
1991, p. 350. Adapted by permission of Prentice Hall, Englewood Cliffs, NJ 07632.

tially and inevitably through the stages (this follows directly from the presumed
correspondence of the life cycle with the experience curve for average industry
prices).[7]

The classic life cycle postulated that each of the stages was distinct and that
the challenges they brought sellers were different. This implied that the marketer must continually adapt the marketing focus at each stage. Mickwitz, for
example, postulated that the response elasticity of the various marketing tools
changed over the life cycle.[8] He suggested that advertising had the highest
elasticity during the growth and decline stages and that price had the highest
elasticity in maturity.

Levitt talked of the need for "life extension" and "market stretching" activities at the maturity stage to stave off decline.[9] Others, such as Kerr and Donaldson, spoke of the need to assign managers and adapt the structure of the
organization on the basis of the product life cycle.[10] Many scholars developed
normative prescriptions for managerial action at each of the stages of the life

[7] George Day, *Analysis for Strategic Market Decisions* (St. Paul, MN: West Publishing Co., 1986), p. 59.
[8] Gosta Mickwitz, *Marketing and Competition* (Finland: Helsinfors, Centraltrycheriet, 1959).
[9] Theodore Levitt, "Exploit the Product Life Cycle," *Harvard Business Review*, 42, no. 6 (November-
December 1965), 81–94.
[10] Jeffrey Kerr, "Assigning Managers on the Basis of the Life Cycle," *Journal of Business Strategy*, 2,
(spring 1982), 58–65; Lex Donaldson, "Organization Design and the Life-Cycle of Products," *Journal
of Management Studies*, 22, no. 1 (January 1985), 25–37.

cycle and presented them in tables.[11] One article catalogued 567 recommended strategies for the five life-cycle stages over seven functional business areas.[12]

While impressive, the typical strategies called for in these articles cannot in any sense be termed true or immutable. One critic characterized them as checklists that indiscriminately listed all possibilities.[13] In fact, there are some who doubt that any such prescriptions are possible. One recent empirical study, for example, found that there was no unique success strategy associated with any life-cycle stage.[14]

The Validity of the Classic Life Cycle

The product life-cycle concept is, at best, a simplistic view of reality. The concept that a single S-shaped, time-based curve with a fixed number of stages can represent the reality that any product will experience is naive. Gardner, in a major review of the literature, tested the concept against a number of criteria used to evaluate classificational models such as the PLC.[15] His assessment was that it had a noticeable absence of conceptual validity or rigorous empirical support. He pointed to the many variations of the shape of the curve that are found in the literature and the confusion about whether the model described behavior at the level of the product class, product form, or brand. He presented two telling arguments: (1) that the PLC was a tautology in that it used sales to determine the stage of the life cycle, which then was used to predict sales; and (2) that time was the only causal factor used to explain the shape of the sales curve.

His conclusion was that the concept did not even meet the minimum criteria for acceptance of it as a classification scheme. As a recent article put it,

> the typically generalized descriptions and prescriptions in the product life cycle literature would be unlikely to find empirical support because key assumptions are flawed and important dimensions of evolutionary processes are overlooked.[16]

AN EVOLUTIONARY MODEL OF THE LIFE CYCLE

At the end of his review of the classic product life cycle, Gardner suggests that the concept of the *product evolutionary cycle*, as suggested by Tellis and Crawford,

---

[11] See, for example, Kotler, *Marketing Management*, p. 367, or Day, *Analysis for Strategic Market Decisions*, p. 90.

[12] David R. Rink and John E. Swan, "Product Life Cycle Research: A Literature Review," *Journal of Business Research*, 78, no. 3 (September 1979), 219–242.

[13] Colin Camerer, "Redirecting Research in Business Policy and Strategy," *Strategic Management Journal*, 6, no. 1 (January–March 1985), 1–16.

[14] R. A. Thietart and R. Vivas, "An Empirical Investigation of Success Strategies for Businesses along the Product Life Cycle," *Management Science*, 30, no. 12 (December 1984), 1405–1423.

[15] David M. Gardner, "The Product Life Cycle: A Critical Look at the Literature," in Michael J. Houston, ed., *Review of Marketing* (Chicago: American Marketing Association, 1987), pp. 162–195.

[16] Mary Lambkin and George S. Day, "Evolutionary Processes in Competitive Markets: Beyond the Product Life Cycle," *Journal of Marketing*, 53, no. 3 (July 1989), p. 8.

might form a more appropriate conceptual basis for the study of the dynamics of product and market interaction.[17] The following discussion explores the concept of biological evolution as the basis for a life-cycle theory.

The Evolutionary Approach

Crawford and Tellis note that the PLC is based on the pattern of birth-growth-maturity-death intrinsic to all individual biological specimens—the individual horse, human being, dog, etc. They propose, instead, that the evolutionary cycle from biology be used. The evolutionary cycle is used to explain the growth and proliferation of species (groups of individual specimens that can breed within but not outside each group, such as horses, dogs, etc.).

Evolution is a scientifically rigorous construct—it is used to designate gradual, continuous change that is

Cumulative, each change building on the previous one;
Motivated by *generative* (creates variety and change), *selective* (favors variations better suited to the environment), and *mediative* forces (intervenes in the process of the first two forces);
Directional, the linear sequence of changes characterized by increasing diversity, efficiency, and complexity;
Patterned, evidenced by five distinct patterns of which only the first (the emergence of a new species) and the last (extinction) need to occur in fixed sequence.

The analogies are apt. Viewing products not as individual, isolated entities but as part of an overall dynamic and evolving pattern gives new insights. For example, change in products is clearly cumulative. As Tellis and Crawford put it,

> We can trace a continuous line of history of the clothes washing machine as it evolved from the first crude hand- and foot-driven models to the present sophisticated versions with variable speeds, temperatures, and timing facilities. The changes undergone were cumulative, much like that of species in nature.[18]

Product changes seem directional, as evidenced by increasingly diverse, more efficient, and more complex product forms stemming from a given original form (or technology). New products are frequently offered in only one size and form as they begin their life (e.g., the Sony Walkman®). Over time, the basic product technology and form becomes adapted to meet the differing needs of the various customer groups and applications.[19] The Walkman® and its imitators

---

[17] Tellis and Crawford, "An Evolutionary Approach to Product Growth Theory."
[18] Tellis and Crawford, "An Evolutionary Approach," p. 127.
[19] It has been observed that two seemingly opposite moves actually occur as markets develop. First, product differentiation among competing suppliers tends to diminish over time due to competitive imitation. Second, product differentiation across segments increases simultaneously as competitors strive to satisfy customer needs more precisely. See Derek Abell and John S. Hammond, *Strategic Marketing Planning* (Englewood Cliffs, NJ: Prentice-Hall, Inc., 1979), p. 57.

EXHIBIT 7-1

"If It Ain't Broke, Don't Fix It": Product Saturation,
Managerial Action, and Product Evolution

One researcher in marketing had an interesting insight. He hypothesized that since managers operated according to the philosophy, "if it ain't broke, don't fix it," they would not act as long as the sales of the established product form continued to rise. He hypothesized specifically that managers would act to introduce product enhancements or new products only once the saturation for an existing product exceeded some critical level, at which time additional sales growth became increasingly difficult. Only then would firms start to think of ways to spur sales.

He tested his idea in the market for televisions and VCRs over the past several decades. He pointed out that although color television had been around since the 1950s, it was not until the saturation level of black and white televisions reached 75% in 1964 and sales began to plateau that serious marketing of color televisions began. By 1976, the sales of color television began to slump as its saturation level exceeded 70%. In 1976, Sony introduced its Betamax system to the United States. Although the technology had been available since the early 1960s, it was not until predictions of a stagnating color television market surfaced that Sony introduced the VCR. This researcher further pointed out that when VCR saturation reached 40% in 1986 and sales began to slow, it was then that manufacturers chose to make wireless remote controls and other features available.

This supply-side theory of market development is important, for it reminds one that the evolution of products and markets does not just happen. It is caused by managers responding to signals from the marketplace in terms of sales and profits. If those signals are good, the existing competitors see no reason to act any differently. Only when there is a slowing are managers spurred to enhance their products or to leapfrog them with even better product forms.

SOURCE: Adapted from William P. Putsis, Jr., "Product Diffusion, Product Differentiation and the Timing of New Product Introduction: The Television and VCR Market 1964–85," in *Managerial and Decision Economics*, 10, 37–50, copyright © 1989 by John Wiley & Sons, Ltd. Reproduced by permission of John Wiley and Sons, Limited.

are now available in a wide variety of sizes, shapes, colors, and with numerous special features. Exhibit 7-1 explores the process by which managers are stimulated to introduce newer and better product forms.

In terms of evolutionary theory, the process of change is motivated. Managerial and entrepreneurial activities are the **generative** force. Actions of individuals and firms create and deliver new offerings into the marketplace. Consumers and competitors are the **selective** force. Their acceptance or rejection of the new products offered determines whether the products will flourish and prosper and for how long. Government and other agencies are the **mediative** force in the evolution of products. By setting the rules of the marketplace, they mediate the actions of both the firms and the customers.

Product change can be characterized by the same **patterns** of change as biological species are. Table 7-1 compares the five distinct patterns of change identified in biology with their marketplace counterparts. Tellis and Crawford suggest that these patterns can be used to characterize different **patterns** of product growth which offer insights different from those suggested by the time-related stages of the PLC.

Figure 7-2 presents the evolution of the U.S. tobacco industry as it would be portrayed in evolutionary terms.

In contrast to the traditional product life cycle, the evolutionary approach is dynamic and open ended. A product need not go through stages in a predetermined order. More importantly, the evolutionary cycle is one in which development is a function of the interaction of the product with the environment. The firm does not simply respond to change in the environment, it is an active participant in the process. As Tellis and Crawford point out,

> This approach assumes that products are in a state of constant evolution motivated by market dynamics, managerial creativity, and government intervention, and that the evolution proceeds in a direction of greater efficiency, greater complexity, and greater diversity.[20]

A POPULATION ECOLOGY MODEL OF COMPETITIVE MARKETS

Whereas the product evolutionary concept focuses on the processes by which product offerings evolve over time, the population ecology model uses the same biological perspective to provide insight into the population of competing organizations and their strategies.[21] It is a supply-side theory of market evolution that includes

A *population growth process* that accounts for differences in the competitive environment over time, particularly in the intensity of competition.

A *typology of strategies* for competing in new markets that recognizes the diversity of resources and skills among the business population, as well as differences in their order of entry.

An *integrative model* that provides predictions about the likely success of different generic strategies as the product-market evolves through different stages.[22]

---

[20] Tellis and Crawford, "An Evolutionary Approach," p. 131.
[21] Lambkin and Day, "Evolutionary Processes in Competitive Markets." Lambkin and Day summarize and adapt to a marketing perspective the organization ecology model developed by Michael T. Hannan and John Freeman, "The Population Ecology of Organizations," *American Journal of Sociology*, 82, no. 5 (March 1977), 929–964.
[22] Lambkin and Day, "Evolutionary Processes," pp. 9 and 10.

TABLE 7-1   *Patterned Change in Biological and Product Evolution*

BIOLOGICAL PATTERNS	PRODUCT PATTERNS
1. Cladogenesis is the divergence of a new species from an evolutionary line, triggered by some environmental stimulus.	1. Divergence is the start of a new product type. TV may be considered an evolutionary divergence from radio and motion pictures.
2. Anagenesis is a pattern of adaptation by a species to its environment characterized by increasing complexity and numbers of members of the species.	2. Development is the pattern in which a new product's sales increase rapidly and the product is increasingly improved to best suit consumer needs.
3. Adaptive radiation refers to a period of increasing variations among members of a particular species, leading to the formation of subspecies, each adapted to a particular niche in the environment.	3. Differentiation occurs when a successful product is differentiated to serve the varying needs of consumers in different segments.
4. Stasigenesis refers to a period of stability or stagnation when there is not much change in the numbers or variation of a species.	4. Stabilization refers to the period in which there are few and minor substantive changes in the category.
5. Extinction is the dying out of a species that can no longer cope with environmental change.	5. Demise occurs when a product fails to meet consumer needs and can no longer satisfy consumer demands.

SOURCE: Gerard J. Tellis and C. Merle Crawford, "An Evolutionary Approach to Product Growth Theory," in *Journal of Marketing,* 45, no. 4 (fall 1981), pp. 128 and 129. Reprinted by permission of the American Marketing Association.

Population Growth

The model defines the population as the group of businesses serving a given product market. Such a population begins when there has been a substantial shift in the definition of the business (either in product technology, customer function, or customer group) that is outside the scope of existing suppliers and such that new ventures are required to exploit and serve it.

The population growth process specified in the model is a logistic one (S-shaped curve) in which there is some natural rate of increase (r) and an upper limit or carrying capacity (K):

$$\frac{dN}{dt} = rN\left(\frac{K-N}{K}\right).$$

The model is such that when the population is small relative to its carrying capacity (potential), there is exponential growth in the number of organizations and the reverse when the population approaches or exceeds the carrying capacity.

Strategy Typologies

Ecologists have constructed a typology of strategies that show the time at which an organization enters the new resource space (market). In their terminology, these strategies are described in terms of the growth equation, as either r strategies (early entrants) or K strategies (those entering later when the population of competitors is larger). The typology proceeds through three additional con-

Figure 7-2 Product evolution as a patterned process

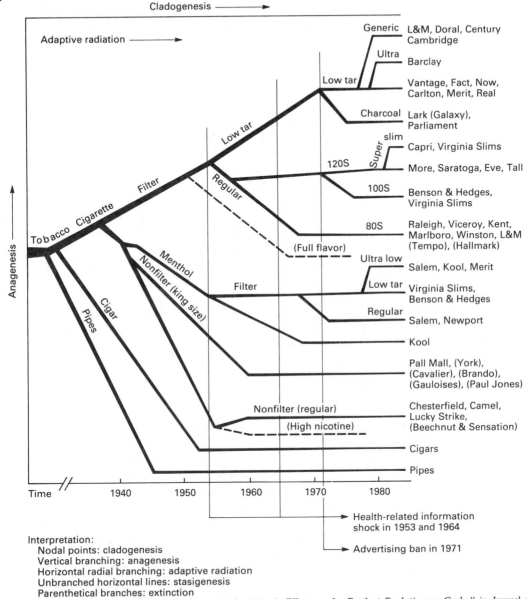

Interpretation:
Nodal points: cladogenesis
Vertical branching: anagenesis
Horizontal radial branching: adaptive radiation
Unbranched horizontal lines: stasigenesis
Parenthetical branches: extinction

SOURCE: Susan L. Holak and Y. Edwin Tang, "Advertising's Effect on the Product Evolutionary Cycle," in *Journal of Marketing*, 54, no. 3 (July 1990), p. 20. Reprinted with permission of the American Marketing Association.

cepts: (1) density dependence, (2) environmental niches, and (3) niche width strategies.

Density dependence says that competitive conditions in any population are a function of the number of organizations competing for the finite level of resources available. When there are few organizations, competition is indirect and diffuse; when population density increases it becomes difficult to avoid direct competition in the sense of a zero-sum game.

Most important in this model is that it points out that each entrant faces a unique set of resources and competitive conditions when it enters—that its strategy must contend with a different strategic problem than that faced by prior or subsequent entrants. An *r*-strategy firm (early entrant), for example, enters a competitive arena in which a small number of firms is working to develop a market on the basis of product performance versus that performance provided by some alternative product form or technology. A *K* strategist, on the other hand, must contend with a larger number of competitors, each of which is saying that its offering is better or cheaper than the others' offerings.

The *concept of niches* defines a niche as each unique combination of resources and competitive conditions sufficient to support any one type of organization. While a single resource space (market) generally contains several overlapping niches, competition is likely to constrain the ability of an individual organizational form to flourish in its chosen niche(s). Since it is difficult to identify the boundaries of a fundamental niche (a theoretical abstraction), ecologists define realized niches in terms of the characteristics of the organizations that occupy them. To the extent that there are different organization types in existence, each type is assumed to occupy a distinct niche.

Since organizations are built based on the set of resources available in the resource space (and the number of firms competing for that resource set) at the time of their founding, those founded at the same time are more similar in structure in comparison to those formed at other times. Since each faced a different strategic problem at its time of entry, their solutions will have been different. Ecologists therefore speak of *waves of organizing* as different types of organizations appear in each stage of the market's development.

Finally, since organizations exhibit structural inertia—the tendency to preserve their original form—their ability to adapt to changing environmental conditions is impeded. This provides the opportunity for new organizations to emerge. A mature population, therefore, contains a variety of organizational forms, each a function of its time of entry and suited to certain niche conditions.

The *concept of niche width* defines the extent to which an organization chooses to spread its resources across a broad spectrum of the environment (hopefully to balance its risks) or concentrates on a narrow segment (to earn a high return). Specialists are depicted as smaller entrants which rely on their ability to exploit first-mover advantages in new markets (*r* specialists) or new segments in mature markets (*K* specialists).

Generalists tend to be larger and possess more extensive resources. However, they are slower moving because of their inertia—explaining why they are

TABLE 7-2 *Strategy Typologies*

NICHE CONFIGURATION	EMBRYONIC	DEVELOPING	MATURING
Population density	Low	Increasing	High
Size and rate of environmental change	High	Reducing	Low
Predominant organization form	r specialists	K generalists	K generalists
Other forms	r generalists	Polymorphists	K specialists
Best performers	r specialists	K generalists	K generalists

NOTE: r specialists are small-scale pioneers and r generalists are large-scale pioneers. K generalists are early followers with established businesses in related markets. Polymorphists are early followers with widely diversified portfolios. K specialists are small-scale late entrants occupying narrow market segments.

SOURCE: Mary Lambkin and George S. Day, "Evolutionary Processes in Competitive Markets: Beyond the Product Life Cycle," in *Journal of Marketing*, 53, no. 3 (July 1989), p. 12. Reprinted by permission of the American Marketing Association.

more likely to be early followers. Their size allows them to invest heavily to achieve competitive efficiency and to dominate markets. Polymorphists are a special form of generalists which lack direct synergy between existing markets and technologies and the new opportunity. They do, however, typically have managerial and financial resources that enable them to develop the necessary technological and market skills needed. Table 7-2 contains the full typology based on the model.

Natural Selection

Success in ecological terms can range from *viability* (the best-performing surviving competitor) to simple *survival* (the worst-performing surviving competitor) to *mobility* (an organization so transformed that it is no longer in its original form) to *failure* (either withdrawal or dissolution). Ecologists view success or failure to be a function of the fit between an organization and its environment; it can be viewed as a game of chance in which the organization chooses a strategy (specialism or generalism) and then the environment chooses an outcome (by tossing a coin, say). "If the environment 'comes up' in a state favorable to the table organizational form it prospers; otherwise, it declines."[23]

Two factors determine the state of the environment: the rate of change and the magnitude of the change. Change which is minor (or of very short duration relative to the lifetime of the organization) and which comes infrequently indicates a stable (and some might say benign) environment. An environment which frequently undergoes radical change is difficult to operate in.

According to this theory, then, when changes are extreme and rapidly paced, such as in the emergent phase of a new market, a specialist's strategy is optimal because the cost of maladaptation for a generalist's strategy is higher because of its much larger required investment.[24] When change is frequent but

[23] Michael T. Hannan and John Freeman, "The Population Ecology of Organizations," *American Journal of Sociology*, 82, no. 5 (March 1977), p. 952.
[24] It must be remembered that maladaption, at its extreme point, means the demise of the organization. A statement that some strategy would have been the best long-run strategy (based on averaging the positive and negative returns over a long period) makes no sense if the string of results contains one that was sufficiently negative to cause the firm to fail at an early point.

minor, large-scale generalists are preferred because they have the capacity to ride out the small shocks that smaller specialist firms lack.

Minor and infrequent change also favors generalists because of their competitive efficiency; however, as the environment becomes increasingly stable, specialists again become favored because, in their chosen niches, they can outperform the generalists (the stability assures their survival). Environments in which change is infrequent but radical require a hybrid strategy, polymorphism, in which one of the number of federated specialists is always attuned to a particular environment.

An Ecological Approach to Market Evolution

The processes that occur during a market's evolution are analogous to those described by the population ecology model: (1) New markets attract increasing numbers of competitors until the density becomes such that, relative to the size of the resource space, a shakeout occurs; (2) each wave of entrants is structured differently and pursues different strategies depending on the resources available at their time of entry; and (3) risk and uncertainty about the nature and size of the resource space diminish over time as competitive intensity increases.

Emerging (embryonic) markets have great uncertainty about the nature and level of market demand, and the development of that demand is a matter of trial and error and rapid change. As the population ecology model suggests, *r* specialists predominate to exploit first-mover advantages. Their size is not a drawback because the market is not large and the population density (and therefore competitive intensity) is low. Risk comes from the inherent uncertainty of demand, the inexperience of the entrants, and the possibility of future competition from fast followers. Firms that survive this stage have generally been able to create and exploit first-mover advantages such as the establishment of their offering as the industry standard, cost advantages through experience in production, and the ability to reinvest their monopoly profits into plant capacity and product improvements.

The rapid growth of a market beyond the embryonic stage is itself a major reduction in the uncertainty about demand that existed earlier. The ultimate size of the resource space is better understood, and experience with customers and operations provides firms with opportunities to improve efficiency and standardize products. The increasing population density and corresponding competitive intensity reward competitive efficiency favoring larger, more efficient, *K*-generalists organizations. Such entrants are typically organizations in related or overlapping markets. Remaining *r* specialists are either those which have used their first-mover advantages to transform themselves into *K* generalists (as did Apple Computer) or are sought after as merger partners or acquisitions either by *K* generalists seeking volume or by polymorphists seeking rapid entry.

Maturing markets are marked by a low level of uncertainty about the nature and size of the resource space and by a population of competitors that approaches the ability of the resource space to support them. While *K* generalists predominate, they are unable to cater to all of the needs of the marketplace, leaving niches for specialists to exploit without significant competition. As stability increases, moreover, the diffusion of technological knowledge on the supply side and about markets on the demand side tend to stimulate a third wave of *K* specialists which tailor themselves to fit very narrow niches. Customers or suppliers to the industry may backward or forward integrate, and very-low-cost producers with almost nonexistent overhead are created to serve steady, large-volume, plain-vanilla markets.

Whereas the evolutionary model emphasizes the product aspect of market evolution, the population ecology model takes one step back to explain how product evolution is the natural outgrowth of the strategies that firms develop to solve the strategic problems they face. Together, these two biologically based models provide a strong theoretical basis for the descriptive models discussed next.

MODELS OF COMPETITIVE ENTRY AND STRATEGY

Two models of the competitive evolution of markets have been offered which provide additional insight into the strategic issues faced over a product or market's evolution. The first is termed the *competitive life cycle* and is built on the observation of the development of many industrial markets. The second model, termed *competitive market strategies*, covers all markets and focuses on how the choices of one competitor lead others to make their choices.

The Competitive Life Cycle

The competitive life cycle refers to the analysis of the impact of competitive entry on the evolution of the life cycle.[25] The competitive life cycle is shown in Figure 7-3. The impact of competition and competitive strategies have a major effect on the evolution and structure that a market takes over time. The competitive cycle is an idealized model of the competitive process useful for quickly gaining an overview of the dynamics of competitive evolution.

Innovative Entry.   Product markets begin when a firm introduces a product based on a new technology to a market. As noted earlier, that new product invariably gains sales from some older product form or technology that had been satisfying the same or close functional need. The new product gains acceptance because it performs the function better and/or less expensively than the product it is replacing.

The new product is priced in relation to the older product on the basis of the value-in-use it provides. Compared to the new product's investment and costs

[25] John B. Frey, "Pricing and the Life Cycle," *Chemtech* (January 1985), 40–43.

Figure 7-3   The competitive life cycle

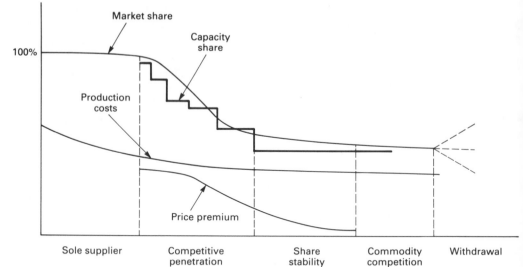

SOURCE: John B. Frey, "Pricing and the Product Life Cycle," given at the annual Marketing Conference of The Conference Board.

and some notions of what constitutes a normal return, the new product is frequently able to command a premium price. It can achieve this because the new technology allows it to perform the same function as the old at a lower cost (or perform better at the same cost).

Market growth for the new product (or displacement of the old, depending on how you view it) is a function of both how much value is created by the new product and how much of that created value is shared with users by the innovating firm. A skimming price strategy shares just enough of the value with users to induce them to switch at a rate sufficient to satisfy the growth and volume objectives of the innovating firm. The innovating firm is able to skim because it has no direct competition—except for that of the old technology.[26] In other words, the innovator has a temporary monopoly and can act accordingly.

A penetration price, on the other hand, is low in comparison to the former product and provides a large motivating force for buyers to adopt the new product and for the firm, therefore, to achieve rapid growth, and ultimately, high volume. By converting potential users into actual users quickly, the firm is able to leave less room in the market for new entrants.

Competitive Penetration.   Monopolies seldom last long, however. In fact, the greater the innovator's success, the more potential competitors will do to try to

---

[26] The analysis here assumes that the displaced product can do little to offset the inroads of the new. In reality, of course, the incumbent products are defended vigorously by their firms. See the examples cited in A. Cooper, E. Demuzzio, K. Hatten, E. Hicks, and D. Tock, "Strategic Responses to Technological Threats," paper no. 431 (November 1973), Institute for Research in the Behavioral, Economic, and Management Sciences, Krannert School of Industrial Administration, Purdue University.

enter the market.[27] At some point, one or more competitors will enter, selling an essentially equivalent product. This is called the competitive penetration phase. Typically, the new entrant achieves entry by pricing lower than the first entrant for some equivalent performance level.[28]

Upon competitive entry, the focus for value-in-use calculations moves from the new-technology product versus the old-technology product (which yielded a high value-in-use for the new) to the original new-technology product versus the second entrant's new-technology product (which provides a much smaller value-in-use figure). As the proven supplier of a product of known quality, the original entrant provides values that new entrants cannot, and therefore can obtain a premium price in comparison to those obtained by later entrants.[29] By definition, as new entrants arrive, the first entrant's market share falls from 100% as does its share of industry capacity.

As shown in Figure 7-3, the original producer's shares of market and capacity continue to decline through this phase. Early capacity additions have the potential to overshoot demand as new entrants' additions are large as a percentage of the existing, installed capacity. This is one of the key supply-side risks of new markets, for the added capacity can quickly become overcapacity and cause price levels to fall precipitously if expected demand does not grow as fast as anticipated or if a recession reduces the overall level of demand.

Over time, this process erodes the original entrant's price premium. This occurs because customers' experiences with the new competitors and their products offset the pioneer's reputational advantage.

Share Stability and Commodity Competition.   At some point, growth slows and industry demands begin to stabilize. Because the market is now very large, capacity additions no longer bring on large percentage increases in total industry capacity, and their potential to disrupt the market is therefore diminished. Depending on the aggressiveness of competitors, shares may stabilize while the price premium accorded to the original entrant continues to lessen.

Ultimately, the market reaches commodity status, as demonstrated by a lack of any perceived value differences among suppliers by buyers.[30] Price premiums at this stage are accorded only to superior performance. The originator has no lead that competitors have not been able to match and receives no price premium. Finally, as growth slows to a rate less than or equal to the gross national product (GNP) growth rate, competitive pressures begin to take their toll.

---

[27] This description assumes that the innovator does not have ironclad patent protection and that one or more competitors will have the right combination of technology, assets, financing, and market access to allow them to enter. Given the small number of instances in which monopolies exist over long periods, it is generally a good assumption that competitors will somehow find a way of entering.

[28] In some instances where marketplace demand for the new product is very high relative to the innovator's ability to supply, the second entrant may not find it necessary to offer a discount to gain acceptance in the market.

[29] The ability of an existing competitor to offer value in the form of proven product and supplier performance that a new entrant cannot provide is one of the factors which account for pioneering advantage, a concept explored in chapter 8.

[30] To quote one strategy consultant, "In the long run, all products become commodities."

Weaker, higher-cost competitors may exit the market, especially during periods of oversupply or extended recessions.

Competitive Market Strategies

Derek Abell's study of competitive strategy led him to a unique and useful way of characterizing the problems and strategies available to a firm as a market evolves.[31] He saw companies in a dynamic game, almost like children playing, as they each attempted to gain advantageous positions.

Abell characterized infancy as posing the first entrant into the market with two interesting strategic questions: which segments of the market it should target and how broad or narrow that entry should be. The temporary monopoly gives the entrant the opportunity to preempt competitors in the most attractive segments, but the firm pays a strategic price whether it chooses to serve either a broad or narrow slice of the market.

The broader the target it chooses, the more it will cost the firm in marketing costs and, more importantly, the more average its offering needs to be to serve the necessarily more diverse needs of the larger, more general customer grouping. This average offering leaves room for competitors to provide more exact offerings to those parts of the market for whom the average product is a marginal fit with real needs. For example, a product for the entire family (an average offering) can often be beat out by products designed specifically for children or for adults (exact offerings).

On the other hand, a strategy which focuses the firm's product development and marketing resources on a narrow segment requires a smaller investment to commercialize the new product and allows the firm to better tailor its offering to customer needs. The problem with this strategy is that the firm leaves the other segments unserved, almost inviting competitors to fill the void.

Chain bookstores, for example, have chosen to serve the broad, general market. Waldenbooks and B. Dalton, the largest of these discounters, locate in large malls and shopping centers, necessitating high inventory turnover to pay for the high rents. Their inventories must be limited, therefore, and focused only on books of widespread interest. This strategy choice necessarily leaves unserved the more narrow segment of book buyers who desire less popular books. Independent booksellers such as the Tattered Cover in Denver and Oxford Books in Atlanta serve this latter market profitably by choosing low-rent locations which enable them the large space necessary to house their much wider selections. For example, whereas a chain bookstore averages 3,000 square feet and 20,000 titles, the new independents are large, about 40,000 square feet, with 110,000 titles in stock.[32]

---

[31] Derek Abell, "Competitive Market Strategies: Some Generalizations and Hypotheses" (Cambridge, MA: Marketing Science Institute Report No. 75-107, April 1975).
[32] Edwin McDowell, "Bookstore Thrives on Independence," *The New York Times,* July 17, 1989, pp. D1 and D9.

The choices made by the innovating firm in infancy presage the strategic questions faced in the growth stage. These involve establishing new positions and defending old ones. Competitors can choose either to heel nip or to leap-frog the innovator. Heel nipping involves confronting the innovator in its home markets by outperforming it in either cost or product performance. Leapfroggers, on the other hand, compete by not competing (i.e., by finding new segments of primary demand unserved by the innovator). Faced with such competition, the innovator faces the question of whether to protect and defend its home base against the heel nipper, heel nip the leapfrogger by in-vading its segment, or leapfrog itself into yet another unserved segment (if such exists).

The choice of the strategy with which to respond involves issues of fighting selective demand battles (buy mine vs. theirs) versus creating new primary demand (my product is the only one that can fill your need). The resolution of that strategic question depends on what it is that the firm is able to do that is better than competitors can do. A firm better at marketing might, for example, choose to fight the selective demand battle under the assumption that it has a better chance of winning that way. A firm stronger in R&D might pursue prod-uct development while other firms would forge strategies based on their own unique competencies.

As the market approaches maturity and new primary demand slows, the strategic issue becomes one of jostling for advantage. As the market's evolu-tion makes clear the positions that are available in which the competitive ad-vantage in creating value can be achieved—necessary to survive into maturity—rivals begin to compete against each other to achieve those posi-tions and avoid the shakeout of those who do not.[33] In this they are not unlike children as they jostle for the best place in the movie line or in a game of musical chairs. Since leadership in product performance, variety, cost, or in some specific segment is needed to achieve long-run competitive advantage, many different strategies evolve. Each competitor seeks a protected position along some dimension.

At maturity, all that remains is to slug it out. The protected positions achieved during the prior stages offer some protection, but competitive imitation erodes many of the major differences. After all, only those with some advantage have made it this far. The others have exited or failed at an earlier stage. The real concern is to find ways of competing that do not destroy the market's profit-ability.

The aforementioned models provide accurate, if terse, descriptions of the generic process of competitive entry. These descriptions are prototypical—useful for understanding and visualizing the more complex process of a product mar-ket's evolution.

---

[33] For empirical evidence on shakeouts, see Gary Willard and Arnold Cooper, "Survivors of Industry Shakeouts: The Case of the U.S. Color Television Industry," *Strategic Management Journal*, 6, no. 4 (October-December 1985), 299–318; and Michael Gort and Stephen Klepper, "Time Paths in the Diffusion of Product Innovation," *The Economic Journal*, 92, no. 367 (September 1982), 630–653.

THE DYNAMICS UNDERLYING A PRODUCT'S
EVOLUTIONARY CYCLE

As the models demonstrate, the evolution of product markets is a complex phenomenon. The following discussion provides additional insight into the process by examining four aspects of product evolution. The first topic is to address the level at which the evolution occurs. The second and third topics are concerned with demand-side influences on product market evolution, specifically the issues of how a new product technology displaces an old and the social nature of customer tastes and needs. The fourth topic again deals with a supply-side issue as it examines the interactions among product market growth and evolution, product strategy, and cash flow.

The Level of Product Market Evolution

The levels at which one may examine the evolution of a product market range from the very broad (the technology level) to the very specific (the brand level), as shown in Figure 7-4. For example, one may speak of technology itself as a product. Large-scale integrated circuits, for example, have replaced discrete semiconductor components, which themselves replaced vacuum tube components. Figure 7-5 shows how records were supplanted by cassettes as the dominant technology for recorded music in 1983 and how compact disc technology in turn is challenging cassettes.

There are problems with this level of analysis, however. Primary among these is the definition of a technology per se. While technology occasionally precedes in step-change fashion and one can easily differentiate one technology from another, more often technological improvements emerge continuously. More telling, however, is that for the most part, a technology is not a product.[34] Seldom do managers manage technologies, per se. Finally, most products benefit from numerous technologies in their creation and production. To do the analysis at the technology level would not generally yield useful insights.

At the next level is the industry. While there are instances in which an industry is identical with a product or a technology, those are exceptions. For the most part, industries produce a large number of noncompeting products. The soap and detergent industry, for example, produces a wide range of cleaning products. From an industry standpoint this may be logical, as the different products may share the same technology base, the same raw materials, the same distribution channels, and same customer base, or some other commonality which yields advantage. While industry dynamics and firm resources are important factors in competition, firms do not compete for customers, sales, or profits at the firm or industry level but at the product level. Industry-level analysis is useful and industries do evolve; however, they evolve primarily through their activities at the product level.

[34] Except when the creator of a technology sells that technology by transferring patent ownership or licenses others to operate under its patents.

Figure 7-4   The levels at which product market evolution may be examined

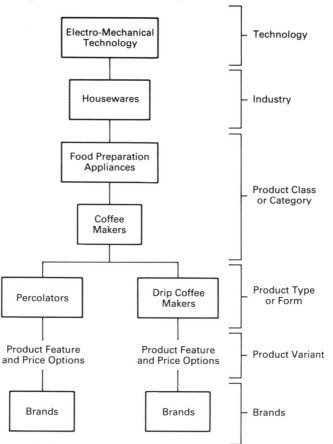

The question then becomes, which product level? It is argued that the brand or product variant level is too micro to reflect the factors that shape the evolutionary cycle. Generally, so too is the product type or form level, except when those distinctions reflect basic differences in product or production technology (or customer type or function) such that each is truly a separate product or business. Hair dryers for home use, for example, evolved through several different forms, from soft bonnets to miniature salon types to styling dryers to pistol dryers. Since the basic technology, customer base, and customer function remained the same, however, each would be viewed as simply part of the evolutionary process occurring within the overall evolution of the hair dryer. New entrants would not have sustainable strategic advantage over existing competitors as the basic structural factors which determine success or failure would not have changed.

Consensus is that the most useful level is the product class level (e.g., hair

Figure 7-5   Demand-technology-product life cycle

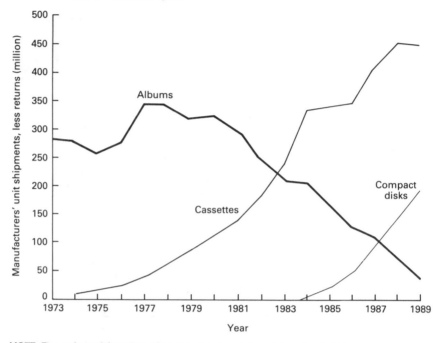

NOTE: Figure derived from Recording Industry Association of America statistics.

SOURCE: Andrew Pollack, "Recording Enters a New Era, And You Can't Find It on LP." Copyright © 1990 by The New York Times Company. Reprinted by permission.

dryers for home use). At this level, the differences in strategy are played out most tellingly and strategic advantage can be most strongly employed and experienced. At the product class level, the structural factors that govern competition have their effect.

The Process of Market Penetration and Saturation

One of the key processes underlying the emergence of a new product type is that of technological substitution—one product technology replacing another product technology. While this typically means a new technology replacing an old technology (electronic calculating technology replacing electromechanical calculating), the process may also be initiated by a shift in the economics (or other structural factor) affecting the utility yielded by a product in use. For example, the major increases in energy costs during the 1970s and early 1980s rekindled interest (and sales) in wood-burning stoves for household heating.

Although it is difficult to prove, virtually every new product displaces some other product or activity as it gains acceptance by users. That displacement may be directly observable and almost one to one, as in the preceding examples, or more difficult to observe.[35] The concepts of market penetration and market saturation are key in understanding the dynamics of this displacement process and, therefore, the sales growth for the new product.

The process known as the diffusion of innovation, discussed in chapter 6, is a key determinant of the rate by which this process occurs. The characteristics of the innovation, such as relative competitive advantage, perceived risk, and communicability, together with the social characteristics of the market are major factors affecting its acceptance. Our concern here is not with that process per se, but with the results of that process as seen through the eyes of the strategist.

Penetration is a measure of the extent to which the new has been accepted by the market. In those instances where one technology is directly substituting for an older technology, the penetration curve is matched by a displacement curve, which tracks the decline in usage of the old. This process is shown in Figure 7-6. At time *a* on the *x* axis, 100% of the productive capacity for glass was accounted for by the hand cylinder process. At time *b*, the hand cylinder's share of productive capacity was declining as it was being replaced by Lubber's mechanical cylinder process. Three processes were in use at time *c*, when the continuous sheet-drawing process emerged. By the time *d*, the continuous process had replaced both competitors and dominated the industry.

The growth rate for the new product is a function of two factors: (1) the demand it obtains by replacing the old technology, and (2) the amount that it obtains by its ability to expand the market through its superior performance or economics. It achieves this in two ways: (1) by converting a larger percentage of the potential users for the existing product to actual users, and (2) by increasing the population of potential users. The latter demand component comes from activating latent demand that the prior product technology was unable to satisfy. Together, these provide the new product with phenomenal growth.

Growth typically slows as the substitution process begins to near 100%. There are three reasons underlying this result. First, as predicted by diffusion theory (and economic theory), early buyers are typically those for whom the product has greatest utility. Almost by definition, later buyers have less need for that utility (or experience less utility from the product) and therefore exert a smaller driving force for penetration.

Second, the remaining unconverted users have formed a strong attachment to the old technology.[36] Diffusion studies have shown that laggards adopt later for attitudinal reasons as much as for rational utilitarian reasons. For example, many writers and reporters initially rejected the replacement of manual typewriters with electrics in spite of the many advantages that electric typewriters had. They cited the lack of the satisfying feel to which they had become accustomed with their manual typewriters (conveniently forgetting their predeces-

---

[35] It may be one to one if only by the fact that $1 spent on one product means, by definition, that there will be $1 less spent on some other product.

[36] The term *attachment* is used to indicate a nonutilitarian preference for a product. *Nonutilitarian* means that the preference is for some less-than-objectively-useful aspect of a product.

Figure 7-6 Technology substitution: three generations of glass-making technology

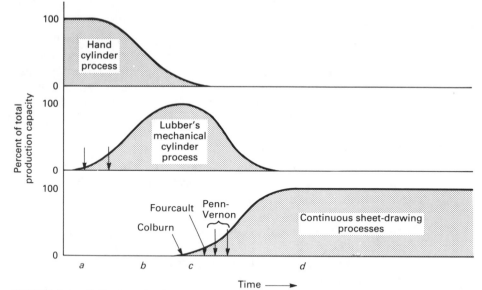

SOURCE: James R. Bright and Milton E. F. Schoeman, eds., *A Guide to Practical Technological Forecasting*. Reprinted by permission of James R. Bright, p. 108. Published by Prentice Hall, Englewood Cliffs, NJ 07632.

sors, who had probably said much the same about the difference between pens and the early typewriters). Some diet soft drink users have gotten used to the taste of saccharin and reject products which use aspartame, even though it is a superior-tasting sugar substitute. There is, for example, a devoted body of Tab® drinkers for just this reason.

The third explanation is that the remaining unconverted users may have needs that the new technology simply does not satisfy. The old product technology has typically had many years in which its products were adapted to fill the needs of the many special applications that exist in the corners of all markets. It takes time for the new product technology to be adapted to meet and serve all of these special needs.

In fact, it is entirely possible that pockets of demand for products based on the old technology may exist for extended periods of time because of the inability of the new technology to perform in certain applications. While computer-based word processing systems have all but replaced typewriters in most applications, there has still been demand for portable typewriters among those who write and travel. It now appears that the advent of portable laptop and notebook computers may finally allow word processing to replace the typewriter in even those applications.

Saturation is a science term which refers to the amount of moisture a gas can absorb, almost in the way that one can think of the capacity of a sponge to absorb water. At some point, adding water to either the air or a sponge causes an equal amount to be released. A market for a product can be said to be saturated when all of the potential buyers are using the product, when the market has absorbed all of the product it can use or consume.

The concept underlying market maturity is that the market has reached some maximum level of product saturation; further growth in sales is unlikely to come from the existing market of buyers (although population growth may cause increases in the number of buyers and, therefore, the product's sales). In some real sense, everyone who is a realistic prospect for the product is already buying and using it.

One can distinguish between theoretical and practical potential markets as well as between those in which the market size estimates are based on hard reality versus those in which hard reality is a difficult concept. Consider, for instance, the markets for electric kitchen ranges and soft drinks. The potential market for electric kitchen ranges is, theoretically, one per each dwelling unit that contains a kitchen. In practical terms, however, that potential can be qualified to include only those dwelling units which have electric power, or even more finely, those which have (or can afford to have installed) a 220-volt electrical circuit in the kitchen. Table 7-3, for example, shows the percentage of American households that owned various kinds of consumer electronics products in 1986 and 1990. While the penetration of television did increase, its movement was small in comparison to that experienced by the other products shown.

Calculating the theoretical and practical market potential for a product like soft drinks, however, is more difficult. Is the theoretical potential simply a measure of the number of individuals who could ever have a soft drink, that number times the number of occasions on which a soft drink might have been consumed, or something else? How one estimates the practical potential in the soft drink market is no easier. While soft drinks have apparently been successful in displacing other beverages (soft drinks now account for one fourth of all beverage consumption in the U.S; in 1989, consumption was more than 46 gallons of soft drinks for every man, woman, and child[37]), it is difficult to say what some upper limit penetration might be.

The concepts of penetration and saturation are of more than academic interest. They are hard measures of a product's progression through its evolutionary cycle. Such indicators, on an overall and segment basis, provide management with an assessment of performance and potential beyond those given by simple sales figures.

Social and Fashion Influences

While it is technology that makes products possible and the activities of businesses that make them available, it is only the approval of society that allows consumers to feel free to buy, use, and consume them. As noted in chapter 6, the rapid-growth stage of the life cycle is due to social acceptance through such processes as word of mouth and social imitation. The purpose of this discussion

---

[37] PepsiCo Annual Report, 1989, p. 80.

TABLE 7-3 *Penetration of Consumer Electronics in American Households*

	PERCENTAGE OF AMERICAN HOUSEHOLDS WITH EACH TYPE OF CONSUMER ELECTRONICS PRODUCT	
	1990	1986
Color television	96%	92%
Videocassette recorder	69	40
Answering machine	35	15
Cordless telephone	28	16
Compact disk player	22	5
Camcorder	11	2

SOURCE: Copyright © 1990 by The New York Times Company. Reprinted by permission.

is to indicate some of the ways that the evolutionary cycle is affected by factors which transcend the strictly economically utilitarian.

Virtually all products and services are subject to social influence. While clothing typically comes to mind first because of the well-known fashion phenomenon, there are few product categories that are immune to social influence. Exhibit 7-2 describes the limits to which the fashion phenomenon (acceptable one day, unacceptable the next) can go. Most highly influenced are those categories in which the aesthetic component is important. Such products as automobiles, houses, furniture and home furnishings, entertainment and music, and even foods and restaurants exhibit what can best be termed "fashion-oriented behavior."[38] To assume that fashion is concerned solely with aesthetics is to oversimplify the idea, however, for fashion-oriented behavior has been observed in even such esoteric pursuits as science, education, managerial thinking, and literature.

Fashion products seem to exhibit behavior similar to that predicted by the traditional classic life cycle. Few products have life cycles as distinct as fashions. Note that the focus is on the demand for an individual style currently in fashion (which varies), not the demand for the underlying functional good. People continue buying clothing, furniture, cars; but they buy only those items in the style corresponding to that which is currently fashionable.[39]

Fashions are temporary cyclical phenomena adopted by consumers for a particular time and situation.[40] Other definitions of fashion are also useful. Some have termed fashion the pursuit of novelty for its own sake, while others more simply regard it as the current mode of consumption behavior.[41]

Fashions are generally seen to have a slow rise to popularity followed by a period of continuing popularity with a rather abrupt decline. A single fashion cycle may last for several years, sometimes even as long as five to ten

[38] George B. Sproles, "Analyzing Fashion Life Cycles—Principles and Perspectives," *Journal of Marketing*, 45, no. 4 (fall 1981), 116–124.

[39] A style is a distinctive aesthetic expression which may or may not be fashionable at any given point in time.

[40] George B. Sproles, *Fashion: Consumer Behavior toward Dress* (Minneapolis, MN: Burgess Publishing Company, 1979).

[41] Dwight E. Robinson, "Fashion Theory and Product Design," *Harvard Business Review*, 36, no. 6 (November-December 1958), 126–138.

Fashion Hits Fruits and Vegetables

The two young men dressed in khaki slacks and sleeves-rolled-to-the-elbow button-down shirts were examining the fruit at Fairway on Broadway and 74th Street. Sandra S. Smith was there, too, and this is what she overheard:

First man: Would you like some nectarines?
Second man: Nectarines are yuppie.
First man: What about peaches?
Second man: Peaches are O.K.
First man, eyeing the MacIntoshes: Apples?
Second man: Not Granny Smith. They're yuppie. But Macs are O.K. Raspberries are yuppie, strawberries just pass. But be careful of melons. Watermelon is O.K., except for the round yuppie variety. Cantaloupes pass. Honeydews are tricky. Small is yuppie, you know.

Ms. Smith hadn't known. By now the two were out of earshot. She headed for the vegetables.

SOURCE: Copyright © 1989 by The New York Times Company. Reprinted by permission.

years.[42] Fads, on the other hand, enjoy equally rapid ascents and declines with no stable period in between. Some recognize a third category—the classic, which is never out of style but never the rage.[43]

Socially, fashion behavior exists in the tension between the human need to imitate and be one of the group and the opposite need to be different and unique. Underlying both drives is a need for variety and novelty in experiences. Fads are easily adopted styles and activities in which the novelty drive is dominant and whose very success, therefore, is the source of their rapid fall from favor.

Those who study fashion point out that fashions follow an inexorable cycle. As one noted authority put it,

In their shortsighted obsession with their own era, people forget that *fashion change is and has been incessant*, at least since civilization emerged from the dark ages. To prove this point for yourself, all you need do is review the history of any art, fine or applied. Has any period of painting, architecture, or literature repeated the style of its predecessor? . . . Of course not. Once stated, the law is obvious. Yet over and over again, people think and act as though it didn't exist. At every moment we tend to think that the ultimate in design has somehow been reached.[44]

[42] Sproles, "Analyzing Fashion Life Cycles."
[43] Chester R. Wasson, "How Predictable are Fashion and Other Life Cycles," *Journal of Marketing*, 32, no. 3 (July 1968), 36–43.
[44] Dwight E. Robinson, "Style Changes: Cyclical, Inexorable, and Foreseeable," *Harvard Business Review*, 53, no. 6 (November-December 1975), p. 122.

Two kinds of fashion cycles seem to operate. The first, of which the afore-mentioned author is speaking, is the long run. Consensus is that fashion follows a principle of historical continuity—each new fashion being an outgrowth of the previously existing fashion. New fashions, therefore, make only small styling changes rather than revolutionary or visually dramatic changes.[45] Figure 7-7 gives one example: the fifty-year progression to longer and lower cars. The car roof has steadily become lower and lower, by about half an inch in the typical year, from approximately 75 inches to about 50 inches in the mid 1970s. As the researcher noted,

> It is tempting to speculate how many billions of dollars every single inch of this mighty downward compression has cost. . . . It is as though fashion were a heavy hammer pounding the car body ever flatter. Perhaps in the beginning all the designer needed to do was lower the roof a few inches, sacrificing a little headroom. But it soon became all too evident that, in order to wage the campaign for the very longer, lower look, car designers could not leave the mechanics of the automobile to the engineers.[46]

But long-run forecasts are of value only once one can live through the short run. And short-run fashion forecasts are notably more difficult. For while the long-run trend in the height of a car (or skirt lengths—another focus of fashion researchers) may be apparent when years of data are observed as a whole, the data also show more randomness on a year-to-year basis. Beyond this, the long range forecasts concentrate on the big picture, the silhouette of the car or clothing article. There are innumerable other important elements—ornamentation, color, texture, and the like—which exhibit substantial variation from year to year. In short, there is little of a scientific nature that can help the decision maker.

One cannot overestimate the impact that social influence has on the life cycle of products. Society's definition of acceptable behavior and acceptable products is all powerful. For some years now, for example, society has been favoring white distilled alcoholic beverages over brown beverages. More simply put, fashion has preferred vodka over whisky—whiskey's share of the U.S. alcoholic beverage market has declined from 48.8% in 1978 to 39.6% in 1988[47] Taste is a socially formed characteristic, and it makes little difference whether it is the rise in the popularity of vodka, jogging, and seafood or the decline in whiskey, tennis, and beef—the manager needs to be able to anticipate and respond.

PROFITS, CASH FLOW, AND THE LIFE CYCLE

The success of products and services in the marketplace is due not only to their competitive superiority but to the ability and willingness of the business to invest in their growth. As noted in our discussion of the PEC approach, market

[45] Sproles, "Analyzing Fashion Life Cycles."
[46] Robinson, "Style Changes," pp. 124, 125.
[47] *Business Week*, "What Stirs the Spirit Makers: Vodka, Vodka, Vodka," June 12, 1989, pp. 54, 55.

Figure 7-7   Fifty-year progression to longer and lower cars

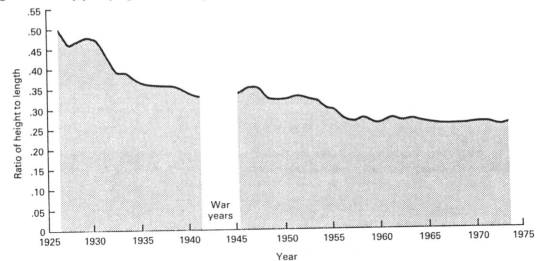

SOURCE: Reprinted by permission of *Harvard Business Review*. An exhibit from "Style Changes: Cyclical, Inexorable, and Foreseeable" by Dwight E. Robinson, November/December 1975. Copyright © 1975 by the President and Fellows of Harvard College; all rights reserved.

growth is as much a function of what the firm does as it is the tapping of latent demand for a product. In a very real sense, the cash flow and access to cash that a business possesses is as important to a product's success as is the product's characteristics.

Think, for a minute, about two different businesses. Assume that the owners of one of these businesses are uniformly well off. All have other incomes and assets sufficient to take care of their financial needs. Let's assume that the second business, on the other hand, is owned and managed by individuals for whom the business is their only source of income. The first business is obviously advantaged. It can forgo current income to invest in such business-building activities as continuing product development, intensive promotion, and market development activities that the second firm cannot afford.

A product's profitability and cash flow, therefore, are both a cause and an effect of the actions and results observed over the life of an individual product or product category. The start-up of a new product business, its market entry, and the rate of the growth or decline of that business all have different impacts on profitability and cash flow, which, in turn, either constrain or open up present and future strategies and actions.

The manager needs to understand the nature of the relationships involved and the magnitude of the effects that are observed. Just as an army is said to march on its stomach, a business needs profits and cash to keep going. Even in the current highly leveraged era, cash management is still important. In general, the relationships of concern are simple:

1. Start-up and entry always result in negative profits and cash flow.
2. Rapid growth is a cash drain; slow or negative growth produces cash.

3. Cash needs are a function of the market environment and business strategy.
4. Large-share businesses generate relatively more cash than small-share businesses in the same environment.[48]

Start-up and Entry

A business or product is most financially vulnerable at the point of start-up and market entry. The immediate and cumulative effects of R&D expenditures, capital investment in facilities, working capital investments in the form of raw materials and finished goods inventories, expenses in the form of advertising and sales force training and selling materials, all in the absence of any income from sales, naturally produce negative cash flows. Figure 7-8 depicts the profit and cash relationships generally observed in the early stages of the life cycle.

Empirical reality supports this theory. Table 7-4 shows the results of a study of sixty-eight new ventures launched by *Fortune* 200 companies compared to a sample of older businesses drawn from the PIMS database.[49] The median new business earned a negative 40% ROI in each of the first two years following start-up and a negative 14% in each of the next two years. In other words, whatever investment had been incurred prior to start-up was increased by losses in an amount equal to 80% of the initial investment in the first two years and another 28% by the end of the fourth year.

No business in the sample had a positive cash flow in the first two years, and only six in the sample had a positive cash flow in the second two years. Cash flow for the median business did not become positive in the first eight years. The breakeven point for cumulative cash flow, therefore, is further into the future.

As seen in Table 7-4, profitability was no better, with the median new business still generating losses into its eighth year. A few businesses in the sample achieved profits in the first two years (twelve of the sixty-eight, or about 18%). By year four, the number had increased to 38% of the sample. Interestingly enough, seven of the twelve businesses profitable at the end of their second year were no longer profitable in the fourth year. Apparently, gaining early profitability does little to improve continued profitability.

These data are for new venture start-ups, which involve more than the simple addition of a new product to an existing product line. They were defined as a business marketing a product that the parent company had not previously marketed and that required new equipment, new people, or new knowledge.

---

[48] These four points and the following discussion are based on Bradley T. Gale and Ben Branch, "Cash Flow Analysis: More Important Than Ever," *Harvard Business Review*, 59, no. 4 (July-August 1981), 131–136.

[49] Ralph Biggadike, "The Risky Business of Diversification," *Harvard Business Review* 57, no. 3 (May-June 1979), pp. 103–111.

Figure 7-8 Revenues, expenditures and cash relationships of a product

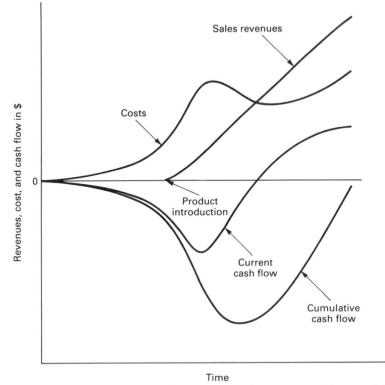

Time

SOURCE: Adapted from C. Merle Crawford, *New Product Management* (Homewood, IL: Richard D. Irwin, Inc., 1983), p. 491.

This definition is similar to that used to designate the start of a new product market in the population ecology model.

Growth Rates and Cash Flow

Mathematically, cash flow is inversely related to the rate of growth. Cash flow is positive when growth is slow or negative and is lowest when sales growth is fast. (The mechanisms that cause this behavior were discussed in the preceding section.)

In fact, if one understands the relationship between the capital requirements of a business and sales growth, then one can calculate the ROI needed to break even on a cash-flow basis for any given growth rate. If one makes the assumption, for example, that there are no long-run scale economies in the capital requirements of a business (i.e., investment grows at the same rate as sales; 20% in sales growth requires a 20% growth in assets), then the breakeven ROI is calculated as

TABLE 7-4   *Median Financial Performance for a Sample of New Business Ventures from Start-up through Adolescence: A Comparison with Mature Businesses*

	START-UP		ADOLESCENCE		MATURITY
PERFORMANCE RATIO	YEARS 1 AND 2	YEARS 3 AND 4	YEARS 5 AND 6	YEARS 7 AND 8[b]	AVERAGE AGE ABOUT 18 YEARS
Return on investment	−40%[a]	−14%	−8%	+7%	+17%
Cash flow—sales	−90	−29	−13	−4	+3
Pretax profit—sales	−39	−10	−5	−4	+9
Gross margin—sales	+15	+28	+19	+22	+26
Number of businesses	68	47	61	61	454

[a]Performance of the median business is shown because the sample performance was spread over a wide range. The median is not affected by extreme cases and is therefore less likely to mislead.

[b]Profit-to-sales is negative, while ROI is positive because these averages are medians, not means (mean ROI is +5% and mean profit-to-sales is +1%).

SOURCE: Reprinted by permission of *Harvard Business Review*. An exhibit from "The Risky Business of Diversification by Ralph Biggadike, May/June 1979. Copyright © 1979 by the President and Fellows of Harvard College; all rights reserved.

$$\text{Breakeven ROI (pretax, preinterest)} = \frac{2g}{1 + g}$$

where g is the growth rate expressed as a decimal.[50]

Figure 7-9 compares this theoretical calculation with the average actual ROI achieved by the businesses in the PIMS database. As can be seen, if a business earns an average ROI, it will be able to generate a positive cash flow up to about a 15% growth rate.

Two points should be noted. First, the preceding formula assumes that assets grow one to one with the growth of the business. If, on the other hand, there are scale economies in the capital investment or inventory requirements of a business (the ratio of investment to sales declines as the business gets larger), then the ROI needed to break even on cash flow will be lower than that shown.

The second point to be noted is that the cash flow being discussed is achieved at the operating level—before taxes, interest payments, or dividends. A highly leveraged, tax- and interest-paying business will find it needs a far greater return to break even on cash at the business level.

Cash Flow, the Environment, and Strategy

Cash is a function of the growth rate inherent in the opportunity and the inflation rate (both environmental factors) and the business's strategy. Figure 7-10 shows how these are related. It has already been shown how increases in unit demand require cash. Inflation can have a similar effect independent of real unit

[50] S. J. Q. Robinson, "What Growth Rate Can You Achieve?" *Long Range Planning*, August 1979, pp. 7–12. For example, if $g = .10$, then the ROI for a breakeven cash-flow rate = $\frac{2(.10)}{(1 + .10)} = 18\%$.

Figure 7-9 ROI for breakeven cash-flow increases with sales growth

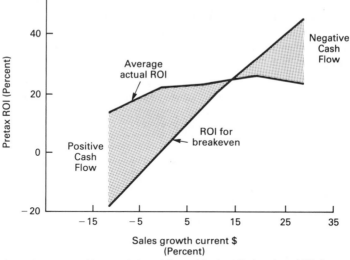

Figure 7-10 Relationship between cash needs, environment, and strategy

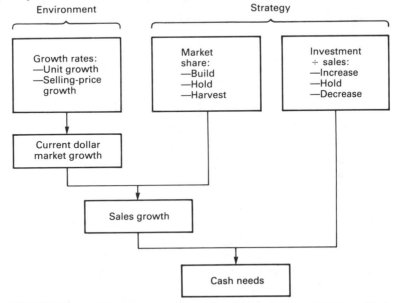

growth. Few businesses are able to grow their prices fast enough to offset the growth in the prices of their input factors.[51] In dollar terms, the market growth rate is the result of real unit growth plus inflationary growth.

The business's strategy interacts with this opportunity by its market-share strategy and the decisions the firm makes about the kind of relationship it will maintain between investment and sales. A decision to grow share always uses cash (except in markets where share increases are offset by declines in market size). A decision to grow share in an environment characterized by high real unit growth and inflation rates uses a lot of cash.

The strategy the firm uses to grow share can have a powerful impact on cash flow. For example, one way businesses grow share is to speed up delivery and/or to increase product variety (colors, sizes, etc.). Both typically require growth in inventories, unfavorably (from a cash viewpoint) changing the investment-to-sales ratio. A hallmark of competition that one observes over time in a market is an increase in product variety and a decrease in delivery time.

SUMMARY

Product markets and the competition that occurs within them are best understood in dynamic rather than static terms. They reflect the continual change that occurs in customer needs and tastes, competitor strategies, the pace of fashion and technological change, and the ambition and creativity of those managing the competing businesses. This means that the war is never won—that competition in product markets is best conceived of as a continuing series of skirmishes and battles.

The strategist has several models of that process which help in understanding the nature, shape, and likely future courses of those skirmishes. The classic product life cycle is a simplistic conception of the process based on the biological analogy of the life cycle of an individual member of a species. The product evolutionary cycle uses instead the evolutionary cycle from biology, which explains the growth and proliferation of species. This model provides a useful conception of the process by which a new product form evolves into an increasingly diverse, efficient, and complex family of products serving a wide variety of users and applications.

The population ecology model provides a strong theoretical basis for the process by which the population of supplying firms grows to serve a market and how, based on the different strategic problems that each faces on entry, they develop unique competitive strategies. The model shows the relative advantages that accrue to the different strategic choices available—early versus later entry and specialist versus generalist segment scopes.

Two models provide more managerially tuned interpretations of market evolution in accord with the theoretical models. The competitive life cycle dem-

---

[51] A retail business is a good illustration of this phenomenon. Goods bought at preinflationary prices (even when sold at inflated prices) must be replaced in stock with those costing even more.

onstrates how initial penetration and later competition is based on the value-in-use a buyer obtains from the product and its supplier and why the first supplier can obtain a premium for its product. The model of competitive strategies explicitly demonstrates the strategic choices available to competitors in the form of a choice between strategies that aim to win primary or selective demand battles. It further points out how almost any strategy chosen leaves open some other part of a market for competitors—that having it all may be impossible strategically.

This chapter ended with a discussion of some of the dynamics underlying the models. It showed how the insights were best applied at the level of the product category rather than the technology or industry level or the brand or variant level. Penetration and saturation were shown to be useful concepts and measures of market development, and the impact of social influence was explored to add greater depth to the process. Finally, it was shown how both cash flow and profits varied over the evolution of a product market. Cash flow was shown to be simultaneously a result, a constraint, and a strategic weapon.

8

CREATING STRATEGIC CHANGE
IN EVOLUTIONARY MARKETS

The bases of competition in a given product market seldom stay the same over time. Change occurs in all three of the major forces affecting a product's strategy: (1) Competitors learn to imitate and offset the strategies of successful firms, (2) the needs and marketplace power of customers evolve, and (3) the economic and political environment changes continually. This chapter deals with how the firm can create strategies which anticipate and adapt to the changing bases of competition over a product market's evolution. It begins with a theory which identifies the natural points for achieving significant strategic change. It then examines the key strategic issues at each of the key stages of the evolutionary development of a product market.

A THEORY OF STRATEGIC CHANGE

As markets evolve, the requirements needed for success change.[1] For example, in the early stages of the development of a product market, the focus is on the product and its application to customer needs. This requires expertise in R&D and applications engineering issues. In the rapid-growth stage, production issues start to become more important and obtaining the capital necessary to fund the capacity expansions needed to keep pace with rapid growth becomes a critical issue. As noted in chapter 6, in the maturity stage the key success factor in many industries is clearly manufacturing process superiority. As an industry evolves, therefore, the basic nature of competition within it evolves accordingly.

The theory of strategic change is simple: During transition periods between evolutionary stages or phases, the leading firms in an industry have no special advantages over competitors.[2] The logic of this is compelling. The leading firm

[1] Charles W. Hofer and Dan Schendel, *Strategy Formulation: Analytical Concepts* (St. Paul, MN: West Publishing Company, 1978); and Jorge Alberto Sousa De Vasconcellos E Sa and Donald C. Hambrick, "Key Success Factors: Test of a General Theory in the Mature Industrial-Product Sector," *Strategic Management Journal*, 10, no. 4 (July-August 1989), 367–382.
[2] Hofer and Schendel, *Strategy Formulation*, p. 107.

must have been exceptionally strong in the key success factors needed up to the transition point for it to be successful. Its leading position validates that observation. However, during the transition period those skills no longer retain potency, as success during the next phase will require a new set of skills. Except for the advantages gained by its possession of the leading market share, the leader therefore is on a par with its competitors when it comes to possessing the key skills needed in the new competitive environment. In fact, the organizational inertia inherent in a heretofore successful business (discussed in chapter 7) suggests that the leader may find change more difficult to accomplish than others.

Theoretically, then, during these transitional periods alert followers and new entrants can displace leaders. They can accomplish this by being the first to develop the strategies that will be the most effective in addressing the needs of the future competitive environment. Consider, for example, the transition from small-scale production to mass production that must occur to support large-volume markets. Figure 8-1 (seen earlier as Figure 5-11) demonstrates the relationship between production technology and the evolution and growth of a product market. To gain strategic advantage, it is not enough for the firm to move down the diagonal in lockstep with other producers.

Strategic advantage comes only from having the insight and willingness either to lead the pack down the diagonal or to move off the diagonal. For example, the first firm in a rapidly growing market to adapt its product offerings to large-volume production methods gains strategic advantage by having adapted to the success requirements of the new competitive stage before competitors. This way, the firm has both volume and cost positions while competitors struggle to meet the market's volume requirements at a high cost.

Alternatively, the firm that moves off the diagonal (or the accepted mode of the industry) can also gain strategic advantage. For example, the business that retains small-scale production technologies while competitors have all moved on to large-volume methods can serve markets for special and custom products more easily and gain competitive advantage in that manner.

Once it has gained competitive advantage, the firm must use that advantage. It must not be content just to increase profitability. It must use that advantage to gain share (perhaps by lowering prices to levels competitors find difficult to match) or by building barriers to effective competition (perhaps by using its profits to fund product R&D). Since competitors will imitate the firm's actions in an effort to neutralize its competitive advantage, the firm must take all actions which will make its actions difficult to imitate or, alternatively, continue to improve its products and processes such that even if competitors are able to duplicate its present position, the firm will be even farther ahead.

Hofer and Schendel state that major changes are easiest during the development, shakeout, and decline stages of a product market's evolution.[3] They feel that major shifts during other periods can occur only (1) if the industry

---

[3] Hofer and Schendel, *Strategy Formulation*, p. 107.

Figure 8-1   Relationship between product technology and evolution of a product market

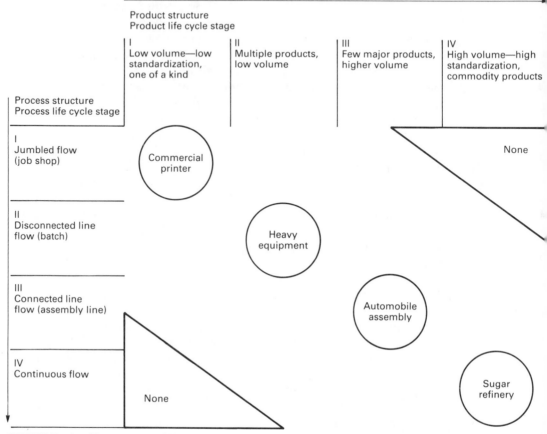

SOURCE: Reprinted by permission of *Harvard Business Review*. An exhibit from "Linking Manufacturing Process and Product Life Cycles" by Robert H. Hayes and Steven C. Wheelwright, January/February 1978. Copyright © 1978 by the President and Fellows of Harvard College; all rights reserved.

leader commits a major blunder, (2) through a major investment program by a well-positioned follower, (3) through acquisition of one or more existing competitors, or (4) through the accretion of many small, consistent incremental advantages over a long period of time. While such efforts can indeed result in major strategic change, as happened when Philip Morris bought Miller Beer and gave it the funds necessary to launch an all-out attack on the beer market, they are more difficult and more expensive than those opportunities which arise naturally during evolutionary transitions.

Strategic Windows

The term *strategic windows* is used to "describe the limited periods during which the 'fit' between the key requirements of a market and the particular competencies of a firm competing in that market is at an optimum."[4] The key is to recognize when change is incremental and therefore attainable by existing competitors and when it introduces a **discontinuity** that favors only some subset of the incumbents or even new entrants. The same change can represent an opening window of opportunity to one firm at the same time that it closes that same window for others.

Consider the personal computer business, for example. Its creation and acceptance by the market opened a strategic window for a myriad of small entrepreneurial computer manufacturers who were able quickly to design, manufacture, and market small computers and thus capitalize on the rapidly growing market. However, after several years of success, volume had grown to the point that another strategic window opened. This second strategic window advantaged firms that could manufacture at low cost and at high volume and that had the kind of reputation and staying power needed for larger businesses to accept PCs. That strategic window favored IBM, whose PC model became the dominant design. While the arrival of IBM closed the strategic window for many small computer manufacturers, it opened one for assemblers in Hong Kong and Singapore, who were able to capitalize on IBM's dominant design and hurriedly designed and shipped IBM-compatible PC clones.

Two strategic windows arise in market evolution that are difficult to recognize. The first of these is the development of *new primary demand* opportunities whose requirements for success differ considerably from those needed in serving existing market segments. In the PC example, the original growth in the market came from technically sophisticated hobbyists, a market well known to the original firms in the business. But the next wave of growth came from customers who were not technically sophisticated, from customers who needed more hand holding and the assurance of low risk that came from a well-known and accepted supplier such as IBM.

The second less obvious kind of strategic window is that caused by *market redefinition.* Market redefinition occurs when competing suppliers attempt to redefine the direction a product market is taking by the products it chooses to offer. The cold-remedies market, for example, has been redefined several times. Early offerings treated single symptoms such as headaches, coughs, congestion, and fever, for example. The next generation offered products in which several ingredients were mixed to alleviate multiple symptoms. The third generation created products designed for specific situations such as coughs and colds or sinus and allergies. Each shift in definition favored some brands at the expense of others.

When automatic teller machines (ATMs) were first introduced, they were successfully sold by their originator as stand-alone, offline components. As acceptance grew and computer firms such as Burroughs, IBM, and Honeywell were attracted to the market, they tried to redefine the market to favor their competencies. In essence, this meant to make the ATM part of the bank's entire

[4] Derek F. Abell, "Strategic Windows," *Journal of Marketing*, 42, no. 3 (July 1978), p. 21.

on-line Electronic Funds Transfer System (EFTS). Such a redefinition, of course, favored the computer firms' competencies (the ability to design intelligent units and to integrate them into a customer's online information system) and disadvantaged those who made stand-alone components.

The concept of a strategic window is of value. It reminds managers of two important facts: the importance of timing and the importance of fit. It is not enough to recognize or have one without the other.

STRATEGY IN THE EARLY PHASES OF PRODUCT MARKET EVOLUTION

A host of sayings in society stress the importance of early actions and positions. From "The early bird gets the worm" to "As the twig is bent so groweth the tree" and "Mighty oaks from tiny acorns grow," we are exhorted to pay close attention to being first and to the actions we take during those early stages. These same sayings appear to apply to market entry and the importance of the positions taken during the early stages of a market's development. This discussion reviews what is important to the development of competitive product strategy during the early stages of the development of a product market.

The Pros and Cons of Early Entry into Rapidly Growing Markets

It is almost axiomatic that growth markets are attractive. To be in on the ground floor of a new and growing product market is, in many markets at least, a seeming prerequisite to participation in its later stages. Yet participation in growth opportunities is not without its risks. As economists are fond of noting, "no risk, no reward." The arguments for early entry, presented next, are followed by a discussion of the major risks of early entry.[5] Much theoretical and empirical work on the advantages which accrue to pioneers has been done in the last ten years. That work is examined later in this chapter.

Arguments for Early Entry

It Is Easier to Gain Share in Growing Markets. Two arguments are advanced for early entry into rapidly growing markets. The first argument is that since the market is growing rapidly, there are large numbers of new users who have yet to establish relationships with any supplier. It is not as difficult or necessary, therefore, to woo them away from a competitor's product as it would be if the firm were to enter at a later stage of its development.

The second argument in favor of rapid entrance is that it is easier to grow share because, while your actions may have caused competitors to lose share, the speed of the market's growth may allow them to achieve dollar and unit volume gains and therefore not react as strongly. In comparison, share gains in

---

[5] This discussion is adapted from David A. Aaker and George S. Day, "The Perils of High Growth Markets," *Strategic Management Journal*, 7, no. 6 (November–December 1986), 409–421.

stagnant or slow-growth markets always result in declines in competitors' dollar and unit volumes. Since many businesses manage more on dollars than share points, the argument goes, competitive response will be less strong in the growth case than in the stagnant case.

SHARE GAINS IN GROWING MARKETS HAVE GREATER LONG-RUN VALUE.   The key assumption in this argument is that once gained, the share will be held through subsequent periods. If the assumption is true, then the dollar value of a share point in a rapidly growing market increases over time and is, therefore, worth more in comparison to a share point gained in a flat market whose value remains constant.[6] Early entrants do have an advantage over later entrants in retaining share, as some have noted.[7] However, it is important to note that share which is bought by promotions or low-ball pricing is less likely to be retained.

GROWTH MARKETS EXPERIENCE LESS PRICE PRESSURE.   Rapid growth is a clear sign that the market places a high value on the product. Buyers are not being deterred by existing price levels (by definition, why else the rapid growth?) and are less likely to put pressure on prices. Furthermore, there is typically an excess of demand over supply, adding to the support for premium pricing. As noted in the foregoing discussion of the competitive cycle, early entrants can maintain a premium over later entrants because they provide customers with lower risk since they provide known quality and performance. Of course, this state of affairs seldom lasts forever. Premium prices are one sure way of attracting competitors who bring additional capacity and, sooner or later, reduce prices overall.

EARLY ENTRANTS GAIN EXPERIENCE ADVANTAGES.   As discussed in chapter 5, the experience curve can provide cost advantages to early entrants, who can achieve large market shares and therefore accumulate experience faster than competitors. However, if all competitors are attempting similar strategies, the results may be a ruinous level of competition instead of competitive advantage. Nonetheless, in industries and markets where there are strong scale and learning economies, the firm may have little choice but to enter early and take those risks if it is to participate in the industry.

Such a strategy can work, however, if the experience curve effect is significant *and* the firm can keep its learning proprietary (secret). In this case, entry barriers are kept very high and, as a simulation of the situation showed, fewer than a handful of firms can exist in an industry when the learning curve lies in the normal range of 70% to 90%.[8] However, this circumstance is unlikely. Some have suggested that 60% to 90% of all learning ultimately diffuses outside the

[6] Aneel Karnini, "The Value of Market Share and the Product Life Cycle: A Game Theoretic Model," *Management Science*, 30, no. 6 (June 1984), 696–712.
[7] Richard Schmalensee, "Product Differentiation Advantages of Pioneering Brands," *American Economic Review*, 72, no. 3 (June 1982), 349–365.
[8] Marvin B. Lieberman, "The Learning Curve, Diffusion, and Competitive Strategy," *Strategic Management Journal*, 8, no. 5 (September-October 1987), 441–452.

firm and that in many industries (e.g., chemical products), learning occurs primarily on an industry-wide basis.[9]

EARLY ENTRANTS GAIN TECHNOLOGICALLY.   In many state-of-the-art markets, much technological knowledge is created in the application of the technology to real customer problems. Since customers are seldom willing to work with more than one supplier, later entrants not only lose out on the technological knowledge created but also have difficulty finding customer sites at which to gain the necessary applications experience. While first-generation products are frequently leapfrogged in such rapidly advancing technologies, those with market contacts and experience are, nonetheless, still in the best position to catch up.

On a behavioral note, experienced managers in technology-based businesses point out that there is a real difference in R&D productivity with and without the pressure of an actual operating business. They note that while it is wise to wait until the critical inventions are made before actually entering a business, the problems inherent in commercializing any technology are never solved without the pressure of an operating business demanding their solution. In simple terms, the firm does not learn as much through R&D when there is no burning need to achieve as it does when immediate business pressures force solutions.

EARLY ENTRY CAN DETER POTENTIAL COMPETITORS.   A major concern underlying many decisions is "what's the other guy gonna do?" Early entry into a market is not simply a signal of a firm's intentions with respect to a market, it is a commitment. Actions say more about a firm's real intentions than any announcement, press conference, or contract signing. The very presence of a firm in a business makes entry less attractive to others. Aggressive entry in the form of large production facilities and ambitious advertising and sales force expenditures sends a message to competitors that the entrant intends to win.

There are two keys to how well this strategy works. The first is whether early entry allows the firm (and is perceived by competitors) to erect strong barriers to subsequent competitive entry. The strongest barrier is to build sufficient capacity to serve the market before a competitor can, which effectively renders uneconomic any subsequent investment on the competitor's part. As Judge Learned Hand wrote in the famous antitrust judgment against Alcoa,

> It was not inevitable that it [Alcoa] should always anticipate increases in demand for ingot and be prepared to serve them. Nothing compelled it to keep doubling and redoubling its capacity before others entered the field. It insists that it never excluded competitors but we can think of no more effective exclusion than progressively to embrace each new opportunity as it opened, and to face each new comer with new capacity already geared into a giant organization."[10]

Economic analyses are clear about this strategy. In one analysis, it was shown that if the growth of a market is foreseen, it will always pay existing firms

[9] Marvin B. Lieberman, "The Learning Curve and Pricing in the Chemical Processing Industries," *Rand Journal of Economics*, 15, no. 2 (summer 1984), 213–228.

[10] *U.S. v. Aluminum Company of America et al.*, 44F.Supp.97(1941) 148F, 2d 416(1945), p. 431.

to preempt the market by building new plants before the time when it would first pay new firms to enter. Further, and interestingly, if the existing monopoly firm does not add that capacity, the competition among the potential new entrants will lead to the addition of the unneeded capacity at virtually the save time that the monopolist would have added it.[11]

The second key to the success of a preemptive entry strategy is the perceived importance of the market to potential competitors. If a market is of critical importance to a competitor's long-run strategy, entry into it by a rival may simply spur the competitor to enter sooner rather than later.

ENTRY IS A CHEAP OPTION.   Given a large potential payoff from a new technology or market, a high level of uncertainty in the direction it will take, the combination of skills it will take to win, and the necessity to participate if one is to have any chance in the market, early entry can, in effect, be equivalent to buying a financial option. Buying the option gives the firm the right to play and the option to make the next move.[12] What drives the entrants is the philosophy that, as one observer put it, "Early birds are not always winners in product markets, but late comers are almost always losers."[13]

The value of any potential losses that may be incurred if the first step does not bring results may be insignificant compared to the potential gains if it does. While this lottery-style argument may not sound managerial, there are instances in which it is sound statistically and financially. The key is to know when to cut the losses.

Arguments against Early Entry.   Just as there are sound arguments in support of early entry into new, rapidly growing markets, so too are there arguments which stress the negative aspects—arguments which remind one that the difference between an opportunity and a problem is one of perspective. Many of the problems of emerging, technologically based growth industries were covered thoroughly in chapter 6, so this discussion will avoid repetition.[14]

TOO MANY COMPETITORS MAY ENTER.   New markets with a great deal of promise often attract more competitors than they may ever be able to support. Consider the computer Winchester (hard) disk drive business, for example.[15] In 1978, sales were $27 million, but analysts forecasted revenue growth to reach $700 million in 1983 (twenty-six times 1978 volume), a figure which they shortly revised to $1.1 billion (forty times 1978 volume). At that, they expected 1984

[11] B. Curtis Eaton and Richard G. Lipsey, "The Theory of Market Pre-Emption: The Persistence of Excess Capacity and Monopoly in Growing Spatial Markets," *Economica*, 46 (May 1979), 149–158. For another view, see Ram C. Rao and David P. Rutenberg, "Preempting an Alert Rival: Strategic Timing of the First Plant by Analysis of Sophisticated Rivalry," *The Bell Journal of Economics*, 10, no. 2 (autumn 1979), 412–428.

[12] Robin Wensley, Patrick Barwise, and Paul Marsh, "Strategic Investment Decisions," in Jagdish N. Sheth, ed., *Research in Marketing*, vol. 8 (Greenwich, CT: JAI Press, 1987).

[13] William A. Sahlman and Howard H. Stevenson, "Capital Market Myopia," *Journal of Business Venturing*, 1, no. 1 (winter 1985), p. 8.

[14] See Francisco-Javier Olleros, "Emerging Industries and the Burnout of Pioneers," *Journal of Product Innovation Management*, 3, no. 1 (March 1986), 5–18.

[15] Sahlman and Stevenson, "Capital Market Myopia," p. 18.

volume to grow a further 36%, to $1.5 billion. Prospects such as that are tempt-ing to any potential entrant.

By 1984, some forty-three different manufacturers had entered the business assisted by $400 million from professional venture capital firms and over $800 million raised in public offerings of common stock. In the middle of 1983, the market valuation of the top twelve companies was $5.4 billion. However, by the end of 1984 that valuation had fallen to $1.4 billion. The reason for this precipi-tous drop was that the aggregate net income of those twelve firms in the quarter ended September 30, 1984, was only $2.3 million compared to an average of $24.2 million in each of the previous three quarters. In the words of those who have studied this situation, "The industry attracted so many resources that the growth had high probability of being unprofitable. Excesses in the capital market turned an opportunity into a disaster."[16]

TECHNOLOGY MAY CHANGE.   The early entrant that necessarily makes a commitment to a technology may find itself leapfrogged by a wait-and-see com-petitor who learns from the early entrant's mistakes and launches a superior technology. Priam, one of the earliest (1978) start-ups in the computer hard disk drive industry, for example, originally intended to produce 14-inch, 34-megabyte drives. However, before production could even begin, competitors announced competitive 8-inch products and Priam was forced to start a parallel develop-ment for an 8-inch line of drives. Within a year, Seagate (a 1979 start-up) an-nounced a 5.25-inch drive, which it began delivering in July 1980.

Every entrant in the computer hard disk drive business learned something from previous entrants in terms of how to manufacture and the best available technologies. Later entrants also benefited from better knowledge about the nature of the industry and could better tailor plans to match emerging customer needs.

RESOURCE NEEDS ARE HIGH.   Those early entrants who do succeed face the problems of coping with the resource needs success poses. Many fast-growing firms are simply unable to generate sufficient cash to finance their growth, and they enter bankruptcy or are bought out. Others lose control of costs as the firm experiences hypergrowth. Still others cannot keep pace with the need for quality people.

This is the classic dilemma of a growth industry. Unless a business staffs, builds, and finances for growth, it can never achieve it. However, if it prepares for growth which falters or does not arrive on schedule, it is faced with the painful and sometimes permanently damaging task of scaling back people and assets. In such situations, according to those who know, it always seems that the next $1 million is all the firm needs, but history shows that this is unlikely to be the case.[17]

THE PROMISED GROWTH MAY NOT ARRIVE.   There are countless examples of promised market growth which just does not materialize. As someone once put

[16] Sahlman and Stevenson, "Capital Market Myopia," p. 7.
[17] Sahlman and Stevenson, "Capital Market Myopia," p. 23.

it, forecasting is difficult, especially when it involves the future. In one study of ninety new product, market, and technology announcements which appeared in the *Wall Street Journal, Business Week,* and *Fortune* from 1960 to 1979, the growth forecasted failed to materialize in 55% of the cases.[18] As noted earlier, the firm which has planned and staffed for growth may be in serious trouble when such growth fails to materialize. Docutel, the creator of automatic teller machines, expanded its sales force from seventeen to fifty people in 1973 but, when expected market growth failed to occur in 1974, found its reputation was seriously damaged as it cut back on sales personnel.[19]

KEY SUCCESS FACTORS MAY CHANGE.   As noted earlier in this chapter, as markets evolve over time the skills and resources needed to be successful change. One of the more common is the switch in focus from product technology to process technology as the volume in an industry grows and products become standardized. This change is behind the classic shakeout observed in many growing industries as the small pioneers that have been unable to shift into the large-scale, capital-intensive mode fail or are bought out.

Equally common is the switch in market focus required for success. The failure of the three pioneering firms in the personal computer industry (MITS, IMSAI, and Processor Technology) seems to have stemmed from a failure to understand how the nature of their markets necessarily changed as demand grew. When these firms started, they served what could be termed a specialty market made of technically sophisticated computer buffs. As the market grew, it became more mass and was composed of relatively unsophisticated, demanding, and price-sensitive individuals. The pioneering three, however, could be described as technology driven and could not accommodate the new thinking required to serve the different market. In two years, from 1976 to 1978, they disappeared and were replaced by three new entrants capable of understanding the needs of mass markets—Radio Shack, Commodore, and Apple.[20]

REWARDS TO SUCCESSFUL PIONEERS: THE THEORY[21]

It has been long observed informally that successful pioneers seem to enjoy long-term benefits. Conventional marketing wisdom has noted that me-too products—those claiming equivalent performance to an original entrant—seldom achieve either the same share or are able to command the same price as the original. Work done at the Federal Trade Commission (FTC) found, for example, that pioneering brands of prescription drugs enjoy long-lived advan-

[18] Steven P. Schnaars and Conrad Berenson, "Growth Market Forecasting Revisited: A Look Back at a Look Forward," *California Management Review,* 28, no. 4 (summer 1986), 71–88.
[19] "Docutel Corp.," Harvard Business School Case 9-578-073.
[20] Olleros, "Emerging Industries."
[21] Much of the following discussion is based on the study of successful pioneers—those who survive. Until longitudinal studies are performed which study both those who survive and those who do not, much of this discussion should be read with that in mind.

tages over later entrants that even lower price cannot overcome. In this study, only by being different—offering distinct therapeutic benefits—could later entrants overcome that advantage.[22]

Bain, whose early work on entry barriers in the mid-1950s formed the basis of much current strategic thinking, found that "the advantage to established sellers accruing from *buyer preferences* for their products as opposed to potential entrant products is on average larger and more frequent in occurrence at large values than any other barrier to entry" (emphasis added).[23] His work led him to believe that there were some fundamental consumer processes at work which resulted in the development of strong and stable product preference patterns in the favor of those who were first to market.[24]

Schmalensee, an economist, was prompted by these precedents to explore the issue from a theoretical basis. He created a relatively simple model of the process which was built around the concept of "experience goods"—those products for which the only way a consumer can resolve uncertainty about quality is to purchase a brand and try it. His model had a number of strong assumptions which subjected the preference and quality notion to a tough test. He assumed (1) that products either worked or they did not, (2) that the second entrant was objectively equal to the first, (3) that the pioneer does not respond competitively to the entrance of the second, and (4) that there was no advertising. These four conditions are such that, objectively, buyers should divide purchases equally between the two suppliers since the only difference between the two is the time of entry.

The result of the model, however, is to show that the pioneering brand can, equally objectively, obtain a long-run price advantage because, once buyers use the product, they will be willing to pay more for it, if it works, because they are not certain the second product will work. In Schmalensee's model, the second entrant must offer a price reduction to persuade consumers to try the product and, therefore, learn about it. "When consumers become convinced that the first brand in any product class performs satisfactorily, that brand becomes the standard against which subsequent entrants are rationally judged. It thus becomes harder for later entrants to persuade consumers to invest in learning about their qualities than it was for the first brand."[25]

Schmalensee notes several generalizations from his model:

- The effect should be operative in most markets for experience goods;
- It is not of central importance in many markets, however;

---

[22] R. S. Bond and D. F. Lean, "Sales, Promotion, and Product Differentiation in Two Prescription Drug Markets," Staff Report to the U.S. Federal Trade Commission, Washington, 1977; and "Consumer Preference, Advertising, and Sales: On the Advantage from Early Entry," Working Paper 14, Bureau of Economics, U.S. Federal Trade Commission, Washington, October 1979.
[23] Joe S. Bain, *Barriers to New Competition* (Cambridge, MA: Harvard University Press, 1956), p. 217.
[24] For further insight into the sources of the pioneer advantage, see Marvin B. Lieberman and David B. Montgomery, "First Mover Advantages," *Strategic Management Journal*, 9 (summer 1988), 41–58.
[25] Richard Schmalensee, "Product Differentiation Advantages of Pioneering Brands," *American Economic Review*, 72, no. 3 (June 1982), 360.

- The effect may be more pronounced in situations where performance risk is high relative to unit cost and in low-purchase-frequency situations (because buyers have had little opportunity to try out products);
- First-entrant advantages are greater for products with low unit costs and for convenience goods for which retailers do not provide much information;
- In markets where this mechanism is important, a me-too strategy (identical product at a lower price) is especially unattractive to potential later entrants;
- Successful later entrants in such markets will generally have differentiated themselves sufficiently from their predecessors as to appear pioneering to at least a sizable segment of buyers;
- After a new and *ex ante* risky brand has become established, its trademark performs the valuable function of transmitting information that is not easily transmitted in other ways—it is something like a patent with infinite life.[26]

The "Defender" model formulated by Hauser and Shugan examines defensive strategy through a strategy model that uses the positioning of the second entrant to determine share.[27] In their approach, the ability of the pioneering brand to maintain high sales levels depends on how well it designed its product to meet heterogenous consumer preferences.[28] If the pioneer chose the best positioning (the combination of product attributes that best satisfies some large segment of consumers), then later entrants will have lower market shares because, if they want to differentiate, they have only inferior positions available. If, on the other hand, the first product was poorly positioned because the firm did not fully understand consumer preferences at the time of its entry (a possible result in a new product category), then the second entrant could achieve that better (or best) positioning and earn a greater share.[29] Exhibit 8-1 examines yet another explanation of the pioneer's advantage, one based on how consumers learn about and form preferences for products.

REWARDS TO PIONEERS: THE EVIDENCE

Pharmaceuticals and Cigarettes

A number of studies have been undertaken to explore pioneering advantages. The FTC study of prescription drugs, mentioned earlier, found that neither

---

[26] Schmalensee, "Product Differentiation Advantages," pp. 360–361.

[27] John R. Hauser and Steven M. Shugan, "Defensive Marketing Strategies," *Marketing Science*, 2, no. 4 (fall 1983), 319–359; see also John R. Hauser, "Theory and Application of Defensive Strategy," in L. G. Thomas, ed., *The Economics of Strategic Planning* (Lexington, MA: Lexington Books, 1986).

[28] *Heterogeneous* means that there is not just one perfect product that meets all customers' needs (homogeneous preference) but that consumer preferences for the configuration of product features that are needed are distributed across a product space.

[29] Depending on the shape of customer demand preferences, there are instances in which the second entrant may indeed have an advantage over the pioneer. See Avijit Ghosh and Bruce Buchanan. "Multiple Outlets in a Duopoly: A First Entry Paradox," *Geographical Analysis*, 20, no. 2 (. 111–121.

EXHIBIT 8-1

Preference Formation and Pioneering Advantage:
A Supply-Side Theory

Two researchers, Greg Carpenter and Kent Nakamoto, were dissatisfied with existing explanations of the pioneer's advantage.[30] First they summed up the three basic arguments put forth in support of pioneering advantages:

1. The early entrant preempts later entrants by adopting the best product position leaving competitors with smaller or less attractive market segments;
2. Later entrants' products are perceived as riskier by buyers if trial is necessary to verify product performance or quality, forcing those entrants to reduce price or otherwise enhance the value of their offering to offset that risk;
3. Switching costs caused by brand-specific user learning require later entrants to offer inducements to offset the costs that consumers experience in switching

They then noted the existence of situations in which later entrants could reposition and in which user skills and switching costs were minimal. In these instances, they reasoned, later entrants should be able to offset the pioneer's advantage. The problem was that this did not happen—they pointed to Miller's Lite Beer, Wrigley's chewing gum, and Coca Cola as examples of products where the pioneer's advantage should have eroded but did not.

This led them to believe that the advantage must have arisen from some other sources. The theory they advanced has two arguments:

> First, in the early stages of many markets, consumers know little about the importance of attributes or their ideal combination. For example, 100 years ago few people were likely to have strong opinions about how sweet or carbonated a cola should be. A successful early entrant can have a major influence on how attributes are valued and on the ideal attribute combinations. Coca Cola, for example, may have had a significant impact in its early years on the formation and evolution of individuals preference for colas. This influence can shift individuals' preferences to favor the pioneer over later entrants, leading to a market share advantage.
>
> Second . . . the pioneer can become strongly associated with the product category as a whole and, as a result, become the 'standard' against which all later entrants are judged. Kleenex, Xerox, and Jello are obvious examples. Being strongly representative, the pioneer is *competitively distinct*, which makes competing away its high share difficult for later entrants, especially for low-priced copies or so-called 'me-too' brands.[31]

They pointed out that this argument, however, holds only for multiattribute products and services in which the combination of attributes or features to

---

[30] Gregory S. Carpenter and Kent Nakamoto, "Consumer Preference Formation and Pioneering Advantage," *Journal of Marketing Research,* XXVI, no. 3 (August 1989), 285–298.
[31] Carpenter and Nakamoto, "Consumer Preference Formation," p. 286.

EXHIBIT 8-1 (cont.)

overall brand value (or even the ideal attribute combination) is ambiguous. Soft drink flavors and the features of computer software programs are examples. In neither category were there a priori definitions of the benefits and attributes that defined the highest level of product performance. In these instances, therefore, the sequential entry of products into the market favors the first entrant as consumers learn and evolve their preferences toward the combination offered by the successful pioneer.

Carpenter and Nakamoto conducted two experiments which supported their theory. In their experiments (the first used a simulated computer software program; the second the down quilt market), they rotated the first product to which their subjects were exposed. As predicted, they found that whichever product they presented first, their subjects shifted their taste distribution toward its position. Second, they varied the type and pricing of the second product to which their subjects were exposed—whether a me-too or a distinct entry at the same or lower prices. By then asking their subjects to make purchase choices and to rank order still other hypothetical entrants (which were either more or less me-too products or distinct), they were able to isolate some of the processes by which the pioneer advantage worked.

They found that the pioneer is able to protect its position because it has a central role in category preference formation and, therefore, becomes prototypical of brands in the category. When this happens, they found that the closer the me-too was to the pioneer, the more the me-too lost sales. Further, they found that pioneers were least sensitive to the prices of competitors that are the most similar.

They suggested that, in developing a theory of pioneering advantage, an important extension was to understand how to overtake the pioneer. Their work suggests that only by positioning itself away from the pioneering brand, segmenting the market, can a later entrant achieve significant success. Exactly how this can be done, however, is unclear.

Perhaps their most important contribution, however, lies in the insight into the supplier/consumer relationship in the design of truly new products. In such instances, since the product has never existed before, the right combination of attributes and their relative importance is unknown to either party. The pioneer then achieves competitive advantage by influencing consumer tastes as much as it responds to them. Once this occurs, the pioneer possesses a valuable asset—a consumer preference structure built on its attributes.

heavy promotional outlays nor low price was able to dislodge the pioneer brands. Only by offering novel therapeutic benefits (and heavy promotional expenditures) did later entrants achieve substantial sales. In their own words, "large scale promotion of brands that offer nothing new is likely to go unrewarded."[32] In another FTC study, of seven cigarette submarkets, similar results were obtained.[33] This study showed, however, that not only could brands that were significantly differentiated from the pioneer gain substantial share, but close followers in rapidly growing markets could attain similar results.

Consumer Products

Urban et al. performed several studies of pioneer entry rewards across a large number of consumer product categories and brands (over 100 brands across 36 categories).[34] The products in their samples were from tightly defined and well-established categories of frequently purchased goods such as liquid detergent, instant freeze-dried coffee, and the like. In their data set, the average time in the market for second entrants was almost twenty-six years, third entrants about twenty years, down to sixth entrants around six years.

The model estimated the ratio of a brand's sales to that of the pioneer as a function of (1) its entry order, (2) preference for the product (termed positioning by Urban), (3) its advertising over the prior three years in comparison to the first entrant's advertising, and (4) the number of years between its entry and the prior entrant's entry. The model allowed the testing of the relative effects of the various strategic choices. For example, a second entrant whose positioning and preference was no better than the pioneer's and whose advertising was at parity would not be predicted to surpass the pioneer's share. In the model, share is reduced by the order effect (the later the entry, the lower the share) and modified by the positioning effect (the better the preference, the greater the share). It is possible for a late entrant to gain a dominant share when it has a superior positioning—one potent enough to overcome the order-effect penalty.[35] Superior positioning and aggressive advertising spending would be the most likely cause of dominance by a later entrant in this model.

The results of the model were generally as hypothesized. Entry order did result in higher shares, all other things being equal. In Figure 8-2, entry order is shown on the x axis, and the ratio of the followers' shares to that of the pioneer is depicted on the y axis. A share index greater than 1.0 indicates that the follower's share exceeded that of the pioneer; a share index of less than 1.0

[32] Bond and Lean, "Sales, Promotion, and Product Differentiation," p. vi.

[33] I. T. Whitten, "Brand Performance in the Cigarette Industry and the Advantage of Early Entry 1913–1974," Federal Trade Commission, Bureau of Economics, June 1979.

[34] Glen L. Urban, Theresa Carter, and Zofia Mucha, "Market Share Rewards to Pioneering Brands An Exploratory Empirical Analysis," in H. Thomas and D. Gardner, eds., *Strategic Marketing and Management* (New York: John Wiley and Sons, 1985); and Glen L. Urban, Theresa Carter, Steven Gaskin, and Zofia Mucha, "Market Share Rewards to Pioneering Brands: An Empirical Analysis and Strategic Implications," *Management Science*, 32, no. 6 (June 1986), 645–659. For a less quantitative approach, see Steven P. Schnaars, "When Entering Growth Markets, Are Pioneers Better Than Poachers?," *Business Horizons*, 29 no. 2 (March-April 1986), 27–36.

[35] This effect may account for the rapid and frequent turnover in leadership in the fax machine market, in which the top five firms in 1982 were deposed by 1986 and, of the five leaders in 1986 only three remained in the top five by 1988. Frederick H. Katayama, "Who's Fueling the Fax Frenzy," *Fortune*, October 23, 1989, pp. 151–156.

Figure 8-2 The effect of entry order, preference, and advertising on market share: actual and predicted results

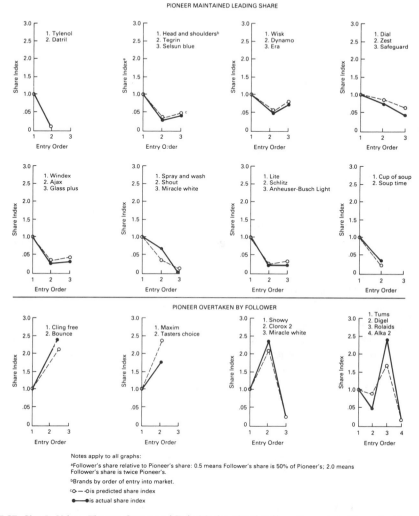

Notes apply to all graphs:
[a]Follower's share relative to Pioneer's share: 0.5 means Follower's share is 50% of Pioneer's; 2.0 means Follower's share is twice Pioneer's.
[b]Brands by order of entry into market.
[c]○ – –○ is predicted share index
●——● is actual share index

SOURCE: Glen L. Urban, Theresa Carter, and Zofia Mucha, "Market Share Rewards to Pioneering Brands: An Exploratory Empirical Analysis," in H. Thomas and D. Gardner, eds., *Strategic Marketing and Management* (New York: John Wiley and Sons, 1985), pp. 246 and 247; and Glen L. Urban, Theresa Carter, Steven Gaskin, and Zofia Mucha, "Market Share Rewards to Pioneering Brands: An Empirical Analysis and Strategic Implications," *Management Science*, 32, no. 6 (June 1986), p. 658.

indicates that the follower's share was less than that of the pioneer. As can be seen, the pioneer's share was highest in six of the eleven categories shown as predicted by the model (compare the solid line, which shows actual performance, with the dotted line, which plots the model's predictions).

However, positioning, preference and advertising were also found to have positive share effects. In five of the cases shown, at least one of the later entrants

TABLE 8-1   *Order of Entry Penalty[a]*

ENTRY ORDER	SHARE RELATIVE TO PIONEERING BRAND	SHARES					
		1ST	2ND	3RD	4TH	5TH	6TH
First	1.0	100	—	—	—	—	—
Second	0.71	58.5	41.5	—	—	—	—
Third	0.58	43.6	31.0	25.4	—	—	—
Fourth	0.51	35.7	25.4	20.8	18.1	—	—
Fifth	0.45	30.8	21.9	17.9	15.5	13.9	—
Sixth	0.41	27.3	19.4	15.9	13.8	12.4	11.2

[a]Assumes that products are equal, all advertise at the same level as the pioneer, and there is one year or less between entrances.

SOURCE: Glen L. Urban, Theresa Carter, Steven Gaskin, and Zofia Mucha, "Market Share Rewards to Pioneering Brands: An Empirical Analysis and Strategic Implications," *Management Science*, 32, no. 6 (June 1986), p. 654.

was able to surpass the pioneer. As can be seen, these instances were all correctly predicted by the model. For example, Rolaids, the third entry in the antacids market, was predicted to have a leading share and achieved a share higher than that predicted in spite of its rank as third entrant. According to the researchers, Rolaids's values for both advertising and positioning were quite high, which compensated for the order of entry decline.

Table 8-1 presents an interesting use of Urban et al.'s estimates. It shows the decreases in share that later entrants experience in terms of relative and absolute shares based on the actual marketplace data. In effect, the table represents the average of the actual shares received by all entrants in the thirty-six product categories studied. The conclusion that one draws from the table is that a follower strategy is not an optimal one as measured by market share. While it is possible to surpass the pioneer (as shown in Figure 8-2), on the average the second entrant will achieve only 71% of the share achieved by the pioneer.

PIMS-Based Studies

Two studies based on the PIMS database found similar results.[36] Table 8-2 shows the advantages that pioneers hold in both consumer and industrial markets. Pioneers in both have an average market share of approximately 29%. As the data show, early followers and later entrants in industrial markets take somewhat less of a share penalty than do their consumer counterparts.

The findings of these two studies, summarized in Table 8-3, are as follows:

• Pioneers' higher shares are due to their higher product quality and broader product lines, even though they charge essentially the same price as late entrants.

[36] William T. Robinson and Claes Fornell, "Sources of Market Pioneer Advantages in Consumer Goods Industries," *Journal of Marketing Research*, XXII, no. 3 (August 1985), 305–317; and William T. Robinson, "Sources of Market Pioneer Advantages: The Case of Industrial Goods Industries," *Journal of Marketing Research*, XXV, no. 1 (February 1988), 87–94. See also Mary Lambkin, "Order of Entry and Performance in New Markets," *Strategic Management Journal*, 9 (summer 1988), 127–140.

TABLE 8-2 *Pioneer Advantages in Consumer and Industrial Markets*

	MATURE INDUSTRIAL PRODUCTS	MATURE CONSUMER PRODUCTS
Pioneer average market share	29%	29%
Early follower market share	21	17
Late entrant market share	15	12
% of market share variation explained by order of market entry	9	18
% of ROI explained by market share	9	21

SOURCE: Adapted from William T. Robinson, "Sources of Market Pioneer Advantages: The Case of Industrial Goods Industries," *Journal of Marketing Research*, XXV, no. 1 (February 1988), p. 89. Also adapted from William T. Robinson and Claes Fornell, "Sources of Market Pioneer Advantages in Consumer Goods Industries," *Journal of Marketing Research*, XXII, no. 3 (August 1985), p. 310.

- The share advantage for consumer products is larger initially (total of 23% vs. 17% for industrial) but not permanently (total advantage for consumer and industrial after twenty years is almost equal at 13% and 12.75%, respectively).
- Product quality advantages deteriorate significantly over time; in consumer markets so too do the advantages due to product line breadth while the deterioration of that advantage in industrial markets is modest.
- Pioneer share advantages are greater in industries with higher value added but are negative in industries in which new products compose a high percentage of total sales.

TABLE 8-3 *Market Pioneer Advantages in Industrial and Consumer Goods Industries*

	PIONEER MARKET SHARE POINT ADVANTAGE OVER LATE ENTRANTS	
	INDUSTRIAL	CONSUMER
Business characteristics		
Relative product quality		
Pioneer	4.27	8.01
20-year pioneer	1.95	1.71
Relative product line breadth		
Pioneer	3.83	9.42
20-year pioneer	3.20	5.23
Industry characteristics		
Pioneer industry value added/sales	3.64	8.49
Pioneer industry new product sales/sales	−1.46	−3.44
Large and infrequent purchases		
Pioneer purchase amount	4.29	
Pioneer purchase frequency	NS[a]	
Consumer information/intensive distribution		
Pioneer low purchase amount		6.75
Total average share advantage		
Pioneer	17.16	23.56
20-year pioneer	13.01	12.75

[a]NS = not statistically significant.

SOURCE: Adapted from William T. Robinson, "Sources of Market Pioneer Advantages: The Case of Industrial Goods Industries," in *Journal of Marketing Research*, XXV, no. 1 (February 1988), p. 92. Reprinted with permission of the American Marketing Association.

- Pioneer advantages in industrial markets increase with purchase amount (es pecially those greater than $100,000), whereas in consumer markets the oppo site is the case—the share advantage increases for purchases less than $10.

STRATEGY IN THE TRANSITION PERIOD

The period during which an industry changes from rapid growth to maturity is particularly sensitive. The key success factors in the business are undergoing change, and the period is, therefore, ripe for major strategic moves on the par of competitors. In some industries, this may also be when the first shakeout based on firm size, occurs.

The transition to maturity is not easily defined or discerned, especially on a real-time basis. Conceptually, it is the period when the growth rate in the in dustry begins to slow as a prelude to the stable, GNP-like growth rate of a mature industry. The transition is easy to see after the fact. However er, the slow ing a manager sees at any given point in time could just be a momentary dip— and for the manager to act like it was a permanent dip might result in a self fulfilling prophecy. One sure way of slowing the growth of a product market is to begin reducing product innovation, withholding marketing resources, and the like.[37] Table 8-4 lists some of the indicators that a market is maturing.

Changes in the Transition Period

Managers need to cope with the transition period and the changes it brings Some of those changes are discussed next.[38]

Market-Share Competition Intensifies. As growth slows, a firm can either slow with it or attempt to maintain its old, higher growth rate by increasing its share. Since few firms are willing to accept the former alternative, share battles are not unusual as all strive to maintain higher growth rates. For many, espe cially those in new industries which have never experienced anything but growth, intense share competition is a new phenomenon which requires learn ing about how to compete and about how competitors will compete.

Experienced, Repeat Buyers Are the Norm. Industries begin the maturation process when repeat buyers and their volume become the larger part of total sales. As their expertise and numbers grow, they demand a change in selling strategy from "buy this new set of product performances" to "my set's price performance ratio is better than theirs."

Price Competition Begins to Replace Performance Competition. As a technol ogy begins to mature, the performance delivered by the competitors in the

---

[37] Nariman K. Dhalla and Sonia Yuspeh, "Forget the Product Life Cycle Concept," *Harvard Business Review*, 54, no. 1 (January-February 1976), 102–112.
[38] This discussion is based on Michael Porter, *Competitive Strategy* (New York: Free Press, 1980) chapter 11.

TABLE 8-4　*Leading Indicators of a Maturing Market*

- Evidence of saturation (as evidenced by a declining proportion of new-trier versus replacement sales)
- Increasing rate of decline in real prices and profit margins
- Industry overcapacity levels that cannot be accounted for by short-run economic fluctuations
- Appearance of substitute technologies and related products
- Changes in the ratio of exports and imports, due to growing off-shore sourcing and production
- Declining responsiveness of sales to advertising, promotion, and sales efforts, in conjunction with increasing price sensitivity.
- Increasing reluctance of buyers to pay for technical services
- Decreasing profitability and reduced risks of backward integration by customers

SOURCE: Reprinted by permission from p. 82 in *Analysis for Strategic Marketing Decisions* by George S. Day. Copyright © 1986 by West Publishing Co. All rights reserved.

business starts to homogenize, forcing competition to the areas of price and service. It is not easy for a firm which has succeeded on the basis of product performance to refocus toward price or service.

The Threat of Overcapacity Is Real.   When growth slows, it is easy for competitors to overshoot in adding capacity relative to demand. Until this point, overcapacity in the industry was quickly alleviated by rapid growth, and the key to firm success was the ability to add capacity promptly and thereby preempt competitors. Gaining this new perspective is not easily achieved, and prolonged periods of overcapacity frequently occur with the severe price competition it occasions.

New Product Development Economics Evolve.   Much of the growth in the early stages of the life cycle comes from new product performance capabilities and the application of the product technology to new uses and markets. The returns on the R&D dollars allocated to these activities decline, and the firm needs to reassess the direction and funding of those activities.[39]

Profitability Pressures Mount.   Potential overcapacity, sophisticated buyers, competition for share, and strategic changes are the causes of a temporary, and sometimes long-run, decline in profits. While such woes typically affect all firms, smaller-share firms are frequently hardest hit. In some instances, this may result in a shakeout and industry restructuring.

Channel Relationships Change.   In industries which do not sell direct, channel members frequently take cuts in margins due to price competition for some period before manufacturers' profits are squeezed. This results in the attrition of many in the channel—often of those handling smaller-share entrants. As a result, channel power increases because good outlets are now in short supply.

[39] Richard N. Foster, *Innovation: The Attacker's Advantage* (New York: Summit Books, 1986).

Managing the Transition

Significant strategic advantage accrues to the first to accommodate the new environment. Merely making the same changes as competitors on the same timetable only perpetuates competitive parity. Those who lag in adjusting to the new environment lose position rapidly. There are three steps that need to be taken during the transition to maturity.

Step 1: Forecast the Competitive Environment at Maturity.   During the transition phase, two questions face managers. One is whether to continue in the industry; the second concerns the strategies available to do so. By the transition period, the economics that should prevail at maturity can generally be discerned and the ability of the firm to survive the industry's transition estimated. Constructing scenarios of the likely industry development is one method by which one can gain an understanding of the firm's ability to compete at maturity and the strategies available to the firm.[40]

If it has not already done so, the firm needs to choose or reaffirm its basic competitive strategy. The three basic strategies—overall cost leadership, differentiation, or the focus version of each—diverge sharply at this point in a market's evolution. From this point forward, the market will reward only those who have taken a clear position to gaining competitive advantage.

Step 2: Establish Clear Segment Targets.   Most industries are composed of segments and subsegments defined along a variety of dimensions. The key to competing during the transition period is to be able to identify those segments which are growing and/or have good customers, and to focus the firm on serving those segments better than any competitor.

By focusing its efforts on growth segments, of course, the firm has figured out how to avoid competing in the slower-growth main market, which is the idea. The essence of strategy is precisely that—to choose conducive places to compete. Such a selection process, however, requires more than simply listing and thinking about segments. Detailed breakdowns of industry statistics by the relevant segmentation variable(s) is needed and is seldom publicly available. This requires staff work—the acquisition of primary market data, its analysis, and the formulation and testing of hypotheses about how best to segment and approach the market—which may be a new activity to some firms.

Choosing good customers is another approach. Customers with the largest volume requirements and the most forgiving performance needs are often among the first to put pressure on suppliers for price concessions. They are also frequently the most competed for. Identifying buyers with whom the firm has competitive advantage and catering to their needs is a positive strategy for avoiding the otherwise fierce competition that begins during the transition phase.

Competitors will, of course, be pursuing a similar strategy. However, the

[40] See Michael Porter, *Competitive Advantage* (New York: Free Press, 1985), chapter 13.

firm that is first to focus gains more than a temporary advantage. It gains the ability to shape the nature of competition to its advantage. Those who follow must necessarily walk in the leader's footprints.

Step 3: Rationalize the Product Line.   Since one of the keys to the growth of an industry is its product variety, firms frequently arrive at the transition phase with broader product lines than necessary, especially if production cost becomes of concern. Given the reaffirmation of its basic strategy and selection of its target segments, the firm can begin to shape its product line.

Most important in any strategy is the need to understand product profitability. Such techniques as average product costing or the use of averaged allocations for overhead unnecessarily penalizes some products as it favors others. These accounting practices often result in high sales of the underpriced items and low sales of the overpriced items as the market cherry picks the mix. The result, of course, is profit and sales underperformance.

The relationship between product variety and product cost is a key focus. Typically, in most production technologies there is an adverse relationship between the two. In some industries, there is a positive relationship between price and product variety. The firm that, during the transition phase, can best tailor these relationships to its strategy for the future can gain a strategic jump on competitors.

STRATEGY AT MATURITY AND DECLINE

Most businesses are operating in the mature phase of their industry's evolutionary cycle. Much of what is discussed in basic marketing texts involves the day-to-day issues of marketing in an ongoing business. There are generally few natural opportunities for strategic repositioning at maturity. The decline phase, in contrast, poses major strategic issues. This discussion first examines the strategic issues faced in maturity and how they affect the firm's posture for the decline stage. Next, it explores the end-game strategies available to the firm in the decline stage of an industry's evolution.

Maturity

At the mature stage of an industry's evolution, the general assumption is that the industry has reached some sort of equilibrium in which the forces that have shaped it maintain stability. Unlike the introduction and growth stages, in which there are naturally occurring opportunities for strategic action, maturity is not generally thought to be ripe for change.

After the struggles to survive until maturity, the winners are generally assumed to be happy not to challenge the status quo. Competitors are typically in stable positions, their investments in plant and equipment are well depreciated, cash flow is positive, the wars and shakeouts are behind them, and each is well aware of the others' competitive strengths, weaknesses, and hot buttons. For most, maintaining position and the industry's profitability is the desirable outcome. As all major competitors in a mature industry said to the author during one consulting project, "We don't want change. We like this business the way it is."

Success Strategies in Maturity

The mature stage of an industry is not easy, however. The forces of supply and demand and competition have forced margins down considerably compared to the earlier stages of the industry's evolution. In one study of some twenty-three industries, for example, it was found that real prices for product declined consistently as the market evolved. In the five-stage model used in the study, average prices declined 13.6% in the first stage, 13% in the second, and 7.2%, 9%, and 5.2% in the remaining three stages.[41] This effect forces competitors to continue to improve the efficiency with which their businesses are run.

In another study of eight mature, slow-growth industries, it was found, however, that maturity need not mean poor returns.[42] In fact, its author found that the top two firms in each of these industries were able to earn returns on equity that placed them within the top 20% of the *Fortune* 1,000 industrials. The secret to their success was very basic, according to the author. It was their continuous, single-minded determination to achieve either or both

> the lowest delivered cost position relative to competition, coupled with both an acceptable delivered quality and a pricing policy to gain profitable volume and market share growth.
> . . . the highest product/service/quality differentiated position relative to competition, coupled with both an acceptable delivered cost structure and a pricing policy to gain margins sufficient to fund reinvestment in product/service differentiation.[43]

Table 8-5 lists the eight industries and the firms that achieved either or both of these positions, and Figure 8-3 positions the competitors in the heavy-duty truck industry according to the same two criteria.

Ford, which positioned its business as the low-cost producer of average performance trucks, received a 25% return on assets (ROA); and Paccar, which produces trucks with the highest relative performance but has only an average production cost position, earned a 30% ROA. White Motor and International Harvester, in contrast, earned only 4.7% and 9% ROAs, respectively. Figure 8-3 also divides the product space into four subgroups, which suggest the outcomes that can be expected for each combination of cost and differentiation.

---

[41] Michael Gort and Steven Klepper, "Time Paths in the Diffusion of Product Innovations," *The Economic Journal*, 92 (September 1982), 630–653.

[42] William K. Hall, "Survival Strategies in a Hostile Environment," *Harvard Business Review*, 58, no. 5 (September-October 1980), 75–85.

[43] Hall, "Survival Strategies," pp. 78, 79.

TABLE 8-5   *Strategies Used to Succeed in Maturity in Eight Basic Industries*

INDUSTRY	ACHIEVED LOW DELIVERED COST POSITION	ACHIEVED "MEANINGFUL" DIFFERENTIATION	SIMULTANEOUS EMPLOYMENT OF BOTH STRATEGIES
Steel	Inland Steel	National	
Tire and rubber	Goodyear	Michelin (French)	
Heavy-duty trucks	Ford	Paccar	
Construction and materials handling equipment		John Deere	Caterpillar
Automotive	General Motors	Daimler Benz (German)	
Major home appliances	Whirlpool	Maytag	
Beer	Miller	G. Heilman Brewing	
Cigarettes	R. J. Reynolds		Philip Morris

SOURCE: Reprinted by permission of *Harvard Business Review*. An exhibit from "Survival Strategies in a Hostile Environment" by William K. Hall, September/October 1980. Copyright © 1980 by the President and Fellows of Harvard College; all rights reserved.

Figure 8-3   Successful strategies in U.S. heavy-duty truck manufacturing

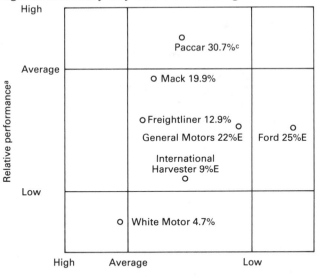

[a]Based on customer and industry interview data.

[b]Based on manufacturing and distribution cost analysis, evaluating economies of scale, and vertical integration profiles.

[c]Operating return on assets; E = estimated from industry sources.

SOURCE: Reprinted by permission of *Harvard Business Review*. An exhibit from "Survival Strategies in a Hostile Environment" by William K. Hall, September/October 1980. Copyright © 1980 by the President and Fellows of Harvard College; all rights reserved.

Creating Strategic Change at Maturity

Generally speaking, in maturity the forces that determine strategic advantage are on the side of existing competitors. The economics of depreciated investments, experience curve effects, customer and channel commitments, and the like make it difficult for new firms to enter the industry. These same factors also make it difficult for existing competitors to create strategic change. Barring major environmental change, there are really only two basic scenarios under which strategic change can be accomplished.

Knockout Economics.   A firm that can deliver comparable product performance at economics that allows it to profit at a price lower than that of existing competitors' variable costs can revolutionize a mature industry. The term *knockout* refers to the ability of a firm with such economics to knock out existing competitors if it wishes.

While such breakthroughs seldom occur, their results are potent. By viewing the entire world as their market and building world-scale manufacturing facilities, Japanese motorcycle manufacturers reduced costs to a level at which the U.K. motorcycle industry could not compete. Their low costs also gained them substantial shares of the European and U.S. markets during the 1960s and 1970s.

Knockout Performance.   Knockout product performance, once experienced, renders existing products obsolete. This is typically unlikely within the framework of existing product technology, but it can happen. The reliability of Savin copiers in comparison to Xerox's machines during the late 1970s and early 1980s (detailed in chapter 6) was such that the latter's machines were almost uneconomic purchases. The fit, finish, and mechanical reliability of Japanese automobiles in the 1970s and 1980s forced American automobile manufacturers into major redesigns and restructurings to avoid large volume losses.

Decline

Understanding the major forces behind a decline in demand is important to the firm's end-game strategy.[44] There are three basic causes of the decline of an industry:[45]

1. *Technological obsolescence.* The major force underlying the death (and birth) of industries is technological change. Chapter 6 discussed this cause extensively.
2. *Decline in customer population.* Many markets shrink or disappear simply because their customer base (or, in the case of industrial markets, their customers' customer base) declines in numbers. As the baby-boom generation has aged, for example, the demand for blue jeans has declined from over 500 million pairs per

---

[44] Kathryn Rudie Harrigan and Michael E. Porter, "End Game Strategies for Declining Industries," *Harvard Business Review*, 61, no. 4 (July-August 1983), 111–120.
[45] Porter, *Competitive Strategy*, chapter 12.

year in 1981 to less than 400 million pairs in 1988.[46] Firms which were suppliers to such shrinking industries as the steel industry or consumer electronics manufacturers in the United States suffered as severely as did their disappearing customers during the last twenty years.

3. *Changes in customer needs.* Tastes change and needs change and even disappear. The market for men's and women's hats simply evaporated during the 1950s. No other product replaced hats. Beef producers have been battling the major shift in tastes that cut their demand, while egg producers are searching for a way to overcome the health concerns causing their decline.

Creating the Strategic Response

While it may seem strange, it is not axiomatic that a declining industry be unprofitable or inhospitable to competitors. For some, such as GTE Sylvania, which is the last U.S. producer of flashbulbs, a declining market can be a highly profitable place because of the relative absence of competition. The issue is one of understanding the cause of the decline and interpreting that for its implications for competition.

Table 8-6 lists the factors that determine the basic attractiveness of a declining market. Four of these are worth special attention because they interact with the causes of the decline to determine attractiveness.

Uncertainty.   Uncertainty is a key issue is determining competitors' strategies. A clear, unambiguous signal of a market's demise (such as occurred with slide rules) is preferable to one in which the true long-run status of the product is unknown. In the former case, capacity withdrawal can be more orderly than in the latter, in which many competitors linger in the hopes of a resurgence. The market for chlorinated fluorocarbons, once used as a propellant in aerosols and until recently the refrigerant of choice, has had clear shutdown dates set in the U.S. and the European Economic Community (EEC) because of fluorocarbons' damage to the ozone layer.

Rate and Pattern of Decline.   It is difficult, a priori, to say exactly what rate or pattern is good or bad except in the most general terms. Erratic patterns and very steep declines are probably the least desirable—the former because they interact with uncertainty and cause competitors to hang in longer than they should; the latter almost by definition because many or most participants will have to take large writeoffs. Perhaps the worst is an erratic decline in an industry whose sales have been inherently erratic or cyclical. Participants have no way of knowing for sure the market's future. However, industry participants can influence the shape of the decline by their actions.

Structure of Remaining Demand Pockets.   While the last television set containing vacuum tubes was manufactured in 1974, there is a large population of

---

[46] Andrew Pollack, "Jeans Fade but Levi Strauss Glows," *The New York Times*, June 26, 1988, pp. D1 and D4.

TABLE 8-6 *Structural Factors That Influence the Attractiveness of a Declining Market*

STRUCTURAL FACTORS	ENVIRONMENTAL ATTRACTIVENESS	
	HOSPITABLE	INHOSPITABLE
CONDITIONS OF DEMAND		
Speed of decline	Very slow	Rapid or erratic
Certainty of decline	100% certain predictable patterns	Great uncertainty, erratic patterns
Pockets of enduring demand	Several or major ones	No niches
Product differentiation	Brand loyalty	Commodity-like products
Price stability	Stable, price premiums attainable	Very unstable, pricing below costs
EXIT BARRIERS		
Reinvestment requirements	None	High, often mandatory and involving capital assets
Excess capacity	Little	Substantial
Asset age	Mostly old assets	Sizable new assets and old ones not retired
Resale markets for assets	Easy to convert or sell	No markets available, substantial costs to retire
Shared facilities	Few free-standing plants	Substantial and interconnected with important businesses
Vertical integration	Little	Substantial
Single product competitors	None	Several large companies
RIVALRY DETERMINANTS		
Customer industries	Fragmented, weak	Strong bargaining power
Customer switching costs	High	Minimal
Diseconomies of scale	None	Substantial penalty

SOURCE: Reprinted by permission of *Harvard Business Review*. An exhibit from "End-Game Strategies for Declining Industries" by Kathryn Rudie Harrigan and Michael E. Porter, July/August 1983. Copyright © 1983 by the President and Fellows of Harvard College; all rights reserved.

TVs and other-lived electronic products in existence which contain vacuum tubes. The cost of replacing a receiving tube relative to the cost of a new set is such that tube manufacturers are assured of a sizable, price-insensitive market for some time. In other markets where the remaining demand is for the basic, commodity-like product types, competition can be vicious.

Exit Barriers.   Exit barriers are the inverse of entry barriers.[47] They make it expensive or difficult for firms to leave an industry. Long-lived and single-purpose assets (plant and equipment that cannot be used to do anything except make and polish widgets, for example), may simply be of little value to anyone. While the firm may be earning a poor return on its investment, that return is better than the prospect of no return at all (which would be the case were it to shut down the business). In contrast, a business whose assets may be redeployed can exit more easily. Businesses part of an internal company vertical chain are especially difficult to shut down, as are those whose production, warehousing, or marketing is interrelated with other company products. The emotional resistance of top management to withdrawal is cited as an especially high exit barrier.

[47] Kathryn Rudie Harrigan, "The Effect of Exit Barriers upon Strategic Flexibility," *Strategic Management Journal*, 1, no. 2 (April-June 1980), 165–176.

TABLE 8-7   *Strategies for Declining Businesses*

	HAS COMPETITIVE STRENGTHS FOR REMAINING DEMAND POCKETS	LACKS COMPETITIVE STRENGTHS FOR REMAINING DEMAND POCKETS
Favorable industry structure for decline	Leadership or niche	Harvest or divest quickly
Unfavorable industry structure for decline	Niche or harvest	Divest quickly

SOURCE: Reprinted by permission of *Harvard Business Review.* An exhibit from "End-Game Strategies for Declining Industries" by Kathryn Rudie Harrigan and Michael E. Porter, July/August 1983. Copyright © 1983 by the President and Fellows of Harvard College; all rights reserved.

The Strategies

Four basic strategies exist in the decline phase: (1) rapid divestment, (2) harvest, (3) niche, or (4) leadership. Table 8-7 suggests how they fit as a function of the firm's competencies and the structure of the industry's decline.

Rapid divestment is a rational strategy for a competitor who is able to see the inevitability of decline before others do and to receive, therefore, a higher price than it would if it waited. It may be the only route for a firm lacking the specific competitive advantages needed to succeed in the end game. There is some evidence that the stock market overvalues those companies that are willing to bite the bullet by divesting businesses quickly.[48]

Niching assumes that some durable pockets of demand exist and that the firm has enduring competitive advantages in serving the chosen niches. Niching is neither easy nor always rewarding, however. Unless the business has an assured lock on some sizable niche, it will still most likely have to downsize its operations.

Leadership is a strategy that can prove rewarding. Its goal is placing the firm as one of the remaining few in the industry, at which time it can better manage a harvest strategy until the inevitable end. Contrary as it may seem, this requires the company to be a proactive competitor and strategist as it seeks to speed the exit of undesirable competitors. Some approaches include aggressive pricing or advertising to convince competitors of the market's unattractiveness, or the introduction of new products which would force competitors to make uneconomic investments to hold their sales. Buying and scrapping competitors' capacity is not infrequently an economic decision. *Runners' World* magazine, for example, bought out its competitor as advertiser demand declined and was insufficient to support two entrants. *Gourmet* magazine bought out *Cuisine* under similar circumstances.

A *harvest* strategy may be appropriate. This strategy seeks a controlled, orderly withdrawal from a market with the intent of increasing cash flow and profits.[49] Essentially, the strategy assumes that the firm's only choice is to run the business into the ground in the most financially advantageous manner. In

---

[48] Kathryn Rudie Harrigan, "Strategies for Declining Industries," *Journal of Business Strategy*, 1, no. 2 (fall 1980), 20–34.

[49] Laurence P. Feldman and Albert L. Page, "Harvesting: The Misunderstood Market Exit Strategy," *Journal of Business Strategy*, 5, no. 4 (spring 1985), 79–85.

some instances, this may mean cutting all investment, marketing support, R&D, plant maintenance, and any other discretionary expenditure. In other situations, where a long-term market decline is expected, for example, the strategy may actually call for investment and continued marketing support. Not all businesses can be harvested, and the strategy may be more easily conceived than executed in many instances.

SUMMARY

The ability to create effective strategies and to initiate strategic change is a function of the development of the product market. In general, the strategic window is open widest during the development, shakeout, and decline stages of market evolution. More specifically, later entrants or followers have the best opportunity to wrest control of a market's leadership during those periods in which the key success factors in the business are changing. At this time, the firm which can anticipate what the competitive structure will reward in the future can accommodate itself to that new regime before competitors, whose prior successes have made them more resistant to change.

Clearly, one of the most rewarding strategies is for a firm to initiate a new product market. It is also one of the most risky. Several empirical studies have shown that the rewards to pioneers can be real and long lasting, enabling pioneers to receive premium prices and large market shares for long periods. In general, these pioneer advantages have been found in both consumer and industrial markets and have been found to be due to the pioneer's ability to choose the best position for its entry (leaving only smaller segments for its followers), the higher risk that consumers perceive in later entrants' products (for experience goods), and the costs for consumers to switch in terms of the usage skills required. In addition, pioneers of products for which the contribution of product attributes to overall value is ambiguous (as in the case of many new-to-the market products) benefit because, *if they are successful,* buyers shift their ideal points—their definition of the ideal product—in the direction of the pioneer. Further, the pioneer becomes the prototypical product, achieving perceptual prominence, which insulates it from me-too competitors.

Strategic change during the transition from rapid growth to the slower growth phase that precedes maturity is very important. Seldom do mature markets' economics allow competitors the same freedom that they enjoyed during the growth period. Success at this transition phase has been empirically shown to be the result of strategies which have provided the firm with a sustainable competitive advantage. With such a strategy, it is possible to be profitable even in many declining markets, but this depends on the rapidity and nature of the decline.

9

ANALYZING COMPETITION

At the heart of a free market system is competition—the idea that society's need for goods and services is maximized by requiring suppliers to vie for customers' patronage by varying the terms and attractiveness of their offerings. Although marketplace competition is an ever-present activity in modern societies, most would be hard pressed to define it. It is likely that even fewer truly understand it.

This chapter analyzes competition because understanding competition is necessary to creating effective competitive strategies. It begins by analyzing economic competition itself. Next, it uses economic analysis to define different types of competitive markets and to demonstrate the long-run effectiveness of the competitive system in eroding competitive advantage. Third, it introduces game theory as one technique for analyzing competitive interaction. It closes with an analysis of the long-run sustainability of supranormal profits.

PERSPECTIVES ON MARKETPLACE COMPETITION

The ability of exchange to create value for both participants is at the heart of the economic system. As noted in earlier chapters, buyers compete with other buyers, and sellers compete with other sellers to be partners in marketplace exchanges. How this competition occurs and how it can be viewed is the focus of this discussion.

Economists' Perspective on Competition[1]

Competition is at the heart of the economic system. It is the independent striving for patronage by the various sellers in a market—the pursuit of self-interest channeled and controlled by competition—that results in an optimization of a

---

[1] A good perspective on the evolution of economists' views can be found in David J. Teece, "Contributions and Impediments of Economic Analysis in the Study of Strategic Management" in James W. Frederickson, ed., *Perspectives on Strategic Management* (New York: Harper & Row, 1990).

society's economic performance. Competition, so defined, is the "invisible hand" to which Adam Smith referred.[2]

Curiously, economists have poor definitions of competition. They have extremely rigorous definitions of competitive markets but none of the concept of competition itself.[3] In their concern with the efficiency of markets, economists instead created the concept of perfect competition as the ideal case in which the welfare of the entire society was maximized, and then defined it in terms of the market structure that gave rise to it.

An industry can be said to be purely competitive "only when the number of firms selling a homogeneous commodity is so large, and each individual firm's share of the market is so small, that no individual firm finds itself able to influence appreciably the commodity's price by varying the quantity of output it sells."[4] A perfectly competitive market is "the *result* of the free entry of a large number of formerly competing firms . . . to the point where no *further* competition . . . is possible."[5]

Perfect competition involves "no presumption of psychological competition, emulation, or rivalry."[6] Paradoxically, in perfect competition there is no competition—the atomistic structure of the market assures that. In fact, in economic theory, every act of competition by a business is evidence of some degree of monopoly power.[7]

Schumpeterian Competition. Schumpeter perceived aspects of competition that other economists overlooked.[8] He described a process in which the flywheel of economic growth was fueled by a competition process in which technological innovation was key. He made two large contributions through his work. The first of these was on the technical side, when he conceived a technological change as occurring in the three steps of *invention, innovation,* and *imitation* (or diffusion). Invention he associated with the technical aspects of creating a new product or process. **Innovation,** to him, however, was even more important. Innovation is the entrepreneurial function required to bring that invention into economic reality. It involves identifying the market, raising the capital, developing the market, and the like. To Schumpeter, innovation is the important act, for the innovator frequently takes more risks than does the inventor.

[2] F. M. Scherer and David Ross, Industrial Market Structure and Economic Performance, 3rd ed. (Boston: Houghton Mifflin, 1990), p. 15.

[3] See Paul J. McNulty, "Economic Theory and the Meaning of Competition," *Quarterly Journal of Economics*, 82, no. 4 (November 1968), 639–656.

[4] Scherer and Ross, *Industrial Market Structure and Economic Performance*, p. 6.

[5] McNulty, "Economic Theory and the Meaning of Competition," p. 642.

[6] Frank H. Knight, "Immutable Law in Economics: Its Reality and Limitations," *American Economic Review*, 36, no. 2 (May 1946), 93–111.

[7] "A weird consequence is that the same behavior which the businessman sees as hallmarks of competition are viewed by many economists as indicia of monopoly." See Joel Dean, "Competition as seen by the Businessman and by the Economist," in Harvey W. Huegy, ed., *The Role and Nature of Competition in Our Marketing Economy* (Bureau of Economic and Business Research, University of Illinois, 1954), p. 10.

[8] J. A. Schumpeter, *The Theory of Economic Development* (Cambridge, MA: Harvard University Press, 1934).

Imitation or **diffusion** is the process by which the invention gains widespread use and, ultimately, is imitated by other firms.

Schumpeter's second contribution was to describe competition in ways closely related to the everyday meaning of the term. The process he describes is both dynamic and personal. For him, the "joys of the struggle and the hope of recognition as a winner may be more significant motivational considerations than the pecuniary rewards on which economists normally focus."[9] In this kind of competition, temporary supranormal profits are the reward for the successful innovator.[10] Since growth typically depends on profitability, a successful innovating firm will grow relative to other firms and may become dominant. In this way, one can see winners emerging from the competitive struggle.

Rivalry versus Competition. Economists' definition of competition varies from the behaviors that ordinary people describe as competition. In everyday business usage, competition means a conscious striving against other sellers for customers. That competition may involve price but more generally is conceived to include any of the attributes of an offering. "Competition, to the businessman, is whatever he has to do to get business away from his rivals and whatever they do to take sales away from him."[11] Economists term this activity *rivalry*.

The concept of rivalry contains two elements: goal incompatibility and the awareness of that incompatibility. Two firms bidding for a contract have incompatible goals. Only one will be awarded the business, and the loser will have lower sales as a result. Further, both firms are aware of that incompatibility. Under this distinction, then, it is possible to have vigorous rivalry that does not meet economists' definition of competition as well as to have pure competition without rivalry. In the former case, IBM, Unisys, Apple, and other computer manufacturers are rivals in an industry that is not perfectly competitive. In the latter case, neighboring farmers growing wheat or corn can be good friends because, while they are in competition, they are not rivals. Exhibit 9-1 provides a good insight into the concept of rivalry.

From a practical, managerial, and strategic viewpoint, rivalry is of greater interest. In comparison to the impersonal nature of pure (or monopolistic) competition, rivalry is personal, antagonistic, immediate, and identifiable. Its effects are not automatic and impersonal but are due, instead, to the actions of others who could have acted otherwise had they chosen to cooperate instead of to compete.

Oligopolistic competition is characterized by such mutual awareness and is the situation in which many decision makers find themselves. We explore the full implications of rivalry under oligopolistic competition later in this chapter.

---

[9] Richard R. Nelson and Sidney G. Winter, "Forces Generating and Limiting Concentration Under Schumpeterian Competition," *The Bell Journal of Economics*, 9, no. 2 (autumn 1978), p. 525.
[10] Those supranormal profits are temporary since the success of the innovating firm inevitably brings imitation by competitors, resulting in lowered profitability.
[11] Joel Dean, "Competition as Seen by the Businessman and by the Economist," p. 8

EXHIBIT 9-1

Portrait of Rivalry

A few days before Edwin Artzt was named CEO of Procter & Gamble . . . one of his colleagues snuck into his office and left a plaque on his desk: "It is not enough that I win; all others must lose." That sentiment, lifted from *The Leadership Secrets of Attila the Hun*, tells a lot about the competitive drive of the company's new leader. Says he: "Winning is the only result that matters. You have to establish benchmarks for yourself and then beat your own benchmarks."

SOURCE: Brian Dumaine, "P&G Rewrites the Marketing Rules," *Fortune*, © 1989 The Time Inc. Magazine Co. All rights reserved.

The Rationale for Competition.   At the root of economists' obsession with pure competition are three arguments. The first argument is political. In societies with competitive markets, power is diffused and the allocation of resources and distribution of income is solved through the impersonal mechanism of supply and demand. Neither government bureaucrats nor self-interested monopolists can exercise power over the marketplace or individuals' freedom to use their talents and skills as they prefer. This idea has strong intellectual and popular support. Apart from the economic issues they raise, most monopolies are simply disliked by their customers.

The second argument in favor of competitive markets is that they are efficient. In the long run (at equilibrium), no producer or industry is obtaining a return above that necessary to induce them to keep their investment at the level necessary to produce the industry's output efficiently. In simple terms, capital does not earn a surplus return. Further, in competitive markets price is equal to average total cost (including the aforementioned "rental" of the capital used) leading to efficiency in the allocation of resources in the economy (discussed later). Finally, firms that cannot operate at the lowest total cost lose money and are driven from the industry. Competitive markets give no shelter to inefficient producers.

The third major argument in support of competitive markets is that monopoly power leads to inefficiently allocated resources in the sense that the economy does not operate at maximum effectiveness in satisfying consumer wants. Without getting into all of the economics involved, there are two major effects from monopoly pricing. The first is simply that the profit-maximizing monopolist produces a smaller quantity of goods at a higher price than would happen in a competitive market. When the monopolist stops producing, there are still customers who would be willing to pay a higher price for the product than the monopolist's marginal cost. The problem is that to serve those customers the monopolist would have to reduce its price to all of those who would have paid a higher price, and thereby reduce its total profits. Had the monopolist done so, however, a larger number of individuals would have had their needs satisfied. The monopolist sacrifices social good for private good.

When that happens, fewer of the monopolized goods are produced than could be usefully consumed, and this too is the case with the total output of the economy. This happens because productive resources are allocated in a way that fails to maximize the value of the overall output bundle to society. In essence, if the monopolized industry were competitive, additional investment would move into it from other industries (or individuals), and this reallocation of productive investments would result in a higher total output for the economy. Monopoly distorts the allocation of investment in industries that is necessary to optimize total output.

Market Power.   Market power, also called monopoly power, is the ability of a firm to affect the price of its output relative to the price of the products of other producers in the general product class. Clearly, if a firm can affect its price, it is not in a perfectly competitive market. The only instance is which a seller does not possess at least some market power is under conditions of pure competition.

The source of market power is product differentiation. If offerings are truly perceived as identical (homogeneous) in all respects, then any increase by one supplier over the going price will reduce that supplier's unit volume sold to zero. Product differentiation exists when, for any reason, a seller is able to raise the product's price without sacrificing its entire sales volume. The strategist can estimate the degree (and value) of differentiation perceived by the market by observing the price the market is willing to pay for one product relative to the going price for the average product.

The following is an excerpt from an actual company document in which such an approach is discussed. The quotation is exact except that the terms *our differentiated product* and *standard product* replace the real product name used in the original document.

> The rapidly changing market conditions have made it increasingly difficult to promote our differentiated product at the originally planned pricing. A year ago in a shortage situation the market valued our differentiated product at 8 to 10 cents over the standard product. At present, however, the market is not prepared to pay more than a premium of between 2 and 8 cents depending on the market area and exact product involved. . . . The net result is that the market is putting a value on our differentiated product, a value that we have to live with and accept.

Differentiation can be achieved in any of the factors presented in chapter 3. Physical attributes, in-use performance benefits, pre- or post-sale service, delivery consistency, and supplier reputation are just some of the differences which a market may value sufficiently to warrant paying more than it does for the generic, homogeneous product. Putting it another way, the concept of value is inherent in differentiation. It is not enough that a product be different to be differentiated; that difference must be valued by the market.

Strategic Implications of Market Power.   In its present form, the science of economics is judgmental in the presence of market power. All it sees in its analyses are the inefficiencies and the less than optimal allocation of resource such marketplace imperfections cause. The reality, of course, is that the ideal of perfect competition will never be achieved. The assumption of full foresight, the absence of barriers to entry, and the full mobility of productive resources make perfect competition more of a base point for estimating economic efficiency than a realistic goal. Markets will be forever imperfect.

For the strategist, however, supranormal profits (or the potential to obtain supranormal profits) are a sign of opportunity. The strategist sees them as the market's way of attracting investment by indicating that customers highly value the good in question and that those who produce it will be rewarded. Barring an absolute lock on product or process technology by the monopolist, sooner or later those profits will attract someone who will find a way to copy, imitate, and compete with the monopolized product—even if only by luring away its customers with a substitute. In the real world, that kind of behavior makes markets more competitive. Firms that search for supranormal profits are fulfilling the market's imperative—filling needs that have yet to attract sufficient investment to satisfy customer needs.

MODELS OF COMPETITION[12]

In reducing real-world economic behavior into its basic elements and structures economists have been able to isolate, define, and predict many facets of competitive behavior. While their analyses may not always be of immediate help to the assistant product manager contemplating the relative efficacy of consumer couponing versus a trade deal to make this quarter's numbers as demanded by management, the understanding they provide of the underlying structure of competitive behavior is a valuable preparation in devising the overall competitive strategy for the brand of the firm's efforts in a product category. Exhibit 9-2 examines the nature of competition in many aspects of daily life and provides a good counterpoint to the discussion of economic competition.

The Basic Structure of Markets

The foregoing definition of pure competition included two key elements: the number of firms and product homogeneity. If these two elements are varied, a wide variety of market types can be differentiated. Table 9-1 classifies market structures based on whether there are one, few, or many sellers in the market and on product type—homogeneous or differentiated.

While this two-fold classification gives us five basic types of markets based on the type of competition they engender, in reality there are many more. The distinctions contained in Table 9-1 as categories are actually continuous vari

---

[12] An overview relevant to marketers is presented in Jehosua Eliashberg and Rabikan Chatterjee "Analytical Models of Competition with Implications for Marketing: Issues, Findings and Overlook," *Journal of Marketing Research*, 22 (August 1985), 237–261.

EXHIBIT 9-2

Competition

According to traditional usage, *competition* identifies a situation in which two or more people vie for a prize, honor, or advantage. . . . John Thompson, the highly successful Georgetown basketball coach, summed up a lot of fashionable thinking when he remarked, "Life is *about* competition."

The fuss over competition is a revival of some older conceits about the survival of the fittest and the laws of the jungle. The idea is that competition is the behavioral equivalent of gravity, a force that makes the world go 'round—the point being that life is shaped by individuals and species continually battling one another for food, space, sex and various luxury items. In the process, goes the theory, the minds and bodies of some individuals or species are greatly improved, and they become winners. The less able or less lucky—the dinosaur, the dusky seaside sparrow—are eliminated like early losers in a tennis tournament. With regard to the human species and its internecine struggles, this is called social Darwinism.

Indeed, it all sounds as if it has a lot to do with the realities of evolution and zoology, but it does not. The trouble with the theory of direct, unrelenting competition as a long-range force in a nature is that such a scheme always has fewer winners than losers. Thus the win-or-drop-dead, tennis-tournament model of evolution is at odds with the fact that, through the aeons, life-forms on Earth have become increasingly numerous and various. The multitude of species reflects the evolutionary drive to find a small edge—a niche, zoologists call it—that enables creatures to go about their business without always fighting with others with the same appetites.

Humans have long had a high regard for niches, which allow us to occupy positions in which competition is completely eliminated or greatly reduced. To this end we have invented such things as tariffs, tenure, the American Medical Association, and monopolies. A prominent college football coach once explained the attraction of monopolies in relation to the recruiting policies of his school: "We don't want just enough good football players. We want them all. If I have the six best quarterbacks in this great republic tied down at my school, anyone I play against will be going with no better than the seventh best. You follow my meaning?"

Good monopolies, however, are easier to fantasize about than to find. As a practical matter, cooperation is the tactic most commonly used to get what we want. Groups of people agree to divvy up desirable things, just as other species do natural resources and the NFL does draft picks. Individuals may not get everything they yearn for, but few are shut out completely. As a matter of historical record, many of the most notable human accomplishments—cathedrals, constitutions, college athletics departments—are monuments to co-operative behavior. So, while we may in principle praise the virtues and joys of

EXHIBIT 9-2 (cont.)

head-on competition, we are much less enthusiastic about it in practice. Getting what we want by taking it from somebody else in an overt contest is usually for us, as for other species, a last resort.

SOURCE: The following article is reprinted courtesy of *Sports Illustrated* from the May 16, 1988 issue Copyright © 1988, Time Inc. "Competition: Is It What Life's All About?" by Bil Gilbert. All rights reserved.

ables. While a product either is or is not homogeneous, there can be many gradations of differentiation. The same may also be said about the number of firms: The case for monopoly is clear but the dividing line between a few and many is not. The strategist seeking insight must remember this: The distinctions made are abstractions of reality; they are not reality.[13]

Monopoly, Oligopoly, and Monopolistic Competition

Like the case with product homogeneity, it is easy to identify monopoly and not monopoly. Where oligopoly ends and pure or monopolistic competition begins is a more difficult distinction, however. In the case of pure competition, each seller is so small relative to the total market that it can act as if its output has no effect (for all practical purposes) on market price (and be good friends with neighbors, therefore).[14] This perception (that the seller can sell as much as it wants at the market price) is the key to identifying the dividing line between oligopoly and pure competition.

The difference between few and many is behaviorally defined: If the firm feels that its fortunes are perceptibly affected by specific others' actions and that its actions can significantly affect specific others, then that market can be termed oligopolistic. Sellers who consider themselves conscious rivals, defined as those who recognize that one's gains are losses to some specific other seller, are therefore oligopolists.

Monopolistic competitors, in contrast, can seldom identify those who lose when they gain, or vice versa.[15] The clothing and fashion industries exemplify

[13] A key element is completely absent from this classification—the number of buyers. There is such a thing as buyer power (monopsony), and that does influence sellers' actions. One could make the case that the table should be three dimensional to take this into account.

[14] This creates the classic catch 22 of perfect competition. Each atomistic producer therefore expands output, and the price plummets as a result of the excess supply.

[15] According to Scherer and Ross (*Industrial Market Structure and Economic Competition*), monopolistic competition exists when competitors are small relative to the market for their general class of products and entry into the market is free. Two versions of the concept exist, however. One terms it *monopolistic competition* and emphasizes product differentiation. The other terms it *imperfect competition* and stresses market imperfections such as firm location, differences in sales skills, reputation, or advertising. See William L. Baldwin, *Market Power, Competition and Antitrust Policy*, (Homewood IL: Richard D. Irwin, Inc. 1987) pp. 196–197.

TABLE 9-1 *Principal Seller's Market Structure Types*

	NUMBER OF SELLERS		
	ONE	A FEW	MANY
Homogeneous product	Pure monopoly	Homogeneous oligopoly	Pure competition
Differentiated product	Pure monopoly	Differentiated oligopoly	Monopolistic competition

SOURCE: F. M. Scherer and David Ross, *Industrial Market Structure and Economic Performance*, 3rd ed. Copyright © 1990 Houghton Mifflin Co. Used with permission.

monopolistic competition. While there are undoubtedly specific industry segments that are oligopolistic in nature, the large numbers of sellers with widely varying styles, colors, and qualities in most sectors exemplifies the impersonality of monopolistic competition.

Moreover, monopolistic competition is characterized by two conflicting forces: differentiation and imitation (or ease of entry). These forces work at both the industry and firm level. If the entire industry earns economic profits, then new firms will enter and reduce those profits to the risk-adjusted level. If an individual firm in the industry is able to create an offering for which the market is willing to pay high prices, then existing or new producers will imitate it as quickly as they are able, thereby reducing the excess profits by their imitation or entry. The computer hard disk drive business described in chapter 8 is a good example. Some forty-three firms entered the business in four years.

To understand the importance of ease of entry, consider the fashion-oriented clothing business and the confections (candy) business. At the industry level, there is relatively easy entry and exit. As the fortunes of the industry fluctuate, the number of participants in both goes up and down. At the individual firm or product level, however, the picture is different. Knock-offs (line-for-line copies of successful designers) are common in the fashion business. Hot items, fast-selling styles, are quickly imitated and just as quickly reduce the size of the monopoly profits that the originator can claim.

At the product level in the candy business, however, that ability to duplicate the preferred or fast-selling style is hampered by the importance of branding. A Baby Ruth® or Snickers® bar may be physically duplicated, but consumers consistently prefer the branded item. Similar entry barriers at the product level exist in the toy business. As the market demonstrated several years ago, even four, five, and six year olds were able to tell the difference between original and imitation Cabbage Patch® dolls and rejected the imitators.

Contestable Markets. As noted earlier, economists have historically equated the efficiency of markets with their structure. Only perfectly competitive markets, by their analyses, could be efficient. The traditional wisdom, moreover, was that efficiency was a function of the number of competitors. With the worst case being an unregulated pure monopoly, relative efficiency in resource allocation was expected to increase in parallel with the number of competitors.

Recent work, however, has challenged this. Work by Baumol, Panzar, and Willig has indicated that a new type of market may be conceptualized—termed a *perfectly contestable market*—which can yield the same, socially desirable results even though its structure may be characterized as monopoly or oligopoly.[16] "A contestable market is one into which entry is absolutely free, *and exit is absolutely costless.*"[17] Intuitively, the reason for this is easy to understand. Under such conditions, incumbent competitors must act with an eye toward the potential of hit-and-run entry, and therefore do all of the things that ensure economic efficiency. In short, this means to price in a way that does not create the economic profits that would attract such a competitor.

Although the case of monopoly is not as clear, once a second producer emerges and the necessary conditions for contestability exist, any contestable market must behave ideally in every respect. As Baumol notes, economic "optimality is *not* approached gradually as the number of firms supplying a commodity grows . . . two firms can be enough to guarantee optimality."[18]

Perfect contestability is as much an ideal case as is perfect competition. It is, however, a more general concept, a broader ideal with wider applicability than the concept of perfect competition since it removes the constraint that there be a large number of competitors to achieve the desired economic efficiency.

The necessary conditions for a contestable market deserve some discussion. *Freedom of entry* does not imply the absence of costs or of ease. It means that the entrant is able to practice the productive technology such that it suffers no cost disadvantage nor real or perceived product quality disadvantage relative to incumbents. *Absolutely costless exit* means that the firm can leave the industry without impediment; it can recoup any costs incurred in its entry either by selling assets or reusing them with no cost other than those attributable to normal wear and tear or depreciation.

Under such conditions, then, any risk of entry is eliminated. Further, with such conditions, the only consideration in the entry decision is the preentry prices of the incumbents. Markets like this exist. Consider the case of airline competition between city pairs. Assume that there are two airlines, one flying between points *a* and *b*, the other airline with gates in those same two cities but with no direct service between the two. If the monopolist prices like a monopolist, the second airline will quickly move in, price to capture the volume and profits available, and move on when the monopoly profits disappear. Entry and exit were costless. From a strategic viewpoint, the idea of contestable markets suggests the overriding importance of barriers to entry as a condition of true profitability.

Oligopoly Theory

Oligopoly theory is in many ways the most interesting and useful model of competition simply because, in contrast to the other competitive states, the

---

[16] William J. Baumol, John C. Panzar, and Robert D. Willig, *Contestable Markets and the Theory of Industry Structure* (San Diego, CA: Harcourt Brace Jovanovich, 1982).

[17] Baumol, "Contestable Markets: An Uprising in the Theory of Industry Structure," p. 3.

[18] Baumol, "Contestable Markets: An Uprising," p. 2.

oligopolist has the most difficult competitive situation. In monopoly, the firm has no direct competition; the demand curve it faces is the market demand curve. In perfect competition, each firm can sell all it can produce at the market-determined price. It must simply compete straightforwardly.[19] In oligopoly, on the other hand, the firm's actions influence its competitors' actions. It needs to predict not only what customers will do in response to its actions but what its competitors will do. Further, the firm can choose any of a number of competitive orientations. It can compete aggressively, it can be docile and follow the lead of some other firm, or it can seek to avoid competition.

The problem with oligopoly is that there is no determinate solution to the problem of how to act. While economists have developed numerous theories of behavior under oligopolistic conditions—from simple to mathematically complex—none can explain or predict all of the diverse behavior actually observed. Anything can and does happen. Some oligopolies hold prices up as high as one would expect from an unregulated monopolist, while in others there are intense price wars.

Understanding Competitive Behavior in Oligopoly

Cournot's Insights.   Augustin Cournot was an economist who worked in the first half of the nineteenth century. His analysis of rivalry in a duopoly (the two-firm case of oligopoly) assumes that the competitors move only after having seen the other's move. At the heart of the model is the actor's assumption that the competitor will not respond, specifically that it will hold its price. The following example differs somewhat from Cournot's original but retains its essential flavor.[20]

Imagine two firms in a duopoly, each of which makes products that while functionally equivalent are nonetheless different. One could make red dresses, for example, the other green dresses. While that difference does not translate into any direct qualitative or performance advantages or disadvantages, it is sufficient to allow both to sell in the market at different prices. When prices are equal, both share the market equally; when the price of one is lower than the other, its share is larger as a function of the percentage difference between the two prices. The market is responsive to the industry's weighted average price as well. Higher average prices reduce total unit volume; lower prices increase total unit volume.

In such a situation, while it is clear to both that if the rivals were to collude or simply refuse to compete on a price basis where they could share the market

---

[19] To compete straightforwardly does not mean that there are no decisions to make or that the task is easy. It does mean, however, that the firm focuses its attention on producing the best possible offering to the market with no regard to the possible actions of any specific competitor. In oligopoly, on the other hand, the interdependence between the competing firms makes it necessary for each to consider the possible moves that the others could take before choosing its actions.

[20] The example is essentially one offered by Scherer and Ross, *Industrial Market Structure and Economic Performance*, pp. 200–208.

at a high price and with high profits, it is also clear to both that if one were to cut its price and the other did not respond,[21] the price cutter would make even more than it would be maintaining price equality. In such a situation, then, the two engage in a price-cutting and counter-cutting sequence. This little dance continues until neither firm can unilaterally increase its profits by further downward price changes.

The irony of this sequence is that, at the end, both are earning a smaller profit than they would had they been able to hold to the original price or had they acted jointly. What prevents them from acting jointly to raise price, however, is the same assumption that led them down their price spiral: the myopic assumption that their rival's price is fixed. Under this assumption, if one rival were to consider raising its price, it would have to assume that the other would hold its existing price and that the price raiser will therefore lose share and profits.

Cournot used this analysis to conclude that a determinate and stable price/quantity equilibrium exists for any industry. Further, he concluded that the equilibrium price is a function of the number of sellers—with price decreasing as the number of sellers increased until it reached the competitive level.

Clearly, the assumption made at every move, that the rival will not respond, is flawed. The rival's continuing responses demonstrate the incorrectness of the assumption, yet each continues to hold to the assumption and to continue its behavior. Edwin Chamberlain took steps to improve the analysis.

Chamberlain's Contributions.   Chamberlain made his analysis with the understanding that any rational business executive would soon realize that his or her assumption that the rival would not respond was unreal. As he put it,

> If each seeks his maximum profit rationally and intelligently, he will realize that when there are only two or a few sellers his own move has a considerable effect upon his competitors, and that this makes it idle to suppose that they will accept without retaliation the losses he forces upon them. Since the result of a cut by any one is inevitably to decrease his own profits, no one will cut, and although the sellers are entirely independent, the equilibrium result is the same as though there were a monopolistic agreement between them.[22]

The point that Chamberlain makes is simple: Monopoly pricing follows naturally from the very structure of an industry. The argument is based on the fact that once firms recognize their mutual self-interest (especially in a high

---

[21] One need not assume that the other will not respond for the analysis to work. Simply imagine a market in which daily, real-time volume is high and that it takes one day for the other firm to respond. The price cutter will gain a net addition of one day's sales at the higher market-share rate before the other can restore equilibrium through its own price action. Price changes in the airline and commodity petrochemicals industries are often described and justified in such terms. See, for example, James E. Ellis, "The Airlines Just Don't Know How to Stay Out of Fights," *Business Week,* October 23, 1989, p. 55.

[22] E. H. Chamberlain, *The Theory of Monopolistic Competition* (Cambridge, MA: Harvard University Press, 1933), p. 48.

price), the only reasonable assumption is that they will indeed behave accordingly. This is his main contribution: When sellers are few and products standardized, formal collusion is not necessary to establish a monopoly price.

There are several exceptions to this result which serve to explain commonly observed behavior. The first is that as the number of sellers in the market increases, there comes a point at which the recognition of mutual interdependence unravels. In fact, if it becomes clear that one seller is likely to begin an independent pricing policy, even a fully rational oligopolist may decide to be the first on the bandwagon.[23] Such behavior can happen abruptly, and the price can rapidly slide down to the competitive price.

The point at which this slide occurs is unknown. There is some evidence that the existence of a third firm (large relative to the two leaders) may be sufficient in some instances to reduce prices and returns. In a study of industries with high two-firm concentration ratios (the share of market held by the two largest firms), profit margins declined sharply when there was a large third firm. The researcher noted that "equality of size among three large firms appears to breed a rivalry capable of simulating competitive performance levels."[24] While there is some question about the study and the generalizability of its findings, such an effect is at least plausible, given the more recent theoretical work on contestable markets cited earlier in this chapter.[25]

The second common exception occurs when there are substantial time lags between the point at which one competitor cuts price and the other matches it. In very large markets where vast amounts are sold daily, the firm that undercuts the monopoly price can gain considerable extra share in the interim period before parity is restored. Given a slow enough response time and a high enough cost of capital (which makes the time-adjusted value of a sale today worth much more in comparison to a sale tomorrow), it is possible that such behavior may make economic sense. Of course, such reasoning causes prices to slide. If every seller is convinced that it can win if it is the "first down and last up," then the monopoly price will seldom hold.[26]

Air travel pricing seems at times to follow such behavior. Since air travel involves high fixed costs, almost infinitesimal variable costs, and a very perishable product,[27] a cutter can gain financially in even the few days it takes for competitors to restore parity. While it is tempting to say that the price would not have fallen had the cutter not acted, the price-cutting firm likely reasoned that since, in its analysis of supply and demand, the price was unlikely to hold anyway, it might as well be the first to cut it and to achieve the temporary advantage. It is for this reason that airlines constantly monitor each other's fares

[23] Baldwin, *Market Power, Competition, and Antitrust Policy*, p. 193
[24] John E. Kwoka, "The Effect of Market Share Distribution on Industry Performance," *Review of Economics and Statistics*, 61, no. 1 (February 1979), 101–109.
[25] See the comments in Baldwin, *Market Power, Competition, and Antitrust Policy*, p. 313.
[26] Attempting to be "first down and last up" is the stated objective of the pricing policies of many firms in large, commodity-like markets.
[27] Perishability in this case refers to the fact that whenever a plane takes off with an empty seat, the opportunity to sell it disappears.

and have managers and staffs capable of quickly responding to price cuts on constant duty.

A third exception is centered around the existence of differences in each firm's costs and market shares.[28] The existence of such differences may make it difficult for the industry to choose a profit-maximizing price. For example, the optimal price for the firm with a large market share and low marginal costs would be lower than for a smaller firm with low overhead and high variable costs. The end result is that although the industry's members share the common goal of maximizing industry profits, their profit structures are sufficiently different that it will be difficult to set a price which is attractive to all members. In cases like this, it is possible to observe very aggressive, myopic, and profit-destroying behavior.

For example, in the early 1980s, there were major cost differences between the traditional airlines and the newer, nonunion, low-fixed-cost airlines such as People's Express. Those cost differences were sufficient to result in drastically different ideas about the proper price. The low-cost airlines, in fact, were able to use a classic strategic rule: Put your competitors on the horns of a dilemma. As the vice president of a big airline was quoted, "Either we don't match [prices] and we lose customers, or we match [prices] and then, because our costs are so high, we lose buckets of money."[29] In 1989, the story was much the same, except that it was the weak competitors' needs for cash that impelled them to discount fares during the traditionally slow (for nonbusiness travel) fall season. As a senior vice president put it, "This is a least common denominator business where the weakest company sets the pricing."[30]

Game Theoretic Approaches to Oligopoly

At the root of the problems of oligopolistic competition is the gulf between competitive and cooperative behavior. While all parties understand that cooperation is better than competition, in the absence of binding collusion or enforceable sanctions it requires a leap of faith for one of the competitors to take the first cooperative step, because by so doing it becomes vulnerable to the others' possibly competitive actions.

The rules of strategy enumerated in chapter 1 were clear on this matter: The only sure strategy is one of invulnerability and assume that your competitor will take the actions that result in the worst possible outcome for you. For example, given Procter & Gamble's reputation ("The only good competitor is a dead competitor" is rumored to be P&G's motto), one would have to have a death wish to knowingly and voluntarily take any action that would leave one vul-

---

[28] For a full exposition of these differences, see Scherer and Ross, *Industrial Market Structure and Economic Performance*, pp. 238–248.

[29] William M. Carley, "Rough Flying: Some Major Airlines Are Being Threatened By Low-cost Rivals," *The Wall Street Journal*, October 12, 1983, p. 23.

[30] James E. Ellis, "The Airlines Just Don't Know How to Stay Out of Fights," *Business Week*, October 23, 1989, p. 55.

nerable to its actions. Game theory offers insights that lead to a better understanding of such situations.

The Basic Elements.   Game theory is an extremely rigorous and powerful technique for the analysis of certain kinds of competitive situations.[31] It is at its strongest in the analysis of two-person, zero-sum games. This limitation frustrates somewhat the high early expectations that game theory promised, but for strategy-making purposes game theory is sufficient to allow decision makers to gain insights into many types of competitive situations.

In a zero-sum game, what one gains, another loses. Figure 9-1 presents a simple payoff matrix which illustrates the basic concepts. Player A can play any of the three strategies, 1, 2, and 3. The three strategies have the payoffs to A as shown in the matrix as a function of the moves of player B (whose payoffs are the negative of A's). If A chooses strategy 1 and player B chooses its strategy 1, then A wins 8 and B loses 8. The problem each faces, however, is that both must move simultaneously (neither knows what the other's move will be) and that there will be only one play of the game.

Von Neuman and Morgenstern were able to demonstrate mathematically that there is a strategy rule by which both will maximize their outcomes given such a situation.[32] If the players follow a pure strategy of either *minimax* or *maximin*, such an outcome will be realized. A minimax strategy is one in which the player minimizes the maximum loss; maximin strategy is one in which the player maximizes the minimum gain.

If one examines A's rows, the principle will be clear. While the row 1 strategy would allow A to make as much as 8, it could also cause it to lose as much as 10; a row 2 strategy would allow a gain of 6 and a loss of 2; a row 3 strategy allows a win of only 5 but the smallest possible loss of the three strategies—only 1. By minimizing the maximum loss, taking a row 3 strategy, A has immunized itself from the actions of its competitor—the worst that can happen to it is the one-point loss.

It can do this because it is intelligent; it assumes that B is rational and that it will be playing its best possible strategy, the one that gives B the best possible outcome whatever move A makes. That strategy is B's column 2—whatever action A takes, B will never make less than one point. The strategy is stable; for A to have moved to another strategy would have caused it to lose more (-2 or -5). A similar analysis for B shows that given A's strategy, it could not have done better, either. Neither has cause to regret its choice.

There is no incentive for cooperation in the particular zero-sum game illus-

---

[31] See Jean-Pierre Ponssard, *Competitive Strategies* (Amsterdam: North Holland Publishing Company, 1981); and Avinish Dixit and Barry Nalebuff, *Thinking Strategically: The Competitive Edge in Business, Politics, and Everyday Life* (New York: W. W. Norton, 1991).

[32] This statement requires two very basic assumptions: (1) that the players are rational and therefore maximize their subjective expected utility; and (2) that they are intelligent and therefore recognize the other firm's rationality. This means that they can analyze the other firm's position and reason from its viewpoint. See K. S. Moorthy, "Using Game Theory to Model Competition," *Journal of Marketing Research*, 22, no. 3 (August 1985), 262–282.

Figure 9-1   Zero-sum game

		B'S STRATEGIES		
		B₁	B₂	B₃
	A₁	8	−5	−10
A'S STRATEGIES	A₂	0	−2	6
	A₃	4	−1	5

CELL ENTRIES REFLECT A'S PAYOFFS.

SOURCE: F. M. Scherer and David Ross, *Industrial Market Structure and Economic Performance*, 3rd ed. Copyright ©
1990 Houghton Mifflin Co. Used with permission.

trated. Player A is going to lose unless player B is irrational. There is nothing
that A can do to induce any other behavior on the part of B.

Variable-sum Games. The problem with the application of such strategies to
oligopolistic competition is that the zero-sum assumption seldom operates.
While a market-share war looks like a zero-sum game, transforming it into a
game in which profits rather than market share form the payoffs is more realistic. The problem is that while a minimax strategy is unbeatable in a zero-sum
game, it is not an optimal strategy in variable-sum games. The crux of the
problem in playing such games is to recognize how to transform them and to
induce cooperative behavior.

The *prisoners' dilemma* is a particularly relevant illustration of the issue. We
first examine it in its original form and then translate it into a business example.

Imagine that you and a partner have committed a crime and have been
apprehended as suspects. The problem for the authorities is that although they
have good reason to know that you are the perpetrators, they have no proof and
can only prosecute you on minor charges unless one of you confesses. Your
problem is that the authorities are holding each of you in separate cells, unable
to communicate with each other, and that they have offered each of you a deal
(unknown to the other), illustrated by the payoff matrix in Figure 9-2.

The first figure in each cell of the matrix is your payoff; the second is your
partner's payoff. The term for the minor charges is one year—if neither of you
confesses, that is the worst that can happen. On the other hand, if both of you
confess, each of you gets six years. The offer you have been made, however, is to
turn state's evidence and confess—that way, you get off free, but your partner
gets ten years in prison. What would you do? What will your partner do?

For whatever reason, you will likely confess. Whether you argue that you
absolutely cannot abide incarceration and value highly any opportunity to get off
free or alternatively argue that you simply do not trust your partner, you
confess—and so does your partner, and you both serve six years. In game terms,
the confess strategy dominates the don't-confess strategy.

To translate this into a business situation, simply change the strategy titles
to low price and high price and you have the classic problem of a duopoly. The
low-price strategy seems to have an irresistible magnetism. Because of the nature of the situation, either because of rare opportunism or lack of trust, both
rivals end up with lower profits.

Figure 9-2   Prisoners' Dilemma

		YOUR PARTNER'S STRATEGIES:	
		DON'T CONFESS	CONFESS
YOUR STRATEGIES:	DON'T CONFESS	−1, −1	−10, 0
	CONFESS	0, −10	−6, −6

SOURCE: F. M. Scherer and David Ross, *Industrial Market Structure and Economic Performance*, 3rd ed. Copyright © 1990 Houghton Mifflin Co. Used with permission.

There are three reasons why this outcome occurs. The first is one of communication and information. If the rivals cannot communicate, the probability of defection is high (that's why the police interrogate prisoners separately). Second is the potential existence of lags in response. If one rival thinks that there is a real possibility that some time may elapse before the other responds, he or she may act to gain the interim benefits.

The third source of the outcome is the structure of the game. In a one-trial game (games which have but one play, as in the prisoners' dilemma) or in games with a known finite number of trials, rivals must assume opportunistic behavior of the other. Opportunistic behavior simply means that the individual will take that action which maximizes individual utility. Since there is to be but one play of the game, there is no incentive to cooperate.

In a continuous game (or one with an unknown, indefinite duration), on the other hand, two effects occur: (1) Repetitive experiences under stable conditions provide the rivals with the opportunities to learn to trust and cooperate; and (2) repetition allows each to threaten the other with damaging retaliation tomorrow if opportunistic behaviors are chosen today. Exhibit 9-3 provides insight into the ways cooperation can be elicited even in such noncooperative settings.

Using Game Theoretic Approaches to Analyze Oligopolistic Competition.
Business situations are well suited to analysis by game theoretic approaches because rationality and rewards can generally be defined in economic terms.[33] Intelligent firms can therefore put themselves in the other firms' positions and reason from their points of view. Once this is done, the firm can make the strong assumption that actions that competitors will take and those of the firm itself will be driven by the rational seeking of the rewards which maximize the utility function.[34] One of the problems with this analysis is its assumption that the competitive reactions will take place in the same product market. This need not be the case as Exhibit 9-4 demonstrates in its discussion of the cross-parry.

MARKET ENTRY DECISIONS.   An example will clarify this logic. Figure 9-3 presents an extensive form representation of a hypothetical payoff matrix facing

[33] This is not to say that management always acts in ways that maximize shareholder wealth. However, in comparison to other situations in which participants' utility functions may be totally unknown and even vary considerably among players, businesses pay at least nominal attention to the profit criterion.

[34] This assumes that both firms share a common view of the available strategies and their payoffs. If this is the case, then the strategies each takes will not only be given in the sense that to do otherwise would be irrational but will also be an equilibrium in that neither would unilaterally change its strategy. See Moorthy, "Using Game Theory to Model Competition," pp. 264–266.

EXHIBIT 9-3

TIT FOR TAT:

The Emergence of Cooperation in a Competitive Environment

The Prisoner's Dilemma precisely describes the central problem of competing in a duopoly or oligopoly. Both parties acknowledge the advantages of avoiding ruinous behavior but are wary of initiating cooperative behavior for fear of being exploited by the other. This same behavior underlies many issues in international relations, the arms race, and even those between two individuals.

One researcher, Robert Axelrod, decided to explore how cooperation evolved in such settings through the use of the Prisoner's Dilemma. He invited experts in game theory to create computer programs for use in an iterated Prisoner's Dilemma tournament. In an iterated Prisoner's Dilemma, the participants "play" a long series of the game rather than just one trial. The winner in such a tournament is the one who accumulates the largest number of points. Since there are two ways of winning (to confess when the other cooperates or when both cooperate), the game is a good test of cooperative versus competitive strategies. Two rounds of the tournament were run. In the first, some fourteen entries plus a simple random rule were run against each other in a round robin tournament. The results of that tournament were circulated together with an invitation for another round for which 62 entries from six countries were received. In each tournament 200 trials were run.

Surprisingly, the winner was the same both times and was the simplest and "nicest" of the strategies submitted. *Nice* means that it is never the first to confess. The strategy, termed TIT FOR TAT, was submitted by Anatol Rapopor of the University of Toronto. The strategy was to start with a cooperative move and thereafter to do what the other player did on the previous move. What is interesting is that all of the players in the second tournament knew of this strategy's success in the first tournament yet the strategy still succeeded.

There appear to be four properties of TIT FOR TAT that make it successful

1. It avoids unnecessary conflict by cooperating as long as the other player does
2. It responds immediately (on the next move) to an uncalled-for defection by the other (by making a non-cooperative move—confessing),
3. It forgives immediately on the next move (by reverting to the cooperative mode)
4. Its behavior is clear—the other player can learn its pattern of action.

Two insights into competition can be gained from this research. First, it leads to an understanding of how competition can become more or less intense in oligopolistic markets through the continued interactions of the competitors in the marketplace. It demonstrates how a competitive equilibrium can be reached without direct communication or collusion among the competitors. It is as Chamberlain predicted.

EXHIBIT 9-3 (cont.)

The second insight strikes at the heart of the theory of competitive strategy which requires that every analysis begin with the assumption that your competitor will take that action which results in the worst possible outcome for you. It may be that unless there will be but one play of the game or the stakes are small enough that *preparing for the worst but acting cooperatively may bring better returns*. It is possible to be too competitive, in other words.

SOURCE: From *The Evolution of Cooperation* by Robert Axelrod. Copyright © 1984 by Robert Axelrod. Reprinted by permission of Basic Books, a division of HarperCollins Publishers Inc.

a possible new entrant into a business or market. As shown in the figure, if the firm does not enter the incumbent does not respond. If it enters, however, then the incumbent can either decide to fight the entry (increase advertising or couponing, decrease price) or to acquiesce to the new competitor's entry.

Knowledge of the payoff matrix allows one to understand the likely behavior of the two firms. For example, if the potential entrant can be assured of acquiescence by the incumbent, then it should enter. On the other hand, if the incumbent will fight entry, then the entrant should not enter. For the incumbent, the best would be for the entry not to occur, but if the entry is going to happen, it is better to give in (acquiesce) rather than fight. At this point, rationality and intelligence have their effect.

In reality, the entrant which is aware of the true payoffs faced by the incumbent and which is reasonably assured that the incumbent is rational should not hesitate to enter. The apparent fight strategy is a spurious threat—the incumbent will not fight if actually confronted with entry (it can make more money by not fighting). On the other hand, if the potential entrant is uncertain about the true payoffs (and the incumbent is aware of this uncertainty), fighting becomes a real threat. The entrant knows that there are situations in which the payoff from an incumbent's fighting a new entrant makes economic sense, and it is unable to rule out that possibility.

ADVERTISING COMPETITION.   Advertising competition in an oligopoly presents some interesting insights into competitive behavior. The forces that Chamberlain spoke of, the recognition of mutual interdependence that is the hallmark of oligopolistic competition, should work in the same manner as in the price arena. Yet there is reason to believe that firms may behave otherwise.

Figure 9-4 presents a prisoners' dilemma game matrix of such a situation (the payoffs to A are listed first, payoffs to B are second). If one were to make a prediction based on oligopoly theory, then one would expect that the two firms should spend $4 million each on advertising—the joint profit-

EXHIBIT 9-4

Multiple-Point Competition, Competitive Harassment, and the Cross-Parry

Most economic theory describes competition within a given product market. But modern firms compete across many different product markets across varying geographical marketplaces, and the forms of competition match that diversity. One seldom discussed form of economic competition is called competitive harassment, the cross-parry, or, more technically, multiple-point competition. In its most obvious military form, it is known as attacking a competitor's supply lines rather than directly confronting his attacking troops. Without supplies, the troops soon stop attacking and the objective is achieved without a direct confrontation at the point of attack. Similar forms of competition exist in the marketplace as well, as the following examples show.

In 1988, when the Clorox Company began test marketing a line of laundry detergents, a market it had not been in, it soon found Procter & Gamble test marketing a new liquid bleach positioned directly against Clorox bleach under P&G's well-known Comet brand name. While many in the industry didn't dispute that P&G had long been interested in entering the bleach business, they found it too coincidental with the possible entry of a Clorox laundry detergent. "Procter views Clorox's bleach business as the cash generator for funding [Clorox's] efforts into other household product areas," said Jay Freedman, household products analyst at Kidder Peabody. "P&G most likely is trying to take some of that profit away, deflecting Clorox's attention from laundry detergents."[35] Clorox was not to be deterred, however, and continued to test its laundry detergent until, in 1991, it decided the attempt was not profitable enough to continue. The company took a $125 million writeoff on the venture.[36]

In the 1980s, Eastman Kodak was having difficulty defending itself against the Japanese onslaught. Fuji Photo Film attacked the American and European markets, in which Kodak was the dominant force in color film. Kodak's margins were squeezed and it was forced into a defensive cost-cutting effort to prop up profits. But once they had admitted to themselves that Fuji's global challenge was real, Kodak executives decided that the best strategy was to attack Fuji's source of cash, the Japanese market where it had a 70% share. Kodak entered the market in 1984 with 15 people, and by 1990s Kodak's sales in Japan had reached $1.3 billion in spite of fierce resistance from the entrenched Fuji. In fact some of Fuji's best executives were pulled back to Tokyo to aid in the battle, and its domestic margins have been squeezed. Fuji has proved to be as vulnerable to attack in Japan as Kodak was in America.[37]

---

[35] Laurie Freeman and Wayne Walley, "Bleach Battle Spills Out," *Advertising Age*, March 7, 1988, p. 4. See also "A Washout for Clorox?" *Business Week*, July 9, 1990, pp. 32, 33.
[36] "Clorox, in Revamping, to Drop Detergent," *The New York Times*, May 18, 1991, p. 37.
[37] "The Revenge of Big Yellow," *The Economist*, November 10, 1990, pp. 77, 78.

After BIC had revolutionized the ballpoint pen business with its throw-away pen and mass-merchandising techniques, it found itself being attacked by Gillette's entry into the market with its own formidable array of merchandising skills. Since BIC's primary business centered on its disposable pens, it needed to respond in a way that would force Gillette to pay attention. BIC's counterattack took the form of entry into the disposable razor market, which offered it two advantages: It not only directly attacked Gillette's source of cash but also represented a good business expansion strategy in its own right.[38]

What are the rules governing this kind of competition? The essence of the strategy requires that there be differences between the rivals in the importance of the markets and segments in which they participate such that what is profitable to one not be so to the other. This difference allows one to threaten the other with little risk or cost to oneself. P&G was not in the liquid laundry bleach market, so it was not concerned if its actions lowered profitability in that market. Kodak had not been in the Japanese film market, so it cared little if its entry ruined that market's profitability. Disposable razors would be only a small percentage of BIC's business, whereas they represented the core profit and cash machine for Gillette.

---

maximizing price. Scherer, however, notes three reasons why the competitors are likely to end up spending $6 million each and receiving lower profits as a result:[39]

1. Price cuts can be matched almost instantaneously, whereas it may take an extended period to retaliate to advertising, during which time the initiator may enjoy market share and profit gains;
2. Success in advertising involves both the amount of advertising spending and its creative content. While any competitor can match the dollar spending, it is not always apparent how to counteract clever advertising.[40]
3. Given the absence of price cutting in oligopoly, managers may use nonprice competition as an outlet for their competitive instincts.

Empirical evidence suggests that the prisoners' dilemma may be a good model for analyzing such competition.[41] Congress banned television and radio advertising by tobacco companies as of January 1, 1971. This was analogous to

[38] This example is cited in Aneel Karnani and Birger Wernerfelt, "Multiple Point Competition," *Strategic Management Journal*, 6 (1985), 87–96.
[39] F. M. Scherer, *Industrial Market Structure and Economic Performance*, 2nd ed. (Boston: Houghton Mifflin, 1980), p. 388.
[40] Scherer and Ross note that one key to this is the self-image of the contestants. "In this unpredictable clash of creative power sellers often tend to overestimate their own ability to make market share gains and underestimate their rivals' ability to retaliate successfully, exhibiting little concern for mutual interdependence." See Scherer and Ross, *Industrial Market Structure and Economic Performance*, p. 595.
[41] Other models are possible. See, for example, Gary M. Erickson, "A Model of Advertising Competition," *Journal of Marketing Research*, 12, no. 3 (August 1985), 297–303.

Figure 9-3   Payoff matrix for a new entrant

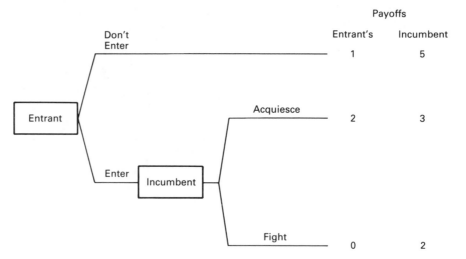

SOURCE: Sridhar Moorthy, "Using Game Theory to Model Competition," in *Journal of Marketing Research*, XXII, no. 3 (August 1985), p. 270. Reprinted with permission of the American Marketing Association.

a legislated move from the $6 million to the $4 million level in the matrix shown in Figure 9-4. Just as profitability improves in our example, so too did the tobacco companies'. Advertising dropped by $63 million in that first year and profits rose by $90 million.[42]

THE INDUSTRIAL ORGANIZATION APPROACH

Industrial organization economists are concerned with the performance of markets and, thereby, the economic system. In their terms, performance has several dimensions: (1) that it be efficient (does not waste resources) and responsive (provides qualities and quantities consumers want); (2) that producers use emerging technologies to further the long-run growth of real per-capita income; (3) that full employment should be facilitated by producers' actions; (4) that income is distributed equally—especially that producers not receive rewards in excess of those necessary to call forth their services and capital.[43]

Figure 9-5 depicts the basic paradigm industrial organization economists use in their research. Performance is postulated to be a function of the conduct of the sellers in a market. That conduct, in turn, is dependent on the structure of the market. Both market structure and performance are influenced by the basic

---

[42] Quoted in Scherer and Ross, *Industrial Market Structure*, p. 596. The higher profit figure is credited to an increase in cigarette consumption, which accelerated because the advertising ban also eliminated counteradvertising that stressed the health hazards of smoking.

[43] Scherer and Ross, *Industrial Market Structure*, p. 4.

Figure 9-4 Prisoners' Dilemma: advertising Expenditures

		FIRM B SPENDS EACH YEAR ON ADVERTISING	
		$4 MILLION	$6 MILLION
FIRM A SPENDS	$4 MILLION	10.0, 10.0	6.0, 12.0
	$6 MILLION	12.0, 6.0	8.7, 8.7

SOURCE: F. M. Scherer, *Industrial Market Structure and Economic Performance,* 2nd ed. Copyright © 1980 by Houghton Mifflin Co. Used with permission.

conditions of supply and demand noted in the figure. An earlier school of thought held that one could formulate direct, empirical links between structure and performance and deemphasize conduct accordingly. More recent research pays more attention to conduct variables.

The economist Joe S. Bain, who typifies the earlier school, postulated that

Figure 9-5 Basic paradigm used by industrial organization economists

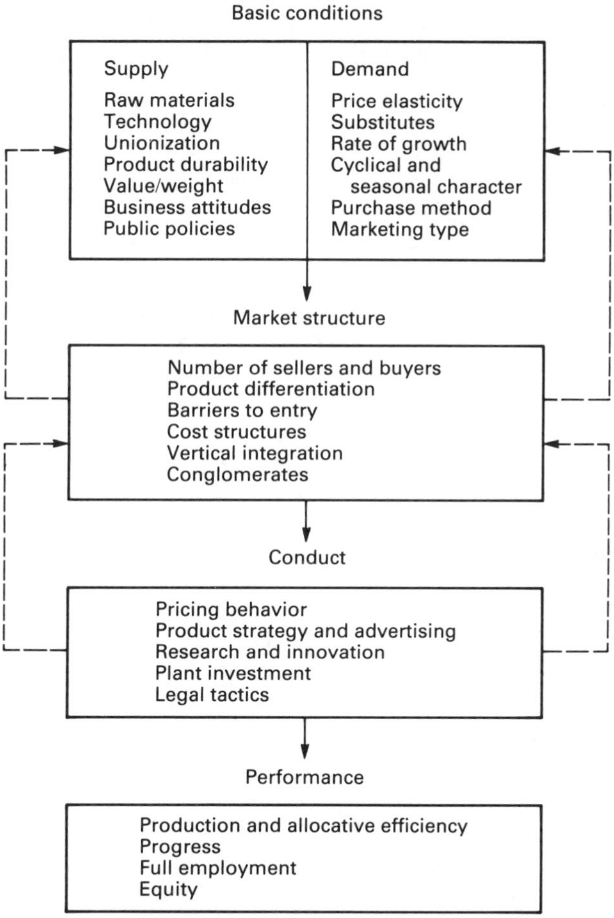

SOURCE F. M. Scherer and David Ross, *Industrial Market Structure and Economic Performance,* 3rd ed. Copyright © 1990 by Houghton Mifflin Co. Used with permission.

there were three key dimensions of market structure: (1) producer concentra
tion, (2) product differentiation, and (3) barriers to entry.[44] By this perspective
one can predict the relative profitability of markets. For example, a concentrated
market (few competitors control a large market share), with differentiated prod
ucts (some buyers willing to pay a premium for the product of one produce
versus a rival's) and with high barriers to entry, is hypothesized to lead to higher
than normal profits for the producers.

Concentration

Perhaps one of the key elements in industrial organization economics is the
hypothesized linkage between concentration ratios and profitability. The hy
pothesis is clear and intuitively logical: Given the kind of pricing behavior that
one would expect in a monopoly or an oligopoly with few producers, the prof
its attained by firms in highly concentrated industries should be higher than
those of firms in either less concentrated or atomistically structured indus
tries.[45]

In the 1950s, Joe Bain performed two studies which seemingly confirmed
this hypothesis. In one study he found that the return on stockholders' equity
was substantially higher in industries whose eight-firm concentration ratios ex
ceeded 70% (the proportion of output controlled by the eight largest firms in an
industry) than it was in those industries with concentration ratios below 70%. In
the second study, he found a positive correlation between profitability and the
concentration ratio and a subjective measure of entry barriers. Following his
work, numerous researchers found similar results. As recently as 1980, for ex
ample, Scherer summarized the literature by noting,

> There is considerable statistical support for industrial organization theory's predic
> tions of a relationship among profitability, seller concentration, and barriers to entry
> This conclusion must be leavened with appropriate caveats, for the results are no
> uniform, the data have many shortcomings, the statistical tests leave much mor
> variation in profitability unexplained than they explain.[46]

Scherer's "appropriate caveats" have gained ascendancy, however, as nu
merous studies threw Bain's central hypothesis further into question.[47] Contras
Scherer's 1980 statement with what he says in 1990:

[44] Richard Schmalensee, "The New Industrial Organization and the Economic Analysis of Moder
Markets," in W. Hildebrand, ed., *Advances in Economic Theory* (Cambridge England and New York
Cambridge University Press, 1982), pp. 253–285.
[45] For a complete exposition of the argument, see Scherer and Ross, *Industrial Market Structure*
chapter 11.
[46] F. M. Scherer, *Industrial Market Structure and Economic Performance*, 2nd ed. (Boston: Houghto
Mifflin, 1980), pp. 294–295.
[47] Bradley T. Gale and Ben S. Branch, "Concentration Versus Market Share: Which Determine
Performance and Why Does It Matter?," *Antitrust Bulletin*, 27, no. 1 (spring 1982), 83–105; David I
Ravenscraft, "Structure-Profit Relationship at the Line of Business and Industry Level," *Review o*

However, recent work has demonstrated that most, if not all, of the correlation between profitability and concentration found by Bain and his descendants . . . was almost surely spurious—the result of aggregating a positive relationship between sellers' market shares and profitability to the industry level.[48]

Another researcher suggests that the earlier findings came from what is termed "omitted variable bias."[49] This means that if in a mathematical study the true cause of some result is left out of the equation, the mathematics will nonetheless ascribe that result to whatever variables are in the equation to the extent possible. This researchers' study found that concentration had no effect on profitability; that "competition may be just as intense among a few large competitors as between many small competitors."[50]

This is not to say that concentration does not have some effects, just that those effects do not seem to filter down to the bottom line. Numerous studies, for example have found that an increase in seller concentration does tend to raise prices. Many of these studies have been conducted in the banking industry, where the effect of product differentiation is smaller than in other industries. These studies have uniformly shown, for example, that the prices that consumers pay for money (loan interest) tend to be higher and the prices consumers receive for money (interest received on accounts at banks) tend to be lower the more concentrated is the local banking market.[51]

Entry Barriers

A second key element in the industrial organization paradigm is the concept of barriers to entry. For monopolies and oligopolies to exist, there must be some impediment to the entry of competition. Otherwise, those industries would soon resemble pure or monopolistic competition as new competitors, attracted by the prospect of higher profits, entered and competed away any excess profits. Table 9-2 lists nineteen of the entry barriers most frequently noted in the literature.

Caves and Porter pioneered the concept of exit barriers, which may have an equally important effect on competition.[52] Where profits are poor and exit barriers low, the reverse of the entry process occurs (competitors exit the industry)

Economics and Statistics, 65, no. 1 (February 1983), 22–31; Richard Schmalensee, "Do Markets Differ Much? " *American Economic Review*, 75, no. 3 (June 1985), pp. 341–351.

[48] Scherer and Ross, *Industrial Market Structure*, p. 411.

[49] Robert Jacobsen, "The Persistence of Abnormal Returns," *Strategic Management Journal*, 9, no. 5 (September-October 1988), 415–430.

[50] Jacobsen, p. 428

[51] Scherer and Ross, *Industrial Market Structure*, p. 440.

[52] Richard E. Caves and Michael E. Porter, "Barriers to Exit," in David P. Qualls and Robert T. Mosson, ed., *Essays in Industrial Organization in Honor of Joe S. Bain* (Cambridge, MA: Ballinger, 1976), chapter 3. See also Kathryn Rudie Harrigan, "The Effects of Exit Barriers Upon Strategic Flexibility," *Strategic Management Journal*, 1, no. 2 (1980), 165–176.

TABLE 9-2 *Most Frequently Cited Market Entry Barriers*

BARRIERS	IMPLICATIONS
Cost advantage	One of the most important entry barriers, and usually results from economies of scale and learning curve effects.
Product differentiation of incumbents	Established firms have brand identification and customer loyalties due to advertising, being first in a market, customer service, or product differences.
Capital requirements	Need to invest in large financial resources to compete or enter a market constitutes barrier to entry and is higher in capital-intensive industries.
Customer switching costs	Switching costs prevent the buyer from changing suppliers, and technological changes often raise or lower these costs.
Access to distribution channels	First or early market entrants use intensive distribution strategies to limit the access to distributors for the potential market entrants.
Government policy	Government limits the number of firms in a market by requiring licenses, permits, etc.
Advertising	Heavy advertising by firms already in the market increases the cost of entry for potential entrants and affects brand loyalty as well as the extent of economies of scale by causing cost-per-dollar revenues to decline.
Number of competitors	Market entry is expected to be more likely during periods of increasing incorporations and less likely after a lag, during periods when high numbers of business failures occur.
Research and development	This barrier is usually short lived. Incumbent firms may prevent the entry of new firms by investing effectively in R&D, which increases technological scale economies and forces the ongoing industry to evolve in a way that would make subsequent attempts to enter even more ineffectual.
Price	Price warfare can be a significant deterrent to entry, particularly in industries where firms are more likely to lower their prices to fill underutilized plants.
Technology and technological change	Usually present in high-technology industries and can actually raise or lower economies of scale, which are one of the major sources of cost advantages.
Market concentration	The influence and impact of concentration on entry appear to be minimal.
Seller concentration	Entry is unlikely to be as easy in highly concentrated as in less concentrated markets. The higher the degree of concentration, the greater the effect of barriers on profit; the lower the degree of concentration, the lower the effect of barriers on profit.
Divisionalization	Only expected in exceptionally profitable oligopolistic industries. Incumbent firms create new independent divisions more cheaply than potential entrants, who must incur additional overhead costs for entry.
Brand name or trademark	New entrants to an industry are denied the benefits of brand name created by others as a result of the exclusive rights to use given with a trademark. Usually a weak barrier.
Sunk costs	Contribute to entry barriers that can also give rise to monopoly profit, resource misallocation, and inefficiencies.
Selling expenses	Shifts in demand functions can result from selling efforts, making market entry endogenous.
Incumbent's expected reaction to market entry	May deter market entry only if the incumbent firms are able to influence potential entrants' expectation about the post-entry reaction of the incumbents
Possession of strategic raw materials	Access to strategic raw materials contributes to firm's absolute cost advantages.

SOURCE: Adapted from Fahri Karakaya and Michael J. Stahl, "Barriers to Entry and Market Entry Decisions in Consumer and Industrial Goods Markets," in *Journal of Marketing*, 53, no. 2 (April 1989), p. 81. Reprinted by permission of the American Marketing Association.

and their exit allows the remaining competitors a better chance to profit. Where exit barriers are high, on the other hand, competitors do not exit the industry when profits are poor because they reason that any return on their unrecoverable investment is better than no return at all.

Empirical evidence of the relationship between barriers and results is difficult to obtain. It is difficult to quantify the concept of barriers sufficiently objectively to allow research similar to that found with respect to the concentration hypothesis. Beyond that, there are other problems involved in measuring the effect. Simultaneity is one. Not only does the entry or exit of firms influence profitability, but profitability can be expected to influence entry and exit. Disentangling these two simultaneous forces is difficult.

One recent study, however, gained some insight into how entry barriers were evaluated by managers. The study asked managers to make hypothetical market entry decisions.[53] In the scenario describing each decision, six different entry barriers were embedded: (1) the cost advantage of incumbents, (2) product differentiation of incumbents, (3) capital requirements, (4) customer switching costs, (5) access to distribution channels, and (6) government policy.

The results of the study showed the cost advantage of incumbents barrier to be the most critical for all market entry decisions, followed by the capital requirements barrier. The third most important barrier was the product differentiation of incumbents. In industrial markets, customer switching costs were fourth in importance, whereas in consumer markets access to distribution channels ranked fourth.

Natural Market Structures

One of the topics studied by industrial organization economists is the size distribution of the firms in an industry. These studies have shown, without exception, that these distributions are all highly skewed, with a small number of very large firms and many small ones in every industry or specific product category. What is curious about these distributions is first that they are all very similar; second, the distributions are identical with the distributions that would have been generated by chance; and third, with one exception, they exhibit a leveling process over time in which the smaller gain share at a faster rate than the large. These empirical results have led one researcher to wonder if these distributions reflect some sort of "natural" market structure.[54]

Table 9-3 shows what is meant by a skewed size distribution. It shows the distribution of the market shares of the producers in the ready-to-eat cereal industry in 1974 and 1987. The distribution of market shares fits what is known

[53] Fahri Karakaya and Michael J. Stahl, "Barriers to Entry and Market Entry Decisions in Consumer and Industrial Goods Markets," *Journal of Marketing*, 53, no. 2 (April 1989), 80–91.
[54] See Robert D. Buzzell, "Are There 'Natural' Market Structures?" *Journal of Marketing*, 45, no. 1 (winter 1981), 42–51.

TABLE 9-3   *Equilibrium and Actual Market Share Distributions in the Breakfast Cereal Industry, 1954–1964, 1969–1974, and 1987*

FIRM RANK	EQUILIBRIUM DISTRIBUTION	AVERAGE ACTUAL 1954–1964	AVERAGE ACTUAL 1969–1974	ACTUAL 1987
1st	41.0%	40.8%	40.3%	42%
2nd	24.5	24.4	24.3	21
3rd	14.6	14.6	14.7	13
4th	8.7	8.8	8.9	8
5th	5.2	5.2	5.4	5.5
6th	3.1	3.1	3.3	5.5
Others	1.8	1.9	2.0	5

SOURCE: William E. Cox, Jr., "Product Portfolio Strategy, Market Structure and Performance," in Hans B. Thorelli, ed., *Strategy + Structure = Performance* (Bloomington, IN: Indiana University Press, 1975), p. 87; and "The Energized Cereal Industry," *The New York Times*, December 30, 1987, p. D4.

as the semilogarithmic distribution, in which each firm's share is a constant proportion of the share of the next higher-ranking firm.[55] In the cereal industry, this proportion is approximately 0.6. The share of each competitor is about six tenths of the next larger competitor's share. It has been suggested that this constant proportion or size ratio is useful in summarizing a market's structure because there is generally a close relationship between the ratio's value and the number of significant competitors in a market.

In a sociobiological sense, one might say that each industry has its own pecking order. Work on the PIMS database shows that the typical size ratio is approximately 0.6. The actual market share distributions showed the average leading competitor's market share to be 32.7% and shares for the second to fourth largest to be 18.8%, 11.6%, and 6.9%. This and the breakfast cereal data conform well to Kotler's hypothetical market structure, shown in Figure 9-6, in which 40% is in the hands of a market leader, 30% in the hands of a market challenger, 20% is held by a market follower, and 10% by market nichers. It is also in accord with what the Boston Consulting Group called "The Rule of Three and Four."[56] By this rule, stable markets have only three significant competitors whose shares are in the proportions 4:2:1, which is a size ratio of 0.5. If one assumes that fringe competitors have a total of 10% market share, then the shares of the leading competitors in the normal market would approximate 50%, 25%, and 13%.

Causes of the Skewed Distribution.   In contrast to the work demonstrating the phenomenon, little has been done to isolate the causes of the skewed size distributions. One hypothesis is that such distributions are simply the result of pure historical chance.[57] If one simply creates an industry on a computer in

[55] For a full explanation of the mathematics, see Buzzell, "Are There 'Natural' Market Structures?," p. 43.
[56] Boston Consulting Group, "The Rule of Three and Four," *Perspectives*, No. 187 (Boston: Boston Consulting Group, 1987).
[57] Scherer, *Industrial Market Structure*, pp. 145–150.

Figure 9-6   A comparison of the average PIMS market structure with Kotler's hypothetical structure and the Boston Consulting Group's Rule of Three and Four

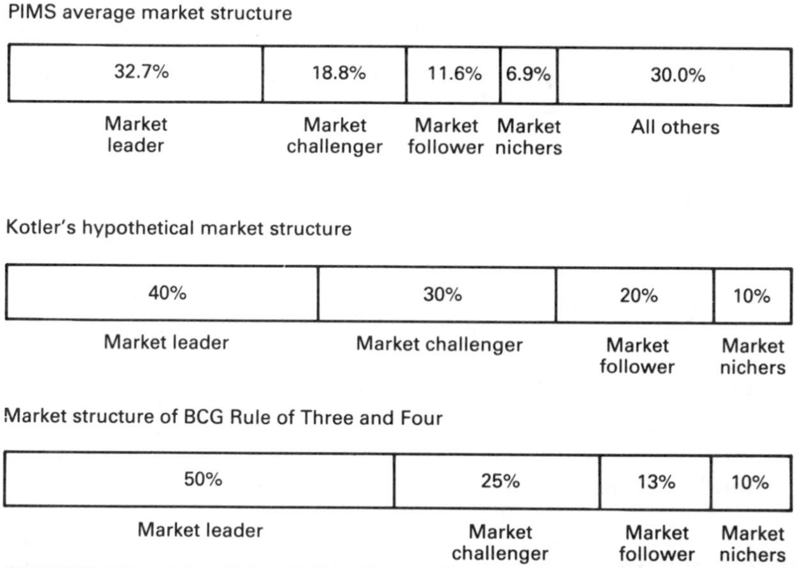

PIMS average market structure

32.7%	18.8%	11.6%	6.9%	30.0%
Market leader	Market challenger	Market follower	Market nichers	All others

Kotler's hypothetical market structure

40%	30%	20%	10%
Market leader	Market challenger	Market follower	Market nichers

Market structure of BCG Rule of Three and Four

50%	25%	13%	10%
Market leader	Market challenger	Market follower	Market nichers

SOURCES: Adapted from Robert D. Buzzell, "Are There 'Natural' Market Structures?," *Journal of Marketing*, 45, no. 1 (winter 1981), p. 46; Philip Kotler, *Marketing Management: Analysis, Planning, Implementation, and Control* (Englewood Cliffs, NJ: Prentice Hall, 1977), p. 319; and "The Rule of Three and Four," *Perspectives*, no. 187 (Boston: The Boston Consulting Group, 1976).

which the year-to-year growth rate for each firm is random but from the same probability distribution, then it will generate concentrated market-share distributions indistinguishable from those actually observed. Even if all firms have the same probabilities of growth in any given year, some will experience very low growth purely by chance and others very high growth purely by chance. A few fortunate firms will experience exceptionally high growth rates for a few years running, which then puts them out in front of the pack, a position they are likely to hold.

One cannot easily dismiss the effects of random good luck, even in a book dedicated to the conscious manipulation of the strategic variables that shape competitive results. The head start that luck brings may well account for much observed success. One need only a few years of luck to give the lucky firm resources markedly superior to those of competitors, after which time the superior resources enable the firm to continue its dominance.

Another view is that every industry has its own set of economic laws that determine its structure. One of those, for example, might be the minimum techno-economic scale required to be able to produce and profit at the current market price. In markets in which the minimum economic scale is small in comparison to the size of the total market, the size ratio will be large as will the number of significant competitors (as in gasoline refining). In contrast, in markets such as automobile manufacturing, the minimum scale is large in comparison to the size of the market, and there will be a relatively small number of competitors. Much research needs to be done to identify such factors.

The Relationship Between Growth and Size. One of the problems with the chance hypothesis is that it assumes that every firm has an equal probability of growth, on the average. The PIMS data, on the other hand, demonstrate that this is not the case. As can be seen in Table 9-4, average growth rates are systematically lower for large market-share businesses than for small-share businesses. The only exception to this seems to be in markets undergoing very rapid growth (those with real unit growth exceeding 10% per year), in which case the growth rates appear equal across competitors of all sizes.

One explanation for this phenomenon is based on costs. If the relationship between share and costs (large shares imply lower costs) is less pronounced in more mature than in youthful markets, then the disparity in costs between large- and small-share competitors is smaller and the large-share competitors will be more vulnerable to the small-share competitors' actions. This results in markets tending to become less concentrated over time.

MANAGERIAL APPROACHES
TO MARKET STRUCTURE

In addition to understanding the underlying economic models determining how an industry competes, the manager must be able to apply those concepts more concretely. This discussion provides some insight on how to achieve that end

There are a few important insights about an industry's structure that a manager needs to know:

1. Where is the market on a consolidated to fragmented continuum? Where has it been and where is it headed?
2. How stable is that market structure? What factors are likely to increase or decrease its stability?
3. What are the competitive dynamics in the industry? What are the relative sizes, shares, and growth rates of the individual competitors?
4. What do the trajectories of the various competitors over time tell us about their strategies and goals?

Figure 9-7 presents one approach to understanding the structure of an industry in a form known as a *sector chart*, which crosses relative market share on the horizontal (x) axis with growth rates on the vertical (y) axis.[58] The horizontal line shows the overall industry growth rate, and the centers of the circles lie on the individual firms' growth rates. The size of the circle represents the firm's size

The vertical line dividing the rectangle is placed on the point of 1.5 times relative market share. This is based on the observation that stability in a market

[58] This discussion is based on Marcus C. Bogue III and Elwood S. Buffa, *Corporate Strategic Analysis* (New York; Free Press, 1986), chapter 3.

TABLE 9-4 *Market Share, Market Growth Rate, and Sales Growth Rate for PIMS Businesses (Average Annual Real Growth Rates)*

	MARKET SHARE—BEGINNING OF PERIOD				
REAL MARKET GROWTH RATE	Under 10%	10%– 15%	15%– 25%	25%– 40%	Over 40%
	REAL SALES GROWTH RATE				
−5% or less	+0.1%	−5.9%	−3.5%	−5.5%	−6.9%
−5% to zero	+3.8	+0.3	−1.6	−1.8	−2.4
Zero to +5%	+8.8	+6.6	+4.3	+1.1	+1.7
+5% to +10%	+10.4	+10.9	+7.2	+8.1	+5.5
Over +10%	+19.2	+20.3	+21.3	+22.2	+18.1

SOURCE: Robert D. Buzzell, "Are There Natural Market Structures?" in *Journal of Marketing*, 45, no. 1 (winter 1981), p. 49. Reprinted by permission of the American Marketing Association.

Figure 9-7   Sector charts

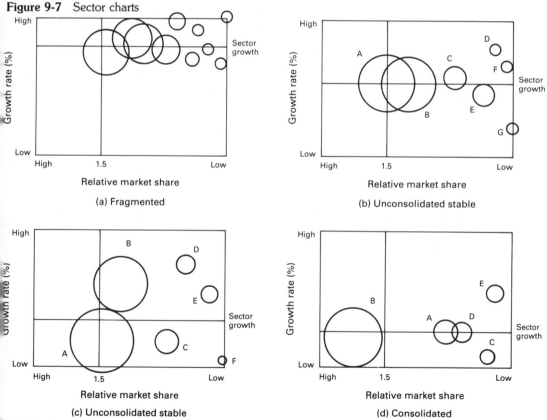

(a) Fragmented

(b) Unconsolidated stable

(c) Unconsolidated stable

(d) Consolidated

SOURCE: Marcus C. Bogue III and E. Buffa, *Corporate Strategic Analysis* (New York: Free Press, 1986), p. 52.

is a function of the relative difference between leader and followers in a market. Henderson, for example, has stated that, based on empirical observation, a ratio of 2 to 1 in market share between two competitors seems to be an equilibrium.[59] One is thereby able visually to determine the extent to which the leader has such a position by its relationship to the vertical dividing line.

Figure 9-7a depicts a fragmented, high-growth market. Such a structure is not unusual in the early stages of market development. While there is no clear leader, the high growth rate ensures that major competitive activity is directed to new primary demand rather than zero-sum share battles. Such a market may mature to resemble either Figure 9-7b or 9-7d. Figure 9-7d shows a typical stable, consolidated market with a single dominant competitor. Figure 9-7b is stable based on factors not shown on the graph. Competitors A and B each lead different and clearly separate geographical segments. They are therefore not in direct competition, although their relative sizes are such that no other competitor could challenge them.

Figure 9-7c is unstable because firm B has challenged the former market leader and is growing rapidly at the expense of both firms A and C. It is unstable because the competition between A and B is still a very close battle between almost equal-size firms, and either could still end up dominant in the end, perhaps based on purely random factors. The market is unstable because the heavy competition between the two giants will end up harming not only whichever loses but all of the smaller competitors, too. As the old saying goes, "When the elephants fight, it is the ants that get trampled." This is what happened in the U.S. beer industry as Anheuser-Busch was challenged by Miller beginning in the late 1960s. Exhibit 9-5 tells the story as it unfolded over two decades.

COMPETITION AND SUPRANORMAL PROFITS

The goal of competitive strategy in any setting is to win. In economic competition, true winning is the earning of a supranormal return. Supranormal returns, however, can occur in both the long and short terms. Management's task is not only to generate supranormal profits in the short run but to ensure their persistence in the long run. However, according to one researcher, "Conditions under which abnormal rates of return do not dissipate seem pathological, if present at all."[60]

The Impact of Competitive Entry

Economic theory is clear on the results of high profitability. It is the signal that additional investment is needed to satisfy customer demand. As that additional investment comes on stream, supply catches up to demand and profitability returns to competitive levels. Real life and the literature is full of stories detailing this effect.

---

[59] Bruce Henderson, *Henderson on Corporate Strategy* (Cambridge, MA: Abt Books, 1979), p. 90.
[60] Jacobsen, "The Persistence of Abnormal Returns," p. 428.

EXHIBIT 9-5

The Changing Structure of the U.S. Beer Industry:
1968–1988

THE U.S. BEER MARKET

1968–1972 (Exhibit Figure A)

The beer industry from 1968 to 1972 was unconsolidated and fairly stable. Competitive market activities were minimal until Philip Morris purchased Miller, a minor player with less than 5% market share. With Philip Morris's backing, Miller adopted an unconventional competitive strategy for the brewing industry. Instead of lowering prices, it increased costs by increasing advertising expenditures, thereby forcing competitors to follow suit.

EXHIBIT FIGURE A

Beer market sector chart, 1968–1972

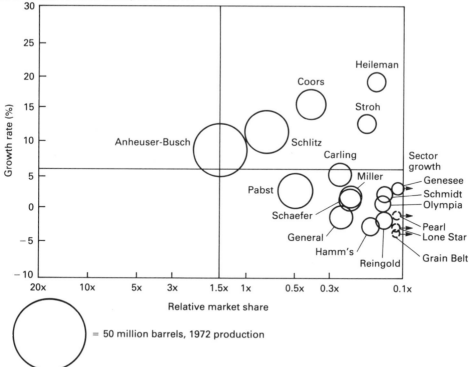

SOURCE: Bogue and Buffa, *Corporate Strategic Analysis*, p. 57.

EXHIBIT 9-5 (cont.)

1972–1976 (Exhibit Figure B)

This new competitive dynamic affected Miller's and Anheuser-Busch's margins and market shares dramatically. Miller's investment spending on advertising reduced its operating margins from 5.8% to less than zero by 1973 before its increased market share pulled it back to over 9% in 1976. Although Anheuser-Busch's share continued to grow, its growth was slightly below the industry's growth rate. Miller's growth rate was 36%, bringing it from 20% the size of Anheuser-Busch, to almost 70%.

EXHIBIT FIGURE B

Beer market sector chart, 1972–1976

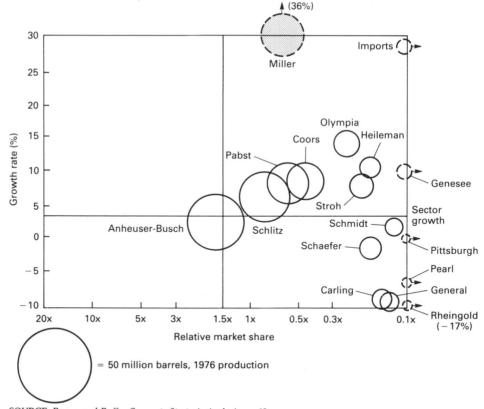

SOURCE: Bogue and Buffa, *Corporate Strategic Analysis*, p. 60.

EXHIBIT 9-5 (cont.)

1976–1979 (Exhibit Figure C)

During this period, Anheuser-Busch responded to Miller's aggressive growth. It invested heavily in advertising and increased its growth rate from less than 4% to above 16%, slowing Miller's growth to less than 25%. Since the industry growth rate was only 4%, the battle between the two industry leaders forced many brewers (Coors, Pabst, Stroh) to negative growth. Heileman was the only other large brewery that continued to grow faster than the industry.

EXHIBIT FIGURE C
Beer market sector chart, 1976–1979

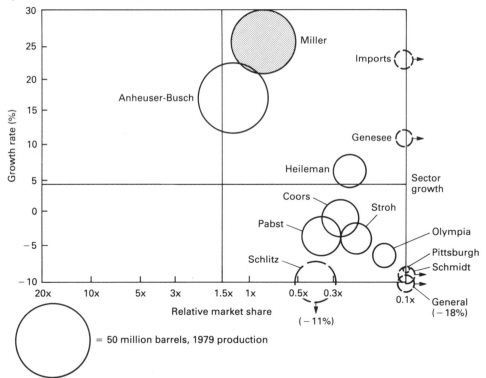

SOURCE: Bogue and Buffa, *Corporate Strategic Analysis*, p. 61.

EXHIBIT 9-5 (cont.)

1979–1983 (Exhibit Figure D)

As Anheuser-Busch fought back, it grew faster than Miller to 1.5 times Miller's size. The entire industry suffered from Miller's initiative. Of the ninety-three U.S. breweries in 1970, fifty had either gone out of business or been driven into mergers with stronger partners by 1984. Anheuser-Busch emerged the winner of the industry's drive toward consolidation.

EXHIBIT FIGURE D
Beer market sector chart, 1979–1983

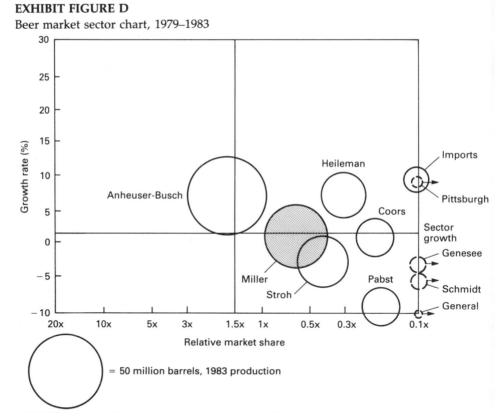

SOURCE: Bogue and Buffa, *Corporate Strategic Analysis*, p. 62.

EXHIBIT 9-5 (cont.)

1983–1988 (Exhibit Figure E)

By the mid to late 1980s, the structure of the beer market looked very different than it did in the early 1970s. There are now many fewer players. While overall consumption increased by only 1.2%, per-capita consumption decreased by nearly 3%. Only Anheuser-Busch, Miller, and Coors showed increases during this period. Anheuser-Busch has consolidated its dominance over the industry. With total industry growth at only 0.9% in 1988, Anheuser-Busch's and Miller's over 3% growth rates are but a small fraction of their earlier performance.

EXHIBIT FIGURE E
Beer market sector chart, 1983–1988

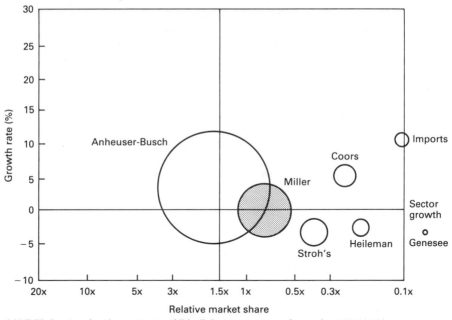

SOURCE: Reprinted with permission of Edgell Communications. Copyright © 1989–1990 Annual Manual, Beverage Industry Magazine.

The Reynolds International Pen Corporation pioneered the ball point pen business in 1945. The pens which cost it 80 cents each to manufacture were being sold in retail stores late that year for $12 to $20 (yielding factory prices of $6 to $10 if one assumes a 50% gross margin on the retail price). Its success led to the entry of some 100 competitors and its own exit by 1948.[61]

[61] Scherer, *Industrial Market Structure*, p. 240.

A study of the German cartel experience found that most of the thousands of cartels formed between 1873 and 1933 collapsed quickly. The reason for their demise was typically due to their own success in raising prices. As soon as this occurred, new firms entered the industry, undercut the cartel price which led to a decline in sales by the cartel and a collapse of the cartel. As one economist put it, the members of cartels often found themselves "holding the umbrella over outsiders and getting increasingly wet feet."[62]

The Winchester (hard) disc drive industry grew from $27 million in sales in 1978 to $1.3 billion in 1984. In that period, some 43 different manufacturers had entered the business. In the second half of 1984, however, sales of leading firms dropped by as much as one-half and industry-wide profitability fell from an average of $24.2 in the prior three quarters to $2.3 million in the third quarter of 1984.[63]

The Xerox Corporation's first entry in the copy machine business was with the model 914 in 1959. These machines were directed to the low- and medium-volume segments in which its economic advantage versus a competing process that used coated paper was essentially nil. The firm priced high to maximize short run profit and its actions attracted 29 firms into that segment in the 1961 to 1967 period. However, in the very high-volume segment the Xerox products had an unassailable economic advantage versus competition and a strong patent position. In this segment it was able to charge monopoly-like prices for almost a decade without experiencing appreciable entry.[64]

The Nutrasweet Company's artificial sweetener, aspartame, has had very high profits since 1982, its first year of major sales. Operating profits in 1988 totaled $330 million on sales of $736 million for an almost 45% return on sales. In the U.S. large customers pay $55 per pound while small ones pay up to $90 per pound. Its patents have begun expiring however. European and Canadian patents expired in 1987 and U.S. patents expire in 1992. Since the expiration of the European patents, prices there have fallen by two-thirds, to $27 per pound.[65]

The Impact of Substitution

Substitution effects limit supranormal profits as surely as does competitive entry. While a single monopolist or small group of firms with monopoly power can extract high prices and profits in the short run, in the long run buyers generally have alternatives. The behavior of substitution among raw materials such as steel, aluminum, wood, polyethylene, fiberglass, and a host of similar materials is almost a universal economic phenomenon. While each material may have unique advantages one versus another in certain specific applications, there is

[62] Fritz Machlup, *The Economics of Sellers' Competition* (Baltimore, MD: Johns Hopkins, 1952), pp. 527–529.

[63] William A. Sahlman and Howard H. Stevenson, "Capital Market Myopia," *Journal of Business Venturing*, 1, no. 1 (winter 1985), 7–30.

[64] Scherer and Ross, *Industrial Market Structure*, p. 368.

[65] Eben Shapiro, "Nutrasweet's Bitter Fight," *The New York Times*, November 19, 1989, p. F4.

almost always some price/performance combination which will tempt the user to switch in the long run. In many applications, performance is defined simply as price per cubic inch.

Examples of such switching are many. The actions of OPEC in increasing oil prices led consumers to turn to alternate sources of energy and to insulation and conservation. Prodded by the government, consumers bought smaller, more fuel-efficient automobiles and appliances. As a result of high copper prices in the mid-1960s, American automobile manufacturers reduced the copper content of their vehicles, displacing it from even such application strongholds as radiators. High sugar prices in the 1970s led soft drink manufacturers to switch to corn syrup and to displace a million tons of sugar demand per year. In the 1980s, high paper prices led stores and supermarkets to replace paper bags with plastic bags. In short, strategies aimed at short-run profit maximization frequently send customers seeking for substitutes to offset the monopolist's power.[66]

Strategies for Gaining Long-Term Supranormal Profits

Research has found that three strategies seem to be associated with the slowing of the long-run convergence of supranormal profits to a normal rate of return: (1) high vertical integration, (2) market share, and (3) marketing expenditure intensity.[67] These factors do not necessarily cause high profitability in and among themselves, but rather slow the return of high profits to competitive levels. In addition, the effects are small, although since they work over a period of years their cumulative impact may be important.

High vertical integration works to diminish the competitive forces that suppliers and customers can have on profitability. It can also serve as a credible threat to existing channel members and thereby dissipate some of their market power. Finally, it makes it difficult for new entry to occur since the firm has secured at least some of the resources which new entrants would need. In this way, the firm has diminished some of the major forces that help drive profits back to the competitive level.

Intense marketing expenditures help the firm to differentiate its product from the competition and thereby slow the return of profits to the normal level. The researcher suggests that this works to reduce the attractiveness of substitutes and thereby the effectiveness of price competition and makes competitive entry more difficult due to the substantial advertising expense required to establish a new brand. Marketing expenditure intensity itself is negatively related to ROI—that is, high marketing expenditure intensity reduces profitability. Among those firms with supranormal profits, however, those profits are more persistent

---

[66] Porter provides a full exploration of substitution effects. See Michael Porter, *Competitive Advantage* (New York: Free Press, 1985), chapter 8.
[67] Jacobsen, "The Persistence of Abnormal Returns."

among firms with high marketing intensity than among firms with low market
ing expenditure intensity.

High market share was also found to induce a greater persistence in high ROI
While the author is careful to note that market share is not a causal factor ir
achieving that ROI, it does allow it to be retained for a longer period of time
suggesting that a brand leader could be considered an annuity since bran
leadership is sustainable.[68] The author noted three reasons why this effect ma¥
work: (1) Higher market shares are associated with economies of scale (or scope
and bargaining power to better deal with competitive forces; (2) markets with ¿
high market-share competitor may discourage potential entrants; and (3) sup
pliers and buyers are less likely to have market power versus the firm tha
accounts for a large share of the industry.

Marketing pioneering was not included in the aforementioned study, but it
effects on market share were cited in chapter 8. There is evidence that pioneer
may also be able to sustain a price premium versus followers for some extendec
period, even in industrial markets.[69] *Product differentiation* is another often citec
factor leading to higher profits. Work with the PIMS data set indicate highe¥
ROIs for higher-quality products.[70]

Avoiding the Effects of Competition

Economists are clear about supranormal profits. They attract competition, anc
except the aforementioned effects, which allow them to persist longer than the¥
might otherwise, supranormal profits always dissipate in the long run. The choice
faced by those planning strategy is depicted in Figure 9-8. One can pursue either
short-run profit maximization (price high, gain supranormal profits, and attrac
new entrants) or long-run profit maximization (price to limit competitive entr¥
and expand output to meet demand). These two strategies correspond to the mar
keter's skimming and penetration pricing strategies, respectively, which wer€
discussed in chapter 3.

The basic concept underlying this idea is to leave no room for potentia
entrants to earn economic profits. The firm needs to close off to competition th€
major alternate routes by which competitors can create value and steal the firm'
market. In practice, this may be achieved not only by the practice known as limi
pricing (pricing at that level which does not yield potential entrants an accept

---

[68] This distinction is important. In an earlier article, the author determined that market share itsel
did little to cause high profitability; that the findings relating the two were the result of not con
trolling for some unmeasured common factors such as luck and management quality. See Rober
Jacobsen and David A. Aacker, "Is Market Share All That It's Cracked Up to Be?" *Journal of Mar
keting*, 49, no. 4 (fall 1985), 11–22.

[69] John B. Frey, "Pricing and the Product Life Cycle," *Chemtech*, 15, no. 1 (January 1985), 40–43

[70] Robert D. Buzzell and Bradley T. Gale, *The PIMS Principles: Linking Strategy to Performance* (Nev
York: Free Press, 1987), chapter 6; see also Lynn W. Phillips, Dae Chang, and Robert D. Buzzell
"Product Quality, Cost Position, and Business Performance: A Test of Some Key Hypotheses,'
Journal of Marketing, 47, no. 2 (spring 1983), 26–43.

Figure 9-8 Comparison of profit streams over time

Short-run profit maximization[a]

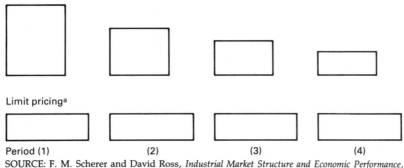

Limit pricing[a]

Period (1)   (2)   (3)   (4)

SOURCE: F. M. Scherer and David Ross, *Industrial Market Structure and Economic Performance,* 3rd ed. Copyright © 1990 by Houghton Mifflin Co. Used with permission.

able ROI on their investment), but also by product differentiation or proliferation and preemptive capacity and location strategies.[71] All of these strategies, however, require forgoing at least some of the supranormal profits that might otherwise be gained. The concept of product proliferation is sometimes also termed market fortification. Consider, for example, the clothing manufacturer who makes clothing in a one-size-fits-all mode.[72] Even though he or she may be pricing to limit competition entry, it would be no surprise to find a competitor entering with a "small, medium, large" (or even more exact) sizing strategy, perhaps even at a higher price.[73] Similar strategies work in a geographical dimension. A firm which pursues a location strategy in which it places large outlets across a market on 40-mile centers—say every 40 miles along an area's major highways—should not be surprised to find a competitor building smaller outlets in spaces in between to gain geographical advantage.

A product proliferation strategy allowed General Motors to win over Ford's Model T strategy (one size, one color, very low price) in 1921. As Alfred Sloan stated,

> It seemed to me that the intelligent approach would be to have a car at every price position, just the same as a general conducting a campaign wants to have an army at every point he is likely to be attacked. . . . One of the first things we did was to develop a line of products that met competition in the various positions in which competition was offered.[74]

---

[71] Scherer and Ross discuss these strategies in depth in chapter 10 of *Industrial Market Structure.*

[72] This is an unrealistic but easily understood example.

[73] In an investigation of competition in markets in which product specifications are infinitely variable, it was found that "it is never optimal to produce any good at minimum average cost, but always better to increase variety at the expense of average cost when any good reaches this level of output." See Kelvin Lancaster, "Competition and Product Variety," *Journal of Business,* 53, no. 3, pt. 3 (July 1980), S79–S103.

[74] Quoted in Alfred Chandler, Jr., *Strategy and Structure: Chapters in the History of the American Enterprise* (Cambridge, MA: MIT Press, 1962), p. 143.

Each of these strategies, however, reduces returns. The question of which is correct depends on financial and personal factors. The financial factors concern the firm's cost of capital. If it is high, it means that future profits are discounted back at a high rate and the discounted present value of the income stream shown in the upper half of Figure 9-8 is therefore higher than that obtained by a long-run strategy. Large firms often have lower costs of capital than smaller ones and therefore the capacity to pursue strategies with longer payouts.

The risk aversion of the decision maker (or the reward structure of the firm) is the personal factor involved. A standard strategy under conditions of uncertainty is to discount the future heavily. Choosing a strategy that may yield higher profits but only five or ten years in the future is a tough decision for any decision maker. There are arguments on both sides. Corporate reward structures typically reward current accomplishments and therefore put bonus dollars in the pockets of those who bring in big profits today. Further, top executives have heard untold managers promise big returns tomorrow if only they let them "investment spend" today. It's a tough argument to make: Forgo profits today to stave off the entry of yet unseen competition tomorrow.

On the other hand, one way to ensure the future is to get large numbers of customers, which is the result of a long-term strategy. As one economist argued,

> All entrepreneurs . . . have in mind the vast uncertainties of a relatively distant future. The best method of insuring against them is to attach to oneself by ties of goodwill as large a market as possible as quickly as possible. If one can get a substantially larger market by earning no more than a normal profit than one could get by earning a surplus profit . . . one may well choose to do the former, as an insurance against future uncertainties.[75]

CHOOSING THE FIRM'S COMPETITIVE ORIENTATION

The type of competition and the level of competitive intensity that exists in an industry does not just happen. It is the result of the interaction among the personal and firm-level models of competition that each of the competitors uses to guide their actions. At the heart of the problem is the choice of competitive orientation along the competition to cooperation dimension. Should the firm attempt cooperatively oriented strategies, or should it be intensely competitive, taking every opportunity to seize the advantage from its competitor?[76] BankAmerica's switch to an intensely competitive orientation is described in Exhibit 9-6.

The difficulty is that competition is somewhat like an arms race—each com-

[75] R. F. Harrod, *Economic Essays* (London: Macmillan, 1952), pp. 147, 174.
[76] Some of the issues here are dealt with by Richard P Nielsen, "Cooperative Strategy in Marketing," *Business Horizons*, 30 (July-August 1987), 61–68. See also Eric von Hippel, "Cooperation Between Rivals: Informal Know-How Trading," *Research Policy*, 16 (1987), 291–302.

EXHIBIT 9-6

Combat Banking

"I want my people to destroy our competitors, I want them to kill and crush them," barks Thomas Peterson, a BankAmerica Corp. executive vice president and chief of its far-flung branch network.

Standing in a 43rd-floor conference area in BankAmerica's downtown tower, the former army sergeant adds, "This is the war room." Charts bearing zigzagging red and blue lines compare BankAmerica's performance with those of its main California rivals, Wells Fargo & Co., Security Pacific Corp. and First Interstate Bancorp. On one wall hangs a cartoonlike painting of BankAmerica executives riding in a tank and waving a banner reading "Annihilate the competition."

These days, a retail-banking war is rumbling with the big talk and loud hype more traditional on a used-car lot. Recent months have seen the rise of late-night banking, Saturday banking, Sunday banking, 24-hour-a-day loan-by-phone dial-a-banker banking, African-safari sweepstakes banking. BankAmerica has been leading the pack, handing out free checking accounts and pushing credit lines with no up-front charges. Its Seattle-based Seafirst Corp. unit is offering five bucks to any customer who has to wait in line more than five minutes (it's paid out about $2,000 so far).

This "combat banking," as some at BankAmerica call it, has played a key role in the biggest turnaround in U.S. banking history. A little more than two years ago, BankAmerica's survival was in doubt; now, largely on the strength of retail profits and remarkably low domestic loan losses, its net income is up 114% for the 1989 first half, to $579 million, or $2.88 a share. After losing $1.8 billion from 1985 through 1987, BankAmerica is expected this year to post record net income of more than $1 billion.

SOURCE: Charles McCoy, "Combat Banking: Slashing Pursuit of Retail Trade Brings BankAmerica Back," *The Wall Street Journal*, October 2, 1989, p. A1.

petitor, afraid to be vulnerable to the others, spends more and more on its offensive and defensive capabilities. In the end, each has wasted vast amounts of resources without changing the competitive lineup. In international politics, the only winners of such a race are the arms merchants. In business, the winners are the customers (when competition centers on price and product quality) or the advertising agencies and the media (when competitive activity is directed into advertising and promotion).[77]

Unrestrained competition makes little sense for the competitors. Seldom do any of the firms engaged in intense competition profit by it. The question is to

[77] See, for example, the description of the intense competition among credit card issuers in Bill Saporito, "Melting Point in the Plastic War," *Fortune*, May 20, 1991, pp. 71–78.

choose the appropriate type and level of competition for the firm. To do so requires that the individual manager have a good grasp of those firm- and industry-level factors that shape industry competition and, based on them, choose the appropriate competitive orientation for the firm. The four prototypical competitive orientations discussed next illustrate what is meant by the term *competitive orientation*.

One-on-One Combat

The mental picture of this competitive orientation shows competitors facing off against each other, ready to do hand-to-hand battle with their fists, guns, armies, or products. Competition in this perspective is oriented toward what each competitor gets versus what every other competitor gets (e.g. "I've got to beat the competition. It doesn't matter what my score is, if my competitors have a larger score, I've lost."). Market share is a key element in this competitive perspective. By its zero-sum nature, there can be but one winner in a market-share battle.

The logic of an alternate, more general argument supporting this competitive orientation is shown in Figure 9-9.[78] In this view, marketplace competition is perceived as a struggle among firms for prizes, of which customers are the most valuable prize. Because the number of prizes grows only slowly and sometimes erratically if at all, firms naturally work to defend their hold on those customers they have won and to win prizes away from vulnerable competitors. The game is to identify those businesses which are the firm's closest rivals and capitalize on their vulnerabilities while at the same time minimizing the firm's own vulnerabilities.

There are drawbacks to a intensively competitive orientation. Prime among these is that the preoccupation with "what the other guy's got" instead of "Are we satisfied with what we've got?" can lead the firm to focus on imitating and countering competitors' strategies instead of forging its own strategic path.[79] Second, by setting the tone for the industry, the firm may raise the competitive level to the point that customers (or advertising agencies and the media) become the main beneficiaries of the competition. Third, by training competitors to anticipate its intense competitive responses, the firm can unwittingly create the equivalent of an arms race in which no competitor, including itself, can dare to take a less competitive or more cooperative stance.

I Do the Best I Can

The mental picture for this competitive orientation depicts two street vendors, each actively wooing customers, many of whom buy from both vendors. Competition in this perspective lies in the parallel attempts to provide customers

---

[78] This argument and the subsequent argument supporting the customer orientation are based on Alfred R. Oxenfeldt and William L. Moore, "Customer or Competitor: Which Guideline for Marketing?," *Management Review*, 67 (August 1978), 43–48.

[79] Kenichi Ohmae makes this point well when he says that strategy is not about beating the competition; it is about serving customers' real needs. See his article, "Getting Back to Strategy," *Harvard Business Review*, 66, no. 6 (November-December 1988), 149–156.

Figure 9-9   Means/end chain for competitor orientation

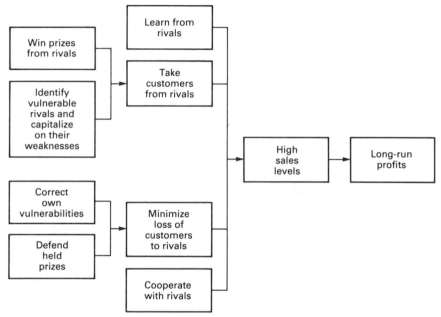

SOURCE: Alfred R. Oxenfeldt and William L. Moore, "Customer or Competitor: Which Guideline for Marketing?" Reprinted by permission of publisher from *Management Review*, August 1978, Copyright © 1978. American Management Association, New York. All rights reserved.

with offers of valued goods and services, of which the prospects may buy several. The thinking behind this orientation is, "If I can provide customers with sufficient value, they'll choose my offer enough times to be profitable. It doesn't matter what happens to my competitors; I can't control their actions or the needs of customers. All that matters is whether my strategy for satisfying customers is the best one I can devise to maximize the earning potential of my abilities. Profitable sales are my measure of success, and I get those by carefully choosing and serving customers."

The marketing concept, a customer orientation, envisions marketplaces in which customers work hard to identify offerings that satisfy their needs and then patronize those firms that offer them. As depicted in Figure 9-10, the logic of this approach to competition is clear: Find out what customers want and value, design products and services that deliver those attributes, and deliver them consistently to get satisfied customers, high sales, and long-run profits.

The problem with this competitive orientation is that it requires a sometimes heroic set of assumptions. As Oxenfeldt and Moore noted, it presupposes that

- Customers know what they want.
- Marketing research can determine what it is that they want.
- Satisfied customers will reward marketers with repeat purchases and favorable word-of-mouth mentions.

Figure 9-10   Means/end chain for customer orientation

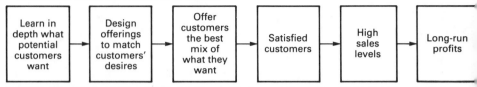

- Brand decisions are important enough that customers will seek an optimum product, rather than just a satisfactory one.
- Competitive offering differences are great enough to be important to the customers.[80]

Further, it assumes that the technology is such that the firm can simply create to customers' expressed desires rather than leading customers by choosing its offerings to optimize its strategic position within the competitive framework. These assumptions do not always hold.

We're All in the Same Boat

The mental picture for this competitive orientation puts us in Judge Elbert H. Gary's (Chairman of United States Steel) smoke-filled dining room early in the century while he is having dinner with steel industry leaders and discussing how to avoid destructive competition in their industry.[81] This discussion goes "Competition is something to be avoided. It merely gives customers a larger share than they deserve of the value created by our investments." By carefully coordinating industry actions, customers can be better served by the resulting strong, profitable industry. A stable market is the measure of industry success and the route to individual business profitability.

The argument for the anticompetitive cartel concept says that commodity products, differentiable only by price, and an oligopolistic market structure in which price decreases are immediately matched by nervous competitors but in which price increases are seldom followed, cry out for the coordination of competition (at least to their participants). A too-competitive firm can quickly ruin such an industry (and its own profitability) in the pursuit of additional sales.[8] If all competitors refuse to reduce prices—or at least to compete only on

---

[80] Oxenfeldt and Moore, "Customer or Competitor," p. 44.

[81] See, for example, the description of Judge Gary's and other industrialists' views of competition at the turn of the century in Ron Chernow, *The House of Morgan* (New York: Atlantic Monthly Press, 1990). A more contemporary example, of course, would have us in an OPEC meeting, hammering out production quotas and minimum prices.

[82] Porter makes this point well in a section of his book, *Competitive Advantage*, titled "What Makes 'Good' Competitor?," pp. 212–218.

nonprice basis—then the same volume of product will still be sold and all competitors will profit.

There are three main drawbacks to such an orientation. The first is that it assumes that the present state of affairs is more profitable for the industry than a more competitive state would be. That may not be the case if demand is price elastic, as proved to be the case with air travel. Second, such a state of affairs shelters the inefficient firms and keeps them and their capacity alive for longer than they should. Third, to the extent that the cartel is able to provide stable profits for its members, unless it is able to create barriers to entry those very profits invite further entry into the business by new firms, putting further pressure on all.[83]

Competition without Competition

The relevant mental picture in this instance is that of a small, wiry kid in a tough neighborhood whose continued existence is dependent on his or her ability to avoid conflict by blending into the background, avoiding contact with the big kids, or simply by fast running. Competition in this perspective has only downsides—either because competitors have the edge or because there are other, just as valuable prizes to be had without the risks of direct competition. The thinking goes, "Competitors and competition is something we try to avoid. If we can't avoid competition by running out ahead of the crowd in performance terms, then we'll avoid them by working the corners of the market." Careful picking, choosing, and structuring of the competitive arena is the hallmark of this approach: "Why compete if we can get what we need without fighting?"

There are two basic logics in support of competitive avoidance. The first is simply that monopoly is an inherently more profitable (at least in percentage terms) competitive position. The firm that runs out ahead of competitors in terms of product performance can obtain monopoly profits until such time as competitors catch up, by which time the firm will have its next generation of performance available. Such a strategy clearly follows Sun Tzu's advice, quoted in the first chapter: The smartest strategy in war is that strategy which avoids a battle. The second logic does not deny the monopoly argument but adds that the resources of the firm are sufficiently limited that it is better for it to serve smaller niches than to attempt to compete in the broader and larger arenas.

Competitive avoidance may make sense as a general principle but does have its drawbacks. First, it locks the firm out of the big volume markets, almost by definition. Second, by avoiding competition entirely, the firm passes up those opportunities in which it could have beaten competitors. Third, the firm gets the reputation as one that can be scared away by aggressive competitors. Since competition is based first of all on the perceptions of competitive strength, the firm may find itself bluffed out by aggressive actions rather than the reality of competitive advantage.

---

[83] In effect, the greater the success the cartel has in creating profits for its members, the greater the incentive for firms to enter.

SUMMARY

While scoring in the game of economic competition is always dependent on offering differential value to the market, there are several leagues in which the typical competitive behavior of the players differs considerably. The strategist that can discern the current and potential forms that competition will take in the firm's chosen strategic arena will be advantaged.

The overall thrust of the economic system is toward efficiency through competition. The self-seeking actions of the individual competitors inevitably move all markets and industries closer to the most efficient form of perfect competition. This happens even though each competitor is always seeking out the highest return possible and attempting to gain some form of market power through every means at its disposal. There is evidence that even cartels or two-competitor markets may not be able to restrain for long the forces working to level all economic profits to the competitive level. Empirical evidence shows that there are few situations in which supranormal profits are sustained in the long run.

Real or potential competitive entry is the lever that restricts competitors from overreaching in their actions. While oligopoly theory teaches that competitors have strong incentives to cooperate instead of to compete, the results that accrue from cooperation attract new entrants. The key to understanding the likely moves of competitors is to understand their payoff matrix. Since the game's score is dominated by economic rewards, the actions and strategies of intelligent and rational competitors can often be predicted with some accuracy.

10

ANALYZING COMPETITORS

Competitive strategies are strongest either when they position a firm's strengths against competitors' weaknesses or choose positions which pose no threat to competitors. As such, they require that the strategist be as knowledgeable about competitors' strengths and weaknesses as about customers' needs or the firm's own capabilities. This chapter is designed to help the strategist understand how to gather and analyze information about competitors that is useful in the strategy development process. It begins by discussing the goal of competitive analysis and proceeds through the processes involved in identifying important competitors and information needs, gathering necessary information, and interpreting this information. It closes with a discussion of the need for a competitive intelligence system—since strategy is dependent on its intelligence inputs, the system that provides that input is critical to good strategizing.

THE GOAL OF COMPETITOR ANALYSIS

The goal of competitor analysis is to know enough about a competitor to be able to think like that competitor so the firm's competitive strategy can be formulated to take into account the competitors' likely actions and responses. As Sun Tzu said,

> Know the enemy and know yourself; in a hundred battles you will never be in peril. When you are ignorant of the enemy but know yourself, your chances of winning or losing are equal. If ignorant of your enemy and yourself, you are certain in every battle to be in peril.[1]

In one abstract sense, the goal is to be able to fill in a game theory matrix with competitors' actual financial and personal outcomes.[2] The strategist must be able to

---

[1] Sun Tzu, *The Art of War*, translated and with an introduction by Samuel B. Griffith (New York: Oxford University Press, 1963), p. 84.

[2] *Personal outcomes* refers to the effects that the success or failure of a strategy has on the decision makers in the firm.

1. Estimate the nature and likely success of the potential strategy changes available to a competitor;
2. Predict each competitor's probable responses to important strategic moves on the part of the other competitors; and
3. Understand competitors' potential reactions to changes in key industry and environmental parameters.[3]

IDENTIFYING COMPETITORS

Identifying competitors for analysis is not quite as obvious as it might seem. Two complementary approaches are possible. The first starts with customers, questioning whom and what they consider when making their purchase choices in the marketplace. The second approach identifies competitors as those firms whose competitive strategies conflict with the firm's. In either case, there exists a core set of competitors who may be termed *direct*.

However, direct competitors are not the only ones with which the firm must be concerned. When it first emerged, television was not considered to be a direct competitor by the movie industry, yet television came close to destroying the industry in the 1950s. Metaphorically, the firm must pay attention not only to today's immediate competitors but also to those that are just over the horizon (such as television was to movies or personal computers were to typewriters). Figure 10-1 provides a framework for recognizing the sources and types of the direct and less direct competitors to which the firm must also attend. In intelligence terms, the circles represent the areas of influence, the contiguous area, and the areas of interest.

- The *area of influence* is the territory, market, business, or industry in which the firm is directly competing for business. It is the arena in which ABC, CBS, and NBC television networks compete with each other; where Sony competes with Panasonic in consumer electronics.
- *Immediately contiguous areas* are those in which competition is close but not as direct. This contiguousness may be conceptual (motion pictures versus television) or geographical (two regional competitors whose geographical boundaries abut one another).
- *Areas of interest* are those longer-term threats or opportunities that lie just over the horizon. Direct satellite broadcasting, for example, is a long-term threat both to cable operators and local broadcasters. With the advent of glasnost, the large, highly skilled, and currency-starved workforce in the Eastern Bloc countries poses a threat to competitive advantage of the Asian countries such as Malaysia, Korea, and Taiwan.

This chapter explores both this supply-side approach to identifying relevant competitors as well as the more technically difficult task of market definition—

---

[3] Michael Porter, *Competitive Strategy* (New York: Free Press, 1980), chapter 3.

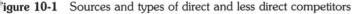

Figure 10-1 Sources and types of direct and less direct competitors

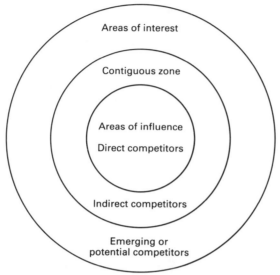

SOURCE: William L. Sammon, Mark A. Kurland, and Robert
Spitalnic, *Business Competitor Intelligence: Methods for Collecting,
Organizing and Using Information*. Copyright © 1984 John Wiley &
Sons, Inc. Reprinted by permission of John Wiley & Sons, Inc.

that is, competitor definition as defined by the customer. A product need not be
identical or even of the same material or technology to be considered a competitor. Competitor analysis should include the makers of those products that customers would consider identical, interchangeable, or substitutable in a given
customer application.

Business Definition

The most direct competitor competes for the exact same customers in exactly the
same way as the subject firm. It sells the same product made by the same
technology to the same customers via the same channels. If the firm cannot win
customer patronage versus such an identical competitor, then it is unlikely that
it can do any better competing against its less direct competitors. The reasoning
behind this is not difficult. If the firm's exact counterpart can win in direct
competition, then that same competitor should also win more against the less
direct competitors.

More generally, a firm's competitors are those firms whose strategies conflict
with those of the subject firm. There are two approaches to identifying the
degree to which two firms' strategies conflict. The first approach is based on the
work of Derek Abell, who suggests that a business can be defined along a
number of dimensions such as customer group, product technology, and the

function served by the product.[4] The more similar the definitions of the busi
ness, the closer the firms are judged to compete. The second approach takes on
step back, as it were, and achieves a similar end by examining other firms
strategies per se to define strategic groups of competitors.[5]

Abell's Approach.   A business is defined in terms of a number of key dimen
sions, which reflect the ways and places in which it has chosen to compete
Primary among these are the products it offers and the types of customers t
whom it chooses to sell.

The products a firm offers can be defined along three dimensions: functions
technology, and materials.

- *Customer function* is concerned with what need is being satisfied. This is the
  most natural way to think about a product. Electromechanical devices, fo
  example, can frequently be designed to satisfy any size set of function
  from very narrow to very wide. For example, some cooking appliances ar
  single function (microwave ovens), others are dual function (combinatio:
  convection-microwave ovens), while others are multifunction (combina
  tion convection-microwave-conventional ovens). Another example concern
  over-the-counter medications which, although identical in ingredients, may b
  positioned or sold for the relief of colds or allergies or sinus symptoms. Oth
  ers, such as Nyquil, are sold for even more specific usage applications (night
  time cold relief).
- *Technology* tells how the customer function(s) are being satisfied. For example
  kitchen ranges may use two sources of thermal energy (gas or electric) o:
  alternatively, microwave energy to cook. X rays, computerized axial tomogra
  phy (CAT scan machines), and NMR (nuclear magnetic resonance) are thre
  different technologies used in medical diagnostic imaging.
- The *materials* used in the manufacture of the product may also differ, produc
  ing slight differences in products that are otherwise identical. Cabinets may b
  made of chipboard versus plywood; bottles of glass or of such plastics as PET
  polypropylene, or polyethylene; and beverage cans of aluminum or steel.

The customer group being served (who) is a key dimension. Automobil
parts manufacturers, for example, may choose to serve either the original equip
ment manufacture (OEM) market or the automotive aftermarket, or both. On
competitor may focus on serving urban markets, another rural markets. Wa
Mart's initial success came from its focus on serving small, rural markets tha
traditional discounters had thought too small and too poor to serve. In contras:

---

[4] See Derek F. Abell, *Defining the Business: The Starting Point of Strategic Planning* (Englewood Cliff
NJ: Prentice Hall, 1980); and Derek F. Abell and John S. Hammond, *Strategic Market Planning* (E:
glewood Cliffs, NJ: Prentice Hall, 1979), chapter 8.
[5] Porter, *Competitive Strategy*, chapter 7. For a good description of the development of the strateg
group concept, see John McGee, "Strategic Groups: A Bridge Between Industry Structure an
Strategic Management?," in H. Thomas and D. Gardner, eds., *Strategic Marketing and Manageme:*
(London: John Wiley & Sons Ltd., 1985).

J.C. Penney has defined its customers as those households in the middle 80% of the U.S. income distribution. Lane Bryant stores cater to women in need of larger sizes. There are obviously many ways of defining a firm's targeted customer groups.

VISUALIZING THE BUSINESS. A given business, then, is defined by how it participates along the aforementioned dimensions: customer group, customer function and technology. In this way, it is possible to visualize the business in three-dimensional space, as shown in Figure 10-2. The vertical dimension shows the particular customer functions the firm serves, the left-hand axis the technologies it uses to serve those needs, and the horizontal dimension the customer groups it serves. The single cell pictured depicts a firm filling one function via one technology for one customer group.

Figure 10-3 shows how it is possible to visualize two different, but competing, businesses. It depicts the business definitions of two competitors in the laboratory oven business.[6] One type makes and sells ovens based on two technologies (electric and microwave) to three customer groups (laboratories, institutions, consumers). The second type sells only to laboratories but provides them with a wide range of laboratory equipment and apparatus (incubators, baths, pumps, instruments, etc.), of which ovens are just one product. The first type defines itself broadly in terms of customer groups and technology, whereas the second defines its customer group narrowly (it sells only to laboratories) but broadly by the customer functions it serves.

The Strategic Group Approach. The strategic group approach to identifying competitors is based on the differences in firms' strategies for competing in an industry. As such, it is a more general concept than Abell's approach to business definition. Like the business definition approach, the concept is intuitively appealing and understandable. For example, a hypothetical industry may be composed of three strategic groups:

1. A set of large firms pursuing a strategy of low-cost production of a full line of standardized products through mass-market outlets;
2. Another set of firms whose strategy emphasizes high-quality, differentiated, and branded products sold through specialty shops; and
3. A group of smaller firms which have gained strategic advantage by specializing in serving either specific customer groups or producing a very narrow range of products.[7]

[6] This example is based on one in Abell and Hammond, *Strategic Market Planning*, p. 394.

[7] This hypothetical industry, in fact resembles the home appliance industry in the 1960s as described by Michael S. Hunt in his dissertation. Hunt coined the phrase "strategic groups" to explain the differences in profitability he observed within the industry. Michael S. Hunt, "Competition in the Major Home Appliance Industry, 1960–1970" (unpublished doctoral dissertation, Harvard University, 1972).

Figure 10-2 Visualizing the business along three key dimensions

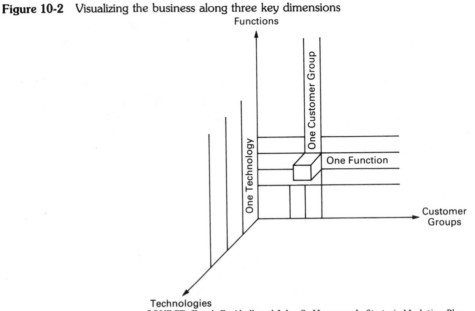

SOURCE: Derek F. Abell and John S. Hammond, *Strategic Marketing Planning: Problems and Analytical Approaches,* © 1979, p. 395. Adapted by permission of Prentice Hall, Englewood Cliffs, NJ 07632.

Figure 10-3 Two different business definitions in the market for laboratory ovens

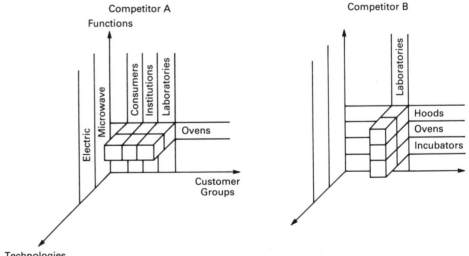

SOURCE: Derek F. Abell and John S. Hammond, *Strategic Marketing Planning: Problems and Analytical Approaches,* © 1979, p. 395. Adapted by permission of Prentice Hall, Englewood Cliffs, NJ 07632.

The strategic group concept is useful in identifying and analyzing competitors because members of a strategic group not only resemble each other but are also affected similarly by any given event or change in the environment. The commonality in their strategies means that they will likely respond in a similar manner to competitive threats or moves.

A further point should be noted about strategic groups. While all of the firms in an industry are in competition at a broad level, those in the same strategic group compete more closely among themselves than with those in other groups.[8] Further, the competition between and among groups is not equal—the various pairs of groups may compete more or less intensely. By observing the successes of the different strategic groups, one can better understand the inherent strengths and weaknesses of one strategy versus another.

FACTORS DETERMINING STRATEGIC GROUP MEMBERSHIP.   At the broadest level, any strategic factor or group of strategic factors can form the basis for the existence of strategic groups in an industry. Table 10-1 lists almost a dozen such strategic choices available to a business which, individually or in combination, could form the basis for a strategic group. The first step in analyzing an industry is to use these dimensions to describe the strategies of significant competitors.

Key to uncovering an industry's strategic groups is the ability to identify the few critical factors which differentiate among the various strategies being pursued by the competitors. Figure 10-4 portrays a hypothetical petrochemical industry in which the degree of product/market specialization (along a commodity-specialty continuum) and the degree of vertical integration (from those basic in crude oil to those purchasing raw materials) serve to differentiate among competitors' strategies. Discussions with long-time industry observers can often aid in identifying those key factors.

Alternatively, a focused analysis would start with the analysis of those firms which are considered to be the business's most direct competitors. In some businesses, this might yield several competitors who are pursuing identical strategies with very similar resources and competencies. The analyst could then work outward, selecting as the anchor for the next grouping that firm or firms whose strategic choices made them one step away from the original target grouping. This stepwise process would continue until the strategies of the firms examined are distant and no longer competitive with the focal firm. Essentially, this stepwise approach helps the analyst to recognize the key similarities and differences which cause the firms to cluster strategically.

In one study, Porter used an interesting methodology to identify strategic groups quickly.[9] He made the assumption that being an industry leader or an

---

[8] The biological analogy predicts this. As Bruce Henderson noted, "The more similar competitors are to each other, the more severe their competition. This observation was made by Darwin in *The Origin of Species*." Bruce Henderson, "The Anatomy of Competition," *Journal of Marketing*, 47, no. 2 (spring 1983), p. 8.

[9] Michael E. Porter, "The Structure Within Industries and Companies' Performance," *Review of Economics and Statistics*, 61, no. 2 (May 1979), 214–227.

TABLE 10-1 *Typical Strategic Options Available*

Product Line
Specialization: along such dimensions as line width/breadth, variety of segments served, application areas, geographic scope
Quality: including basic value position, perceived and conformance quality, relative performance emphasis
Offer Breadth: the extent of customer service from engineering design stage to post-sales, inventory and credit policies

Marketing Strategy
Branding: focusing on the choice of generic versus branded promotion and the mix of personal selling and advertising
End-User Orientation: the extent to which consumed demand is created directly (pull) versus by channel members (push)
Channel Choice: direct sales versus representation; choice of channels, broad versus selective distribution

Technology and Manufacturing
Leadership: leader or follower position in process or product technology; areas of focus and specialization
Vertical Integration: choice of position along entire value chain from basic in raw materials through to retail or end-user
Cost and Responsiveness: trade-offs made between cost minimization, product variety and quality, and the speed of manufacturing responsiveness to market changes.

---

industry follower (in terms of market share) was a rough proxy for membership in one or another strategic group and then performed separate regression analyses which explained each group's financial performance. The explanatory variables in the regression then could be interpreted as the factors differentiating one strategic group from the other. For example, the two groups had different advertising to sales ratios, indicating a different emphasis on advertising as one major difference between the groups' strategies. Others have attempted to develop similar statistical approaches to defining strategic groups.[10]

---

[10] Karel Cool and Dan Schendel, "Strategic Group Formation and Performance: The Case of the U.S Pharmaceutical Industry, 1963–1982," *Management Science*, 33, no. 9 (1987), 1–23; and Karel Cool and Dan Schendel, "Performance Differences Among Strategic Group Members," *Strategic Management Journal*, 9, No. 3 (May–June 1988), 207–223. More recent work is by Wayne DeSarbo, Kamel Jedidi, Karel Cool, and Dan Schendel, "Strategic Groups, Conduct, and Goal Asymmetry: The Stratgroup Methodology" (unpublished research working paper no. 89-AV-5, Graduate School of Business Administration, The University of Michigan); and Pam Lewis and Howard Thomas, "The Linkage Between Strategy, Strategic Groups, and Performance in the U.K. Retail Grocery Industry," *Strategic Management Journal*, 11 (1990), 386–97.

Figure 10-4   Strategic groups in a hypothetical petrochemical industry

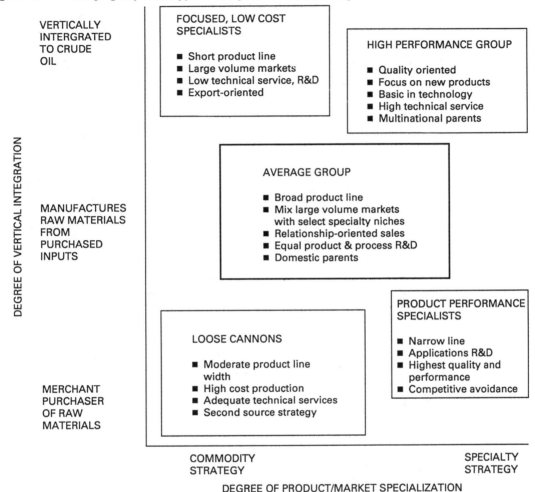

Identifying Competitors at the Product Market Level

The foregoing discussions of identifying competitors focused primarily on the industry and firm levels. The essentially supply-oriented techniques described are fine for the individual concerned with competition at the business, strategic business unit, SBU, or category level but lack the specificity required by the product manager. The product manager needs to understand the exact extent of competition among the products available on the market. At this level, competitors are best identified by customers—the demand side—rather than by supply characteristics.

Substitution-in-use.   Current thinking about identifying the competitive structure for any given product is based on the idea of substitution-in-use. Three
premises underlie the idea:

1. People seek the benefits that products provide rather than the products per se.
2. The needs to be satisfied and the benefits which are being sought are dictated by
   the usage situations or applications being contemplated.
3. Products and technologies are considered part of the set of substitutes if they are
   perceived to provide functions which satisfy the needs determined by intended
   usage.[11]

Determining a product's direct competition, then, may provide an answer
that says, "It depends." It depends on (1) the number of separate and different
uses or applications for the products in the market; (2) the number of different
usage situations which customers encounter; and (3) user characteristics, including the number of product types or brands that a customer would evoke and
choose among.[12]

Some markets are relatively simple because the offerings within them provide only a single function for one or a few uses. Travelers checks or bathroom
tissue are two such products. Other examples include home pasta makers or
irons, both of which perform a specific function across a small number of different usage situations. At the other extreme are complex markets in which each
customer has many uses for the product and many alternatives to consider.
Financial services have been cited as one such example.

Srivastava, Alpert, and Shocker performed a study which illustrated this
discussion. They defined a product market to be "the set of products judged to
be substitutes within those usage situations in which similar patterns of benefits
are sought by groups of customers."[13] In their study, upscale customers were
asked to judge the appropriateness of twenty-four different financial services
across each of twelve different usage situations. One such usage situation was
described thus: While you are out of town on a trip you have some unexpected
problems with your car. The repair bill, at a small independent garage, is about
$100 and must be paid immediately.[14]

There are two ways of analyzing such a market. The first, hierarchical clustering, groups products together based on the perceived similarity in their use
across different situations. In this method, each product can be grouped in only

---

[11] George S. Day, "Strategic Market Analysis: Top-Down and Bottom-Up Approaches" (Cambridge,
MA: Marketing Science Institute, Report No. 80-105, August 1980), p. 14.
[12] Day, "Strategic Market Analysis," p. 20; see also Glen L. Urban, Philip L. Johnson, and John R.
Hauser, "Testing Competitive Market Structures," *Marketing Science*, 3, no. 2 (spring 1984), 83–112.
[13] Rajendra K. Srivastava, Mark I. Alpert, and Allan D. Shocker, "A Customer-Oriented Approach
for Determining Market Structures," *Journal of Marketing*, 48, no. 2 (spring 1984), p. 32.
[14] Srivastava, Alpert, and Shocker, "A Customer-Oriented Approach for Determining Market Structures," p. 32.

one cluster. The results of the analysis is shown in Figure 10-5. Services that are perceived to be most similar are grouped together first (savings certificates and stocks and bonds; overdraft protection and cash advance credit card), and as one moves up the chart the dissimilarity of the products groups increases. The higher up two services are joined together, the more dissimilar they are (a bank installment loan and a checking account, for example, are perceived to be very dissimilar and therefore do not directly compete).

The problem with the hierarchical technique is that each product can only be placed in one cluster, whereas in real life a given product may serve several different functions across a number of different situations. To depict this reality accurately, a second technique was used which allows for overlapping clusters. The analysis showed six interpretable clusters (for clarity, only clusters 3 to 6 are shown in Figure 10-6). Cluster 3, for example, consisted of products likely to be used in in-town retail settings requiring larger amounts of money, and as can be seen in Table 10-2, it is a subset of the first cluster.

Using Purchase Behavior to Identify Competitors.   No matter how much logical sense an analysis such as the foregoing makes, it is based on what customers say, not on what they do. Several researchers have developed techniques which are based on actual purchase data. Figure 10-7, for example, depicts the competitive structure of the toothpaste and bathroom tissue markets estimated on the basis of supermarket scanning data.[15] In this instance, the map positions products on the basis of their attributes on a per-dollar basis consistent with the discussion in chapter 4.

As the map shows clearly, all toothpastes are not alike. Customers preferring taste over anticavity qualities are more likely to buy Close-Up® or Aim® than they are Crest®. Furthermore, Close-Up® and Aim® are in closer competition than either is with Crest. The bathroom tissue market shows a similar positioning along its two primary dimensions: absorbency and softness. To say that Scott® and White Cloud® compete is true and not true at the same time. One might better say that Scott® and Northern® are in closer competition than either is with White Cloud® or Charmin®.

Identifying Potential Competitors

Depending on the purposes of the competitive analysis, it may also be important to identify potential competitors. This task is not as difficult as it may seem. The process starts by identifying firms for whom the various barriers to entry to the industry are low or easily surmountable. These may include the following:

[15] Steven M. Shugan, "Estimating Brand Positioning Maps Using Supermarket Scanning Data," *Journal of Marketing Research*, XXIV (February 1987), 1–18; see also Steven M. Shugan, "Brand Positioning Maps from Price/Share Data: The Case of Bathroom Tissue" (unpublished working paper, University of Chicago Graduate School of Business, July 1986, Revised) and Terry Elrod, "Choice Map: Inferring a Product-Market Map from Panel Data," *Marketing Science*, 7, no. 1 (winter 1988), 21–39.

Figure 10-5 Hierarchical clustering of financial services

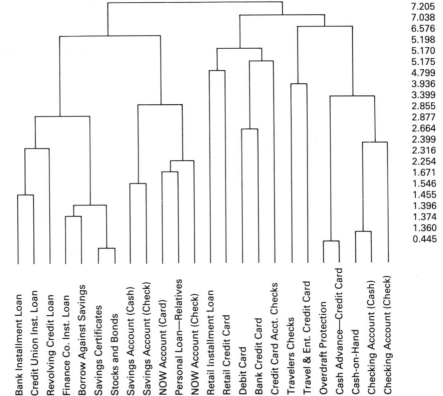

SOURCE: Rajendra K. Srivastava, Mark I. Alpert, and Albert D. Shocker, "A Customer-Oriented Approach for Determining Market Structure," in *Journal of Marketing*, 53, no. 3 (July 1989), p. 40. Reprinted by permission of the American Marketing Association.

- *Technology:* Firms which possess the technologies necessary to operate in an industry represent one source of potential competitors. Communications, computing, and microelectronics technologies are sufficiently similar that an analysis in the 1970s would have listed AT&T as a potential competitor in the computer industry before it actually entered. Analysis of patent activity frequently signals intentions well prior to actual entrance.

- *Market access:* In businesses where market access is a key factor for success, firms with that access frequently attempt to leverage it by acquiring additional product lines to be sold in that channel or to those customers.

- *Reputation and image:* Brand extension strategies are based on the use of a firm's reputation in one product area to leverage its entry into another. Clairol used its reputation in hair coloring to enter into the hair dryer business; Borden and Lipton used their names to challenge the dominance of the Tang® brand in instant breakfast beverages.

Figure 10-6   Financial services market structure (overlapping clusters)

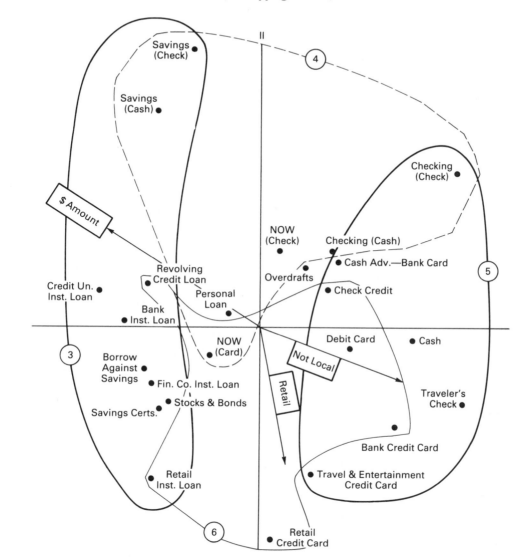

SOURCE: Rajendra K. Srivastava, Mark I. Alpert, and Albert D. Shocker, "A Customer-Oriented Approach for Determining Market Structure," in *Journal of Marketing*, 53, no. 3 (July 1989), p. 41. Reprinted by permission of the American Marketing Association.

Operating knowledge and skills: Regional competitors in a business often expand geographically. Entenmann's Bakeries moved into the Florida and Midwestern markets from their original Northeastern base, similar to the path taken by Thomas's English Muffins. Folger's coffee was originally a regional brand on the West Coast until purchased by Procter & Gamble which expanded its distribution nationwide.

TABLE 10-2 *Interpretation of the six overlapping clusters of financial services*

USAGE SITUATION

FINANCIAL PRODUCT	1. Products likely to be used when large amounts are required (local use)	2. Products likely to be used when low/medium amounts are required in retail settings	3. Products likely to be used when large amounts are required in retail settings (local use)	4. Products likely to be used when low/medium amounts are needed in nonretail settings (local use)	5. Products likely to be used when low/medium amounts are required in out-of-town settings	6. Products likely to be used when medium amounts are required in retail settings while out of town
Cash on hand		X			X	
Checking (cash)		X		X		
Checking (check)		X		X	X	
Debit card		X			X	X
Savings (cash)	X		X	X		
Savings (check)	X		X	X		
NOW account (check)	X			X		
NOW account (cash card)	X			X		X
Savings certificate	X		X			
Stocks and bonds	X		X			
Borrow against savings	X		X			
Traveler's check		X			X	
Cash advance bank card		X		X	X	
Overdraft checking		X		X		
Check credit bank card		X			X	X
Bank credit card		X			X	X
T&E credit card		X			X	
Retail credit card		X				X
Personal loan—relative	X			X		
Bank installment loan	X		X			
Finance co. installment loan	X		X			
Credit union installment loan	X		X			
Retail installment loan			X			X
Revolving credit loan	X		X			X

SOURCE: Rajendra K. Srivastava et al., "A Customer-Oriented Approach for Determining Market Structure," in *Journal of Marketing*, 53, no. 3 (July 1989), p. 32. Reprinted by permission of the American Marketing Association.

Figure 10-7   Brand positioning for the toothpaste and bathroom tissue markets

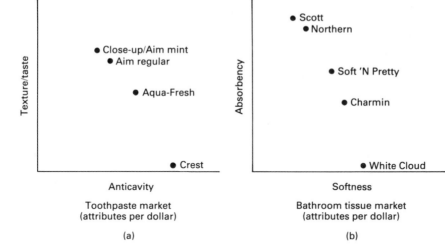

SOURCE: Adapted from Steven M. Shugan, "Estimating Brand Positioning Maps Using Supermarket Scanning Data," *Journal of Marketing Research*, XXIV (February 1987), p. 8; and "Brand Positioning Maps From Price/Share Data: The Case of Bathroom Tissue" (unpublished working paper, University of Chicago Graduate School of Business, July 1986), p. 21.

Less obvious potential entrants are those whose present strategies (and therefore the firm's long-term viability) are challenged by the success of the subject industry. Union Camp, for example, is essentially a forest products company whose product mix is focused on paper. However, as its traditional outlets for kraft and other papers declined (bags for supermarkets and general merchandise stores) due to the switch to plastic bags, Union Camp entered into the plastic bag business. The analyst seeking to identify potential competitors needs to identify companies in positions similar to Union Camp.

IDENTIFYING INFORMATION NEEDS

The goal of competitor analysis is to be able to predict a competitor's probable future actions, especially those made in response to the actions of the focal business. Exhibit 10-1 makes clear the reasons for this. This requires information which is both quantitative and factual (what the competitor is doing and can do) as well as that which is qualitative and intentional (what the competitor is likely to do).

What the Competitor is Doing and Can Do

At the base of any competitive analysis is the quantitative and factual information about what a competitor is capable of, what it has or possesses, what it is doing, and with what results. While a complete delineation of every possible

EXHIBIT 10-1

What You Should Expect from Competitor Analysis

Underneath all of the complexities and depth of competitor analysis are some simple and basic practical questions, of which the following are typical:

- Which competitors does our strategy pit us against?
- Which competitor is most vulnerable and how should we move on its customers?
- Is the competitor's announced move just a bluff? What's it gain if we accept it at face value?
- What kind of aggressive moves will the competitor accept? Which moves has it always countered?

---

type and category that would be included is beyond imagination, Table 10-3 offers as complete a listing as can be expected.

A more focused approach would be to focus specifically on those areas in which competitive advantage has its sources. Table 10-4 provides a useful conceptual approach in which the data are based both on customer and competitor assessments. Doing marketing research on one's own performance with customers versus the performance of selected competitors can provide a valuable insight not available in other ways.

More important than the gathering of data and facts, however, is the evaluation and interpretation of what is obtained. *Evaluation* means to judge each aspect of the competitor's business—distribution; marketing and sales; manufacturing and operations; research, development and engineering; cost positions; financial positions and capabilities; organization structure and morale; leadership ability and depth; and business portfolio—in terms of its strengths and weaknesses. Operationally, an area of strength is one in which the firm is admired by customers and feared by competitors; a weakness is the opposite. For example, an analysis of competitors' financial performance, such as found in Exhibit 10-2, provides insights not otherwise obvious.

Interpretation takes the base facts and their evaluation as strengths and weaknesses and asks of them some key, penetrating questions:

- *What are the competitor's core capabilities?* What are its capabilities in each functional area? Which is it best at? Worst at? Do these capabilities match up with its announced or inferred strategy? What changes seem to be occurring in them for better or for worse?
- *What is the competitor's ability to grow?* Which capabilities will be stretched by growth? What is the competitor's capacity to grow in terms of physical or human resources? Given present financials, what is its sustainable growth rate

TABLE 10-3 *Outline of Basic Data Needed for Competitor Analysis*

Strategic Background
1. Overall competitive position within core industry
     General reputation
     Management reputation
     Major qualitative strengths
     Major qualitative weaknesses
2. Comparative financial performance (last five years)
     Profitability trend vs industry averages (sales margin, asset turnover, return on operating assets)
     Key growth rates (sales S&A, cost of goods, R&D, profit margins, etc.)
     Capital structure, earnings pattern, and stock performance
3. Business portfolio analysis/investment strategy
     Product mix by segment
     Distribution of operating assets by segment
     Comparative analysis of segment financial performance
       Sales and profitability trends
       Funds deployment trends (funds used/funds generated)
4. Geographic balance
     Domestic versus international
     Foreign subsidiaries
5. Corporate culture and history
     Historical perspective—growth pattern/development milestones
     Core organizational values and business mission/vision
     Managerial/operational style

Corporate Strategy
1. Announced objectives and strategies
2. Inferred goals—domestic and international
3. Past strategies—consistency/continuity
4. Short term—long-term constraints and tradeoffs
5. Competitors' reaction
6. planning and implementation capabilities
7. Capital investment program
8. Acquisition and divestment pattern
9. Relative emphasis on growth through acquisitions versus interval development

Business-Unit Strategies
1. Segment #1   Products/market share rank/demand assumptions
2. Segment #2   Capabilities, goals, actions
3. Segment #3   Relationship to corporate strategy
4. Segment #4

Joint Ventures
1. Type and purpose
2. Trends

Functional Analyses
1. Sales and marketing
     Key products, market share, commitment
     Product quality, customer reputation
     Pattern of product introductions

TABLE 10-3   (cont.)

Pricing tactics
Distribution
Sales force caliber/reputation compensation
Market research capability
Technical service
Major accounts/key customers
Marketing image—overall, by key businesses and/or products
2. Manufacturing and operations
Production thrust/operations
Competitive cost position (geographic and by major product lines)
Facility profiles
  a. Location, capacities, bottlenecks
  b. Production mix
  c. Capacity utilization trends
Expenditure patterns
Capacity expansions/reductions
Raw materials
Supply relationships
Quality control
Union issues
Regulatory concerns
3. Research and development
Technological focus, priorities, and innovativeness
R&D mix
Track record and reputation of research labs and staff
Key product development projects
Corporate financial support (levels and trends)
Strategic priority
Major patents and proprietary areas
Security issues
4. Financial
Overall financial management ability
Credit ratings, borrowing capacity
Lender relationships
Business growth and development funding strategies
5. Organizational
Senior management control/decision-making process
Corporate structure
  Line operations/support staff
  Business units/product lines
  Global/country teams
  Centralization/decentralization
Congruence with corporate values
Informal structure and sources of influence
  Dominant functions
  Strongest business units
Human resources/personnel strategies
Employee talent, morale, turnover, productivity
6. Legal/governmental issues

TABLE 10-3 (cont.)

Management
1. Overall reputation and accomplishment
       Background, experience, functional orientation
       Flexibility/adaptability
2. CEO profile
       Abilities, tenure, reputation
       Succession
3. Other key decision-makers
       Dominant role models
       Sources of influence
       Value consensus
4. Depth and continuity
5. Outside board of directors

Strategic Net Assessment
1. Capabilities/weaknesses recap
       Best at
                   operations and functions
       Worst at
       Trends, capacity for change and/or growth
2. Evaluation of perceived strategy
       Management commitment
       Coherence and consistency (compatible goals)
       Congruence with managements' assumptions, industry trends, business unit strategies, and
       stated corporate goals
       Financial ability
       Match between company capabilities and strategic objectives
       Timing and implementation problems
       Probability of success (expected performance)
3. Probable competitive reactions and company response
4. Strategic implications (for your company)
       Threats
       Opportunities
       New issues

SOURCE: William L. Sammon, Mark A. Kurland, and Robert Spitalnic, *Business Competitor Intelligence: Methods for Collecting, Organizing and Using Information.* Copyright © 1984 John Wiley & Sons, Inc. Reprinted by permission of John Wiley & Sons, Inc.

without external financing? How capable is it of increasing share before additional capacity is needed?

• *What is the competitor's ability to respond and change?* Does the competitor have the wherewithal to respond quickly in terms of financial, physical, and human resources? Has it demonstrated the managerial and organizational willpower to do so? How does the business's ratio of fixed to variable costs drive its short-term responses? How does its need to make fixed debt or other payments influence its actions? Does its response ability vary across its functions? Are there other barriers to action or exit that constrain it, such as joint ventures or large undepreciated assets?

• *What is the competitor's ability to tough it out?* How close to the edge is the competitor skating? Can it survive a protracted recession? A major industry con-

TABLE 10-4 *Methods of Assessing Advantage*

COMPETITOR CENTERED	CUSTOMER FOCUSED
A. Assessing sources (distinctive competences)	
1. Management judgments of strengths and weaknesses	
2. Comparison of resource commitments and capabilities	
3. Marketing skills audit	
B. Indicators of positional advantage	
4. Competitive cost and activity comparisons	5. Customer comparisons of attributes of firm vs. competitors
a. Value chain comparisons of relative costs	a. Choice models
b. Cross-section experience curves	b. Conjoint analysis
	c. Market maps
C. Identifying key success factors	
6. Comparison of winning vs. losing competitors	
7. Identifying high leverage phenomena	
a. Management estimates of market-share elasticities	
b. Drivers of activities in the value chain	
D. Measure of performance	
	8. Customer satisfaction surveys
	9. Loyalty (customer franchise)
10a. Market share	
	10b. Relative share of end-user segments
11. Relative profitability (return on sales and return on assets)	

SOURCE: George S. Day and Robin Wensley, "Assessing Advantage: A Framework for Diagnosing Competitive Superiority," in *Journal of Marketing*, 52, no. 2 (April 1988), p. 9. Reprinted by permission of the American Marketing Association.

frontation? Are stockholders and the financial community behind management? How big of a cut in internally generated cash flow can the business take without major dislocation?

What the Competitor Is Likely To Do

From a strategic perspective, however, information about where a business currently stands is somewhat like accounting data are to a potential purchaser of a company's common stock—it describes the past, when what is really needed is information about the future. Predicting the future can take two shapes. In a literal sense, it may mean the specific actions a competitor will take; in a more general sense, it may mean knowing about what it is that the competitor is trying to accomplish. Exhibit 10-3 suggests one way an analyst can detect changes in a company's strategy.

It would generally be better to be able to predict what it is a competitor is trying to accomplish. If one understands a competitor's intentions, then forecasting the range of actions that may be used to implement those intentions is a

EXHIBIT 10-2

Analyzing Financial Performance of Strategic Groups and the Individual Competitors in Them

Analyzing the financial performance of strategic groups and the competitors within them can provide insights that more microanalytic analyses may not. Exhibit Figures A through D position both the strategic groups in the forest products industry and the competitors within each of the three strategic groups in that industry in a two dimensional space based on their operating margin (in % terms) and their asset turnover. The product of the two is Return on Assets (ROA) and, as the curved lines show, there are many combinations of operating margin and turnover that will yield the same ROA. A high margin combined

EXHIBIT FIGURE A
Strategic groups

Forest Products Industry—Strategic Groups
Four Year Average
Results: 1978–1981

Group	Cos	$Sales (MM)	ROA =	Turnover
Paper	7	$12398	13%	1.31
Wood Products	4	11288	12%	1.10
Balanced	5	12154	12%	1.50
Industry	16	$35840	12%	1.30

Operating Profitability Matrix:
Operating Margin × Asset Turnover = Return on Assets

SOURCE: William L. Sammon, Mark A. Kurland, and Robert Spitalnic, *Business Competitor Intelligence: Methods for Collecting, Organizing, and Using Information*, p. 107.

EXHIBIT 10-2 (cont.)

with low asset turnover can produce the same ROA as a low margin combined with a fast turnover. More of both, of course, produces a higher ROA.

The industry shown is the forest products industry and the strategic groups shown are simple ones based solely on the composition of the product lines of the firms. In this industry, competitors' product lines can be heavily weighted to paper products (kraft linerboard, newsprint, printing and fine papers) or to solid wood products (lumber, plywood, logs) or the mix can be equally balanced between the two product types. The data used to position the groups and the individual competitors are the average of four years' results to reduce the effect of year-to-year variability. The author of the analysis analyzes them thusly:

EXHIBIT FIGURE B

Paper strategic group

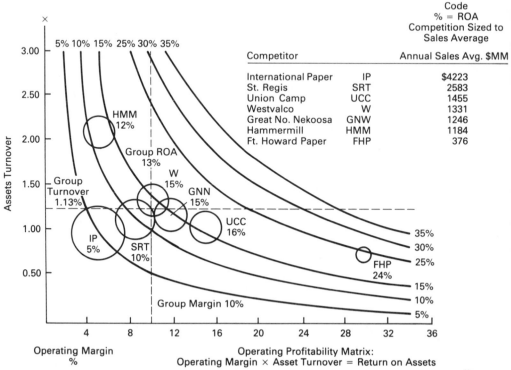

Forest Products Industry—Paper Strategic Group
(1978–1981)

Competitor		Annual Sales Avg. $MM
International Paper	IP	$4223
St. Regis	SRT	2583
Union Camp	UCC	1455
Westvalco	W	1331
Great No. Nekoosa	GNW	1246
Hammermill	HMM	1184
Ft. Howard Paper	FHP	376

Code
% = ROA
Competition Sized to
Sales Average

Operating Profitability Matrix:
Operating Margin × Asset Turnover = Return on Assets

SOURCE: William L. Sammon, Mark A. Kurland, and Robert Spitalnic, *Business Competitor Intelligence: Methods for Collecting, Organizing, and Using Information,* p. 108.

EXHIBIT 10-2 (cont.)

- The paper strategic group enjoys the highest ROA—13 percent—of the three groups despite the fact that it includes one of the industry's largest but least profitable competitors. Does a product mix oriented towards paper lines confer a strategic advantage in the current economic environment?
- In the wood products group, large competitors have achieved a financial performance markedly superior to the group's smaller competitors. The reverse is the case in the paper group where size seems to be a strategic disadvantage. Why?
- With one or two exceptions, the balanced strategic group has the weakest group of competitors in the industry. In their attempt to straddle both the wood and paper sectors, have they ended up with half-measure strategies and suffered a financial penalty as a consequence?
- What explains the exceptional outlying performance of Ft. Howard Paper, one of the industry's smallest competitors, yet its most profitable by far?

EXHIBIT FIGURE C

Wood products strategic group

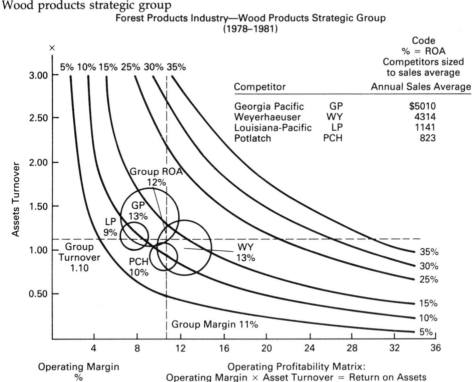

Forest Products Industry—Wood Products Strategic Group
(1978–1981)

Competitor		Annual Sales Average
Georgia Pacific	GP	$5010
Weyerhaeuser	WY	4314
Louisiana-Pacific	LP	1141
Potlatch	PCH	823

Code
% = ROA
Competitors sized
to sales average

Operating Margin
%

Operating Profitability Matrix:
Operating Margin × Asset Turnover = Return on Assets

SOURCE: William L. Sammon, Mark A. Kurland, and Robert Spitalnic, *Business Competitor Intelligence: Methods for Collecting, Organizing, and Using Information*, p. 109.

EXHIBIT 10-2 (cont.)

EXHIBIT FIGURE D

Balanced product line strategic group

Forest Products industry—Balanced Product Line Strategic Group
(1978–1981)

Code
% = ROA
Competitors sized
to sales average

Competitor		Annual Sales Avg. $MM
Champion Int'l	CHA	$3746
Crown Zellerbach	CZZ	2880
Boise Cascade	BCC	2904
Mead	MEA	2624
Willamette	WMTT	888

Operating Margin
%

Operating Profitability Matrix:
Operating Margin × Asset Turnover = Return on Assets

SOURCE: William L. Sammon, Mark A. Kurland, and Robert Spitalnic, *Business Competitor Intelligence: Methods for Collecting, Organizing, and Using Information*, p. 110.

- Three competitors—Hammermill (paper group), Mead (balanced group), and Crown Zellerbach (balanced group)—have asset turnover ratios far above the industry norm of 1.30. This suggests that they have a product line and/or at least one business segment that is not capital intensive—unusual in a "smokestack" basic manufacturing industry like forest products. What are these segments or product lines and, in terms of ROA, is this an effective strategy for increasing overall profitability while reducing the capital intensity of a company's business portfolio?

SOURCE: William L. Sammon, Mark A. Kurland, and Robert Spitalnic, *Business Competitor Intelligence: Methods for Collecting, Organizing and Using Information*. Copyright © 1984 John Wiley & Sons, Inc. Reprinted by permission of John Wiley & Sons, Inc.

natural result. More specifically, if one understands the goals that a competitor has and the relevant assumptions that the competitor holds, then the competitor's decision process can be reproduced and its future actions forecast. In a theoretical sense, the process is much like understanding a customer's utility function. If you can understand what a customer values, then you can predict his or her potential purchase behavior.

Understanding Competitors' Goals. Achieving knowledge and understanding about a competitor's goals is one of the more difficult tasks of competitive intelligence. One reason for this is the sheer volume of information required and the necessity of interpretation to make it usable. A second reason is that there is no single, simple overriding set of goals driving the organization. Rather, the analyst needs to be able to infer, from the goals held by the various levels across each of the areas of concern (shown in Figure 10-8), what the resultant goal vector is that drives firm strategy and action. The following discussion first examines the areas of concern and then the issues related to the various levels.

Financial goals are always of importance. Understanding the firm's goals with respect to short- and long-run performance, to the trade-off between profit growth and cash flow or revenue growth, to short-run performance versus stability in performance, is key to understanding what drives a competitor. Knowing the financial indicators for which there are goals provides almost as much insight as knowing what the numerical targets are.

Strategic goals, on the other hand, may override financial goals (at least in the short run) since the achievement of such strategic goals as market share, cost position, and other measures of competitive advantage causes the firm's financial results. Knowledge of the major indicators of strategic position used to measure goal achievement is key to understanding a competitor's future actions.

Cultural goals indicate a business's tendency to value certain kinds of actions over others. What is the organization's culture? What shared values and beliefs unite its managers? Does the firm believe that success comes from technology, superior product quality, tough managers, intimidating competitors, marketing savvy, penny pinching, or going first class? What actions have always worked, which kind have caused failures?

Organizational goals are indicated by those activities that the organization rewards. What kinds of incentive systems drive the organization? The firm's organization structure, the levels at which the various functions report into upper management, the background of those occupying top positions, and even the composition of the board give clues to the goals that drive the organization itself.

How does the firm integrate goals across organizational levels? To assume that goals remain constant across the various business units or even across the different managerial levels or functional units within a given business unit is naive. Understanding the differences can provide as much insight as can the similarities. Knowing the function of each business unit in the corporate portfolio, for example, can allow one to predict its future actions. Understanding a

EXHIBIT 10-3

Identifying Changes in a Firm's Strategy

One researcher, George Tassey, hypothesized that a method for identifying strategic groups in an industry or for characterizing the strategy of a given firm would be to analyze the ratio of the firm's "demand-acquiring strategies" over time. In his conception, there are two activities that a firm performs that are used to generate increases in the firm's sales. One is R&D. The firm that invests in R&D can consistently produce innovative products and thereby gain sales increases in that manner. Alternatively (or in addition), firms invest in marketing to increase their sales.

EXHIBIT FIGURE A
Annual R&D and advertising expenditures for selected drug companies

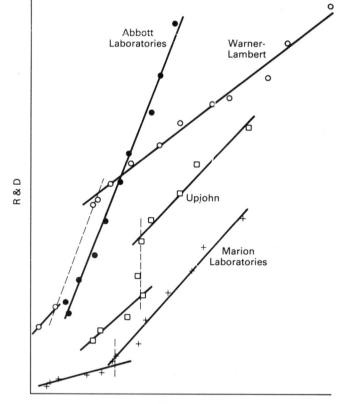

SOURCE: Reprinted by permission of the publisher from "Competitive Strategy and Performance in Technology-Based Industries," by George Tassey, *Journal of Economics and Business*, 35, no. 1, p. 31. Copyright © 1983 by Elsevier Science Publishing, Inc.

EXHIBIT 10-3 (cont.)

In Tassey's conception, one can envision two opposite strategies. The firm that invests heavily in R&D is able to create products whose performance characteristics are so superior to existing products that they sell themselves to a large extent. This firm would have a high ratio of R&D to marketing. Imitators, on the other hand, pay a price for not being first. They have to overcome the initial success of the leader by spending more on marketing to convey information about their own version of the new product and to persuade buyers of its acceptability. They have a low ratio of R&D relative to marketing.

Exhibit Figure A shows how one can use this relationship to compare the strategies of different firms as well as to identify shifts in the strategy of a given firm. The data depict four drug companies in the period from 1970 to 1980 (additional, earlier data for some allow as much as a fourteen-year time series). Only Abbott Laboratories has held a consistent ratio through the period; the other three all changed slope (and therefore their strategies) during the period. Based on the apparent relationships in this figure, one would say that Abbot had a more research-intensive strategy than its competitors (Tassey warns, however, that comparison between the firms' slopes on this graph should not be attempted because different scales were used to be able to depict adequately all four plots on the same graph). Performing such comparisons would obviously be of great interest, however.

SOURCE: Reprinted by permission of the publisher from "Competitive Strategy and Performance in Technology-Based Industries," by George Tassey, *Journal of Economics and Business*, 35, no. 1, pp. 21–40. Copyright © 1983 by Elsevier Science Publishing, Inc.

generational split in goals within management's ranks indicates that future directions may veer sharply from the present course.

Understanding Competitors' Assumptions.   Future behavior is a function both of a competitor's goals and of the assumptions it holds. It matters little what objective reality is. Action is based on perceived reality. The useful competitor analysis seeks to identify the assumptions that the competitor holds about itself and the industry.

Knowledge about a competitor's assumptions can prove useful, especially if those assumptions are wrong. There are competitors in many industries which believe that customers are driven by the price/performance ratio. Their assumption is that customers prefer strategies that reduce price at the expense of product performance as long as the price/performance ratio is improved. If the reality, however, is that customers actually prefer strategies which increase product performance more than the price increases necessary to create that improved performance, then a strategic opportunity exists. The astute competitor can take

Figure 10-8 The levels and types of goals

TYPE OF GOALS MANAGERIAL LEVEL	FINANCIAL	STRATEGIC	CULTURAL	ORGANIZATIONAL
CORPORATE LEVEL				
BUSINESS UNIT 1 TOP MANAGEMENT MIDDLE MANAGEMENT				
BUSINESS UNIT 2 TOP MANAGEMENT MIDDLE MANAGEMENT				

advantage of the blind spot by improving product performance, secure in the knowledge that the competitor will respond inappropriately and ineffectively.

One should attempt to assess competitors' assumptions across most key functional areas. Key topics in which assumptions are important include beliefs about competitors' relative cost positions, the factors that drive industry growth, the reasons for previous company success, and the relative importance of product performance and price to customers.

The Competitor's Response Profile

The combination of this analysis of competitors' goals and assumptions together with competitors' current strategies and capabilities allow one to estimate their response profiles. A response profile tells one what kinds of actions a competitor is likely to take, if any, in response to the firm's own actions. A good competitor described in Exhibit 10-4, will take actions that preserve industry profitability.

Calculating the Response Profile. It may sound simplistic, but one of the most powerful determinants of a competitor's future actions is the set of economic outcomes that would result from each different competitive response. To the extent, then, that one can calculate the financial results that would flow from different actions, one should be able to predict competitors' actions.

Theoretically, the issue is complex. Economists use the term *conjectural variation* to refer to what is known about the likelihood and the intensity of competitors' responses. Specifically, a conjectural variation is what is believed about the relationship between a firm's own behavior and the corresponding return-maximizing action that will be taken by the competitor.[16] The interesting aspect is that estimating a competitor's actions requires the recognition that the competitor's decision involves more than simply choosing the action that yields it the highest relative financial result from among the set of actions available to it. This is because those financial results themselves are simultaneously affected by the competitor's own conjectures concerning the acting firm's response profile

---

[16] Raphael Amit, Ian Domowitz, and Chaim Fershtman, "Thinking One Step Ahead: The Use of Conjectures in Competitor Analysis," *Strategic Management Journal*, 9, no. 5 (1988), 431–442.

EXHIBIT 10-4

Are Your Competitors "Good" Competitors?

While there are many marketers for whom the only good competitor is a dead competitor, the fact is that competition and competitors are inescapable. Some competitors, however, are better for the firm than others. Strategically, the goal is to recognize the hallmarks of a good competitor and to behave differently toward good competitors than to bad competitors.[17]

Good competitors compete and thereby keep the firm on its toes but have characteristics which incline them toward a mutually attractive competitive equilibrium rather than toward aggressive and expensive warfare. These characteristics are logical. The good competitor provides an acceptable alternative to customers and is strong enough to deter potential entrants. It has recognized weaknesses that inhibit expansionary objectives, plays by the existing rules (which favor incumbents), makes realistic assumptions about the industry and itself, and knows its costs. In other words, it is not a dumb competitor. Its strategy improves industry structure rather than destroys its profit potential and is inherently self-limiting in that its objectives do not conflict with those of the firm. In addition, its goals are reconcilable with those of the firm—the actions that improve its profitability are the same as those that improve the firm's profitability.

Good competitors have only moderate strategic stakes in the industry that do not require drastic improvement in competitive position and are interested in maximizing ROI rather than some other goal. Competing against state-owned industries whose objectives are foreign exchange and jobs instead of ROI has prematurely removed all profit from many industries. Good competitors are satisfied with current profitability and often interested in generating cash flow, both of which inhibit aggressive tendencies. Finally, the good competitor is risk averse and satisfied with its position relative to the risks of acting to improve it.

to its response. Some research has been undertaken which indicates that the problem can be solved mathematically and, in simple cases, empirically estimated.[18]

In more practical terms for the analyst, this means working two moves ahead—estimating whether the competitor would see its action choices as leading to more or less effective countermoves. Game theory, discussed in chapter 9, provides one framework for analyzing the situation. The main point, however, is to attempt to calculate the relative financial implications of the competitor's possible responses.

[17] The idea of the "good" competitor is Michael Porter's. See his *Competitive Advantage* (New York: Free Press, 1985), pp. 212–215.
[18] Amit, Domowitz, and Fershtman, "Thinking One Step Ahead: The Use of Conjectures in Competitor Analysis."

A second approach suggests that one analyze the past effectiveness of the competitor's marketing mix elements (e.g., price, advertising, product performance). As theory would suggest, a competitor's response to, say, the market entry of a new competitor will be to use the weapon that has shown the greatest response elasticity in the past. Recent empirical research has shown this to hold with the entry of two new brands into a four-brand over-the-counter gynecological product category and with the entrance of a new airline into a city previously served by three competitors.[19] Advances in knowledge about competitive response will grow in the future as researchers study the issue further.[20]

ASSESSING AND INTERPRETING COMPETITIVE SIGNALS AND MOVES

Analyzing competitors is more than a static activity. It involves more than the creation of a comprehensive report detailing the apparent strategies of the key industry competitors. It often means having only an hour or two to interpret the meaning of a competitor's 10% across-the-board price cut and to formulate a response. Exhibit 10-5 tells of one such incident in the beer industry. It often means being able to predict the reaction of competitors to your announcement of a major joint venture with the technology leader from an adjacent industry or to your preannouncement of a major new product.[21] It means being able to understand what the leading competitor's chief executive means when quoted as saying of his company, "We must absolutely be as competitive as we possibly can." Is the message intended to rally the troops or to warn competitors?

Interpreting Competitive Signals

Table 10-5 presents a more or less complete picture of the domain of competitive signaling. Interpreting a competitor's message requires that one simultaneously consider the form of the message, its probable function, the forum or medium in which it is communicated, and the probable veracity of the message.

Message Form. Prior announcements are perhaps the most often used form of competitive signaling because of their absolute versatility and ambiguity. One can announce with complete truthfulness the intention to expand capacity at some future point in time and change one's mind at some point thereafter. Prior announcements admit to the largest range of purposes and forums.

Announcements of accomplished fact or results, on the other hand, admit to

[19] Hubert Gatignon, Erin Anderson, and Kristiaan Helsen, "Competitive Reactions to Market Entry, Explaining Interfirm Differences," *Journal of Marketing Research*, XXVI (February 1989), 44–55.
[20] William T. Robinson, "Marketing Mix Reaction to Entry," *Marketing Science*, 7, no. 4 (fall 1988) 368–385.
[21] Jehoshua Eliasberg and Thomas S. Robertson, "New Product Preannouncing Behavior," *Journal of Marketing Research*, XXV (August 1988), 282–92.

EXHIBIT 10-5

A Warning Shot From the King of Beers

It looked like an all-out war. Breaking with its traditional reluctance to cut prices too much or too often, Anheuser-Busch Cos. said on Oct. 25 that it would start matching the steep discounts its competitors were offering in some markets. The nation's No. 1 brewer warned that its earnings growth was likely to slow as a result of the decision. . . . But instead of launching the Beer Wars that Wall Street feared, Anheuser may have been craftily setting the stage for a cease-fire. And if it was a gambit, it seems to be working. Sources close to the company say that Anheuser's announcement was meant as a warning to its rivals that they would pay dearly if they continued the price-slashing that sent prices down as much as 22% in some markets last summer. Now, although the industry is moving into a time of seasonal promotions, wholesalers and retailers say that prices have stabilized. . . . "This is the price war that hasn't happened," said one large retailer.

SOURCE: *Business Week,* "A Warning Shot from the King of Beers," December 18, 1989, p. 124.

TABLE 10-5 *The Domain of Competitive Signaling*

FORM	PURPOSE (UNDERLYING OSTENSIBLE)	VERACITY	FORUM OR MEDIUM	MESSAGE CONTENT
Prior announcement Announcement after the fact Public discussion of industry Discussion of own moves	• Preemption • Communicate strategic advantages • Threat of contingent action • Express pleasure or displeasure • Test of competitors' sentiments • Minimize provocative potential of own action • Avoid simultaneous actions • Inform financial community • Gain internal support	• True/untrue • Bluff • Misleading • Over/understated	• Broad, prestigious industry audience • Financial analysts meeting • Interview in major industry/business publication • Press release • Letter to customers or suppliers • Private communication with competitor	• Firm's goals • Internal situation of firm • Firm's intention • Expectations of competitor behavior • Rules of game/nature of dilemma

a smaller range of application perhaps, but gain in the willingness of the receiver to believe that what has been announced has actually happened. Of course, this belief does not necessarily extend to swallowing whole the exact numbers, market shares, etc. that are offered in the announcement.

Public discussions of the state of the industry or competition within it rival prior announcements in their frequency and breadth of purpose. Speeches made at industry conferences, especially those attended exclusively by the top brass, are carefully crafted to convey messages to participants and just as carefully dissected by rivals. Some, of course, need little interpretation. Note the following comments by Lee Iacocca in an interview reported in *U.S.A. Today*:

> Incentives are hurting carmakers' profits. . . . If [General Motors] had built fewer cars, we wouldn't be having this problem. It's that simple. [Car buyers] are like Pavlov's dogs, and we made 'em that way. . . . Now it's going to be very difficult to get away from incentives. . . . Incentives are scheduled to expire in October. Whether they return later is up to GM.[22]

Discussing one's own move in terms of its intent or rationale happens with less frequency than prior announcements but possibly with greater impact. The apparent openness with which a competitor discusses the rationale underlying a given strategic move adds the luster of truth to the message, especially if it is shared in whispered tones with key customers or suppliers over cocktails and dinner. Few public relations campaigns can spread news through an industry faster than sharing a strategy "in confidence, of course," with a customer whose greatest benefit is served by keeping competition for his or her business at a high pitch.

Message Function.   The range of functions served by signaling is wide, and any given message may fulfill several simultaneously. Attempts to preempt competitors are certainly a leading function. During periods of shortages, industry publications are full of competitors trying to preempt others from adding capacity by announcing their own capacity additions first. Announcing the future availability of major product developments to postpone customer purchase of competitors' products is another form of preemption. To the extent that it can be achieved, preemptive announcements are also used as the occasion to communicate strategic advantage to discourage less advantaged competitors from cluttering up the playing field.

Communicating threats or expressions of displeasure (or pleasure) are usually less direct. Exhibit 10-6 discusses several of these more subtle threats. Anheuser-Busch's announcement of its intent to match competitive price cuts certainly said no more than that. However, in interviews with business writers more of its intent was indicated:

> "So price as a tool for our competition is no longer there anymore," said Mr. Busch one day recently in his office here. "It is no longer effective." Anheuser is

---

[22] *U.S.A. Today,* September 10, 1986.

hoping competitors will recognize that price cutting is futile and relent. Mr. Busch said he has already spotted some higher pricing in several Texas markets. His expectation is that other markets will follow, until bargains begin to evaporate by the end of next summer.[23]

Some messages are intended to minimize competitive provocation by explaining the rationale behind projected actions which could otherwise be interpreted as aggressively competitive. A price cut taken to clear out bloated inventories, for example, might be announced as such with the intent of avoiding a permanent across-the-board price reduction in the industry (of course, this would not work if competitors thought that the announcement was simply a ploy to gain time before competitive retaliation).

Some external signals are given to gain internal support. Announcements in the public press by a company's president or chairman of its new drive to provide the highest level of quality are frequently more credible to employees than many internal communications programs. A variation is the external announcement that is made to cut off further internal discussion of a given strategy or specific action. Along the same line, some announcements are made primarily to communicate indirectly with the financial community. Signals such as these may indeed carry little of import for competitors.

Message Content.   The actual content type of the message is important. One researcher has studied the various messages allowed in experimental studies of negotiation, cooperation, and competition built around the various forms of the prisoner's dilemma and was able to discern five different types of content.[24] Communication about the firm's goals has the potential to remove the dilemma in a situation in which the motivations are not clear. For example, if both are cooperatively disposed and both are aware of that, the obvious choice is to cooperate. Signals which communicate information about the internal situation of the firm, its health, success, and feelings about its outcomes and situation give others that knowledge necessary to infer its payoff matrix.

Signals about a firm's intentions give competitors information about how best to plan their own actions; this is especially so if the statement reveals commitment as well. Such knowledge is clearly important if the goal is to chart nonintersecting strategies. Communications or signals which state expectations of the competitor's behavior may be helpful in situations in which competition or cooperation are the choices and it is not clear to others how they should act.

It has been said that discussing the rules of the game and nature of the dilemma is particularly relevant in competitive interfirm situations because this message content contains more information than any of the others do. Not only are statements about the nature of the game the most innocuous, but a coop-

---

[23] N. R. Kleinfield, "The King of Beers Raises the Ante," *The New York Times*, December 24, 1989, sec. 3, pp. 1 and 11.
[24] Marian Chapman Bourke, "Signalling and Screening: Tactics in Negotiations Across Organizations" in Blair Sheppard, Max Bazerman, and Roy Lewicki, eds., *Research on Negotiations in Organizations* (Greenwich, CT: JAI Press, 1988).

EXHIBIT 10-6

The Value of a Tough Reputation

When Procter & Gamble introduced Folger's coffee in the northeast it met ferocious competition from Maxwell House. . . . Though this strategy was more costly to Maxwell House than letting Folger's in, it presumably signalled to P&G the likely response if other regions were invaded. When Union Carbide test-marketed a disposable diaper in Bangor, Maine, P&G flooded the market with promotions and price discount coupons for its Pampers diapers. . . . [It is reported] how IBM "mistakenly" underpriced its 4300 mainframe computers by 5–7 percent. A year later the company "admitted" its mistake and raised prices. However, the true intentions of IBM were never made clear. . . .

It is difficult to know whether the firms in these examples are actually tough types or are weak types mimicking tough types. However, as long as there is a small probability that tough-type firms exist, reputation-building behavior by weak firms can be rewarding.

SOURCE: Keith Weigelt and Colin Camerer, "Reputation and Corporate Strategy: A Review of Recent Theory and Applications." Copyright © 1988 John Wiley & Sons Limited. Reproduced by permission of John Wiley & Sons Limited.

erative equilibrium typically requires that competitors share a common view of how the game is played. Ultimately, of course, all competitors must limit their competitive behavior, and public discussions about how the buyer is the only winner in price wars are one way of signaling the need to cool the competitive state.

Forum or Medium.   Where and how a message is delivered is of key importance in its interpretation. Messages delivered before prestigious industry audiences or to a formal meeting with financial analysts are taken to contain a higher truth content than those delivered in other forums. This is simply because both groups have good memories and require relationships based on personal trust.

Interviews in industry and business publications, on the other hand, are taken for what they are—the attempt by the competitor to deliver a carefully crafted message to a specific audience. The reality of the situation is that no executive has to consent to be interviewed and that consent is only given when there is some purpose to be served. Press releases are in a similar category. Letters to customers, on the other hand, carry a lot of weight. Private direct communication should always be taken with a grain of salt. There is no reason for it to be anything but self-serving.

Veracity.   Truth in strategic communication is indeed a relative concept. While a communication may indeed be just what it is and says, the analyst is better off asking how it would benefit the sender if it were to be accepted as true by the receiver.[25] Some signals are bluffs which will not be implemented if the bluff is successful in deterring competitive action but probably would not have been implemented anyway. Too many bluffs, however, and all parties suspend belief and the firm has lost a valuable tool through overuse.

More often, the content of communications contains some aspects that are misleading or simply over or understated.[26] These aspects require the analyst to cross-check all numbers and to analyze every statement for possible alternative interpretations. Sometimes ambiguity is intentional to allow one to read a possible worst-case scenario into an otherwise innocuous message. Some signals carry as much contradictory and hidden meaning as the gambits and contrivances one finds in the best of the Cold War spy novels.

COLLECTING COMPETITIVE INFORMATION

Once relevant competitors have been identified and information needs understood, the data collection process may begin.[27] There are innumerable sources and types of competitive information, but the most useful initial breakdown is into published (or secondary) and field (or primary) data.[28] The reader is cautioned, however, not to mistake information for intelligence. This distinction is explained in Exhibit 10-7.

Published sources are the first place to search for information. Major categories in which useful competitor information can be found include the following:

Industry studies exist in many forms. One common form is the multiclient study performed by industry-focused consulting and research businesses. These studies are typically done on some regular schedule and cover competitors, their economics and products, and industry forecasts. Often, scholarly studies of industries may have been performed and available as published books. One valuable source of industry studies are securities firms, whose researchers frequently assess industry profitability trends and the viability of the various competitors in an industry.

Trade publications are a second source of industry information. In some business areas these publications may produce their own industry studies (for distribution to their advertisers, who need to understand the publication's target market) or compilations of industry statistics. In addition to the hard data they

---

[25] There are times, however, when things are just what they seem. Remember, Freud once said that "sometimes a cigar is just a cigar."

[26] As one master of the art put it, "I never lie, but if someone chooses to misinterpret my carefully crafted words that's not my fault."

[27] Data collection should be just one aspect of a comprehensive, ongoing competitor intelligence effort. See, for example, Sumatra Ghoshal, and D. Eleanor Westney, "Organizing Competitor Analysis Systems," *Strategic Management Journal*, 12, no. 1 (January 1991), 17–31; and William L. Sammon, Mark A. Kurland, and Robert Spitalnic, eds., *Business Competitor Intelligence: Methods for Collecting, Organizing, and Using Information* (New York: Ronald Press, 1984).

[28] For a particularly good guide to competitive data sources, see Murray A. Young, "Sources of Competitive Data for the Management Strategist," *Strategic Management Journal*, 10, no. 3 (May-June 1989), 285–293.

EXHIBIT 10-7

Information and Intelligence

A basic but often misunderstood principle is that intelligence does not equal information. Information is the raw material of the intelligence process. It is unevaluated, unanalyzed data derived from every possible source of information—financial statements, trade show gossip, union newsletters, marketplace rumors, product brochures, executive speeches, and so on. The bits and pieces of competitor information that flow by in a constant stream may be true or false, relevant or irrelevant, confirmed or unconfirmed, positive or negative, deceptive or insightful. In its undigested state, this voluminous competitor information, 90 percent of which is publicly available, may be vaguely interesting and occasionally intriguing, but however glittering it is essentially an unusable and potentially dangerous resource.

Within this disorganized, confused stream of competitor information there is, however, a pattern of knowledge that if pieced together and analyzed can be very revealing and strategically significant. *Intelligence is the analytical process that transforms disaggregated competitor data into relevant, accurate, and usable strategic knowledge about competitors' position, performance, capabilities, and intentions.* With this intelligence—this knowledge about competitors' strategy—the uncertainty that confronts executives who make strategic decisions is reduced, and the probability of making the right decision is increased."

SOURCE: William L. Sammon, Mark A. Kurland, and Robert Spitalnic, *Business Competitor Intelligence: Methods for Collecting, Organizing and Using Information.* Copyright © 1984 John Wiley & Sons, Inc. Reprinted by permission of John Wiley & Sons, Inc.

---

contain about current events in the industry, these publications are especially useful in understanding the mind set and values of their readers.

Trade associations are a third major source of data. In many industries, they are the collectors and disseminators of industry statistics. Some operate industry libraries and information clearinghouses and, even if they do not, are typically aware of the major sources of available information on the industry.

Company documents, such as annual reports, 10Ks, prospectuses, and presentations before financial analysts, are valuable sources of information. Product brochures, literature, instruction and repair manuals, and advertising material all contain information of use in competitive analysis. The analysis of a firm's patent activity gives insight not only into its technical direction but into the organization and identity of key R&D personnel.[29]

---

[29] While patent applications (as opposed to granted patents) are secret in the U.S., patent applications are published in Europe, Japan, and a growing number of other countries. Competitive surveillance efforts, therefore, pay special attention to patent activity in those countries as a closer-to real-time indicator of a competitor's R&D direction.

Government sources can provide insights not obtainable otherwise. The Freedom of Information Act, for example, has opened up many sources of data. One firm monitors the actions of the pollution control boards of the states in which its competitors do business, and by analysis of the emissions data they must provide has received advance notice of expansions and insight into the processes involved. Census data are another source of useful insight. There are firms which specialize in advising on and locating pertinent data from government sources.

Field research is an important part of any competitive data-gathering endeavor. It is important not only because published data are limited and need to be augmented with live data but also because it is sometimes the only way of identifying the existence of published materials. Table 10-6 depicts the major external and internal sources of primary information about competitors.

Conducting field research is an art.[30] It involves in-person or telephone interviews with individuals among a competitor's customers and suppliers and others tangential to the industry who have insight into its workings. Given the expense of primary data gathering, it should not be undertaken without a clear understanding of the data sought. However, some advise that field interviews with key industry or competitor observers should be among the earliest activities undertaken because of their usefulness in framing the issues and questions to be addressed.

One point that few mention is that competitors can be approached directly for data in certain instances.[31] While there are competitors who discourage and refuse all contact with and assistance to competitors, the reality is that not all do. Further it is not illegal per se for competitors to talk or share information, as long as the nature of the discussion cannot be construed to be collusive.[32] Obviously, such a contact provides the competitor with knowledge that another firm is interested in it, as does the specific nature of the questions. Further, as with all field research, the competitor may choose to mislead or misdirect the investigator intentionally, but that is part of the game.

Using consultants or other intermediaries to perform the field work is a frequently chosen option. Few firms have the ability to staff a comprehensive competitive information group capable of doing all of its own data gathering. Use of a consultant further shields the exact identity of the firm seeking the information (although many respondents will typically require some vague information about the type of client before agreeing to cooperate). In some in-

---

[30] For a good introduction to field collection of data, see Connie Cox, "Planning in a Changing Environment: The Search for External Data," in William D. Guth, ed., *Handbook of Business Strategy* (Boston: Warren Gorham & Lamont, 1986), pp. 5–1 to 5–9. Porter also provides a useful introduction to field research in Appendix B ("How to Conduct an Industry Analysis") of his book *Competitive Strategy*.

[31] See, for example, Eric von Hippel, "Cooperation Between Rivals: Informal Know-How Trading," *Research Policy*, 16 (1987), 291–302.

[32] Sharing information about prices and customers, for example, is generally discouraged or prohibited by most companies' legal advisors because of its potential for such use.

TABLE 10–6 *Major External and Internal Sources of Primary Competitive Information*

SOURCE	EXAMPLES	COMMENT
Government	Freedom of Information Act	1974 amendments have led to accelerating use.
	Government Contract Administration	Examination of competitor's bids and documentation may reveal competitor's technology and indicate his costs and bidding philosophy.
	Patent filings	Belgium and Italy publish patent applications shortly after they are filed. Some companies (e.g., pharmaceutical) patent their mistakes in order to confuse their competitors.
Competitors	Annual reports and 10Ks	FTC and SEC line of business reporting requirements will render this source more useful in the future.
	Speeches and public announcements of competitor's officers	Reveal management philosophy, priorities, and self-evaluation systems.
	Products	Systematic analysis of a competitor's products via back engineering may reveal the competitor's technology and enable the company to monitor changes in the competitor's engineering and assembly operations. Forecasts of a competitor's sales may often be made from observing his serial numbers over time.
	Employment ads	May suggest the technical and marketing directions in which a competitor is headed.
	Consultants	For example, if a competitor has retained Boston Consulting, then portfolio management strategies become more likely.
Suppliers	Banks, advertising agencies, public relations firms, and direct mailers and catalogers, as well as hard goods suppliers	Have a tendency to be more talkative than competitors since the information transmitted may enhance supplier's business. Can be effective sources of information on such items as competitor's equipment installations and on what retail competitors are already carrying certain product lines. Suppliers biases can usually be recognized.
Customers	Purchasing Agents	Generally regarded as self serving. Low reliability as a source.
	Customer engineers and corporate officers	Valued sources of intelligence. One company taught its salespersons to perform elementary service for customers in order to get the salespersons past the purchasing agent and on to the more valued sources of intelligence.
Professional Associations and Meetings	Scientific and technical society meetings, management association meetings	Examine competitor's products, research and development, and management approach as revealed in displays, brochures, scientific papers, and speeches.
Company Personnel	Executives, sales force, engineers and scientists, purchasing agents	Sensitize them to the need for intelligence and train them to recognize and transmit to the proper organizational location relevant intelligence which comes to their attention.
Other Sources	Consultants, management service companies, and the media	Wide variety of special purpose and syndicated reports available

SOURCE: David B. Montgomery and Charles B. Weinberg, "Toward Strategic Intelligence Systems," *Journal of Marketing*, 43, no 3 (fall 1979), p. 46.

stances, well-connected and networked consultants can provide better data faster and less expensively than internal staffers.

The Need For a Strategic Intelligence System

The need for a strategic intelligence system is more than academic. The strategist and the strategies devised are both the result and the prisoner of the available intelligence. Incomplete, untimely, or incorrect data result in poor or incorrect decisions. As one operating manager put it, "When it comes to competitor information, it always seems that I never have the information I need and the information I do have is never what I need."

There is little consensus on the exact form that a strategic intelligence system should take in a company, but there is on the functions that such a system needs to perform. Figure 10-9 depicts the traditional intelligence cycle in terms that fit the business strategist's understanding.[33] Experienced practitioners note that the real issues with reference to strategic intelligence systems is not in the collection phase—obtaining data—but in identifying what to collect and in linking the system to the users and the purposes to which the data are intended. Top management and other key strategic decision makers are responsible for directing the efforts and, as chief users, cannot delegate that responsibility.

The Outputs of an Intelligence System

It is useful to think of competitive intelligence as consisting of four categories, as shown in Figure 10-10:[34]

1. *Strategic net estimates* are the end result of the gathering and analysis. They are the final summing up of a competitor's strategies and performance, capabilities and vulnerabilities, strategic goals, and probable future actions and reactions. Such a work product contains as much interpretation as it does information.
2. *Periodic intelligence,* the first aggregation and collation of competitor information into preliminary intelligence, is best thought of as a hybrid between an intelligence newsletter and a competitive activity scorecard. It focuses on the reporting of a small number of key indicators of comparative performance, activities, and trends.
3. *Base case intelligence* is the research core of the intelligence process that details the past, outlines the present, and suggests the future. It is the constantly updated aggregation of the essential information available about a given competitor,

---

[33] *Intelligence cycle* is a term developed in the military, where formal intelligence systems are of life or death importance. For a good overview, see Herbert E. Meyer, *Real World Intelligence* (New York: Weidenfeld & Nicholson, 1987), or Sammon, Kurland, and Spitalnic, eds., *Business Competitor Intelligence.* See also Montgomery and Weinberg, "Towards Strategic Intelligence Systems," *Journal of Marketing,* 43, no. 3 (Fall 1979), pp. 41–52.

[34] The following is based on Sammon, Kurland, and Spitalnic, *Business Competitor Intelligence.*

Figure 10-9   The intelligence system

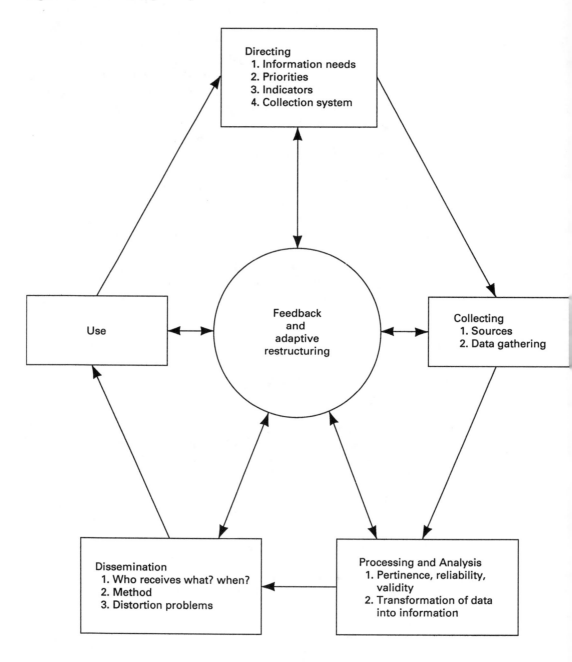

SOURCE: David B. Montgomery and Charles B. Weinberg, "Toward Strategic Intelligence Systems," *Journal of Marketing* 43, no. 3 (fall 1979), p. 44.

Figure 10-10 Four categories of competitive intelligence

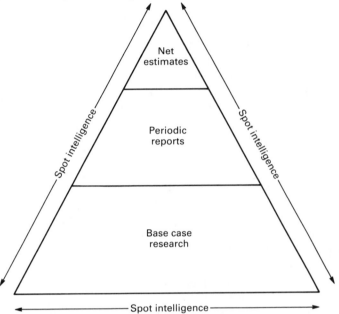

SOURCE: William L. Sammon, Mark A. Kurland, and Robert Spitalnic, *Business Competitor Intelligence: Methods for Collecting, Organizing and Using Information.* Copyright © 1984 John Wiley & Sons, Inc. Reprinted by permission of John Wiley & Sons, Inc.

covering all aspects of a competitor's business including its full range of capabilities, strengths, and weaknesses.

4. *Spot intelligence* cuts across the three aforementioned types to address specific "need it yesterday" or narrowly-focused project-based information needs.[35] Spot or project intelligence can focus on the gathering and interpretation of any information type or level, depending on the immediate needs of the decision makers requesting it.

SUMMARY

Competitive product strategy requires that the strategist position the firm's offerings such that they minimize direct competition either by choosing vulnerable competitors or by pitting strength against weakness. The goal of competitor analysis is to provide the strategist with the intelligence needed to achieve that result.

Competitor analysis begins by being able to identify relevant direct, indirect, and potential competitors. Direct competitors are those whose products and customers are identical with the firm's. Indirect competitors are those who serve

[35] See, for example, John E. Prescott and Daniel C. Smith, "A Project-Based Approach to Competitive Analysis," *Strategic Management Journal,* 8, no. 5 (1987), 411–423.

either related customer groups or functions with closely related but not identical products. More generally, the strategic group concept allows the strategist to identify competitors whose strategies conflict with those of the firm in spite of minor differences in tactical implementation.

If the goal of competitive analysis is to be able to predict the future actions of competitors, then one must be able to find out competitors' present capabilities—both their strengths and their weaknesses—their future goals, and the assumptions they hold. To do so requires a wide variety of information, from the firm's marketing capabilities to its financial structure and the backgrounds of its key decision makers.

But competitive analysis is more than collecting, sifting, analyzing, and communicating competitive assessments to decision makers. It is also the ability to interpret the real-time competitive signals that competitors send directly via their announcements and indirectly through their actions in the marketplace. Careful analysis of the medium, content type, message form, identity of the sender, probable function, and the result to the sending firm of acceptance of the message as true will allow the strategist to decipher its real meaning for strategic purposes.

If competitive information is such a key element in strategy formulation, then the strategist is the prisoner of the strategic intelligence system. If the information is not collected or transmitted to the decision maker in a timely fashion, then the decisions made are likely to be flawed. Successful strategy decisions demand effective intelligence systems as much as the information they produce.

11

DEVELOPING AND ANALYZING
STRATEGIC OPTIONS

The strategic problem is not an easy one—seldom does any firm have truly optimal choices. There is rarely one strategy that maximizes competitive advantage, volume growth, margins, market share, cash flow, and return on investment in both the short and long runs while simultaneously minimizing investments, risk, and competitive retaliation. This chapter provides a number of tools and techniques for developing and analyzing strategic options and choices in ways that enable the strategist to understand the broader implications of each strategy. The chapter begins with an analysis of such generic strategy options as invest, harvest, and grow. Following that discussion, the chapter presents a number of the key strategy analysis and evaluation methods, including both portfolio and matrix techniques.

GENERIC STRATEGY OPTIONS

When faced with a threatening situation, most life forms face a simple generic strategy option: fight or flight. Business organizations have an expanded but similar range of options. When faced with a new competitive situation, a business can decide to defend, to exit, or to counterattack. Since all strategies are implemented by the application of resources behind a given course of action, managers frequently use a shorthand way of speaking in which they characterize strategies in terms of their resource implications rather than the actions themselves. For example, one hears of such generic strategies as *invest to grow* or *milk for cash*.

Whether these are indeed strategies is an interesting question. Competitive advantage is the result of superior skills and superior resources, as discussed earlier (Figure A in Exhibit 2-1, reproduced here as Figure 11-1). Superior resources are as critical as superior skills, and both reinforce each other through their combined ability to create superior profit performance which, in turn, further increases the resources available to invest in improved skills and performance, and so on. This is why leading businesses are so difficult to dislodge.

Figure 11-1   Competitive advantage is the result of skills and superior resources

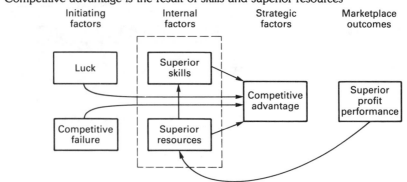

Their superior profitability allows them to do more R&D, create more and better products, and improve and expand productive capacity, which allows them to increase further their lead over competitors. Since one definition of strategy is the planning of the conquest of enemies through the deployment of resources, one can indeed make the argument that *invest to grow* is a strategy.

Some, however, feel that an investment strategy is a separate issue, that a business's strategic thrust has two components: the specification of the source of competitive advantage and the investment strategy, as shown in Figure 11-2. In this view, the strategic thrust specifies how the business intends to compete. The investment strategy then specifies the funding required to implement the chosen strategic thrust and the financial results that are expected.[1] Some term this aspect of strategy its *financial mission,* while others use the terminology *strategic role.*[2]

It is not easy or necessary to choose between the two views. The issue has been raised, however, because strategies ultimately consume and generate funds, because there are generic aspects of strategies which exist somewhat independently of the specific competitive advantage being sought, and because it is easy to confuse an investment strategy with a strategy for gaining competitive advantage (this chapter contains many of the generic, investment-type strategy prescriptions). The strategist needs to be clear about those instances in which the application of resources is an integral part of the strategy and be able to recognize when such terminology obscures the underlying strategic concept.

Table 11-1 compares the two generic resource strategy prescriptions. The *investment strategy* approach is commonly used. The prescriptions for action it contains are seen often through this chapter. The *strategic roles* approach is somewhat less commonly seen but still representative of the generic thought patterns that managers use in characterizing their resource options. The prove viability role, for example, is often seen in practice when managers are given an opportunity (and sometimes even a modest infusion of funds) to turn a business

[1] George S. Day, *Strategic Market Planning* (St. Paul, MN: West Publishing Company, 1984), p. 34.
[2] See, for example, Ian C. MacMillan, "Seizing Competitive Initiative," *The Journal of Business Strategy,* 2, no. 4 (spring 1982), 43–57.

Figure 11-2 Strategy includes both competitive advantage and resource components

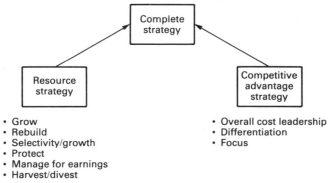

- Grow
- Rebuild
- Selectivity/growth
- Protect
- Manage for earnings
- Harvest/divest

- Overall cost leadership
- Differentiation
- Focus

around. While somewhat lacking in substantive strategic content, it has no less substantive content than does a build or a harvest strategy. Finally, these generic moves represent more than just armchair strategizing. Empirical evidence suggests that these approaches capture well the thrust of different strategic directions.[3]

PORTFOLIO TECHNIQUES FOR STRATEGY GENERATION, ANALYSIS, AND EVALUATION

For many, the concept of strategy revolves around the use of various strategy analysis techniques. Most common among these are portfolio techniques. They are termed portfolio techniques because they allow managers to evaluate their portfolio of products and markets on a common basis, much like an investment manager evaluates an investment portfolio. The logic underlying these approaches is that not all products or businesses are in equally strong strategic positions, and managers need a logical approach to identifying the differences that separate them. This discussion begins with the Boston Consulting Group (BCG) product portfolio, then presents the business screen matrices, and finishes with a description of the PIMS program's approach to strategy analysis.

The BCG Product Portfolio[4]

The Boston Consulting Group's product portfolio is perhaps the most well-known strategy planning model. Its ability to illuminate the strategic issues in

[3] Craig Goldbraith and Dan Schendel, "An Empirical Analysis of Strategy Types," *Strategic Management Journal*, 4, no. 2 (April-June 1983), 153–173.

[4] Core material for this discussion is found in Bruce D. Henderson, "The Experience Curve—Reviewed. IV. The Growth-Share Matrix of the Product Portfolio," *Perspectives*, no. 135 (Boston: The Boston Consulting Group, 1973); extended discussions may be found in George S. Day, "Diagnosing the Product Portfolio," *Journal of Marketing*, 41, no. 2 (April 1977), 29–38; George S. Day, *Analysis for Strategic Market Decisions* (St. Paul, MN: West Publishing Co., 1986), chapter 6; and Derek F. Abell and John S. Hammond, *Strategic Market Planning* (Englewood Cliffs, NJ: Prentice-Hall, 1979), chapter 4.

TABLE 11-1A   *Investment Strategy Categories*

- *Invest to enter.* Here, resources are allocated to entry into a business or business segment that is new to the company. This might entail a separate unit or may be undertaken within the structure of an existing unit. When a new market is being created, the investment requirements and corresponding risks are especially large.

- *Invest to build aggressively or gradually.* A business or segment in this category uses resources both to grow the market and to enhance or gain a leadership position. The rate and breadth of building may be aggressive with a view to preempting competition, or may be more gradual to moderate the risk exposure.

- *Invest to rebuild aggressively or gradually.* This investment strategy is indicated when the goal is to reestablish a leadership position that has been allowed to erode. These catch-up efforts are often costly, especially if results are expected quickly.

- *Build selectively.* In this category, the goal is still overall growth, but the investment will be highly focused in selected areas in which differential gains can most readily be obtained. The business may be expected to fund the necessary investments from current earnings.

- *Protect current position.* This thrust implies taking aggressive steps to maintain a strong position but not to grow any faster than the market. Depending on the competitive and technological turbulence and rate of growth of the market, the investment demands may be substantial.

- *Selectively manage for earnings.* Here, the business will limit and focus investment deployments on a few specific segments, with the priority given to maintaining and improving current earnings.

- *Harvest.* Investments in these businesses will be limited, with emphasis on generating maximum short-term cash flows. Modest harvesting is typical of leaders in maturing and declining industries in which competitive pressures have abated or stabilized. Harvesting can be rewarding because it contributes cash and profits that can be used elsewhere. Too often, it is falsely equated with surrender, through permitting market position to erode rapidly. This does not have to be a consequence unless a conscious decision has been made to exit the industry because intense competitive pressure has eroded the competitive position.

- *Exit/divest.* Here, management concludes that the long-run problems overwhelm any promise of profits and wishes to channel its efforts and resources elsewhere. This is normally a zero investment option, although selective investments may enhance the selling price.

SOURCE: Reprinted by permission from p. 26 of *Strategic Analysis: The Pursuit of Competitive Advantage* by George S. Day. Copyright © 1984 by West Publishing Co. All rights reserved.

TABLE 11-1B *Strategic Role Categories*

- *Build aggressively.* The business is in a strong position in a highly attractive, fast-growing industry, and management wants to build share as rapidly as possible. This role is usually assigned to an SBU early in the life cycle, especially where there is little risk that this rapid growth will be sustained.
- *Build gradually.* The business is in a strong position in a very attractive, moderate-growth industry, and management wants to build share, or there is rapid growth but some doubt as to whether this rapid growth will be sustained.
- *Build selectively.* The business has some good positions in a highly attractive industry and wants to build share where it feels it has strength, or can develop strength, to do so.
- *Maintain aggressively.* The business is in a strong position in a currently attractive industry, and management is determined to maintain that position aggressively.
- *Maintain selectively.* Either the business is in a strong position in an industry that is getting less attractive, or the business is in a moderated position in a highly attractive industry. Management wishes to exploit the situation by maximizing the profitability benefits of selectively serving where it best can do so, but with the minimum additional resource deployments.
- *Prove viability.* The business is in a less than satisfactory position in a less attractive industry. If the business can provide resources for use elsewhere, management may decide to retain it, but without additional resource support. The onus is on the business to justify retention.
- *Divest/liquidate.* Neither the business nor the industry has any redeeming features. Barring major exit barriers, the business should be divested.
- *Competitive harasser.* This is a business with a poor position in either an attractive or highly attractive industry and where competitors with a good position in the industry also compete with the company in other industries. The role of competitive harasser is to sporadically or continuously attack the competitor's position, not necessarily with the intention of long-run success. The object is to distract the competition from other areas, deny them revenue from other businesses, or use the business to cross-parry when the competition attacks an important sister business of the strategic aggressor. Such competitive harassers are popular in the chemical industry.

SOURCE: Reprinted from *Journal of Business Strategy* (New York: Warren, Gorham & Lamont), Copyright © 1982 Warren, Gorham & Lamont Inc. Used with permission.

complex, multiproduct (or multibusiness) situations gave it a great deal of popularity, as did the apparent face validity of the prescriptions for action it offered. Like all such simplifications of reality, however, the product portfolio's prescriptions were more severely limited than was first recognized, and the assumptions on which it rested more sensitive than many managers realized. The importance it accorded market share, for example, was interpreted by many to mean simply "more is better" when, in reality, the how and why one obtained that large market share was the more important issue. This issue is examined closely in

Exhibit 11-3, presented on pp. 390–91. Properly understood, however, the product portfolio remains a useful conceptual approach.

The question of how to think of the portfolio concept is important. At the broadest conceptual level, the product portfolio helps one to think about strategic issues in a new way that both suggests alternate strategies and objectives for products and business units. But the portfolio is also useful as a **diagnostic aid.** The positioning of a product in the matrix helps managers to diagnose the factors that contribute to its present position. Finally, the portfolio can be used to generate **normative prescriptions** for action. If all of the assumptions inherent in the model are met, then the portfolio is capable of identifying actions that should be taken.

The Growth-Share Matrix: An Overview.   At the heart of the concept is the growth-share matrix on which each product in the firm's portfolio is positioned, as shown in Figure 11-3. For each product, the display shows

- The sales of the product in dollar terms (represented by the area of the circle);
- The market share the product holds relative to that of the largest competitor in the market (as shown by its position horizontally);
- The growth rate of the market in which each product competes (indicated by the location of the product vertically).

The manager thus has a depiction of each product in the firm's portfolio together with some measure of each's future potential as well as its current competitive position. There are three concepts inherent in the model, around which the following discussion is structured: (1) the inherent attractiveness of different markets for investment, (2) the relative competitive strength of products or businesses, and (3) the contribution that a given product (or business) makes to the larger business (or corporation).

Market Attractiveness.   The product portfolio was created to help managers allocate resources among a portfolio of products. As such, some measure of market attractiveness was required. The market growth dimension provides that perspective. Shown as the vertical dimension, market growth rate provides a measure of the inherent attractiveness of the opportunity for investment. Overall, growth markets are posited to be more attractive for a number of reasons

1. A market's growth rate is a good measure of where it is in its growth and evolutionary cycle;
2. If one assumes that, once gained, a share point can be held, then an investment to gain a share point in a growing market will be worth more in the long run than making the same investment to gain a share point in a nongrowth market,
3. Since demand frequently exceeds supply in rapidly growing markets, competition among the entrants is assumed to be less vigorous, and prices and profits consequently are more attractive;
4. The entrance and presence of a firm with a competitive advantage in a growth

Figure 11-3 A growth-share matrix for General Food Corporation, 1980–1982

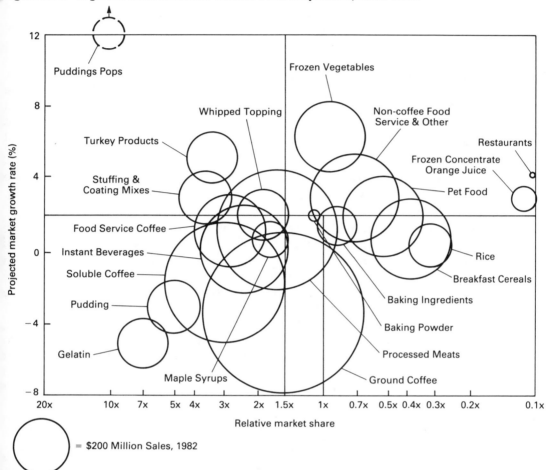

SOURCE: Marcus C. Bogue III and Elwood S. Buffa, *Corporate Strategic Analysis* (New York: Free Press, 1986), p. 15.

market is itself a strategic act that discourages further entrance by additional competitors;

5. Early entrants into growth markets have a head start down the experience curve at a time when cost differences among competitors are highest;
6. Conventional wisdom is that it is easier to attract new, first-time customers who have no prior purchase experience than it is to switch customers who already have a relationship with a supplier—this is one of the reasons that many believe it is easier to gain share in a growing market than in a stagnant market.

Two things must be noted about the vertical dimension. First, it measures the attractiveness of the opportunity—the growth rate for the product market itself, not the growth rate of the specific product entrant. The growth rate of the product may be higher or lower than the growth rate of the market. While this generally makes sense, it does cause problems when there is but one entrant in the product market. In this instance, there is no independent growth rate for the product to participate in—growth does not exist independently of what the firm does.

The second issue concerns what constitutes high growth versus low growth. When the scale is shown in nominal terms (current dollars not corrected for inflation), then the cutoff point is generally thought of as 10%. This works out to GNP growth (e.g. 2% to 4%) plus inflation (e.g. 3% to 6%) plus real incremental growth roughly equal in magnitude to GNP growth (e.g. 2% to 4%). In simple terms, rapid growth is defined to be about twice the growth of the economy after correction for inflation.

Relative Competitive Strength.   The growth-share matrix equates competitive advantage with market-share dominance. The horizontal dimension visualizes relative competitive strength as a function of the share of the firm's product relative to the share of the largest competitor.[5] In a two-firm market, then, where one firm holds a 66% share and the other 33%, the leader would be said to have a $2\times$ relative share (66%/33% = 2); the other firm's relative share would be $0.5\times$ (33%/66% = 0.5). The vertical center line in the matrix is typically set at 1.0—the point at which the two leading competitors would have equal market shares, neither being dominant.[6]

The choice of relative market share expressed in multiples is directly tied to the experience curve, in which costs are postulated to decrease as a function of the doubling of cumulative experience. In the preceding example, if there were an 80% cost curve for the industry, then the leading firm with its 66% market share would have twice the experience of the smaller share firm, and its relative costs would be 20% lower. Since the larger market-share firm accumulates experience at a faster rate over time, it has the best opportunity to exploit that cost advantage. Beyond the experience curve, the largest-share firm in a product market typically has other advantages such as lowered marketing costs per unit because of scale economies and a more favorable brand reputation.

The equating of market-share dominance with competitive advantage through the mechanism of the experience curve is the most critical assumption in the classic product portfolio. As one BCG executive put it, "The largest competitor in a particular business area should have the potential for the lowest unit costs and hence greatest profits."[7] It may sound trite, but if there is no competitive cost advantage to be gained through market-share dominance, then the portfolio is of far less usefulness than usually assumed.

---

[5] The largest competitor's relative share is its share relative to the next largest competitor's share.
[6] Mathematically, only one firm in any business can be located to the left of that vertical center line. Additionally, growth-share matrices are often divided by a vertical line at the $1.5\times$ relative market-share point to reflect the belief that true competitive dominance is not established unless the business is at least 50% larger than its closest competitor.
[7] Barry Hedley, "A Fundamental Approach to Strategy Development," *Long Range Planning*, 9, no. 6 (December 1976), 2–11, at p. 11.

The Product's Contribution to the Business.   The growth-share matrix shows the product's dollar-volume contribution to the larger business directly (through the relative size of the circles). The manager-strategist can see the firm's entire portfolio of products and their relative contributions to total sales. The most important implications of the matrix, however, are not shown directly—those are the implications it has for cash flow from each product and for the portfolio as a whole.[8] To understand those implications, several observations need to be made:

- *Products with dominant market shares have higher contribution margins than those with lesser shares in the same market.* If one assumes that the dominant product can command the going market price and that it has lower costs as a result of the experience curve effects, this must be the case.[9]
- *Products in fast-growing markets require cash to finance additional production capacity and working capital.* Cash needs vary directly with the growth rate. Products in rapidly growing markets need more cash than those in slower-growth markets.
- *Products which are gaining share also use cash.* They need cash to finance their share-gaining tactics (increased advertising, sales force expenditures, improved product quality, lowered prices) as well as to expand the production capacity and working capital needed to support the higher sales level.
- *Products which are gaining share in fast-growth markets require the most cash.* This follows from the prior two points. The reverse is also true—products which are giving up share or are in negative-growth markets (or both) are assumed to throw off the most cash.

CONTRIBUTIONS OF EACH QUADRANT TO THE BUSINESS.   The most popular aspect of the growth-share matrix is the analysis of the products in each of the four quadrants in terms of their cash-flow characteristics (shown in Figure 11-4).

Cash cows have dominant shares in low-growth markets. Their dominant shares give them higher gross margins than others in their market and, because market growth is slowing or low, their needs for additional investment should be small.[10]

Stars have dominant shares in high-growth markets. While a star's dominant market position provides it with large margins, its growth rate requires cash to support that growth. Netted out, the star should be cash neutral but may require additional cash depending on the product's exact capital intensity.

Question marks (or problem children or wildcats) are low-share products in fast-growth markets. As such, their margins are not as large as the star's in their market, while their capital needs on a per-unit basis are identical. This means that question marks are cash users. This tendency to use cash is magnified if the

---

[8] The product portfolio/growth-share matrix analysis says nothing directly about profitability per se. It treats only volumes, growth rates, and relative market shares.

[9] In fact, in many markets the dominant brand can frequently command a higher price in the marketplace than lesser brands, thereby accentuating the increased margin it earns by virtue of its lower costs.

[10] In some businesses, the cash-generating ability of cows may be magnified by the existence of depreciation charges which are in excess of capital spending and thereby shield income from taxes.

Figure 11-4   Cash-flow characteristics of the quadrants of the growth-share matrix

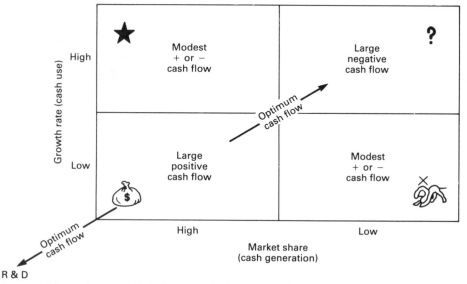

SOURCE: Adapted from Derek F. Abell and John S. Hammond. © The Boston Consulting Group, Inc., 1970.

question mark tries to gain share to better its position in the market.[11] If the question mark cannot attain a dominant position before the market growth slows, it becomes a dog.

Dogs are low-share products in slow-growing markets. They have low shares and therefore low gross margins, but since they are in low-growth markets they do not require large amounts to invest in additional capacity. Depending on the exact cost penalty incurred as a result of its low share, the dog may or may not produce free cash flow. Those which do not are called cash traps because, while they may be technically profitable, they are unlikely ever to be a significant source of free cash flow.

Exhibit 11-1 discusses less derogatory terms for these characteristics.

Empirical Evidence of the Growth-Share Matrix.   Two studies using the PIMS database explored the validity of the cash-flow implications of the growth-share matrix. The first, mentioned in chapter 7, essentially reproduced the growth-share matrix as shown in Figure 11-5.[12] The figure shows the average cash-flow-rate contour lines (expressed as a percent of investment) across the growth-share matrix. On the average, cash cows in the PIMS database generate an average positive cash flow (as a percent of investment) of 9%, while dogs generate a negative 3%. The authors note, however, that market growth rate and relative share together account for only about one tenth of the variation in

---

[11] Recall that the absolute dollar value of the experience curve effect is greatest at the early stages of a market's development, magnifying the cash-flow difference between a star and a question mark.
[12] Bradley T. Gale and Ben Branch, "Cash Flow Analysis: More Important Than Ever," *Harvard Business Review* (July-August 1981), 131–136.

EXHIBIT 11-1

A Rose by Any Other Name

Managers and others have made fun of the labels coined by BCG for cells of the product portfolio. The terms *cash cow* and *dog* are considered to be derogatory by some. In response to this criticism, the Mead Corporation is reported to have renamed the cells, using titles which more accurately suggest the financial missions they fulfill. The following are their terms for the four quadrants (with the BCG labels in parentheses) and the characteristics of each business type:

Savings account (star)
- Growing businesses
- Self-financing
- Medium risk
- High profit
- Should maintain cost-effectiveness

Bond (cash cow)
- Mature business
- Net cash generator
- Low risk
- High profit
- Cost-effective

Sweepstake (question marks)
- Developing businesses
- Net cash user
- Extremely high risk
- Low profit
- Not cost-effective

Mortgages (dogs)
- Mature business
- Should be net cash generator
- Medium risk
- Low profit
- Probably not cost-effective

SOURCE: Francis J. Aguilar, *The Mead Corporation: Strategic Planning.* Boston: Harvard Business School Case 379070111. Copyright © 1978 by the President and Fellows of Harvard College; all rights reserved.

Figure 11-5   Cash-flow-rate contour lines for the growth-share matrix

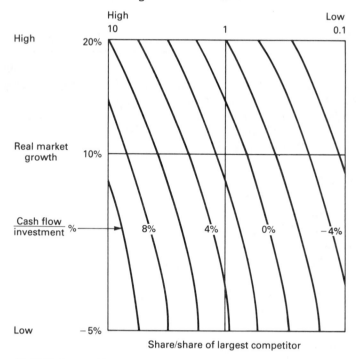

cash-flow rates that is actually observed. As shown in Figure 7-10, cash-flow is a result of a number of additional factors.

The second study also used the PIMS database and found similar results, except for the dog category.[13] Table 11-2 shows the average return on investment, cash flow, and a measure of return per risk for the four cells of the matrix. The study, which used four-year average values for all measures to smooth out year-to-year variability, found that the four types each have significantly different tendencies to consume or generate cash. Cash flow, expressed as a percent of investment, varies from just over 10% for cows to −2.67% for question marks. Stars are closest of the four to breaking even on cash flow, equal to 0.74% of investment.

The dog category in this study differs from the BCG analysis and the first study just mentioned. In this study, dogs had an average net positive cash flow on investment of 3.4%, even while holding share. The authors note that this cash flow should be enough to meet the cash needs of the average question mark

[13] Donald C. Hambrick, Ian C. MacMillan, and Diana Day, "Strategic Attributes and Performance in the BCG Matrix—A PIMS-Based Analysis of Industrial Product Businesses," *Academy of Management Journal,* 25, no. 3 (September 1982), 510–531.

TABLE 11-2 *Performance Levels of Businesses in the Four Cells of the BCG Matrix[a]*

PERFORMANCE MEASURE	QUESTION MARKS (N = 181)	STARS (N = 114)	CASH COWS (N = 315)	DOGS (N = 418)
Return on investment	20.55	29.58	30.00	18.48
	(24.53)	(22.59)	(22.67)	(21.68)
Cash flow on investment	−2.67	.74	10.01	3.41
	(18.79)	(18.26)	(17.03)	(16.17)
ROI/ROI variability	2.37	3.96	4.57	2.80
(return per risk)	(3.53)	(5.20)	(4.15)	(4.68)

[a] Means are reported with standard deviations in parentheses.
SOURCE: Adapted from Donald C. Hambrick, Ian C. Macmillan, and Diana L. Day, "Strategic Attributes and Performance in the BCG Matrix—A PIMS-based Analysis of Industrial Product Businesses," in *Academy of Management Journal*, 25, no. 3 (September 1982), p. 518.

in the study (−2.67%).[14] They also note that, with a standard deviation on that average of 16%, some dogs produced quite high cash flows (while some, of course, produced significantly negative cash flows).[15]

As predicted, market dominance pays. Return on investment (ROI) for cows (30.0%) and stars (29.58%) exceeded that of dogs (18.48%) and question marks (20.55%). The authors also attempted to measure the risk inherent in each business by an index which they called "return per risk." The index took each firm's own four-year average ROI and from this calculated the difference between that average ROI and each year's observed ROI. It then summed the four differences and computed the index by dividing the average ROI by that sum of the differences to obtain the "average ROI for each point of variability in year-to-year ROI." A small number means that there is a larger variability in ROI relative to the average ROI, whereas a larger number shows that variability is small relative to the average ROI. Dominance helps on this measure, too. Cows and stars have the lowest variability, followed by dogs and question marks.

Implications for Managing the Portfolio

Recall that the purpose of the growth-share matrix is to help the manager-strategist analyze the product portfolio to be able to maximize its value. Exhibit 11-2 lists the six typical steps such an analysis takes. By the analysis, however, it becomes apparent that there are only two things that the manager can manipulate in the context of the model: market share and the uses to which the cash generated are devoted). The market growth rate is assumed to be exogenous.

The key point of the model is to achieve synergy in the portfolio by the appropriate managing of the cash-flow characteristics of the individual products. This means to create a balanced portfolio in which there are products

[14] If one assumes that fledgling question marks are one half the size of a dog business, then a dog could support two question marks.
[15] Technically, assuming the data are normally distributed, one would expect to find two thirds of the sample averages to fall between one standard deviation above and one standard deviation below the sample average or 3.41 − 16.17 = (12.76), 3.41 + 16.17 = 19.58.

EXHIBIT 11-2

Six Steps in Analyzing a Product Portfolio

1. *Check for internal balance.* The largest-selling products should be cash cows or stars; there should be few question marks because of their funding needs and risk. Dogs should be reasonable in number and contributing cash. Overall, the cash balance should be appropriate. This analysis should generate ideas for improving the portfolio.

2. *Look for trends.* Compare the growth-share matrix of five years prior with the current and projected matrix for the next five years based on current managerial philosophies for the products. Has the portfolio improved? Are trends favorable?

3. *Evaluate competition.* Analyze competitors' portfolios by creating growth-share and growth-gain matrices for significant competitors. What is their apparent cash-flow position? Is it possible to infer their strategies from the analysis? Which of our products are close to dominance and positioned against competitors' weaknesses? Which of their products are cash cows that are likely to be vigorously defended? Are there competitive products that are losing share and possibly being underfunded?

4. *Consider additional strategic factors.* Not all relevant strategic factors can be captured in the matrices, and the analyst should recognize those that change the apparent position of products in the matrices or add insight. A dog product, for example, may have an extremely low-cost source of raw materials that makes it profitable in spite of its apparent dog position. The existence of entry or exit barriers is an example of the other factors which would add depth to an analysis.

5. *Develop possible target portfolios.* At this point, the analyst is ready to create several alternative portfolio configurations and to identify the generic strategies needed to achieve them. Care must be taken with this step so such generic actions as "invest to gain share" and the like are not confused with the actual strategic moves that would be taken to implement such an objective. The question in evaluating such alternative portfolios is the existence of strategies which allow for the implementation of the generic prescriptions. This step requires rigorous creativity on the part of the analyst—the matrices cannot prescribe action.

6. *Check financial balance.* As a final step, the strategy choices are evaluated and revised based on cash-flow projections. Care must be taken to ensure that products receive objectives and actions which coincide with their strategic positions. Second, a portfolio which is cash balanced may be desirable but may also be too conservative, especially if competitive analysis shows competition to be using more financial leverage to support products positioned against the firm's. Third, at this point the issue of focus becomes critical. Can the firm be even more successful if it reduces the number of entrants it fields to increase the cash support available to the critical few winners and potential winners?

SOURCE: Derek F. Abell and John S. Hammond, *Strategic Market Planning: Problems and Analytical Approaches*, © 1979, pp. 186–190. Adapted by permission of Prentice Hall, Englewood Cliffs, NJ 07632.

which generate cash and those which use cash to support long-run growth in the value of the portfolio. Figure 11-4 portrays the idea. Cash, primarily coming from cash cows, is used to fund the growth rate of problem children toward stardom and to fund R&D to create new stars.

This idea is demonstrated in Figure 11-6, which shows two disaster sequences and one success sequence. In the latter case, a question mark receives sufficient funding to push it to stardom, which it holds until the market matures and it becomes a cash cow. In the disaster sequences, the products are mismanaged and thereby lose the source of their competitive advantage. In one instance, a star product loses its initially dominant position to become a question mark, which at maturity becomes a dog. In the other instance, a cash cow loses its dominant position to become a dog. These disaster sequences would be avoided if management followed some simple rules:

- *Focus resources appropriately.* Strategy is implemented through the application of resources to specific products and businesses, and firms which win do so by allocating more resources to supporting a product than their competitors. It is better to have a smaller number of well-supported entrants than a larger number of cash-starved products.
- *Maintain market-share dominance.* Cash cows and stars achieve their competitive advantage by virtue of their market-share dominance. Loss of that position means the loss of the advantage. Cows should not be milked of cash to the detriment of their dominant position; stars should receive the funding needed to maintain position and growth.
- *Invest cash wisely.* Cows should not receive any more cash than that necessary to maintain dominance. Question marks should either receive enough funding to achieve star status or should be divested. Dogs should receive only that funding necessary to maximize long-run cash flow.
- *Create a balanced portfolio.* Too many cash cows can be just as bad as a portfolio with all stars. In the former case, the firm has no long-term future; in the latter it is likely that each product will receive less support than is needed to maintain the leading position required to hold that position into maturity.
- *Manage strategically.* Use the four major strategic moves at the portfolio level: (1) Increase market share, (2) hold market share, (3) harvest, (4) withdraw or divest. Bold actions are needed to achieve strategic results; timidity and subtlety is not rewarded. Figure 11-7 shows the ideal positioning of a firm's product portfolio on a growth-gain matrix.[16]

Critical Issues in Portfolio Analysis

There are two critical issues in the use of portfolio analysis of which the user must be aware. The first of these is the question of how to define the relevant market on which to base the relative market-share comparison. The second

---

[16] The growth-gain matrix positions a product on the basis of its growth rate relative to the growth of the category in which it participates. A product which holds its share grows just as fast as the market and is positioned on the 45-degree line. A product which is losing share will be positioned above the 45-degree line; one gaining share will be positioned below the line.

Figure 11-6   Product dynamics in the portfolio chart

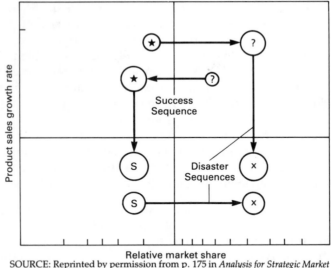

Relative market share

question concerns the validity of the cash and profit projections that the method generates.

Defining the Relevant Market.   Key to the insights of the portfolio approach is that market-share dominance confers strategic advantage through the experience curve effect. High-share firms have low costs relative to their lower-share competitors and therefore enjoy higher gross margins and cash flow. The goal of

Figure 11-7   Product growth rate: ideal portfolio distribution

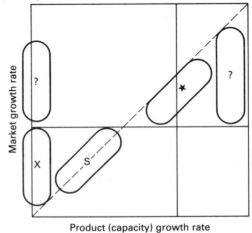

Product (capacity) growth rate

market definition for the purposes of portfolio analysis is to correctly define the market—the competitive arena—such that these cost differences are accurately captured.

Market share is the elusive concept.[17] One can obtain a very low share of market if one defines the market in the broadest terms possible; a very high share if the market is defined narrowly. Häagen Dazs' share of market increases as the market in which it participates is narrowed from dairy products to frozen desserts to premium ice creams. While it is likely that dairy products is too broad a definition, without additional specific information it is not clear whether frozen desserts or premium ice creams is the better definition. The test of the definition is whether it captures the sources of competitive advantage that come from market share. Abell and Hammond suggest that typically the answer lies in the broader market definition. However, to the extent that by focusing on a more finely defined segment the firm is able to gain real cost and performance advantages versus the more broadly defined competitors, a narrow definition may be the correct one.[18]

Validity of the Cash Projections.   Everything that the product portfolio says about cash and cash flow comes from two key assumptions: (1) Dominant share products will be able to generate stronger cash flows; and (2) rapidly growing markets require more cash than slow-growth markets. There are instances in which these assumptions do not hold.

The relationship between share dominance and cash flow may be weak because (1) a small-share competitor may have access to low-cost raw materials or labor that offset its share deficit; (2) smaller competitor(s) may be using superior operations technology or a higher proportion of their productive capacity than the dominant firms; or (4) the leader's product quality may be such that it sells at a discount to followers' products, thereby giving away the value of its cost advantage. These exceptions are frequent enough that care should be taken to make sure that the dominant share/lowest cost assumption is justified.

The relationship between market growth rate and cash flow may be weak because (1) the business is of low capital intensity and capacity expansion is therefore easy financially; (2) the product creates high value and competition is not intense such that the product earns the very high gross margins that enable it to self-fund its own growth and still generate free cash flow; and (3) price competition or rapid inflation of major raw materials prices in maturity reduces profits and cuts into the cash flow normally expected from a cash cow. The cash-flow assumption is not as critical as the market dominance assumption yet should always be tested.

---

[17] For a particularly good review of the issues involved in measuring market share, see Yoram Wind and Vijay Mahajan, "Market Share: Concepts, Findings, and Directions for Further Research," in Ben M. Enis and Kenneth J. Roering, eds., *Review of Marketing, 1981* (Chicago: American Marketing Association, 1981), pp. 31–42.
[18] Derek F. Abell and John S. Hammond, *Strategic Market Planning*, p. 186.

EXHIBIT 11-3

The Controversy over Market Share

In the mid-1970s, a number of articles were published based on either the PIMS database or the experience of the Boston Consulting Group which demonstrated, seeming convincingly, the direct contribution of market share in determining profitability. The *Harvard Business Review* in 1975 carried an article titled "Market Share—a Key to Profitability" in which the authors reported that a 10% difference in market share is accompanied by a 5% difference in ROI.[19] In 1976, an employee of the Boston Consulting Group published a widely cited article that stated, "the largest competitor in a particular business area should have the potential for the lowest unit costs and hence greatest profits."[20] The chairman of the Boston Consulting Group, Bruce Henderson, made the following unequivocal statement:

> Market share is very valuable. In a competitive business it determines relative profitability. If it does not seem to do so, it is nearly always because the relevant product market sector is misdefined or the leader is mismanaged.[21]

A 1981 article in the *Harvard Business Review* opened on an equally positive note:

> Past data analyses have consistently demonstrated that most high-share businesses enjoy above-average profit margins and rates of return on investment, while most small-share businesses have below-average margins and ROI.[22]

In the same time frame, other articles and publications based on the PIMS database were published supporting the same relationship, that a 1% increase in market share leads to a 0.5% or 0.6% increase in ROI.[23]

Jacobson and Aaker were the first to challenge what, by this time, had almost become accepted wisdom. In a 1985 article, they argued that the association could be spurious:[24]

---

[19] Robert D. Buzzell, Bradley T. Gale, and Ralph G. M. Sultan, "Market Share—a Key to Profitability," *Harvard Business Review*, 53 (January-February 1975), 97–106.

[20] Barry Hedley, "A Fundamental Approach to Strategy Development," *Long Range Planning*, 9, no. 6 (December 1976), 2–11, at p. 11.

[21] Bruce D. Henderson, *Henderson on Corporate Strategy* (Cambridge, MA: Abt Books, 1979), p. 94.

[22] Robert D. Buzzell and Frederik D. Wiersema, "Successful Share-Building Strategies," *Harvard Business Review* (January-February 1981), p. 135.

[23] Bradley T. Gale, Donald T. Heany, and Donald S. Swire, "The Par ROI Report: Explanation and Commentary on Report" (Cambridge, MA: Strategic Planning Institute, 1977); Ben Branch, "The Laws of the Marketplace and ROI Dynamics," *Financial Management*, 9 (summer 1980), 58–65; and Bradley T. Gale and Ben S. Branch, "Concentration versus Market Share: Which Determines Performance and Why Does It Matter?," *The Antitrust Bulletin*, 27 (spring 1982), 83–103.

[24] Robert Jacobson and David A. Aaker, "Is Market Share All That It's Cracked Up To Be?," *Journal of Marketing*, 49, no. 4 (fall 1985), 11–22.

EXHIBIT 11-3 (cont.)

1. The classic argument is that market share improves ROI through its effect on experience, scale, or market power.
2. However, what if both market share *and* ROI were both being jointly influenced by some third factor(s)?
3. One such factor could be management quality, which first produced an attractive product line and effectively marketed it, thereby gaining share, and second, was also able to control costs and thereby achieve a high ROI.
4. Another factor of equal importance could be chance, which enables a business to stumble onto one or more products or strategies that prove to be successful.

To test their hypotheses, Jacobson and Aaker used the same PIMS database, replicated the earlier positive findings with respect to the positive effect of market share, and then introduced another factor into the equation to serve as a proxy for luck and skill. The result was to lower the estimate of market-share effect on ROI from 0.5% ROI for every 1% in market share to 0.1% for every 1% in market share.

In subsequent research, Jacobsen further refined his mathematical techniques and was able to address specifically the two competing theories:

> Is the association due to large market share creating advantages (e.g., lower costs resulting from economies of scale) that enable the firm to be more profitable or is it the result of firms with advantages (e.g., better management) growing larger and being profitable? . . . Distinguishing among the competing theories is essential because of their drastically different strategic implications.[25]

The analysis in this case showed any market-share effect to be indistinguishable from zero. Jacobson found, moreover, that the findings are consistent with a model in which ROI is influenced by unmeasured firm-specific factors and by strategic factors. Where does this leave us? Is market share itself the cause of profitability? The answer seems to be no—market share is more likely the result of a good strategy (or luck).

Interestingly enough, even if market share were a direct cause of profitability, it probably would not be a useful strategic insight anyway. This is because the strategy's simplicity would lead all businesses to try to maximize share, and the resulting intense competition would lower the profits of all. As Jacobson puts it, any "well-understood, unsuccessful strategy will be imitated until its return premium is exhausted."[26]

Summary of the Product Portfolio

At the time of its creation, the product portfolio/growth-share matrix was considered to be a major advance in the process of thinking about strategy and

[25] Robert Jacobson, "Distinguishing Among Competing Theories of the Market Share Effect," *Journal of Marketing*, 52, no. 4 (October 1988), p. 69.
[26] Jacobson, "Distinguishing Among Competing Theories," p. 78.

the resource allocation decisions it requires. Today, its specific usefulness has been recognized to apply mostly to large, capital-investment-intensive businesses in which there is a strong experience curve effect. Nonetheless, it remains a major conceptual contribution. Its usefulness remains in terms of thinking about a firm's products in portfolio terms, in advancing the understanding of financial synergy, in analyzing strategy at a level that focuses attention on strategic factors, and in providing a tool for analyzing competitors' goals and strategies.

Industry Attractiveness/Business Position Matrices

The underlying assumptions of the growth-share matrix are that a market's growth rate is a good proxy for the idea of market attractiveness and that relative market share is a good proxy measure of **a business's competitive position.** The following discussion describes a class of portfolio models that are based on the direct assessment of market attractiveness and the relative competitive position a business holds. Three such models have been described in the literature: the GE/McKinsey Business Screen, the Directional Policy Matrix advanced by Shell Chemical, and the A. D. Little Industry Maturity/Competitive Position Matrix.[27] This discussion first presents a generic matrix which incorporates features of the first two approaches, and then describes the A. D. Little approach.

Overview of the Market Attractiveness/Competitive Position Matrix

The strategic concepts underlying the matrix are straightforward: first, that investments should be made in accordance with the long-run profit potential inherent in an opportunity; second, that firm-level profitability is a function of its relative competitive position. These two ideas are combined into a matrix depicted in Figure 11-8, in which business position is crossed with industry attractiveness, not unlike the growth-share matrix. These matrices are typically 3×3 matrices in which each dimension is rated high-medium-low.

Obtaining the ratings for products requires that management identify the factors that determine the attractiveness of the market and those that measure the company's relative competitive position. Once the products have been classified, the generic strategies are applied. The key to the process is identifying the factors that make a market attractive and that measure a firm's relative competitive position.

[27] See William E. Rothschild, *Putting It All Together* (New York: AMACOM, 1976), chapter 8; S. J. Q. Robinson, R. E. Hitchens, and P. E. Wade, "The Directional Policy Matrix—A Tool for Strategic Planning," *Long-Range Planning*, 11, no. 3 (June 1978), 8–15; and Peter Patel and Michael Younger, "A Frame of Reference for Strategy Development," *Long-Range Planning*, 11, no. 2 (April 1978), 6–12. An extended discussion of the A. D. Little matrix can be found in Arnoldo C. Hax and Nicolas S. Majluf, *Strategic Management* (Englewood Cliffs, NJ: Prentice-Hall, 1984), chapter 9.

Figure 11-8   The directional policy matrix

Prospects for Market-Sector Profitability

	Unattractive	Average	Attractive
Weak	Disinvest	Phased Withdrawal	Double or Quit
		Proceed with Care	
Average	Phased Withdrawal	Proceed with Care	Try Harder
Strong	Cash Generator	Growth	Leader
		Leader	

Company's Competitive Position

SOURCE: Reprinted with permission from *Long-Range Planning*, II, no. 4, August 1978, p. 3, by D. E. Hussey, "Portfolio Analysis: Practical Experience with the Directional Policy Matrix." Copyright © 1978, Pergamon Press plc.

Applying the Market Attractiveness/Business Position Technique[28]

Figure 11-9 shows the six steps required to use the matrix technique. As shown, the process has two phases: situation assessment and strategy development.

In the strategy assessment phase, establishing the unit of analysis is the first step. The analysis can be performed at the SBU level, major units within an SBU, or at the product-line level. Two points need to be noted about this choice. First, there is much to be gained by performing the analysis at several different levels of the business or across different geographical subsets. Second, regardless of the level, the unit analyzed should be one for which relatively independent decisions and resource allocations can be made.

The second step is the critical one: identifying the relevant factors that make markets attractive and that measure a business or product's competitive position. This requires management to develop a valid theory which explains why some markets are more attractive than others and how the firm becomes competitively advantaged. It is important to recognize that there is no magic formula for identifying those factors as there is in the growth-share matrix, where one factor on each dimension is all that is required.

Table 11-3 contains a listing of some of the factors which could be considered. In some product markets, the exact identity of the factors that drive prof-

---

[28] This discussion is based on George S. Day, *Analysis for Strategic Market Decisions* (St. Paul, MN: West Publishing Company, 1986), chapter 7.

Figure 11-9   Six steps in using the market attractiveness/business position matrix technique

Situation assessment	Step 1: Establish the level and units of analysis (business units, segments, or product markets).
	Step 2: Identify the factors underlying the market attractiveness and competitive position dimensions.
	Step 3: Assign weights to factors to reflect their relative importance.
	Step 4: Assess the *current* position of each business or product on each factor, and aggregate the factor judgments into an overall score reflecting the position on the two classification dimensions.
Strategy development	Step 5: Project the future position of each unit, based on forecasts of environmental trends and a continuation of the present strategy.
	Step 6: Explore possible changes in the position of each of the units, and the implications of these changes for strategies and resource requirements.

SOURCE: Reprinted by permission from p. 195 of *Analysis for Strategic Market Decisions* by George S. Day. Copyright © 1986 b West Publishing Co. All rights reserved.

itability are well known; in others they may have been the subject of continuing intense management debate; while in other instances the question may have never been asked. One technique that has been suggested is to contrast product or businesses about which there is general agreement about their attractiveness or unattractiveness. What factors distinguish one from the other? Practice has shown that obtaining management's buy-in (acceptance) of the factors identified is crucial. For this reason, this aspect of the process may and should take some time.

The final step in this situation assessment phase is to assign weights to the identified factors based on their relative importance. Seldom are all of the factor identified of equal import in determining attractiveness or competitive position Even if not explicitly reduced to a numerical rating of the factor, managers are always unconsciously applying qualitative weights to the factors. The extent to which this step is performed through to the assignment of explicit weights is a factor of the managerial environment. However, as an exercise which makes explicit different managers' implicit weightings, it is invaluable. Forcing man agers to try to assign weights and then defend those assignments reveals the hidden assumptions different managers are using and aids the process of reaching consensus.

Assessing the current position of each unit on the matrix is the fourth and final step in the situation assessment phase. If weights have been assigned and scores calculated, then the product can be positioned in exact locations. Quali tative assessments, on the other hand, would probably result in more broad brush assessments, with products simply being assigned to one of the nine boxe shown in Figure 11-8. It is possible to use circles with areas equal to the size of th business (similar to those used in the growth-share matrix) to achieve an idea c the relative impact of each product. One method then shades a pie wedge in eac circle proportional to the product's market share and uses an arrow to indicate th product's trend. In this way, three additional pieces of data (size, share, trend regarding the product can be communicated on the one matrix.

There are two steps in the strategy development phase. The first of these i

TABLE 11-3 *Factors Contributing To Market Attractiveness and Business Position*

ATTRACTIVENESS OF YOUR MARKET	STATUS/POSITION OF YOUR BUSINESS
Market factors	
Size (dollars, units, or both)	Your share (in equivalent terms)
Size of key segments	Your share of key segments
Growth rate per year:	Your annual growth rate:
Total	Total
Segments	Segments
Diversity of market	Diversity of your participation
Sensitivity to price, service features, and external factors	Your influence on the market
Cyclicality	Lags or leads in your sales
Seasonality	
Bargaining power of upstream suppliers	Bargaining power of your suppliers
Bargaining power of downstream suppliers	Bargaining power of your customers
Competition	
Types of competitors	Where you fit, how you compare in terms of
Degree of concentration	products, marketing capability, service, produc-
Changes in type and mix	tion strength, financial strength, management
Entries and exits	Segments you have entered or left
Changes in share	Your relative share change
Substitution by new technology	Your vulnerability to new technology
Degrees and types of integration	Your own level of integration
Financial and Economic Factors	
Contribution margins	Your margins
Leveraging factors, such as economies of scale and experience	Your scale and experience
Barriers to entry or exit (both financial and nonfinancial)	Barriers to your entry or exit (both financial and nonfinancial)
Capacity utilization	Your capacity utilization
Technological factors	
Maturity and volatility	Your ability to cope with change
Complexity	Depths of your skills
Differentiation	Types of your technological skills
Patents and copyrights	Your patent protection
Manufacturing process technology required	Your manufacturing technology
Socio-political factors in your environment	
Social attitudes and trends	Your company's responsiveness and flexibility
Laws and government agency regulations	Your company's ability to cope
Influence with pressure groups and government representatives	Your company's aggressiveness
Human factors, such as unionization and community acceptance	Your company's relationships

SOURCE: Derek F. Abell and John S. Hammond, *Strategic Market Planning: Problems and Analytical Approaches,* © 1979, p. 214. Adapted by permission of Prentice Hall, Englewood Cliffs, NJ 07632.

simply to project out the future based on a continuation of current strategy and environmental trends. This projection is typically for three to five years but may be longer or shorter depending on the rate at which the industry changes. This is not an easy task. It requires managers to spell out their assumptions about the future and to accept the implications about the future of the business were there to be no change in strategy. At this point, the reality of the strategic positions is first truly felt and the strategic issues surface. Like the immediately preceding step (strategy assessment), this is not a technical task that can be done off line. It requires the full participation of the managers involved.

In the final step, different changes in strategy are evaluated. From a technical viewpoint, the task is clear: Trace through the changes each strategy requires in resources and test them for feasibility and reasonableness. The tough task is to get to the strategies. Each position in the matrix implies one or more generic strategies, which need to be interpreted into actual strategies for the specific product or business. Table 11-4 gives definitions for the eight generic strategies in the Shell version of the matrix. Figure 11-10 presents another set suggested by Kenichi Ohmae. Using these generic strategies can be of help in clarifying and coalescing managerial opinions about the general direction that strategy should take but does little to identify exactly what actions need to be taken. This is why operating managers need to do strategy. Only they are capable of creating true strategies to support the generic investment strategies that the matrix contributes.

The Life-Cycle Portfolio Matrix

The life-cycle portfolio matrix was created by the consulting firm A. D. Little as one part of its multistep strategic planning methodology.[29] Like the growth-share matrix and the market attractiveness/business position matrix, the life-cycle portfolio matrix positions the products or businesses of the firm on a two-dimensional matrix. One of the dimensions measures competitive position similar to the other portfolio techniques; the other dimension measures the state of the market or industry on the basis of life-cycle descriptors. This latter dimension differs from the other portfolio techniques, which instead use industry attractiveness.

The Industry Evolution Dimension.   The life-cycle portfolio matrix is shown in Figure 11-11. It uses a four-stage life-cycle model to capture industry evolution. The stages are determined by an evaluation of eight descriptors: (1) growth rate, (2) market growth potential, (3) breadth of product lines, (4) number of competitors, (5) the distribution of market share among competitors, (6) customer loyalty, (7) entry barriers, and (8) technology. An embryonic industry, for example, is typically characterized by rapid change. In addition to its rapid growth, there are frequent changes in technology, the market shares among the competitors, and the size and composition of the customer base. A growth industry

[29] A complete description of the methodology can be found in Arnoldo C. Hax and Nicholas S. Majluf, *Strategic Management* (Englewood Cliffs, NJ: Prentice-Hall, 1984), chapter 9. This discussion is based on that description.

TABLE 11-4 *Generic Strategies Recommended by the Shell Directional Policy Matrix*

- *Disinvestment.* Products falling in this area will probably be losing money—not necessarily every year, but losses in bad years will outweigh the gains in good years. It is unlikely that any activity will surprise management by falling in this area since its poor performance should already be known.
- *Phased withdrawal.* A product with an average to weak position with low unattractive market prospects, or a weak position with average market prospects, is unlikely to be earning any significant amount of cash. The indicated strategy is to realize the value of the assets on a controlled basis to make the resources available for redeployment elsewhere.
- *Cash generator.* A typical situation in this matrix area is when the company has a product which is moving toward the end of its life cycle and is being replaced in the market by other products. No finance should be allowed for expansion, and the business, so long as it is profitable, should be used as a source of cash for other areas. Every effort should be made to maximize profits since this type of activity has no long-term future.
- *Proceed with care.* In this position, some investment may be justified but major investments should be made with extreme caution.
- *Growth.* Investments should be made to allow the product to grow with the market. Generally, the product will generate sufficient cash to be self-financing and should not be making demands on other corporate cash resources.
- *Double or quit.* Tomorrow's breadwinners among today's R&D projects may come from this area. Putting the strategy simply, those with the best prospects should be selected for full backing and development. The rest should be abandoned.
- *Try harder.* The implication is that the product can be moved toward leadership by judicious application of resources. In these circumstances, the company may wish to make available resources in excess of what the product can generate for itself.
- *Leader.* The strategy should be to maintain this position. At certain stages, this may imply a need for resources to expand capacity. A leader may need cash exceeding that which the product itself generates, although reported earnings should be above average.

SOURCE: Reprinted with permission from *Long-Range Planning*, II, no. 4, August 1978, p. 3, by D. E. Hussey, "Portfolio Analysis: Practical Experience with the Directional Policy Matrix." Copyright © 1978, Pergamon Press plc.

on the other hand, may still be fast growing, but technology, market shares, and customers are tending toward more stability. Entry barriers are stronger as a result.

The Competitive Position Dimension. The methodology also provides criteria for the evaluation of the firm's competitive position. It defines the criteria as follows:[30]

---

[30] Hax and Majluf, *Strategic Management*, p. 192.

Figure 11-10   The strategic implications of each position of the attractiveness/strength matrix

	Low	Medium	High
High	**Serious entry into the market** Opportunistic position to test growth prospects; withdraw if indications of sustainable growth are lacking.	**Selective growth** Select areas where strength can be maintained, and concentrate investment in those areas.	**All-out struggle** Concentrate entire effort on maintaining strength; if necessary, maintain profit structure by investment.
Medium	**Limited expansion or withdrawal** Look for ways of achieving expansion without high risk; if unsuccessful, withdraw before involved too deeply.	**Selective expansion** Concentrate investment, and expand only in segments where profitability is good and risk is relatively low.	**Maintenance of superiority** Build up ability to counter competition, avoiding large-scale investment; emphasize profitability by raising productivity.
Low	**Loss-minimizing** Prevent losses before they occur by avoiding investment and by lowering fixed costs; when loss is unavoidable, withdraw.	**Overall harvesting** Promote switch from fixed to variable costs; emphasize profitability through value analysis and value engineering of variable costs.	**Limited harvesting** Reduce degree of risk to a minimum in several segments; emphasize profit by protecting profitability even if loss of market position is involved.

Market attractiveness

Corporate strengths

SOURCE: From Kenichi Ohmae, *The Mind of the Strategist: Business Planning for Competitive Advantage.* Copyright © 1978 by McGraw-Hill Inc. Reprinted with permission of McGraw-Hill, Inc.

- *Dominant:* Dominant competitors are rare. Dominance often results from a quasi-monopoly or from a strongly protected technological leadership.

- *Strong:* Not all industries have dominant or strong competitors. Strong competitors can usually follow strategies of their choice, irrespective of their competitors' moves.

- *Favorable:* When industries are fragmented, with no competitor clearly standing

- *Tenable:* A tenable position's profits can usually be maintained through specialization in a narrow or a protected market niche. This can be a geographic specialization or a product specialization.

- *Weak:* Weak competitors can be intrinsically too small to survive independently and profitably in the long term, given the competitive economics of their industry; or they can be larger and potentially stronger competitors, but suffering from costly past mistakes or from a critical weakness.

Figure 11-11   The life-cycle portfolio matrix

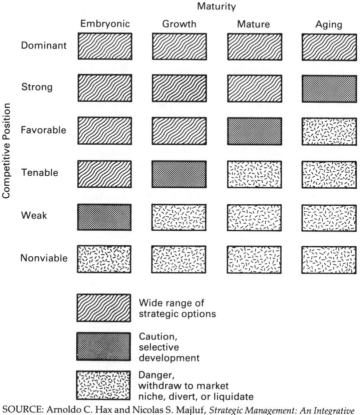

SOURCE: Arnoldo C. Hax and Nicolas S. Majluf, *Strategic Management: An Integrative Perspective*, © 1984, p. 145. Adapted by permission of Prentice Hall, Englewood Cliffs, NJ 07632.

These descriptions deserve some additional comment. A dominant position, for example, can be held by only one firm. Dominant competitors are often cited for their ability to set the technological and business standards by which the market or industry competes. Firms such as Kodak, IBM, and Boeing typify dominant competitors. According to these criteria, a **strong** competitor would have a relative market share exceeding 1.5× and be described as having a definite advantage over competitors. Favorable competitors often have a distinctive competence in one area that allows them to excel in that domain. Tenable businesses are those which, although they may exhibit some weaknesses, are worthy of management's full attention and are capable of improvement.

Strategic Directions Provided by the Life-Cycle Portfolio Matrix

The methodology provides several levels of strategic direction based on the product or business's position in the matrix. The first, broad level is shown in

Figure 11-11. Given the unit's position, a specific thrust is then chosen from among those contained in Table 11-5. In the favorable range, for example, these thrusts can be summarized as follows:

- *Start-up* is applied in the embryonic stage when a business in a strong competitive position can quickly gain a position of strength.
- *Growth with the industry* is a strategy to be used when the firm has little to be gained from changing its position and holding share is called for. Dominant or strong firms in the later stages of the life cycle, for example, might choose this strategy.
- *Gain position gradually* would be applicable for a business in a favorable position which could be aided by an increase in market share to solidify its position.
- *Gain position aggressively* is a strategy called for by tenable or weak units beginning to be squeezed out of an attractive industry which is starting to mature.
- *Defend position* applies when a firm in a dominant or strong position is being attacked in the early stages of maturity.
- *Harvest* is a strategy to be used in the aging stage.

Summary of the Life-Cycle Portfolio Matrix

As a methodology, the technique is a well-thought-out and integrated strategy planning system. On a conceptual level, it makes a contribution through its explicit consideration of the process of market and industry evolution. In this respect, it matches the growth-share matrix (in which the market's growth rate reflects market and industry evolution). On the other hand, by not explicitly providing a methodology by which to identify favorable and less favorable markets at any given stage of evolution, it may lead some not to consider that question.

The PIMS Program's Approach to Strategy Analysis[31]

Both the growth-share matrix and the market attractiveness/business position matrix use assessments of competitive advantage and the attractiveness of markets to make theory-based recommendations for investment and competitive strategy. In contrast, the PIMS program uses empirical measures of management's strategy in addition to those of its competitive position and the structure of the market to estimate financial performance, as depicted in Figure 11-12. The core of the PIMS program is a mathematical model which uses quantitative measures of the experiences of several thousand businesses on each of 100 variables to estimate the likely outcomes of strategic moves. It compensates for its lack of a display matrix with sophistication and the flexibility to perform a wide variety of what-if analyses. This discussion first gives

---

[31] This discussion is based primarily on Robert D. Buzzell and Bradley T. Gale, *The PIMS Principles* (New York: Free Press, 1987).

TABLE 11-5   *Strategic Positioning in Terms of Both Market Share and Investment Strategies Suggested by the Life-Cycle Portfolio Matrix*

	SHARE AND POSITION STRATEGIES			
	EMBRYONIC	GROWTH	MATURE	AGING
Dominant	All Out Push For Share Hold Position	Hold Position Hold Share	Hold Position Grow With Industry	Hold Position
Strong	Attempt to Improve Position All Out Push For Share	Attempt to Improve Position Push For Share	Hold Position Grow With Industry	Hold Position or Harvest
Favorable	Selective or All Out Push for Share Selectively Attempt to Improve Position	Attempt to Improve Position Selective Push For Share	Custodial or Maintenance Find Niche and Attempt to Protect	Harvest or Phased Withdrawal
Tenable	Selectively Push For Position	Find Niche and Protect it	Find Niche and Hang on or Phased Withdrawal	Phased Withdrawal or Abandon
Weak	Up or Out	Turnaround or Abandon	Turnaround or Phased Withdrawal	Abandon
	INVESTMENT STRATEGIES*			
	EMBRYONIC	GROWTH	MATURE	AGING
Dominant	Invest Slightly Faster Than Market Dictates	Invest to Sustain Growth Rate (and Preempt New Competitors)	Reinvest as Necessary	Reinvest as Necessary
Strong	Invest as Fast as Market Dictates	Invest to Increase Growth Rate (and Improve Position)	Reinvest as Necessary	Minimum Reinvestment or Maintenance
Favorable	Invest Selectively	Selective Investment to Improve Position	Minimum and/or Selective Reinvestment	Minimum Maintenance Investment or Disinvest
Tenable	Invest (Very) Selectively	Selective Investment	Minimum Reinvestment or Disinvest	Disinvest or Divest
Weak	Invest or Divest	Invest or Divest	Invest Selectively or Disinvest	Divest

* The terms invest and divest are used in the broadest sense and are not restricted to property, plant & equipment

SOURCE: Arnoldo C. Hax and Nicolas S. Majluf, *Strategic Management: An Integrative Perspective,* © 1984, p. 186. Adapted by permission of Prentice Hall, Englewood Cliffs, NJ 07632.

Figure 11-12   The conceptual organization of the PIMS data base

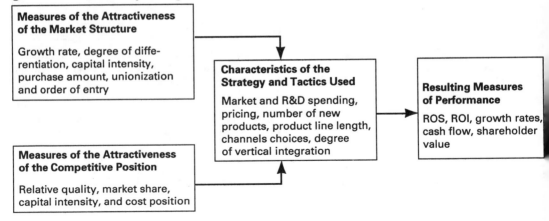

an overview of the PIMS program and then reviews its methodology for analyzing strategic moves.

Overview of the PIMS Program

The PIMS (Profit Impact of Market Strategy) program was started in 1972 as an outgrowth of work begun in the 1960s by General Electric. The program is housed at the Strategic Planning Institute (SPI), a nonprofit organization owned by its member companies. Since its beginning, over 450 companies have contributed information on more than 2,600 strategic business units for periods that range from two to twelve years.[32]

The PIMS program works to identify strategy principles based on documenting the experiences of a wide variety of different businesses across an equally wide assortment of market and competitive settings. It collects three kinds of data:

1. A description of the market conditions in which the business operates. Such data include the number and size of customers, market growth rate, distribution channels, and the like. Table 11-6 lists the measures used.
2. The business unit's competitive position in the marketplace. These measures include market share, relative product quality, costs, prices, and the degree of vertical integration, as listed in Table 11-7.
3. Measures of the unit's financial and operating performance on an annual basis.

These data are organized conceptually, as shown in Figure 11-13. Market attractiveness is measured by the relative profitability of the given market as compared to the other markets in the PIMS database. The pluses and minuses listed next to each variable show the variable's influence on profitability. A

[32] A complete description of the PIMS program can be found in chapter 3 of Buzzell and Gale, *The PIMS Principles.*

TABLE 11-6   *PIMS Measures of Major Market and Industry Influences on Business Performance*

MARKET AND INDUSTRY FACTORS	MEASURES
Market growth	• Average rate of change in real market volume
Stage of market evolution	• Age of product or service category
	• Life-cycle stage
Inflation	• Average rate of change in selling prices
Unionization	• Percent of employees unionized
Import competition	• Imports and exports, percent of industry sales
Suppliers	• Percent of purchases from largest suppliers
Product/service standardization	• Standardization vs. customization of products and services
Importance of products to customers	• Typical transaction size
	• Purchases of product class, percent of customer's total purchases

SOURCE: Robert D. Buzzell and Bradley T. Gale, *The PIMS Principles: Linking Strategy to Performance*, p. 44.

rapidly growing market, for example, positively affects profitability (the measure of market attractiveness), whereas it is less attractive if it requires capital intensity.

Competitive position determines the profitability of the firm relative to the others in the market. This is measured by such variables as relative product quality, prices, and market share. Production structure variables straddle both

TABLE 11-7   *PIMS Measures of Major Competitive Position and Strategy Dimensions[a]*

ELEMENTS OF POSITION	POSITION MEASURES	CHANGE MEASURES
Competitive standing	• SBU market share (MS)	• Change in MS
	• SBU market share rank	• Change in MS ranking
Product and service policies	• Index of quality, relative to leading competitors	• Change in quality index
	• New products and services as a percent of sales, and relative to competitors	• Change in new product or service (%)
Pricing	• Index of SBU relative prices (average of competitors = 100)	• Change in relative price index
Marketing programs	• Marketing expense, % of sales	• Change in marketing or sales
Investment strategy	• Value of plant and equipment relative to (1) sales, (2) value added, (3) employment	• Change in fixed asset ratios
	• Newness of plant and equipment (net book value, % of gross book value)	• Change in newness
	• Labor productivity (Valued added per employee)	• Change in productivity
	• Inventory, % of sales	• Change in inventory or sales
Vertical integration	• Value added, % of sales (adjusted)	• Change in value added or sales
	• Vertical integration relative to competitors (more/less/same)	• Change in relative vertical integration
Research and development	• R&D expense, % of sales	• Change in R&D or sales

[a] Adjusted to remove above-average or compensate for below-average net profits.

SOURCE: Robert D. Buzzell and Bradley T. Gale, *The PIMS Principles: Linking Strategy to Performance*, p. 41.

Figure 11-13 Determinants of profitability

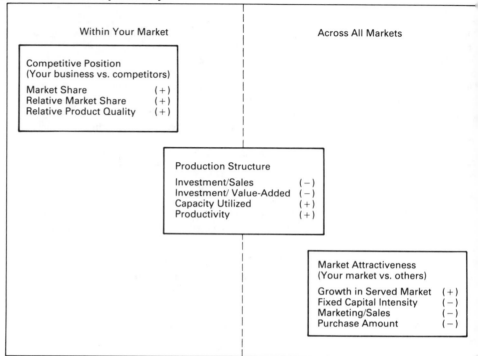

ideas in that they measure the relative efficiency with which the firm runs the business within the economic and technical framework required to serve the type of market in which it competes. A business which runs at over 90% of its capacity will earn more than one using only 70%; a business that uses $1 of investment to yield $1 in sales will earn a lower ROI than one that requires only $0.30 (all other things being equal).

These variables are contained in a multiple regression equation and linked to each other, as shown in Figure 11-14.[33] Since one can obtain any given ROI by either a high turnover together with a low margin or a low turnover and a high margin, it can be seen that the model could be termed *compensatory*—there is not just one way to achieve success. A low price, for example, could be offset by an even lower relative cost to achieve the same margin. This is how it is in real life—competitive advantage can come from any source in the business.

Participants in the PIMS program use the database to compare the ROI potential of existing or potential businesses by inputting their data to the program. The program then calculates what the ROI of a business with that profile

---

[33] Figures 11-12 and 11-13 are simplified and note only a few key illustrative variables. The database on each business contains approximately 100 such variables.

Figure 11-14 Business strength: what variables account for relative profitability?

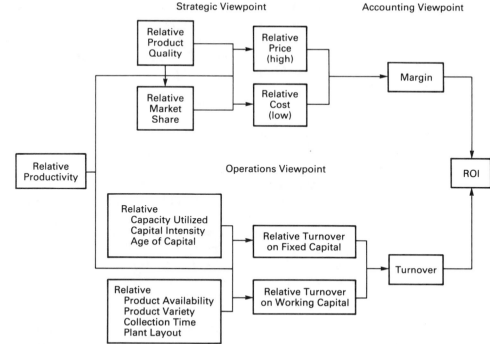

SOURCE: Reprinted by permission from p. 120 of *Analysis for Strategic Market Decisions* by George S. Day. Copyright © 1986 by West Publishing Co. All rights reserved.

should be if it performs like the businesses in the database. The output identifies the variables that contributed to higher or lower ROI performance than expected. The strategist can see what happens if the strategy is changed—if, for example, product quality is improved, market share is increased, or any other similar alteration in the strategy or operations.

How Managers Use the PIMS Program to Develop Strategy

Manager-strategists use two kinds of PIMS-based input: (1) the generic principles which have emerged from analysis of the PIMS database; and (2) a set of services that the PIMS program provides its members.

PIMS principles have emerged from scholarly analysis of the PIMS database. From the beginning, the program has sought to uncover basic strategy principles in addition to the custom strategy evaluation services provided to members. Over 100 reports and articles using the database have been published by affiliated and independent researchers.[34] The most accessible compilation of these findings is in *The PIMS Principles*, by Robert Buzzell (a Harvard Business School professor who has actively researched the database) and Bradley Gale (formerly

[34] See the "Select Bibliography" in Buzzell and Gale, *The PIMS Principles*, for an extended listing.

Managing Director and CEO of the Strategic Planning Institute, which houses the PIMS program). Table 11-8 summarizes Buzzell and Gale's major PIMS findings on the strategic and market factors related to business profitability.

The PIMS database is used to provide four different kinds of analyses which are useful to the strategist: (1) the PAR Report, (2) a similar report based on look-alikes, (3) a LIM (Limited Information Model) report, and (4) a Strategy Analysis Report.

The PAR Report is the basic PIMS analysis. It takes the set of data that a business submits to the program which quantitatively describes the business (the variables shown in Tables 11-6 and 11-7) and, using a regression model estimated on the PIMS database, asks the question, What ROI (or cash flow) should a business like this generate given what is known about how all of the businesses in the database have actually performed? In simple terms, "PAR ROI is a benchmark of what profitability level is normal, given a business unit's profile of strategic characteristics."[35]

The PAR Report then cites the actual calculated ROI for the business and compares it to the PAR ROI. The report contains diagnostic information as well. It identifies the individual factors which contributed to the deviation of the actual ROI from the PAR ROI (either positive or negative). For example, a firm's lower relative product quality and high receivables may each have contributed to an actual ROI that was lower than the PAR ROI.

The cash flow that a business may reasonably expect to have is separately reported. It also contains diagnostic information. It reports, for instance, the portion of the actual cash flow experienced that is attributable to management's decisions (such as a decision to increase market share), that which is forced (the need to keep up with real market growth), and that which comes from differentiation from competitors (relative price and relative quality), among other factors.

The Report on Look-Alikes allows a business to compare itself directly (not through a mathematical model) to other businesses that are close in structure to itself. The strategist can select any reasonable combination of factors on which to select these look-alikes. The large number of businesses in the database makes it possible to find out how other companies in positions similar to the subject business's situation performed in reality.

The *Limited Information Model* is a shortened version of the PAR ROI model that is especially useful in estimating the position of competitors. It requires only eighteen factors to estimate a business's ROI. While the model explains only 60% of the variability in ROI compared to the approximately 70% explained by the full model, its required inputs are considerably easier to estimate from outside of a firm.

The *Strategy Analysis Report* simulates the effect of strategic moves on profits, cash, and investments. It takes the current position of the business and management's assumptions about the future environment. From this it esti-

---

[35] Buzzell and Gale, *The PIMS Principles*, p. 159.

TABLE 11-8　*The Impact of Competitive Position, Market Factors, and Industry Influences on ROI and ROS*

COMPETITIVE POSITION AND STRATEGY FACTORS	IMPACT ON	
	ROI	ROS
	(+ = POSITIVE;	− = NEGATIVE)
Market share	+	+
Relative product or service quality	+	+
New products, % of sales	−	−
R&D expenses, % of sales	−	−
Marketing expense, % of sales	−	−
Value added, % of sales[a]	+	+
Fixed assets, % of sales (at capacity)	−	−
Newness of plant and equipment	+	+
Labor productivity	+	+
Inventories, % of sales	−	−
Capacity utilization rate	+	+
FIFO inventory valuation	+	+
MARKET AND INDUSTRY INFLUENCES		
Real market growth rate (annual %)	+	+
Stage of market evolution		
Growth state	+	+
Decline stage	−	−
Rate of inflation in selling prices	+	+
Concentration of suppliers with few purchasers	+	(+)[b]
Typical customer purchase amount		
Small	+	+
Large	−	−
Importance of product purchase to customer		
Low	+	+
High	−	−
% of employees unionized	−	−
Industry exports	+	+
Industry imports	−	−
Standardized products (vs. custom produced)	+	+

[a] Value added is adjusted to remove above-average or compensate for below-average net profits.

[b] Relationship not statistically significant.

SOURCE: Adapted from Robert D. Buzzell and Bradley T. Gale, *The PIMS Principles: Linking Strategy to Performance*, pp. 46–47.

mates such performance measures as ten-year profits (discounted net income), ten-year cash flow, a five-year average pretax ROI, and the residual economic value of the business.

Issues in Using PIMS-Based Analyses

While the PIMS program contains perhaps the best extant collection of real business data and programs with which to analyze those data for managerial purposes, there are limits to its usefulness. Strategists intending to use PIMS-based analyses in generating and evaluating strategic alternatives must acquaint themselves with those limits.

One source of those limits is the mathematical model at the heart of the methodology. It is a multiple regression model and, like all such, is subject to numerous issues. For example, there is an issue termed *multicollinearity*, which is of concern when two variables are both highly correlated with each other as well as with the dependent variable the model is trying to explain, such as ROI. When this occurs, the mathematics are unable to discern which variable is really contributing to ROI.[36] There is multicollinearity in the model, but it is felt to be mild.[37]

A second issue is that the core PIMS model is based on combining the data from all industries. If there are significant differences in the way that different industries work, then such a combination can obscure what is actually occurring. One set of researchers estimating the relationships between product quality, cost position, and performance, for example, found it useful to separate the PIMS sample into six different industry groups to achieve acceptable estimates of the true relationships among the variables.[38]

The impact of yet a third issue is almost impossible to assess: that the model may not have included important variables. If this is the case, then the results will be distorted, attributing importance to other variables beyond their actual significance. While most would say that the model seems to include most of import according to existing economic, accounting, and management theory, there is always a possibility that the combined effects of some indirect variable(s) may be significant.

A related issue concerns the use of accounting identities, especially ratios such as return on investment, turnover (sales divided by investment), and the like. Unless the modeler takes great care, it may be possible to have the same piece of information contained in both independent and dependent variables.[39] The use of return on investment (return divided by investment) as a dependent variable makes suspect any explanation of it by its relationship to supposedly independent variables such as turnover (which is sales divided by investment). Having investment on both sides of the question is equivalent to regressing investment on itself. For example, when this is corrected for, the relationship between return on investment and market share is demonstrated to be due to the improvement in return on sales (ROS), not turnover (sales/investment). This focuses management attention in a whole new direction.

In addition to the mathematical and modeling issues (which are real but acceptable if understood), there are issues with the data that is input into the model. This is termed *measurement error*. PIMS data are submitted by different

---

[36] See the discussion on this point in Day, *Analysis for Strategic Market Decisions*, pp. 132, 133.

[37] Mark J. Chussil, "Responses to PIMS: Fact or Folklore?" *Journal of Business Strategy*, 4, no. 1 (spring 1984), 93–96.

[38] Lynn W. Phillips, Dae R. Chang, and Robert D. Buzzell, "Product Quality, Cost Position, and Business Performance," *Journal of Marketing*, 47, no. 2 (spring 1983), 26–43.

[39] For an extended discussion of this point, see Paul W. Farris, Mark E. Parry, and Frederick E. Webster, Jr., "Accounting for the Market Share-ROI Relationship" (Cambridge, MA: Marketing Science Institute, Report No. 89-118, November 1989).

individuals in different firms, and there can be differences in the extent to which the definitions are interpreted, differences in accounting systems across the firms, and differences among the individuals. Recent research has focused on this question by comparing the findings produced by the PIMS database with the findings produced by the Federal Trade Commission's line-of-business database.[40] Since the two databases have had different criticisms leveled at them, it is highly unlikely that comparable results would be obtained if the quality of either or both data sets was deficient. The study showed that "the data sets generally produce highly comparable descriptive and relational results."[41]

The final limit is in the application of the model. Since the model is estimated on what is termed cross-sectional data, true causality cannot be assessed. The results will always be based on the observation of *association* between variables, not the observation that one *caused* the other. The strategist must be especially careful of putting too much faith in the results. There are two aspects to this. First, whether measurement error, causality, or whatever, any such model has limitations. The apparent validity and accuracy must be understood within those limits.

Second, there is more to strategy than one finds in the model. There is the specific identity of those one is actually competing against; there are the strong elements of personality that are involved in the making of strategy; and there is the push and shove of power politics in strategy, none of which are measured in the model. When all of the players are similarly equipped to compete, it is not what they have but how they use it that determines who wins. For example, recognizing and acting on opportunity before competitors is a significant factor in real-world strategy. An otherwise parity competitor who acts first may find that sustainable competitive advantage flows from the success that being first created rather than the other way around. All of these factors suggest caution in the use of the PIMS model.

PORTFOLIOS AND PIMS: A SUMMARY

Both portfolio and PIMS approaches to the generation and analysis of strategic action offer much within their own limits.[42] Portfolio models continue to assist in identifying the issues in strategy generation for the individual product or business and the issues that accompany the strategic management of a portfolio of entries. While the specific prescriptions contained in the growth-share matrix are best narrowly restricted to large-volume, technology- and capital-intensive

---

[40] The FTC line-of-business data set was compiled from 1974 to 1977 under a law that required approximately 500 large, U.S.-based manufacturing firms to submit data to the FTC. See Cheri T. Marshall and Robert D. Buzzell, "PIMS and the FTC Line-of-Business Data: A Comparison," *Strategic Management Journal*, 11, no. 4 (May-June 1990), 269–282.

[41] Marshall and Buzzell, p. 269.

[42] For a description of how managers actually use portfolio techniques, see Philippe Haspeslagh, "Portfolio Planning: Uses and Limits," *Harvard Business Review* (January-February 1982), 58–73; and Richard G. Hammermesh, "Making Planning Strategic," *Harvard Business Review* (July-August 1986), 115–120.

businesses, the technique does highlight the important advantages that accrue to a leader in a business. If nothing else, portfolio techniques focus management attention on the two critically important questions in strategy decisions: Is the prize worth winning? and Do we have a good chance of winning it?

By forcing managers to refine their thinking and to recognize the quantitative financial impact of their decisions, the PIMS methodology brings reality to the strategy development process. It allows strategists to work through the numbers and to confront the real probabilities of success in the situations they face.

SUMMARY

This chapter reviewed five distinct methodologies for generating and evaluating strategy. It began with a discussion of generic strategy prescriptions, noting the difficulty in separating competitive strategy from investment strategy.

Then the Boston Consulting Group's product portfolio and growth-share matrix was reviewed extensively. Its contributions are the view it provides of a firm's products as a portfolio and the concept of quantifying and presenting market attractiveness and a product's competitive position on one simple display. While the exact prescriptions are misinterpreted by many and more limited than originally thought, the underlying ideas inherent in the technique—the use of cash, the value accruing to market leadership, among others—remain as major conceptual contributions.

Two forms of the market attractiveness/business position were presented. Both generalized models with which to analyze multiproduct businesses, they provide a solid basis for analysis.

The PIMS program, the fifth methodology in the chapter, is perhaps the only methodology available with which to test market strategies empirically. Subject to numerous qualifications, the PIMS program allows a strategist to test a strategic approach against the results actually achieved by other business units. Its findings have shaken many strategists' prior beliefs.

12

STRATEGIZING:
UNDERSTANDING THE PROCESSES
OF STRATEGY FORMULATION
AND STRATEGIC THINKING

Learning to think strategically is a natural stage in the development of expertise in any endeavor. Think about the last time you learned a game or sport. In the early stages, it was all you could do to learn and remember the rules, techniques, and moves. The concept of strategy (e.g., in tennis) was irrelevant to you until you could be reasonably assured that you could hit the ball and make it go where you wanted it to go. Even then, the strategic aspect of the game was not immediately apparent until someone pointed out to you that mistakes made at the higher, strategic level in the game were more important to winning than the technical issues concerning your forehand or backhand.

Now that the basic concept of strategy and the content of competitive strategy has been studied, we look at the process in which that content is used—the process of strategizing. This chapter contains two major sections—the first devoted to developing an understanding of both the normative concepts of strategy and the reality of strategic decision making in organizations; the second devoted to gaining skills in thinking strategically.

We are all prisoners of the concepts we use to give structure to the phenomena in the world around us. The dominant conceptions of strategy used so far in this book have been simple, suggested by battlefield strategy and the concept of the economic or biological survival of the fittest, and based on the idea of competitive advantage in creating value. Given that simple concept, this book has examined those aspects of economic competition that can give rise to competitive advantage. We now turn our attention to the process by which that substantive knowledge is used. The *strategy formulation process* is the term we use to describe how strategy is created and implemented in an organization. We look first at a normative model of strategy formulation and then at several alternative views.

THE NORMATIVE MODEL OF STRATEGY AND
STRATEGY FORMULATION

The normative model of strategy and strategy formulation starts from the assumptions that the goals of the firm are to maximize its present market value and that the most important element in achieving that end is to be able to differentially create value for customers. All of this book has been directed toward that end. It is a strongly economic and rational approach. Those assumptions stand out clearly in Kenichi Ohmae's definition of strategy and the creation of strategy:

> In making strategy. . . . First comes painstaking attention to the needs of customers. First comes close analysis of a company's real degrees of freedom in responding to those needs. First comes the willingness to rethink, fundamentally, what products are and what they do, as well as how best to organize the business system that designs, builds, and markets them . . . strategy takes shape in the determination to create value for customers. It also takes shape in the determination to *avoid* competition whenever and wherever possible.[1]

The Content of Normative Strategy

The concept of what strategy is and what it contains has evolved since its emergence as a concept in the 1960s. Early statements about it were not overly specific. For example, in 1965 two books were published that dealt with strategy. One, a book combining text and cases, defined it as follows:

> Strategy is the pattern of objectives, purposes, or goals and major plans and policies for achieving these goals, stated in such a way as to define what business the company is in or is to be in and the kind of company it is or is to be.[2]

The second book never actually defined strategy but described it as the common thread that ties together the firm's activities. That thread includes the scope of the products and markets in which the firm is active, the direction in which the firm plans to grow, the source of competitive advantage, and the synergy that results.[3]

The idea about what constitutes the content of strategy is much clearer today. The first content item is the ideas of pure strategy, as described in chapter 1 of this book and reflected in the preceding quotation by Ohmae, in which he refers to the determination to avoid competition. The second content item is the specification of how the firm will gain competitive advantage in creating value (as discussed in chapter 2). At the level with which this book is primarily concerned, the product market unit or the focused business unit, most conceptions of the content of strategy include the following elements:

1. The product market in which the firm chooses to compete;
2. The investment strategy that combines both the way in which finances are to be used as a tool and the direction in which cash is to flow;

[1] Kenichi Ohmae, "Getting Back to Strategy," *Harvard Business Review* (November-December 1988), p. 149.

[2] Kenneth Andrews, Edmund Learned, C. Roland Christensen, and William Guth, *Business Policy: Text and Cases* (Homewood, IL: Richard D. Irwin, Inc., 1965), p. 107.

[3] H. Igor Ansoff, *Corporate Strategy: An Analytic Approach to Business Policy for Growth and Expansion* (New York: McGraw-Hill, 1965).

3. The competitive advantage(s) and the source(s) of that advantage that allow the firm to differentially create value;
4. The supporting functional programs that are necessary in implementing the strategy.[4]

When the more than one product market unit or focused business is involved in the strategy, there are two other elements necessary to the complete strategy:

5. The allocation of resources across the different product market or business units;
6. The specification of how synergy is achieved among the collection of businesses.

These six elements constitute the core of the content of strategy in the normative strategy model.[5]

Given the assumptions with which we started, this content is to be expected. The elements specified are key to accomplishing the task of maximizing the present worth of the firm. They are internally consistent and, if achieved, should allow the firm to succeed. These are not the only strategic routes available to a business, however, as Exhibit 12-1 illustrates.

The Process of Normative Strategy

In chapter 1, we suggested that Varro lost to Hannibal because his planning process was deficient and did not provide him with the intelligence needed to position his cavalry correctly. This means that the process of strategy creation is important to the creation of good strategy. While it is indeed possible that a good strategy process can yield poor strategy, that outcome is far less likely than getting a poor strategy from a poor strategy process. In more managerial terms, one cannot easily manage the creative process involved in strategy determination. One can manage, however, the process by which the issues and information are provided to those responsible for strategy determination.

In overview terms, the process of strategy formulation in the normative tradition is seen as having four main steps, as shown in Figure 12-1.[6] These are as follows:

---

[4] Elaboration of these elements can be found in David A. Aaker, *Strategic Marketing Management*, 2nd ed. (New York: John Wiley & Sons, 1988), chapter 1; George S. Day, *Strategic Market Planning* (St. Paul, MN: West Publishing Company, 1984), chapter 2; and Dan E. Schendel, "Strategic Management and Strategic Marketing: What's Strategic About Either One," in H. Thomas and D. Gardner, eds., *Strategic Marketing and Management* (New York: John Wiley & Sons, 1985), chapter 1.3.

[5] Some would argue that the setting of objectives is another critical element in the complete strategy statement. Aaker, in *Strategic Market Management*, and Day, in *Strategic Market Planning*, both include the setting of objectives as key elements. Hofer and Schendel do not include objectives, but only after much discussion. (Charles W. Hofer and Dan Schendel, *Strategy Formulation: Analytical Concepts* (St. Paul: West Publishing, 1978).)

[6] There are many different (but similar) models of the process, some quite elaborate. Hofer and Schendel, *Strategy Formulation: Analytical Concepts*, chapter 3, contains an extensive collection of examples. Our overview of the normative process is based on the discussion found in Day, *Strategic Market Planning*, chapters 1 and 3, and in Schendel, "Strategic Management and Strategic Marketing: What's Strategic About Either One?"

EXHIBIT 12-1

Comparing Three Models of Strategy

While strategy in the military sense seems straightforward, the interpretation of the idea for businesses and other formal organizations is not as simple. Ellen Chaffee has studied the many meanings of strategy and suggests that three models can be discerned, as shown in Exhibit Table A.

EXHIBIT TABLE A

VARIABLE	LINEAR STRATEGY	ADAPTIVE STRATEGY	INTERPRETIVE STRATEGY
Sample definition	"Determination of the basic long-term goals of an enterprise, and the adoption of courses of action and the allocation of resources necessary for carrying out these goals"	"Concerned with the development of a viable match between the opportunities present in the external environment and the organization's capabilities and resources for exploiting those opportunities"	Orienting metaphors constructed for the purpose of conceptualizing and guiding individual attitudes of organizational participants
Nature of strategy	Decisions, actions, plans Integrated	Achieving a match Multifaceted	Metaphor Interpretive
Focus for strategy	Means, ends	Means	Participants and potential participants in the organization
Aim of strategy	Goal achievement	Coalignment with the environment	Legitimacy
Strategic behaviors	Change markets, products	Change style, marketing, quality	Develop symbols, improve interaction and relationships
Associated terms	Strategic planning, strategy formulation and implementation	Strategic management, strategic choice, strategic predisposition, strategic design, strategic fit, strategic thrust, niche	Strategic norms
Associated measures	Formal planning, new products, configuration of products or businesses, market segmentation and focus, market share, merger/acquisition, product diversity	Price, distribution policy, marketing expenditure and intensity, product differentiation, authority changes, proactiveness, risk taking, multiplexity, integration, futurity, adaptiveness, uniqueness	Measures must be derived from context, may require qualitative assessment

[a] A. D. Chandler, Jr., *Strategy And Structure* (Cambridge MA: MIT Press, 1962), p. 13.

[b] C. W. Hofer, "Some Preliminary Research on Patterns of Strategic Behavior," *Academy of Management Proceedings* (1973), pp. 46–59.

EXHIBIT 12-1 (cont.)

In *linear strategy*, the leaders of the organization plan how they will deal with competitors to achieve their organization's goals. It views the environment as a necessary nuisance "out there" that is composed mainly of competitors. In this view of strategy, the key ideas involve the integration of decisions, actions, and plans to achieve organizational goals, including such activities as strategic planning, strategy formulation, and strategy implementation. The model emphasizes top managers going through a prototypical rational decision-making process starting with goals, the generation of alternatives, the selection of strategies, and the implementation and control of those strategies.

In *adaptive strategy*, on the other hand, the organization views the environment, especially the market, as a force with which it needs to be aligned. The organization therefore changes proactively or reactively with consumer preferences. In contrast to the linear model, change is a continuous process in which alignment with the environment is itself the goal, strategy making is less centralized, and the boundaries between the firm and the environment are highly permeable. The dominant metaphor is the biological model, which emphasizes the organization's ability to cope with the environment or to inhabit a particular niche in it.

In *interpretive strategy*, organizational representatives convey meanings that are intended to motivate stakeholders in ways that favor the organization. Rather than the biological model, the interpretive model views an organization as based on a social contract—a collection of cooperative agreements entered into by individuals. Existence, therefore, depends on the organization's ability to attract enough stakeholders to cooperate in mutually beneficial exchange. Whereas the adaptive model emphasizes the need to change with the environment, the interpretive model mimics linear strategy in its emphasis on dealing with the environment. The focus of interpretive strategy is to shape the attitudes of participants toward the organization and its outputs rather than make physical changes in the outputs.

SOURCE: Adapted from Ellen Earle Chaffee, "Three Models of Strategy," in *Academy of Management Review*, 10, no. 1 (1985), pp. 89–98.

- *Situation assessment* is the step in which the current strategy of the business is specified and evaluated in light of the environment and competition. This step is essentially analytical and incorporates most of the techniques presented in this book to understand the totality of the strategic situation in which the firm finds itself. It includes the specification of the opportunities and threats facing the firm (identified by examining the environment and competitive situation) and the business's strengths and weaknesses (identified by comparing the business's capabilities with those of competitors).

Figure 12-1 The strategy formulation process

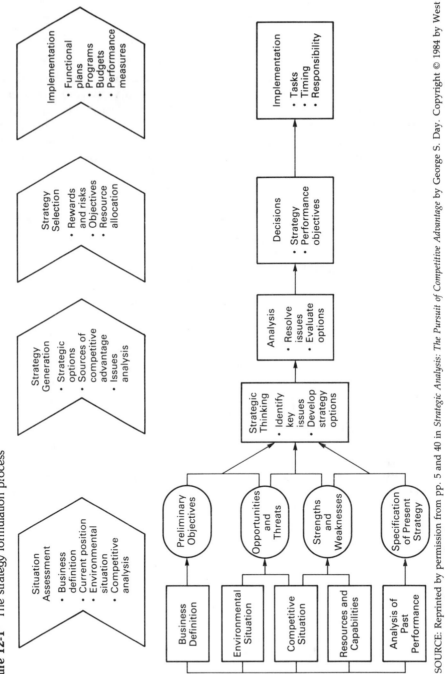

SOURCE: Reprinted by permission from pp. 5 and 40 in *Strategic Analysis: The Pursuit of Competitive Advantage* by George S. Day. Copyright © 1984 by West Publishing Co. All rights reserved.

416

- *Strategy generation* is the second, creative, step. The goal of this step is to develop strategy options for dealing with the key issues surfaced in the prior step. At the analytical stage, strategy options are evaluated based on their risk/ reward ratios relative to the objectives and in light of the resources available.
- *Strategy selection* is the third step in the process. Strategy decisions involve not only the selection of a strategy but also the setting of the objectives by which its accomplishments will be judged and controlled.
- *Implementation* is the fourth step in the process. Implementation involves working out the plans, programs, and budgets by which the strategy's concepts are turned into actions. It involves setting of specific time-related performance measures and assigning responsibilities.

Summing Up the Normative Model

Both the content and process implied by the normative model of strategy formulation are logical, rational, and comprehensive. Since the process is predominantly analytical (with the exception of the admittedly central creative strategy generation step), the process can be well defined, managed, and even delegated to a large extent. In fact, in many large formal organizations there are formal planning processes which do just that. If someone follows the steps rigorously, they should not go too far wrong in formulating strategy if one assumes at least some ability in the creative strategy generation step. For someone learning about strategy, the normative model provides a useful mental construct by which to organize the concepts and techniques central to making strategy.

BEHAVIORAL MODELS OF STRATEGY AND STRATEGY FORMULATION

For all of its apparent logic and utility, however, there is a real concern that the normative model neither captures the true essence of the content of strategy nor usefully describes the process by which it is made. In essence, many would say, to think about strategy in the normative sense is to carry around a concept that is seriously flawed. There have been many arguments about why this is so and, if we were to recount them all here, we could easily spend more time discussing what *is not* the case than providing useful positive concepts, techniques, and insights. Accordingly, this discussion focuses on alternative behavioral models, which provide insights that go beyond those provided by the normative approach.

A Constituency-Based Model of Strategy

Strategy is the thinking that forms the "link between the goals and objectives the organization wants to achieve and the various functional area policies and operating plans it uses to guide its day-to-day activities."[7] In simple terms, strategy serves the purpose of choosing the best path to reach some given set of objectives. The objective assumed in the normative model of strategy is that the goal of the firm is to maximize its net present value—profitability, in other words.

As Anderson has noted, however, that goal does not reflect the realities of organizational functioning or goals.[8] For one, since many modern managers are not the owners of their firms, their actions do not always reflect the best interests of the stockholders. This tendency was put into high relief by the activities of the managers involved in the buyout of RJR Nabisco, described in the book *Barbarians at the Gate*.[9] To account for this reality, organization theorists have suggested two models of the firm: the *behavioral* model and the *resource dependence* models. In these models, both based on the observation of real behavior, firms are viewed as coalitions of individuals with differing interests. One result of these coalitions is that the firm pursues multiple goals, and to speak of a single common goal which the firm seeks to maximize is to ignore reality. In fact, goals are seen more as constraints to be met as each coalition seeks its own interests. As one author put it, "It is hard to imagine middle managers, let alone blue collar employees, waking up each day with the sole thought of creating more shareholder wealth."[10]

This means that to construct an internally consistent strategy framework around profit maximization is to ignore reality. If one is to build a framework for understanding strategy and the strategy formulation process, it is necessary to understand how a business really acts and what its real goals are. Anderson suggests that a better theory on which to base our understanding of strategy formulation is one which focuses on the roles performed by the various functional areas found in the modern business. He terms this a *constituency-based* theory of the firm.

This constituency-based theory suggests that the major functional areas be viewed as specialists in providing particular resources for the firm from external sources. The primary objective of the functional areas is to provide an uninterrupted flow of resources from the external coalition each represents, and in so doing each function needs both to serve and manage those constituencies. The marketing function, for example, sees its responsibility as satisfying the long-run needs of its customer coalition if it is to provide the sales revenue resource to the firm—just as purchasing must satisfy suppliers to provide raw materials, human resources must attract and satisfy people, and so on. Each function, moreover, is constrained by the needs of every other function in attempting to achieve its objectives.

The objectives of the firm in this view are negotiated among the various functions, and the function whose resource responsibility is most important is

---

[7] Hofer and Schendel, *Strategy Formulation*, p. 13.

[8] This discussion is based on the work of Paul F. Anderson, "Marketing, Strategic Planning and the Theory of the Firm," *Journal of Marketing*, 46 (spring 1982), 15–26.

[9] Bryan Burrough and John Helyar, *Barbarians at The Gate: The Fall of RJR Nabisco* (New York: Harper & Row, 1990).

[10] Gary Hamel and C. K. Prahalad, "Strategic Intent," *Harvard Business Review* (May-June 1989), p. 66.

likely to have relatively greater power in that negotiation. The dominance of production and finance in the early part of the twentieth century is credited to the fact that nearly all vital resource exchanges in that period were negotiated by those areas. As Anderson notes, "In this regard, the marketing area's desire to promote the marketing concept as a philosophy of the entire firm may be interpreted by the other functional areas as a means of gaining bargaining leverage by attempting to impress them with the survival value of customer support."[11]

If strategy is to reflect the objectives of the business then, it must be seen not as simply aiding the firm in maximizing the profit objective but as reaching the objectives that emerge from the bargaining process among the functional areas. Since each functional area is important in providing resources, each has the right to lobby the firm to move toward what it views as the preferred position for long-term survival. This requires the strategist to understand the contributions, technologies, and true relative importance of each function to success in the short and long run. Recent research on one of these relationships, that between the marketing function and the R&D function, validates this need.[12]

Marketing's role in the negotiation process is to identify the optimal long-term positions that will assure customer satisfaction and support and to develop the strategies that will capture those preferred positions. In this view, marketers need to recognize that their role and function is but one of several important functions—that marketing needs to negotiate with the other functions if its preferred strategies are to be implemented. To be successful in this task, marketing must be able to communicate the true meaning of its viewpoint in terms which the other coalitions in the firm can comprehend. This role is clearly seen in research which has traced the interactions over time among the several functions in devising strategy for new offerings within an existing business.[13] The managers who built the new businesses within the firm established strong informal connections first with the R&D function and then with the other functions before the programs even became formally recognized efforts.

As a model by which to understand the content and formulation of strategy, Anderson's constituency theory is superior to the normative model. It is superior in the way it conceptualizes the objectives which strategy is to serve, and it is superior in its contribution to an understanding of the process by which strategy is formulated. As anyone who has participated in strategy discussions in a business will attest, it is not only a realistic but enlightening model.

---

[11] Anderson, "Marketing, Strategic Planning," p. 22.

[12] One aspect of this is the quality of the relationship that exists between the marketing and the R&D functions within the firm. See, for example, Ashok K. Gupta, S. P. Raj, and David Wilemon, "A Model for Studying the R&D–Marketing Interface in the Product Innovation Process," *Journal of Marketing*, 50 (April 1986), 7–17; W. E. Souder, "Disharmony Between R&D and Marketing," *Industrial Marketing Management*, 10 (February 1981), 67–73; J. D. Weinruch and P. Anderson, "Conflicts Between Engineering and Marketing Units," *Industrial Marketing Management*, 11 (1982), 291–301; and Robert W. Ruekert and Orville C. Walker, Jr., "Interactions Between Marketing and R&D Departments in Implementing Different Business Strategies," *Strategic Management Journal*, 8, no. 3 (1987), 233–248.

[13] Michael D. Hutt, Peter H. Reingen, and John R. Ronchetto, Jr., "Tracing Emergent Processes in Marketing Strategy Formulation," *Journal of Marketing*, 52 (January 1988), 4–19.

The Proactive Model of Strategy

One of the concerns that many have with the normative model is that its logic, rigorousness, and discipline does not and cannot capture the proactive essence of strategy. The emphasis on quantification in the normative model frequently seems to direct strategists toward reactive modes of thinking (serving an existing market versus creating a market) and a short time horizon. One influential article, for example, argued that the emphasis on marketing research and short-term financial control measures has led to the decline of American firms.[14] Market research, for example, has limitations in that it is typically better at identifying a market's current desires than it is in assessing future needs. This leads to strategies based on forecasts (what do we think is going to happen) rather than on visions (what do we want to happen?).[15]

The criticism is valid. Planning processes typically act as a feasibility sieve in which a strategy is accepted or rejected on the basis of the precision with which managers can document the how as well as the why of their plans. Questions about milestones, adequacy of skills and resources, competitive reactions, and market-based data admonish the manager to be realistic.[16] John Kotter calls this the difference between leading and planning.[17] Leading creates visions and strategies, not plans.

The Means-Ways-Ends Approach.   Several positive concepts are advocated to offset the inherent conservatism of the normative model of strategy formulation. The first is Hayes's concept of reversing the usual ends-ways-means logic of normative strategy formulation.[18] He suggests that the alternative logic of means-ways-ends is worth exploring. He believes that the firm should invest in the development of its capabilities—the means it has available. In this he includes the firm's human resources as well as its assets and technologies. Then, as these capabilities develop and as technological and market opportunities appear, he suggests that the company encourage managers well down in the organization to exploit matches wherever they occur (ways). As he puts it, "the logic here is, Do not develop plans and then seek capabilities; instead, build capabilities and then encourage the development of plans for exploiting them."[19]

The Leverage Approach.   This view is echoed by others who advocate building and leveraging the "core competence" of the business and then set out to le-

---

[14] Robert H. Hayes and William J. Abernathy, "Managing Our Way to Economic Decline," *Harvard Business Review*, 58 (July-August 1980), 67–77.

[15] Robert H. Hayes, "Strategic Planning—Forward in Reverse?" *Harvard Business Review* (November-December 1985), 111–119.

[16] Gary Hamel and C. K. Prahalad, "Strategic Intent," *Harvard Business Review* (May-June 1989), p. 66.

[17] John P. Kotter, "What Leaders Really Do," *Harvard Business Review* (May-June 1990), 103–111.

[18] Hayes, "Strategic Planning—Forward in Reverse?" p. 112.

[19] Hayes, "Strategic Business—Forward in Reverse?" p. 118.

verage that competence through a clearly articulated "strategic intent."[20] Table 12-1 details the main differences between this proactive leverage approach to strategy and the more common adaptive model of strategy. This recalls the point noted in the first chapter of this book, that strategy is best constructed on unique strengths rather than on the correction of weaknesses. Andrall Pearson, who was the president of Pepsico for fifteen years in the 1960s through the 1980s, agrees with that idea. He tells of the success Pepsi had in the 1970s when it focused on improving the sales of its strongest products in its strongest markets with its strongest distributors and then using the resulting payoffs to help fund the search for future edges. He contrasts this strategy with the strategy Pepsico followed in the 1960s, when the company spent so much of its money trying to prop up weaker markets, products, and channels that it lacked the resources to go all out in its stronger areas. As Pearson points out, building on strength, your core competency, keeps competitors "so busy responding to your initiative that they have less time to launch their own."[21]

The importance of this proactive stance based on the business's core strengths cannot be overemphasized. As one executive has consistently stressed to his managers, strategy is the leveraging of capabilities to their best advantage. It is not waiting for things to happen, it is taking actions that make them happen. Good poker or bridge players, for example, do not wait for the perfect hand. They actively work to maximize the value of whatever cards they have been dealt. As soon as a poker player senses an advantage, he or she actively bets—not only to maximize the size of the reward but to induce potential rivals to drop out and improve the odds of winning. Effective strategy formulation processes search for opportunities to be proactive.

Learning Models of Strategy Formulation

Studies of actual strategy processes uniformly find them to be best characterized as a process of organizational learning and describe the process using words such as "evolutionary," "incremental," and "emergent."[22] This view is aptly summed up in the following two quotations:

[20] C. K. Prahalad and Gary Hamel, "The Core Competence of the Corporation," *Harvard Business Review* (May-June 1990), 79–91; and Gary Hamel and C. K. Prahalad, "Strategic Intent," *Harvard Business Review* (May-June 1989), 63–76. Empirical research has been able to identify distinctive competencies and relate them to corporate performance. See Michael A. Hitt and R. Duane Ireland, "Corporate Distinctive Competence, Strategy, Industry and Performance," *Strategic Management Journal*, 6, no. 3 (July-September 1985), 273–293.

[21] Andrall E. Pearson, "Six Basics for General Managers," *Harvard Business Review* (July-August 1989), p. 97.

[22] This discussion is based on the works of Henry Mintzberg and James Brian Quinn, both of whom have done extensive research into the process of strategy formulation. Mintzberg's ideas are summed up in his articles "The Design School: Reconsidering the Basic Premises of Strategic Management," *Strategic Management Journal*, 11 (1990), 171–195; "Crafting Strategy," *Harvard Business Review* (July-August 1987), 66–75; and "Strategy Formulation—Schools of Thought," in James W. Frederickson, ed., *Perspectives on Strategic Management* (New York: Harper Business, 1990), chapter 5. Two key articles which capture Quinn's ideas are "Strategic Change: Logical Incrementalism," *Sloan Management Review*, 20 (spring 1978), 7–21; and "Managing Strategic Change," *Sloan Management Review*, 22 (summer 1980), 3–20.

TABLE 12-1   *Strategic Intent: Key Differences in the Adaptive Versus the Leverage Models of Strategy*

ISSUES	ADAPTIVE	LEVERAGE
Strategy	Maintain strategic fit with environment	Leverage existing resources to maximum value
Competing with limited resources	Trim ambitions to match available resources	Leverage resources to reach seemingly unattainable goals
Competitive advantage	Search for inherently sustainable advantages	Accelerate learning to outpace competitors in creating new advantages
Competing vs. larger competitors	Search for niches or do not challenge larger competitor	Search for new rules that devalue incumbent's advantages
Reduction in risk	Build balanced portfolio of cash-generating and cash-using businesses	Create balanced and broad portfolio of advantages
Allocating resources across organization	Allocate to product market units where relatedness is in common products, channels, customers	Invest in core competencies and then allocate across product market units
Achieving consistency in action	Financial objectives, standard operating procedures, defining served market	Allegiance to firm's strategic intent; consistency achieved by pursuit of intermediate-term challenges and goals

SOURCE: Adapted from Gary Hamel and C. K. Prahalad, "Strategic Intent," *Harvard Business Review* (May-June 1989), p. 65

The full strategy is rarely written down in any one place. The processes used to arrive at the total strategy are typically fragmented, evolutionary, and largely intuitive. Although one can usually find embedded in these fragments some very refined *pieces* of formal strategic analysis, the real strategy tends to evolve as internal decisions and external events flow together to create a new, widely shared consensus for action among key members of the top management team. Far from being an abrogation of good management practice, the rationale behind this kind of strategy formulation is so powerful that it perhaps provides the normative model for strategic decision making—rather than the step-by-step "formal systems planning" approach so often espoused.[23]

Imagine someone *crafting* strategy. A wholly different image likely results, as different from planning as craft is from mechanization. Craft evokes traditional skill, dedication, perfection through the mastery of detail. What springs to mind is not so much thinking and reason as involvement, a feeling of intimacy and harmony with the materials at hand, developed through long experience and commitment. Formulation and implementation merge into a fluid process of learning through which creative strategies evolve. My thesis is simple: the crafting image better captures the process by which effective strategies come to be. The planning image, long popular in the literature, distorts these processes and thereby misguides organizations that embrace it unreservedly.[24]

[23] Quinn, "Strategic Change: "Logical Incrementalism," p. 7.
[24] Mintzberg, "Crafting Strategy," p. 66.

The Learning Approach.   These views are in response to the excessive rationalism that the normative approach implies. Mintzberg, for example, makes four simple but profound criticisms of the normative, design approach to strategy.[25] The first is that it promotes thinking versus learning. The process captured in the normative model is one in which thinking is emphasized and the task of creating strategy is equated with an act of conception. To Mintzberg, the idea of separating thought from action is unrealistic. Since strategic action, if it is not simply to be a copy of someone else's actions, necessarily involves new experience, taking risks, entering unknown territory, testing cause-and-effect linkages never before attempted, then how can one know beforehand what will happen? A learning process, on the other hand, recognizes the limitations of thought divorced from action and proceeds step by step, constantly linking thought and action. Learning necessarily involves trial-and-error and experimentation. Exhibit 12-2 demonstrates how this approach works in real life.

Mintzberg's second criticism is the premise that structure follows strategy. Reminiscent of Hayes's ends-ways-means reversal, Mintzberg argues that not only do means and structure typically preexist the strategy issue but, more important, their existence constrains the strategy process to incremental change. Strategy, in other words, is seldom if ever written on a clean slate.

Third is the criticism that explicit strategy may promote inflexibility. Key to the normative, thinking school of strategy is that only explicit, articulated strategies can be argued, tested, or debated and that only a stated strategy can serve to unite the organization in coordinated action. While that may be true, it also implies that the environment is stable and that, once set, the strategy need not evolve. This is counter to a learning approach and may make firm that which is merely speculative or temporary. As Mintzberg puts it, "When strategists are not sure, they had better not articulate strategies . . . [and] while strategists may be sure for now, they can never be sure forever."[26]

Last is the criticism that separating strategy formulation from implementation detaches thinking from acting. Think first, then do is the rationalist's dictum. Yet to separate strategy formulation from implementation is to assume that the strategist can truly know the realities of what is happening and capable of happening at the doing level. To think of the two, formulation and implementation, as separate and separable entities is to close off entire realms of reality. Learning, opportunism, and improvisation depend on the close linkage of the two. The highly successful strategy that the Honda Motor Company used to conquer the United States motorcycle industry in the 1960s was not brilliantly deliberate but rather one that its executives "backed into."[27] Rather than being the result of a carefully thought-out plan, the company kept changing its approach until it found a strategy that worked. The success of the Pepsi Free® decaffeinated cola is due in part to the perception of a strategic opening with

---

[25] Mintzberg, "The Design School: Reconsidering the Basic Premises of Strategic Management."
[26] Mintzberg, "The Design School," p. 184.
[27] R. T. Pascale, "Perspectives on Strategy: The Real Story Behind Honda's Success," *California Management Review* (spring 1984), 47–72.

EXHIBIT 12-2

Trial and Error in Strategic Decision Making at Pepsico

Andrall Pearson, then President and Chief Operating Officer at Pepsico, responded to a question in an interview by describing how strategic decisions were made at the company:

> The difference between a Strategy that works and one that never gets beyond paper is *feedback*. You've got to get out there and see if it works. If you do it on a small scale you don't have to build the facility-of-a-lifetime or commit yourself to a $100 million expansion. You get out there and you try something and you find out that what you're trying doesn't work, but here's what will. And then your status becomes a lot more clear, and it also permits you to act with a great deal more conviction, than if you divine a world class strategy and commit yourself to [a] $100 million sort of venture company kind of thing on the basis of analysis alone. . . . that's why getting into action is important. You've got to get something out there that is physical and in the marketplace, to see what it does.

SOURCE: Walter Kiechel, Andrall E. Pearson, and Thomas Peters, "Reconciling Strategic Thinking with What Managers Actually Do: A Panel Discussion," in *Advances in Applied Business Strategy,* vol. 1 (Greenwich CT: JAI Press, 1984).

respect to Coca-Cola® that Pepsi capitalized on opportunistically by significantly accelerating Pepsi Free's launch to achieve first-mover advantages.[28]

Deliberate strategy is the term Mintzberg uses to describe what has here been called normative strategy. Figure 12-2 shows how Mintzberg visualizes the process of strategy. Intended strategy has two components: an unrealized component and an emergent component. Realized strategy is what is intended minus that which is unrealized plus that which emerges.

Mintzberg uses the term *emergent strategy* to describe strategies which just form without conscious attention.[29] To cite an example he studied extensively, the National Film Board of Canada (NFB) has a by now well-known strategy of sponsoring outstandingly creative feature films.[30] That strategy, however, emerged from a fortuitous event. The NFB's original strategy was to focus its resources on short documentaries in which there was little competition and in which it was expert. Some years back, however, it funded a filmmaker on a project that ran unexpectedly long. To distribute this project, the NFB turned to theaters and inadvertently gained experience in marketing feature-length films. Other filmmakers caught onto the idea, and eventually the NFB found itself with

[28] Kiechel, Pearson, and Peters, "Reconciling Strategic Thinking with What Managers Actually Do."
[29] Mintzberg, "Crafting Strategy," p. 68.
[30] A complete description of the process by which the strategy was developed, or emerged, can be found in Henry Mintzberg and Alexandra McHugh, "Strategy Formulation in an Adhocracy," *Administrative Science Quarterly*, 30, no. 2 (1985), 160–197.

Figure 12-2 Strategy types: intended, deliberate, emergent, and realized

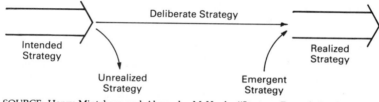

SOURCE: Henry Mintzberg and Alexandra McHugh, "Strategy Formulation in an Ad-hocracy," *Administrative Science Quarterly*, 30, no. 2 (1985), 162.

a new strategy—a pattern of producing such films. The strategy was not planned; it emerged from serendipitous events which shaped a series of small decisions which, in total, resulted in a new direction for the organization. Mintz-berg's point is simple: Strategies can form as well as be formulated.

The Logical Incrementalism Approach. Quinn uses the term *logical incremen-talism* to describe how firms manage to handle the real cognitive and organiza-tional limits that conscious attempts to make strategy decisions entail.[31] This concept emerged to describe the strategy formulation processes he observed operating across ten different large companies he studied in the late 1970s.[32] In many ways, the concept addresses the aforementioned criticisms. As Quinn sees it, logical incrementalism entails keeping early decisions and commitments broadly formative, tentative, and subject to review. In instances in which there is insufficient knowledge to understand the implications of alternative actions, testing and adaptive learning is called for. The extended quotation in Exhibit 12-3 gives an idea of how the process feels to one executive responsible for creating strategy.

Quinn created the flow chart shown in Figure 12-3 to describe in conceptual terms the strategy formulation process he observed. Managers involved in mak-ing strategy who have studied this chart report that they have changed their behavior and thereby become more effective as a result.[33] The steps it contains are described as follows:[34]

- *Leading the formal information system* means that the strategists created networks to provide objective information in advance of that provided by the company's formal information sources, which short-circuited the formal organization's ten-dency "to tell the top only what it wanted to hear." Words like *sensing, uneasi-ness,* and *anomalies* describe the feelings that caused proactive strategists to begin the process.

[31] James Brian Quinn, "Formulating Strategy One Step at a Time," in Roger A. Kerin and Robert A. Peterson, eds., *Perspectives on Strategic Marketing Management*, 2nd ed. (Boston: Allyn & Bacon, Inc., 1983), p. 456.

[32] The ten companies he studied were General Mills, Inc., Pillsbury Company, Exxon Corporation, Continental Group, Xerox Corporation, Pilkington Brothers, Ltd., General Motors Corporation, Chrysler Corporation, Volvo AB, and Texas Instruments, Inc.

[33] Personal reports to the author.

[34] These steps are described more fully in Quinn, "Formulating Strategy One Step at a Time," pp. 471–474.

EXHIBIT 12-3

How Strategy Is Made: One Executive's Description

Typically you start with a general concern, vaguely felt. Next, you roll around an issue until you think you have a conclusion that makes sense for the company. Then you go out and sort of post the idea without being too wedded to its details. You then start hearing the arguments pro and con, and some very good refinements of the idea usually emerge. Then you pull the idea in and put some resources together to study it so it can be put forward as more of a formal presentation. You wait for "stimuli occurrences" or "crises" and launch pieces of the idea to help in these situations. But they lead you toward your ultimate aim. You know where you want to get. You'd like to get there in six months. But it may take three years, or you may not get there at all. And when you do get there, you don't know whether it was originally your own idea—or somebody else had reached the same conclusion before you and just got you on board for it. You never know. The president would follow the same basic process, but he could drive it much faster than an executive much lower in the organization.

SOURCE: Quoted in James Brian Quinn, "Formulating Strategy One Step at a Time," in *Perspective on Strategic Marketing Management*, pp. 470–471.

- *Amplifying understanding*, broadening out the focus to avoid too early or too narrow definition of the issue, was an important step. This often meant generating a broad range of alternatives, delaying adoption of even seemingly acceptable alternatives, and seeking out challenging objective data to test understanding of the issue.
- *Building awareness* followed so key players did not kill potential changes before potential supporters were fully informed and able to bring their interests to bear on the issue. Managers avoided directive processes, preferring to study, challenge, question, and listen instead of seeking commitment at this stage.
- *Changing symbols* was a step taken to signal the coming change to the organization before specific solutions or strategies were even formulated. Highly visible symbolic actions communicated more and better than words could that change was needed and coming.
- *Legitimizing new viewpoints* takes time. Creating discussion forums to allow the organization to talk through issues and buy into the idea and work out its implications made the change seem less risky, whereas change that is too quick or is pushed down from the top of the organization can be strongly resisted.
- *Tactical shifts and partial solutions* are a step often taken in advance of a totally new strategic direction. Part of the learning and risk reduction effort, they allow managers to experiment with new approaches without high risk to the business.
- *Broadening political support* is a step achieved through the creation of task forces, committees, and managerial retreats, often with carefully selected agendas and

Figure 12-3 Some typical process steps in logical incrementalism

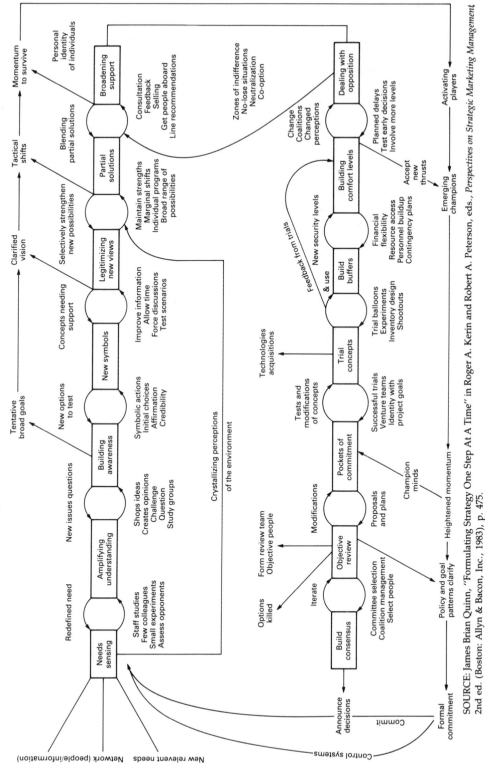

SOURCE: James Brian Quinn, "Formulating Strategy One Step At A Time" in Roger A. Kerin and Robert A. Peterson, eds., *Perspectives on Strategic Marketing Management,* 2nd ed. (Boston: Allyn & Bacon, Inc., 1983), p. 475.

memberships to result in a desired outcome. While primarily designed to bring those out of step into the emerging consensus, the interactive nature also improved the quality of the decisions in the process.

- *Overcoming opposition* was almost always necessary in spite of the preceding steps. In addition to seeking support from key executives, successful strategists sought no-lose situations which honored legitimate differences among the players. Early opponents often shaped change in more effective directions and became supporters of the new strategy.

- *Structuring flexibility* into the process and strategy was key. The inability to predict everything in advance or to prepare for all possible contingencies made this an essential part of the proactive strategy system. It allowed strategy to emerge incrementally as knowledge developed.

- *Trial balloons* were a logical part of the incremental process. Broadly stated and without real commitment behind them, executives tried out concepts to stimulate the organization's own creativity without fear of rejection by line managers.

- *Creating pockets of commitment* was achieved by the initiation of several exploratory projects representing the strategy options, none of which the executive was closely identified with. This allowed learning to take place without damage to the strategist's credibility yet allowed him or her to select those that were successful (while quietly allowing the others to lapse). The successful project then provided the decision maker a core team of people within the organization who were deeply committed to the idea.

- *Crystallizing focus* was essential, but only when the executive saw consensus emerging around a desired formulation or thrust, rather than earlier in the process when it might have provided a common focus for otherwise fragmented opposition or prematurely centralized the organization or preempted other interesting options.

- *Managing coalitions* was a key task as the strategy developed. Since there are often legitimate differences among executives in strategic decisions where there is no objectively right answer, maneuvering coalitions toward solutions they can actively support is an essential step and talent.

- *Formalizing commitment* is possible only at this stage and was often accompanied by the empowerment of a champion, who felt responsible for its execution and took over its thrust.

- *Continuing dynamics and eroding consensus* were final stages that those who had guided the process now took to ensure that the new direction was not too inflexible. Effective executives purposely continued the change process by introducing new people and stimuli to continually hone the edge of the new thrust.

Behavioral Models: A Summary

The behavioral models add much to our understanding of the real process of strategy formulation. They should not, however, cause us to discard the formal normative model. In fact, leading researchers tend to describe good strategy formulation processes as those which blend both models, using the normative planning model for the ongoing fine tuning of existing strategies and as the support system for the incremental approach used when new strategies or major changes in strategic direction are needed. As Mintzberg notes, "all strategy making walks on two feet, one deliberate, the other emergent. For just as purely deliberate strategy making precludes learning, so purely emergent strategy making precludes control."[35]

Even in those instances and companies in which Quinn's concept of logical incrementalism best described the process, there were still formal planning systems. While those systems did not formulate the organization's most central strategy, they did provide important process support. They created an information base that would have otherwise not been available, regularly forced managers into thinking in longer time frames, rigorously communicated goals and strategic issues, systematically taught managers about the future, provided managers with the comfort to plan beyond the comfortable short term, and periodically stimulated special studies and scenarios which could serve the needs of specific strategic decisions.[36]

ORGANIZATION STRATEGY AS BUSINESS STRATEGY

An alternative view of strategy content and formulation suggests that that organization itself is the important element. In this view, organization strategy comes first; it is the overriding construct that determines the content of business strategy.[37] The argument for this view is simple. It is built around the concept of the organization's ability to adapt its strategy to its environment and the appropriateness of its internal processes to its strategy.

This can be summarized in the concept of *fit* among the organization's strategy, structure, and management processes.[38] Organizations that are successful are able to achieve strategic fit with their market environment, and their organization structures and managerial processes support (i.e., fit) their strategies. If an organization is a misfit for a prolonged period, it will fail. The organization that has a tight fit (externally and internally) is typically associated with excellence, while the organization that can achieve early fit is associated with supranormal performance. In this context, early fit describes the firm that is first to discover and implement a new pattern of strategy, structure, and process, perhaps in the form of a new organization form.

At the heart of this view is the *adaptive cycle*, which is diagrammed in Figure

[35] Mintzberg, "Crafting Strategy," p. 69.

[36] Quinn, "Formulating Strategy One Step at a Time," pp. 466–467.

[37] Terminology in this area is unclear. The terms *organizational strategy*, *organizational strategy type*, *strategic orientation*, and *strategy type* are often used interchangeably. See Daryl O. McKee, P. Rajan Varadarajan, and William M. Pride, "Strategic Adaptability and Firm Performance: A Market Contingent Perspective," *Journal of Marketing*, 53 (July 1989), p. 22.

[38] This discussion is based on the works of Raymond E. Miles and Charles C. Snow: *Organization Strategy, Structure, and Process* (New York: McGraw-Hill, 1978); and "Fit, Failure and the Hall of Fame," *California Management Review*, XXVI, no. 3 (spring 1984), 10–28.

12-4. Organizational adaptation requires the simultaneous solution of three intricately interwoven problems: entrepreneurial (which product market domain), engineering (which production and distribution technologies), and administrative (the formalization of technological learning into organization structure and process and articulation of direction). Any adjustment of these three in a given time period tends to become an aspect of tomorrow's structure, and the adjustment cycle can be initiated or triggered in any of the three areas.

The contribution which Miles and Snow made is to recognize the existence of patterns in the ways in which organizations act to adapt themselves to the forces of change. In their view, managers consciously develop and seek consensus on an organizational self-definition (or image) that identifies how and why the organization's structure and process reflect previous decisions about the market and about the future. This consensus is the firm's organizational strategy.[39]

While the possible combinations among the three problem areas are infinite, patterns of behavior emerge which suggest that these self-definitions can be reduced to several archetypes—each of which defines a particular strategy for adaptation and consists of a particular configuration of technology, structure, and process consistent with that adaptation strategy. Miles and Snow identified four such organization types, three of which are successful (defenders, prospectors, analyzers) and one of which is an unsuccessful type (reactors):[40]

- *Defenders* work to create a stable domain by developing a highly cost-efficient single-core technology with the aim of cornering a narrow segment of the total potential market. Top managers are highly expert in within the business's limited scope and do not scan outside of present domains for new opportunities. Defenders grow through market penetration and, over time, are able to carve out and maintain a small niche, which competitors are able to penetrate only with difficulty.

- *Prospectors* are proactive organizations which trade off efficiency for innovation. They maintain broad and continuously developing domains while continually searching for and experimenting with new market opportunities and trends. Thus, they are often the creators of change to which their competitors must respond. Structurally, they tend toward low formalization and decentralized control to achieve flexibility.

- *Analyzers* are fast followers who maintain a firm base of traditional products and customers (with stable technologies and formalized structures and processes) while simultaneously locating and exploiting new product and market opportunities (using more flexible technologies and structures). In the latter area

---

[39] A similar research approach was taken by Miller and Friesen, who used factor analysis to determine ten archetypes in a study of eighty-one published business cases. These included such categories as "Impulsive Firms" and "Stagnant Bureaucracies." See Danny Miller and Peter H. Friesen, "Strategy-Making in Context: Ten Empirical Archetypes," *Journal of Management Studies*, 14, no. (October 1977), 253–280.

[40] The following descriptions are adapted from Miles and Snow, *Organizational Strategy, Structure, and Process*, p. 29, and Eli Segev, "A Systematic Comparative Analysis and Synthesis of Two Business-Level Strategic Typologies," *Strategic Management Journal*, 10 (1989), p. 502.

Figure 12-4 The adaptive cycle

SOURCE: From Raymond E. Miles and Charles C. Snow, *Organization Strategy, Structure and Process.* Copyright © 1978 by McGraw-Hill, Inc. Reprinted with permission of McGraw-Hill, Inc.

managers watch competitors closely for new ideas and rapidly adopt the most promising.

- *Reactors* perceive the change and uncertainty in their environments but are unable to respond effectively. This can be the result of an unclear definition of their strategy, an inability to shape structure and processes to fit the strategy, or maintaining a strategy inappropriate to a changed environment until forced to change by outside pressures.

The four archetypes can be easily understood if one thinks of them as points on a continuum which measures adaptive capability or, more specifically, entrepreneurial effort.[41] Prospectors are the most entrepreneurial or adaptable, followed by analyzers, defenders, and finally reactors. This insight led several researchers to examine the relationship between organization strategy and per-

[41] The entrepreneurial linkage is suggested by Robert W. Ruekert and Orville C. Walker, Jr., "Interactions Between Marketing and R&D Departments in Implementing Different Business Strategies," *Strategic Management Journal*, 8, no. 3 (1987), 233–248.

formance (although in their original work Miles and Snow had suggested that there would not be any differences among the types). The hypothesis is that the relationship between performance and adaptive capability would be positive, up to a point, and then negative as the trade-off between the advantages of maintaining adaptive capability versus its costs balanced. Analyzers, which maintain a balance between adaptive capability and efficiency, were hypothesized to perform best.[42] The results are shown in Figure 12-5. The two empirical studies validated the shape of the hypothesis although with greatly varying estimates of the actual empirical impact.[43] This work adds confidence to the construct of organizational strategy.

Summary of the Organizational Strategies Model

The organizational strategies model moves the view of strategy content and formulation a considerable distance from that described by the normative model. It suggests first that the strategist is more constrained in his or her deliberations than the normative model even begins to suggest, and second that the real strategy decisions are located several conceptual levels higher—at the point when the organization itself is creating its own adaptation strategy by its choice of the structure and processes which define it.

THINKING STRATEGICALLY

Closely aligned with the issues of how to think about strategy and strategy formulation is the question of learning to think strategically. As our discussion so far has demonstrated, strategic thinking requires more than that implied by the normative model of strategy content and formulation. It requires a deep understanding of the organization, its technology, and the marketplace coupled with a particular set of analytical and creative skills. As Bruce Henderson, founder of the Boston Consulting Group (BCG) put it, it requires the "(1) ability to understand competitive behavior as a system in which competitors, customers, money, people, and resources continually interact; [and] (2) ability to use this understanding to predict how a given strategic move will rebalance the competitive equilibrium."[44] It requires the ability to think at a conceptual level and at a practical level simultaneously.[45] It requires individuals who can deal

---

[42] Linel J. Bourgeois, III, "Strategy and Environment: A Conceptual Integration," *Academy of Management Review*, 5, no. 1 (January 1980), 25–39.
[43] Daryl O. McKee, P. Rajan Varadarajan, and William M. Pride, "Strategic Adaptability and Market Performance: A Market Contingent Perspective," *Journal of Marketing*, 53 (July 1989), 21–35; and C. C. Snow and L. Hrebiniak, "Strategy, Distinctive Competence, and Organizational Performance," *Administrative Science Quarterly*, 25, no. 2 (June 1980), 317–336.
[44] Bruce D. Henderson, "The Origin of Strategy," *Harvard Business Review* (November-December 1989), 139–143.
[45] Andrall E. Pearson, "Six Basics for General Managers," *Harvard Business Review* (July-August 1989), 94–101.

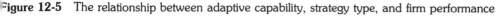

Figure 12-5 The relationship between adaptive capability, strategy type, and firm performance

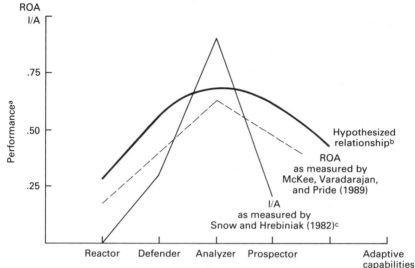

[a] ROA = returns on assets. I/A = income/assets.

[b] L. J. Bourgeois, III, "Strategy and Environment: A Conceptual Integration," *Academy of Management Journal*, 5, no. 1 (January 1980), 25–39.

[c] C. C. Snow and L. G. Hrebiniak, "Strategy, Distinctive Competence, and Organizational Performance," *Administrative Science Quarterly*, 25, no. 2 (June 1980), 317–336.

SOURCE: Adapted from Daryl O. McKee, P. Rajan Varadarajan, and William M. Pride, "Strategic Adaptability and Firm Performance: A Market-Contingent Perspective," in *Journal of Marketing*, 53, no. 3 (July 1989), p. 24. Reprinted by permission of the American Marketing Association.

with the reality of the environment as it is, not as they hope it can be.[46] This requires the ability to think analytically, competitively, and strategically.

Thinking Analytically

Thinking analytically is the core competence of the strategist. At the heart of analytical thinking is the ability to identify the underlying causal origins of observed, concrete phenomena. This is achieved by rigorous, logical thinking aided by some skill at data analysis and a healthy dose of skepticism, with which to locate and test assumptions. This skill is not an intuitive one, especially for managers whose careers have been built on action instead of reflection. On the other hand, it is a skill that can be learned with practice.

The key technique is to learn how to move from the concrete to the abstract and then back to the concrete. The methodology is pictured in Figure 12-6. The first step is to list all of the concrete phenomena (or symptoms) that gave rise to the analysis. This might include such items as "decline in market share," "de-

---

[46] Noel Tichy and Ram Charan, "Speed, Simplicity, Self-Confidence: An Interview with Jack Welch," *Harvard Business Review* (September-October 1989), 112–119.

Figure 12-6   Strategic analysis of problems

STEP	IDENTIFICATION OF CONCRETE PHENOMENA AND SYMPTOMS	GROUPING OF RELATED ITEMS BY TYPE OF ISSUE	DIAGNOSIS OF THE UNDERLYING CAUSE	SPECIFICATION AND ANALYSIS OF CONCEPTUAL LEVEL SOLUTIONS	TRANSLATION INTO CONCRETE ACTIONS
SKILLS NEEDED	Insight Dissection of problems into symptoms	Pattern recognition in symptoms	Abstraction Diagnosis of critical issue in group	Rational analysis Creative reintegration	Validation of solution hypotheses Organization of formal plan Implementation
EXAMPLE	Increased employee turnover (b) Increased supply costs (a) Constraints in capacity (c) Decrease in ROI (d) Lower employee productivity (b,c) Higher distribution costs (a) Decreased morale among managers (b) Delay in new product development (d) Increased mfg. costs (a, c) Increase in unprofitable products (d)	Cost problems (a) Personnel problems (b) Equipment/ process technology (EPT) problems (c) Strategic problems (d)	Costs high compared to competitors Lack of motivations EPT outmoded Product line diverse and outdated	Lower costs Increase training and benefits Update EPT Establish focus and streamline product line	Renegotiate contracts with suppliers/distributors or find new ones Create formal training programs Stock options for managers Formulate capital expenditure plan Revise strategic goals and approach

SOURCE: From Kenichi Ohmae, *The Mind of the Strategist: Business Planning for Competitive Advantage.* Copyright © 1978 by McGraw-Hill, Inc. Reprinted with permission of McGraw-Hill, Inc.

cline in number of distributors," "falling average realized unit price," or "sales force dissatisfaction with incentive compensation."

The second step is to physically rearrange (or group) the symptoms into categories based on the similarity of their underlying issues.[47] For example, one might group together items which deal with distribution issues, sales force issues, product issues, etc. This grouping process is not always easy. It requires some insight and the ability to recognize patterns. The result of this grouping process is to focus the investigation—the analysis—toward a few broad catego

---

[47] A similar approach is described by David W. Nylen in *Marketing Decision Making Handbook* (Englewood Cliffs, NJ: Prentice-Hall, 1990), chapters 3 and 5.

ries of problem types or categories rather than a broad listing of simple symptoms. In so doing, not only has the focus been narrowed but it has also moved up one conceptual level from concrete reality. Instead of finding remedies for symptoms, the process brings us one step closer to identifying solutions to real problems.

Now that categories of issues have been identified, the real work can begin: the analytical task of uncovering the underlying causes of the observed symptoms. In medical terminology, it is the task of diagnosis. In broad terms, this is accomplished by identifying the potential cause-effect relationships (as hypotheses) and obtaining the data and performing the analyses that test each relationship for validity. The approach is not unlike that used by a medical doctor. The answers at this level will be yet one step higher in conceptual terms than the prior. They will take the form of statements such as "low relative product performance" or "insufficient product R&D." There is a set of techniques that are regularly used in this step, discussed later in this chapter.

Given the identification of underlying causes, the fourth step is to specify the conceptual-level solutions to the underlying problems and to analyze them for the appropriateness. This is accomplished using the same kind of techniques that are used to generate and test the possible causal origins of the problem. Following this step (or concurrent with it) is the job of linking conceptual solutions to real concrete actions, the fifth step in the process prior to choosing the most appropriate solution and beginning the process of testing and implementing that solution. If one follows this process, one will avoid the most common managerial mistake: applying bandages to symptoms before one has determined their underlying cause.

The process just described requires the ability to move between the concrete, doing level, and the abstract, thinking level. The idea underlying this process is that by moving up from the level of concrete phenomena to the conceptual level, not only is one more easily able to identify the true causal origin of the problem but one can also more easily manipulate the problem and its possible solutions. Then, once theoretical solutions have been identified, one moves back to search for the concrete analogs to the ideas. Next, this process is demonstrated as the techniques that are useful in the process are explained.

Useful Analytical Techniques.   Identifying or diagnosing the underlying cause of concrete phenomena is not unlike the general scientific process. One observes phenomena, proposes hypotheses that might explain that which is observed, and then obtains data that allow one to test the hypotheses. There are two important rules in this type of thinking for strategy purposes:

1. Every analysis should always try to estimate the effect of the action on profitability in dollars and cents terms. Since the ultimate score of the game is in those terms, the more that the strategist tries to drive every analysis in the dollars and cents direction, the closer he or she will be to uncovering a good solution.
2. The task needs to be done in writing—no mind can hold the complex information arrays required. Working in writing is essential. It is estimated that the

human mind can focus on eight facts at a time and that our ability to calculate probabilities, especially to combine two or more, is low.[48] Experienced strategists always work out ideas on paper—whether working alone or with a group.

The class of techniques described here is based on the concept of decomposition—the separating of a given entity into its component parts.[49] The easiest way to understand this is to think about a frequently asked question: how to improve profitability. As shown in Figure 12-7, profitability can be improved in two ways: sell more or spend less.[50] Selling more, increasing sales revenues, can be achieved by increasing volume or increasing price, and so on. One can go through a similar exercise on the cost side. An elegant version of this technique is termed *gap analysis* and is shown in Figure 12-8.[51] While the techniques used look different, they are in effect the same thing: a logical decomposition of a phenomenon into its component parts.

Such techniques can take many forms. Many have in common the ability to provide the user with a comprehensive array of the available choices and to thereby require a sometimes painful recognition of reality. Two-way comparison tables can add much insight into analyses. Consider the example shown in Figure 12-9. It depicts the four choices facing managers depending on the outcome of a tear-down, and comparison of a leading competitor's product versus the firm's own product. There is little doubt about the actions that need to be taken.

Figure 12-10 shows a similar exercise based on a firm which was attempting to devise a competitive strategy for a new business based on an as-yet uncompleted R&D program which had the potential to reduce investment and operating costs significantly at the same time it could potentially offer significant product performance advantages. With limited R&D resources, however, the strategy team had to decide on the allocation of R&D resources and effort between the two quite different directions. Based on the conceptual-level analysis shown, the team proceeded to quantify the dimensions. They obtained estimates of the R&D resources required to achieve differing levels of cost improvement versus product performance. This information, combined with market based information on the relative value of price versus product performance enabled them to determine the relative slope of the profitably contours and move forward toward a strategy in line with profitability goals and the realities of their relative ability to achieve differing levels of the two types of competitive advantage.

The key to learning the decomposition technique is to think in simple terms. Look at Figure 12-7, for example. It is nothing more than a simple-minded

---

[48] Amitai Etzioni, "Humble Decision Making," *Harvard Business Review* (July-August 1989), 122–126.
[49] See, for example, James M. Hulbert and Norman E. Toy, "A Strategic Framework for Marketing Control," *Journal of Marketing*, 41, no. 2 (April 1977), 12–20.
[50] Actually, profitability may mean either to earn more total dollars or a greater percentage of the sales dollar. This analysis does not differentiate between the two.
[51] John A. Weber, *Growth Opportunity Analysis* (Reston, VA: Reston Publishing, 1976).

Figure 12-7 Analysis by successive decomposition

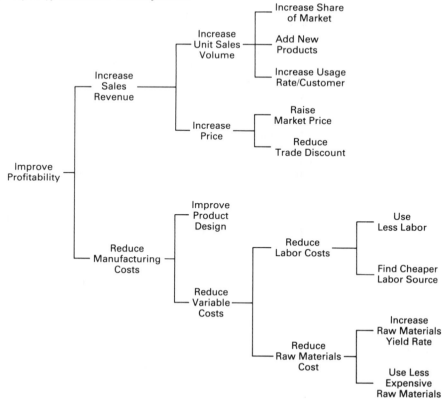

analysis of reality, yet it lays out clearly the paths available to the manager. In trying to apply the idea to a specific problem, the analyst should look at the concrete phenomena and ask the question, According to economic theory, what is the process that must be working to achieve this observed result?

Thinking Competitively

Learning to think competitively is the second skill the strategist needs. This is a skill the normative model omits and not even analytical thinking necessarily provides. It requires the ability to think first in terms of competitive interaction; second in dynamic terms. On occasion, it helps to think in military terms, also.

Competitive Interaction. The first lesson here is the most important: In competitive situations, success comes not only from what you do but from how your competitors respond to your actions. In other words, *strategic decisions are interactive in nature.* You win market share not only because of your own actions but because your competitors have voluntarily stopped short of a maximum effort to acquire share themselves.

Figure 12-8   Gap analysis

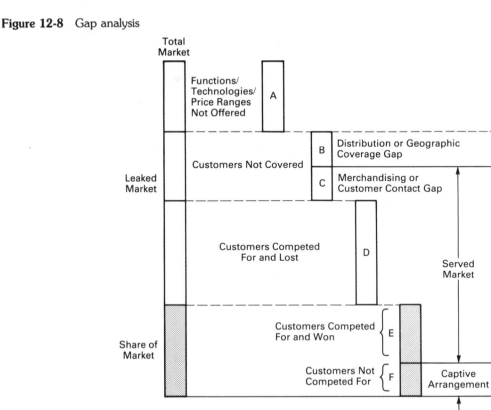

In games in which one's gain is another's loss, there is, therefore, almost no distinction between competition and cooperation. Your competitive success comes from convincing competitors not to compete to the utmost but to compromise on their ambitions; to cooperate to their own best advantage. Your words and actions, must therefore

- Communicate to rivals what they can gain if they cooperate and what it will cost them if they do not.
- Avoid actions which will arouse competitors' emotions, since it is essential that they behave in a logical, reasonable fashion.
- Convince opponents that you are emotionally dedicated to your position and are completely convinced that it is reasonable.[52]

[52] This is based on the ideas of Bruce D. Henderson contained in his book, *Henderson on Corporate Strategy* (Cambridge, MA: Abt Books, 1979), pp. 27–33.

Figure 12-9 Product change options after competitive tear-down

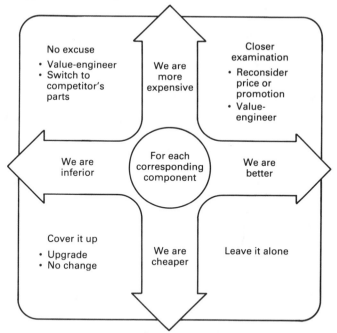

Actions toward competitors, therefore, have both logical and nonlogical components. As shown in Table 12-2, points 1, 2, and 3 are terribly logical but 4 and 5 are not. It is important that the strategist understand the basis for the nonlogical component. This basis begins by recognizing that any competition which does not eventually eliminate a competitor requires the competitor's cooperation to stabilize the situation. There is a point in all competitive situations at which both competitors can gain more or lose less from peace than they can hope to gain from further competition—cooperation is more profitable than conflict. But the gain is not necessarily equal for both, especially if one is trying to change the status quo. The aggressor is the one trying to get more than it currently has. The question is to determine how to share the benefits of cooperation. From this viewpoint, the goal of strategy is to produce a stable relationship favorable to you with the consent of your competitors.

At the base of this is the recognition that each competitor can hurt the other by continuing to compete. Agreement depends on three things: (1) each party's willingness to accept the risk of punishment, (2) each party's belief that the other party is willing to accept the risk of punishment, and (3) the degree of rationality in the behavior of each party. The first result of this state of affairs is that the competitor which is unwilling to accept the risk of punishment—the first to back down—is almost certain to elicit either the punishment or progres-

Figure 12-10   Profitability and strategic flexibility as a function of product performance and manufacturing cost advantage achieved

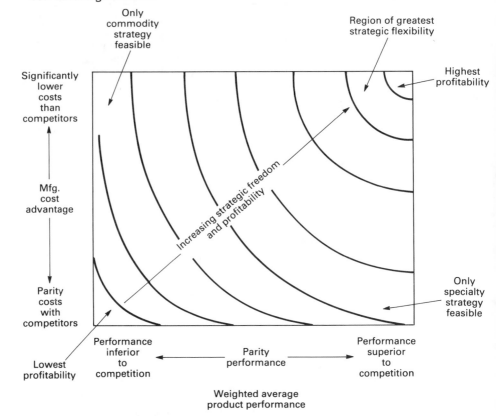

sively more onerous conditions for cooperation (provided that the opponent knows of this unwillingness).

The second insight that comes from the mutual punishment perspective is that beliefs about a competitor's future behavior or response determine competitive cooperation. It is not so much the judgments about actual capability but of the probable use of that capability that count. This leads to the third point: The less rational or less predictable the behavior of a competitor appears to be, the greater the advantage that competitor possesses in establishing a favorable competitive balance. This advantage is limited only by the need to avoid forcing opponents into an untenable position or creating an emotional antagonism that will lead the opponent to be as emotional and irrational as the competitor.

This is not unlike the art of diplomacy, which has been described as the ability to be unreasonable without arousing resentment. The goal of diplomacy is like that of business competition as it has been described here—inducing cooperation on terms more favorable to you than to your opponent without the actual use of force. As Bruce Henderson puts it,

TABLE 12-2 *The Rules of Competitive Brinkmanship*

I. You must know as accurately as possible just what your competition has at stake in their contact with you. It is not what you gain or lose, but what they gain or lose that sets the limit on their ability to compromise with you.

II. The less the competition knows about your stakes, the less advantage they have. Without a reference point, they do not even know whether you are being unreasonable.

III. It is absolutely essential to know the character, attitudes, motives, and habitual behavior of a competitor if you wish to have an advantage.

IV. The more arbitrary your demands are, the better your relative competitive position—provided you do not arouse an emotional reaction.

V. The less arbitrary you seem, the more arbitrary you can in fact be.

SOURCE: Adapted from Bruce D. Henderson, *Henderson on Corporate Strategy*, Abt Books, 1979.

> More business victories are won in the minds of competitors than in the laboratory, the factory, or the marketplace. The competitor's conviction that you are emotional, dogmatic, or otherwise nonlogical in your business strategy can be a great asset. This conviction on his part can result in an acceptance of your actions without retaliation, which would otherwise be unthinkable. More important, the anticipation of non-logical or unrestrained reactions on your part can inhibit his competitive aggression.[53]

This push-and-shove aspect of competition is real, it exists, it is important. Competition is not only about what you deserve but about what you can take and get away with. One year after the deregulation of the airline industry, the Civil Aeronautics Board granted Eastern Airlines the coveted New York to Los Angeles route, previously the domain of only United Airlines, TWA, and American Airlines, effective June 1, 1980. In a move designed to grab a large piece of this market as quickly as possible, Eastern announced it would offer a $99 one-way fare during the month of June. To protect their market share, the others were forced to match this fare. At a rate well below operating costs, it was estimated that the planes would have to fly at 150% capacity to make a profit. While all the airlines posted operating losses for that quarter and several laid off substantial numbers of employees, they were determined to fight for that route. As the CEO of United's parent company, Richard J. Ferris, said at the time, "You'll have to take me out of that market feet first. We'll protect it to our dying breath."[54]

Strategy Dynamics. Strategy is not a static problem; it is a dynamic one. Short of an absolute, sustainable competitive advantage (which is almost impossible to attain), competitive advantages are generally short lived.[55] In fact, the larger and more successful the advantage, the harder competitors work to neutralize it. The

[53] Henderson, *Henderson on Corporate Strategy*, pp. 32–33.
[54] *Forbes Magazine*, July 21, 1980, p. 80.
[55] Pankaj Ghemawat, "Sustainable Advantage," *Harvard Business Review*, 64 (September-October 1986), 53–58.

manager's goal, therefore, is not just to gain a competitive advantage but to predict how competitors will likely act to counter that advantage; the manager must also think about how to play in the next round of the game.

In industries in which product performance improvement is the key factor for success, for example, the rule for the leader is not only to have the best-performing product in the market but to have its replacement on the shelf and yet the third-generation product in R&D. In this way, by the time competition has caught up with the product in the marketplace, the leader is ready to move to an even higher level of performance. The competition between American and Japanese automobile makers in the late 1980s and early 1990s seems to resemble that model. Every time the Americans catch up to the Japanese on performance, durability, or pure value, the Japanese have already moved on to a new, higher level of performance.

The basic technique for addressing the dynamics of competition is to create diagrams which capture the successive iterations of the game, beginning with your action and then listing the competitors' possible responses, your possible counters to those, and so on. The market entry game diagrammed in Figure 9-3 is one simple example. Clearly, such a task can get out of hand, although the application of logic can keep the task manageable by allowing elimination of nonfeasible branches and concentration on more likely responses. Once completed, four questions can be addressed of each response branch:

1. How likely is the response?
2. How soon would this response be implemented?
3. How effective would this response be as a counter to our action?
4. Can we influence the probability that this response will occur?

Thinking Militarily.   One can frequently obtain insights into competitive situations by thinking in the terminology of warfare. While the analogy is not always perfect, there are times when it yields new ways of understanding situations. Table 12-3 lists some of the questions one would ask in this type of analysis.

The basic idea of attacker/defender, understanding which opponent is choosing the weapons or has the initiative, is useful in understanding the physics of the situation as described in chapter 1. Questions like "who deserves to win?" force the strategist to remove the specifics of the situation and to concentrate on such factors as relative strengths and what it takes to overcome an entrenched competitor. Simply lining up two competitors' characteristics in adjoining columns frequently gives one an estimate of the likely outcome of the battle. In one analysis, for example, the comparison showed that firm A, the defender, should be the winner. A's product substantially outperformed its opponent's, it outspent the opponent 5 to 1 on advertising, had wider distribution, A itself was a much larger firm with strong cash flow than was B, and the like. Firm A deserved to win but was losing share rapidly. This showed that the matching of competitive strengths was missing an important competitive element in the battle (or else the laws of economic warfare were being broken). This

TABLE 12-3   *Thinking Militarily: Questions That Define the Battle*

---

1. Who is attacking or defending?
2. Who is taking the initiative, selecting the battlefield, and choosing the weapons?
   —How is the contested market defined?
   —Which weapons are being used?
   —Which opponent is more proficient in the use of the chosen weapons?
3. How big is the prize?
4. Who now holds the prize?
5. What is the type of attack?
   —More and better of the same across the board?
   —Focused resources on segment or niche?
   —New game strategy industry-wide?
   —Selective game strategy?
6. What are the relative strengths at the point of attack?
7. What are the key elements of the attack?
   —Improved performance and satisfaction of existing needs?
   —Better price for equivalent performance?
   —Satisfaction of previously unmet needs?
8. What is the source of the attacker's advantage?
   —Product technology?
   —Process technology?
   —Marketing, sales, or distribution technology?
   —Superior resources or lower need for profit?
   —Pioneer advantages (timing)?
   —Market position?
   —Knowledge of market needs?
9. Can the advantage be duplicated or countered?
10. Do the attackers or defenders have sufficient resources to maintain their attack or defense? What is the source of those resources?
11. Where or how is the opponent vulnerable?

---

led for a search for the weapon that was being used. Once found, the understanding firm A gained of its vulnerability enabled it to formulate a strategy which not only allowed it to fight off the attacker but ultimately to build a larger and more profitable business. Thinking militarily does not always add to the analysis, but it is a technique that deserves to be tried.

Thinking Strategically

Analytical and competitively oriented forms of thinking are the basis of strategic thinking. But strategic thinking differs from those two. Strategic thinking uses those forms as tools in the quest for the means to upset existing competitive relationships. It does that by thinking systematically, in terms of value creation, and at the structural level.

Systemic Thinking.   Thinking in terms of biological evolution, strategy is equivalent to the manipulation of the forces of natural competition. It is like trying to understand how to change the rabbit so it chases the fox. It is like trying to understand what would happen to other elements of the system as a result of the change in the competitive system. What would happen to the vegetation the rabbit usually consumed? What would happen to the other animals the fox had hunted as the population of foxes declined?

Strategy is based on understanding the entire competitive system. Strategic thinking seeks to identify the key elements in the system that define and drive the competitive system. The Fidelity group of mutual funds was created by Ned Johnson, who was able to envision the system in which individual investors made their decisions about mutual funds. He saw the problems which hampered the mutual fund industry: (1) Fund managers lived or died on the basis of last year's performance, since competition was based on who had performed best recently; and (2) customers constantly shifted funds based on either poor performance or poor service. His solution was to create a supermarket of fifty to sixty funds which offered customers every conceivable investment focus plus superior service. In this way, customers have a choice, and if the particular fund chosen does not have a good year customers blame themselves, not the fund manager. Fidelity has created a system in which customers can easily switch among the entire range of funds. With such a large number of funds, Fidelity always has four or five winners for the customer to switch to.[56]

A key concept here is the identification of what are termed the *key factors for success* and the focusing of resources on those factors to excel in them. Assume a situation in which distribution was the key factor for success. If all competitors allocated resources identically, $x\$$ to advertising, $y\$$ to product R&D, and $z\$$ to distributor relations, then no firm would have a competitive edge. If one firm, however, allocated resources $0.5x\$$ to advertising, $0.5y\$$ to product R&D, and $2z\$$ to distributor relations, that firm would win because it would do twice as well as the others in the key, success-determining factor.

A key factor for success is a source of advantage in which a change in the firm's performance would have a large impact on its ability to deliver value in the marketplace.[57] This necessarily means an element in which the change it achieves can be sizable and which competitors would have a difficult time neutralizing or outperforming. Key success factors can be located anywhere in the whole vertical chain of the business system involved, which is why strategic thinking needs to be systemic. They may be located in the cost or quality of raw materials acquisition or anywhere through to the cost and quality of postsales service. Since the linkages among the variables are complex, somewhat like a

---

[56] Andrall E. Pearson, "Six Basics for General Managers," *Harvard Business Review* (July-August 1989), 94–101.

[57] See the discussion in Ohmae, *The Mind of the Strategist*, chapter 3. For alternative views, see Andrew C. Boynton and Robert W. Zmud, "An Assessment of Critical Success Factors," *Sloan Management Review*, 25, no. 4 (summer 1984), 17–27; and Joel K. Leidecker and Albert V. Bruno, "Identifying and Using Critical Success Factors," *Long-Range Planning*, 17, no. 1 (February 1984), 23–32.

tangled ball of string, the analyst must be able to penetrate the system to see its overall pattern.

Successful firms do not necessarily trace through every string but instead choose to concentrate on one key function early and use the funds generated by that success to move on to another function. Those that have studied the matter state that all of today's industry leaders, without exception, began by bold deployment of strategies based on key success factors.[58] The key to understanding the use of key success factors is summed up in the phrase *bold deployment*. At the strategic level, success does not come from small, marginal changes; it comes from changing the structure of the situation. That requires bold action.

Value Creation.   The rule that determines winners and losers in the game of economic competition is that of value creation. The competitor who best creates value for customers wins.

There are two models for thinking about value creation. The first model is the competitive model. It says that the way to deliver the most value to customers is simply to beat the competition. Figure 9-9 diagrammed the logic of this philosophy. If the competitor's coffee pot brews coffee in ten minutes, then designing one to brew coffee in seven minutes is what you do. If the competitor's coffee pot uses x watts of electricity, then design yours to use $0.5x$ watts. There is an inherent logic there: By beating competitors, you will satisfy customers better. The reverse is certainly true. Building products that perform less well than competitors' products will certainly not win the game. But beating competitors is not always the best model. First, strategically it plays the game as the competitors have defined it. It is the game they have chosen to play because they are good at it (possibly even because you are not so good at it). That is not a good strategic idea.

The second reason that beating competitors is not always a good model is that it obscures the real idea of creating value and directs thinking toward well-worn paths instead of toward the new. Kenichi Ohmae tells the story of the Japanese home appliance company trying to develop a coffee percolator.[59] Executives were wondering which competitor's it should resemble—General Electric's, Philips's? Instead of answering that question, Ohmae asked them the following questions: Why do people drink coffee? What are they looking for when they do it? He reasoned that if the objective is to serve the customer better, then the answers would help to answer the question of what kind of percolator to make.

The answer to those questions ("good taste") led Ohmae to ask another question: What influences the taste of a cup of coffee? That was an answer none knew. They went out and researched the question. Of all of the factors they found, two made the greatest difference: (1) water quality, and (2) the quality of the grinding of the beans and the time between grinding and brewing. Armed with this information, the company was able to design a new type of coffee

[58] Ohmae, *The Mind of the Strategist*, p. 49.
[59] Ohmae, "Getting Back to Strategy."

percolator. This machine had a dechlorinating function built in to improve water quality and a built-in grinder that worked just before the start of the brewing process.

Only by thinking in terms of creating value—a better-tasting cup of coffee, in this example—could such an answer have been developed. It is an answer that takes the initiative away from the competition and puts it in your hands. You can win because you played the customer's game, not the competitors'.

Structural-Level Thinking.   One of the hallmarks of strategic thinking is that it addresses the elements of competition that are enduring and not easy to change. Strategic decisions affect the stance the company takes; the bricks and mortar and manufacturing process decisions that, once taken, are not easily changed. There are two interesting insights regarding structural-level thinking. First, the competitor that fashions its structural decisions in the same mold as its competitors is constrained to play the same game as they are playing. Second, once a competitor makes those structural decisions, it is committed and thereby vulnerable to attacks that do not depend on those structures.

For example, Union Carbide's Linde Division long dominated the industrial gas market. Its gas separation plants were of large scale and located to minimize transportation costs. The company had a large fleet of rail and truck carriers that efficiently carried the gases to its customers. The economies it enjoyed were not only in its plants but in the entire complex business system it had so carefully built. Competitors had difficulty competing. But one competitor did succeed. It succeeded, however, not by playing Union Carbide's game but by creating a new game. The company, Air Products, reconceptualized the business and built on-site industrial gas production facilities to service large industrial customers. Even though these production units cost more per unit of gas produced, that cost was offset by the elimination of transportation costs, especially the capital required to finance the large fleet of special rail cars and trucks.

In another example, in a two-year period in the late 1970s, Savin copiers won from Xerox 40% of the low-end (less than forty copies per minute) plain-paper copier market in the United States.[60] It did this by changing the entire business system, from initial technology choice through distribution and service. Where Xerox chose the dry xerography technology, which gave high copy quality, Savin chose liquid toner (which, although yielding only medium-quality copies, was more reliable and foolproof in comparison to Xerox's complex, failure-prone design). Savin's machine was built with standard components for lower costs and was sold and serviced by office supply dealers instead of leased through a company sales force. This not only increased Savin's cash flow but focused attention on the small account, which tended to get second-class treatment from Xerox salespeople, who were more interested in their large accounts.

The underlying principle behind Air Products's and Savin's successes is shown in Figure 12-11. Rather than choosing to compete in the same way as

[60] Roberto Buaron, "New Game Strategies," *The McKinsey Quarterly* (spring 1981), 24–40.

Figure 12-11 The strategic gameboard

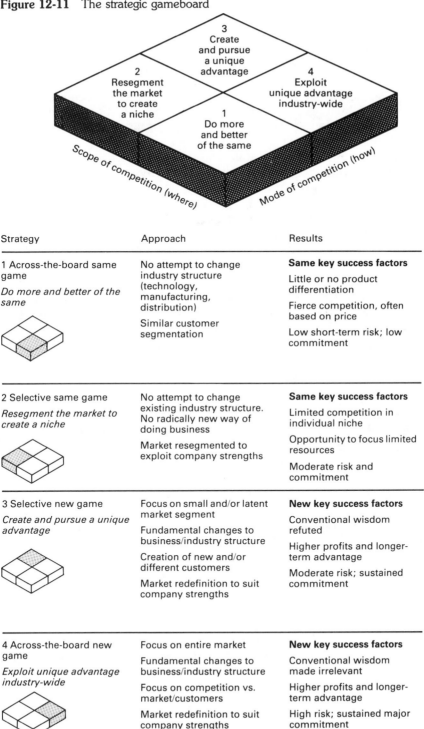

Strategy	Approach	Results
1 Across-the-board same game *Do more and better of the same*	No attempt to change industry structure (technology, manufacturing, distribution) Similar customer segmentation	**Same key success factors** Little or no product differentiation Fierce competition, often based on price Low short-term risk; low commitment
2 Selective same game *Resegment the market to create a niche*	No attempt to change existing industry structure. No radically new way of doing business Market resegmented to exploit company strengths	**Same key success factors** Limited competition in individual niche Opportunity to focus limited resources Moderate risk and commitment
3 Selective new game *Create and pursue a unique advantage*	Focus on small and/or latent market segment Fundamental changes to business/industry structure Creation of new and/or different customers Market redefinition to suit company strengths	**New key success factors** Conventional wisdom refuted Higher profits and longer-term advantage Moderate risk; sustained commitment
4 Across-the-board new game *Exploit unique advantage industry-wide*	Focus on entire market Fundamental changes to business/industry structure Focus on competition vs. market/customers Market redefinition to suit company strengths	**New key success factors** Conventional wisdom made irrelevant Higher profits and longer-term advantage High risk; sustained major commitment

existing competitors, both chose to compete in new ways. There is a different logic and a different thinking required in the formulation of strategy, depending on whether you are playing the same-game or the new-game approach:

- Same-game thinking is deductive and analytical. It takes the existing environment and business system as given. It seeks to optimize within those constraints by identifying and targeting particular segments and shaping approaches to those segments.
- New-game thinking is intuitive and opportunistic. In its quest for new combinations, it looks for ways to change the environment, redefine the business system, or reshape market behavior to fit the company's strengths.[61]

Strategists learn to think in terms of the business system and regularly challenge the assumptions of even their own system. They look for new operations technology that could change existing cost structures, view head-on battles between major competitors as opportunities to do things differently, examine changes in the environment for differential effect on competitors, test every new technology for its ability to challenge the existing order, and see the excellence that present industry leaders demonstrate in implementing the existing system as vulnerabilities to be capitalized on.

SUMMARY

Good strategies seldom just appear. Strategy is as much a function of the process by which it gets created as it is of the inherent constraints and opportunities that exist in the environment. This chapter outlined the key conceptions of the content of strategy, strategy formulation, and the thought processes used in the creation of strategy.

The key differentiation is between the normative model of strategy and those models constructed on the observation of actual behavior. While the normative approach contributes to a comprehensive approach to understanding the strategy-making process, it has its drawbacks. Chief among them is that it is seldom observed in practice. In the so-called real world, the process is nonlinear and recursive, its goals are broader than simply maximizing the economic value of the firm, and it resembles more of a trial-and-error learning process than an intellectual exercise. The hallmark of real-world strategy is its proactive stance—its will to make the world into a shape that suits it rather than the other way around.

Thinking strategically has three components: analytical, competitive, and strategic. Good strategists do not necessarily need a formal strategy-planning system, but they do need those modes of thinking. All three can be learned and better strategy created as a result.

---

[61] Buaron, "New Game Strategies."

13

EVALUATING, VALUING, AND IMPLEMENTING STRATEGY

A good strategy has three characteristics: (1) Its actions can be put into effect, (2) the strategy works as planned, and (3) the strategy results translate into economic rewards for the company. The problem is to determine the probability that these things will happen *before* the strategy is adopted. This final chapter is about assessing the probability that a strategy will work. It discusses evaluating strategy, valuing strategy, and implementing strategy.

EVALUATING STRATEGY

In chapter 1 of this book, two criteria were discussed for evaluating strategy: effectiveness and efficiency. Effectiveness was defined as the answer to the question, "Will it work, will it enable us to reach our objective?" Efficiency, on the other hand, took effectiveness as a given and asked, "Is it the most cost-effective method of achieving the objective?" Effectiveness is the dominant criterion of the two, but both questions need to be answered. We begin by examining objectives, since effectiveness makes sense only in the light of some given set of objectives.

Strategy Objectives

In chapter 1, we defined objectives to be the concrete, measurable, and time-related achievements necessary to reach the goals of the organization. For profit-seeking firms, the goals are profitability and competitive advantage, since both are necessary for the continued existence of the organization. As we have defined them, goals are open ended, so one can never truly achieve them. Can one ever have enough profit or be truly secure? Objectives are what we measure to tell us how we are performing in reaching those goals.[1] It is assumed that such

---

[1] The terminology of objectives and goals is confused in the literature. Some authors would reverse the meanings used here. See, for example, Peter Lorange and Richard F. Vaneil, *Strategic Planning Systems* (Englewood Cliffs, NJ: Prentice-Hall, 1977), p. 5.

things as market share, cash flow, and the like are good measures of progress toward goals.

The choice of objectives is a critical one. It is critical first because objectives differ in their information content; they each measure different underlying phenomena relative to reaching the firm's goals. The objective(s) chosen need to reflect desired progress. Second, since managers tend to work to achieve that which is measured (especially if compensation is tied to quantifiable measures of performance), then the measures chosen will drive managerial behavior to reach the objective. The choice of an incorrect objective, in other words, will result in incorrect strategies and actions. The following discussion of possible objectives highlights their appropriateness for different situations.[2]

Measures of Competitiveness. The key competitiveness measure is *market share*. Market share tells how the firm's offering is doing relative to the offerings of competitors. A loss in market share indicates either a loss in relative perceived value or a failure of the firm's relative ability to deliver that value to customers. Either way, in a biological sense, losses in market share raise questions about the continued viability of the offering since, by definition, it means competitors' offerings are being chosen over the firm's offering. A second point concerns whether market share is measured in revenues or in units. Since needs are measured in units (the share of individuals, households, businesses, or other consumption units), many would argue that unit market share is the better measure of long-run competitive position. For example, an increase in revenue market share together with a decrease in unit market share is a mixed signal which could indicate a long-term deterioration in relative position.

In contrast to market share, *growth* as an objective contains less information about competitive position within a market. In comparison with other measures, however, it can provide useful information. At the product market level, growth measures indicate the relative importance of the category in the overall hierarchy of consumption needs. A market that is growing more slowly than the economy is actually shrinking in relative terms. At the business or firm level, growth also measures the relative ability of the firm to perform in meeting society's needs. Firms that are growing faster than GNP or population are more effective in meeting society's needs than those that are not.

There are many other types of objectives that measure a strategy's competitive effectiveness before it is demonstrated in market share or some other summary measure. One key objective which is emerging from the increasing acceptance of the quality concept and the drive to become market driven is *customer satisfaction*.[3] Since satisfaction explicitly and implicitly measures the

---

[2] For a good discussion of the broad issues with respect to objectives, especially as applied to not-for-profit organizations, see William E. Rothschild, *Putting It All Together: A Guide to Strategic Thinking* (New York: AMACOM, 1976), chapter 10. Another source is in David A. Aaker, *Strategic Market Management*, 2nd ed. (New York: John Wiley & Sons, 1988), chapter 8.

[3] For an understanding of the implications of being market driven, see George S. Day, *Market Driven Strategy* (New York: Free Press, 1990), chapter 14.

performance of a firm and its offerings in comparison with competitive alternatives in creating value for customers, it is a direct measure of a strategy's success.

Other objectives may be even more competitive in nature—the acceptance by competitors of the firm's new entry, a competitor's withdrawal from a market, or the reduction of excessive promotional efforts by competitors are some of the objectives that may be set for a strategy.[4] Strategists need to be explicit about their objectives with respect to competitive behavior.

Measures of Efficiency. Except for absolute profits, most measures of profitability such as return on sales (ROS) or gross margin percentage measure the efficiency with which the firm is able to convert revenues into profits.[5] Alone, however, neither ROS nor gross margin have much informational content; informational content almost always depends on historical or competitive comparisons. Cash flow, on the other hand, does not need comparisons. It is a measure of the business's ability to generate revenues in excess of the capital investments necessary to support them. At the business or product level, such measures are often used since the variables that contribute are typically within management's control.

Measures that reflect the utilization of resources such as return on investment (ROI), return on capital (ROC), return on equity (ROE), or any of their variations are subject to considerable debate. The traditional concerns have held that these objectives are more useful at the corporate level than at the business or product level. The reason for this is that only at the corporate level is there full control of the major decisions that affect both the numerator and denominator of the ratio. More recently the concern has been that the measures themselves are flawed approximations of the concept of economic return. Second, the use of traditional accounting data introduces error into measurement to the point that they do not accurately measure that which they purport to. (The section on valuing strategy later in this chapter expands on this discussion.)

Measuring the Strategy[6]

"Will it work?" is the key question underlying a strategy. This discussion explores the four key criteria, shown in Table 13-1, which help the strategist address that question: fit with the environment, consistency within the strategy,

---

[4] There is some question as to the usefulness of the setting of objectives with respect to the behavior of competitors. One strategist's firm, for example, was adamant that all strategy objectives be attainable solely as the result of the firm's own actions and not depend in any way on competitors' behavior. A good strategy in its terms was one that could succeed regardless of what competitors did. This may be an extremely conservative view.

[5] Return on sales is equal to net income divided by sales expressed as a percentage. It may be expressed either as pre- or posttaxes or interest, depending on the situation. Gross margin percentage is much the same except that none of the firm's fixed or overhead costs are deducted. Gross margin is often defined as the amount available to pay for overhead and profits.

[6] The key ideas in this discussion are found in Seymour Tilles, "How to Evaluate Corporate Strategy," *Harvard Business Review*, 41, no. 4 (July-August 1963), 11–121; and Richard Rumelt, "The Evaluation of Business Strategy," in William F. Glueck, ed., *Business Policy and Strategic Management*, 3rd ed. (New York: McGraw-Hill, 1980), pp. 359–367.

TABLE 13-1   *Four Key Questions in Assessing Strategy*

Does the strategy fit the changing environment?
  A good strategy addresses the real needs in the marketplace, both current and future, and does so better than
  do competitors' offerings. It takes account of trends in the industry value chain both up- and downstream and
  fits with the economic, social, and political environments.

Is the strategy internally consistent?
  Good strategies have actions that are mutually reinforcing and produce the desired competitive advantage. The
  objectives of the strategy match the objectives set for the managers who will implement the strategy, and the
  achievement of those objectives will bring the desired competitive advantage.

Does the strategy fully exploit the firm's resources and distinctive competencies?
  The best strategy is one which gets the most out of what the firm has. Not only does the firm have the resource
  necessary to implement the strategy, but the strategy is built around the business's unique competencies so
  others cannot easily duplicate the advantage.

Are the strategy's risks consistent with its rewards?
  Good strategies take good risks—risks that avoid creating vulnerability beyond the ability of the business to
  control; they hedge financial risks and avoid strategic risk. Good strategies estimate risk dynamically, estimating that which emerges beyond competitors' first countermoves.

feasibility of the strategy in terms of its resource needs, and risks to which the strategy exposes the business.

Environmental Consistency.   The first criterion of any strategic option is "Does it address the changes in the environment?" This question is concerned with the issue of fit or suitability. A good strategy fits the existing and future environment and demonstrates that it can create or maintain competitive advantage in that environment. The evaluation needs to address the width of the environmental conditions under which the strategy is expected to work— whether the strategy will work only within a narrow range of conditions or in a wide range of environments. A strategy dependent on low energy prices, for example, needs to specify the upper limit of prices under which the strategy will work and be tested against conditions such as prevailed during the Arab Oil Embargo from 1973 to 1974 or following the Iraqi invasion of Kuwait in 1990.

Since the environment also contains competitors, the question of fit and suitability requires a similar test of the width of competitive actions under which the strategy will work. In this endeavor, there is no methodology for guaranteeing that all possible competitive actions can be forecast. Of all the issues that confront the strategist, this is the most crucial yet is least amenable to objective verification. The weakness of this testing lies in the assumption of economic rationality on the part of competitors. Since economic rationality is in the eye of the beholder, actions that appear irrational and uneconomic to the strategist (and which are therefore discounted or not analyzed) may look eminently reasonable to a competitor with its back to the wall.

This highlights that the issue of fit hinges on the validity of the assumptions made about the future environment. King suggests a strategy for dealing with assumptions that is simple and useful.[7] He suggests that they be plotted along the two dimensions of certainty and importance, as depicted in Figure 13-1. Assumptions located in the upper right quadrant (labeled A)—those that are relatively important and highly certain—are the bedrock assumptions of the strategy. Those located in the upper left quadrant (labeled B) must be carefully assessed for their impact, and alternative strategies need to be developed for them.

Two methods may be used to handle the uncertain but important assumptions. The *contingency approach* builds a basic strategy based on both the A and B assumptions but then formulates contingency strategies that will be considered should one or more of the B assumptions prove invalid. The *dialectic approach* involves the development of a feasible counterstrategy to the basic strategy. King suggests that the counterstrategy be based on the bedrock assumptions (A) and counterassumptions (directly opposite assumptions) for the B assumptions previously used. This provides a plan and a counterplan. He suggests that the usefulness of this approach is not actually to choose between the two but to aid the search for some combined strategy.

Tough-minded strategists list the assumptions underlying every facet of their strategies and continually test them for their validity. Good strategy documents continually key every number and statement of fact to its source so the testing can be continual. Data which purport to describe competitors is especially prone to error. One syndrome is to overestimate competitors' capabilities by ascribing to them the theoretical potential linked to their technology and market position, while underestimating the full potential of the analyst's own firm because the analyst is aware of the reality (and the warts) of its performance.

Internal Consistency. An internally consistent strategy is one whose actions (1) reinforce one another, (2) fit with the thrust of the competitive advantage they are to produce, and (3) match the objectives set for the strategy and those by which its managers will be evaluated. For example, a strategy which calls for an increase in both the number of new products and an across-the-board increase in product quality is not reinforcing operationally; the actions do not reinforce each other. In most manufacturing or operations systems, the two are traditionally opposites—a high rate of new product introduction stretches most organizations' ability to control quality. Similarly, reducing R&D expenses does not fit the thrust of a strategy calling for leapfrogging competitors' product performance. The explanation that R&D will work smarter and still produce product performance improvements in spite of its budget reductions is a fallacy. If that were the case, R&D would have already produced the leapfrogging product performance called for by the strategy.

While obvious to an outsider, such inconsistencies in objectives regularly

---

[7] William R. King, "Strategic Issue Management," in William R. King and David I. Cleland, eds., *Strategic Management and Planning Handbook* (New York: Van Nostrand Reinhold Company, 1987), pp. 252–264.

Figure 13-1 Assessing strategic assumptions

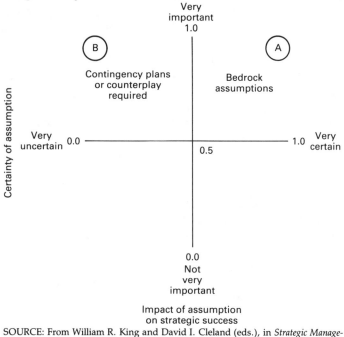

SOURCE: From William R. King and David I. Cleland (eds.), in *Strategic Management and Planning Handbook.* Copyright © 1987 by Van Nostrand Reinhold. Reprinted by permission of the publisher.

creep into strategies. Jack Welch, chairman and CEO of General Electric, sees this as the result of organizations not fostering candor. To him, candor is "facing reality, seeing the world as it is rather than as you wish it were."[8] He is trying to instill that virtue in GE, to get managers to see and speak about reality rather than what they think their bosses want. It is hard to tell the Emperor that he has no clothes on.

The more difficult inconsistency is between a strategy and either its stated measurable objectives or those by which its managers are evaluated. Many strategies seemingly call for positive improvements in all measures of performance—the objectives call for increasing share and cash flow simultaneously, increasing R&D and ROS in the same period, and so on. In most industries and theoretically, such objectives require trade-offs of one for the other. The actions which increase share, for example, are opposite of those which increase cash flow.[9] Share increases come from investing in additional sales and advertising efforts, broadening distribution, adding performance to products, and increasing inventories and working capital, all of which require

---

[8] Quoted in Noel Tichy and Ram Charan, "Speed, Simplicity, Self-Confidence: An Interview with Jack Welch," *Harvard Business Review,* 67, no. 5 (September-October 1989), p. 113.

[9] For empirical work which demonstrates these trade-offs, see Terence A. Oliva, Diana L. Day, and Wayne S. DeSarbo, "Selecting Competitive Tactics: Try a Strategy Map," *Sloan Management Review,* 28, no. 3 (spring 1987), 5–15.

cash expenditures in advance of the subsequent sales and share increase. Mathematically such measures reduce cash flow.

Mismatches between strategies and the measures used to evaluate managers are similarly frequent. One manager, for example, was implementing a strategy which called for long-term market development in which the task was to obtain acceptance of the product across a number of high value-added segments and applications. This required a high level of technical support and the trading off of volume for product variety in the manufacturing operation. However, the manager's compensation plan—standard for the company—made compensation a function of traditionally defined profitability. Instead of the defined strategy, which would have significantly lowered the manager's income, he concentrated on earnings (his and the product's) by reducing technical service and by focusing on a few high-volume products. To have done otherwise would have involved a voluntary and significant sacrifice of his own well-being for that of the company, not a rational choice by most definitions.[10]

Feasibility. There are really two questions here. The first is the traditional, "Do we have the resources necessary to implement the strategy?" The second question asks instead, "Does the strategy fully exploit the resources and distinctive competencies the firm possesses?" We will address the traditional question first.

There are three resources most frequently identified as critical to a strategy: money, competence, and physical resources. Of the three, money is the most flexible and, in many ways, the least constraining. Money can be used to support any kind of strategy, whereas physical and competence resources are area specific. An electrical engineer skilled in the design of computer memories cannot easily be used in support of a fashion strategy in the junior sportswear clothing business; a steel plant cannot be used as a supermarket. Cash (or debt capacity), however, can serve any strategy.

Money is (or should be) the least constraining resource in the firm. One philosophy states that, if the opportunity is sufficiently attractive, there are always sources of money for it. The firm may have to share control or profits, lease facilities, or pledge revenues to obtain the funding, but the financing can be found for attractive strategies. This is not to say that cash is not or should not be a constraint that may force the strategist to limit his or her ambitions; simply that it is less constraining than competence or facilities.

Competence, that combination of know-how incorporated into individuals and organizations, is the most constraining of a firm's resources. There are three questions in this regard:

- *Has the organization demonstrated that it has the abilities and special competencies called for by the strategy?* Note that the question specifies *demonstrated*, not *possesses*.

---

[10] The example is not unusual. See, for example, the illustrations in Steven Kerr, "On the Folly of Rewarding A, While Hoping for B," *Academy of Management Journal*, 18, no. 4 (December 1975), 769–783.

Many organizations possess very bright and intelligent people who are theoretically capable of accomplishing a wide range of activities. This capability is vastly different, however, from the demonstrated ability to run a rapidly changing fashion business or, conversely, a low-cost commodity business. Too many businesses state, "Our people can accomplish anything" and embark on strategies that prove them wrong.

- *Has the organization demonstrated the coordinative and integrative skills called for by the strategy?* Beyond the individual skill level is an organizational-level competence that involves the knitting together of disparate skills, functions, and geographic locations to create the coherent actions that implement the thrust of a strategy. Strategies that require different kinds of integration or response rates from those the business has demonstrated need to be carefully assessed.

- *Does the strategy challenge and motivate key personnel?* Key personnel are one of any organization's distinctive resources. If they are unmoved or unconvinced by a strategy, then the organization is underutilizing the resources and creating a situation in which the strategy will not likely get the support it needs. Any strategy which underestimates its need for managerial commitment to its goals and methods will fail.

The third component of feasibility concerns the applicability of the firm's physical facilities and assets. Many strategies are twisted by the apparent need to use existing assets whose value to the thrust of the strategy is simply tangential. Assets have little inherent value except as they are able to provide earnings or unique locational advantages not available to competitors.

In many ways, the most interesting question in the feasibility area is whether the strategy exploits the firm's distinctive competencies—those things the firm has more and better of than competitors. The problem with the environmental fit approach to strategy is that the ideal strategies created by looking outward seldom fit the firm's competencies as well as they do market needs. As a result, the firm all too often tries to change itself and to acquire competencies different from those it possesses. It is far more difficult to build or acquire competencies than it is to buy physical assets. Strategists evaluating strategy, therefore, need continually to ask the question, "Does the strategy center on the firm's distinctive competencies?" A strategy which does so only tangentially is as infeasible as one for which the firm lacks the finances or skills.

Risk and Vulnerability.   Risks are the firm's assessments that any given outcome might happen; vulnerability is the consequence of that occurrence. The risks inherent in any given strategy can be assessed through an analysis of the importance and certainty of the key assumptions on which it is based, as described earlier in Figure 13-1.

Two key risk elements in the strategy arena are (1) the uncertainty surrounding the continued availability of key resources critical to the strategy, and (2) the duration of the commitment inherent in the strategy. Key to many savings and loan and real estate developers' strategies in the 1980s was the value of the properties on which they lent and borrowed. The overbuilding and subsequent slump caused many, including the highly visible Donald Trump, to fail because of the severe reduction in the value of their assets, which had been the source of the financial resources they needed to carry out their strategies. Any analysis of strategy needs to examine rigorously the factors that could lead to a withdrawal or disappearance of the resources critical to the strategy. This caution extends to the human element. Businesses built on the unique creative or personal leadership talents of individuals are especially vulnerable.

Strategies which take a long time to pay off are especially risky. As analyzed in chapter 1, slow-to-be-realized strategies are vulnerable to changes in the fundamental environmental factors that favored the strategies at their inception. What started out as a good bet in year 1 can easily turn out to resemble a crapshoot in the changed environment of five or ten years later. Electrical and communications utilities with their long lead-time capital projects are one type of firm that must be able to deal with such risks. Other industries with long construction or design and development horizons are similarly affected. Boeing and others in the commercial airframe industry have had to commit to development projects of long durations, the success of which depend on favorable economic environments for their airline customers in the future.

But it is not the risk itself which is important, it is the consequences of the undesirable result. This is the real concept of vulnerability. The consequences can be financial and/or strategic. On the financial front, the size of the amount at risk is, of course, a paramount concern. Perhaps equal in importance to size is the amount at risk relative to the firm's total resources. A sum generally agreed to be large in absolute size (e.g., $500 million) could be lost and not cripple a GE, Exxon, or IBM as it would most other firms.

The consequences must be examined in a dynamic sense, also. In rapidly growing markets, the analysis must include not only the initial amount but the size of the follow-on investments that need to be made to maintain position. A market growing at 30% or 40% per year requires the ability to commit to grow the firm's productive capacity similarly (and inventories and working capital) just to hold share.[11] A second, nonfinancial consequence in such a situation is that the market which was of low interest to the biggies because of its initial small size becomes more interesting to them as it grows, just when the needed financial commitments begin to stretch those in the market from the beginning. Not all firms in such situations are able to be acquired. In many instances, the superior resources of the larger firms enable them to better serve the now larger market and to outcompete the pioneers.

Equal in importance to the financial risks are the strategic risks. Firms that sell through channels (e.g., a consumer packaged goods company like P&G or Pillsbury) are successful in gaining trace acceptance of their new products and strategies in part because of their past successes. A failed strategy or product weakens their ability to gain the acceptance they need in the future. In industrial or business markets, a similar process is at work among a company's direct customers. A visible strategic failure gives customers cause to question the firm's

---

[11] The 30% or 40% growth is on a constantly increasing base, therefore magnifying the effect.

abilities at the same time as it gives competitors the courage to challenge it in the future. That is the meaning of vulnerability.

VALUING STRATEGY

The ultimate measure of a strategy in economic terms is its financial consequences. In financial terminology, the goal is to maximize shareholder value. That is the focus of this discussion. Remember, however, that the creation of shareholder value rests first on the creation of competitive advantage, which provides for profitability and growth into the future, as shown in Figure 13-2. The ability to measure those three concepts accurately, however, becomes more difficult as one moves from the level of competitive advantage up to the level of shareholder value.

The underlying reasons for this increasing difficulty are based in both practical and theoretical concerns. Figure 13-3 shows the three main sources of error in valuing strategies. The first, incorrect assumptions, was discussed earlier in this chapter. The concern here is practical—there is a limit to the accuracy of any forecast, especially one based on achieving strategic change in competitive relationships. Biased judgments on the part of managers, the second source of error, are discussed in Exhibit 13-1. This is also a practical issue based in the recognition that there are limits to human judgment.[12]

The third source of error lies in the choice of economic evaluation methodologies used to evaluate the effect of the strategy on shareholder value. The problem here is theoretical and practical. Simply stated, the issue concerns the choice of techniques which best match the theoretical concept of shareholder value and the practical concerns of obtaining the data to implement those techniques. In approaching this issue, we first discuss the theoretical issues encountered in the use of such traditional measures as earnings, earnings growth, return on investment (ROI), and return on equity (ROE). Next, we describe two methodologies which better fit the theoretical construct of shareholder value.

Traditional Measures of Profitability[13]

Economic Returns versus Book Income.   Business strategies have as their goal the creation of economic returns for shareholders. These returns are equal to the cash dividends the business distributes plus the increase in the value of the company (measured as the increase in share price) that results from the strategy. In more technical terms, this would be described as the discounted cash-flow

---

[12] For further insight into this issue, see Jean-Claude Larreche and Reza Moinpour, "Managerial Judgment in Marketing: The Concept of Expertise," *Journal of Marketing Research*, XX (May 1983), 110–121.

[13] The following discussion of traditional measures of profitability and the shareholder value approach follows that found in Alfred Rappaport, *Creating Shareholder Value* (New York: Free Press, 1986), chapters 2 and 3. For additional insight into the issues of valuing strategy, see Patrick Barwise, Paul R. Marsh, and Robin Wensley, "Must Finance and Strategy Clash?" *Harvard Business Review*, 67, no. 5 (September-October 1989), 45–57.

Figure 13-2   The hierarchy of objectives in evaluating strategic results

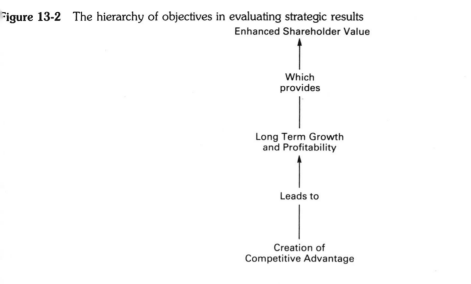

Enhanced Shareholder Value

↑

Which
provides

Long Term Growth
and Profitability

↑

Leads to

Creation of
Competitive Advantage

(DCF) return (also known as the internal rate of return) for an investment. This is simply this year's cash flow plus the change in value of the asset or business over the year, divided by the value at the beginning of the year. The change in the present value of the business is the net of its present value at the end of the year minus the present value at the beginning of the year.

$$\text{DCF return} = \frac{\text{cash flow} + \text{change in present value}}{\text{present value at beginning of year}}$$

The significance of this number lies in its relationship to the business's cost of capital. If the DCF return is greater than the cost of capital, then the firm has created economic value for its owners.

Accounting income, often termed *book income,* is a different entity altogether.

Figure 13-3   The sources of error in valuing strategy options

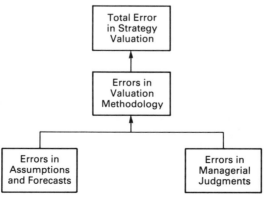

Total Error
in Strategy
Valuation

↑

Errors in
Valuation
Methodology

↑

Errors in
Assumptions
and Forecasts

Errors in
Managerial
Judgments

Book income is the sum of net cash flow plus the investments made in real capital and working capital minus depreciation and other noncash charges, such as deferred income taxes.[14] This number does not purport to measure the value of a business in the economic sense—as an asset capable of generating a stream of income in the future. Rather, it is the result of a commonly agreed on set of accounting conventions.[15]

These conventions can yield a wide variety of results depending on which are being used. The use of last-in, first-out (LIFO) versus first-in, first-out (FIFO) conventions for computing the cost of sales can yield widely varying book income figures. Depreciation, for example, is charged on the basis of a schedule, frequently on a straight-line method for book purposes (to show larger current earnings) and on an accelerated basis for tax purposes (to reduce current earnings and therefore the taxes due in the current period). Neither necessarily represents the actual economic value of the assets being depreciated. For these reasons, valuing the effect of a strategy in book income terms is as likely to reflect the accounting conventions used as it is the true economic value of the strategy option.

Economic Performance and ROI.   The result of the aforementioned difference in book income versus the concept of economic return is most pronounced in the use of ROI data to evaluate different courses of action. To begin with, ROI uses accounting data in its computation and is therefore subject to all of the aforementioned shortcomings (FIFO versus LIFO, depreciation schedules, and so on). Second, there is no single theoretically sound method for computing ROI. Instead, there is a wide variety of techniques for calculating ROI—some firms use gross book value of plant and equipment, others use it net of accumulated depreciation; some capitalize the value of leased assets in the investment base while others do not.

Research which has compared calculated ROI with DCF rate of returns (internal rate of returns) have concluded that ROI is not an accurate or reliable estimate of the DCF return.[16] At the base of this discrepancy is the length of the project and the company's treatment of depreciation. Since ROI is a single period measurement (another conceptual flaw in comparison to the concept of economic return), the ROI of any investment increases over time as the asset value is depreciated. Further, the ROI figure is subject to the firm's policies with respect to depreciation. Firms which capitalize more assets at the margin will have lower ROIs because the denominator will be larger than companies which tend to expense more investments, which reduces the size of the denominator.

---

[14] This definition is different from those to which the reader may be accustomed because it is stated in cash terms rather than sales revenues minus costs, etc. The result is the same.

[15] For a full explanation of this issue, see Franklin M. Fisher and John J. McGowan, "On the Misuse of Accounting Rates of Return to Infer Monopoly Profits," *American Economic Review*, 73, no. 1 (March 1983), 82–97.

[16] See Ezra Solomon, "Return on Investment: The Relations of Book-yield to True Yield," in *Research in Accounting Measurement* (Chicago: American Accounting Association, 1966), reprinted in Alfred Rappaport, *Information for Decision Making* (Englewood Cliffs, NJ: Prentice-Hall, 1982).

EXHIBIT 13-1

Sources of Bias in Managerial Judgments

In making strategy, the hard facts only go so far. Human judgment converts a set of hard data, assumptions, and forecasts into their implications for the future, and human creativity structures a response by which the firm intends to win in the predicted future environment. These subjective processes are a major component in the formulation and evaluation of strategy. If the processes or judgments are faulty, so too will be the strategy. Psychological research has studied how the general rules—called heuristics—we use to make such judgments can lead to persistent biases in our judgments.

The concept of *availability* describes the tendency for individuals to judge an event as likely or frequent if instances of it are easy to imagine or recall. However, availability is also affected by factors unrelated to the frequency of occurrence. Recent events, for example, tend to dominate strategic planning more than their relative frequency of occurrence would indicate simply because the organization is sensitive to them. An organization that has recently had cash-flow problems, for example, will carefully scrutinize strategic options for their cash-flow implications. In a reverse sense, the unavailability of a certain issue in managers' minds may mean that out of sight out of mind will rule.

Hindsight is a judgmental bias of which we all are aware. It is the tendency after an event has occurred to feel that the event was inevitable and should have been apparent in foresight. Because of this tendency, when we review past decisions we focus on the factor which "caused" the outcome and assign a higher probability that the event will occur again. We do this because we have "seen it work" in the past. After seeing a competitor turn an apparently minor scientific invention into a multimillion dollar business (like the Xerox copying machine), we make sure that such an opportunity does not escape our notice in the future and sink millions into attempting to commercialize what, in reality, turn out to be simply scientific curiosities.

Misunderstanding sampling and probabilities affects even the most scientific minded. Decision makers necessarily act on small and limited samples of past results and behavior. Studies of scientists have shown that they consistently overvalue, make biased judgments on the basis of a few initial data points; have undue confidence in early data trends; and rarely attribute a deviation from expectations to sampling variability. This lack of understanding can be critical to the strategist using the PIMS database, for example. The PIMS data set is a sample, after all, and one that is not random.

Confusing correlation and causality is another judgmental problem. There is a world of difference between correlation (knowledge of one variable enables a prediction of the other) and causality (one variable causes the other to occur). Most mathematical models used in forecasting are based more on correlation than causality. The user, however, may impute causality which does not exist.

EXHIBIT 13-1 (cont.)

Moreover, if one has some prior expectation about a relationship between two variables, one is likely to perceive some correlation that does not really exist. This tendency is termed *illusory correlation*.

In spite of (or in ignorance of) these judgmental biases, individuals are typically very confident about the judgments they make. The psychological basis for this unwarranted certainty seems to be people's insensitivity to the tenuousness of the assumptions on which their judgments are based. Such confidence is dangerous—it indicates that we often do not realize how little we know and how much additional information we need.

One simple example is to compare two companies (or business strategies) one R&D intensive and the other not R&D intensive. Since R&D is expensed even though economically its results are an asset on which the firm earns returns, the R&D-intensive firm will show a higher ROI than the non-R&D intensive, even though both may be earning identical economic rates of return. To use ROI either as a strategy objective or to evaluate the economic attractiveness of a strategy is to use a theoretically and practically flawed methodology.

Economic Return and ROE. While ROE is seldom used at the business level because of the difficulties involved in allocating debt to individual businesses or SBUs, it is frequently used at the corporate level.[17] In common with ROI, ROE shares all of the problems concerning the use of accounting data. During inflationary periods, for example, ROE is increased simply by the apparent increase which occurs in the turnover of the firm's assets, when inflated sales dollars are divided by the book value of assets and inventories acquired in preinflationary periods.

Further, ROE is responsive to the use of financial leverage—larger proportions of debt (invested at rates larger than the borrowing rate) add to income (the numerator) without adding to the denominator, thereby increasing ROE. Of course, at some point the addition of debt to the balance sheet increases the financial risk borne by the shareholders. ROE calculations make no provision for the absence or presence of risk. The ROE number for a highly leveraged and therefore risky business can be the same as for one which is more conservative in its use of debt and therefore less risky. The concept of economic returns, however, does incorporate risk. The economic value of two businesses with identical projected income streams but which differ in their inherent risk cannot

[17] $$ROE = \frac{\text{net income}}{\text{book value of stockholders' equity}}.$$

be the same. The business with the higher risk is simply worth less than the less risky.

Like ROI, therefore, using ROE as the measure of the value of a given business strategy is flawed. It does not account for the differences in risk among the strategy options and, even if it could, would still be based on all of the vagaries of accounting information.

Shareholder Value Approach

Business strategies should be evaluated by the economic returns they generate for stockholders. The evaluation of strategy options or alternatives begins with a comparison of each alternative's ability to develop and sustain competitive advantage. But since competitive advantage itself has no common unit of measurement, the comparison process measures instead the economics of the business affected by the competitive advantage. This discussion explains the process by which this economic comparison is made.

At the heart of the shareholder value approach to evaluating strategy is the use of cash flow rather than earnings or other accounting-based measures. Cash flow is a concept whose measurement is unambiguous, so the estimates of value are not distorted by the use of different accounting or depreciation techniques. The concept is to compute an initial shareholder value based on a continuation of the present strategy or other baseline measurement and to compare that value with one calculated for each strategy alternative.

Shareholder value equals the value of a business minus any debt that it has. The value of a business is simply the discounted present value of the cash flow expected from the business's future operations. This is usually separated into two components:

1. A period for which cash flows are explicitly forecast based on known and reasonably estimated data. This is typically the period in which the competitive value of the strategy is strongest as measured in growth and profitability. This is termed the *forecast period.*
2. The period following the forecast period, by which time the strategist expects the advantage gained by the strategy to have worn off but during which the business is expected to continue earning money at only a normal rate of return. The earnings during this period are termed the *residual value* of the business.

More explicitly, the value of the business is the present value of the cash flow during the forecast period, plus the residual value, plus or minus any debt or marketable securities held by the business. This requires the ability to estimate (1) cash flow from operations, (2) the cost of capital for the business, and (3) the residual value of the business beyond the forecast period.

Cash flow from operations is the difference between operating cash inflows and outflows. It is an easily calculable number which is driven by the sales level, the sales growth rate, operating profit margin, incremental fixed and working capital investment rates,[18] and the actual cash income tax rate. The formula is

> Cash flow = [(sales in prior year)(1 + sales growth rate)(operating profit margin)(1 − cash income tax rate)] − (incremental fixed plus working capital investment).

Once having calculated each year's cash flow, it is then discounted by the cost of capital, and these figures are then summed to arrive at the cumulative present value.

The competitive advantage of a strategy is captured in its ability to grow sales over the prior period and the operating profit margin it is able to create by its improved prices or lowered costs over the forecast period. The forecast period may be a relatively short three to five years or a longer five plus years, depending on the inherent design-manufacture-market and competitive reaction cycles in the business. Exhibit 13-2 suggests some ways of ensuring that these estimates and forecasts are realistic. Of course, increases in sales may require (or even be caused by) larger inventories and production or operating capacity, which are subtracted each year to produce the net cash flow.

Cost of capital is key in these analyses. At the simplest level, the cost of capital is the weighted average of the costs of the firm's debt and its equity capital. It is a measure of what the suppliers of capital expect to be paid for their investments and is the basis for the minimum acceptable rate of return that management should require on new investment proposals. Investments earning greater than the hurdle rate create value for shareholders; investments providing less than the cost of capital decrease shareholder value.

The cost of debt is generally accepted to be the cost of new debt to the firm, since what is to be financed is prospective, not past. To account for future inflation, the use of a long-term interest rate is advised. Estimating the cost of equity is more difficult since, unlike debt, there is no fixed or contractual rate owed shareholders. Since shareholders provide the risk capital to the firm, the cost of equity is thought of as being composed of a risk-free rate (assumed to be that being paid on long-term Treasury bonds) plus a risk premium.

The risk premium is what investors demand to absorb the risk of investment. It can be estimated by first calculating the market risk premium for equity in general (e.g., the expected rate of return on the S&P 500 stock index in excess of the risk-free rate) and the firm's individual systematic risk (as measured by its Beta coefficient):

> Risk premium = Beta (expected return on market − risk-free rate).

---

[18] These are the rates at which additional investments must be made in fixed assets (such as plant capacity) and working capital (increases in work-in-process and inventories) to support sales increases. The use of a fixed investment rate assumes that the capacity additions may be made continuously rather than in incremental steps. This assumption may not hold, and actual forecast sums for future capacity additions should be used whenever possible.

EXHIBIT 13-2

Testing Strategic Performance Forecasts

Numbers are one of the ways that strategy is evaluated. The numbers represent the units produced, units sold, revenues, costs, you name it. How can you tell if the strategist is cooking the numbers (i.e., making them up to look good)? Or if your own numbers are likely to be achieved? All are familiar with "hockey stick" forecasts—so called because the results graph looks like a hockey stick. "The results have been headed down, boss, but as soon as you approve my strategy they are going to angle up and head for the sky."

You can estimate the likelihood of achieving the numbers by comparing them to those achieved by others. If yours diverge too far from those projected by others, you may be fooling yourself. Three easy questions allow you to test the validity of your projections:

- How well do your projections match those created by knowledgeable industry watchers, analysts, and consultants?
- Are the specific external forces facing your firm and its internal characteristics such that it is reasonable to expect it to operate at the level of the industry?
- In the areas you forecast to outperform the industry, are you sure that your actions are sufficiently strong or the specific environment favorable enough to merit those results?

The Beta of a stock measures its riskiness relative to that of the market by comparing the volatility of its return in relation to that of a market portfolio. In addition to Betas based on a company's past performance, there are multiple factor econometric models which can be used to estimate future Betas.

Residual value is the value of the strategy (or business) attributable to cash flows that occur beyond the forecast period. The largest part of the value of many businesses lies well beyond what happens in the next five or even ten years. In fact, it has been estimated in a study of businesses in the PIMS database that more than one third had negative operating cash flows *before* interest expenses from 1970 to 1979.[19] Any strategy that calls for growth is likely to use cash in the short run to obtain the position that enables it to capture cash in the future.

The strategy's residual value depends first on the size it attains during the forecast period, and second on its competitive position at the end of that period. A business whose assets are technologically obsolete and whose presence in the

---

[19] Bradley T. Gale and Ben Branch, "Cash Flow Analysis: More Important Than Ever," *Harvard Business Review*, 59, no. 4 (July-August 1981), 131–136.

market is negligible at the end of the forecast period may have a residual value equal only to liquidation value. A strategy which brought a product line to technological and marketplace leadership, on the other hand, would be best valued as a going concern. The question is how to value that business.

Underlying the perpetuity method to be described here is the assumption that abnormal rates of return—returns above the cost of capital—are seldom sustained for long periods. As discussed in earlier chapters, few businesses can erect barriers to competitive entry sufficient to deter competition forever. The competition that excess returns attracts will drive returns down to the minimum acceptable rate—the cost of capital. What this means for the estimation of residual value is that the best estimate of earnings beyond the forecast period is that the business will earn no more than the cost of capital.

An important aspect of this assumption is that it is equivalent to saying that after the forecast period the business will invest in strategies whose net present value is, on average, zero. Period-by-period differences in cash flows therefore do not change the value of the business. The business can, of course grow, but as long as the additional investments are assumed to earn only the cost of capital the value of the business does not change. This sounds curious but makes sense if you remember that only investments made at rates of return in excess of the cost of capital increase the value of a business. This simplifying assumption makes calculating residual value easy.

The present value of a perpetuity is equal to its annual cash flow divided by the rate of return. Using this method, the residual value of a business is equal to dividing its cash flow by the cost of capital:

$$\text{Residual value} = \frac{\text{perpetuity cash flow}}{\text{cost of capital}}$$

This does not imply that future managers will not find or create strategic opportunities to invest at higher rates to increase the value of the business. It assumes only that the value of a present strategy is best measured by the size and position in which it leaves the business at the end of the forecast period.

The market-to-book ratio is an alternative technique for the computation of residual value.[20] In this approach, the residual value is the book value of the business at the end of the forecast period times an estimate of the market-to-book (M/B) ratio. The technique rests on the meaning that the market value of common stock has in economies with efficient capital markets. The assumption is that stock price is a consensus of the present value assigned by investors to the expected cash flow from present and future investments to be made by a firm. The argument is that the M/B ratio allows one to measure the economic and financial performance of the business (Is it earning in excess of its cost of cap-

---

[20] For a complete description of the methodology, see Arnoldo C. Hax and Nicholas S. Majluf, *Strategic Management: An Integrative Perspective* (Englewood Cliffs, NJ: Prentice-Hall, 1984), chapter 10.

ital?) as well as its competitive performance (Is its M/B ratio as good as its competitors in the same industry?).

There are two major concerns in using the M/B technique. The first is that book value is an accounting item, subject to all of the criticism of accounting numbers mentioned earlier. As one description puts it,

> When we refer to book value, we assume that all distortions induced by accounting rules have been corrected, mainly the ones produced by inflation and the charges of certain investments as expenditures in one period (most notably R&D and advertising).[21]

How this restatement is accomplished is not addressed. The second concern is the lack of market values for business units within firms as opposed to the M/B ratios of firms per se. There are several methods for estimating M/B ratios for business units which may offset this deficiency.[22] Since the conceptual heart of the technique lies in its belief in the ability of efficient markets to value firms' future earnings prospects, however, the use of non-market estimators of market value seems contradictory.

Using shareholder valuation techniques is accomplished by comparing the value of the forecasted strategy with the prestrategy value. The prestrategy value is the value of the business as it is, assuming that no additional value is created. That value is generally the residual value of the most recent period of historical data. However, the choice of the base case against which to compare strategy options is often as important as the techniques used, and it is not always clear that the most recent period is the best choice.

Hayes and Garvin give an example which illustrates the point.[23] In their story, two companies share the market in a price-sensitive industry. In the beginning, both use the same production processes and consequently have similar cost structures. A new manufacturing process, however, emerges which will reduce variable costs significantly. Each company goes through the ritual of calculating the value of the proposed new investment. Company A rejects the innovation as being insufficiently profitable, perhaps in part because it has a higher investment hurdle rate than Company B, which decides to buy the technology.

Once B has installed the new technology, it naturally proceeds to use its competitive advantage by competing aggressively for market share with lower prices. The new process, after all, does require high production volumes to achieve the lowest unit costs. Company A has a difficult time responding. Its now outdated production technology has higher costs, and the resulting lower profitability makes the business unattractive to management. Further, at its smaller market share the new technology makes even less sense than initially,

---

[21] Hax and Majluf, *Strategic Management*, p. 211.
[22] For a complete description, see Hax and Majluf, pp. 229–238.
[23] Robert H. Hayes and David A. Garvin, "Managing as If Tomorrow Mattered," *Harvard Business Review*, 60, no. 3 (May-June 1982), 71–74.

especially in light of the fact that it will take more than simply matching B's prices to win customers back. Every delay means more lost market share, but the numbers just do not add up. Company A is now stuck with an unprofitable business and only apparently unprofitable ways out.

Company A could be said to have gone wrong when it selected its base case. It compared the case of the new technology with that of the ongoing business, which was healthy. It took the last historical period's numbers, applied the perpetuity method, and found that the new technology did not create value. Had it compared either (1) the value of its adopting the technology while B did not or (2) the value of its business if B adopted the new technology and it did not, the answer would have been quite different. The question is also raised as to whether the analysis is still being performed correctly. Since the value of the business appears to be bottoming, perhaps nearing liquidation value (or salvage value, more likely, since the assets have little earning value as they stand), it may be that the additional investment may make economic sense by creating value for shareholders in comparison to the value destruction of the current strategy.

Valuing strategy is more an art form than a science. As discussed in Exhibit 13-3, the purpose of the valuation exercise is to try to understand what the economics of the strategy mean for the firm. The philosophy of the process is to see if under a reasonable set of assumptions (as reasonable as those under which other options are valued) the economic formula for the business is indeed capable of creating value. In other words, is the competitive advantage sufficiently advantageous?

IMPLEMENTING STRATEGY

The difference between intended strategy and realized strategy is well recognized in the literature.[24] As one observer noted in a *Fortune* magazine article,

> Consultants used to counter criticism of their concepts with what might be termed "the implementation problem." The strategy was perfectly good, they would say, the client just couldn't implement it. . . . For some folks, including some consultants, a small disturbing voice began to whisper, "Doesn't the fact that hardly anyone can carry it out say something about the value of the strategy?"[25]

For von Clausewitz, the military strategist mentioned in chapter 1, the slippage that occurred between the idea and the reality of what was achieved on the battlefield was due to "friction." That friction might have its source in the weather, the skills of field officers, the motivation of the troops, or even the

[24] Henry Mintzberg and Alexandra McHugh, "Strategy Formulation in an Adhocracy," *Administrative Science Quarterly*, 30, no. 2 (1985), 162.
[25] Walter Keichel, III, "Corporate Strategists Under Fire," *Fortune*, December 27, 1982, pp. 37 and 38.

EXHIBIT 13-3

The Philosophy of Valuing a Strategic Alternative

The process and philosophy underlying the economic analysis of strategic options eludes many people who see in it little more than cooking the numbers long enough to create a set of results that management will buy. Nothing could be further from the truth.

The purpose of economic analysis is to try to understand what the economics of the strategy mean for the firm. The philosophy of the process is to see if under a reasonable set of assumptions (as reasonable as those under which other options are valued) the economic formula for the business does create value for shareholders. To do this requires an evaluation of the economic advantages the competitive advantage provides. Will the strategy:

- create enough value to attract customers and convince them to buy a unit volume
- at a price sufficiently distant from variable cost that
- the resulting gross margin contribution will pay (after allowing for fixed costs) a rate of return higher than the risk-adjusted rate of return on the funds invested
- even after the inevitable worst-case competitive response occurs?

Key to the right approach to the process is understanding the importance and role of the three key sources of the numbers: (1) measured or researched values, (2) forecasts, and (3) assumptions. This bears on the probability of obtaining false positives (analysis shows a strategy to make money when it really won't) or false negatives (analysis shows a strategy to be not profitable when it would be). Given the tendency for strategists to seek best-case analyses, the probability of false positives is more likely. Negative results, therefore, are more likely to be real negatives than false negatives. In effect, this means that while a negative result is probably true, a positive result is most likely a maybe at best.

---

expectations of the strategist; the source mattered little to von Clausewitz because the lesson was clear: Only realized strategy can have any impact. The only good strategy, therefore, is one which can be realized and which works even though its implementation is only ordinary.

In this discussion, we will see the process by which strategies are translated into actions in the marketplace. In doing this, we will examine the general problem of relating the organization to the strategy. In addition, we will look at the issues involved in marketing implementation.

A Model of Strategy Implementation[26]

One way of looking at strategy is that a strategy decides what the business should look like in the future. In that framework, then, implementation is deciding how to get the business to look like you want it, given where the business is today. Two problems intervene in accomplishing this. The first is that any ongoing organization has adapted itself to the needs of the strategy it is currently pursuing. A new strategy, by definition, will require it to change in some manner. The second problem is that organizations are not simply mechanical transmission devices in which pulling a lever at one end causes a certain and predictable movement at the other end. Organizations are complex organisms composed of systems, structures, and people which combine to define their own unique structure.

Figure 13-4 presents one model useful in organizing the issue. The first element in the model, strategy formulation, is not only concerned with the right economic answer but also with the organization's ability to implement the strategy. As noted earlier in this chapter, a strategy needs to fit and to be feasible in terms of the organization and its capabilities. The second element in the model is the organization which is described in terms of its *culture, structure, human resources,* and *managerial processes.*

Culture is of overriding importance in implementing strategy. An organization's culture, just like a society's, sets the unwritten rules of what is important, what can be done, what will be done. The culture in an organization has a direct impact on how well and even if a particular strategy can be implemented.

Think about the kind of changes that AT&T and local telephone companies have had to go through over the course of the deregulation process. Since their businesses were first started, they have been highly service-oriented regulated utilities dedicated to treating all customers alike and to providing their customers what the company determined was good and economically rational for them. Deregulation's impact was probably felt more at the cultural level than at any other level in the organization. Engineers, scientists, and operating people uniformly found difficult the concept that customers could have the freedom to decide what kinds of services and equipment they wanted instead of the company deciding what kind they needed. "But what if what customers want is not what we know customers need?" they would ask again and again. The term *Ma Bell* indeed described the culture.

Clearly, a culture can inhibit the success of a particular strategy, as it may have in the telephone companies just described. Just as important, however, is that by recognizing and building on the strengths of an organization's culture a strategy can become even more potent. What is important is cultural awareness—being able to understand what the culture is, how well it matches

---

[26] The following discussion is built on the ideas contained in Paul J. Stonich, ed., *Implementing Strategy: Making Strategy Happen* (Cambridge, MA: Ballinger Publishing Company, 1982). For an expanded view of this issue, see Jay R. Galbraith and Robert K. Kazanjian, *Strategy Implementation: Structure, Systems, and Process,* 2nd ed. (St. Paul, MN: West Publishing Company, 1986).

Figure 13-4 Implementing strategy: the model

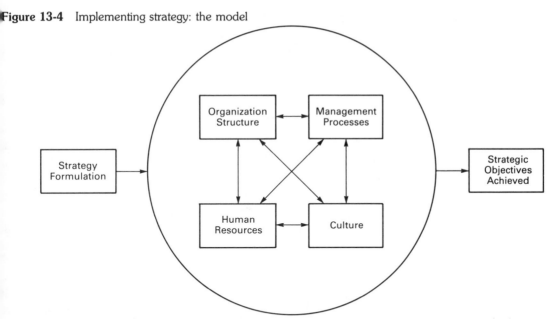

SOURCE: Paul J. Stonich, ed., *Implementing Strategy: Making Strategy Happen* (Cambridge, MA: Ballinger Publishing Company, 1982), p. xviii.

the existing strategy, and what aspects of it need to be considered before the new strategy can be implemented. Since culture plays such a central but unseen role in defining what an organization is to itself, changing it is difficult except when there is little choice, as in the telephone company case. Most managers would be advised to "manage around" cultural impediments to strategy.

Structure is more amenable to change than is culture. It is formal, it is visible, it is nominally rational in its basis, it was invented and can therefore be reinvented as necessary. Structure, because of its visibility, was the earliest focus of those studying strategy implementation. The earliest work in this regard is Alfred Chandler's 1962 book titled *Strategy and Structure.*[27] His study of seventy firms' strategies and their structures led him to conclude that structure is dictated by strategy. While that statement is still considered to be the norm, it should also be recognized that structure also affects strategy. Once a primary structure is chosen, its nature constrains future decisions at the operating level.[28]

As a result, trying to gain the essential fit between the implementation needs of the strategy and the structure is neither automatic nor easily accomplished. The basic character of the different business functions fosters ingrained behaviors that are not easily changed. According to Hammermesh, "Manufacturing's drive for standardization, marketing's for customer responsiveness, engineering's for innovation, and finance's for cost control are all very natural functional

---

[27] Cambridge, MA: MIT Press, 1962.
[28] For an extended discussion of this point, see Lawrence G. Hrebiniak and William F. Joyce, *Implementing Strategy* (New York: Macmillan Publishing Company, 1984), pp. 87–91.

postures that extend deep into each functional area."[29] These functional biases must be overcome for a strategy to be achieved.

The traditional view is that structural decisions are made after the strategy is formulated and selected. Following the principle of minimum intervention, for example, organization theorists would suggest that managers should change only what is necessary and sufficient to produce an enduring solution to the strategic problem being addressed.[30] However, it has been noted by others that by the time the new structure is fine tuned, it is likely that another, newer strategy will be on the way. Some advocate, therefore, that structural issues should be thought of in more dynamic terms—that organization structure issues be part of the strategy formulation process from the beginning.[31]

The choice of formal structure for an organization is considered to be a contingency decision—one that depends on the exact balance needed between specialization and coordination. The three key forms—centralized functional, divisional, and matrix—are linked to the key variables which determine their selection in Table 13-1.

Human resources are the third part of the organization that needs analysis. The issue of human resources is not always of concern in strategy but, when it is, it can be critical. For example, as shown in Figure 13-5, small changes at the margin of the existing strategy base of the business probably do not require new human resource skills. A business with a basic strategy of being a differentiated product producer serving broad markets could begin to shift to a focus strategy by adding segment-specific products without needing skills it did not already possess. That would not be the case if that same firm were required by environmental changes to become more commodity-like in its approach to the market. That change is large in comparison to the prior strategy and does require a different set of skills in all areas of the business.

The question of how to acquire those skills depends on the rate of change. A "make" strategy, for example, is suitable only in those instances when the change in skill requirements is minor and not immediate. Education or training programs to grow the right skill base over time can provide the talent needed. In situations where the change is great, however, internal development programs will not work because the existing skills do not currently exist in the organization. It is difficult for individuals in a commodity-oriented business, for example, to learn how to pursue a differentiated product strategy without a model to follow. In such situations, a "buy" or convert strategy is needed. Buying talent from outside the firm has advantages in terms of getting the right skill base quickly but, depending on the organization, outside hires are a high risk in terms of fitting in or being accepted. Converting existing managers via training and consultation can be accomplished but has its own set of problems. It is difficult in three or four days of training to change someone whose whole

[29] Richard G. Hammermesh, *Making Strategy Work: How Senior Managers Produce Results* (New York: John Wiley & Sons, 1986), p. 45.
[30] Hrebiniak and Joyce, *Implementing Strategy*, pp. 8 and 9.
[31] This is the view put forward by Stonich, *Implementing Strategy: Making Strategy Happen*, chapter 3.

TABLE 13-1   *Strategic Conditions, Strategy, and Primary Structure*

STRATEGIC CONDITIONS, PRODUCT AND MARKET FACTORS, AND OTHER KEY VARIABLES	STRATEGIES	PRIMARY STRUCTURE
I Commodity-type products Small numbers of products and services High degree of production and market relatedness Need to focus on efficiency criteria, cost reduction, or economies of scale	Volume expansion (horizontal growth) Geographical expansion	Functional organization (process specialization) Central administrative unit

II   As in I above, plus
 	
  High stability or low demand volatility for products
 	
  Prospect of adding new products with high production or technological relatedness
 	
  High proportion of potential new productive capacity being absorbed by existing or new products
	As in I above, plus
	
	  Vertical integration
		As above in I, plus
		
		  More sophisticated operating structures

III Large numbers of products or services Low production relatedness Low market relatedness Excess productive capacity (distinctive competence) Slack resources Need to reduce coordination costs	Product diversification	Multidivisional organization (purpose specialization by product, customer, or geography) Strategic business units (discrete units, highly self-contained) Holding companies and conglomerates
IV Need for dual focus—products and functions Scarcity of resources, with opportunity for cross-fertilization or synergy across products or projects High uncertainty, complexity, and interdependence, increasing need to process information and make decisions more efficiently	As in I, II, or III above	Matrix organization

SOURCE: Reprinted with permission of Macmillan Publishing Co. from *Implementing Strategy* by Lawrence Hrebiniak and William Joyce. Copyright © 1984 by Macmillan Publishing Co.

background has focused on cost reduction as the route to profitability to focus on revenue enhancement instead.

Changing existing managerial styles and skills can therefore be as frustrating as attempting to change an organization's culture. As a result, there has been quite a bit of interest in matching specific managerial styles with specific strategies. Some of the descriptors used to define different sets of managerial skills include such terms as *growers, caretakers,* and *undertakers; pioneer, conqueror, level-*

Figure 13-5   Four types of strategic changes dictating different approaches to filling human resource needs

Large	*Type A: Slow Overhaul* Situation: The way the firm conducts business will change greatly, but over a long period of time.	*Type B: Rapid Overhaul* Situation: The change to an extremely different way of doing business must be undertaken quickly.
Small	*Type C: Steady at the Helm* Situation: The nature of the business is relatively predictable and stable. Most environmental change is transitory or evolving slowly.	*Type D: Full Speed Ahead* Situation: A very fluid and competitive environment, but one in which the firm's lines, resources, and tactics are frequently adjusted.

Difference from Previous Strategy (vertical axis label)

Long   Short

Time Frame for Change

SOURCE: Paul J. Stonich, ed., *Implementing Strategy: Making Strategy Happen* (Cambridge, MA: Ballinger Publishing Company, 1982), p. 72.

headed, administrator, economizer, and *insistent diplomat; entrepreneur, sophisticated market manager,* and *opportunistic milker.*[32] There is some evidence to suggest that these skill sets may be enduring.

Managerial processes is the fourth area of the organization that needs to be reviewed for fit with the new strategy. Two aspects of this process are of concern: (1) the generic process by which strategies get translated into actions, and (2) the capabilities of current managerial processes with respect to the specific needs of the particular strategy.

Figure 13-6 outlines the basic activities involved in translating a strategic plan into real actions. The strategic plan typically specifies the sources of ad vantage, the targets of that advantage, the resource weighting supporting the strategy, and the objectives to be achieved. That plan is then translated into the set of strategic programs necessary to achieve the tasks and objectives specified in the plan. This might include, for example, programs designed to achieve product performance, cost, and timing targets; programs for the acceptance by channels of new activities or changes in channel relationships; programs to develop and qualify new suppliers; or programs to achieve new sales and service performance levels.

These programs need to be integrated into functional plans. Functional managers translate the program needs into the skills, timing, and other resources that do the program's work (as well as the ongoing tasks of the function) and, simultaneously, work to establish their implications for budgets. The budget is the ultimate and fundamental tool that is used to convert strategic thinking and planning into action. Finally, control systems track and control performance of the programs and, ultimately, the strategic plan itself.

---

[32] For a good review of the studies in which these terms were used, see Jay R. Galbraith and Robert K. Kazanjian, *Strategy Implementation: Structure, Systems, and Process,* 2nd ed. (St. Paul, MN: West Publishing Company, 1986), chapter 6.

Figure 13-6 The managerial process of strategy implementation

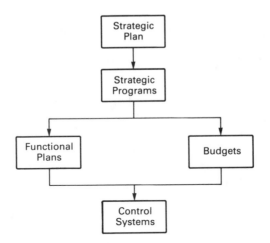

The ability of the organization to act strategically is a function of the adequacy of the managerial planning process in which the aforementioned activities take place. Systems which limit the coordination needed to think in terms of cross-functional strategic programs, or budgeting systems which force managers to choose between current profits from ongoing activities and the pursuit of strategic objectives, are some of the common obstacles. Strategies whose implementation requires coordination, planning, or budgeting requirements beyond those which the existing system is capable of may not succeed unless those responsible for the strategy's implementation can either change the system or find ways around the existing system. This is why successful managers need to understand the capabilities of their businesses and the way they work. Accomplishing work that goes beyond the repetitive tasks to which the organization is accustomed is critical in implementing strategy.

Control systems are the last of the management processes that can aid or retard strategic implementation. Effective control systems include timely and objective feedback from operations and the marketplace that is tied to performance standards, which define acceptable and unacceptable performance, trigger corrective actions, and are tied to managerial reward systems. The process starts with the selection of objectives for the strategy that are appropriate to the tasks that each manager is responsible for. Objectives for operating managers, for example, may specify such hard measures as on-time delivery performance or the opening of new sales accounts. Higher-level managers may have to meet revenue or cost targets, while profitability or gross margin targets are the responsibility of the business unit manager.

Especially difficult in this respect is establishing control and reward systems which achieve the correct balance between long- and short-run goals and between business unit and firm-wide performance. Current thinking suggests that control systems need be crafted carefully to achieve the desired balance. This crafting must be differentiated by the role that the business unit is to play in the corporate portfolio (e.g., growth versus cash) and the cross-unit (or cross-functional) coordination and support needed.[33]

The Individual's Perspective on Implementation[34]

It is important to understand the influence that the organization has on the successful implementation of strategy. It is equally important for the individual strategist to understand his or her own role in achieving that implementation. Ultimately, the individual has the greatest amount of control of his or her own behavior, and that is where successful implementation must start. To be a successful implementer, the individual needs

- Diagnostic skills to recognize that an implementation or execution problem exists;
- The ability to assess the level in the firm at which the problem is occurring;
- An understanding of the specific skills necessary for effective execution.

Diagnosing Implementation Problems.   Diagnosis can be seen as a two-step process. The first step is to determine whether the source of the problem is in the strategy itself—is it appropriate? The second step is to examine the implementation—has it been excellent or poor? These two factors combined to produce four kinds of strategy implementation problems, as shown in Figure 13-7.

Figure 13-7 demonstrates an important fact about strategy and implementation: Poor implementation can disguise good strategy. When both are on target, the strategist and company have done all that they can. Any shortcomings in results are not in management's control. In the opposite corner, however, when both strategy and implementation are questionable, diagnosis is especially difficult. The manager who rushes to correct problems without adequate diagnosis will likely be wasting energy on the wrong question.

In the lower left-hand cell, inadequate implementation of a sound strategy (the "trouble" cell), management will only worsen the situation by changing the strategy. The diagonal situation, poor strategy/excellent execution, can go either way. Excellent execution will speed its demise. Hence the "rescue or ruin" description. When in doubt as to the source of problems, the best rule is to start with examining the strategy's execution.

---

[33] This discussion, of course, assumes a rational control process. Experience shows, however, that success may be better defined as the results obtained versus management's expectations about results. See Thomas V. Bonoma, "Marketing Performance—What Do You Expect?," *Harvard Business Review*, 67, no. 5 (September-October 1989), 44–47. See also Robert Simons, "Strategic Orientation and Top Management Attention to Control Systems," *Strategic Management Journal*, 12, no. 1 (January 1991), 49–62.

[34] The material in this section is built on work of Thomas V. Bonoma, "Making Your Strategy Work," *Harvard Business Review* 62, no.2, (March-April 1984), 68–76 and Thomas V. Bonoma, "Note on Marketing Implementation," *Harvard Business Review School*, #0-582-135, 1982.

Figure 13-7 Marketing strategy and implementation problem diagnosis

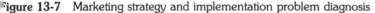

Strategy

		Appropriate	Inappropriate
Marketing implementation	Excellent	**Success** Targets for growth, share, and profits are met.	**Rescue or ruin** Good execution may mitigate poor strategy and give management time to correct it, but good execution of poor strategy may hasten failure.
	Poor	**Trouble** Poor execution hampers appropriate strategy; management may conclude that its strategy is inappropriate.	**Failure** Cause of failure is hard to diagnose because poor strategy is masked by inability to execute.

SOURCE: Reprinted by permission of *Harvard Business Review*. An exhibit from "Making Your Marketing Strategy Work" by Thomas V. Bonoma, March/April 1984. Copyright © 1984 by the President and Fellows of Harvard college; all rights reserved.

Assessing the Implementation Level. Execution problems can exist at (1) the functional level, (2) the program level, or (3) at the policy level. The type of problem and the ease of its correction depend on the level at which it occurs.[35] The strategist must be able to assess the level in the firm at which the strategic blockage is occurring to take corrective action.

The functional level is the basic doing level in the organization. Problems that have their source at the level of the function are the most common. In the marketing function, for example, there are a number of subfunctions such as sales force management, pricing, and the management of distributors, each of which must be performed well.

In larger organizations, specialists manage each of these, and higher- or program-level managers must start with the assumption that the tasks are being performed well. Yet like any task, things can go awry—bad assumptions about the marketplace can cause problems that affect the success of the strategy. In one strategy aimed at a business market that called for low prices, for example, there were two ways that the price concept could be implemented: low list prices with very small discounts off the price, or higher prices with larger discounts to end up at the same net price. The subfunction manager chose the low list price approach only to meet with less than expected sales. On investigation, it was discovered that the buyers of the firm's products were evaluated by their managers on the basis of the size of the discounts they were able to negotiate. The subfunction manager's assumption about the marketplace was incorrect.

Structural contradictions and resource allocation issues are two frequent sources of execution problems at the functional level. Managers often create plans that seemingly call for the simultaneous achievement of contradictory

---

[35] The examples used here are primarily marketing based. The type of analysis, however, can be extended to any of the business functions.

goals. A sales manager who indicates that the sales force size can be reduced while it simultaneously opens a large number of new accounts and increases the call frequency on existing accounts is promising contradictory results. Whether it is promised because of management pressure for performance or simply wishful thinking matters little. The result—fewer than required new accounts and decreased call frequency on existing accounts—is the cause of the failure to achieve the strategy's promise.

Allocation issues are similarly frequent. Many programs fail because the critical function in the strategy (e.g., new product development) gets the same budget increases and managerial attention as do the sales force, promotion and advertising, and distribution management. All of those functions, therefore, are performed at an adequate level when what is needed is for new product development to be done at an outstanding level and the remaining functions to be performed merely competently. Functional allocations responsive to the strategic thrust are needed. Attempts to attain global excellence more often result in global mediocrity and failure to achieve the strategic result.

Programs are plans which coordinate the actions of several functions or subfunctions to implement the idea underlying the strategy. Program-level failures can be traced to issues in the design of the program or to the cross-functional coordination needed for implementation. In the design case, programs are too often empty promises with no changes in the resources, plans, or budgets necessary to achieve what the program promises. This is reminiscent of the children's story in which the king of a rural country visits a modern society and is taken by the wondrous postal system. On returning to his country, he installs mailboxes and is disappointed when nothing happens. The core of the story is the king's recognition that it took more than mailboxes to deliver mail; that there had to be people, sorting, and transportation systems behind the mailboxes. Successfully implementing strategic programs requires the existence and application of the resources they call for. Strategic programs require that the functions go beyond business as usual.

Programs demand not only resources but the coordinated use of those resources across the different functions that comprise the business. Cross-functional coordination requires joint planning and the managerial control and reward systems that reinforce its importance. The program designer cannot simply assume that the functional managers will get together and move ahead. It is the program designer's responsibility to provide the framework by which the coordination will be achieved and to create the checkpoints at which the achievement of the program targets will be measured. It is also the designer's responsibility to see that reward systems reinforce the behaviors and actions that the strategy requires. Too many strategies fail because the control systems do not reward functional managers' pursuit of strategic rather than functional goals.

Above the programs and functions that make strategic actions happen are the policies from which they get their direction and guidance. Most policy-level failures in Bonoma's research were due to the absence of clear policies. The policies he found critical were those that articulated a clear marketing theme and a sense of focus in terms of what management is good at and what it is not.[36] Strategic programs fail when management fails to define, communicate, and instill in others its vision of what the firm does, and how. In the absence of such thematic guidance, it is difficult to create the culture in which programs are implemented as clear extensions of that theme. Implementation problems which have their source at the policy level are especially difficult to correct.

Understanding Personal Implementation Skills.   Ultimately, the implementation of strategy rests on the individual's personal skills. The self-critical manager is aware of his or her performance and always searching to identify those skills critical to the particular implementation problem. There are four skills critical to effectiveness: interacting, allocating, monitoring, and organizing.

People skills, the basic *interaction* skill, is essential to strategic implementation. Since strategic action requires the wholehearted support of the functions through which it is implemented, Theory X approaches seldom work.[37] The ability of the manager to communicate, interact, motivate, and influence is the essence of the issue and, unlike other areas of expertise, it is not a skill that can be delegated to a specialist.

Allocating resources—not only money and people but the manager's own time and energy—is a skill that can be learned. In the allocation skill, there is one central rule to be learned—that of concentration. As in strategy itself, the key to the achievement of strategic goals lies in the unequal allocation of resources. Key programs, key functions, key issues require concentrated resources; allocate to them what they need to achieve success and then divide the rest to the less critical programs, functions, or issues.

Skill in *monitoring* requires the ability to select the important measures to follow, the creation of the systems to provide the measures, and the personal will to use the measures in controlling the strategy's implementation. This last point may be most important—measures that are never used quickly become just another useless exercise invented by management to bedevil the functions.

The importance of skill in *creating organizations* depends on the situation. In implementing strategy that differs little from what already exists, it is probably of little import. In introducing a major strategic change or the creation of a new free-standing unit, it is central. The organizing skill is a personal one which requires cultivation. The ability to think in terms of a system needs to be blended with the realization that the system must reflect the capabilities of the people available to staff it, and such a skill cannot be learned overnight or through books. It comes from spending time staffing and managing and thinking about the process.

[36] Bonoma, "Note on Marketing Implementation," p. 4.
[37] For more information on Theory X, see Douglas McGregor, *The Human Side of Enterprise* (New York: McGraw-Hill, 1960), pp. 33–58.

SUMMARY

The three separate but overlapping processes described in this chapter—evaluating, valuing, and implementing strategy—bring this book to a close. While earlier chapters focused on the factors that must be analyzed in creating strategy, this chapter has focused on the analysis of the strategy itself.

Evaluating strategy is concerned first with the issue of effectiveness—will it work? Effectiveness is a function of the strategy's fit with the environment. A strategy that takes into account the critical economic and competitive forces shaping the industry is only halfway there, though. The second issue is the strategy's fit with the firm. Is the strategy built on the unique competencies of the firm? Has the firm demonstrated the specific competencies required by the strategy? Issues of feasibility blend with those of risk assessment. The key to competitive advantage is the ability to take actions that are risky for other firms but not for the firm in question because its specific competencies allow it to say, "no problem."

Ultimately, evaluating strategy means finding out if it has a good probability of making money. Recent thinking severely faults traditional measures of profitability such as earnings growth, return on investment, and return on equity as true or good measures of the creation of economic value for shareholders. Cash-oriented approaches promise a better approximation of the concept without relying on the vagaries of accounting-based data. The shareholder approach essentially estimates the value on the basis of two periods: (1) in which the firm has a competitive advantage which allows it to earn a return above the firm's cost of capital, and (2) in which the firm's performance is reduced to the risk-adjusted rate by competitive forces.

The best strategy in the world will fail, however, if it cannot be implemented. An organization consists of four subsystems through which strategic action is created: the organization's culture, its human resources, managerial processes, and structure. The strategy and the organization must mesh for implementation to occur. While in the best of all worlds the two match perfectly, frequently both must adjust to accommodate the strategic objective. Strategists need exceptional levels of organizational knowledge and personal skills to be able to translate the promise of competitive advantage into the reality of effective action.

INDEX

SUBJECT